PENGUIN 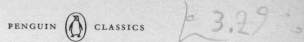 CLASSICS

WILLIAM SHAKESPEARE: FOUR COMEDIES

WILLIAM SHAKESPEARE

Four Comedies

THE TAMING OF THE SHREW
edited by G. R. HIBBARD

A MIDSUMMER NIGHT'S DREAM
edited by STANLEY WELLS

AS YOU LIKE IT
edited by H. J. OLIVER

TWELFTH NIGHT
edited by M. M. MAHOOD

PENGUIN BOOKS

PENGUIN BOOKS

Published by the Penguin Group
Penguin Books Ltd, 27 Wrights Lane, London w8 5TZ, England
Penguin Books USA Inc., 375 Hudson Street, New York, New York 10014, USA
Penguin Books Australia Ltd, Ringwood, Victoria, Australia
Penguin Books Canada Ltd, 10 Alcorn Avenue, Toronto, Ontario, Canada M4V 3B2
Penguin Books (NZ) Ltd, 182–190 Wairau Road, Auckland 10, New Zealand

Penguin Books Ltd, Registered Offices: Harmondsworth, Middlesex, England

This edition of *The Taming of the Shrew* first published in the New Penguin Shakespeare 1968
This edition of *A Midsummer Night's Dream* first published in the New Penguin Shakespeare 1967
This edition of *As You Like It* first published in the New Penguin Shakespeare 1968
This edition of *Twelfth Night* first published in the New Penguin Shakespeare 1968
This collection first published 1994
1 3 5 7 9 10 8 6 4 2

Introduction and notes to *The Taming of the Shrew* copyright © G. R. Hibbard, 1968
Introduction and notes to *A Midsummer Night's Dream* copyright © Stanley Wells, 1967
Introduction and notes to *As You Like It* copyright © H. J. Oliver, 1968
Introduction and notes to *Twelfth Night* copyright © M. M. Mahood, 1968
This edition copyright © Penguin Books, 1967, 1968, 1994
All rights reserved

Set in 10.5/12.5 pt Monophoto Garamond
Filmset by Datix International Limited, Bungay, Suffolk
Printed in England by Clays Ltd, St Ives plc

Contents

These plays and the accompanying editorial apparatus are faithful reproductions of the original New Penguin Shakespeare editions. The text has been reset, with the textual notes placed at the bottom of the pages for ease of reference, but the text itself is unchanged.

THE TAMING OF THE SHREW

Introduction

The note that is sounded in such a line as 'The course of true love never did run smooth', that haunting lyrical expression of sentiment which is such a pronounced feature of much Shakespeare comedy, is not to be heard in *The Taming of the Shrew*. There are no songs in this play, apart from the snatches of ballads that Petruchio sings after he has arrived home with his bride; and the one moment of real tenderness in it drops like a casual parenthesis between a concession and a plea, taking the form of a simple monosyllabic jingle. It comes at the end of the first scene of Act v when, under pressure from Petruchio, Katherina at last kisses him, saying as she does so, 'Nay, I will give thee a kiss. Now pray thee, love, stay.' At this point the long struggle between them has reached its end. Katherina has finally accepted her natural role as a wife; hostility, petulance, and recalcitrance have been replaced by affection, good humour, and partnership. In the final scene, which follows immediately on this action, husband and wife face the rest of the world as allies, not enemies, working together to score a signal triumph over it. And their triumphant alliance is sealed by the longest and most eloquent speech in the entire comedy, Katherina's proclamation of the submission of wife to husband as a law of nature, something essential to the harmonious working of the universe, and therefore to be accepted gladly, not rebelled against grudgingly.

This explicit statement of the play's moral has, however, something of the set piece about it, as has Petruchio's direct address to the audience, at the end of iv.i, in which he takes them into his confidence, explains in considerable detail, and with evident gusto, the methods he intends to use in order to bring his newly married wife to her senses, and then invites anyone who knows of a better way of proceeding to speak up and tell it. Indeed, there is more of this same set excogitated quality about the other passages that linger in the mind when the play is over: Biondello's description, in III.2, of the broken-down nag, a prey to all the diseases that horse-flesh is heir to, on which Petruchio arrives in Padua for his wedding; Gremio's graphic account, in the same scene, of the wildly indecorous marriage ceremony; and Petruchio's abuse of the wretched Tailor in IV.3. All these are bravura pieces, conscious displays of the rhetorical arts of grotesque description, farcical narrative, and inventive vituperation. Language is being deliberately exploited for effect; and what, in another context, might well appear cruel, outrageous, or offensive is transformed into comic exuberance by a linguistic virtuosity that delights in the exercise of its own powers. There is, in fact, much in this play that is reminiscent of the manner of Shakespeare's younger contemporary, Thomas Nashe, whose pamphlets, such as *Pierce Penilesse his Supplication to the Devil* and *Strange News*, both published in 1592, were arousing a good deal of interest about the time when *The Taming of the Shrew* was written. Couched in a lively virile prose full of verbal extravagance and ingenious tricks of style, these works must have attracted Shakespeare's attention, and probably encouraged him to make experiments of his own in the same direction. The description of the horse looks very much like an attempt to outdo Nashe at his own game. This vigour and this assurance in the use of the rich resources of Elizabethan English are, however, confined to certain parts of the play. They appear in the Induction, where Christopher Sly's every word smacks of the Warwickshire countryside, and in the story of Petruchio and Katherina. By comparison with them most of the writing in that section of the play that deals with Bianca and her various wooers seems generally insipid, often over-ornate, and at other times flat and even clumsy, though there is one flash of truly memorable spontaneous comic utterance as Biondello tells his master Lucentio, at the end of IV.4, 'I knew a wench married in an afternoon as she went to the garden for parsley to stuff a rabbit.'

There is a good reason why the best writing in the play should be rhetorical in nature, for the main concern of *The Taming of the Shrew* is, as the title indicates, with a process – indeed, with more than one process – of conditioning. In it people are persuaded by words, and compelled by actions, all of which have been carefully planned and calculated for the purpose, to see themselves in a new light, to take on a fresh personality, and to assume a different role in life from that which they have had previously. Sly's experience in this respect anticipates and prefigures Katherina's. There is also a good reason why the writing employed in the tale of Bianca and her suitors should be comparatively tame and conventional, for here words, like actions, are not intended to create something new or reveal something latent, but to serve as a form of disguise for characters who seek to hide what they are, or to take on an identity that is not their own, in order to get what they want.

The contrast in style between the different parts of the play is, then, functional; but recognition of this fact provides little incentive for the reader who, deprived of the bustle and animation of the stage, may well find it hard to develop any very lively interest in the elaborate intrigues of Tranio, Lucentio, Gremio, and Hortensio, particularly as their names, disguises, and disguise-names make it far from easy to keep one distinct from another. He will discover much support for his dissatisfaction in the writings of those critics who have approached the play through the study rather than through the theatre, for, until fairly recently, the general reception they have given it has been either apologetic or openly hostile. Some have felt that it cannot be wholly from Shakespeare's hand, and have assigned the story of Bianca to one or another of his contemporaries; some have described it as brutal and barbarous; others have concluded that it is certainly not for all time but very definitely a thing of its own age, only intelligible in terms of attitudes to women that have long disappeared, and, even so, badly in need of special pleading. Writing in 1929, John Bailey said of it: 'It is rather strange that the play is still acted, for it is, to tell the truth, an ugly and barbarous as well as a very confused, prosaic and tedious affair' (*Shakespeare*, pp. 100–101). A year earlier Sir Arthur Quiller-Couch, in his Introduction to the New Cambridge edition of the play, had been even more outspoken. After reproaching it for being 'unforgivably coarse when it puts some of its grossest words into the mouth of Katharina', he continues:

'Let us put it that to any modern civilised man, reading . . . *The Shrew* in his library, the whole Petruchio business . . . may seem, with its noise of whip-cracking, scoldings, its throwing about of cooked food, and its general playing of "the Devil amongst the Tailors", tiresome – and to any modern woman, not an antiquary, offensive as well. It is of its nature rough, *criard* [noisy]: part of the fun of those fairs at which honest rustics won prizes by grinning through horse-collars' (pp. xv–xvi).

Yet Quiller-Couch is forced to admit, with a surprised regret that outdoes Bailey's, that 'the trouble about *The Shrew* is that, although it reads rather ill in the library, it goes very well on the stage' (p. xxv). It does indeed. More than three and a half centuries after it was written, *The Taming of the Shrew* still remains today one of the most popular of all Shakespeare's comedies in the theatre, the place for which its author intended it. Thousands of men – not to mention women who are not antiquaries – go to see it every year, not only in the English-speaking countries but also on the Continent, where it is a great favourite. Nor are the reasons for its wide international appeal far to seek. They lie in its main theme: that battle of the sexes which is as old as the Garden of Eden and as new as the latest love-affair – and in the way in which this theme is worked out. Precisely because Shakespeare's central concern in this particular play is with action, characters, and ideas, rather than with poetry and atmosphere, and because the play relies for its effect on broad and obvious contrasts between characters and attitudes instead of subtle discriminations between them, it loses much less in the process of translation than do such comedies as *A Midsummer Night's Dream, As You Like It*, or *Twelfth Night*. Essentially of the theatre and for the theatre, *The Taming of the Shrew* goes on living because it has, in the first place, that necessary quality of all good drama, a delight in vigorous events subjected to the discipline of a coherent, well organized, and significant plot.

2

It is no exaggeration to say that the first audience to witness a performance of the play (in 1594 or possibly two years before that – the exact dating of it is difficult and uncertain) were seeing the most elaborately and skilfully designed comedy that had yet appeared on the English stage. In what was probably his earliest piece of comic writing, *The Comedy of Errors*, Shakespeare had used two main stories, one of them, which he drew from medieval narrative, serving as a framework for the other, which he took from Latin comedy. In *The Taming of the Shrew* he employed three stories, not two, and related them to one another in a far more complex fashion. The first of them – *The Waking Man's Dream*, as it is called in one version – is at least as old as *The Arabian Nights*, where one of the stories tells how the Caliph Haroun Al Raschid has a poor man called Abu Hassan, whom he finds in a drunken stupor, carried to his palace. There Abu Hassan is dressed in fine clothes and, when he awakens, is persuaded that he is really a great man who has been suffering from temporary insanity. From whatever intermediate source Shakespeare derived this tale, he shaped it to his own purposes with consummate artistry. The beggar is transformed into Christopher Sly, a drunken tinker from the part of England that Shakespeare knew best. The concise account of his chequered career that Sly gives when he wakes up in the second scene of the Induction describes a life such as many a man born in the Cotswolds must have had, and some of the drinking cronies whom he mentions later have good Warwickshire names. Solid, earthy, and addicted to ale, Sly is a thoroughly convincing character, and he makes the perfect link between the world of the audience, to whom he would be a familiar figure, and the world of the play. Moreover, he is placed in a realistic setting. The Hostess, the hunting scene, the great house to which he is transported, with its musty rooms that need airing, and its mythological pictures or tapestries – all these carry the conviction of people and places that have been observed and absorbed by a sharp eye and a retentive memory, as for that matter does the scene in which the players arrive at the Lord's mansion.

But far more is involved than the setting of a scene and the telling of a tale. The brief yet vigorous altercation between Sly and the Hostess with which the Induction begins is a little curtain-raiser for the struggle between Petruchio and Katherina that is to follow, while the Lord's instructions to his page Bartholomew as to the behaviour he is to assume when he appears disguised as Sly's wife adumbrate the main theme of the play proper. Bartholomew is told that he must do the drunkard 'duty'

> *With soft low tongue and lowly courtesy,*
> *And say 'What is't your honour will command,*
> *Wherein your lady and your humble wife*
> *May show her duty and make known her love?'*
>
> Induction 1. 112–15

These lines are a succinct sketch of the ideal of wifely conduct that Katherina will ultimately acknowledge. More interesting still, there is a marked resemblance between what the Lord does to Sly and what Petruchio does to Katherina. Like Petruchio the Lord is a countryman, fond of sport, something of an actor, and much given to practical jokes. He takes Sly in an unguarded moment, and by using the varied resources that are at his disposal – his servants, his house, and so forth – succeeds in imposing a new identity on the tinker. Similarly Petruchio, through his ability to act a part, manages to alter Katherina's nature, or rather her outlook; for she and Sly have this much in common, that each of them is in some measure predisposed to take up the new role that is offered to them. It is plain from Sly's muddled attempt to impress the Hostess by saying 'Look in the Chronicles, we came in with Richard Conqueror' that he has vague delusions of grandeur and aristocratic descent which leave him open to the Lord's practices. In the same way there are evident indications early in the play proper that Katherina is not so strongly opposed to the idea of marriage as she pretends to be.

The Induction, then, lives up to its name in the sense that it does indeed lead into the play that follows. But it also has a unique interest of its own, because in no other of his plays does Shakespeare make use of this particular device. Adopted, it seems likely, from medieval narrative poetry, where it was extensively used to introduce a story in the form of a dream, the Induction was a common feature of many plays written around 1590. In most cases, however, it amounted to little more than a prologue. The two outstanding examples, prior to *The Taming of the Shrew*, of plays in which the Induction is set in a thematic relationship to the action that succeeds it are to be found in Thomas Kyd's *The Spanish Tragedy*, which was written about 1587 and is referred to on more than one occasion by Sly, and in George Peele's *The Old Wives' Tale*, which probably dates from about 1590. The echoes of *The Spanish Tragedy* placed in Sly's mouth suggest that Shakespeare had the Induction to that play in mind when writing his own, which reads like a parody of it. In Kyd's Induction the Ghost of Don Andrea relates that when he reached the underworld, after being slain in battle, Proserpine intervened with Pluto on his behalf, and obtained leave for him to return to earth. He then sits down, with the figure of Revenge by his side, to witness a bloodthirsty tragedy. Sly, on the other hand, is thrown out of the only heaven he has known hitherto, the tavern, goes to sleep on the cold ground, and awakens to find himself in a heaven on earth, where the drink is free and plentiful. There he is presented with a comedy. The Ghost of Don Andrea is passionately involved in the events that are staged for his benefit, and ultimately, after many disappointments with the way they seem to be going, expresses deep satisfaction with their outcome. Sly, in contrast, is so little taken with what is offered to him that he nods off during the first scene, and then, with a grand but despairing gesture towards aristocratic politeness, utters his damning opinion of it, "Tis a very excellent piece of work, madam lady. Would 'twere done!'

These are his last words. The stage direction at this point shows that he remains in his place for the next scene at least, but no more is heard from him or of him. Having served his purpose as a lead-in from the reality of everyday life to the imagined world of the play, he is quietly dropped. There may, however, be more practical reasons for the suppression of his part, along with those of the other two 'Presenters'. These three roles in the Induction would require actors of ability; and only a very flourishing company could have afforded the luxury of having three of its leading performers, including a boy who could play female parts, largely immobilized on the upper stage while the main action of the play continued below. The Earl of Pembroke's Men, for whom *The Taming of the Shrew* was probably written, were in anything but a prosperous state in 1592–4; in fact, they were disintegrating. It is more than likely that Shakespeare, in characteristic fashion, has made dramatic capital out of theatrical necessity.

3

Sly's disappearance from the action is well timed, because it coincides with the moment when he might be expected to sit up, take notice, and even, perhaps, begin to make a nuisance of himself, for his final utterance immediately precedes the arrival of Petruchio and his man Grumio in Padua, and the beginning of a tale fit for a tinker. The shrewish wife had long been established as a comic figure on the English stage when Shakespeare wrote his play, with a history going back at least as far as the miracle-plays on the subject of Noah. In poetry Chaucer had immortalized her in the formidable shape of the Wife of Bath, and numerous *fabliaux* about her were circulating during the sixteenth century. Comedy delights in the clash of theory with inescapable fact. Nowhere in life was this clash more evident than in the matter of the position of women. The official doctrine, inherited from the Middle Ages and proclaimed by the Elizabethan Church in its *Book of Homilies*, was that woman is by nature and by divine ordinance inferior to man, and that the wife is therefore subject to her husband. She owes him obedience 'in the respect of the commandment of God, as St Paul expresseth it in this form of words: *Let women be subject to their husbands, as to the Lord; for the husband is the head of the woman, as Christ is the head of the church.* Ephes. v.' This is the explicit statement on the matter that Shakespeare and his contemporaries heard when 'The Sermon of the State of Matrimony' was read in church. But life obstinately refused to be ordered by doctrine and theory. The struggle for mastery in marriage remained as a fact of existence, and also as a standing topic for writers of all kinds, some serious and some humorous, because they knew that it had a powerful appeal both for the reading public of the time and for those who frequented the theatre. Moreover, attitudes to women were gradually changing, and throughout Elizabeth's reign a long controversy was carried on between those who thought of women as the daughters of Eve, and therefore the primary cause of human troubles and miseries, and those who took a more enlightened view of them. Some of the pamphleteers involved even went so far as to write on both sides of the question in order to keep the paper battle going. An offshoot of this controversy was the large body of satirical writing, both in prose and verse, on the subject of extravagant fashions in women's dress. This is well represented in the play. Petruchio's flamboyant diatribes against Katherina's cap and gown, in IV.3, would have had a familiar ring to the ears of the original audience. They had heard the like from many a pulpit.

Before he wrote *The Taming of the Shrew*, which has the right sort of catchpenny title for a contribution to a popular debate, Shakespeare had already touched on the controversy in *The Comedy of Errors*. In II.1 of that play the two sisters, Adriana and Luciana, discuss the position of women in marriage. Adriana, who has been turned into something of a nagger by her husband's casual and unfair treatment of her, speaks up for a greater degree of equality between the sexes, while Luciana, who is unmarried, puts the more orthodox view, that men 'Are masters to their females, and their lords', in a speech which foreshadows Katherina's lengthier enunciation of the same doctrine at the end of *The Taming of the Shrew*. In *The Comedy of Errors*, however, the whole issue remains a subsidiary one and can never rise above the level of debate, because in this play of mistaken identities husband and wife hardly ever meet. In the story of Petruchio and Katherina it receives full dramatic treatment.

Whether Shakespeare adapted some existing tale to his purposes, or whether he invented the plot himself, the first thing that distinguishes his handling of the taming theme from any of its predecessors is the sophistication, the subtlety, and the ingenuity of the methods by which Petruchio achieves his end. The traditional means of subduing a shrewish woman was by the use of physical force. In the old play *Tom Tyler and His Wife* (*c*. 1560) the domineering wife is given a thorough drubbing by her husband's friend Tom Tayler disguised as her husband. An even more cruel beating is meted out to a provocative wife by her long-suffering husband in *The Ballad of the Curst Wife Wrapt in a Morell's Skin* (c. 1550). Petruchio goes to work in a very different fashion. Only once does he so much as offer to use violence. This occurs during the course of his first meeting with Katherina in II.1, when she strikes him and he retorts 'I swear I'll cuff you, if you strike again.' But at this point he has momentarily been jolted out of his predetermined plan by her spirited and witty resistance. He has no further lapses of this kind, and adheres to the course he has set for himself.

His main line of attack is psychological. He perceives that Katherina, whom the men of Padua see as a devil and whom her father calls 'thou hilding of a devilish spirit', is in fact a woman of spirit who has become spoiled and bad-tempered because she has never met a man who is her equal and capable of standing up to her. He diagnoses the cause of her bad temper with immediate insight and great accuracy when, at his first meeting with her father in II.1, he says:

> *I am as peremptory as she proud-minded;*
> *And where two raging fires meet together,*
> *They do consume the thing that feeds their fury.*
> *Though little fire grows great with little wind,*
> *Yet extreme gusts will blow out fire and all.*
>
> lines 131–5

The 'little wind', that has made Katherina the firebrand that she now is, is the weak and ineffective opposition from others that her will has so far encountered. Very much the sportsman and the soldier, ever ready to take on an opponent or to lay a wager, Petruchio recognizes a kindred spirit in the spoiled girl, and welcomes the chance of meeting an antagonist who will put up a good fight. When Hortensio enters *'with his head broke'* after his ineffectual attempt to teach Katherina how to play the lute, and recounts in a piece of comic narrative what actually happened, Petruchio is filled with admiration for her vigour and cries out:

> *Now, by the world, it is a lusty wench.*
> *I love her ten times more than e'er I did.*
> *O, how I long to have some chat with her!*
>
> lines 160–62

And he means it.

Appreciating Katherina's wild, proud animal spirits, Petruchio equates her with another fierce difficult creature he is familiar with, the haggard or wild falcon. Falcons, which were much prized by the Elizabethans who used them for hunting, were tamed – and still are for that matter, as anyone who has read T. H. White's book *The Goshawk* will know – by being denied sleep. The tamer watches the bird continually until it is subdued and eventually gives way in the battle of wills that takes place between it and its would-be master, to whom, if he succeeds in his purpose, it then becomes very attached, or, as one Elizabethan writer on the subject puts it, 'very loving to the man', which is just what Petruchio wishes Katherina to be. This part of his programme – the most obvious and elementary part of it, and the one that comes closest to the traditional methods of shrew-taming – he explains to the audience at the end of IV.1 when he makes his entrance after seeing Katherina to bed. In the course of the scene he and his newly married wife have arrived at his country house, after he has hurried her away from her father's without allowing her to partake of the wedding feast. The journey has been cold, dirty, and unpleasant, and at the end of it Katherina has been packed off to bed without any supper under the pretext that the food provided is unfit to eat. Taking the spectators into his confidence, Petruchio then says:

> *My falcon now is sharp and passing empty,*
> *And till she stoop she must not be full-gorged,*
> *For then she never looks upon her lure.*

Another way I have to man my haggard,
To make her come and know her keeper's call,
That is, to watch her, as we watch these kites
That bate and beat and will not be obedient.

lines 176–82

Two other aspects of Petruchio's plan are much subtler and, in the end, far more important. Both call for considerable acting ability from the player who takes the part. A clue to the first of them is given by the servant Peter, who observes of his master's behaviour, just before Petruchio reappears to make the speech of which part has been quoted above, 'He kills her in her own humour.' What Peter means by this is that Petruchio is deliberately outdoing his wife in his displays of perversity and bad temper. The beginnings of it are to be seen at their first meeting, where, acting in accordance with the scheme he announces immediately before Katherina appears, Petruchio takes everything that she says in the reverse sense. It goes much further in the wedding scene, III.2, where he flouts all the normal conventions, arriving late, on a horse that is a disgrace to any gentleman, dressed in clothes more suitable for a scarecrow, behaving scandalously and outrageously in church, and rushing off in the most unceremonious and impolite manner as soon as the wedding is over. When he reaches his own home, his conduct is even worse. The house is admirably run, and his servants are models of efficiency, yet he continually finds fault with everything they do, rating and beating them for actions that are his, not theirs. Tyrannical, violent, and capricious, he rejects the cap and the dress he has ordered for his wife, and abuses the Haberdasher and the Tailor without restraint or mercy.

The entire proceedings are, of course, an act. Petruchio has more than a little in common with Richard III, who is pretty much his contemporary in terms of Shakespeare's career as a playwright. Both of them adopt roles in order to achieve their ends, both take a delight in doing so, and both inform the audience by direct address what their plans and purposes are. Petruchio's aim is to make himself a kind of mirror – a mirror that exaggerates – to Katherina. His displays of temper are a caricature of hers. Absurd and unreasonable, they enlist her sympathies for those who suffer under them. When he knocks over a basin of water and then blames the servant for letting it fall, Katherina intervenes on the man's behalf, saying 'Patience, I pray you, 'twas a fault unwilling'; and when he creates an angry fuss about the meat, which, he says, is overcooked, she attempts to calm him and make him take a more reasonable attitude. She is coming to see the value of that order and decency for which she previously had no use, and also, by implication, to see herself as she is. In the same way Petruchio's apparent disrespect for all the normal conventions of social life forces her to appreciate their worth. She discovers the shame and misery of being kept waiting by her bridegroom on the morning of the wedding, the indignity of not being allowed to preside at her own wedding breakfast, the disappointment of being deprived of fashionable clothes. Just as the lack of food and sleep brings her to a recognition of the basic importance of these things which she has always taken for granted, leading her to be conciliatory and gentle to Grumio in the hope of getting something to eat, and to say, after some prompting, 'I thank you, sir' to Petruchio when he eventually provides her with it, so her enforced loss of the woman's customary rights and privileges makes her acknowledge her own femininity.

Not only does Petruchio show Katherina what she is, through his own exaggerated parody of her wild and unreasonable behaviour, but he also shows her what she might be and what he wants her to be, through the way in which he treats her and talks to her. His offensive and outrageous actions and speeches are always directed – ostensibly at least – at others, never at her. In fact, the role he adopts is that of a knight-errant coming to the aid of a damsel in distress. All that he does 'is done in reverend care of her'. The blow he deals the priest who marries them is given in defence of her modesty;

when he carries her off from her father's house he is saving her from a band of thieves who would rob him of her; when he refuses to allow her to eat roast mutton it is out of consideration for her health and temper! As he says himself, when justifying his tactics, 'This is a way to kill a wife with kindness . . .' And, while all this is going on, he also takes care to tell her the things that deep within her she really wishes to hear. Praise of her beauty flows from his lips. She is 'sweet as spring-time flowers', she looks like the goddess Diana; and in a couple of lines that give a vivid impression of how Shakespeare himself must have visualized this fierce, wayward, yet fundamentally likeable and naturally honest creature of his imagination, he tells her

> *Kate like the hazel-twig*
> *Is straight and slender, and as brown in hue*
> *As hazel-nuts and sweeter than the kernels.*
>
> II. 1.247–9

Before the end of the play is reached, all that in Katherina's character which had been warped by her faulty upbringing and by the circumstances in which she found herself has become as straight as her body. And she knows how the change has been brought about, for in IV.5, the scene in which she and Petruchio on their way to Padua encounter old Vincentio, she uses her husband's methods against him. Having been forced by him to say that the sun is the moon, she is then told by him that it is the sun after all. Thereupon she retorts:

> *Then, God be blessed, it is the blessèd sun.*
> *But sun it is not, when you say it is not,*
> *And the moon changes even as your mind.*
>
> lines 18–20

She has now taken his measure, and, understanding his games, is ready to join in them, which is what she does for the rest of the play.

4

For the third element that goes to make up the elaborate plot of *The Taming of the Shrew* Shakespeare went to an entirely different source from those which he had used for the other two. In 1509 the great Italian poet Ludovico Ariosto had written a comedy called *I Suppositi*, a title that means 'The Substitutes' or 'The Impostors'. This had been translated into English by George Gascoigne, one of the pioneers of Elizabethan literature, in 1566, under the title of *Supposes*. Following Ariosto's example, Gascoigne used prose as the vehicle for his translation, and *Supposes* has the distinction of being the first prose drama in English. Moreover, Gascoigne's prose is good; varied in style, well articulated, and liberally sprinkled with quibbles, it revealed something of the potentialities that the new medium offered to the playwright. Modelled, like the main plot of Shakespeare's own *Comedy of Errors*, on the comedies of Plautus and Terence, *Supposes* is a lively and fast-moving play of intrigue. It is about that perennial theme of Latin comedy, the efforts of a young man, aided by a clever servant, to outwit the old men who stand in the way of his obtaining, or rather in this case retaining, the girl of his choice. When it opens, the heroine Polynesta, who appears only in the first scene and takes no part in the subsequent action, is already pregnant by her lover Erostrato, a student at the University of Ferrara. Seeing her in the street on his arrival in the city from his home in Sicily, Erostrato fell in love with her at once, and, in order to gain access to her, changed names and identities with his man Dulipo. For the past two years Erostrato has been a servant in the house of Polynesta's father, Damon, while Dulipo has been taking his place at the University. Polynesta is sought in marriage by Cleander, an old lawyer who wants to beget a son and heir to replace the son whom he lost, years before the action of the play begins, during an attack on Otranto by the Turks. In an attempt to foil Cleander's plans,

Dulipo, who is, of course, known throughout Ferrara as Erostrato and held in some esteem, also becomes a suitor for the
hand of Polynesta. So far as her father is concerned, the only
relevant question in deciding which of the two suitors he shall
give his daughter to – her feelings are not considered at all – is
which of them can provide her with the greater dowry. The
advantage here is very much on the side of Cleander, who is his
own master, whereas any promise made by Dulipo will only be
valid when it receives the approval and blessing of his supposed
father in Sicily. The ingenious Dulipo therefore provides himself with a father. Meeting a Sienese merchant who is just
entering Ferrara, he invents a cock-and-bull story to persuade
the man that Ferrara is a highly dangerous place for him,
because it is almost on the brink of a war with Siena. He then
offers to help the Sienese by taking him to his own house and
giving out that the man is his own father, come from Sicily to
see him. In return for this favour, the Sienese is to guarantee
his supposed son's dowry. At this point two things complicate
the issue: Damon discovers that Polynesta is pregnant by
Erostrato, and casts him into a dungeon; and Erostrato's real
father, Philogano, arrives in Ferrara. There is much confusion
when the real father and the supposed father meet. Each calls
the other an impostor, and Dulipo denies any connexion with
his old master Philogano. Philogano enlists the services of the
lawyer Cleander to put matters right, and as the two of them
talk together it dawns on them that Dulipo is Cleander's long-
lost son. Erostrato is then released, his real father is only too
glad to provide the dowry, Damon is delighted to get the
embarrassment of Polynesta off his hands, and all ends happily.

The value of this play for Shakespeare was threefold. First, it
offered him an intrigue plot which would form an excellent
contrast to Petruchio's wooing of Katherina, which is direct
and open, with Petruchio making a straightforward proposal to
her father Baptista, and telling Katherina herself 'I am he am
born to tame you, Kate'. Secondly, it enabled him to treat the
whole matter of marriage and its social implications much

more fully than he could otherwise have done. Thirdly, it gave him one of the central ideas that he employs to unify the varied elements of which *The Taming of the Shrew* is compounded. As it stood, however, the action of *Supposes* was not sufficiently romantic, even in a surface fashion, which was all Shakespeare required of it, to suit his purposes. Consequently, while retaining the basic structure of this play of mistaken identities, he also modified much of the detail in it, adding some things and suppressing others. In classical style Ariosto had confined his play to the final stages of the action, leaving the story of how Erostrato and Polynesta met, and of its progress through two years, to be briefly recounted in the first scene. But in a romantic play the initial encounter of hero and heroine is a matter of the first importance, and must therefore be enacted, as it is in 1.1 of Shakespeare's play, where Lucentio is transported at the sight of Bianca and expresses his feelings in the stock terms and phrases of conventional Elizabethan love-poetry. Nor would Ariosto's heroine do. Pregnancy is too practical a matter to be romantic, and, in any case, Polynesta's part was much too restricted a one for the kind of comedy Shakespeare was writing, where the women always have a substantial role. Bianca, therefore, is given a much larger share in the action and shows far more initiative than her counterpart in *Supposes*, not only for these reasons, but also because her main function is to act as a contrast to the sister, Katherina, with whom Shakespeare endows her.

There are two other significant alterations. The motive of the lost son who is restored to his father is completely suppressed, perhaps because Shakespeare had just handled it at length in *The Comedy of Errors*, but more probably because he realized that it would be out of place in this comedy of wooing and wedding for which he had designed a very different ending from that of *Supposes*. Then there is an addition to the number of Bianca's wooers in the shape of Hortensio. The main reason for his inclusion is clearly to provide yet more 'supposes' when he assumes the disguise of Licio, the music teacher, and to complicate and enrich the lesson scene, III.1, but he also serves as a useful link between Petruchio and Padua, and is essential to the success of the last scene of all, where three sets of husbands and wives are needed to give the right amount of suspense and climax to the business of the wager. He is, in fact, part of the plot mechanism rather than a coherent character, since his various roles are not consistent with one another.

The comedy that results from these changes is still, when viewed apart from the story of Petruchio and Katherina, very much a comedy of situation, culminating in the riotous fun and muddle of v.1, where the real father of Lucentio arrives unexpectedly in Padua and meets his supposed father, the Pedant. Of its very nature, comedy of this sort works through the activities of type figures who remain unchanged throughout, and whose actions and reactions are entirely predictable: the Pedant, the old pantaloon (Gremio), the father (Baptista), the lover (Lucentio), and the clever, scheming servant (Tranio). Except for Bianca, whose position is different from that of the rest and who is therefore developed along rather different lines, the characters involved in this part of the play can be divided into two groups: the old, who are tricked, and the young, who do the tricking, setting their wits to work to outmanoeuvre the old, and one another as well. In such a situation the most successful man is he who knows the most, and the characters can be arranged according to the extent to which they are aware of what is really happening. The one who knows the least is Baptista, who is consistently mistaken about everything and everybody, so that he does not even understand why Bianca asks his pardon in v.1 when she enters after her secret marriage to Lucentio. Too gullible to be interesting, he is merely the butt for all the intrigues that go on. The character who comes closest to Baptista in his unawareness of the extent to which he is being duped is Gremio, especially when he unwittingly introduces his rival Lucentio into Baptista's house. But Gremio is, it must be added, one of the most satisfactory figures in this section of the play. His character, as the aged suitor who is absurd because he is too old, is admirably sustained and consistent. Foolish in his pretensions as a lover, he is not without shrewdness in other matters, and he certainly gives Tranio a jolt when he tells him, near the end of II.1:

> *Sirrah, young gamester, your father were a fool*
> *To give thee all, and in his waning age*
> *Set foot under thy table. Tut, a toy!*
> *An old Italian fox is not so kind, my boy.*
>
> lines 393–6

When he makes this remark, Gremio is drawing on that stock of proverbial wisdom that contributes so much to the creation of the distinct and distinctive idiom he is endowed with; and his experience in the play is substantially summed up in yet another bit of proverbial lore, which he uses twice: first, when he tells Hortensio 'Our cake's dough on both sides' (I.1.108); and then when he says 'My cake is dough' (V.1.128). It is a wry confession of failure in an action where everyone is busy cooking up plots. The direct opposite to these two, in terms of his knowledge of what is going on, is Tranio, the arch-manipulator, who has all the strings in his hands until the moment when Vincentio turns up, by which time Tranio's main purpose of enabling Lucentio to marry Bianca has been achieved. Tranio, in fact, serves as the brains for his love-besotted master, who is incapable of thinking about anything except Bianca, or rather about his romantic and, as it eventually proves, fatuous and mistaken notion of what Bianca is. Lucentio's bookish and extravagant speeches in praise of his beloved reveal him for the shallow and infatuated type that he is. He is obviously meant to contrast with Petruchio, who has a grasp on things as they are and is not led astray by the workings of his own imagination, just as Bianca provides another contrast, of a rather different kind, with her sister Katherina.

At the level of the action the two stories Shakespeare used for the play proper are firmly linked together by Baptista's first words as he enters in 1.1, where he tells Gremio and Hortensio, the suitors of Bianca:

> *Gentlemen, importune me no farther,*
> *For how I firmly am resolved you know;*
> *That is, not to bestow my youngest daughter*
> *Before I have a husband for the elder.*
>
> lines 48–51

To the modern spectator or reader this decision must sound arbitrary and unreasonable. It would not have done so, however, to those who first saw the play, for it was taken for granted in Elizabethan England that it was a parent's duty to arrange a suitable match for his daughters; and the main criteria of suitability were status and income. Marriage was, in fact, very much a business arrangement, with love and compatibility as decidedly subsidiary factors. Girls looked on it as their proper end in life, and, indeed, as their due, with the result that parents who failed to do their duty in the matter were often censured by their children as well as by their neighbours. Katherina's bitter resentment at her unmarried state is plainly voiced by her in 11.1, and it is not without its representative quality. After Baptista has restrained her when she '*flies after Bianca*', Katherina bursts out with these words:

> *What, will you not suffer me? Nay, now I see*
> *She is your treasure, she must have a husband.*
> *I must dance bare-foot on her wedding-day,*
> *And for your love to her lead apes in hell.*
>
> lines 31–4

She obviously feels that her father has failed her badly in not finding a husband for her, and that it would be a deep personal insult if he were to allow her younger sister to marry before her.

The Taming of the Shrew, unlike most of Shakespeare's other comedies – the nearest to it in this respect is *All's Well that Ends Well* – deals with marriage as it really was in the England that he knew. Whether Baptista is bargaining with Petruchio about his marriage to Katherina, or with Gremio and Tranio about which of them shall wed Bianca, the crucial consideration is the dowry, both in the sense of the money which a father paid to the man who took a daughter off his hands, and in the other sense of the money or property that the bridegroom assured to his wife in case he predeceased her, so that she would not be left without provision for her widowhood. And in each case the bargaining ends with the drawing up of a legal agreement or, in the words of the play, of an 'assurance'. In these circumstances the needy adventurer on the look-out for a profitable match was a common phenomenon, and so was the older man in search of a young wife on whom he might beget an heir. In fact, middle-aged bridegrooms were generally popular with Elizabethan parents, since they were more likely to be settled in life and financially sound than were younger men. Petruchio begins as a variant on the first type, making no pretence about the mercenary motives which have brought him to Padua, and saying quite unashamedly on his arrival:

> *Antonio, my father, is deceased,*
> *And I have thrust myself into this maze,*
> *Haply to wive and thrive as best I may.*

1.2.53–5

He is not, however, needy, because his father has left him well-off. Gremio is a variant on the second, differing from his prototype Cleander in *Supposes* in that he never mentions the begetting of an heir as a motive that carries any weight with him.

But while marriage was primarily a business arrangement, in which parents and guardians took the lead – Petruchio, whose father is dead, enjoys an independence of action that is denied to Lucentio, whose father is alive – changes in attitude were coming about. Many divines and moralists opposed arranged marriages (particularly enforced marriages, which were by no means rare), on the grounds that they were manifestations of parental covetousness and that they led not only to misery but also to adultery and crime. At the same time the poets and writers of romances were extolling true love as productive of happiness and therefore far more valuable than any amount of dirty land. As a result, concessions were being made to the wishes of the young people themselves, who were gradually acquiring the right to say no. The old traditional view and the new attitude, expressed in an outspoken and daring manner, are neatly opposed to each other in *Much Ado About Nothing*, when Antonio, thinking that the Prince is about to propose to Hero, tells her: 'Well, niece, I trust you will be ruled by your father.' Thereupon Beatrice, who has a mind and a will of her own, gives Hero a very different piece of advice, saying: 'Yes, faith; it is my cousin's duty to make curtsy and say, "Father, as it please you". But yet for all that, cousin, let him be a handsome fellow, or else make another curtsy and say, "Father, as it please me"' (II.1.44–9). Even Baptista makes a gesture in the new direction, for after reaching his agreement with Petruchio in II.1, he adds a proviso that the documents are only to be prepared

> *when the special thing is well obtained,*
> *That is, her love; for that is all in all.*

lines 128–9

On the face of it *The Taming of the Shrew* looks like a play made out of these two contrasting attitudes. The old approach to marriage is represented by Petruchio, who states quite bluntly that he wants to marry for money, makes a bargain with Katherina's father before he has so much as seen her, pays no attention whatever to her wishes, carries her off from her father's house as though she were some newly acquired possession, and then proceeds to tame her in the way he would tame a hawk. The story of Bianca and Lucentio is the obverse of this, for here the woman is dominant, enjoying the pleasure of a complex and protracted wooing, followed by a runaway marriage that receives the approval of both fathers.

The trouble with this interpretation is that it simply does not square with one's experience of the play, where not only are Petruchio and Katherina consistently more vital and more interesting than Lucentio and Bianca, but also by the end they, with their old-fashioned match, look much the more promising and stable couple of the two. Yet it seems inherently improbable that the poet who wrote Sonnet 116 –

> *Let me not to the marriage of true minds*
> *Admit impediments* –

could ever have written a play to commend the *mariage de convenance* at the expense of the love-match. And, of course, Shakespeare has not. The second half of II.1 puts the matter beyond all doubt, for it is a most telling piece of comic satire on the subject of the Elizabethan marriage-market. The match between Petruchio and Katherina has no sooner been agreed on by the two parties most intimately concerned in it – not with any enthusiasm from Katherina, but at least she does not say no – than Gremio and Tranio begin to compete for the hand of Bianca, addressing themselves to her father. Each asserts that he loves her far more than does the other, but Baptista wastes no time in bringing the argument down to the practical terms that he understands by saying:

> *Content you, gentlemen, I will compound this strife.*
> *'Tis deeds must win the prize, and he of both*
> *That can assure my daughter greatest dower*
> *Shall have my Bianca's love.*

> lines 334–7

Thereupon something very like an auction ensues in which the two suitors cap each other's bids, until Gremio is 'out-vied'. At this point Baptista settles for Tranio's offer, but takes care to add that the deal will only go through when Tranio's father underwrites his son's promises; otherwise Bianca will be married to Gremio. The mercenary and stupid nature of the whole business has been fully exposed.

How then does the play function, and what is it saying? The plainest indication is to be found in the contrast that it makes between the characters of the sisters, and in the way in which those characters are developed. Each of them at the end of the play produces exactly the opposite impression from that which she made at its beginning. Bianca, who appears at first to be gentle, modest, and submissive, proves to be a difficult and self-willed wife; while Katherina, who begins by being self-willed, shrewish, and intolerable, becomes a model of wifely obedience and duty. But even from the outset there are signs that first impressions may be misleading. Katherina, on her first appearance, plainly resents the manner in which her father offers her to Gremio and Hortensio, and she has nothing but scorn for the dismay with which they recoil from that offer. Her vigorous and outspoken retort to her father:

> I pray you, sir, is it your will
> To make a stale of me amongst these mates?

shows where she stands. It is an assertion of self-respect by a woman who, much as she wishes for marriage, has no intention of allowing herself to be sold to a man for whom she can feel nothing but contempt. As well as being something of a spoiled girl, Katherina is a girl of spirit in revolt against the society she is living in. As Petruchio says in II.1, 'If she be curst, it is for policy'. Her shrewishness is a role she has adopted in self-defence, and it disappears when she eventually meets a man who can not only stand up to her but also appreciates her for what she is and responds to the challenge she offers.

Bianca is slower to reveal her real nature. Up to the opening of Act III nothing is clear about her except that she is her father's darling and that Katherina detests her. There is no means of knowing whether the detestation springs from mere jealousy or whether it is based on sounder reasons. Are her gentleness and submissiveness genuine, or are they part of an act put on to impress others? Left alone with two young men – Lucentio and Hortensio – Bianca soon provides the answer. She thoroughly enjoys this opportunity for carrying on a double flirtation, joins with Lucentio in fooling his rival, and generally behaves like the accomplished minx that she is. More important still, the apparent submissiveness completely disappears. When the two 'tutors' start to wrangle about which of them shall give his lesson first, she promptly puts them in their places by telling them:

> *I am no breeching scholar in the schools,*
> *I'll not be tied to hours nor 'pointed times,*
> *But learn my lessons as I please myself.*
>
> lines 18–20

She is in complete command of the situation, and she remains so, because she has realized that in the society she lives in deception is a woman's most effective weapon. It is not surprising that the plot of which she is the centre should be made up of complicated intrigues.

The Taming of the Shrew depicts two ways to marriage. The road followed by Bianca and Lucentio, though it seems romantic and exciting at a first glance, is in fact unreliable, because at the end of it the husband is altogether in the dark about his new wife's real nature, as the wager scene makes abundantly plain. The other road, taken by Petruchio and Katherina, results in each gaining full knowledge of the other, much as Beatrice and Benedick do through their verbal sparrings in *Much Ado About Nothing*, so that at the end of it they have absolute trust in each other.

5

In addition to being woven closely together by their contrapuntal relationship, the two plots that make up the play proper are connected with each other, and with the Induction, in subtler and less obvious ways. The first – a very strong argument for the view that the entire play is the work of a single hand – is the use Shakespeare makes of the idea of 'supposes'. The primary meaning that this word has in Gascoigne's play is that of 'substitutes' or 'counterfeits', but in his prologue he also plays with its other possible connotations, for he tells his audience:

I suppose you are assembled here, supposing to reap the fruit of my travails, and to be plain, I mean presently to present you with a comedy called 'Supposes', the very name whereof may peradventure drive into every of your heads a sundry suppose to suppose the meaning of our supposes. Some percase will suppose we mean to occupy your ears with sophistical handling of subtle suppositions. Some other will suppose we go about to decipher unto you some quaint conceits, which hitherto have been only supposed as it were in shadows. And some I see smiling, as though they supposed we would trouble you with the vain suppose of some wanton suppose. But understand this our suppose is nothing else but a mistaking or imagination of one thing for another. For you shall see the master supposed for the servant, the servant for the master; the freeman for a slave, and the bondslave for a freeman; the stranger for a well-known friend, and the familiar for a stranger. But what? I suppose that even already you suppose me very fond, that have so simply disclosed unto you the subtlety of these our supposes, where otherwise indeed I suppose that you should have heard almost the last of our supposes before you could have supposed any of them aright.

An elaborate, though somewhat too protracted, piece of word-play such as this cannot but have caught Shakespeare's eye, and there are two direct allusions to the notion of 'supposes' in his play. The first comes in Tranio's final speech in II.1, where after he has out-vied Gremio for the hand of Bianca he says in soliloquy:

> *I see no reason but supposed Lucentio*
> *Must get a father, called supposed Vincentio.*

The second occurs towards the end of the discovery scene, v.1, when Baptista, who is lost in the maze of events, as well he might be, since he has taken every 'suppose' practised on him

at its face value, asks, 'Where is Lucentio?' and receives the
answer from the right man:

> *Here's Lucentio,*
> *Right son to the right Vincentio,*
> *That have by marriage made thy daughter mine,*
> *While counterfeit supposes bleared thine eyne.*
>
> lines 103–6

In both these cases the 'suppose' involved has been the assumption of a false identity as a form of disguise and as a means of
imposing on others; it has not led to any real change in the
person concerned. But Lucentio himself, as he discovers in the
final scene, has been the victim of a much subtler 'suppose'
than any of those that he has had a hand in, because he has
supposed Bianca to be a rather different person from what she
really is. In so far as Christopher Sly is concerned, the 'suppose'
goes much deeper, for the Lord, with the assistance of his
servants and the players, actually succeeds in convincing him
that he is not Christopher Sly the tinker at all, but a member of
the aristocracy and the husband of a charming and obedient
wife. And, since Sly disappears unobtrusively from the action,
one is left in a delightful state of uncertainty, not knowing
whether he eventually discovers the deception that has been
practised on him, whether he comes to think of it all as a
dream, or whether he emerges from it a changed man.

Shakespeare is already very much interested, in this play, in
the working of the imagination which he was to explore
further in *A Midsummer Night's Dream*. The character most
affected by it is Katherina, who ultimately becomes the person
that Petruchio has deliberately 'supposed' her to be, and,
through his clever speeches of admiration for qualities in her
that no one else can recognize, has put it in her head that she
ought to be and wants to be. The whole process is carried to
the limit at which it becomes a parody of itself in iv.5, where
Katherina joins in Petruchio's game and addresses old Vincentio
as 'Young budding virgin, fair and fresh and sweet'. So pro-

found is the alteration in Katherina's behaviour, though it has been predicted by Petruchio in II.1, when he says that 'For patience she will prove a second Grissel', that her father says in amazement, after the wager has been won, that 'she is changed, as she had never been'.

These words of Baptista's point straight to the other unifying idea that underlies *The Taming of the Shrew*, the notion of metamorphosis. Whether at the elementary and obvious level of a transformation of the outward appearance, such as Lucentio and Tranio undergo, or at the deeper one of a psychological change like Katherina's, this idea runs all through the play, and is closely related to its references to Ovid, which are many. The 'wanton pictures' that the Lord and his servants offer to fetch for Sly's delectation all have mythological subjects drawn from Ovid's *Metamorphoses*. At the opening of the play proper Tranio recommends his master to study Ovid as well as Aristotle. And Lucentio takes his advice. When he reads Latin with Bianca, it is the First Epistle in the poet's *Heroides* that they translate; and in the next lesson scene, IV.2, Lucentio acknowledges Ovid as his model and his master when he tells Bianca 'I read that I profess, *The Art to Love*'. '*The Art to Love*' is Ovid's witty mock-manual for lovers, the *Ars Amatoria*, in which he describes himself as *praeceptor amoris*, the Professor of Love. Ovid meant much to Shakespeare, not only because he was such a rich storehouse of legends and such a skilled purveyor of 'the odoriferous flowers of fancy, the jerks of invention', as Holofernes calls them in IV.2 of *Love's Labour's Lost*, but also because there was behind the *Metamorphoses* a philosophical conception of change as the law of the universe, for the fact of change was something Shakespeare was continuously and profoundly aware of. Ovid's pervasive presence in this play, which is so concerned with the changes and transformations brought about by the power of love and, still more, of the skilfully stimulated imagination, is therefore fully justified.

But it is not only the way in which the characters in his play are affected by their own imaginings and by the imaginings of others that interests Shakespeare in *The Taming of the Shrew*: he is also concerned with the effect that the imagination can have on his audience. Time after time in this play some of the characters stand aside to watch the actions of others, and become for a space almost a secondary audience, observing what goes on, without being personally involved in it. This is the position of Petruchio and Katherina, for example, in the central section of v.1, where their amusement at what they witness mirrors that of the spectators. But the most significant figure in this connexion is Christopher Sly. Literally transported out of the world he knows into another environment altogether, he surrenders so completely to the pleasures of the new world which is offered to him that he ultimately becomes lost in it, which is what Shakespeare wishes his audience to do, and employs all his skill to ensure that they do.

6

The Taming of the Shrew is, then, at least in its broad outlines, a significant piece of social comedy that has something to say about marriage in Elizabethan England, and says it in a truly dramatic manner through a contrast of actions and characters. It is also concerned with the inner world of psychological experience, and particularly with the imagination in relation to human behaviour. These two themes, the social and the personal, are intimately connected with each other, so that the total experience becomes a unified whole. The comedy is a complex work of art. The careful reader, however, as distinct from the theatre audience, will also notice that there are some loose ends in it and some bits of detail that do not fit together as they should. Leaving aside for the time being the unexplained disappearance of Christopher Sly, which can be justified as part of the total effect that the play seeks to achieve, the critic is faced with the fact that the part of Hortensio is far from coherent and satisfactory. When he first appears, early in 1.1, it looks as though his role will be an important one. He is Gremio's rival for the hand of Bianca, and it is he who suggests that they bury their differences temporarily and combine together in the task of finding a man to marry Katherina. The next scene confirms this impression, for it is Hortensio that Petruchio comes to visit, and it is Hortensio who offers to help Petruchio to a wife. He seems to be in control of things, manipulating the other characters much as he wishes. In II.1, however, Petruchio, at Hortensio's own request, presents him to Baptista under the disguise of Licio, the teacher of music; and from this point onwards Hortensio becomes a figure of fun. Katherina breaks the lute over his head, while Lucentio and Bianca use him as their butt. Moreover, he is not present when Gremio and Tranio make their bids for Bianca in the latter part of II.1, though Baptista knows perfectly well that he is a suitor. Odder still, Tranio, who has never seen Petruchio until the play begins, takes over Hortensio's original role as Petruchio's friend, apologizing for the bridegroom's delay at the opening of III.2, offering to provide him with more suitable clothes for his wedding, and entreating him to remain for the wedding breakfast. Oddest of all, Tranio, in IV.2, seems to know all about Petruchio's 'taming-school' and can tell Bianca that Hortensio has gone there, though Hortensio has said nothing whatever about the matter to him. On top of all this, Hortensio's sudden announcement in this same scene that he intends to marry 'a wealthy widow', whose very existence has not been mentioned hitherto, looks extremely suspect.

The conclusion to be drawn from all this evidence is inescapable: in an earlier version of the play Hortensio's part was larger than it is now, and Tranio's was correspondingly smaller. The inconsistencies are the result of a change of plan, made in order to exploit the comic potentialities of having two disguised suitors wooing Bianca at the same time. The necessary tailoring of the part has been done quickly but somewhat carelessly. Confirmation that this is, in fact, what happened is provided by *The Taming of a Shrew*, which was published in 1594 under the following title: *A Pleasant Conceited History, called The Taming of a Shrew. As it was sundry times acted by the Right honourable the Earl of Pembroke his servants*. In this text Polidor (Hortensio) is the friend of both Aurelius (Lucentio) and Ferando (Petruchio). He does not adopt a disguise, and, as a result, the part of Valeria (Tranio) is much slighter than it is in the *The Taming of the Shrew*. There are no inconsistencies in Polidor's part. It is he, not Valeria (Tranio), who apologizes for Ferando's (Petruchio's) delay on the morning of the wedding, and it is he who offers to lend the bridegroom some more suitable clothes for the occasion. Moreover, Polidor announces, shortly after the marriage of Ferando and Kate has taken place:

> *Within this two days I will ride to him,*
> *And see how lovingly they do agree.*
>
> scene viii, lines 113–14

Nor is there any sudden and unexpected appearance of 'a wealthy widow' on the scene. In *The Taming of a Shrew* Katherina has two sisters, not one. The elder of them, Philema (Bianca) is beloved by Aurelius (Lucentio), while the youngest, Emelia (the Widow) is beloved by Polidor.

But *The Taming of a Shrew* is, most modern critics, though not all, think, a pirated text, put together from memory by an actor, or several actors, who had once taken part in performances of *The Taming of the Shrew*. To the present editor the evidence for piracy seems quite conclusive. *The Taming of a Shrew* is made up, like *The Taming of the Shrew*, of three elements: the Induction, consisting of two scenes dealing with the 'translation' of Sly; the taming story of Ferando and Kate; and the tale of the intrigues that Aurelius resorts to in order to win the hand of Kate's younger sister. In his handling of the Induction and of that part of the plot that deals with Petruchio and Katherina the reporter does what reporters usually did, though rather less well than most: he remembers the events in rough outline, but he is far from sure about the words. Even when he gets them more or less right, which is rarely, he misses the point of a jest or a quibble; more generally he falls back on something he knows better – usually a passage from one of Marlowe's plays, and particularly *Dr Faustus* – that can be made to fit the occasion. But his version of the intrigue story is so different, with its use of two sisters for Katherina instead of one, from that which is to be found in *The Taming of the Shrew* as published in the Folio, that it must rest on an earlier and somewhat different version of the play.

There is no evidence to show that the author of this earlier version, which was subsequently revised to make *The Taming of the Shrew* as we now know it, was anyone but Shakespeare. In fact, such evidence as there is points the other way. *The Taming of the Shrew* is much closer in the relevant part of its plot to Gascoigne's *Supposes* than is *The Taming of a Shrew*. It preserves and expands the whole business of the aged wooer, which is not represented in the pirated version at all, and it also has some verbal resemblances to Gascoigne's play that are not to be found in *The Taming of a Shrew*. First, there is the use of the word 'supposed' at II.1.400–401 and of 'counterfeit supposes' at v.1.106. Then the unusual verb 'to *sol-fa*', which Petruchio employs at 1.2.17 when he says to Grumio 'I'll try how you can *sol-fa* and sing it,' appears also in a very similar context in IV.2 of *Supposes*, where an old gossip, called Psyteria, says to Crapyno, a servant, 'If I come near you, hempstring, I will teach you to sing sol-fa.' Thirdly, at the end of IV.3 of *Supposes*, when Philogano, the father of Erostrato, arrives in Ferrara and knocks at the door of Dulipo's house, the stage direction reads: '*Dalio cometh to the window, and there maketh them answer.*' Here, clearly, is the origin of Shakespeare's unusual direction at v.1.13, the corresponding point in his play: '*Pedant looks out of the window*'.

The other difference between Shakespeare's first draft of the play, which was pirated as *The Taming of a Shrew*, and the revision of it that was published for the first time in the Folio of 1623, is that in that first draft Sly did not disappear after the first scene of the play. In *The Taming of a Shrew*, he remains on stage up to the point corresponding to the end of v.1 in *The Taming of the Shrew*, by which time he is sound asleep. In the meanwhile, however, he has three times commented on the progress of the action. Before the last scene of the play proper begins, the Lord gives orders that Sly, who is now once again in a drunken stupor, should be dressed in his own clothes and carried back to the side of the alehouse where he was found. And when the play is over, and the characters in it have gone off, it is there that Sly is awakened by the Tapster who threw him out of the alehouse at the beginning. Reluctantly concluding that the whole experience has been a dream – 'the best dream that ever I had in my life' – Sly decides to make use of his newly won knowledge by going home to tame his own shrew.

It is an ending that is not without its attractions, because it rounds the play off so neatly; and some producers have found it irresistible on that account. It also lends further support to the theory that the first draft was the work of Shakespeare in its anticipation of Bottom's reactions when he wakes up at the end of iv.1 in *A Midsummer Night's Dream*. But it is not strictly necessary; there is no warrant for it in the Folio; and it can be argued that the play is better without it. Sly's main function is to lead the spectator into the imaginary world of the play; and, once he has done that, he is no longer required.

Further Reading

(1) *Editions and Editorial Problems*

The most recent scholarly editions of the play are by H. T. E. Perry in *The Yale Shakespeare*, Yale, 1921, revised by T. G. Bergin, 1954, and by Sir Arthur Quiller-Couch and J. Dover Wilson in *The New Shakespeare*, Cambridge, 1928. The most accessible edition of *The Taming of a Shrew* is in *Narrative and Dramatic Sources of Shakespeare*, edited by Geoffrey Bullough, volume 1, London and New York, 1957. C. J. Sisson's *New Readings in Shakespeare*, Cambridge, 1956, has been of great help to the present editor in coping with some of the more difficult and disputed passages.

A concise and judicious summary of the present state of scholarly opinion about the relationship between *The Taming of the Shrew* and *The Taming of a Shrew* appears in *The Shakespeare First Folio*, by W. W. Greg, Oxford, 1955. Those who wish to carry their study of this matter further should turn to *Shakespeare*, by Peter Alexander, London, 1964, where the author restates his view that *A Shrew* is a pirated version of *The Shrew*, and to G. I. Duthie's article '*The Taming of a Shrew* and *The Taming of the Shrew*', *Review of English Studies*, XIX (1943), pp. 337–56, where a more complicated thesis is advanced in a very detailed and closely reasoned argument.

(2) *Sources*

George Gascoigne's *Supposes* is printed by F. S. Boas in *Five Pre-Shakespearean Comedies*, Oxford, 1934 (World's Classics), by Bullough in the work cited above, by J. Quincy Adams in *Chief Pre-Shakespearian Dramas*, New York, 1924, and by J. W.

Cunliffe in *The Complete Works of George Gascoigne*, volume 1, Cambridge, 1907. Bullough also gives one version of the traditional tale that lies behind the Induction. Further material about the background of drama and story out of which the 'taming' plot comes is available in M. C. Bradbrook's 'Dramatic Role as Social Image: A Study of *The Taming of the Shrew*', *Shakespeare-Jahrbuch*, volume 94 (1958), pp. 132–50, and in Richard Hosley's 'Sources and Analogues of *The Taming of the Shrew*', *Huntington Library Quarterly*, XXVII (1964), pp. 289–308. In so far as the play has its 'sources' in the general life of the age in which it was written, a great deal of interesting and valuable information about Elizabethan attitudes to women and to marriage is to be found in Louis B. Wright's *Middle Class Culture in Elizabethan England*, University of North Carolina Press, 1935, and in Wallace Notestein's delightful essay 'The English Woman, 1580 to 1650', published in *Studies in Social History*, edited by J. H. Plumb, London, 1955.

(3) *Criticism*

In one sense, criticism of *The Taming of the Shrew* began very early indeed. Alone of Shakespeare's plays it provoked an answer in dramatic form which was probably staged during his lifetime. Somewhere between 1604 and 1617 – the date most favoured is *c.* 1611 – John Fletcher wrote a comedy entitled *The Woman's Prize, or The Tamer Tamed*. In it Petruchio, now a widower, marries again, and is skilfully subdued by his new wife Maria, ably assisted by her cousin Bianca and her sister Livia. The moral of this play, as set out in the epilogue, is:

> To teach both sexes due equality,
> And, as they stand bound, to love mutually.

The appearance of Fletcher's play is not only a testimony to the popularity of Shakespeare's, but also adds weight to the view that *The Taming of the Shrew* was, among other things, a contribution to the great debate about women and marriage.

Samuel Pepys saw a play, which he calls *The Taming of a Shrew*, on 9 April 1667, when he described it as 'but a mean play', and again on 1 November, when he dismissed it as 'a silly play and an old one'. What he saw, in fact, was not Shakespeare's play at all but a farcical adaptation of it, the first of several such adaptations which held the stage unchallenged right down to 1844, when *The Taming of the Shrew*, as Shakespeare left it, complete with the Induction, was at last played again in London after a lapse of nearly two hundred years. And, even then, another sixty years were to pass before Shakespeare's comedy finally ousted Garrick's condensed version of it, entitled *Catharine and Petruchio*. In these circumstances it is not surprising that the play received little attention from critics during this period, though the more robust of them responded to it. Dr Johnson, in his edition of Shakespeare, published in 1765, shows how little known the play was at that time, and then goes on to express his own pleasure in it in the following words:

Of this play the two plots are so well united that they can hardly be called two without injury to the art with which they are interwoven. The attention is entertained with all the variety of a double plot, yet is not distracted by unconnected incidents.

Dr Johnson on Shakespeare, edited by W. K. Wimsatt,
Penguin Books, Harmondsworth, 1969, p. 111

Hazlitt, in his *Characters of Shakespear's Plays* (1817), not only writes about Petruchio with insight and gusto, but also anticipates much in modern criticism with his acute perception of the true nature of the methods used to subdue Katherina. He says of the play:

It shews admirably how self-will is only to be got the better of by stronger will, and how one degree of perversity is only to be driven out by another still greater. Petruchio is a madman in his senses . . .

The critics of the nineteenth century were, in general, not much enamoured with *The Taming of the Shrew*, because it did

not fit in very well with the wide-spread notion of Shakespearian comedy as being essentially lyrical, nor was it easy to
reconcile with the more accepted, as distinct from the more
prevalent, attitudes to women and to marriage current at the
time. It is significant that Katherina finds no place in Anna
Jameson's *Shakespeare's Heroines* first published in 1832. The
view, originally advanced by Warburton in his edition of
Shakespeare (1747), that the play was Shakespeare's only in
part, was taken up with some relief, and attention centred
largely on the questions of authorship and of the relationship
between the text of the Folio and *The Taming of a Shrew*, which
was widely, though not universally, regarded as the source.
John Masefield was probably speaking for the majority when,
in his *William Shakespeare* (London, 1911), he devoted most of
what he had to say about this comedy to praise of the Induction
for its picture of country life, and summed up the story of
Petruchio and Katherina as a portrayal of 'the tragedy that
occurs when a manly spirit is born into a woman's body'. The
alternative to this view was to classify the play as a farce not
worthy of serious critical attention. These two lines of approach
to this comedy are not mutually exclusive, as Sir Arthur
Quiller-Couch's Introduction to the New Cambridge edition of
it, cited above, and John Bailey's comments on it in his
Shakespeare (London, 1929), amply demonstrate.

Mark Van Doren, on the other hand, puts the play in the
category of farce, not to excuse it or to belittle it, but in order
to bring out the kind of appeal that it can have for an audience
in the twentieth century, and he gives full recognition to the
linguistic vitality of the scenes dealing with Petruchio and
Katherina, though he does not consider the possibility that the
contrast between them and what he describes as 'the insipid
second story of Bianca and her suitors' may be deliberate and
part of the total design of the play (*Shakespeare*, London, 1941).
T. C. Kemp, writing about George Devine's production of the
comedy at Stratford-upon-Avon in 1953, also thinks of it as 'an
old farce', but adds, rather inconsistently, that by the time

Petruchio and Katherina return to Padua we realize 'that this couple have fallen deeply in love' ('Acting Shakespeare: Modern Tendencies in Playing and Production', *Shakespeare Survey 7* (1954), pp. 126–7). (The comments of these two critics are also available in *Shakespeare's Comedies: An Anthology of Modern Criticism*, edited by Laurence Lerner, Penguin Books, Harmondsworth, 1967.) By 1953, however, two writers had done much to alter the light in which *The Taming of the Shrew* was seen. D. A. Stauffer, in *Shakespeare's World of Images* (New York, 1949), while still thinking of it as a farce, had also called attention to the way in which the idea of 'supposes' has a unifying effect on the different stories that go to make up the plot, and had suggested too that the play is very much concerned with the problem of identity. Two years later G. I. Duthie attempted to remove it from the category of farce altogether by stressing the fundamental seriousness of Katherina's final speech, and by relating the conception of marriage that is expressed there to the right working – in Elizabethan terms – of the state and the universe (*Shakespeare*, London, 1951). The lead given by Duthie has been followed up in different ways by J. R. Brown in his book *Shakespeare and his Comedies* (London, 1957), and by the present editor in an article entitled '*The Taming of the Shrew*: A Social Comedy', published in *Shakespearean Essays*, edited by Alwin Thaler and Norman Sanders (Knoxville, 1964), where the argument advanced in section 5 of the Introduction to this edition is developed at greater length and in more detail.

Most recent criticism of the play, however, stems from D. A. Stauffer's work, cited above, and represents a return to the position of Dr Johnson in the emphasis laid on the artistry that has gone into its making. Bertrand Evans in his book *Shakespeare's Comedies* (Oxford, 1960) picks out 'the profound contrast in the dramatic management of the two plots' as the play's most distinctive feature, while Maynard Mack has some suggestive things to say about the manner in which stage illusion is exploited in it for dramatic ends ('Engagement and Detachment in Shakespeare's Plays', in *Essays on Shakespeare and Elizabethan Drama*, edited by Richard Hosley, London, 1963). The most recent and in many ways the most illuminating essay on this comedy is by C. C. Seronsy, who demonstrates the way in which the idea of 'supposes' runs through the entire work and serves to hold it all together, though in the view of the present editor he underrates the importance of the 'taming' theme in the Induction ('"Supposes" as the Unifying Theme in *The Shrew*', *Shakespeare Quarterly*, XIV, 1963, pp. 15–30).

A useful survey of critical problems and opinions is to be found in D. J. Palmer's chapter, entitled 'The Early Comedies', in *Shakespeare: Select Bibliographical Guides*, edited by Stanley Wells (Oxford, 1973); and Peter Alexander's continued interest in the play's beginnings is evidenced by his 'The Original Ending of *The Taming of the Shrew*', *Shakespeare Quarterly*, XX (1969). Two lively discussions of the play as a play are provided by the chapter devoted to it in Alexander Leggatt's *Shakespeare's Comedy of Love* (London, 1974), and Ralph Berry's chapter on it in his *Shakespeare's Comedies: Explorations in Form* (Princeton, 1972).

An Account of the Text

In 1594 a quarto was published, entitled *A Pleasant Conceited Historie, called The taming of a Shrew. As it was sundry times acted by the Right honorable the Earle of Pembrook his servants.* This volume, however, though it was regarded by the publishing trade throughout the rest of Shakespeare's life and, indeed, even as late as 1631, as being commercially identical with *The Taming of the Shrew,* has, it is generally agreed, no authority whatever. The exact nature of its relationship to Shakespeare's play is still a matter of dispute – in the view of the present editor, it is essentially a 'bad quarto', a very garbled version of the original, put together, probably by an actor or actors, from memory, eked out by extensive patches of verse culled from *Dr Faustus* and *Tamburlaine* – but the crucial point is that, no matter what its origin, it does not go back for its text to a Shakespeare manuscript, or to any copy of such a manuscript. In these circumstances, the sole primary text of the play is that given in the Folio of 1623 (F), where it was printed for the first time.

It is very difficult to determine the kind of copy that the printers of the Folio had at their disposal when they came to set up this particular play. It cannot have been the prompt-book used in the playhouse, because neither entrances nor exits are properly or adequately marked. To take a glaring example, the stage direction at the opening of v.2 reads as follows: '*Enter Baptista, Vincentio, Gremio, the Pedant, Lucentio, and Bianca. Tranio, Biondello Grumio, and Widdow: The Seruingmen with Tranio bringing in a Banquet.*' Tranio, who has only four lines to speak, is mentioned twice, while Petruchio and Katherina, much the most important characters in the scene, are not mentioned at all, nor is Hortensio. As a direction to the actors, this is quite useless. Other instances of entrances and exits that have been omitted will be found in the Commentary. Furthermore, the causes that have led to the muddles about who says what, which occur at III.1.46–56 and at IV.2.4–8, would, of necessity, have been cleared up in a prompt-book.

It seems equally impossible that the text can have been set entirely from the author's manuscript. The stage direction at IV.2.5, 'Enter Bianca.', instead of 'Enter Bianca and Lucentio', which is what is required, must be the work of someone who has been misled by the wrong assigning of lines 4 and 5 to *Luc.* into thinking that Lucentio is already on stage. The curious stage direction at the beginning of V.1, 'Enter Biondello, Lucentio and Bianca, Gremio is out before.', is also suspect. The last four words in it, meaning that Gremio comes on before the other three characters, look distinctly like an afterthought by someone, evidently not the author, who has discovered, on reaching line 6, that Gremio has been on stage all the time, though hitherto he has said nothing. Yet there are other features that do point to the author's manuscript. Some of the stage directions are, from a purely theatrical point of view, unnecessarily elaborate and descriptive, rather as though Shakespeare is reminding himself of who is who; which is what he seems to be doing at I.1.45, where we find 'Enter Baptista with his two daughters, Katerina & Bianca, Gremio a Pantelowne, Hortentio sister [for *suitor*] to Bianca. Lucen. Tranio, stand by.' Other directions are of the vague and indefinite sort normal in a manuscript draft, such as 'Enter foure or fiue seruingmen.' at IV.1.94 It is the Servingmen's first entrance, and Shakespeare has not yet made up his mind how many of them he will need.

The most attractive theory to account for, and even to reconcile, these contradictory kinds of evidence (the one pointing to some sort of outside interference with Shakespeare's manuscript and the other to that manuscript itself) is the view that what the printers of the Folio were using was not the manuscript itself, but a transcript of it, made by someone other than Shakespeare. Further support for this theory is to be found in the state of the text itself. The most obvious and troublesome feature of it is the large number of lines of verse that have been made unmetrical by the omission of a small word, or even part of a word. At Induction 2.2, for example, the Folio reads: 'Wilt please your Lord drink a cup of sacke?' which is neither good metre nor idiomatic English. As early as 1632 it was recognized that something was wrong here, and those who were responsible for the preparation of the Second Folio (F2), which came out in that year, put the matter right – much as they did in a number of similar cases – by substituting 'Lordship' for 'Lord'. In prose, errors of this kind are much more difficult to detect, but when Baptista asks Biondello, at III.2.32, 'Is it new and olde too? how may that be?' it is clear that the word 'olde' must have appeared somewhere – it is impossible to be sure exactly where – in Biondello's previous speech, though there is no sign of it in the Folio text. As the compositors who set the Folio were not, to judge from the evidence of other verse plays in it, very prone to this kind of mistake, it follows that the copy they were using was probably at fault. One only has to imagine that they were working from a transcript of Shakespeare's manuscript, made rather hurriedly and carelessly, to see how it could all have come about.

The Taming of the Shrew is closely connected with a period of great turmoil and change in the history of the Elizabethan acting companies. The worst plague of the reign broke out in 1592, and continued, with a short break, right on into 1594. For the greater part of this time the theatres in London were closed, and the companies tried to make ends meet by touring the provinces. Some of them split up, others lost their identity altogether. Among these latter were the Earl of Pembroke's men, for whom this play seems to have been written. A company that was breaking up into two different groups might well need hurried transcripts of the most popular plays in its repertory, so that each group could act them; and, in the final

stages of the company's disintegration, its more indigent members, cut off from all access to its 'books', could easily have
been driven to the expedient of vamping up a text from
memory for some such occasion as that which Shakespeare
depicts in his Induction. The copy used for the Folio text of
The Taming of the Shrew is probably a result of the first process,
and that used for *The Taming of a Shrew*, published in 1594,
perhaps a result of the second.

COLLATIONS

I

The following list contains the substantial additions and alterations that have been made in the present edition to the stage
directions, and Act divisions and speech headings, of the Folio.
The reading of the present text is to the left of the bracket, and
that of the Folio to the right of it.

(a) *Stage directions*

Ind. 1.	0	*Enter Christopher Sly and the Hostess*] *Enter Begger and Hostes, Christophero Sly.*
	8	*He lies on the ground*] not in F
	10	*Exit*] not in F
	71	*Sly is carried away*] not in F
		A trumpet sounds] *Sound trumpets.*
	72	*Exit Servingman*] not in F
	136	*Exeunt*] not in F
Ind. 2.	0	*Enter aloft Sly*] *Enter aloft the drunkard*
	23	*A Servingman brings him a pot of ale*] not in F
	24	*He drinks*] not in F
	97	*Enter Page as a lady, with attendants. One gives Sly a pot of ale*] *Enter Lady with Attendants.*

    100 *He drinks*] not in F

    115 *Exeunt Lord and Servingmen*] not in F

    126 *Enter the Lord as a Messenger*] this editor; *Enter a Messenger.*

    141 *They sit*] not in F

I.I.   45 *suitor*] *sister*

    91 *Exit Bianca*] not in F

    142 *Exeunt Gremio and Hortensio*] *Exeunt ambo. Manet Tranio and Lucentio*

    207 *They exchange garments*] not in F

    247 *coming to with a start*] not in F

I.2. 137 *disguised as Cambio, a schoolmaster*] *disgused.*

    141 *They stand aside*] not in F

    215 *Tranio, bravely dressed as Lucentio*] *Tranio braue*

II.I.   0 *Bianca with her hands tied*] *Bianca.*

    24 *He unties her hands*] not in F

    36 *Exit Katherina*] not in F

    38 *Petruchio, with Hortensio, disguised as Licio; and Tranio*] *Petruchio with Tranio*

    100 *Biondello steps forward with the lute and the books*] not in F

    101 *(opening one of the books)*] not in F

    110 *Exit Servant, conducting Hortensio and Lucentio, followed by Biondello*] not in F

    168 *Exeunt all but Petruchio*] *Exit. Manet Petruchio.*

    215 *She turns to go*] not in F

    216 *He takes her in his arms*] not in F

    234 *She struggles*] not in F

    245 *He lets her go*] not in F

III.I. 83 *Exeunt Bianca and Servant*] not in F

    84 *Exit*] not in F

III.2. 0 *Lucentio as Cambio*] not in F

    26 *followed by Bianca and the other women*] not in F

    122 *with Grumio*] not in F

    126 *followed by Gremio, Biondello, and attendants*] not in F

48]   THE TAMING OF THE SHREW

182   *Grumio, and attendants*] not in F
226   *He seizes her, as though to protect her from the rest of the
        company, to whom he speaks*] not in F
238   *and Grumio*] not in F

IV.1.   30   *He kindles a fire*] not in F
        55   *He boxes Curtis's ear*] not in F
       133   *He strikes the Servant*] not in F
       137   *Exit another Servingman*] not in F
       140   *He knocks the basin out of the Servant's hands*] not in
              F
       141   *He strikes the Servant*] not in F
       151   *He throws the food and dishes at them*] not in F
       153   *Exeunt Servants hurriedly*] not in F
       173   *Exeunt*] not in F

IV.2.   5   *and Lucentio as Cambio*] not in F
        10   *They court each other*] not in F
        43   *Exit*] not in F
        71   *Exeunt Lucentio and Bianca*] not in F

IV.3.   40   *He sets the dish down*] not in F
        86   *Exit Haberdasher*] not in F
       180   *(to Grumio)*] not in F
       192   *Exeunt*] not in F

IV.4.   0   *Pedant, booted, and dressed*] Pedant drest
        17   *Lucentio as Cambio*] Lucentio: Pedant booted and bare
              headed.
        58   *He winks at Lucentio*] not in F
        66   *Exit Lucentio*] not in F
        93   *He turns to go*] not in F

V.1.   3   *Exeunt Lucentio and Bianca*] Exit.
         5   *Exit*] not in F
        52   *Exit*] not in F
        53   *Exit from the window*] not in F
        82   *Enter an Officer*] not in F
       129   *Exit*] not in F

V.2.   0   *Petruchio with Katherina, Hortensio*] not in F
        48   *Exeunt Bianca, Katherina, and Widow*] Exit Bianca.

104   *Exit Katherina*] not in F
121   *She obeys*] not in F
186   *Exeunt Petruchio and Katherina*] *Exit Petruchio*
188   *Exeunt*] not in F

(b) *Act divisions and speech headings*

                Induction] *Actus primus. Scœna Prima.*

Ind. 1.   1   SLY] *Begger.*
          3   (and before all subsequent speeches) SLY] *Beg.*
       80   FIRST PLAYER] 2. *Player.*
       86   FIRST PLAYER] *Sincklo.*
    2.   99   (and in all subsequent speeches) PAGE] *Lady.*
      127   LORD] this editor; *Mes.*

I.I.   0   I.I] not marked in F
    246   LORD] this editor; *1. Man.*
II.I.   0   II.I] not marked in F
III.I. 46–9 How fiery and forward our pedant is . . . mistrust]
                 assigned to *Luc.* in F
    50–51 LUCENTIO] *Bian.*
      52   BIANCA] *Hort.*
      80   SERVANT] *Nicke.*
IV.I.   0   IV.I] No Act division here in F
      23   CURTIS] *Gru.*
IV.2.   4   HORTENSIO] *Luc.*
       6   LUCENTIO] *Hor.*
       8   LUCENTIO] *Hor.*
      71   Take in your love, and then let me alone] F heads
                 this line *Par.*
IV.3.   0   IV.3] *Actus Quartus. Scena Prima.*
      63   HABERDASHER] *Fel.*
IV.4.   5   Where we were lodgers at the Pegasus] assigned to
                 Tra. in F
V.I.   0   V.I] no division here in F
V.2.   0   V.2] *Actus Quintus.*

2

The following list is of words that have been added to, or, more rarely, omitted from, the text of the Folio, in order to regularize the metre or improve the sense. Most of these changes were first made in the seventeenth and eighteenth centuries – many of them in one or the other of the three seventeenth-century reprints of the Folio (F2, F3, and F4); these are noted. The reading to the left of the bracket is that of this edition; that to the right, of the Folio.

Ind. 1.	62	he is Sly, say] he is, say
2.	2	lordship] F2; Lord
I.2.	45	this's a] this a
	72	she as] F2; she is as
	119	me and other] me. Other
II.1.	8	charge thee tell] F2; charge tel
	79	unto you this] vnto this
III.2	16	Make feast, invite friends] Make friends, inuite
	28	a saint] F2; a very saint
	29	of thy impatient] F2; of impatient
	30	such old news] such newes
	90	Were it not better] Were it better
	127	But, sir, to love] But sir, Loue
	129	As I before] As before
	165	rose up again] F2; rose againe
IV.2.	60	I'm] I am
	86	are newly] are but newly
	121	Go with me, sir, to] F2; Go with me to
IV.3.	81	it is a paltry] F2; it is paltrie
	88	like a demi-cannon] F2; like demi cannon
IV.5.	78	she be froward] F2; she froward
V.1.	115	arrived at last] F2; arriued at the last

3

Below are listed other departures in the present text from that of the Folio. Obvious minor misprints are not noted, nor are changes in lineation and punctuation unless they are of special significance, nor cases in which the Folio prints verse as prose, or prose as verse. Most of these emendations were made by editors in the eighteenth century. Those suggested by modern editors are gratefully acknowledged. The Folio reading is to the right of the bracket.

The Characters in the Play] not in F

Ind. 1. 9–10 thirdborough] Headborough
          15 Breathe] (C. J. Sisson, 1954); Brach F
Ind. 2. 52 wi'th'] with
          72 Christophero] F2; Christopher
         135 I will. Let them play it. Is not] I will let them play, it is not
1.1.   13 Vincentio come] *Vincentio's* come
        17–18 study | Virtue] studie, | Vertue
           25 *Mi perdonato*] *Me Pardonato*
          106 There! Love] Their loue
          204 coloured] F3; Conlord
          241 your] F2; you
1.2.   18 masters] mistris
           24 *Con tutto il cuore ben trovato*] *Contutti le core bene trobatto*
         25–6 *ben venuto, | Molto honorato*] *bene venuto multo honorata*
           51 grows. But] growes but
          170 help me] helpe one
          188 Antonio's] *Butonios*
          222 her too?] her to –
          264 feat] seeke
          279 *ben*] F2; *Been*

II.1.   3 gauds] goods
          75–6 wooing. | Neighbour] wooing neighbors
             90 a suitor] as utor
        104–5 Pisa. By report | I] *Pisa* by report, | I
           186 bonny] F4; bony
           241 askance] a sconce
           323 quiet in] quiet me
           368 Marseilles] Marcellus; Marsellis F2

III.1.   28 and 41 *Sigeia*] F2; *sigeria*
             32 *Sigeia*] F2; *Sigeria*
             79 change true rules for odd] charge true rules for
                    old

III.2.   33 hear] F2; heard
             54 swayed] Waid
             58 new-repaired] now repaired
           152 grumbling] F2; grumlling

IV.1.   42 their white] F3; the white
           128 Food, food, food, food!] J. Dover Wilson, 1928;
                    Soud, soud, soud, soud.

IV.2.   13 none] me
             31 her] F3; them
             71 Take in] Take me
             73 farrer] this editor; farre
             78 Of Mantua? Sir,] Of *Mantua* Sir

IV.3.   177 account'st] accountedst

IV.4.   1 Sir] Sirs
             88 except] expect
             90 *imprimendum solum*] F2; *Impremendum solem*

IV.5.   18 it is] F2; it in
             38 Whither away, or where] F2; Whether away, or
                    whether
             41 Allots] F2; A lots

V.1.   5 master's] mistris
             27 Mantua] *Padua*
             47 master's] F2; Mistris
           135 No, sir] Mo sir

v.2. 2 done] come
     37 ha' to thee] F2; ha to the
     39 butt] But
     45 bitter jest or two] better iest or too
     62 two] too
     65 therefore for] F2; therefore sir
   75–6 That will I. Biondello | Go] this editor; That will I.
         | Goe *Biondello*
   127 a hundred] fiue hundred
   131 you're] your
   147 maintenance; commits] maintenance. Commits

4

The following list contains emendations of the Folio text
which have some measure of plausibility, but which have not
been adopted in this edition. The reading to the left of the
bracket is that of this edition; the reading to the right of it is
the unadopted emendation.

Ind. 1.   15 Breathe] (Brach F); Broach (J. Dover Wilson,
               1928)
      2. 135 comonty] commodity (J. Dover Wilson, 1928)
 1.1.   181 she] he
          202 meaner man] mean man
 1.2.   151 go to] go
          191 O sir] Sir
          206 to hear] to th'ear
          211 yours] ours
 II.1.   109 To my daughters, and tell them both] In to my
               daughters; tell them both from me
          141 shakes] shake F2
          168 I'll] I will
          201 such jade] such a jade
          337 have my Bianca's] have Bianca's F2

III.2.   16 Make feast, invite friends] (Make friends, inuite F);
Make friends invited

        127 But, sir, to love] (But sir, Loue F); But to her love

        165 rose up again] (rose againe F); arose again

        208 tomorrow – not till] (to morrow, not till F); tomor-
row, till

IV.1.   37 wilt thou] thou wilt F2

        56 This 'tis] This is

      106 at door] at the door

IV.5.   26 soft, company] soft, what company

        36 the woman] a woman F2

V.1.   27–8 and here] and is here

V.2.   105 of a wonder] of wonder

        147 maintenance; commits] maintenance commits

THE TAMING OF THE SHREW

The Characters in the Play

INDUCTION

CHRISTOPHER SLY, a drunken tinker
The Hostess of a country alehouse
A Lord
Page, Huntsmen, and Servants attending on the Lord
A company of strolling Players

THE TAMING OF THE SHREW

BAPTISTA MINOLA, a wealthy citizen of Padua

KATHERINA, the Shrew, elder daughter of Baptista
PETRUCHIO, a gentleman of Verona, suitor for the hand of
    Katherina
GRUMIO, Petruchio's personal lackey
CURTIS, Petruchio's servant, in charge of his country house
A Tailor
A Haberdasher
Five other servants of Petruchio

The Act and scene divisions are those of Peter Alexander's edition of the Complete Works, London, 1951. All references to other plays by Shakespeare not yet available in the New Penguin Shakespeare edition are to Alexander.
The Characters in the Play No list of the Characters is given in the Folio. An alternative way of arranging the characters in the play proper, so as to bring out the extent to which they fall into groups, would be to put the three old men (Baptista, Gremio, and Vincentio) together; then the three young men (Petruchio, Lucentio, and Hortensio); then the three young women (Katherina, Bianca, and the Widow); and finally, the rest, who are all servants and tradesmen, or, in the case of the Pedant, a sort of employee.

BIANCA, the Prize, younger daughter of Baptista

GREMIO, a wealthy old citizen of Padua, suitor for the hand of Bianca

HORTENSIO, a gentleman of Padua, suitor for the hand of Bianca

LUCENTIO, a gentleman of Pisa, in love with Bianca

TRANIO, Lucentio's servant and confidant

BIONDELLO, Lucentio's second servant

VINCENTIO, a wealthy citizen of Pisa, father of Lucentio

A Pedant of Mantua

A Widow, in love with Hortensio

Servant attending on Baptista

INDUCTION

Enter Christopher Sly and the Hostess

SLY I'll pheeze you, in faith.

HOSTESS A pair of stocks, you rogue!

SLY Y'are a baggage, the Slys are no rogues. Look in the

Induction The opening of this play is of peculiar interest, because in no other of his works does Shakespeare make use of an Induction (see Introduction, pages 9–10). The setting, it soon becomes plain, is outside an alehouse in the playwright's native Warwickshire, and then, for the second scene, in a large country house. Shakespeare is clearly drawing on direct personal experience in his depiction of country people and their activities. The tang and raciness of the altercation between Sly and the Hostess has the stamp of observed reality about it, making their brief but lively dialogue a fitting prelude to the fuller evocation of life in Elizabethan England that is to follow.

Although it is obviously a separate part of the play, the Induction is not distinguished from the rest of it in the Folio, where the text, like many others, is simply headed '*Actus primus. Scæna Prima.*'

1 (stage direction) *Enter Christopher Sly and the Hostess.* The Folio reads: '*Enter Begger and Hostes, Christophero Sly.*' Sly's speeches are consistently headed *Beg.*, and the Lord refers to him as 'the beggar' at line 39, though according to Sly himself he is in fact a tinker. The distinction between beggars and

tinkers was not a very sharp one, and both were proverbially noted for their fondness for ale. The name Christophero Sly in this initial direction is evidently an afterthought, derived from the text (Induction.2.5), and may well be an addition made by the prompter. The implications of the neutral word *Enter* are well brought out by the corresponding stage direction in *The Taming of a Shrew*, which reads: 'Enter a Tapster, beating out of his doores *Slie Droonken.*'

1 *pheeze you* settle your hash, fix you. Given in the *Oxford English Dictionary* under the commoner spelling *feeze*, this word originally meant 'to drive away or frighten off', but by Shakespeare's time it seems to have taken on an abusive connotation and to have become part of the language of the tavern. It occurs again in *Troilus and Cressida* (II.3.200), where Ajax says of Achilles: 'An 'a be proud with me I'll pheeze his pride', and, with a punning reference to 'vizier', in *The Merry Wives of Windsor* (1.3.10), where the Host calls Falstaff his 'Pheazar'.

3 *Y'are* you are (colloquial)
  baggage good-for-nothing woman, strumpet

Chronicles, we came in with Richard Conqueror. Therefore *paucas pallabris*, let the world slide. Sessa!

HOSTESS You will not pay for the glasses you have burst?

SLY No, not a denier. Go by, Saint Jeronimy, go to thy
cold bed and warm thee.

He lies on the ground

HOSTESS I know my remedy, I must go fetch the third-
10   borough.   *Exit*

---

4 *Richard Conqueror*. Sly's knowledge of
history, like his knowledge of hagi-
ology, is rather shaky. He has confused
Richard Coeur-de-Lion with William
the Conqueror. But his pretensions
to aristocratic descent, though intended primarily to impress the Hostess, also prepare the way for his assumption of a lordly role in the
second scene.

5 *paucas pallabris*. This phrase, which
was something of a cant term in
Shakespeare's England, is a corruption of the Spanish *pocas palabras* (few
words). Its use here may well be a
reminiscence of, or a jesting allusion
to, Thomas Kyd's *The Spanish
Tragedy* (III.14.118), where Hieronimo, the hero of the play, cau-
tions himself against revealing too
much of what he knows by saying:
'*Pocas Palabras*, mild as the Lamb.'

let the world slide let the world go by,
don't worry. The phrase, which was
a proverbial one, was recorded by
John Heywood in 1546 in the following form: 'To let the world wag, and
take mine ease in mine inn.' It sums
up Sly's general attitude to life very
well, and is substantially repeated by
him at Induction.2.141 when he tells
his 'wife' to 'let the world slip'.

Sessa! The precise meaning of this
exclamation, which is also used twice
by Edgar in *King Lear* (III.4.99 and

III.6.73), is uncertain. In all three
cases it appears to be an incitement
to haste, roughly equivalent to 'Off
you go!' or 'Be off with you!'

6 *burst* broken, smashed

7 *denier* pronounced to rhyme with
'many a'. It was a very small French
coin worth one twelfth of a sou.

Go by, Saint Jeronimy. Sly is misquoting from *The Spanish Tragedy*
(III.12.31), where Hieronimo warms
himself against over-hasty action by
saying, '*Hieronimo* beware; go by, go
by.' The words became a popular
catch-phrase. Kyd's editor comments: 'Perhaps no single passage in
Elizabethan drama became so notorious as this. It is quoted over and
over again as the stock phrase to
imply impatience of anything disagreeable, inconvenient, or old-fashioned' (*The Works of Thomas Kyd*, ed.
F. S. Boas, Oxford, 1901, p. 406).
Sly characteristically mixes Hieronimo up with Saint Jerome, as
well he might, since *The Spanish
Tragedy* seems to be his Bible.

7–8 *go to thy cold bed and warm thee*. Precisely these words, which may have
had some proverbial association with
beggars whose 'cold bed' frequently
was the ground, are used by Edgar,
disguised as Poor Tom, in *King Lear*
(III.4.47).

9–10 *thirdborough* petty constable of a

SLY Third, or fourth, or fifth borough, I'll answer him by
law. I'll not budge an inch, boy. Let him come, and
kindly.

>   *He falls asleep*
>   *Wind horns. Enter a Lord from hunting, with his
>   train*

LORD

Huntsman, I charge thee, tender well my hounds.
Breathe Merriman, the poor cur is embossed,
And couple Clowder with the deep-mouthed brach.
Saw'st thou not, boy, how Silver made it good
At the hedge corner, in the coldest fault?
I would not lose the dog for twenty pound.

FIRST HUNTSMAN

Why, Belman is as good as he, my lord.   20

---

township or manor. The Folio reads:
'Headborough' (another name for
the same officer), but Sly's rejoinder
demands the emendation.

11–12 *by law* with judicial proceedings,
in court. Sly is still trying to give the
impression that he is a man of
importance.

12 *budge an inch.* Sly is quibbling on the
literal sense of the phrase and on its
metaphorical sense of giving way on
a matter of principle.

boy servant, inferior (used here as a
term of abuse). Compare *Coriolanus*,
v.6.101–17.

12–13 *and kindly* naturally, of course, by
all means. Sly is being ironical.

13 (stage direction) *Wind horns.* This
command is intended, of course, for
those in charge of the effects in Shakespeare's theatre.

train retinue, followers

14 *tender well* take good care of

15 *Breathe Merriman* give Merriman a

breathing space. 'Breathe' is C. J.
Sisson's emendation of the Folio reading 'Brach' which does not make
very good sense. A 'brach' is a bitch-
hound, whereas Merriman looks like
the name of a dog-hound; the sentence requires a verb at this point to
go with 'couple' in the next line; and
the repetition of 'brach' at the end of
the sentence is ugly and unconvin-
cing. 'Breathing' would be the right
treatment for a hound that was dead
beat. Dover Wilson reads 'Broach',
meaning 'bleed'.

embossed foaming at the mouth (with
exhaustion)

16 *couple* leash together. The Elizabethans took their hounds to and
from the hunt in couples.

17 *made it good* put matters right (by
picking up the scent)

18 *in the coldest fault* at the point where
the scent was almost completely lost.
A 'fault' is a break in the scent.

He cried upon it at the merest loss,
And twice today picked out the dullest scent.
Trust me, I take him for the better dog.

LORD
Thou art a fool. If Echo were as fleet,
I would esteem him worth a dozen such.
But sup them well, and look unto them all.
Tomorrow I intend to hunt again.

FIRST HUNTSMAN
I will, my lord.

LORD
What's here? One dead, or drunk? See, doth he breathe?

SECOND HUNTSMAN
30   He breathes, my lord. Were he not warmed with ale,
This were a bed but cold to sleep so soundly.

LORD
O monstrous beast, how like a swine he lies!
Grim death, how foul and loathsome is thine image!
Sirs, I will practise on this drunken man.
What think you, if he were conveyed to bed,
Wrapped in sweet clothes, rings put upon his fingers,
A most delicious banquet by his bed,
And brave attendants near him when he wakes,
Would not the beggar then forget himself?

FIRST HUNTSMAN
40   Believe me, lord, I think he cannot choose.

SECOND HUNTSMAN
It would seem strange unto him when he waked.

---

21 *cried upon it at the merest loss* yelped
out on the right scent when it was
totally lost
26 *sup them well* give them a good
supper
look unto take care of
31 *a bed but cold* but a cold bed in which
33 *image* likeness. Sly, in his drunken

stupor, looks like a dead man.
34 *practise* play a trick
38 *brave* fine, handsomely dressed
39 *forget himself* lose consciousness of his
own identity
40 *he cannot choose* he must, he is bound
to
41 *strange* incredible, wonderful

LORD

Even as a flattering dream or worthless fancy.
Then take him up, and manage well the jest.
Carry him gently to my fairest chamber,
And hang it round with all my wanton pictures.
Balm his foul head in warm distillèd waters,
And burn sweet wood to make the lodging sweet.
Procure me music ready when he wakes,
To make a dulcet and a heavenly sound.
And if he chance to speak, be ready straight   50
And with a low submissive reverence
Say 'What is it your honour will command?'
Let one attend him with a silver basin
Full of rose-water and bestrewed with flowers,
Another bear the ewer, the third a diaper,
And say 'Will't please your lordship cool your hands?'
Some one be ready with a costly suit,
And ask him what apparel he will wear.
Another tell him of his hounds and horse,
And that his lady mourns at his disease.   60
Persuade him that he hath been lunatic,
And when he says he is Sly, say that he dreams,

46 *Balm* anoint, bathe
    distillèd waters (fragrant liquids, such
    as rose-water, made from flowers and
    herbs)
47 *burn sweet wood to make the lodging sweet.*
    It was a common Elizabethan prac-
    tice to burn sweet-scented wood,
    such as juniper, in a musty room.
    Compare *Much Ado About Nothing*,
    1.3.54–5 where Borachio says, 'as I
    was smoking a musty room'.
48 *Procure me music.* 'Me' is the dative,
    meaning 'for me'.
49 *dulcet* melodious
51 *reverence* bow, obeisance
55 *ewer* (pitcher with a wide spout, to
    bring water for washing the hands)
    diaper towel

60 *disease* disorder of the mind
62 *And when he says he is Sly, say that he
    dreams.* The Folio reads: 'And when
    he sayes he is, say that he dreames',
    which does not make very good
    sense, since there is no point in get-
    ting Sly to admit that he is mad and
    then telling him that he is merely
    dreaming. Dr Johnson's suggestion,
    that the word 'Sly' was omitted by
    the printer because of its similarity
    to the word 'say', has been adopted
    in this edition. It receives strong sup-
    port from Sly's reaction in the next
    scene (lines 16–19) to the statement
    that he is deranged: 'What, would
    you make me mad? Am not I Christo-
    pher Sly . . .?'

For he is nothing but a mighty lord.
This do, and do it kindly, gentle sirs.
It will be pastime passing excellent,
If it be husbanded with modesty.

FIRST HUNTSMAN
My lord, I warrant you we will play our part
As he shall think by our true diligence
He is no less than what we say he is.

LORD
70   Take him up gently and to bed with him,
And each one to his office when he wakes.

Sly is carried away

A trumpet sounds
Sirrah, go see what trumpet 'tis that sounds –

Exit Servingman

Belike some noble gentleman that means,
Travelling some journey, to repose him here.
Enter Servingman
How now? Who is it?

SERVINGMAN   An't please your honour, players
That offer service to your lordship.

---

64 *kindly* naturally, convincingly
  gentle kind
65 *passing* surpassingly, extremely
66 *husbanded with modesty* managed with
  moderation, not carried too far
68 *As* so that
  by as a result of
  true fitting, proper
70 *to bed with him* put him to bed
71 *to his office* go about his duty
  (stage direction) *Sly is carried away*.
  There is no direction for the removal
  of Sly in the Folio, but *The Taming of
  a Shrew* reads: 'Exeunt two with Slie.'
  (stage direction) *A trumpet sounds*.
  The Folio reads: 'Sound trumpets', but
  the following line shows that only

one is required.
75 *An't* if it
77–102 *Now, fellows, you are welcome ...
  nothing that my house affords.* This little
  episode shows the kind of reception
  that an acting company, on tour in
  the provinces, would hope for at a
  great house, even if they did not
  always receive it. It has the further
  interest of anticipating the similar
  but more extended scene (*Hamlet*,
  II.2.416–540), in which Hamlet welcomes the actors to Elsinore. Moreover, there are parallels between the
  Prince's views on acting (III.2.1–44)
  and the Lord's praise of a part that
  was 'naturally performed'.

LORD

Bid them come near.

Enter Players

Now, fellows, you are welcome.

PLAYERS

We thank your honour.

LORD

Do you intend to stay with me tonight?

FIRST PLAYER

So please your lordship to accept our duty.   80

LORD

With all my heart. This fellow I remember
Since once he played a farmer's eldest son.
'Twas where you wooed the gentlewoman so well.
I have forgot your name; but, sure, that part
Was aptly fitted and naturally performed.

FIRST PLAYER

I think 'twas Soto that your honour means.

80 *So please* if it so please. The Folio allots this speech to '2. *Player*', though there has been no mention of a First Player.

86 *I think 'twas Soto that your honour means.* The Folio assigns this speech to '*Sincklo*', and so provides the name of the actor for whom the part was written. John Sincklo or Sincler was a performer of minor roles in Shakespeare's company, and his name turns up on several other occasions. He is first mentioned as a member of the cast that played *The Second Part of the Seven Deadly Sins*, which was probably staged about 1591 and of which only the 'plot' or outline survives. His name appears again in the Folio text of *3 Henry VI* (III.1.1), where he plays a forester; then in the Quarto version of *2 Henry IV* (V.4.0), where he takes the part of the Beadle; and, finally, in the Induction to John

Marston's play *The Malcontent*, which was published in 1604. The remarks made about him by Doll Tearsheet and the Hostess in *2 Henry IV* suggest that he was abnormally thin. Doll calls him 'you thin man in a Censor', 'Goodman death, goodman Bones', and 'you thinne thing'; while the Hostess addresses him as 'you starv'd Blood-hound' and as 'Thou Anatomy, thou'. Other parts which may well have been written with Sincklo's peculiar appearance in mind are those of the Apothecary in *Romeo and Juliet*, Robert Faulconbridge in *King John*, and Starveling in *A Midsummer Night's Dream*. Since Shakespeare thought of the pantaloon as 'lean' (*As You Like It*, II.7.159), it seems likely that Sincklo took the part of Gremio in the main action of *The Taming of the Shrew*.

A character called Soto, who is a

LORD

'Tis very true, thou didst it excellent.

Well, you are come to me in happy time,

The rather for I have some sport in hand

90   Wherein your cunning can assist me much.

There is a lord will hear you play tonight;

But I am doubtful of your modesties,

Lest over-eyeing of his odd behaviour –

For yet his honour never heard a play –

You break into some merry passion

And so offend him, for I tell you, sirs,

If you should smile, he grows impatient.

FIRST PLAYER

Fear not, my lord, we can contain ourselves,

Were he the veriest antic in the world.

LORD

100   Go, sirrah, take them to the buttery,

And give them friendly welcome every one.

Let them want nothing that my house affords.

Exit one with the Players

farmer's son, appears in John Fletcher's play, *Women Pleased*. It is unlikely, however, that Shakespeare is alluding to this particular play here, since it dates from somewhere between 1619 and 1623 – almost thirty years after the composition of *The Taming of the Shrew*, and nearly twenty after the last recorded reference to Sincklo – and since his description of Soto's role does not tally with what happens in *Women Pleased*. Most modern critics are of the opinion that Fletcher's play, which is, for him, rather old-fashioned and not at all well constructed, is probably a revision of a much older play that is no longer extant, and that it is to the part of Soto in this lost play that Shakespeare is referring here. (See

G. E. Bentley, *The Jacobean and Caroline Stage*, volume III, Oxford, 1956, pages 431–2.)

88 *in happy time* just at the right time

89 *The rather for* the more so because

90 *cunning* art, professional skill

92 *doubtful of your modesties* unsure about your ability to control yourselves

93 *over-eyeing of* observing

95 *merry passion* irresistible burst of merriment. Compare 'idle merriment, | A passion hateful to my purposes' (*King John*, III.3.46–7).

97 *impatient* angry, annoyed

98 *contain* restrain

99 *the veriest antic* the most complete buffoon, the oddest and most fantastical fellow

102 *affords* has to offer

Sirrah, go you to Barthol'mew my page,
And see him dressed in all suits like a lady.
That done, conduct him to the drunkard's chamber,
And call him 'madam', do him obeisance.
Tell him from me – as he will win my love –
He bear himself with honourable action,
Such as he hath observed in noble ladies
Unto their lords, by them accomplishèd.   110
Such duty to the drunkard let him do,
With soft low tongue and lowly courtesy,
And say 'What is't your honour will command,
Wherein your lady and your humble wife
May show her duty and make known her love?'
And then with kind embracements, tempting kisses,
And with declining head into his bosom,
Bid him shed tears, as being overjoyed
To see her noble lord restored to health,
Who for this seven years hath esteemèd him   120
No better than a poor and loathsome beggar.
And if the boy have not a woman's gift
To rain a shower of commanded tears,
An onion will do well for such a shift,
Which in a napkin being close conveyed,
Shall in despite enforce a watery eye.

103–4 *Sirrah, go you to Barthol'mew my page . . . a lady.* The Lord is cleverly adapting the Elizabethan stage convention that all female parts were played by boys to the purposes of a practical joke in everyday life. The same trick becomes the central motif of an entire play in Ben Jonson's *The Silent Woman* (1609).
104 *in all suits* in all respects (with a pun on 'suits' in the sense of dress)
106 *do him obeisance* show him the respect due to a superior

108 *honourable action* decent behaviour befitting one of high rank
110 *accomplishèd* performed
112 *lowly courtesy* humble curtsy
117 *with declining head into his bosom* with his head drooping on his chest
120 *esteemèd him* thought himself
123 *commanded* forced, feigned
124 *for such a shift* as an expedient, to serve the turn
125 *close* secretly, covertly
126 *in despite* notwithstanding

See this dispatched with all the haste thou canst,
Anon I'll give thee more instructions.

Exit a Servingman

I know the boy will well usurp the grace,
130   Voice, gait, and action of a gentlewoman.
I long to hear him call the drunkard husband,
And how my men will stay themselves from laughter
When they do homage to this simple peasant.
I'll in to counsel them. Haply my presence
May well abate the over-merry spleen,
Which otherwise would grow into extremes.   *Exeunt*

2   *Enter aloft Sly, with attendants; some with apparel,*
         basin and ewer, and other appurtenances; and Lord

SLY For God's sake, a pot of small ale.

FIRST SERVINGMAN
    Will't please your lordship drink a cup of sack?

---

128 *Anon* soon, immediately afterwards
129 *usurp* counterfeit, assume
130 *action* bodily movements
133 *simple* mere
134 *I'll in* I'll go in. In Elizabethan English the verb of motion was frequently omitted after words implying purpose, such as 'will', 'shall', and 'must'.
Haply perhaps
135 *spleen* impulse to uncontrollable laughter. In Shakespeare's day the spleen was regarded as the seat of any sudden outburst of feeling, whether of mirth or of anger. Laughter and melancholy both came under its control.
136 *grow into extremes* become quite excessive, get out of hand
(stage direction) *Exeunt*. This direction, though it does not appear in the Folio, is clearly implied by the

Lord's remark 'I'll in' (line 134) and by the massed entry, in which he takes part, that follows. *The Taming of a Shrew*, at the corresponding point in its action, has '*Exeunt omnes*'.

2. This scene, in which Sly's attitude changes from one of complete incredulity to an assured assumption of the lordly role that has been thrust upon him, is not only one of the richest and subtlest pieces of comedy that Shakespeare ever wrote, but also one of the most important documents about the Elizabethan stage that we have. The stage direction with which it opens reads as follows in the Folio: '*Enter aloft the drunkard with attendants, some with apparel, Bason and Ewer, & other appurtenances, & Lord.*' The word 'aloft' clearly indicates that the entire scene was played on some kind of upper stage. Where and how

SECOND SERVINGMAN

Will't please your honour taste of these conserves?

THIRD SERVINGMAN

What raiment will your honour wear today?

SLY I am Christophero Sly, call not me 'honour' nor 'lord
ship'. I ne'er drank sack in my life. And if you give me
any conserves, give me conserves of beef. Ne'er ask me
what raiment I'll wear, for I have no more doublets than

was it done? There are 141 lines of dialogue; at least six characters – and probably more, since the Page is accompanied
by attendants when he enters as Sly's
wife – must be on the stage at the same
time; and somewhere, either on the stage
or just off it, there must be a bed or
some indication of one. It seems improbable that a scene of this length and complexity could have been properly or satisfactorily portrayed on the kind of upper
stage that is usually thought of as a
balustraded gallery, forming part of the
façade of the tiring-house. An audience
would surely have found difficulty in
sustaining its interest in a scene of this
length when separated from the actors
by railings and by the large expanse of
unoccupied main stage. An attractive solution to the problem is suggested by C.
Walter Hodges, who thinks that for extended scenes 'aloft', such as this, a temporary structure was employed, jutting
out from the façade of the tiring-house
and in front of the stage gallery. Consisting
essentially of a platform, raised about
seven feet above the floor of the main
stage, this acting area would have needed
nothing more than a single rail around it,
so that there would have been no real obstacle to vision, and it would have served
to bring the action well forward from the
rear wall of the theatre. Attempting to
visualize how this particular scene might
have been produced effectively, yet with a

minimum of properties and without taking up too much space, Mr Hodges writes:

'I will allow myself to imagine the
porch-like booth [the temporary struc-
ture] hung with its arras, standing between the two tiring-house doors [the
two large doors, one on either side of
the main stage at the rear of it, that
provided the chief means of access to it].
It backs up to the gallery floor, where,
behind closed curtains, Sly lies snoring.
A light stairway leads up one side, and
up this from below come the servants
with apparel, basin and ewer. They are
now standing on top of the porch-booth
in front of the curtain which represents
the bed. They draw the curtain. Sly
emerges. "For God's sake," he groans,
"a pot of small ale." And so it begins.'
C. Walter Hodges, *The Globe Restored*,
London, 1953, pages 64–5.
See also pages 56–64.

1 *small ale* (the weakest and therefore
  the cheapest form of the beverage)
2 *lordship*. This reading, essential both
  for sense and metre, comes from the
  Second Folio (1632). The First Folio
  reads: 'Lord'.
  sack (a general name for a class of
  white wines formerly imported from
  Spain and the Canaries)
3 *conserves* candied fruits
7 *conserves of beef* salt beef
8 *doublets* (close-fitting body-garments,

backs, no more stockings than legs, nor no more shoes
10   than feet – nay, sometimes more feet than shoes, or such
shoes as my toes look through the overleather.

LORD

Heaven cease this idle humour in your honour!
O, that a mighty man of such descent,
Of such possessions, and so high esteem,
Should be infusèd with so foul a spirit!

SLY What, would you make me mad? Am not I Christopher Sly, old Sly's son of Burton-heath, by birth a ped-
lar, by education a cardmaker, by transmutation a
bear-herd, and now by present profession a tinker? Ask
20   Marian Hacket, the fat ale-wife of Wincot, if she know
me not. If she say I am not fourteen pence on the score
for sheer ale, score me up for the lyingest knave in
Christendom.

with or without sleeves, worn by
men in Shakespeare's day)
11 *as* that
12 *idle humour* empty fancy, foolish aber-
ration of mind
15 *infusèd with so foul a spirit* inspired by
such mad ideas, filled with such dis-
eased notions
16–23 *Am not I . . . in Christendom.* This
passage is full of references to Warwickshire, and gives the impression
that Shakespeare is drawing on direct
personal experience.
17 *old Sly's son of Burton-heath* old Sly of
Burton-heath's son. Burton-heath has
been identified with Barton-on-the-
Heath, a village about sixteen miles
from Stratford, where Shakespeare's
aunt Joan Lambert lived.
18 *cardmaker* one who made cards – instruments with iron teeth, used for
combing out the fibres of wool by
hand. This occupation might well be
taken up by a boy living at Barton-

on-the-Heath on the edge of the Cotswolds, which were one of the chief
wool- and cloth-producing areas of
the country in Shakespeare's time.
19 *bear-herd* (man who led a performing
bear about the country)
20 *Marian Hacket, the fat ale-wife of
Wincot.* The woman referred to here
may well have been a real person,
since Sara, the daughter of Robert
Hacket, was baptized in Quinton
church on 21 November 1591. The
hamlet of Wincot, four miles south
of Stratford, lay partly in the parish
of Quinton and partly in that of
Clifford Chambers.
21 *on the score* in debt. The score was
originally an account kept by making
notches in a piece of wood; later
chalk marks were used for the
purpose.
22 *sheer ale* ale taken alone without solid
food to accompany it. Compare Hal's
remark about the bill found in Fal-

A Servingman brings him a pot of ale

What! I am not bestraught. Here's —

He drinks

THIRD SERVINGMAN

O, this it is that makes your lady mourn.

SECOND SERVINGMAN

O, this is it that makes your servants droop.

LORD

Hence comes it that your kindred shuns your house,
As beaten hence by your strange lunacy.
O noble lord, bethink thee of thy birth,
Call home thy ancient thoughts from banishment,   30
And banish hence these abject lowly dreams.
Look how thy servants do attend on thee,
Each in his office ready at thy beck.
Wilt thou have music? Hark, Apollo plays,

Music

And twenty cagèd nightingales do sing.
Or wilt thou sleep? We'll have thee to a couch

staff's pocket: 'O monstrous! but one halfpennyworth of bread to this intolerable deal of sack!' (*1 Henry IV*, II.4.522-3). *Score me up* chalk me up

22-3 *the lyingest knave in Christendom.* Humphrey, Duke of Gloucester, addresses the impostor Saunder Simpcox with precisely these words (*2 Henry VI*, II.1.125-6).

23 (stage direction) *A Servingman brings him a pot of ale*. This direction, like the *He drinks* that follows it, is not to be found in the Folio. It seems to be called for, however, for three reasons: first, Sly has asked for a pot of ale (line 1); secondly, he is going to demand a pot of ale 'once again' (line 74); and, thirdly, nothing is more likely to convince him that he

is 'not bestraught' than the appearance of what is to him the most important thing in life.

24 *bestraught* distracted, out of my mind
   Here's —. This sentence, had Sly ever finished it, might possibly have run 'Here's proof.'

26 *droop* feel despondent

28 *As beaten* as if driven, feeling themselves driven

29 *bethink thee of* remember, recollect

30 *ancient thoughts* former manner of thinking

33 *office* place of duty
   beck nod (or other mute signal, indicating a command)

34 *Apollo* (god of music and song in classical mythology)

Softer and sweeter than the lustful bed
On purpose trimmed up for Semiramis.
Say thou wilt walk; we will bestrew the ground.
40   Or wilt thou ride? Thy horses shall be trapped,
Their harness studded all with gold and pearl.
Dost thou love hawking? Thou hast hawks will soar
Above the morning lark. Or wilt thou hunt?
Thy hounds shall make the welkin answer them
And fetch shrill echoes from the hollow earth.

FIRST SERVINGMAN
Say thou wilt course, thy greyhounds are as swift
As breathèd stags, ay, fleeter than the roe.

SECOND SERVINGMAN
Dost thou love pictures? We will fetch thee straight

37 *lustful* provocative of lust
38 *trimmed up* luxuriously prepared
Semiramis (legendary queen of Assyria, proverbial for her voluptuousness and promiscuity)
39 *bestrew* scatter or cover (presumably with rushes)
40 *trapped* caparisoned, decked with an ornamented covering
41 *studded all with* adorned all over with studs of
44–5 *Thy hounds ... hollow earth.* The Elizabethans took much pleasure in the noise their hounds made, and went to some pains to ensure that the cry of the pack was a tunable one. Compare the dialogue between Theseus and Hippolyta (*A Midsummer Night's Dream*, IV.I.104–26).
44 *welkin* sky
46 *course* (the technical word for hunting the hare with greyhounds)
47 *breathèd* long-winded, strong of wind
48–59 *Dost thou love pictures ... are drawn.* The paintings described here are examples of the 'wanton pictures' referred to by the Lord in the previous scene (Induction.1.45). It is not easy to decide whether Shakespeare had

actual paintings in mind when he wrote this passage. The subjects, all of them mythological, were frequently handled by the Italian masters of the late Renaissance, such as Correggio and Giulio Romano, the only Italian artist Shakespeare ever mentions by name (*The Winter's Tale*, v.2.92–3). But there seem to have been very few Italian pictures in this country in the sixteenth century; and there is no reliable evidence that Shakespeare ever visited Italy. He may, of course, have heard something about Italian art from men who had been to that country; but the most likely explanation for the similarity between these descriptions and actual paintings is that the Italian painters, like Shakespeare himself, especially in his early work, were deeply influenced by Ovid. (For fuller discussion of the whole topic than is possible here, see A. Lytton Sells, *The Italian influence in English Poetry*, London, 1955, pages 188–209; and Mario Praz, *The Flaming Heart*, New York, 1958, pages 162–4.)

Adonis painted by a running brook,
And Cytherea all in sedges hid,   50
Which seem to move and wanton with her breath   .
Even as the waving sedges play wi'th'wind.

LORD

We'll show thee Io as she was a maid,
And how she was beguilèd and surprised,
'   As lively painted as the deed was done.

THIRD SERVINGMAN

Or Daphne roaming through a thorny wood,

49–50 *Adonis . . . And Cytherea.* According to Ovid (*Metamorphoses*, x.520–739) Cytherea, more commonly known as Venus the goddess of love, became enamoured of Adonis, a youth who returned her love. Ultimately, however, Adonis, who was even fonder of hunting than he was of Venus, was killed by a boar. Finding his body, Venus changed his blood into a flower – the anemone. Both in this passage and in his elaborate poem on the subject, *Venus and Adonis*, published in 1593, Shakespeare depicts a reluctant and uncooperative Adonis, pursued by a demanding and exigent Venus. His version of the story here was probably influenced by Spenser, who, in *The Faerie Queene* (III.I.34–8), describes a tapestry portraying it in which Venus watches Adonis bathing,

And whilst he bath'd, with her two crafty spies,
She secretly would search each dainty limb.

Indeed, Spenser's imagined tapestry may well be the 'picture' Shakespeare was thinking of.

51 *wanton* behave in an amorous fashion

52 *wi'th'* with the (abbreviated colloquial form)

53 *Io.* Ovid relates (*Metamorphoses*, i.588–600) how Jupiter saw Io, the daughter of the river-god Inachus, and fell in love with her. Io fled from him, but Jupiter pursued her, and raped her under cover of a dense mist, which he created in order to hide his activities from the eyes of Juno.

55 *As lively painted as the deed was done.* Whenever Shakespeare describes a work of art it is verisimilitude that he looks for and praises. Compare lines 49–52 and lines 56–9. Similar views, all stemming probably from the Renaissance commonplace that· poetry was a speaking picture and painting a dumb poem, are to be found in *The Rape of Lucrece* (1371–1442), *Timon of Athens* (I.1.33–41), *Cymbeline* (II.4.68–85), and *The Winter's Tale* (v.2.92–9).

56 *Daphne.* As Ovid tells the story (*Metamorphoses*, i. 452–567), Daphne was the daughter of the river-god Peneus. Cupid, in order to demonstrate his power to the scornful Apollo, caused the god to fall in love with her, but filled her with an aversion for him. As a result, when Apollo wooed her she fled from him, and, as he was about to overtake her, she prayed to

Scratching her legs that one shall swear she bleeds,
And at that sight shall sad Apollo weep,
So workmanly the blood and tears are drawn.

LORD

60   Thou art a lord, and nothing but a lord.
Thou hast a lady far more beautiful
Than any woman in this waning age.

FIRST SERVINGMAN

And till the tears that she hath shed for thee
Like envious floods o'errun her lovely face,
She was the fairest creature in the world –
And yet she is inferior to none.

SLY

Am I a lord and have I such a lady?
Or do I dream? Or have I dreamed till now?
I do not sleep. I see, I hear, I speak.
70   I smell sweet savours and I feel soft things.
Upon my life, I am a lord indeed,
And not a tinker nor Christophero Sly.
Well, bring our lady hither to our sight,
And once again a pot o'th'smallest ale.

SECOND SERVINGMAN

Will't please your mightiness to wash your hands?
O, how we joy to see your wit restored!

---

her father for help. Thereupon she was changed into a laurel.

57 *that one shall swear* so that one must swear, so that one is forced to swear

59 *So workmanly* with such art, so skilfully

62 *this waning age.* The belief that the whole history of man had been a steady degeneration from the state of physical and intellectual perfection that had existed in the Garden of Eden was widely held in the sixteenth and seventeenth centuries. See Spenser, *The Faerie Queene*, v. Proem. 1–9.

64 *o'errun* ran over, flowed over. 'Run' as the form of the past tense is fairly common in Shakespeare's work. Compare:

*The expedition of my violent love
Outrun the pauser reason.*
          Macbeth, II.3.107–8

66 *yet* nevertheless, still, even so
72 *Christophero.* This is the reading of the Second Folio. The First has 'Christopher', which is unmetrical.
76 *wit* understanding, mental faculties
77 *knew but* only knew

O, that once more you knew but what you are!
These fifteen years you have been in a dream,
Or when you waked, so waked as if you slept.

SLY

These fifteen years! By my fay, a goodly nap.   80
But did I never speak of all that time?

FIRST SERVINGMAN

O, yes, my lord, but very idle words,
For though you lay here in this goodly chamber,
Yet would you say ye were beaten out of door,
And rail upon the hostess of the house,
And say you would present her at the leet,
Because she brought stone jugs and no sealed quarts.
Sometimes you would call out for Cicely Hacket.

SLY

Ay, the woman's maid of the house.

THIRD SERVINGMAN

Why, sir, you know no house, nor no such maid,   90
Nor no such men as you have reckoned up,
As Stephen Sly, and old John Naps of Greece,
And Peter Turph, and Henry Pimpernell,

---

80 *By my fay* by my faith
   goodly considerable
81 *of all that time* in all that time
82 *idle* meaningless, empty, silly
83 *goodly* fine, well-proportioned
84 *beaten out of door* driven out of the
   house
86 *present her at the leet* bring her up for
   trial before the manorial court. The
   leet was the equivalent of the modern
   Police Court.
87 *sealed quarts* quart measures officially
   stamped to show that they held the
   correct quantity. Sly is suggesting,
   of course, that the 'stone jugs' are a
   swindle, because they hold less than
   they are supposed to.
88 *Cicely Hacket*. Compare note to Induction. 2.20.

89 *the woman's maid of the house* the mistress of the house's maid, the land-
   lady's maid
   house inn, tavern
91 *reckoned up* mentioned, enumerated
92–3 *Stephen Sly ... John Naps ... Peter
   Turph ... Henry Pimpernell*. These
   could well be the names of real
   people. A Stephen Sly was living at
   Stratford in January 1615. (See E.
   K. Chambers, *William Shakespeare*,
   Oxford, 1930, volume II, p. 144.)
92 *Greece*. It has been suggested that this
   is a misreading of Greet, a hamlet
   not far from Stratford, but there
   were Greeks in England in the sixteenth century, and 'John Naps'
   might be the English version of a
   Greek name.

And twenty more such names and men as these,
Which never were nor no man ever saw.

SLY

Now Lord be thankèd for my good amends.

ALL Amen.

> *Enter Page as a lady, with attendants. One gives Sly a*
> *pot of ale*

SLY I thank thee, thou shalt not lose by it.

PAGE How fares my noble lord?

100 SLY Marry, I fare well, for here is cheer enough.

> *He drinks*

Where is my wife?

PAGE

Here, noble lord, what is thy will with her?

SLY

Are you my wife, and will not call me husband?
My men should call me 'lord', I am your goodman.

PAGE

My husband and my lord, my lord and husband,
I am your wife in all obedience.

SLY I know it well. What must I call her?

LORD Madam.

SLY Al'ce madam, or Joan madam?

LORD

110 Madam and nothing else, so lords call ladies.

---

95 *nor no man* nor any man. Shakespeare frequently uses the double negative for the sake of emphasis.

96 *amends* recovery, improvement in health

97 (stage direction) *One gives Sly a pot of ale*. This direction, which does not appear in the Folio, is called for because Sly has asked for 'a pot o'th'-smallest ale' some twenty lines earlier, and he now thanks one of the servants.

99–100 *How fares . . . I fare well.* There is a quibble here. The Page enquires about Sly's state of health, and Sly replies that he is well supplied with 'fare' in the sense of drink.

100 *Marry.* Derived originally from the name of the Virgin Mary, used as an oath or asseveration, this exclamation meant no more in Shakespeare's day than 'why, to be sure'.

104 *goodman* husband

SLY

    Madam wife, they say that I have dreamed
    And slept above some fifteen year or more.

PAGE

    Ay, and the time seems thirty unto me,
    Being all this time abandoned from your bed.

SLY

    'Tis much. Servants, leave me and her alone.

                    Exeunt Lord and Servingmen
    Madam, undress you and come now to bed.

PAGE

    Thrice-noble lord, let me entreat of you
    To pardon me yet for a night or two,
    Or, if not so, until the sun be set.
    For your physicians have expressly charged,   120
    In peril to incur your former malady,
    That I should yet absent me from your bed.
    I hope this reason stands for my excuse.

SLY Ay, it stands so that I may hardly tarry so long. But I
    would be loath to fall into my dreams again. I will there-
    fore tarry in despite of the flesh and the blood.

        Enter the Lord as a Messenger

---

114 *abandoned* banished

115 (stage direction) *Exeunt Lord and Servingmen.* The Folio provides no direction here, but, as Dover Wilson points out, one is required, because Sly has just expressed his desire to be left alone with his 'wife', and because the upper stage must be cleared of all except the three 'Presenters' · before the play proper can begin.

121 *In peril to incur* on peril of your incurring

123 *stands for* is valid as, can be accepted as

124 *it stands* (a bawdy quibble alluding to the erection of the male organ) *tarry* wait, stay

126 *the flesh and the blood* sexual desire

(stage direction) *Enter the Lord as a Messenger.* The Folio reads: '*Enter a Messenger*'. In this edition the role of the Messenger has been assigned to the Lord for the following reasons: first, the Lord has had the play put on in order to enjoy Sly's reactions to it, and must, therefore, be in a position where he can best observe them; secondly, in *The Taming of a Shrew* it is the Lord who announces the play to Sly in the following words, which are very close to the Messenger's first two lines:

May it please you, your honour's players
    be come
To offer your honour a play,

LORD
Your honour's players, hearing your amendment,
Are come to play a pleasant comedy;
For so your doctors hold it very meet,
130 Seeing too much sadness hath congealed your blood,
And melancholy is the nurse of frenzy.
Therefore they thought it good you hear a play
And frame your mind to mirth and merriment,
Which bars a thousand harms and lengthens life.
SLY Marry, I will. Let them play it. Is not a comonty a
Christmas gambold or a tumbling-trick?
PAGE
No, my good lord, it is more pleasing stuff.
SLY What, household stuff?
PAGE It is a kind of history.
140 SLY Well, we'll see't. Come, madam wife, sit by my side
and let the world slip, we shall ne'er be younger.
They sit

and he remains on the upper stage
until the play is almost done; thirdly,
if the Lord is with Sly and the Page,
the reference to 'The Presenters
above', in the stage direction at
1.1.245 makes much better sense than
it does if he is not; and, finally, who
but the Lord could appear on the
upper stage, and, in his role as
servant to Sly, give the necessary
parallel to the Lucentio – Tranio relationship?

128 *pleasant* merry
129 *For so* because
    meet suitable, fitting, right
130–31 *Seeing too much sadness ... frenzy.*
    For the general attitude to the rela-
    tionship between physical and psy-
    chological states compare *King John*,
    III.3.42–4:

    Or if that surly spirit, melancholy,
    Had bak'd thy blood and made it heavy-

    thick,
    Which else runs tickling up and down the
    veins ...

131 *nurse* nourisher
134 *bars* prevents
135 *Marry, I will. Let them play it. Is not*
    a comonty ...? The Folio reads:
    'Marrie I will let them play, it is not
    a Comontie', which does not make
    satisfactory sense, since 'comonty'
    must be Sly's blunder for 'comedy'.
136 *gambold* frolic, caper
137 *stuff* matter, material (in its literary
    sense)
138 *household stuff* furnishings. Sly, in his
    drunken state, has taken the word
    'stuff' in its most literal sense.
139 *history* story, narrative
141 (stage direction) *They sit.* This does
    not appear in the Folio, though
    clearly demanded by the dialogue.

A flourish of trumpets to announce the play

Enter Lucentio and his man Tranio   I.I

LUCENTIO

Tranio, since for the great desire I had
To see fair Padua, nursery of arts,
I am arrived for fruitful Lombardy,
The pleasant garden of great Italy,
And by my father's love and leave am armed
With his good will and thy good company,
My trusty servant well approved in all,
Here let us breathe and haply institute
A course of learning and ingenious studies.
Pisa renowned for grave citizens   10
Gave me my being and my father first,
A merchant of great traffic through the world,

(stage direction) *A flourish of trumpets to announce the play*. The Folio reads simply: '*Flourish*', and places this direction at the head of what is, in modern editions, I.I.

I.I The opening of this scene is a rather primitive piece of exposition, of the kind that Sheridan guyed so well in *The Critic*. Lucentio tells Tranio many things that Tranio should know already, for the benefit of the audience, who need to know where the scene is and what the two characters are doing there. The scene comes to full dramatic life only with the entrance of Baptista, his daughters, and their suitors. At this point the purveying of information is replaced by action.
(stage direction) *Tranio*. This name appears in Plautus's *Mostellaria*, the character who has it being a wily townsman. It is quite possible that it

was associated in Shakespeare's mind with the word 'train', meaning 'deceit' or 'trickery'.
1 *for* because of, owing to
2 *fair Padua, nursery of arts*. Shakespeare knew what he was writing about. The university of Padua, founded in 1228, was one of the oldest in Europe, and was still in the sixteenth century the main centre for the diffusion of Aristotelian teaching.
3 *I am arrived for* I have arrived in. In Shakespeare's time 'be' as well as 'have' was commonly used to form the past tense of verbs of motion.
8 *breathe* live, settle down *haply institute* auspiciously begin
9 *ingenious studies* intellectual studies, liberal studies
11 *Gave me . . . first* first gave me
12 *of great traffic through* with much business throughout

Vincentio come of the Bentivolii.
Vincentio's son, brought up in Florence,
It shall become to serve all hopes conceived
To deck his fortune with his virtuous deeds.
And therefore, Tranio, for the time I study
Virtue, and that part of philosophy
Will I apply that treats of happiness
20   By virtue specially to be achieved.
Tell me thy mind, for I have Pisa left
And am to Padua come as he that leaves
A shallow plash to plunge him in the deep,
And with satiety seeks to quench his thirst.

TRANIO

Mi perdonato, gentle master mine.
I am in all affected as yourself,
Glad that you thus continue your resolve
To suck the sweets of sweet philosophy.
Only, good master, while we do admire
30   This virtue and this moral discipline,
Let's be no stoics nor no stocks, I pray,
Or so devote to Aristotle's checks
As Ovid be an outcast quite abjured.

---

13   *come of* descended from
14–16 *Vincentio's son, brought up in Flor-
ence,* | *It shall become to serve all hopes
conceived* | *To deck his fortune with his
virtuous deeds.* The sense of this rather
stilted and Latinate sentence is: 'It is
right that Vincentio's son, brought
up in Florence, should fulfil the
hopes men have of him by adorning
his prosperity with virtuous deeds.'
17   *for the time* at present
17–18 *study* | *Virtue,.* The Folio reads:
'studie, | Vertue'. The change in the
position of the comma makes the
statement much more pointed.
19   *apply* pursue, devote myself to
treats of deals with
19–20 *happiness* | *By virtue specially to be*

achieved. The idea of achieving happiness through virtuous action is central to Aristotle's *Ethics.*
23   *plash* pool, puddle
25   *Mi perdonato* excuse me (Italian)
26   *in all affected as* in entire agreement
with
29   *admire* regard with reverence
31   *stoics* rigorists, people who despise
pleasure; *stocks* senseless unfeeling
people. There is a quibble on the
two words.
32   *devote* devoted, addicted
checks restraints, counsels of moderation
33   *As* that
Ovid (Latin poet who lived from 43
B.C. to about A.D. 17. In his *Ars*

Balk logic with acquaintance that you have,
And practise rhetoric in your common talk,
Music and poesy use to quicken you,
The mathematics and the metaphysics
Fall to them as you find your stomach serves you.
No profit grows where is no pleasure ta'en.
In brief, sir, study what you most affect.   40

LUCENTIO
Gramercies, Tranio, well dost thou advise.
If, Biondello, thou wert come ashore,
We could at once put us in readiness,
And take a lodging fit to entertain
Such friends as time in Padua shall beget.

*Enter Baptista with his two daughters Katherina and
Bianca; Gremio, a pantaloon, and Hortensio, suitor to
Bianca. Lucentio and Tranio stand by*

But stay awhile, what company is this?

Amatoria Ovid calls himself *praeceptor amoris*, the Professor of Love,
and it is in this capacity that Tranio
cites him here.)

34 *Balk logic* chop logic
acquaintance acquaintances, friends

35 *common talk* ordinary conversation

38 *to quicken you* to refresh yourself, as
recreation

38 *Fall to them as you find your stomach
serves you* take them up when you feel
so inclined. *Fall to* means literally
'begin eating', and [*when*] *your stomach
serves you* 'when you have an appetite'.
The metaphors indicate the practical
bent of Tranio's mind.

39 *No profit grows where is no pleasure
ta'en*. These words are an adaptation
of Horace's celebrated comment,
which was the foundation of Renaissance aesthetics: *Omne tulit punctum
qui miscuit utile dulci* – the most successful artist is the man who has

contrived to mix the pleasurable with
the instructive (*Ars Poetica*, 343).
ta'en taken (colloquial)

40 *affect* love, enjoy

41 *Gramercies* many thanks (Old French
grant merci)

45 (stage direction) *Katherina*. This name
appears under the forms *Katerina,
Katherina, Katherine*, and, of course,
Kate in the Folio.
(stage direction) *a pantaloon*. The pantaloon (*pantalone* in Italian) was a
stock figure, and indeed the central
figure, in the Italian *Commedia
dell'arte* (Comedy of skill). He was
always portrayed as an old man, a
Venetian by origin and dialect, and
invariably appeared clad in tights, a
red jacket, a long black sleeved
gown, and black slippers. His main
role was to serve as an obstacle to
the lovers. (For a full discussion of
the character and the part see Al-

TRANIO

Master, some show to welcome us to town.

BAPTISTA

Gentlemen, importune me no farther,
For how I firmly am resolved you know;
That is, not to bestow my youngest daughter
Before I have a husband for the elder.
If either of you both love Katherina,
Because I know you well and love you well,
Leave shall you have to court her at your pleasure.

GREMIO

To cart her rather. She's too rough for me.
There, there, Hortensio, will you any wife?

KATHERINA (to Baptista)

I pray you, sir, is it your will
To make a stale of me amongst these mates?

HORTENSIO

Mates, maid, how mean you that? No mates for you
Unless you were of gentler, milder mould.

KATHERINA

I'faith, sir, you shall never need to fear.
Iwis it is not halfway to her heart.
But if it were, doubt not her care should be

lardyce Nicoll, *The World of Harlequin*, Cambridge, 1963, pages 44–55.)
Gremio is explicitly referred to as
'the old pantaloon' by Lucentio at
III.1.36.
47 *show* play, spectacle, pageant
50 *bestow* give in marriage
55 *To cart her.* 'Carting' – undergoing a
whipping while being drawn
through the streets either in, or at
the tail of, an open cart – was the
punishment inflicted on bawds and
whores. There is, of course, a quibble
on 'court' in the previous line.
rough bad-tempered

56 *will you* do you want
58 *a stale of me amongst these mates* a
laughing-stock of me among these
contemptible fellows (with a quibble
on *stale* meaning 'harlot')
59 *Mates . . . No mates* (1) contemptible
fellows; (2) husbands
60 *mould* frame, nature
62 *Iwis it is not halfway to her heart* certainly marriage (with you) is not a
matter that she takes even half
seriously
63 *doubt not her care should be* be sure she
would take care

To comb your noddle with a three-legged stool,
And paint your face, and use you like a fool.

HORTENSIO
From all such devils, good Lord deliver us!

GREMIO
And me too, good Lord!

TRANIO (*aside to Lucentio*)
Husht, master, here's some good pastime toward.
That wench is stark mad or wonderful froward.

LUCENTIO (*aside to Tranio*)
But in the other's silence do I see   70
Maid's mild behaviour and sobriety.
Peace, Tranio.

TRANIO (*aside to Lucentio*)
Well said, master. Mum! And gaze your fill.

BAPTISTA
Gentlemen, that I may soon make good
What I have said – Bianca, get you in.
And let it not displease thee, good Bianca,
For I will love thee ne'er the less, my girl.

KATHERINA
A pretty peat! It is best
Put finger in the eye, an she knew why.

---

64 *comb your noddle* give you a dressing, beat you about the head
65 *paint your face* scratch your face till it bleeds. In *The Taming of a Shrew* (scene v, line 24) Katherina threatens to set her 'ten commandments' (finger-nails) in Ferando's face.
use treat
68 *Husht* be quiet, not a word
toward on hand, about to begin
69 *wonderful froward* incredibly disobedient, perverse
73 *Mum!* keep quiet!

74 *make good* perform, carry out
78–9 *It is best | Put finger in the eye, an she knew why* the best thing she can do is to make herself weep, if she knew of some excuse. 'To put finger in the eye and weep' was a proverbial expression. Shakespeare uses it again in *The Comedy of Errors*, where Adriana says:

Come, come, no longer will I be a fool,
To put the finger in the eye and weep.
                                    II.2.202–3

BIANCA

80   Sister, content you in my discontent.
        Sir, to your pleasure humbly I subscribe.
        My books and instruments shall be my company,
        On them to look and practise by myself.

LUCENTIO (*aside*)
        Hark, Tranio, thou mayst hear Minerva speak.

HORTENSIO
        Signor Baptista, will you be so strange?
        Sorry am I that our good will effects
        Bianca's grief.

GREMIO   Why will you mew her up,
        Signor Baptista, for this fiend of hell,
        And make her bear the penance of her tongue?

BAPTISTA

90   Gentlemen, content ye. I am resolved.
        Go in, Bianca.   *Exit Bianca*
        And for I know she taketh most delight
        In music, instruments, and poetry,
        Schoolmasters will I keep within my house
        Fit to instruct her youth. If you, Hortensio,
        Or Signor Gremio, you, know any such,
        Prefer them hither; for to cunning men
        I will be very kind, and liberal
        To mine own children in good bringing-up.

100   And so farewell. Katherina, you may stay,
        For I have more to commune with Bianca.   *Exit*

---

80 *content you in my discontent* take pleas-
    ure in my sorrow
81 *pleasure* will, command
    subscribe submit
82 *instruments* musical instruments
84 *Minerva* (the goddess of wisdom)
85 *strange* distant, unfriendly
86 *effects* causes

87 *mew her up* shut her up, confine her
88 *for* on account of
90 *content ye* compose yourselves, be
    satisfied
92 *for* because
97 *Prefer* direct, recommend
    cunning well qualified, skilful

KATHERINA
Why, and I trust I may go too, may I not?
What, shall I be appointed hours, as though, belike,
I knew not what to take and what to leave? Ha?   *Exit*

GREMIO You may go to the devil's dam. Your gifts are so
good here's none will hold you. There! Love is not so
great, Hortensio, but we may blow our nails together,
and fast it fairly out. Our cake's dough on both sides.
Farewell. Yet, for the love I bear my sweet Bianca, if I
can by any means light on a fit man to teach her that   110
wherein she delights, I will wish him to her father.

HORTENSIO So will I, Signor Gremio. But a word, I
pray. Though the nature of our quarrel yet never
brooked parle, know now, upon advice, it toucheth us
both — that we may yet again have access to our fair
mistress and be happy rivals in Bianca's love — to
labour and effect one thing specially.

GREMIO What's that, I pray?

HORTENSIO Marry, sir, to get a husband for her sister.

103 *be appointed hours* be given a time-table
105 *the devil's dam* the devil's mother (proverbially thought of as worse than the devil himself and as the archetype of shrews)
gifts endowments, natural qualities
106 *hold* retain, keep *There! Love.* The Folio reads: 'Their loue', which could mean 'the love of women', but confusion of 'their' and 'there' is common in early texts of the plays, and Gremio is fond of 'There' as an exclamation (compare line 56).
106–8 *Love is not so great ... but we may blow our nails together, and fast it fairly out.* The general sense of this passage is: 'Our rivalry over Bianca is not so important that we can't remain on friendly terms while we wait for

things to improve.'
107 *but* but that
blow our nails wait patiently
108 *fast it fairly out* pass our period of abstention from love in a friendly manner
Our cake's dough on both sides our efforts have ended in failure for both of us. 'My cake is dough' was a proverbial way of announcing failure. Gremio uses the phrase again at V.I.128.
110 *light on* find, come across
111 *wish him* commend him, invite him to offer service
113–14 *yet never brooked parle* never yet allowed of negotiations between us
114 *upon advice* on careful reflection
it toucheth it concerns, it is a matter of importance to
117 *labour and effect* strive to carry out

120   GREMIO A husband? A devil.

HORTENSIO I say a husband.

GREMIO I say a devil. Think'st thou, Hortensio, though
her father be very rich, any man is so very a fool to be
married to hell?

HORTENSIO Tush, Gremio. Though it pass your patience
and mine to endure her loud alarums, why, man, there be
good fellows in the world, an a man could light on them,
would take her with all faults, and money enough.

GREMIO I cannot tell. But I had as lief take her dowry
130   with this condition – to be whipped at the high-cross
every morning.

HORTENSIO Faith, as you say, there's small choice in
rotten apples. But come, since this bar in law makes us
friends, it shall be so far forth friendly maintained till by
helping Baptista's eldest daughter to a husband we set
his youngest free for a husband, and then have to't
afresh. Sweet Bianca! Happy man be his dole. He that
runs fastest gets the ring. How say you, Signor Gremio?

GREMIO I am agreed, and would I had given him the best

123 *so very a fool to* such an absolute fool
as to
125 *pass* exceed, go beyond
127 *good fellows* rogues, needy adventurers. Compare Introduction, page 24.
an if, provided that
129 *I cannot tell* I don't know what to
say
as lief as soon, as readily
130 *high-cross* (market-cross in the centre
of a town)
133 *bar in law* legal impediment (Baptista's refusal to allow them to court
Bianca)
134 *it shall be so far forth friendly maintained till* our agreement shall be kept
up in a friendly manner until
136–7 *have to't afresh* let us renew our
rivalry, to battle again
137 *Happy man be his dole* may the best

man win. This proverbial expression
for wishing someone good luck
means, literally, 'may his lot be that
of a happy man'.
137–8 *He that runs fastest gets the ring.*
This proverb is given by John Heywood in 1546 under the following
form: 'Where wooers hop in and
out, long time may bring | Him that
hoppeth best, at last to have the ring
[wedding-ring].' Shakespeare seems
to have given the old saying an original twist here by relating it to the
jousting-game in which each of a
number of riders attempted to carry
off on the point of his lance a circlet
of metal suspended from a post.
139 *would I* I wish that I. Gremio is
continuing with the metaphor of 'running at the ring'.

horse in Padua to begin his wooing that would thor-   140
oughly woo her, wed her, and bed her, and rid the house
of her. Come on.   *Exeunt Gremio and Hortensio*

TRANIO

I pray, sir, tell me, is it possible
That love should of a sudden take such hold?

LUCENTIO

O Tranio, till I found it to be true,
I never thought it possible or likely.
But see, while idly I stood looking on,
I found the effect of love in idleness,
And now in plainness do confess to thee,
That art to me as secret and as dear   150
As Anna to the Queen of Carthage was –
Tranio, I burn, I pine, I perish, Tranio,
If I achieve not this young modest girl.
Counsel me, Tranio, for I know thou canst.
Assist me, Tranio, for I know thou wilt.

TRANIO

Master, it is no time to chide you now;
Affection is not rated from the heart.

141 *woo her, wed her, and bed her.* This is
another proverb, very common in
the sixteenth century, describing the
progress of a love affair from the
wooing to the consummation.
rid free. Gremio has added a bit of
his own to the original proverb.

144 *take such hold* take such firm root,
gain such a hold of a man

148 *love in idleness.* Lucentio is playing
with two ideas: (1) the proverb, 'Idleness begets lust'; (2) 'Love-in-idle-
ness' as another name for the pansy,
or Heartsease, as it was called. Compare Oberon's description of it as 'a
little western flower' (*A Midsummer
Night's Dream*, II.1.166–8).

149 *plainness* frankness

150 *as secret* as intimate, as much in my
confidence

151 *As Anna to the Queen of Carthage
was.* In Virgil's *Aeneid* (IV.8–30)
Dido, Queen of Carthage, confides
to her sister Anna that she has fallen
in love with her guest Aeneas. The
scene between the two sisters had
been dramatized by Christopher Marlowe in his play *The Tragedy of Dido,
Queen of Carthage* (III.1.55–78), published in 1594.

153 *achieve* win

157 *Affection is not rated from the heart*
it's no use trying to expel love from
the heart by scolding it

158 *naught remains but so* there's nothing
left to be done but this

If love have touched you, naught remains but so —
Redime te captum quam queas minimo.

LUCENTIO

160   Gramercies, lad. Go forward, this contents.
The rest will comfort, for thy counsel's sound.

TRANIO

Master, you looked so longly on the maid,
Perhaps you marked not what's the pith of all.

LUCENTIO

O yes, I saw sweet beauty in her face,
Such as the daughter of Agenor had,
That made great Jove to humble him to her hand,
When with his knees he kissed the Cretan strand.

TRANIO

Saw you no more? Marked you not how her sister
Began to scold and raise up such a storm
170   That mortal ears might hardly endure the din?

LUCENTIO

Tranio, I saw her coral lips to move,
And with her breath she did perfume the air.
Sacred and sweet was all I saw in her.

TRANIO

Nay, then 'tis time to stir him from his trance.
I pray, awake, sir. If you love the maid,

159 *Redime te captum quam queas minimo*
free yourself from captivity at the
lowest ransom you can. Shakespeare
took this line from Lily's *Latin Grammar* and not from the original source,
Terence's *Eunuchus* (1.1.30), where it
appears under a slightly different
form.
160 *Go forward, this contents* carry on,
this is the right sort of advice
162 *longly* persistently
163 *marked* noticed
    the pith of all the central issue, the
    main point of it all
165 *the daughter of Agenor* Europa. Ac-

cording to Ovid (*Metamorphoses*, ii,
846–75), Jupiter fell in love with her,
and, in order to win her, appeared to
her as a snow-white bull. He knelt
before her, and behaved so gently
that eventually she mounted on his
back. He promptly rose, rushed into
the sea, and carried her off from
Tyre, where her father was king, to
Crete.
167 *Cretan strand* shore of Crete. It looks
as though Shakespeare thought
Europa had been carried off *from*
Crete, instead of to it.

Bend thoughts and wits to achieve her. Thus it stands:
Her elder sister is so curst and shrewd
That till the father rid his hands of her,
Master, your love must live a maid at home,
And therefore has he closely mewed her up,   180
Because she will not be annoyed with suitors.

LUCENTIO
Ah, Tranio, what a cruel father's he!
But art thou not advised he took some care
To get her cunning schoolmasters to instruct her?

TRANIO
Ay, marry, am I, sir – and now 'tis plotted.

LUCENTIO
I have it, Tranio.

TRANIO   Master, for my hand,
Both our inventions meet and jump in one.

LUCENTIO
Tell me thine first.

TRANIO   You will be schoolmaster,
And undertake the teaching of the maid –
That's your device.

LUCENTIO   It is. May it be done?   190

TRANIO
Not possible. For who shall bear your part
And be in Padua here Vincentio's son,
Keep house and ply his book, welcome his friends,
Visit his countrymen and banquet them?

---

176 *Bend* apply, strain (as in bending a
    bow)
    Thus it stands this is the situation
177 *curst and shrewd* waspish and difficult
180 *closely mewed her up* confined her
    strictly to the house
181 *Because she will not* in order that she
    shall not
    annoyed with molested by
183 *art thou not advised* didn't you notice
185 *marry* indeed, to be sure

186 *for my hand* by my hand
187 *Both our inventions meet and jump in
    one* our two plans concur and operate
    as one
190 *device* scheme, plot
193 *Keep house* entertain in the appropri-
    ate style
    ply his book study
194 *countrymen* fellow-countrymen (na-
    tives of Pisa)

LUCENTIO
   Basta, content thee, for I have it full.
   We have not yet been seen in any house,
   Nor can we be distinguished by our faces
   For man or master. Then it follows thus –
   Thou shalt be master, Tranio, in my stead,
200   Keep house, and port, and servants, as I should.
   I will some other be – some Florentine,
   Some Neapolitan, or meaner man of Pisa.
   'Tis hatched, and shall be so. Tranio, at once
   Uncase thee, take my coloured hat and cloak.
   When Biondello comes, he waits on thee,
   But I will charm him first to keep his tongue.

TRANIO
   So had you need.
         They exchange garments
   In brief, sir, sith it your pleasure is,
   And I am tied to be obedient –
210   For so your father charged me at our parting:
   'Be serviceable to my son', quoth he,
   Although I think 'twas in another sense –
   I am content to be Lucentio,
   Because so well I love Lucentio.

LUCENTIO
   Tranio, be so, because Lucentio loves.

195 *Basta* enough (Italian)
    I have it full I've hit on the answer
200 *port* state, manner of life suiting my
    station
202 *meaner* poorer (than I really am)
204 *Uncase thee* take off your outer gar-
    ments *coloured hat and cloak* (the dress
    of an Elizabethan gentleman, as dis-
    tinct from the 'blue coats', IV.I.81,
    worn by servants)
206 *charm him first to keep his tongue* first
    give him strict orders not to blab
207 *So had you need* you need to. The
    broken line here gives the impression

that there has been a cut, especially
as Tranio does not explain why it is
so necessary to keep Biondello quiet,
but continues his speech with the
inconsequential words 'In brief'.
208 *sith it your pleasure is* since it is your
    will
209 *tied* obliged, bound
211 *serviceable* diligent to serve
212 *in another sense.* It did not occur to
    Lucentio's father that his son would
    require Tranio to change places with
    him.

And let me be a slave t'achieve that maid
Whose sudden sight hath thralled my wounded eye.
    Enter Biondello
Here comes the rogue. Sirrah, where have you been?

BIONDELLO Where have I been? Nay, how now, where
are you? Master, has my fellow Tranio stolen your   220
clothes, or you stolen his, or both? Pray, what's the
news?

LUCENTIO
Sirrah, come hither. 'Tis no time to jest,
And therefore frame your manners to the time.
Your fellow Tranio here, to save my life,
Puts my apparel and my countenance on,
And I for my escape have put on his.
For in a quarrel since I came ashore
I killed a man, and fear I was descried.
Wait you on him, I charge you, as becomes,   230
While I make way from hence to save my life.
You understand me?

BIONDELLO   I, sir? Ne'er a whit.

LUCENTIO
And not a jot of Tranio in your mouth.
Tranio is changed into Lucentio.

BIONDELLO
The better for him, would I were so too!

TRANIO
So could I, faith, boy, to have the next wish after,
That Lucentio indeed had Baptista's youngest daughter.

216–17 *And let me be a slave t'achieve that maid | Whose sudden sight hath thralled my wounded eye.* The paradoxes here are the conventional ones of Elizabethan love-poetry.

217 *Whose sudden sight* the sudden sight of whom
    thralled enslaved

224 *frame your manners to the time* suit your behaviour to the occasion

226 *countenance* manner

229 *descried* seen, observed

230 *as becomes* as is fitting, in the proper manner

231 *make way* go

232 *Ne'er a whit* not in the least

236–41 *So could I . . . Lucentio.* Printed as prose in the Folio, these lines are, in fact, doggerel verse of a kind that is also to be found in *The Comedy of*

But, sirrah, not for my sake but your master's, I advise
You use your manners discreetly in all kind of
      companies.
240   When I am alone, why then I am Tranio,
But in all places else your master Lucentio.

LUCENTIO
Tranio, let's go.
One thing more rests, that thyself execute –
To make one among these wooers. If thou ask me why,
Sufficeth, my reasons are both good and weighty. *Exeunt*
      The Presenters above speak

LORD
   My lord, you nod, you do not mind the play.
   SLY *(coming to with a start)* Yes, by Saint Anne, do I. A
   good matter, surely. Comes there any more of it?

Errors (III.1.11–83) and in *Love's Labour's Lost* (IV.2.21–33).

236–7 *after ... daughter.* These two words, probably pronounced as 'arter' and 'darter', rhymed in Shakespeare's day. Compare the Fool's lines in *King Lear* (1.4.318–22):

A fox, when one has caught her,
And such a daughter,
Should sure to the slaughter,
If my cap would buy a halter.
So the fool follows after.

243 *rests, that thyself execute* remains for you to carry out

244–5 *To make ... weighty* (another patch of doggerel verse)

244 *make one* become one

245 *Sufficeth* it is enough to say, I need only say
(stage direction) *The Presenters above speak.* The presenter, who was a fairly common figure in Elizabethan drama (see, for example, Kyd's *The Spanish Tragedy*, Robert Greene's *James IV*, and Ben Jonson's *Every*

Man Out of His Humour), was the character, either human or allegorical, who was responsible for the presentation or putting-on of a play. He normally sat 'above', and often commented on the progress of the action. In this play the Lord, whose idea it is that the show should be put on before Sly and his 'wife', has the best title to the role, while they can also be considered as 'Presenters' by virtue of their remarks on the play.

246 LORD. The Folio reads: '1. Man.', but no provision has been made for anyone other than a Messenger to be present with Sly and the Page, and neither a Messenger nor a Servant can really be called a 'Presenter'. See note to Induction.2.126.
mind attend to, take notice of

247 (stage direction) *coming to with a start.* Though not in the Folio, this piece of business is obviously demanded by the context.

248 *matter* subject, story
surely no doubt

PAGE My lord, 'tis but begun.

SLY 'Tis a very excellent piece of work, madam lady.   250
  Would 'twere done!

They sit and mark

Enter Petruchio and his man Grumio   I.2

PETRUCHIO

Verona, for a while I take my leave,
To see my friends in Padua, but of all
My best belovèd and approvèd friend,
Hortensio; and I trow this is his house.
Here, sirrah Grumio, knock, I say.

GRUMIO Knock, sir? Whom should I knock? Is there any
man has rebused your worship?

PETRUCHIO Villain, I say, knock me here soundly.

---

249 *but* only just

251 *Would* I would that, I wish
(stage direction) *They sit and mark.*
These words clearly imply that the
three 'Presenters' were to remain in
their places. The problem of why
they say nothing further, especially
after Sly has made his views on it all
so plain, is a difficult one. See Introduction, pages 10 and 36.

I.2 (stage direction) *Petruchio.* The
spelling of this name, with the 'ch'
pronounced as in 'Charles', represents Shakespeare's attempt to find
an English equivalent for the Italian
name *Petruccio.* There is a servant
called *Petrucio* in *Supposes.*
(stage direction) *Grumio.* Shakespeare
may have got this name from Plautus's *Mostellaria*, where one of the
characters, a downright countryman,
is so called, but it could also be the
result of an effort to give the English
word 'groom' an Italian appearance.

1–4 *Verona ... house.* Like Lucentio at
the opening of the previous scene,
Petruchio begins with a bit of self-
explanation, but on this occasion it
is kept down to a bare minimum and
gives way almost at once to dramatic
action. The relationship between
Petruchio and Grumio here forms a
nice contrast to that between Lucentio and Tranio in 1.1.

2 *but of all* but especially, but above all

4 *trow* believe, know
his house. Having come on to the stage
by one of the main doors, Petruchio
and Grumio cross to the other main
door, which now becomes the entrance to Hortensio's house.

5 *knock* rap for admittance. Grumio
takes the word in its other sense of
'beat' or 'strike'.

7 *rebused* (Grumio's mistake for
'abused')

8 *Villain* slave, wretch
knock me here soundly. The *me* here is a
relic of the old dative meaning 'for

GRUMIO Knock you here, sir? Why, sir, what am I, sir,
10   that I should knock you here, sir?

PETRUCHIO
Villain, I say, knock me at this gate,
And rap me well, or I'll knock your knave's pate.

GRUMIO
My master is grown quarrelsome. I should knock you
first
And then I know after who comes by the worst.

PETRUCHIO
Will it not be?
Faith, sirrah, an you'll not knock, I'll ring it.
I'll try how you can *sol-fa* and sing it.
He wrings him by the ears

GRUMIO
Help, masters, help! My master is mad.

PETRUCHIO
Now knock when I bid you, sirrah villain.
Enter Hortensio

20   HORTENSIO How now, what's the matter? My old friend
Grumio and my good friend Petruchio! How do you all
at Verona?

PETRUCHIO
Signor Hortensio, come you to part the fray?
Con tutto il cuore ben trovato, may I say.

---

me' – Grumio, of course, takes it as
the accusative – but by Shakespeare's
time it had become a device for lend-
ing life and colour to a statement
and amounted to 'mark me' or 'I tell
you'.
13–14 *I should knock you first ... worst*
you are asking me to strike you, so
that you can then have an excuse for
giving me a drubbing
16 *an* if

I'll ring it I'll ring. The *it* is superfluous, as it is also in *sing it*, and there is
a quibble on 'ring' and 'wring'.
17 *sol-fa* sing
(stage direction) *He wrings him by the
ears* he twists Grumio's ears
21 *How do you* how are you
23 *part the fray* separate the combatants,
stop the brawl
24 *Con tutto il cuore ben trovato* with all
my heart well met (Italian)

HORTENSIO

Alla nostra casa ben venuto,
Molto honorato signor mio Petruchio.
Rise, Grumio, rise. We will compound this quarrel.

GRUMIO Nay, 'tis no matter, sir, what he 'leges in Latin. If
this be not a lawful cause for me to leave his service,
look you, sir. He bid me knock him and rap him   30
soundly, sir. Well, was it fit for a servant to use his
master so, being perhaps, for aught I see, two and thirty,
a pip out?
Whom would to God I had well knocked at first,
Then had not Grumio come by the worst.

PETRUCHIO

A senseless villain. Good Hortensio,
I bade the rascal knock upon your gate,
And could not get him for my heart to do it.

GRUMIO Knock at the gate? O heavens! Spake you not
these words plain, 'Sirrah, knock me here, rap me here,   40
knock me well, and knock me soundly'? And come you
now with 'knocking at the gate'?

PETRUCHIO

Sirrah, be gone, or talk not, I advise you.

HORTENSIO

Petruchio, patience, I am Grumio's pledge.

25–6 *Alla nostra casa ben venuto,* | *Molto honorato signor mio Petruchio* welcome to our house, most worshipful Petruchio

27 *compound* amicably settle

28 *'leges* alleges
in Latin. Grumio, despite his name, is a good solid English character who does not know the difference between Latin and Italian.

31 *use* treat

32–3 *two and thirty, a pip out.* This is a jesting allusion to the card-game of 'one-and-thirty', the 'pips' being the marks on the cards. According to

John Ray in his *Collection of English Proverbs* (1678), to be 'one-and-thirty' meant to be drunk. It seems more likely to the present editor, however, that Grumio is saying that his master, like a gamester who has overshot the mark by scoring thirty-two instead of thirty-one, is 'not quite right – in the head'.

36 *A senseless* an unreasonable

38 *for my heart* for my life

41–2 *come you now with* do you now come along with

44 *pledge* surety

Why, this's a heavy chance 'twixt him and you,
Your ancient, trusty, pleasant servant Grumio.
And tell me now, sweet friend, what happy gale
Blows you to Padua here from old Verona?

PETRUCHIO
Such wind as scatters young men through the world
50 To seek their fortunes farther than at home,
Where small experience grows. But in a few,
Signor Hortensio, thus it stands with me:
Antonio, my father, is deceased,
And I have thrust myself into this maze,
Haply to wive and thrive as best I may.
Crowns in my purse I have, and goods at home,
And so am come abroad to see the world.

HORTENSIO
Petruchio, shall I then come roundly to thee
And wish thee to a shrewd ill-favoured wife?
60 Thou'dst thank me but a little for my counsel,
And yet I'll promise thee she shall be rich,
And very rich. But th' art too much my friend,
And I'll not wish thee to her.

45 *this's* this is (colloquial). The Folio reads 'this'.
heavy chance sad misunderstanding
46 *ancient* of long standing
pleasant merry, entertaining
51 *in a few* in short, to be brief
54 *maze* chancy business (of looking for a wife)
55 *Haply* with luck, fortunately
to wive and thrive. Two proverbs, both of which help to explain why Petruchio thinks of his enterprise as a *maze*, are relevant here: 'It is hard to wive [get married] and thrive both in a year,' and 'In wiving and thriving a man should take counsel of all

the world, lest he light upon a curse while he seeks for a blessing.' Petruchio takes counsel, but then wisely disregards it.
58 *come roundly* speak plainly
59 *And wish thee to a shrewd ill-favoured wife* and commend you to a sharp-tongued ill-conditioned wife. *Ill-favoured* must mean 'endowed with bad qualities', rather than 'ugly', because at line 85 Hortensio describes Katherina as 'beauteous'.
60 *Thou'dst* thou wouldst
62 *th' art* thou art (abbreviated colloquial form)

PETRUCHIO

    Signor Hortensio, 'twixt such friends as we
    Few words suffice; and therefore, if thou know
    One rich enough to be Petruchio's wife –
    As wealth is burden of my wooing dance –
    Be she as foul as was Florentius' love,
    As old as Sibyl, and as curst and shrewd
    As Socrates' Xanthippe, or a worse,   70
    She moves me not, or not removes at least
    Affection's edge in me, were she as rough
    As are the swelling Adriatic seas.
    I come to wive it wealthily in Padua;
    If wealthily, then happily in Padua.

GRUMIO Nay, look you, sir, he tells you flatly what his
    mind is. Why, give him gold enough and marry him to
    a puppet or an aglet-baby, or an old trot with ne'er a
    tooth in her head, though she have as many diseases
    as two and fifty horses. Why, nothing comes amiss, so   80
    money comes withal.

HORTENSIO

    Petruchio, since we are stepped thus far in,
    I will continue that I broached in jest.

---

67 *burden* (musical accompaniment)
68 *foul* ugly, plain
  Florentius' love. Florentius is a knight
  in Gower's *Confessio Amantis*. His
  life depends on his answering the
  riddle 'what do women most desire',
  and he agrees to marry a loathsome
  old hag on condition that she tells
  him the answer. The same story is
  told by Chaucer in *The Wife of Bath's
  Tale*.
69 *Sibyl*. In the *Metamorphoses* (xiv. 130–
  181) Ovid has the Sibyl of Cumae
  tell Aeneas how Apollo granted her
  as many years of life as the number
  of grains of sand that she could pick
  up in a handful.
  curst and shrewd waspish and shrewish

70 *Xanthippe* (wife of Socrates, notorious for her bad temper)
71 *moves me not* can't make any impression on me, can't alter my plans
71–2 *or not removes at least | Affection's
  edge in me* or at least she can't destroy the keenness of my desire
76 *flatly* plainly, downright
77 *mind* intention
78 *aglet-baby* (small figure, often in the
  shape of a death's-head, forming the
  tag of a lace)
  old trot decrepit old woman, hag
80–81 *so money comes withal* provided
  money comes with it
82 *are stepped thus far in* have gone so far
83 *that I broached* that which I began

I can, Petruchio, help thee to a wife
With wealth enough, and young and beauteous,
Brought up as best becomes a gentlewoman.
Her only fault – and that is faults enough –
Is that she is intolerable curst,
And shrewd and froward so beyond all measure
90   That, were my state far worser than it is,
I would not wed her for a mine of gold.

PETRUCHIO
  Hortensio, peace. Thou know'st not gold's effect.
  Tell me her father's name and 'tis enough.
  For I will board her though she chide as loud
  As thunder when the clouds in autumn crack.

HORTENSIO
  Her father is Baptista Minola,
  An affable and courteous gentleman.
  Her name is Katherina Minola,
  Renowned in Padua for her scolding tongue.

PETRUCHIO
100   I know her father, though I know not her,
  And he knew my deceased father well.
  I will not sleep, Hortensio, till I see her,
  And therefore let me be thus bold with you
  To give you over at this first encounter,
  Unless you will accompany me thither.

GRUMIO I pray you, sir, let him go while the humour lasts.
  O' my word, an she knew him as well as I do, she would
  think scolding would do little good upon him. She may

---

88 *intolerable* intolerably
90 *state* fortune
94 *board* woo. Compare Sir Toby Belch's similarly figurative use of the naval word 'board' when he tells Sir Andrew, '"Accost" is front her, board her, woo her, assail her' (*Twelfth Night*, 1.3.52–3). *chide* scold

95 *crack* go off with a bang (like a gun)
97 *An affable* a polite, kind
103–4 *let me be thus bold with you | To give you over at this first encounter* let me take the liberty of leaving you at this our first meeting
107 *O' my word* on my word
108 *do little good upon* have little effect on

perhaps call him half a score knaves or so. Why, that's
nothing; an he begin once, he'll rail in his rope-tricks.   110
I'll tell you what, sir, an she stand him but a little, he
will throw a figure in her face, and so disfigure her with
it that she shall have no more eyes to see withal than a
cat. You know him not, sir.

HORTENSIO

Tarry, Petruchio, I must go with thee,
For in Baptista's keep my treasure is.
He hath the jewel of my life in hold,
His youngest daughter, beautiful Bianca,
And her withholds from me and other more,
Suitors to her and rivals in my love,   120
Supposing it a thing impossible,
For those defects I have before rehearsed,

110 *an he begin once, he'll rail in his rope-
tricks*. This is one of the most obscure passages in the whole play.
The present editor thinks it means
'if he once begins, he'll scold in
his outrageous rhetoric'. The
nonce-word *rope-tricks* is probably
Grumio's version of 'rope-rhetorics',
a term used by Thomas Nashe in his
pamphlet *Have with You to Saffron-
Walden*, published in 1596. There
Nashe writes of Gabriel Harvey's
'Paracelsian rope-rethorique', apparently meaning 'bombastic rhetoric
for which the author deserved to be
hanged' (*The Works of Thomas Nashe*,
edited by R. B. McKerrow, London,
1904-10, volume III, page 15). In
view of the interest the Elizabethans
had in 'the tropes of rhetoric', it is
quite possible that the word 'trope-
tricks', meaning 'subtleties of rhetoric', may well have existed as a slang
term, though there is no record of it.
If it did, the transition to 'rope-
tricks' would have been an easy one.

111 *stand* face, resist, withstand

111-14 *he will throw a figure in her face,
and so disfigure her with it that she shall
have no more eyes to see withal than a cat.*
The general sense of this passage is
that Petruchio will use figures of
rhetoric to such effect that Katherina
will be quite overcome.

112 *throw a figure in her face.* Grumio is
probably quibbling on two senses:
(1) hurl a figure of speech at her; (2)
subject her to the influence of the
kind of spell-binding figure used by
conjurers and magicians.

disfigure deform, mar. But perhaps
the word is used metaphorically to
mean 'change her attitude'.

113-14 *than a cat.* Shakespeare may be
ridiculing the casual and unthinking
use of terms such as this.

116 *Keep* keeping, custody

117 *hold* safe-keeping

119 *other more* others besides. 'Other'
was a common form of the plural.

122 *For those defects* on account of those
faults

rehearsed recited

That ever Katherina will be wooed.
Therefore this order hath Baptista ta'en,
That none shall have access unto Bianca
Till Katherine the curst have got a husband.

GRUMIO
Katherine the curst,
A title for a maid of all titles the worst.

HORTENSIO
Now shall my friend Petruchio do me grace,
130   And offer me disguised in sober robes
To old Baptista as a schoolmaster
Well seen in music, to instruct Bianca,
That so I may by this device at least
Have leave and leisure to make love to her,
And unsuspected court her by herself.

GRUMIO   Here's no knavery! See, to beguile the old folks,
how the young folks lay their heads together.

*Enter Gremio, and Lucentio disguised as Cambio, a
schoolmaster*

Master, master, look about you. Who goes there, ha?

HORTENSIO
Peace, Grumio. It is the rival of my love.
140   Petruchio, stand by a while

GRUMIO
A proper stripling and an amorous!

They stand aside

GREMIO
O, very well – I have perused the note.
Hark you, sir, I'll have them very fairly bound –
All books of love, see that at any hand –

---

124   *this order* these measures   expense.
129   *do me grace* do me a favour   *proper* fine, handsome
132   *Well seen* well served, well qualified   142   *note* list of the books
139   *the rival of my love* my rival in love   143   *them* the books
       (Gremio)   *fairly* handsomely
141   *A proper stripling and an amorous!*   144   *see that at any hand* see to that in any
       Grumio is being ironical at Gremio's   case

And see you read no other lectures to her.
You understand me. Over and beside
Signor Baptista's liberality,
I'll mend it with a largess. Take your paper too.
And let me have them very well perfumed,
For she is sweeter than perfume itself   150
To whom they go to. What will you read to her?

LUCENTIO
Whate'er I read to her, I'll plead for you
As for my patron, stand you so assured,
As firmly as yourself were still in place,
Yea, and perhaps with more successful words
Than you, unless you were a scholar, sir.

GREMIO
O this learning, what a thing it is!

GRUMIO (*aside*)
O this woodcock, what an ass it is!

PETRUCHIO (*aside*)
Peace, sirrah.

HORTENSIO (*aside*)
Grumio, mum! (*Coming forward*) God save you, Signor
  Gremio.   160

GREMIO
And you are well met, Signor Hortensio.
Trow you whither I am going? To Baptista Minola.
I promised to enquire carefully
About a schoolmaster for the fair Bianca,
And by good fortune I have lighted well
On this young man, for learning and behaviour

145 *read no other lectures* give no other
  lessons
148 *mend it with a largess* improve it with
  a donation
  paper (the 'note' or list of line 142)
149 *them* the books
154 *as yourself were still in place* as if you
  yourself were present all the time
158 *woodcock* dupe, simpleton. The Elizabethans thought of the woodcock as
  a stupid bird.
161 *you are well met* I'm glad to meet you
162 *Trow you* do you know, can you
  guess

Fit for her turn, well read in poetry
And other books – good ones, I warrant ye.

HORTENSIO
'Tis well. And I have met a gentleman
170   Hath promised me to help me to another,
A fine musician to instruct our mistress.
So shall I no whit be behind in duty
To fair Bianca, so beloved of me.

GREMIO
Beloved of me, and that my deeds shall prove.

GRUMIO (aside)
And that his bags shall prove.

HORTENSIO
Gremio, 'tis now no time to vent our love.
Listen to me, and if you speak me fair,
I'll tell you news indifferent good for either.
Here is a gentleman whom by chance I met,
180   Upon agreement from us to his liking,
Will undertake to woo curst Katherine,
Yea, and to marry her, if her dowry please.

GREMIO
So said, so done, is well.
Hortensio, have you told him all her faults?

PETRUCHIO
I know she is an irksome brawling scold.
If that be all, masters, I hear no harm.

GREMIO
No, say'st me so, friend? What countryman?

PETRUCHIO
Born in Verona, old Antonio's son.

167 *turn* needs
170 *help me to* assist me in obtaining
175 *bags* money-bags, wealth
176 *vent* give vent to, utter
178 *news indifferent good for either* news that is equally good for each of us
180 *Upon agreement from us to his liking* on our agreement to conditions that

suit him. The conditions, that Gremio and Hortensio bear the cost of Petruchio's wooing, are mentioned later (lines 212–14).
183 *So said, so done, is well* it's fine when actions come up to promises
187 *What countryman?* where do you come from, where's your home?

My father dead, my fortune lives for me,
And I do hope good days and long to see.   190

GREMIO

O sir, such a life with such a wife were strange.
But if you have a stomach, to't a God's name –
You shall have me assisting you in all.
But will you woo this wildcat?

PETRUCHIO   Will I live?

GRUMIO

Will he woo her? Ay, or I'll hang her.

PETRUCHIO

Why came I hither but to that intent?
Think you a little din can daunt mine ears?
Have I not in my time heard lions roar?
Have I not heard the sea, puffed up with winds,
Rage like an angry boar chafèd with sweat?   200
Have I not heard great ordnance in the field,
And heaven's artillery thunder in the skies?
Have I not in a pitchèd battle heard
Loud 'larums, neighing steeds, and trumpets' clang?
And do you tell me of a woman's tongue,
That gives not half so great a blow to hear
As will a chestnut in a farmer's fire?
Tush, tush, fear boys with bugs!

GRUMIO   For he fears none.

GREMIO

Hortensio, hark.

191 *were strange* would be surprising
192 *if you have a stomach, to't a God's name*
   if you have an inclination to try, get
   on with it in God's name
194 *Will I live?* certainly!
195 *Will he woo her? Ay, or I'll hang her.*
   Compare Feste's remark: 'Many a
   good hanging prevents a bad marriage' (*Twelfth Night*, 1.5.18).
196 *but to that intent* except for that
   purpose
200 *chafèd* annoyed, enraged (the sweat

of the hunted boar being compared
with the foam of a stormy sea)
201 *field* battle-field
204 *'larums* alarums, calls to arms made
   with drum and trumpet
206 *to hear.* So the Folio; but the emendation 'to th'ear', first suggested in the
   eighteenth century, makes good
   sense.
208 *fear boys with bugs* frighten boys with
   bugbears (bogies or hobgoblins)
   fears none is afraid of none

210   This gentleman is happily arrived,
          My mind presumes, for his own good and yours.

HORTENSIO
          I promised we would be contributors
          And bear his charge of wooing, whatsoe'er.

GREMIO
          And so we will – provided that he win her.

GRUMIO
          I would I were as sure of a good dinner.

                Enter Tranio, bravely dressed as Lucentio, and
                Biondello

TRANIO
          Gentlemen, God save you. If I may be bold,
          Tell me, I beseech you, which is the readiest way
          To the house of Signor Baptista Minola?

BIONDELLO He that has the two fair daughters – is't he
220   you mean?

TRANIO Even he, Biondello.

GREMIO
          Hark you, sir, you mean not her too?

TRANIO
          Perhaps him and her, sir. What have you to do?

211 *yours.* So the Folio. The reading has been emended to 'ours' by some editors, so obscuring the dramatic point that Gremio is eager to shift any expense involved on to Hortensio.
213 *charge* expense
215 (stage direction) *bravely dressed.* The Folio reads:
      '*braue*', that is, 'richly attired'.
216 *be bold* take the liberty
217 *readiest* easiest, quickest
219–20 *He that has the two fair daughters – is't he you mean?* Biondello's remark has been prearranged as part of Tranio's opening gambit.

222 *her too?* The Folio reads: 'her to-', denoting either that a word is missing or that the compositor could not make out the sense of what he had printed. If a word is missing, it must be 'woo', but this does not fit Tranio's answer. 'Too' on the other hand, which is interchangeable in Shakespeare texts with 'to', follows naturally on Biondello's 'you mean' (line 220) and fits in perfectly with Tranio's reply.
223 *What have you to do?* what is that to you?

THE TAMING OF THE SHREW I.2   [103

PETRUCHIO

Not her that chides, sir, at any hand, I pray.

TRANIO

I love no chiders, sir. Biondello, let's away.

LUCENTIO (*aside*)

Well begun, Tranio.

HORTENSIO   Sir, a word ere you go.

Are you a suitor to the maid you talk of, yea or no?

TRANIO

And if I be, sir, is it any offence?

GREMIO

No, if without more words you will get you hence.

TRANIO

Why, sir, I pray, are not the streets as free   230

For me as for you?

GREMIO   But so is not she.

TRANIO

For what reason, I beseech you?

GREMIO   For this reason, if you'll know,

That she's the choice love of Signor Gremio.

HORTENSIO

That she's the chosen of Signor Hortensio.

TRANIO

Softly, my masters! If you be gentlemen,

Do me this right – hear me with patience.

Baptista is a noble gentleman,

To whom my father is not all unknown,

And were his daughter fairer than she is,

She may more suitors have and me for one.   240

Fair Leda's daughter had a thousand wooers,

---

224 *at any hand* in any case
233 *choice* chosen, appointed
235 *Softly* gently, just a moment
236 *Do me this right* do me this justice
238 *not all* not altogether
239 *And were his daughter fairer* and even if
his daughter were more beautiful

241 *Fair Leda's daughter* the lovely daughter of Leda (Helen of Troy). The 'thousand wooers' was probably suggested by Marlowe's famous line 'Was this the face that launched a thousand ships?' (*Dr Faustus*, v. 1.97)

Then well one more may fair Bianca have.
And so she shall. Lucentio shall make one,
Though Paris came, in hope to speed alone.

GREMIO

What, this gentleman will out-talk us all!

LUCENTIO

Sir, give him head, I know he'll prove a jade.

PETRUCHIO

Hortensio, to what end are all these words?

HORTENSIO

Sir, let me be so bold as ask you,
Did you yet ever see Baptista's daughter?

TRANIO

250   No, sir, but hear I do that he hath two;
The one as famous for a scolding tongue
As is the other for beauteous modesty.

PETRUCHIO

Sir, sir, the first's for me, let her go by.

GREMIO

Yea, leave that labour to great Hercules,
And let it be more than Alcides' twelve.

PETRUCHIO

Sir, understand you this of me in sooth,

---

242 *one more* one more than she has
already
244 *Though Paris came* though Paris (the
son of Priam, King of Troy, who
stole Helen away from her husband
Menelaus) were to come
in hope to speed alone hoping to be the
winner
246 *give him head, I know he'll prove a jade*
give him free scope, I know he'll
soon tire. The language here is that
of horsemanship – to give a horse its
head is to cease checking it, and a
jade is a poor worthless horse that
soon grows tired.

248 *as ask* as to ask
253 *let her go by* leave her alone
254–5 *Hercules . . . Alcides' twelve.* Hercules, otherwise known as Alcides,
was the legendary hero of classical
mythology who carried out twelve
stupendous tasks, or labours as they
were called. Gremio calls Petruchio
Hercules, and implies that he has
taken on an even greater task.
255 *let it be more than* admit that it
surpasses
256 *understand you this of me in sooth* take
this from me for certain

The youngest daughter whom you hearken for
Her father keeps from all access of suitors,
And will not promise her to any man
Until the elder sister first be wed.   260
The younger then is free, and not before.

TRANIO

If it be so, sir, that you are the man
Must stead us all – and me amongst the rest –
And if you break the ice and do this feat,
Achieve the elder, set the younger free
For our access – whose hap shall be to have her
Will not so graceless be to be ingrate.

HORTENSIO

Sir, you say well, and well you do conceive.
And since you do profess to be a suitor,
You must, as we do, gratify this gentleman,   270
To whom we all rest generally beholding.

TRANIO

Sir, I shall not be slack. In sign whereof,
Please ye we may contrive this afternoon,
And quaff carouses to our mistress' health,
And do as adversaries do in law,
Strive mightily, but eat and drink as friends.

GRUMIO *and* BIONDELLO

O excellent motion! Fellows, let's be gone.

HORTENSIO

The motion's good indeed, and be it so.
Petruchio, I shall be your *ben venuto*.   *Exeunt*

257 *hearken for* lie in wait for, seek to win
263 *Must stead* who must help, who must be of use to
266 *whose hap shall be* he whose good fortune it shall be
267 *so graceless be to be ingrate* be so lacking in all decency as to be ungrateful
268 *conceive* understand the situation
270 *gratify* reward, requite
271 *rest generally beholding* remain without exception under an obligation
272 *slack* remiss, backward
273 *contrive* spend, while away
274 *quaff carouses* drink toasts
277 *motion* proposal
279 *ben venuto* literally, 'welcome' (Italian). Hortensio means that he will pay for Petruchio's entertainment.

II.I   *Enter Katherina, and Bianca with her hands tied*

BIANCA

Good sister, wrong me not, nor wrong yourself,
To make a bondmaid and a slave of me.
That I disdain. But for these other gauds,
Unbind my hands, I'll pull them off myself,
Yea, all my raiment, to my petticoat,
Or what you will command me will I do,
So well I know my duty to my elders.

KATHERINA

Of all thy suitors here I charge thee tell
Whom thou lov'st best. See thou dissemble not.

BIANCA

10   Believe me, sister, of all men alive
I never yet beheld that special face
Which I could fancy more than any other.

KATHERINA

Minion, thou liest. Is't not Hortensio?

BIANCA

If you affect him, sister, here I swear
I'll plead for you myself but you shall have him.

KATHERINA

O then, belike, you fancy riches more.
You will have Gremio to keep you fair.

BIANCA

Is it for him you do envy me so?
Nay then you jest, and now I well perceive

II.1 (stage direction) *Enter Katherina, and Bianca with her hands tied.* The Folio, which has neither Act nor scene heading here, reads: '*Enter Katherina and Bianca*', but Bianca's first speech clearly indicates the state in which she appears.

1 *wrong* (1) harm; (2) disgrace

3 *gauds* pieces of finery, gewgaws. The Folio reads 'goods'.

12 *fancy* like, love

13 *Minion* spoilt brat

14 *affect* love

17 *fair* fine, well dressed

18 *envy* (pronounced with the stress on the second syllable) hate, feel jealous of

You have but jested with me all this while.   20
I prithee, sister Kate, untie my hands.

KATHERINA

    Strikes her

If that be jest, then all the rest was so.

    Enter Baptista

BAPTISTA

Why, how now, dame, whence grows this insolence?
Bianca, stand aside. Poor girl, she weeps.

    He unties her hands

Go ply thy needle, meddle not with her.
(*to Katherina*) For shame, thou hilding of a devilish spirit,
Why dost thou wrong her that did ne'er wrong thee?
When did she cross thee with a bitter word?

KATHERINA

Her silence flouts me, and I'll be revenged.

    She flies after Bianca

BAPTISTA

What, in my sight? Bianca, get thee in.   *Exit Bianca*   30

KATHERINA

What, will you not suffer me? Nay, now I see
She is your treasure, she must have a husband.
I must dance bare-foot on her wedding-day,
And for your love to her lead apes in hell.
Talk not to me, I will go sit and weep,
Till I can find occasion of revenge.   *Exit Katherina*

---

23 *dame* mistress, madam (implying a rebuke)
    whence grows this insolence? what is the reason for this disgraceful behaviour?
25 *meddle not* have nothing to do with
26 *hilding* base wretch, baggage
28 *cross* contradict, annoy
29 *flouts* mocks, shows contempt of
31 *suffer me* let me have my own way
33 *I must dance bare-foot on her wedding-day.* An elder sister who remained

unmarried was supposed to dance bare-foot at her younger sister's wedding. The phrase thus became proverbial for being unmarried.
34 *lead apes in hell.* This is another proverbial occupation of old maids – they led apes in hell because they had no children to lead into heaven. Compare Beatrice's remarks on the same subject in *Much Ado About Nothing*, II.1.34–41.
36 *occasion of* opportunity for

BAPTISTA

Was ever gentleman thus grieved as I?

But who comes here?

> *Enter Gremio, with Lucentio, disguised as Cambio, in*
> *the habit of a mean man; Petruchio, with Hortensio,*
> *disguised as Licio; and Tranio, disguised as Lucentio,*
> *with his boy, Biondello, bearing a lute and books*

GREMIO Good morrow, neighbour Baptista.

40   BAPTISTA Good morrow, neighbour Gremio. God save
you, gentlemen.

PETRUCHIO

And you, good sir. Pray have you not a daughter

Called Katherina, fair and virtuous?

BAPTISTA

I have a daughter, sir, called Katherina.

GREMIO

You are too blunt, go to it orderly.

PETRUCHIO

You wrong me, Signor Gremio, give me leave.

I am a gentleman of Verona, sir,

That hearing of her beauty and her wit,

Her affability and bashful modesty,

50   Her wondrous qualities and mild behaviour,

Am bold to show myself a forward guest

Within your house, to make mine eye the witness

---

37 *grieved* afflicted
38 (stage direction) *Enter Gremio ...*
with Hortensio ... books. The Folio
direction, omitting all mention of
Hortensio, reads as follows: '*Enter*
Gremio, Lucentio, in the habit of a meane
man, Petruchio with Tranio, with his boy
bearing a Lute and Bookes.'
habit of a mean man dress of a
poor man. Compare Lucentio's description of the disguise he intends
to assume, given at I.1.202.
(stage direction) *Cambio* (a significant
name, since it is the Italian for
'exchange')
45 *go to it orderly* go about the business
in a proper orderly manner
46 *give me leave* excuse me
49 *affability* kindness, gentle behaviour

Of that report which I so oft have heard.
And for an entrance to my entertainment
I do present you with a man of mine,
     (*presenting Hortensio*)
Cunning in music and the mathematics,
To instruct her fully in those sciences,
Whereof I know she is not ignorant.
Accept of him, or else you do me wrong.
His name is Licio, born in Mantua.   60

BAPTISTA

Y'are welcome, sir, and he for your good sake.
But for my daughter Katherine, this I know,
She is not for your turn, the more my grief.

PETRUCHIO

I see you do not mean to part with her,
Or else you like not of my company.

BAPTISTA

Mistake me not, I speak but as I find.
Whence are you, sir? What may I call your name?

PETRUCHIO

Petruchio is my name, Antonio's son,
A man well known throughout all Italy.

BAPTISTA

I know him well. You are welcome for his sake.   70

GREMIO

Saving your tale, Petruchio, I pray
Let us that are poor petitioners speak too.
Baccare! You are marvellous forward.

---

54 *for an entrance to my entertainment* as an entrance-fee for my reception, to show that I am in earnest
57 *sciences* branches of knowledge
59 *Accept of* accept
61 *Y'are* you are (colloquial)
62 *for* as for
63 *She is not for your turn* she will not come up to your requirements, she's not the girl for you

65 *like not of my company* don't approve of me
67 *What may I call your name?* what is your name?
71 *Saving* with all respect for, no offence meant to
73 *Baccare!* stand back! give place! A sixteenth-century proverb ran: 'Back-are, quoth Mortimer to his sow.' The word, always used in a jocular

PETRUCHIO
O pardon me, Signor Gremio, I would fain be doing.

GREMIO
I doubt it not, sir, but you will curse your wooing.
(*to Baptista*) Neighbour, this is a gift very grateful, I am
sure of it. To express the like kindness, myself, that have
been more kindly beholding to you than any, freely give
unto you this young scholar (*presenting Lucentio*) that
hath been long studying at Rheims, as cunning in Greek,
Latin, and other languages, as the other in music and
mathematics. His name is Cambio. Pray accept his
service.

BAPTISTA A thousand thanks, Signor Gremio. Welcome,
good Cambio. (*To Tranio*) But, gentle sir, methinks you
walk like a stranger. May I be so bold to know the cause
of your coming?

TRANIO
Pardon me, sir, the boldness is mine own
That, being a stranger in this city here,
Do make myself a suitor to your daughter,
Unto Bianca, fair and virtuous.
Nor is your firm resolve unknown to me
In the preferment of the eldest sister.
This liberty is all that I request –
That, upon knowledge of my parentage,
I may have welcome 'mongst the rest that woo,
And free access and favour as the rest.
And toward the education of your daughters

---

sense, seems to have been made up from the adverb *back* with the addition of *are*, the ending of the Latin infinitive.

74 *I would fain be doing* I am eager for action (probably with a quibble on 'doing' in the indelicate sense)

76 *grateful* agreeable, welcome

80 *Rheims*. The seat of a university founded in 1547.

86 *walk like a stranger* seem to be on your own, not one of the party

93 *In the preferment of* in giving precedence to

95 *upon knowledge of* when you know about

98 *toward* as a contribution to

I here bestow a simple instrument,
And this small packet of Greek and Latin books.   100
        Biondello steps forward with the lute and the books
If you accept them, then their worth is great.

BAPTISTA (*opening one of the books*)
Lucentio is your name? Of whence, I pray?

TRANIO
Of Pisa, sir, son to Vincentio.

BAPTISTA
A mighty man of Pisa. By report
I know him well. You are very welcome, sir.
(*to Hortensio*) Take you the lute, (*to Lucentio*) and you
        the set of books.
You shall go see your pupils presently.
Holla, within!
        Enter a Servant
                Sirrah, lead these gentlemen
To my daughters, and tell them both
These are their tutors. Bid them use them well.   110
                        *Exit Servant, conducting Hortensio
                        and Lucentio, followed by Biondello*
We will go walk a little in the orchard,
And then to dinner. You are passing welcome,
And so I pray you all to think yourselves.

PETRUCHIO
Signor Baptista, my business asketh haste,
And every day I cannot come to woo.

---

102 (stage direction) (*opening one of the books*). This direction, which is not in the Folio, seems necessary in order that Baptista may see Lucentio's name, which has not yet been mentioned, on the fly-leaf.

104 *mighty* illustrious, important, leading

109 *To my daughters, and tell them both.* The line is unmetrical, and something has probably been omitted from it; but it is impossible to say what the missing word was. The Second Folio reads: 'To my two daughters'.

112 *dinner* (the main meal of the day in Shakespeare's England, served between eleven o'clock and noon)
    passing very, most

114 *asketh* requires, demands

You knew my father well, and in him me,
Left solely heir to all his lands and goods,
Which I have bettered rather than decreased.
Then tell me, if I get your daughter's love,
120   What dowry shall I have with her to wife?

BAPTISTA
After my death the one half of my lands,
And in possession twenty thousand crowns.

PETRUCHIO
And for that dowry I'll assure her of
Her widowhood – be it that she survive me –
In all my lands and leases whatsoever.
Let specialties be therefore drawn between us,
That covenants may be kept on either hand.

BAPTISTA
Ay, when the special thing is well obtained,
That is, her love; for that is all in all.

PETRUCHIO
130   Why, that is nothing. For I tell you, father,
I am as peremptory as she proud-minded;
And where two raging fires meet together,
They do consume the thing that feeds their fury.
Though little fire grows great with little wind,
Yet extreme gusts will blow out fire and all.

122 *in possession* in immediate possession
123–4 *for that dowry I'll assure her of |
Her widowhood* in exchange for that
dowry I'll guarantee her her widow's
rights. *Widowhood* here means 'the
estate settled upon a widow' in the
marriage contract.
126 *Let specialties be therefore drawn between us* let explicit detailed contracts
between us therefore be drawn up
130 *father* father-in-law. Petruchio's self-
assurance is splendidly brought out
here.

131 *peremptory* (always accented on the
first syllable in Shakespeare)
133 *the thing that feeds their fury.* The fuel
Petruchio is referring to is Katherina's shrewishness.
134–5 *Though little fire grows great with
little wind, | Yet extreme gusts will blow
out fire and all.* Petruchio makes it
plain, through his use of this analogy, that he thinks Katherina's headstrong temper has been encouraged
by the feeble opposition (*little wind*)
that it has encountered hitherto. His
own opposition (*extreme gusts*) will be

So I to her, and so she yields to me,
For I am rough and woo not like a babe.

BAPTISTA

Well mayst thou woo, and happy be thy speed.
But be thou armed for some unhappy words.

PETRUCHIO

Ay, to the proof, as mountains are for winds,   140
That shakes not though they blow perpetually.

Enter Hortensio with his head broke

BAPTISTA

How now, my friend, why dost thou look so pale?

HORTENSIO

For fear, I promise you, if I look pale.

BAPTISTA

What, will my daughter prove a good musician?

HORTENSIO

I think she'll sooner prove a soldier.
Iron may hold with her, but never lutes.

BAPTISTA

Why then, thou canst not break her to the lute?

HORTENSIO

Why no, for she hath broke the lute to me.
I did but tell her she mistook her frets,

---

of a sterner kind, and so more effective.

138 *happy be thy speed* may the outcome be fortunate for you

139 *unhappy* harsh, inauspicious

140 *to the proof* so as to be invulnerable

141 *shakes* shake (the old plural) (stage direction) *broke* bruised and bleeding

143 *I promise you* let me tell you, I assure you

145 *prove a soldier* (a quibble on (1) become a soldier, and (2) put a soldier to the test)

146 *hold with her* stand up to her handling, not break in her hands

147 *break her to the lute* train her to play the lute (as a horse is broken to the bit). This is the first of a number of analogies in which the taming of Katherina is compared to the taming of a high-spirited animal or bird.

148 *broke the lute to me.* The comic effect of these lines is much increased if Hortensio appears with the broken lute draped round his neck like a horse-collar.

149 *frets* (rings of gut or bars of wood upon the lute to regulate the fingering)

150   And bowed her hand to teach her fingering,
When, with a most impatient devilish spirit,
'Frets, call you these?' quoth she, 'I'll fume with them.'
And with that word she struck me on the head,
And through the instrument my pate made way,
And there I stood amazèd for a while,
As on a pillory, looking through the lute,
While she did call me rascal fiddler
And twangling Jack, with twenty such vile terms,
As had she studied to misuse me so.

PETRUCHIO

160   Now, by the world, it is a lusty wench.
I love her ten times more than e'er I did.
O, how I long to have some chat with her!

BAPTISTA

     Well, go with me, and be not so discomfited.
Proceed in practice with my younger daughter,
She's apt to learn and thankful for good turns.
Signor Petruchio, will you go with us,
Or shall I send my daughter Kate to you?

PETRUCHIO

     I pray you do.   *Exeunt all but Petruchio*
             I'll attend her here,
And woo her with some spirit when she comes.
170   Say that she rail, why then I'll tell her plain

---

152 *Frets* vexations (quibbling)
     fume be in a rage (as in 'fret and fume')
156 *pillory* (an instrument of punishment, consisting of a pair of movable boards raised on a post, with holes through which the culprit's head and hands were thrust so that he appeared to be framed in wood)
157 *rascal* base, good-for-nothing
158 *Jack* (term of contempt used of a base or silly fellow)

159 *As had she studied to misuse me so* as though she had given a lot of careful thought to how she might abuse me so
160 *lusty* merry, high-spirited
164 *Proceed in practice* carry on your lessons
168 *attend* await
170-80 *Say that she rail, why then I'll tell her plain ... married.* Petruchio, to enable the audience to enjoy the ensu-

She sings as sweetly as a nightingale.
Say that she frown, I'll say she looks as clear
As morning roses newly washed with dew.
Say she be mute and will not speak a word,
Then I'll commend her volubility,
And say she uttereth piercing eloquence.
If she do bid me pack, I'll give her thanks,
As though she bid me stay by her a week.
If she deny to wed, I'll crave the day
When I shall ask the banns, and when be married.   180
But here she comes, and now, Petruchio, speak.

    Enter Katherina

Good morrow, Kate – for that's your name, I hear.

KATHERINA

Well have you heard, but something hard of hearing;
They call me Katherine that do talk of me.

PETRUCHIO

You lie, in faith, for you are called plain Kate,
And bonny Kate, and sometimes Kate the curst.
But Kate, the prettiest Kate in Christendom,
Kate of Kate Hall, my super-dainty Kate,
For dainties are all Kates, and therefore, Kate,
Take this of me, Kate of my consolation –   190
Hearing thy mildness praised in every town,
Thy virtues spoke of, and thy beauty sounded,
Yet not so deeply as to thee belongs,
Myself am moved to woo thee for my wife.

---

ing scene to the full, announces his
  plan of campaign.
172 *clear* serenely beautiful
176 *piercing* moving
177 *pack* be gone
179 *deny* refuse
183 *heard . . . hard.* The two words were
  both pronounced 'hard', giving a
  pun.

186 *bonny* fine, strapping
189 *dainties are all Kates* (quibbling on
  'cates' meaning 'delicacies')
190 *consolation* comfort
192 *sounded* proclaimed, praised aloud
193 *deeply as to thee belongs* loudly as you
  deserve
194 *moved* impelled

KATHERINA

Moved, in good time! Let him that moved you hither
Remove you hence. I knew you at the first
You were a movable.

PETRUCHIO   Why, what's a movable?

KATHERINA

A joint-stool.

PETRUCHIO   Thou hast hit it. Come, sit on me.

KATHERINA

Asses are made to bear, and so are you.

PETRUCHIO

200   Women are made to bear, and so are you.

KATHERINA

No such jade as you, if me you mean.

PETRUCHIO

Alas, good Kate, I will not burden thee!
For knowing thee to be but young and light –

KATHERINA

Too light for such a swain as you to catch,
And yet as heavy as my weight should be.

195 *in good time!* indeed, forsooth! Katherina is taking *moved* in its literal sense.

196–7 *I knew you at the first | You were a movable* I recognized you from the start for (1) the piece of movable furniture that you are; (2) a person given to change

198 *A joint-stool* a wooden stool made by a joiner. The proverbial remark used by the Fool in *King Lear*, III.6.51, 'Cry you mercy, I took you for a joint-stool,' was a taunting apology for overlooking a person, as Katherina affects to do here.

199 *to bear* to carry burdens. Petruchio gives the words a bawdy turn in the next line.

201 *jade* a horse (of either sex) that soon

tires. Katherina is impugning Petruchio's virility.

202 *burden* (1) lie heavy on; (2) make accusations against. For the second sense, which is the more important here, compare *The Comedy of Errors*, V.1.209, 'this is false he burdens me withal'.

203 *light* (1) slight, slender; (2) wanton

204 *Too light for such a swain as you to catch* too quick-witted to be caught by a country bumpkin like you

205 *as heavy as my weight should be* the right weight for one of my standing. Katherina has switched the allusion to money. Clipped and counterfeit coins were 'too light'. She is saying that she is good sound currency; her reputation as a woman is untar-

PETRUCHIO

Should be? Should – buzz!

KATHERINA   Well ta'en, and like a buzzard.

PETRUCHIO

O slow-winged turtle, shall a buzzard take thee?

KATHERINA

Ay, for a turtle, as he takes a buzzard.

PETRUCHIO

Come, come, you wasp, i'faith, you are too angry.

KATHERINA

If I be waspish, best beware my sting.   210

PETRUCHIO

My remedy is then to pluck it out.

KATHERINA

Ay, if the fool could find it where it lies.

PETRUCHIO

Who knows not where a wasp does wear his sting?
In his tail.

KATHERINA   In his tongue

PETRUCHIO   Whose tongue?

KATHERINA

Yours, if you talk of tales, and so farewell.

She turns to go

nished, and therefore no charge of lightness can touch her.

206 *Should be? Should – buzz!* Petruchio is quibbling here, first on 'be' and 'bee', and then on 'buzz' as (1) the noise made by bees, and (2) rumour or scandal. In effect he tells Katherina 'You should just hear what is said about you.'

ta'en taken, caught

buzzard (1) useless kind of hawk; (2) according to the O.E.D., 'a worth-less, stupid, or ignorant person'. In the opinion of the present editor, however, 'scandal-monger' or 'tale-bearer' fit this context much better.

A similar use of the word will be found at *Richard* III, 1.1.133, 'kites and buzzards prey at liberty'.

207 *turtle* turtle-dove (the symbol of faithful love)

208 *Ay, for a turtle, as he takes a buzzard.* The best explanation of this difficult passage is given by Dover Wilson, who paraphrases it thus: 'the fool will take me for a faithful wife, as the turtle-dove swallows the cock-chafer [yet another meaning of "buzzard"]'.

215 *tales* rumours, discreditable gossip (with, of course, a pun on 'tails' meaning 'backsides')

PETRUCHIO
What, with my tongue in your tail? Nay, come again.
He takes her in his arms
Good Kate, I am a gentleman –   That I'll try.

KATHERINA
She strikes him

PETRUCHIO
I swear I'll cuff you, if you strike again.

KATHERINA
So may you loose your arms.
220   If you strike me, you are no gentleman,
And if no gentleman, why then no arms.

PETRUCHIO
A herald, Kate? O, put me in thy books!

KATHERINA
What is your crest – a coxcomb?

PETRUCHIO
A combless cock, so Kate will be my hen.

KATHERINA
No cock of mine, you crow too like a craven.

PETRUCHIO
Nay, come, Kate, come, you must not look so sour.

KATHERINA
It is my fashion when I see a crab.

216 *What, with my tongue in your tail?*
Apart from its obvious lewdness, this
means 'What, are you going to turn
tail on my repartee?'
come again (1) come back; (2) let's
renew the combat. Compare *Hamlet*,
v.2.295, 'Nay, come again.'
(stage direction) *He takes her in his
arms*. Not in the Folio, but clearly
indicated by Katherina's remark at
line 219.

217 *try* test, make trial of

219 *loose your arms* (1) relax your hold;
(2) lose your coat of arms (the mark
of a gentleman)

222 *in thy books*. To be in the herald's

books was to be registered as a gentleman, but there is also a pun on being
in someone's good books.

223 *crest* (1) figure or device borne
above the shield and helmet in a coat
of arms; (2) a tuft of feathers or the
like on an animal's head
coxcomb (a fool's cap, like a cock's
comb in shape and colour)

224 *so* provided that

225 *craven* (a fighting-cock that is not
game)

227 *crab* (1) crab-apple; (2) sour-tem-
pered person with a sour-looking
face

PETRUCHIO
  Why, here's no crab, and therefore look not sour.
KATHERINA
  There is, there is.
PETRUCHIO
  Then show it me
KATHERINA   Had I a glass, I would.   230
PETRUCHIO
  What, you mean my face?
KATHERINA   Well aimed of such a young one.
PETRUCHIO
  Now, by Saint George, I am too young for you.
KATHERINA
  Yet you are withered.
PETRUCHIO   'Tis with cares.
KATHERINA   I care not.
PETRUCHIO
  Nay, hear you, Kate –
        She struggles.
        In sooth, you scape not so.
KATHERINA
  I chafe you, if I tarry. Let me go.
PETRUCHIO
  No, not a whit. I find you passing gentle.
  'Twas told me you were rough, and coy, and sullen,
  And now I find report a very liar.
  For thou art pleasant, gamesome, passing courteous,
  But slow in speech, yet sweet as spring-time flowers.   240
  Thou canst not frown, thou canst not look askance,
  Nor bite the lip, as angry wenches will,

231 *Well aimed of such a young one* a good
    guess for one so raw
232 *too young* too strong
234 *scape* escape
235 *chafe* (1) vex, annoy; (2) excite, heat
236 *passing* very, extremely

238 *a very liar* an absolute liar
239 *pleasant* merry
    gamesome sportive, gay
240 *But slow in speech* not a bit sharp-
    tongued
241 *askance* scornfully, with disdain

Nor hast thou pleasure to be cross in talk.
But thou with mildness entertain'st thy wooers,
With gentle conference, soft and affable.

He lets her go

Why does the world report that Kate doth limp?
O slanderous world! Kate like the hazel-twig
Is straight and slender, and as brown in hue
As hazel-nuts and sweeter than the kernels.
250   O, let me see thee walk. Thou dost not halt.

KATHERINA
Go, fool, and whom thou keep'st command.

PETRUCHIO
Did ever Dian so become a grove
As Kate this chamber with her princely gait?
O, be thou Dian, and let her be Kate,
And then let Kate be chaste and Dian sportful.

KATHERINA
Where did you study all this goodly speech?

PETRUCHIO
It is extempore, from my mother-wit.

KATHERINA
A witty mother, witless else her son.

PETRUCHIO
Am I not wise?

KATHERINA   Yes, keep you warm.

PETRUCHIO
260   Marry, so I mean, sweet Katherine, in thy bed.

---

243 *cross* given to contradiction,
    perverse
244 *entertain'st* receivest
245 *conference* conversation
251 *whom thou keep'st command* order your
    own servants about, not me
252 *Dian* (Diana, the goddess of chastity
    and hunting)
    become adorn, grace
255 *sportful* amorous, wanton
256 *study* learn off by heart

257 *mother-wit* natural intelligence
258 *A witty mother, witless else her son* a
    wise mother she must be, for without
    her help her son has no wits of his own
259 *Am I not wise? Yes, keep you warm.*
    The retort is an allusion to the prov-
    erb 'He is wise enough that can keep
    himself warm.' Katherina means that
    Petruchio has the bare minimum of
    intelligence necessary for existence,
    and no more.

And therefore, setting all this chat aside,
Thus in plain terms – your father hath consented
That you shall be my wife; your dowry 'greed on;
And will you, nill you, I will marry you.
Now, Kate, I am a husband for your turn,
For by this light whereby I see thy beauty,
Thy beauty that doth make me like thee well,
Thou must be married to no man but me.
For I am he am born to tame you, Kate,
And bring you from a wild Kate to a Kate   270
Conformable as other household Kates.
          Enter Baptista, Gremio, and Tranio
Here comes your father. Never make denial;
I must and will have Katherine to my wife.

BAPTISTA
Now, Signor Petruchio, how speed you with my daughter?

PETRUCHIO
How but well, sir? How but well?
It were impossible I should speed amiss.

BAPTISTA
Why, how now, daughter Katherine? In your dumps?

KATHERINA
Call you me daughter? Now I promise you
You have showed a tender fatherly regard
To wish me wed to one half lunatic,   280
A madcap ruffian and a swearing Jack,
That thinks with oaths to face the matter out.

PETRUCHIO
Father, 'tis thus – yourself and all the world

263 *'greed* agreed
264 *will you, nill you* whether you will or
    whether you won't
265 *for your turn* to fit your needs, exactly
    right for you
267 *like* love
270 *wild Kate* (with a pun on 'wild-cat')
271 *Conformable* tractable, compliant
    household domestic

274 *how speed you* how are you getting
    on, what progress are you making
276 *speed amiss* not make good progress
277 *In your dumps?* are you feeling down-
    hearted?
278 *I promise you* I can tell you
282 *to face the matter out* to get his own
    way by sheer effrontery

That talked of her have talked amiss of her.
If she be curst, it is for policy,
For she's not froward, but modest as the dove.
She is not hot, but temperate as the morn.
For patience she will prove a second Grissel,
And Roman Lucrece for her chastity.
290 And to conclude, we have 'greed so well together
That upon Sunday is the wedding-day.

KATHERINA
I'll see thee hanged on Sunday first.

GREMIO
Hark, Petruchio, she says she'll see thee hanged first.

TRANIO
Is this your speeding? Nay then, good night our part.

PETRUCHIO
Be patient, gentlemen, I choose her for myself.
If she and I be pleased, what's that to you?
'Tis bargained 'twixt us twain, being alone,
That she shall still be curst in company.
I tell you 'tis incredible to believe
300 How much she loves me – O, the kindest Kate!
She hung about my neck, and kiss on kiss
She vied so fast, protesting oath on oath,
That in a twink she won me to her love.

---

285 *for policy* as a deliberate policy, for
her own purposes
286 *froward* difficult, refractory
287 *hot* violent, passionate
288 *a second Grissel*. The famous story of
Patient Griselda, the model of wifely
obedience, is the subject of Chaucer's
The Clerk's Tale. Borrowed by Chaucer from Boccaccio's *Decameron*, it
was subsequently treated in numerous tales and ballads in English.
Two plays on the theme had been
written by the time Shakespeare was
two years old, and another, entitled
Patient Grissell, by Dekker, Chettle,

and Haughton was first acted in
1600.
289 *Roman Lucrece*. The tale of Lucrece,
the legendary Roman heroine who
committed suicide after having been
raped by Tarquin, is told by Shakespeare himself in his elaborate narrative poem *The Rape of Lucrece*, first
published in 1594.
294 *speeding* success
good night our part farewell to our
share in the business
302 *vied* redoubled. To 'vie' was a technical term in card-playing meaning 'to
raise the stakes'.
303 *twink* twinkling, instant

O, you are novices! 'Tis a world to see
How tame, when men and women are alone,
A meacock wretch can make the curstest shrew.
Give me thy hand, Kate, I will unto Venice,
To buy apparel 'gainst the wedding-day.
Provide the feast, father, and bid the guests.
I will be sure my Katherine shall be fine.   310

BAPTISTA

I know not what to say – but give me your hands.
God send you joy! Petruchio, 'tis a match.

GREMIO and TRANIO

Amen, say we. We will be witnesses.

PETRUCHIO

Father, and wife, and gentlemen, adieu,
I will to Venice – Sunday comes apace.
We will have rings, and things, and fine array,
And kiss me, Kate, we will be married o' Sunday.
                              Exeunt Petruchio and Katherina

GREMIO

Was ever match clapped up so suddenly?

BAPTISTA

Faith, gentlemen, now I play a merchant's part,
And venture madly on a desperate mart.   320

304 *'Tis a world to see* it's a treat to see
306 *meacock* spiritless
   shrew. The sixteenth-century pronunciation of this word is indicated by
   the Folio spelling 'shrow' at v.2.187,
   and confirmed by the rhymes at
   IV.I.196–7 and v.2.28–9.
308 *'gainst* (colloquial form of 'against')
   in readiness for
310 *fine* handsomely dressed, in her
   finery
311–13 *give me your hands . . . witnesses.*
   This brief ceremony before witnesses
   was the essential part of an Elizabethan marriage. Once this pre-con-

tract, as it was called, had been made,
neither party could marry another
person. Compare the Duke's words
to Mariana in *Measure for Measure*,
IV.I.70–1:

   He [Angelo] *is your husband on a pre-*
      contract.
   To bring you thus together 'tis no sin . . .

315 *apace* quickly, soon
318 *clapped up* fixed up in a hurry, arranged in an improvised manner
320 *desperate mart* reckless and chancy
   business arrangement – one that is
   probably doomed to failure

TRANIO

'Twas a commodity lay fretting by you,
'Twill bring you gain, or perish on the seas.

BAPTISTA

The gain I seek is quiet in the match.

GREMIO

No doubt but he hath got a quiet catch.
But now, Baptista, to your younger daughter –
Now is the day we long have looked for.
I am your neighbour, and was suitor first.

TRANIO

And I am one that love Bianca more
Than words can witness or your thoughts can guess.

GREMIO

330   Youngling, thou canst not love so dear as I.

TRANIO

Greybeard, thy love doth freeze.

GREMIO   But thine doth fry.
Skipper, stand back, 'tis age that nourisheth.

TRANIO

But youth in ladies' eyes that flourisheth.

BAPTISTA

Content you, gentlemen, I will compound this strife.
'Tis deeds must win the prize, and he of both

321 *'Twas a commodity lay fretting by you* it
(referring to Katherina) was a piece
of goods that was deteriorating in
value while it remained on your
hands. There is a quibble on *fretting*
(1) decaying through moth and rust;
(2) chafing with vexation.

323 *quiet in.* The Folio reads: 'quiet me',
the compositor having taken 'inne'
for 'me'. The same mistake occurs
again at IV.2.71.

330 *Youngling* stripling, novice

332 *Skipper* light-brained skipping fel-

low. Compare *1 Henry IV*, III.2.60,
where the King contemptuously describes Richard II as 'The skipping
king'.
nourisheth provides the good things
of life

333 *flourisheth* prospers, thrives

334 *compound* compose, make an amic-
able settlement of

335 *deeds* (1) actions; (2) legal deeds,
title-deeds
he of both the one of you two

That can assure my daughter greatest dower
Shall have my Bianca's love.
Say, Signor Gremio, what can you assure her?

GREMIO
First, as you know, my house within the city
Is richly furnished with plate and gold,   340
Basins and ewers to lave her dainty hands –
My hangings all of Tyrian tapestry.
In ivory coffers I have stuffed my crowns,
In cypress chests my arras counterpoints,
Costly apparel, tents, and canopies,
Fine linen, Turkey cushions bossed with pearl,
Valance of Venice gold in needlework,
Pewter and brass, and all things that belongs
To house or housekeeping. Then at my farm
I have a hundred milch-kine to the pail,   350
Six score fat oxen standing in my stalls,
And all things answerable to this portion.
Myself am struck in years, I must confess,
And if I die tomorrow this is hers,
If whilst I live she will be only mine.

TRANIO
That 'only' came well in. Sir, list to me.

336 *dower* (the land and goods which the husband settled on his wife at marriage in order to provide for her widowhood in case she survived him)
340 *plate* utensils of silver
341 *lave* wash
342 *hangings* (draperies with which beds and walls were hung)
343 *crowns* (coins worth five shillings each)
344 *arras counterpoints* counterpanes of Arras tapestry
345 *tents* bed-testers or canopies
346 *bossed* embossed, studded
347 *Valance of Venice gold in needlework*

valances (fringes on the canopy of a bed) adorned with Venetian embroidery in gold thread
348 *belongs* (the old plural)
350 *milch-kine to the pail* cows whose milk goes to the dairy (not to feed calves)
352 *answerable to this portion* corresponding to an estate on this scale
353 *struck in years* advanced in age, old
356 *came well in* was mentioned at the right time, was very apropos – since Tranio now makes great play with the fact that he is an only son
list listen

I am my father's heir and only son.
If I may have your daughter to my wife,
I'll leave her houses three or four as good,
360   Within rich Pisa walls, as any one
Old Signor Gremio has in Padua,
Besides two thousand ducats by the year
Of fruitful land, all which shall be her jointure.
What, have I pinched you, Signor Gremio?

GREMIO

Two thousand ducats by the year of land!
(*aside*) My land amounts not to so much in all.
(*to them*) That she shall have, besides an argosy
That now is lying in Marseilles road.
What, have I choked you with an argosy?

TRANIO

370   Gremio, 'tis known my father hath no less
Than three great argosies, besides two galliasses
And twelve tight galleys. These I will assure her,
And twice as much whate'er thou off'rest next.

GREMIO

Nay, I have offered all, I have no more,
And she can have no more than all I have.
If you like me, she shall have me and mine.

TRANIO

Why, then the maid is mine from all the world

360 *rich Pisa walls* the walls of rich Pisa
362–3 *two thousand ducats by the year* | *Of fruitful land* fertile land bringing in an income of two thousand ducats a year. A ducat was a Venetian gold coin worth about nine shillings.
363 *her jointure* the estate settled on her to provide for her widowhood
364 *pinched you* put you in a tight corner, gained an advantage in the argument
366 *My land amounts not to so much in all* the capital value of my land does not come to that

367 *argosy* (merchant-vessel of the largest size, especially one from Ragusa – whence the name – or Venice)
368 *Marseilles road* the roadstead (sheltered anchorage) at Marseilles. The Folio reads: 'Marcellus roade', and thus indicates the sixteenth-century pronunciation of 'Marseilles'.
371 *galliasses* (heavy, low-built vessels, larger than galleys)
372 *tight* sound, water-tight

By your firm promise. Gremio is out-vied.

BAPTISTA
I must confess your offer is the best,
And let your father make her the assurance, 380
She is your own. Else, you must pardon me,
If you should die before him, where's her dower?

TRANIO
That's but a cavil. He is old, I young.

GREMIO
And may not young men die as well as old?

BAPTISTA
Well, gentlemen,
I am thus resolved. On Sunday next you know
My daughter Katherine is to be married.
Now, on the Sunday following shall Bianca
Be bride to you, if you make this assurance;
If not, to Signor Gremio.
And so I take my leave, and thank you both. 390

GREMIO
Adieu, good neighbour.   *Exit Baptista*
                Now I fear thee not.
Sirrah, young gamester, your father were a fool
To give thee all, and in his waning age
Set foot under thy table. Tut, a toy!
An old Italian fox is not so kind, my boy.   *Exit*

TRANIO
A vengeance on your crafty withered hide!
Yet I have faced it with a card of ten.
'Tis in my head to do my master good.

378 *out-vied* out-bidden. A card-player
was 'out-vied' when he refused to
stake any more on his hand.
383 *but a cavil* merely a captious objec-
tion
393 *gamester* adventurer, gambler. Gremio has picked up the allusion implicit in Tranio's use of the word
'out-vied' at line 378.

395 *Set foot under thy table* live on your
charity
   a toy! sheer nonsense!
398 *faced it with a card of ten* brazened the
matter out by playing a card with
ten pips. To 'outface with a card of
ten' was a proverbial phrase for
bluffing.
399 *'Tis in my head* I have a scheme

400   I see no reason but supposed Lucentio
Must get a father, called supposed Vincentio.
And that's a wonder. Fathers commonly
Do get their children; but in this case of wooing
A child shall get a sire, if I fail not of my cunning. *Exit*

III.1   *Enter Lucentio as Cambio, Hortensio as Licio, and*
            Bianca

LUCENTIO
    Fiddler, forbear, you grow too forward, sir.
    Have you so soon forgot the entertainment
    Her sister Katherine welcomed you withal?

HORTENSIO
    But, wrangling pedant, this is
    The patroness of heavenly harmony.
    Then give me leave to have prerogative,
    And when in music we have spent an hour,
    Your lecture shall have leisure for as much.

LUCENTIO
    Preposterous ass, that never read so far

---

400 *I see no reason but* I see it is necessary
    that
    supposed the pretended, the substitute
402 *wonder* miracle
403 *get* beget
404 *I fail not of my cunning* I don't lose
    my ingenuity

III.1 This scene is headed '*Actus Tertia.*'
in the Folio, though there is no indication there of where the second Act
begins. It shows a side of Bianca's character that has not been apparent up to this
point.

1–3 *Fiddler, forbear, you grow too forward,*
sir . . . withal? From these lines it
looks as though Hortensio, when the

scene opens, is holding Bianca's hand
to 'teach her fingering', as he sought
to do with Katherina at II.1.150.

2 *entertainment* reception

3 *withal* with

4 *But, wrangling pedant, this is.* The line is
metrically defective, but it is impossible to say what has been omitted
from it.

6 *prerogative* precedence

8 *lecture* lesson

9 *Preposterous.* The word is used here in
its literal sense, meaning 'one who
inverts the natural order of things,
one who puts the cart before the
horse'.

To know the cause why music was ordained!   10
Was it not to refresh the mind of man
After his studies or his usual pain?
Then give me leave to read philosophy,
And while I pause serve in your harmony.

HORTENSIO
Sirrah, I will not bear these braves of thine.

BIANCA
Why, gentlemen, you do me double wrong
To strive for that which resteth in my choice.
I am no breeching scholar in the schools,
I'll not be tied to hours nor 'pointed times,
But learn my lessons as I please myself.   20
And, to cut off all strife, here sit we down.
Take you your instrument, play you the whiles—
His lecture will be done ere you have tuned.

HORTENSIO
You'll leave his lecture when I am in tune?

LUCENTIO
That will be never. Tune your instrument.

BIANCA Where left we last?

LUCENTIO Here, madam.
     (He reads)
'Hic ibat Simois, hic est Sigeia tellus,
Hic steterat Priami regia celsa senis.'

BIANCA Construe them.   30

LUCENTIO 'Hic ibat', as I told you before – 'Simois', I am

---

10 *ordained* created, instituted

12 *usual pain* customary toil, normal work

14 *serve in* serve up (Lucentio's way of voicing his contempt for Hortensio and his music)

15 *braves* bravadoes, ostentatious displays of defiance

18 *no breeching scholar in the schools* no schoolboy liable to be flogged

19 *'pointed* appointed

22 *the whiles* the while

25 *That will be never.* Lucentio is deliberately taking 'in tune' in the sense of 'being in a good temper'.

28–9 *Hic ibat Simois, hic est Sigeia tellus ... senis.* These lines from Ovid (*Heroides*, i. 33–4) mean 'Here ran the [river] Simois; here is the Sigeian land [Troy]; here stood the lofty palace of old Priam.'

Lucentio – '*hic est*', son unto Vincentio of Pisa – '*Sigeia
tellus*', disguised thus to get your love – '*Hic steterat*',
and that Lucentio that comes a-wooing – '*Priami*', is my
man Tranio – '*regia*', bearing my port – '*celsa senis*',
that we might beguile the old pantaloon.

HORTENSIO Madam, my instrument's in tune.

BIANCA Let's hear. (*He plays*) O fie! The treble jars.

LUCENTIO Spit in the hole, man, and tune again.

40 BIANCA Now let me see if I can construe it. '*Hic ibat
Simois*', I know you not – '*hic est Sigeia tellus*', I trust you
not – '*Hic steterat Priami*', take heed he hear us not –
'*regia*', presume not – '*celsa senis*', despair not.

HORTENSIO

Madam, 'tis now in tune.

LUCENTIO   All but the bass.

HORTENSIO

The bass is right, 'tis the base knave that jars.
(*aside*) How fiery and forward our pedant is.
Now, for my life, the knave doth court my love.
Pedascule, I'll watch you better yet.

BIANCA

In time I may believe, yet I mistrust.

---

35 *port* state, style

36 *the old pantaloon* Gremio. See note to
    stage direction at 1.1.45.

38 *fie* (an exclamation of disgust)

39 *Spit in the hole, man, and tune again.*
    This is a perversion of the proverb
    that was used to encourage someone
    to make a second attempt, 'Spit in
    your hands and take better hold.'
    Lucentio is showing his ignorance of
    music, because to spit in the sound-
    hole of a lute would not help to tune
    it.

46–56 *How fiery and forward our pedant is
    . . . you both.* In the Folio the speeches
    in this section of the dialogue are
    wrongly assigned as follows:
    Luc. How fiery . . .

                          . . . I mistrust.
    Bian. Mistrust it . . .
                          . . . grandfather.
    Hort. I must . . .
                          . . . you both.
    The prime cause of the confusion
    was probably the use of *Lic.*, the
    shortened form of Hortensio's as-
    sumed name Licio, in the speech
    headings, since *Lic.* would be very
    difficult to distinguish from *Luc.*
    Similar confusion occurs at IV.2.4–8
    (see note).

48 *Pedascule* (a nonce-word coined as a
    contemptuous diminutive of 'pedant'
    on the analogy of '*didaskalos*' – the
    Greek for 'master')

LUCENTIO

   Mistrust it not – for, sure, Aeacides   50
   Was Ajax, called so from his grandfather.

BIANCA

   I must believe my master, else, I promise you,
   I should be arguing still upon that doubt.
   But let it rest. Now, Licio, to you.
   Good master, take it not unkindly, pray,
   That I have been thus pleasant with you both.

HORTENSIO (*to Lucentio*)

   You may go walk, and give me leave awhile.
   My lessons make no music in three parts.

LUCENTIO

   Are you so formal, sir? Well, I must wait –
   (*aside*) And watch withal, for, but I be deceived,   60
   Our fine musician groweth amorous.

HORTENSIO

   Madam, before you touch the instrument
   To learn the order of my fingering,
   I must begin with rudiments of art,
   To teach you gamut in a briefer sort,
   More pleasant, pithy, and effectual,
   Than hath been taught by any of my trade.
   And there it is in writing fairly drawn.

50–51 *Aeacides* | *Was Ajax . . . grand-father.* Ajax Telamonius, one of the Greek heroes in the Trojan War, was also known as Aeacides from the name of his grandfather Aeacus. Lucentio, in an attempt to blind Hortensio with Ovid, has moved on to the next line of *Heroides*, i, which begins '*Illic Aeacides*'.

55–6 *Good master, take it not unkindly, pray,* | *That I have been thus pleasant with you both.* Bianca is addressing Hortensio, who alone has reason to be displeased; and *pleasant with you both* stretches her apology to cover Lucentio's chaff, and her laughter at it.

57 *give me leave* (a polite way of saying 'Please go')

59 *formal* punctilious, concerned for your professional rights

60 *withal* at the same time
but unless

63 *order* method

65 *gamut* the musical scale
briefer sort quicker fashion

66 *pithy* condensed
effectual effective

BIANCA
Why, I am past my gamut long ago.

HORTENSIO
70   Yet read the gamut of Hortensio.

BIANCA (*reads*)
   'Gamut *I am, the ground of all accord* —
   A re, *to plead Hortensio's passion* —
   B mi, *Bianca, take him for thy lord* —
   C fa ut, *that loves with all affection* —
   D sol re, *one clef, two notes have I* —
   E la mi, *show pity or I die.*'
Call you this gamut? Tut, I like it not!
Old fashions please me best. I am not so nice
To change true rules for odd inventions.
      Enter a Servant

SERVANT
80   Mistress, your father prays you leave your books,
And help to dress your sister's chamber up.
You know tomorrow is the wedding-day.

BIANCA
Farewell, sweet masters both, I must be gone.
      Exeunt Bianca and Servant

LUCENTIO
Faith, mistress, then I have no cause to stay.   *Exit*

HORTENSIO
But I have cause to pry into this pedant,
Methinks he looks as though he were in love.

---

71 *ground of all accord* basis of all harmony

74 *ut* (corresponds to the 'doh' of modern usage)

75 *one clef, two notes.* It has been suggested that the 'one clef' is love and the 'two notes' Hortensio's real and his assumed personality.

78-9 *so nice | To change* so capricious as to exchange

79 *odd inventions* fantastical new ideas

80 SERVANT. The Folio heads this speech '*Nicke.*', which some editors have taken as the name of the actor who first played the part. In fact, however, it seems most improbable that Shakespeare would have had a particular actor in mind for a part that only amounts to three lines.

Yet if thy thoughts, Bianca, be so humble
To cast thy wandering eyes on every stale,
Seize thee that list. If once I find thee ranging,
Hortensio will be quit with thee by changing.   *Exit*   90

Enter Baptista, Gremio, Tranio as Lucentio,   III.2
Katherina, Bianca, Lucentio as Cambio, and attendants
on Katherina

BAPTISTA *(to Tranio)*

Signor Lucentio, this is the 'pointed day
That Katherine and Petruchio should be married,
And yet we hear not of our son-in-law.
What will be said? What mockery will it be
To want the bridegroom when the priest attends
To speak the ceremonial rites of marriage!
What says Lucentio to this shame of ours?

KATHERINA

No shame but mine. I must forsooth be forced
To give my hand, opposed against my heart,
Unto a mad-brain rudesby, full of spleen,   10
Who wooed in haste and means to wed at leisure.
I told you, I, he was a frantic fool,
Hiding his bitter jests in blunt behaviour.

87–8 *if thy thoughts, Bianca, be so humble |
To cast* if your inclinations, Bianca,
are so low that you cast
88 *stale* decoy, lure. The metaphor, from
falconry, is carried on in the next
line. Hortensio is beginning to see
Bianca as a hawk that will stoop to
anything.
89 *Seize thee that list* let anyone who
wishes have you
ranging (1) straying (of a hawk); (2)
being inconstant (of a lover or wife)
90 *will be quit with thee by changing* will
get even with you by loving another

III.2 (stage direction) *Enter Baptista ...
Lucentio as Cambio ... Katherina.* The
Folio direction reads: '*Enter Baptista,
Gremio, Tranio, Katherine, Bianca, and
others, attendants.*' The omission of
Lucentio from it is probably due to
the fact that he says nothing until
line 137.
5 *To want* to be without
10 *rudesby, full of spleen* rough unmannerly fellow full of whims and
caprices

And to be noted for a merry man,
He'll woo a thousand, 'point the day of marriage,
Make feast, invite friends, and proclaim the banns,
Yet never means to wed where he hath wooed.
Now must the world point at poor Katherine,
And say 'Lo, there is mad Petruchio's wife,
20   If it would please him come and marry her.'

TRANIO
Patience, good Katherine, and Baptista too.
Upon my life, Petruchio means but well,
Whatever fortune stays him from his word.
Though he be blunt, I know him passing wise,
Though he be merry, yet withal he's honest.

KATHERINA
Would Katherine had never seen him though.
        Exit weeping, followed by Bianca and the other women

BAPTISTA
Go, girl, I cannot blame thee now to weep,
For such an injury would vex a saint,
Much more a shrew of thy impatient humour.

---

14 *to be noted for* in order to be known as, to get a reputation as
16 *Make feast, invite friends, and.* The Folio reads: 'Make friends, inuite, and', which is neither good sense nor good metre. The reading adopted in this edition is based on Petruchio's line at II.1.309 'Provide the feast, father, and bid the guests'.
22–5 *Upon my life, Petruchio means but well . . . honest.* At some stage in the evolution of *The Taming of the Shrew* these lines must have belonged to Hortensio, who is Petruchio's friend and therefore knows a good deal about him. They are out of place in the mouth of Tranio, who, from this point onwards, appears to have taken over much that must originally have been written for Hortensio.

23 *Whatever fortune stays him from his word* whatever accident prevents him from keeping his promise
25 *merry* facetious, a bit of a joker
   honest one who keeps his word
26 (stage direction) *Exit weeping, followed by Bianca and the other women.* The Folio direction '*Exit weeping*' is simpler and more dramatic, since it emphasizes that Petruchio has already met with some success in his effort to make Katherina acknowledge her own feminine nature, but it has to be expanded in order to get the bridal train off the stage.
27 *now to weep* for weeping now
29 *of thy impatient.* The Folio reads: 'of impatient', but the necessary 'thy' appears in the Second Folio.

Enter Biondello

BIONDELLO Master, master, news! And such old news   30
as you never heard of.

BAPTISTA Is it new and old too? How may that be?

BIONDELLO Why, is it not news to hear of Petruchio's
coming?

BAPTISTA Is he come?

BIONDELLO Why, no, sir.

BAPTISTA What then?

BIONDELLO He is coming.

BAPTISTA When will he be here?

BIONDELLO When he stands where I am and sees you   40
there.

TRANIO But say, what to thine old news?

BIONDELLO Why, Petruchio is coming in a new hat and
an old jerkin; a pair of old breeches thrice turned; a
pair of boots that have been candle-cases, one buckled,
another laced; an old rusty sword ta'en out of the town
armoury, with a broken hilt, and chapeless; with two
broken points; his horse hipped – with an old mothy
saddle and stirrups of no kindred – besides, possessed,
with the glanders and like to mose in the chine, troubled   50

---

30 *such old news.* The Folio reads: 'such
newes', but Baptista's comment in
the next speech shows that 'old',
meaning 'good old', or 'rare old',
has been omitted.

42 *what to* what of

44 *jerkin* short outer coat or jacket

45 *boots that have been candle-cases* boots
too old for wear that have been used
to keep candle-ends in

47 *chapeless* lacking a sheath. The 'chape'
was literally the metal plate on a
scabbard that covered the point of a
sword.

48 *points* (tagged laces used for fastening
the hose to the doublet)

hipped lamed in the hip

49 *of no kindred* that don't match, that
are not a pair

49–50 *possessed with* affected by, suffering
from

50 *the glanders* (a contagious disease in
horses, marked by swellings beneath
the jaw and discharge of mucous
matter from the nostrils)
like to likely to
mose in the chine. The word 'mose' is
not known outside this passage and
is probably corrupt. 'To mourn of
the chine' was to suffer from the
final stage of 'glanders', and this is
probably what is meant here.

with the lampass, infected with the fashions, full of
windgalls, sped with spavins, rayed with the yellows,
past cure of the fives, stark spoiled with the staggers,
begnawn with the bots, swayed in the back and shoulder-
shotten, near-legged before, and with a half-cheeked
bit and a headstall of sheep's leather, which, being
restrained to keep him from stumbling, hath been often
burst and new-repaired with knots; one girth six times
pieced, and a woman's crupper of velure, which hath
60   two letters for her name fairly set down in studs, and
here and there pieced with pack-thread.

BAPTISTA Who comes with him?

BIONDELLO O sir, his lackey, for all the world caparisoned

---

51 *lampass* (a disease of horses in which
the fleshy lining behind the front
teeth swells and hinders mastication)
fashions farcy (a horse-disease similar
to glanders)

52 *windgalls* (soft tumours on a horse's
legs just above the fetlocks)
sped with ruined by
spavins swellings of the leg-joints
rayed soiled, befouled
yellows jaundice

53 *fives* strangles (a swelling of the paro-
tid glands)
stark spoiled with absolutely wrecked by
staggers (a horse-disease marked by
giddiness)

54 *begnawn* gnawed at
bots (a disease caused by intestinal
worms)
swayed strained. The Folio reads
'Waid'.

54-5 *shoulder-shotten* with a dislocated
shoulder

55 *near-legged before* knock-kneed in the
front legs

55-6 *half-cheeked bit* bit on which the
cheeks (the rings or side pieces attach-
ing the bit to the bridle) had got
broken

56 *headstall* (the part of the bridle covering the horse's head)
sheep's leather (not so strong as pig-
skin or leather of cowhide, which
were normally used)

57 *restrained* drawn tight

58 *new-repaired*. The Folio has 'now re-
paired', but the context makes it clear
that this operation has been done
not once but time and again.
girth (the leather band going round a
horse's belly and drawn tight to hold
the saddle in place)

59 *pieced* mended
crupper (strap, normally of leather,
ending in a loop which passes under
the horse's tail and prevents the
saddle from slipping)
of velure made of velvet

60 *two letters for her name fairly set down in
studs* her two initials handsomely
marked on it in studs (probably of
brass or silver)

61 *pack-thread* string

63 *for all the world caparisoned* in every
respect harnessed, dressed in trappings exactly

like the horse; with a linen stock on one leg and a kersey
boot-hose on the other, gartered with a red and blue
list; an old hat, and the humour of forty fancies pricked
in't for a feather; a monster, a very monster in apparel,
and not like a Christian footboy or a gentleman's lackey.

TRANIO
'Tis some odd humour pricks him to this fashion.
Yet oftentimes he goes but mean-apparelled.   70

BAPTISTA I am glad he's come, howsoe'er he comes.

BIONDELLO Why, sir, he comes not.

BAPTISTA Didst thou not say he comes?

BIONDELLO Who? That Petruchio came?

BAPTISTA Ay, that Petruchio came.

BIONDELLO No, sir. I say his horse comes with him on
his back.

BAPTISTA Why, that's all one.

BIONDELLO
          Nay, by Saint Jamy,
          I hold you a penny,   80
          A horse and a man
          Is more than one,
          And yet not many.
          Enter Petruchio and Grumio

PETRUCHIO Come, where be these gallants? Who's at
home?

BAPTISTA You are welcome, sir.

PETRUCHIO And yet I come not well?

64 *stock* stocking
   kersey (coarse woollen cloth)
65 *boot-hose* (over-stocking which covers
   the leg like a jack-boot)
66 *list* strip of cloth
   the humour of forty fancies. This must
   be an allusion to some kind of fashionable affectation, but precisely
   what it was no one knows.
66–7 *pricked in't* pinned to it

69 *odd humour pricks* strange whim that
   incites
78 *all one* one and the same thing
79–83 *Nay, by Saint Jamy . . . many.* This
   jingle is printed as prose in the
   Folio.
80 *I hold you* I bet you
87 *I come not well?* I don't arrive oppor-
   tunely? (Petruchio has noticed the
   look of displeasure on Baptista's face.)

BAPTISTA And yet you halt not.

TRANIO Not so well apparelled as I wish you were.

PETRUCHIO

90   Were it not better I should rush in thus?
        But where is Kate? Where is my lovely bride?
        How does my father? Gentles, methinks you frown.
        And wherefore gaze this goodly company
        As if they saw some wondrous monument,
        Some comet, or unusual prodigy?

BAPTISTA
        Why, sir, you know this is your wedding-day.
        First were we sad, fearing you would not come,
        Now sadder that you come so unprovided.
        Fie, doff this habit, shame to your estate,
100   An eye-sore to our solemn festival.

TRANIO
        And tell us what occasion of import
        Hath all so long detained you from your wife
        And sent you hither so unlike yourself?

PETRUCHIO
        Tedious it were to tell, and harsh to hear –
        Sufficeth I am come to keep my word,
        Though in some part enforcèd to digress,
        Which at more leisure I will so excuse

88 *you halt not.* Taking 'come' in the literal sense of 'walk', Baptista points out that Petruchio's entrance has been unceremonious.

90 *Were it not better.* The Folio reads: 'Were it better', which does not make very good sense.

92 *Gentles* gentlefolk, gentlemen

94 *wondrous monument* strange portent

95 *Some comet.* Comets were regarded as omens of disaster. Compare *Julius Caesar*, II.2.30–31:

When beggars die, there are no comets seen;

The heavens themselves blaze forth the death of princes.

prodigy omen

98 *unprovided* unprepared, improperly dressed

99 *habit* dress, outfit
   estate rank, social status

101 *occasion of import* matter of consequence, important reason

105 *Sufficeth* it is enough that

106 *digress* (1) go out of my way; (2) deviate from my promise

As you shall well be satisfied withal.
But where is Kate? I stay too long from her.
The morning wears, 'tis time we were at church.   110

TRANIO

See not your bride in these unreverent robes,
Go to my chamber, put on clothes of mine.

PETRUCHIO

Not I, believe me. Thus I'll visit her.

BAPTISTA

But thus, I trust, you will not marry her.

PETRUCHIO

Good sooth, even thus. Therefore ha' done with words;
To me she's married, not unto my clothes.
Could I repair what she will wear in me
As I can change these poor accoutrements,
'Twere well for Kate and better for myself.
But what a fool am I to chat with you,   120
When I should bid good morrow to my bride,
And seal the title with a lovely kiss.

                                        Exit with Grumio

TRANIO

He hath some meaning in his mad attire.
We will persuade him, be it possible,
To put on better ere he go to church.

BAPTISTA

I'll after him and see the event of this.

                Exit followed by Gremio, Biondello, and attendants

110 *wears* is passing, wears on
111 *unreverent* disrespectful, unseemly
115 *Good sooth* yes indeed, truly
  ha' have (colloquial)
117 *wear* wear away, use up. The allusion is bawdy.
122 *lovely* loving
123–5 *He hath some meaning in his mad
  attire . . . church.* These words, which
  give the impression that Tranio is

about to follow Petruchio, were
almost certainly written for Hortensio in the original version of the
play. There can be little doubt that
the part of Hortensio has been rather
clumsily excised from this scene, and
that his words have not very appropriately been given to Tranio.
126 *event* upshot, outcome

TRANIO

But, sir, to love concerneth us to add
Her father's liking, which to bring to pass,
As I before imparted to your worship,
130   I am to get a man – whate'er he be
It skills not much, we'll fit him to our turn –
And he shall be Vincentio of Pisa,
And make assurance here in Padua
Of greater sums than I have promisèd.
So shall you quietly enjoy your hope
And marry sweet Bianca with consent.

LUCENTIO

Were it not that my fellow schoolmaster
Doth watch Bianca's steps so narrowly,
'Twere good methinks to steal our marriage,
140   Which once performed, let all the world say no,
I'll keep mine own despite of all the world.

TRANIO

That by degrees we mean to look into
And watch our vantage in this business.
We'll overreach the greybeard Gremio,
The narrow-prying father Minola,
The quaint musician, amorous Licio –

127 *But, sir, to love.* The Folio reads:
'But sir, Loue' which does not make
sense. Some editors change this to
'But to her love' which certainly
makes the meaning much clearer.

The abrupt beginning of this
speech, together with Tranio's remaining on the stage after his previous remarks, and with the presence
of Lucentio, who is not included in
the Folio entry at the beginning of
the scene and who has not said a
word hitherto, all point to cobbling.
There is every indication that something has been cut between Baptista's
exit and the beginning of this
speech.

127–128 *to love concerneth us to add | Her
father's liking* it is essential for us to
win her father's good will and join it
to her love for you
131 *It skills not much* it doesn't matter
much, it makes no difference
138 *steps* movements, actions
139 *to steal our marriage* to make a secret
marriage
140 *let all the world say no* even though it
meets with universal opposition
143 *watch our vantage* look out for a favourable opportunity
144 *overreach* dupe, get the better of
145 *narrow-prying* inquisitive
146 *quaint* crafty, scheming

All for my master's sake, Lucentio.

    Enter Gremio

Signor Gremio, came you from the church?

GREMIO

As willingly as e'er I came from school.

TRANIO

And is the bride and bridegroom coming home?   150

GREMIO

A bridegroom, say you? 'Tis a groom indeed,
A grumbling groom, and that the girl shall find.

TRANIO

Curster than she? Why, 'tis impossible.

GREMIO

Why, he's a devil, a devil, a very fiend.

TRANIO

Why, she's a devil, a devil, the devil's dam.

GREMIO

Tut, she's a lamb, a dove, a fool to him.
I'll tell you, Sir Lucentio – when the priest
Should ask if Katherine should be his wife,
'Ay, by gogs-wouns', quoth he, and swore so loud

---

147 (stage direction) *Enter Gremio*. The very short space of time allowed for the marriage – a mere twenty lines – adds to the evidence that the dialogue between Tranio and Lucentio has been heavily cut.

148 *came you* have you come

149 *As willingly as e'er I came from school.* Like much that Gremio says, this expression was a proverbial one.

150 *And is the bride and bridgeroom coming home.* Shakespeare often uses the singular form of the verb when the subject is two singular nouns. Compare 'Hanging and wiving goes by destiny' (*The Merchant of Venice*, II.9.83).

151 *a groom indeed* a really rough individual just like a servingman

156 *a fool* a gentle innocent (term of pity as often in Shakespeare)

157 *Sir Lucentio*. In Shakespeare's day foreigners belonging to the gentry were often addressed as 'Sir'. Lucentio, like Vincentio at IV.2.106, is regarded as a foreigner because he comes from Pisa.

158 *Should ask* asked, came to ask. 'Should' is sometimes used by Shakespeare to denote a reported statement – compare *As You Like It*, III.2.167–8, 'But didst thou hear without wondering how thy name should be hanged and carved upon these trees?'

159 *by gogs-wouns* by God's wounds (a common oath)

160   That all-amazed the priest let fall the book,
And as he stooped again to take it up,
This mad-brained bridegroom took him such a cuff
That down fell priest and book, and book and priest.
'Now take them up', quoth he, 'if any list.'

TRANIO
What said the wench when he rose up again?

GREMIO
Trembled and shook. For why, he stamped and swore
As if the vicar meant to cozen him.
But after many ceremonies done
He calls for wine. 'A health!' quoth he, as if
170   He had been aboard, carousing to his mates
After a storm; quaffed off the muscadel,
And threw the sops all in the sexton's face,
Having no other reason
But that his beard grew thin and hungerly

161 *again to take it up* to take it up again

162 *took him* struck him, gave him

164 *Now take them up.* 'Them' here refers to the bride's dress. Petruchio is explaining his conduct by saying that he suspected the bending priest of trying to interfere with Katherina's underwear – compare Grumio's remarks to the Tailor at IV.3.154–9. Such a suspicion would have some plausibility for an Elizabethan audience, since it was customary after the marriage ceremony for the young men present to rush forward and pluck off the elaborate emblems made of ribbons that the bride wore on her dress, and also to remove her ribbon garters.
if any list if anyone cares to (an obvious threat to any who sought to follow the custom described in the previous note)

165 *rose up again.* The Folio reads: 'rose againe' which is unmetrical. Another way of curing the defect is by reading 'arose again'.

166–82 *Trembled and shook ... minstrel play.* These lines are printed as prose in the Folio.

167 *cozen* cheat, deceive (by some irregularity that would make the marriage invalid)

169 *He calls for wine.* At the conclusion of the marriage service in Shakespeare's time a cup of muscadel (see note below) with cakes or sops in it was drunk by the bride, the bridegroom, and the company.

171 *muscadel* (a sweet wine. Petruchio leaves none for anyone else.)

174 *hungerly* sparsely, having a famished undernourished look

And seemed to ask him sops as he was drinking.
This done, he took the bride about the neck,
And kissed her lips with such a clamorous smack
That at the parting all the church did echo.
And I seeing this came thence for very shame,
And after me, I know, the rout is coming.   180
Such a mad marriage never was before.
Hark, hark! I hear the minstrels play.

> *Music plays*
> *Enter Petruchio, Katherina, Bianca, Baptista,*
> *Hortensio, Grumio, and attendants*

PETRUCHIO
Gentlemen and friends, I thank you for your pains.
I know you think to dine with me today,
And have prepared great store of wedding cheer,
But so it is, my haste doth call me hence,
And therefore here I mean to take my leave.

BAPTISTA
Is't possible you will away tonight?

PETRUCHIO
I must away today before night come.
Make it no wonder. If you knew my business,   190
You would entreat me rather go than stay.
And, honest company, I thank you all
That have beheld me give away myself
To this most patient, sweet, and virtuous wife.
Dine with my father, drink a health to me,
For I must hence, and farewell to you all.

TRANIO
Let us entreat you stay till after dinner.

PETRUCHIO
It may not be.

GREMIO   Let me entreat you.

---

180 *rout* company, crowd of guests   190 *Make it no wonder* don't be surprised
184 *think* expect

PETRUCHIO
   It cannot be.

KATHERINA Let me entreat you.

PETRUCHIO
200   I am content.

KATHERINA Are you content to stay?

PETRUCHIO
   I am content you shall entreat me stay –
   But yet not stay, entreat me how you can.

KATHERINA
   Now if you love me stay.

PETRUCHIO   Grumio, my horse.

GRUMIO Ay, sir, they be ready – the oats have eaten the
horses.

KATHERINA
   Nay then,
   Do what thou canst, I will not go today,
   No, nor tomorrow – not till I please myself.
   The door is open, sir, there lies your way,
210   You may be jogging whiles your boots are green.
   For me, I'll not be gone till I please myself.
   'Tis like you'll prove a jolly surly groom
   That take it on you at the first so roundly.

PETRUCHIO
   O Kate, content thee, prithee be not angry.

KATHERINA
   I will be angry – what hast thou to do?

202 *not stay* not content to stay
    how you can how you may
203 *horse* horses. 'Horse', the old form
    of the plural, was still common in
    Shakespeare's time.
204–5 *they be ready – the oats have eaten the
    horses* the horses are fresh (ready to
    gallop) because they have had more
    oats than they could eat
210 *You may be jogging whiles your boots are
    green* be off while your boots are

fresh (proverbial expression for getting rid of an unwelcome guest)
212 *a jolly* an arrogant, overbearing
213 *That take it on you at the first so
    roundly* since you assume authority so
    unhesitatingly from the outset
214 *content thee* compose yourself, keep
    your temper
215 *what hast thou to do?* what business of
    yours is it, what right have you to
    interfere?

Father, be quiet – he shall stay my leisure.

GREMIO

Ay marry, sir, now it begins to work.

KATHERINA

Gentlemen, forward to the bridal dinner.
I see a woman may be made a fool
If she had not a spirit to resist.   220

PETRUCHIO

They shall go forward, Kate, at thy command.
Obey the bride, you that attend on her.
Go to the feast, revel and domineer,
Carouse full measure to her maidenhead,
Be mad and merry, or go hang yourselves.
But for my bonny Kate, she must with me.

*He seizes her, as though to protect her from the rest of
the company, to whom he speaks*

Nay, look not big, nor stamp, nor stare, nor fret,
I will be master of what is mine own.
She is my goods, my chattels, she is my house,
My household stuff, my field, my barn,   230
My horse, my ox, my ass, my any thing,
And here she stands. Touch her whoever dare!
I'll bring mine action on the proudest he
That stops my way in Padua. Grumio,
Draw forth thy weapon, we are beset with thieves,   ·
Rescue thy mistress if thou be a man.
Fear not, sweet wench, they shall not touch thee, Kate.
I'll buckler thee against a million.

216 *stay my leisure* wait till I'm ready
223 *domineer* feast riotously
226 *for* as for
227 *Nay, look not big, nor stamp, nor stare,
nor fret.* These words are almost a
concealed stage direction to Katherina – it is what she should be doing
– but Petruchio, affecting not to see
her, speaks them angrily to the rest
of the company.

big angry, threatening
229–31 *She is my goods, my chattels, she is
my house ... any thing.* Much of this
echoes the Tenth Commandment.
Petruchio wittily accuses the company of coveting Katherina.
233 *I'll bring mine action on the proudest he*
I'll take legal proceedings against the
proudest man
238 *buckler* shield, defend

Exeunt Petruchio, Katherina, and Grumio

BAPTISTA
Nay, let them go, a couple of quiet ones.

GREMIO
240   Went they not quickly, I should die with laughing.

TRANIO
Of all mad matches never was the like.

LUCENTIO
Mistress, what's your opinion of your sister?

BIANCA
That being mad herself, she's madly mated.

GREMIO
I warrant him, Petruchio is Kated.

BAPTISTA
Neighbours and friends, though bride and bridegroom
      wants
For to supply the places at the table,
You know there wants no junkets at the feast.
Lucentio, you shall supply the bridegroom's place,
And let Bianca take her sister's room.

TRANIO
250   Shall sweet Bianca practise how to bride it?

BAPTISTA
She shall, Lucentio. Come, gentlemen, let's go.   *Exeunt*

---

240 *Went they not* if they had not gone
(subjunctive)
244 *is Kated* has caught the 'Kate' (as
though it were the name of a disease).
Compare Beatrice's remark: 'God
help the noble Claudio! If he have
caught the Benedick, it will cost him
a thousand pound ere 'a be cured'

(*Much Ado About Nothing*, 1.1.81–3).
245–6 *wants | For to supply* are not here to
fill
247 *there wants no junkets* there is no lack
of delicacies
249 *room* place, seat
250 *bride it* play the bride

Enter Grumio

GRUMIO Fie, fie on all tired jades, on all mad masters, and all foul ways! Was ever man so beaten? Was ever man so rayed? Was ever man so weary? I am sent before to make a fire, and they are coming after to warm them. Now were not I a little pot and soon hot, my very lips might freeze to my teeth, my tongue to the roof of my mouth, my heart in my belly, ere I should come by a fire to thaw me. But I with blowing the fire shall warm myself, for, considering the weather, a taller man than I will take cold. Holla, ho! Curtis!

10

Enter Curtis

CURTIS Who is that calls so coldly?

GRUMIO A piece of ice. If thou doubt it, thou mayst slide from my shoulder to my heel with no greater a run but my head and my neck. A fire, good Curtis.

CURTIS Is my master and his wife coming, Grumio?

GRUMIO O ay, Curtis, ay — and therefore fire, fire, cast on no water.

CURTIS Is she so hot a shrew as she's reported?

IV.1 The Folio marks no Act division at this point, though the move to Petruchio's house in the country is the first real change in the location of the action since the play proper began. Shakespeare makes it abundantly plain in Grumio's first speech that the move has taken place, and that this house is a very different place from Padua. Even the weather is on Petruchio's side.

1 *jades* vicious worthless horses

2 *foul ways* dirty roads

3 *rayed* dirtied

5 *a little pot and soon hot*. Grumio is quoting a well-known proverb which means that little men soon grow angry. That Grumio was imagined

by Shakespeare as a little man is also evident from his reference to 'a taller man than I' (line 9) and from Curtis's calling him 'you three-inch fool' (line 23).

7 *come by* get, find

11 *so coldly* like one benumbed with cold

16–17 *fire, fire, cast on no water*. This is a reference to the catch

Scotland's burning, Scotland's burning,
See yonder! See yonder!
Fire, fire! Fire, fire!
Cast on water! Cast on water!

Grumio, unlike Scotland, wants to burn.

18 *hot* angry, violent

GRUMIO She was, good Curtis, before this frost. But thou
know'st winter tames man, woman, and beast; for it
hath tamed my old master, and my new mistress, and
myself, fellow Curtis.

CURTIS Away, you three-inch fool! I am no beast.

GRUMIO Am I but three inches? Why, thy horn is a foot,
and so long am I at the least. But wilt thou make a fire,
– or shall I complain on thee to our mistress, whose hand
– she being now at hand – thou shalt soon feel, to thy
cold comfort, for being slow in thy hot office?

CURTIS I prithee, good Grumio, tell me how goes the
world?

He kindles a fire

GRUMIO A cold world, Curtis, in every office but thine –
and therefore fire. Do thy duty, and have thy duty, for
my master and mistress are almost frozen to death.

CURTIS There's fire ready – and therefore, good Grumio,
the news.

GRUMIO Why, 'Jack boy, ho boy!' and as much news as
wilt thou.

CURTIS Come, you are so full of cony-catching.

GRUMIO Why therefore fire, for I have caught extreme
cold. Where's the cook? Is supper ready, the house
trimmed, rushes strewed, cobwebs swept, the serving-

20 *winter tames man, woman, and beast.*
This is an allusion to the proverb
'Winter and wedlock tame both man
and beast.' Grumio significantly adds
woman to the list.

23 *I am no beast.* By naming himself third
Grumio has equated himself, and
therefore his fellow-servant Curtis,
with the beasts. Hence Curtis's
rejoinder.

24–5 *thy horn is a foot, and so long am I
at the least.* The inevitable retort
–Grumio says that he is big
enough to have made Curtis a
cuckold.

26 *complain on* complain about

28 *hot office* duty of fire-making

32 *Do thy duty, and have thy duty* do thy
duty and take thy due

36 *'Jack boy, ho boy!'* An allusion to a catch
which begins

Jack boy, ho boy, News:
The cat is in the well.

36–7 *as wilt thou* as you could wish

38 *cony-catching* trickery, evasion (perhaps with reference to Grumio's
fondness for catches)

41 *rushes strewed.* The strewing of fresh
rushes on the floor was an essential
part of the preparation for a guest.

men in their new fustian, their white stockings, an
every officer his wedding-garment on? Be the Jacks
fair within, the Jills fair without, the carpets laid, and
everything in order?

CURTIS All ready – and therefore, I pray thee, news.

GRUMIO First know my horse is tired, my master and
mistress fallen out.

CURTIS How?

GRUMIO Out of their saddles into the dirt, and thereby   50
hangs a tale.

CURTIS Let's ha't, good Grumio.

GRUMIO Lend thine ear.

CURTIS Here.

GRUMIO There.

He boxes Curtis's ear

CURTIS This 'tis to feel a tale, not to hear a tale.

GRUMIO And therefore 'tis called a sensible tale; and this
cuff was but to knock at your ear and beseech listening.
Now I begin. *Imprimis*, we came down a foul hill, my
master riding behind my mistress –   60

CURTIS Both of one horse?

GRUMIO What's that to thee?

CURTIS Why, a horse.

GRUMIO Tell thou the tale. But hadst thou not crossed
me, thou shouldst have heard how her horse fell, and
she under her horse; thou shouldst have heard in how
miry a place, how she was bemoiled, how he left her
with the horse upon her, how he beat me because her
horse stumbled, how she waded through the dirt to

---

42 *fustian* (a coarse cloth made of cotton and flax)

43 *Jacks* (1) men-servants; (2) leather drinking-vessels

44 *Jills* (1) maid-servants; (2) metal drinking-vessels
the carpets laid (on tables and chests rather than on the floor, which was strewn with rushes)

52 *ha't* have it (colloquial)

56 *feel* experience, suffer

57 *sensible* (1) capable of being felt; (2) easily understood

59 *Imprimis* first, to begin with (Latin)

61 *Both of* both on

64 *crossed* interrupted

67 *bemoiled* covered with mud and dirt

70 pluck him off me, how he swore, how she prayed that
never prayed before, how I cried, how the horses ran
away, how her bridle was burst, how I lost my crupper
– with many things of worthy memory, which now shall
die in oblivion, and thou return unexperienced to thy
grave.

CURTIS By this reckoning he is more shrew than she.

GRUMIO Ay, and that thou and the proudest of you all
shall find when he comes home. But what talk I of this?
Call forth Nathaniel, Joseph, Nicholas, Philip, Walter,
80 Sugarsop, and the rest. Let their heads be slickly
combed, their blue coats brushed, and their garters
of an indifferent knit. Let them curtsy with their left
legs, and not presume to touch a hair of my master's
horse-tail till they kiss their hands. Are they all ready?

CURTIS They are.

GRUMIO Call them forth.

CURTIS Do you hear, ho? You must meet my master to
countenance my mistress.

GRUMIO Why, she hath a face of her own.

90 CURTIS Who knows not that?

GRUMIO Thou, it seems, that calls for company to countenance her.

CURTIS I call them forth to credit her.

73 *of worthy memory* worthy of remembrance, that ought not to be
forgotten
74 *unexperienced* in ignorance of them
76 *more shrew* more of a shrew (*shrew*
could be applied to either sex)
78 *But what* but why
80 *slickly* smoothly, sleekly
81 *blue coats* (normal uniform of
servants)
82 *of an indifferent knit* of a reasonable
pattern, not too showy
82–3 *curtsy with their left legs* (as a token
of submission – to put the best foot

first was a sign of defiance)
84 *horse-tail* horse's tail
kiss their hands. To kiss one's own
hands was a mark of respect to a
superior.
87–8 *to countenance* to grace, to honour
91 *calls.* This is the second person singular. Shakespeare, who wrote his
words to be spoken, not read, often
avoids the '-est' form.
93 *credit* honour, do credit to. Grumio,
of course, takes the word in the other
sense of 'provide credit for'.

GRUMIO Why, she comes to borrow nothing of them.

Enter four or five Servingmen

NATHANIEL Welcome home, Grumio.

PHILIP How now, Grumio.

JOSEPH What, Grumio.

NICHOLAS Fellow Grumio.

NATHANIEL How now, old lad.

GRUMIO Welcome, you. How now, you. What, you. Fel- 100
low, you. And thus much for greeting. Now, my spruce
companions, is all ready, and all things neat?

NATHANIEL All things is ready. How near is our master?

GRUMIO E'en at hand, alighted by this. And therefore be
not – Cock's passion, silence! I hear my master.

Enter Petruchio and Katherina

PETRUCHIO

Where be these knaves? What, no man at door
To hold my stirrup nor to take my horse?
Where is Nathaniel, Gregory, Philip?

ALL SERVINGMEN Here, here sir, here sir.

PETRUCHIO

Here sir, here sir, here sir, here sir! 110
You logger-headed and unpolished grooms!
What, no attendance? No regard? No duty?
Where is the foolish knave I sent before?

GRUMIO

Here sir, as foolish as I was before.

PETRUCHIO

You peasant swain, you whoreson malt-horse drudge
Did I not bid thee meet me in the park

---

101 *spruce* lively, brisk

103 *All things is ready.* 'All things' is
thought of as a collective equivalent
to 'everything'.

105 *Cock's passion* (a corruption of 'by
God's Passion')

111 *logger-headed* thick-headed, stupid

115 *peasant swain* country bumpkin
whoreson (literally 'son of a whore', but
commonly used as a term of contempt and reprobation)
malt-horse drudge (slow heavy horse,
used to grind malt by working a
treadmill)

And bring along these rascal knaves with thee?

GRUMIO

Nathaniel's coat, sir, was not fully made,
And Gabriel's pumps were all unpinked i'th'heel.
120   There was no link to colour Peter's hat,
And Walter's dagger was not come from sheathing,
There were none fine but Adam, Rafe, and Gregory –
The rest were ragged, old, and beggarly.
Yet, as they are, here are they come to meet you.

PETRUCHIO

Go, rascals, go and fetch my supper in.

Exeunt Servingmen

He sings

Where is the life that late I led?
Where are those –

Sit down, Kate, and welcome. Food, food, food, food!
Enter Servants with supper
Why, when, I say? Nay, good sweet Kate, be merry.
130   Off with my boots, you rogues! You villains, when?

119 *all unpinked* entirely without their proper ornamentation. To 'pink' leather was to decorate it by punching out a pattern on it.
i'th' in the (colloquial)
120 *link* (blacking made of the material of burnt torches, or 'links', as they were called)
121 *sheathing* being fitted with a scabbard
126 *Where is the life that late I led?* This is the first line of a song that is now lost, and *Where are those* appears to be the continuation of it. The existence of the song is known, because an answer to it, entitled 'Dame Beauty's Reply to the Lover late at Liberty', was published in Clement

Robinson's *A Handful of Pleasant Delights*, 1584. The song would be appropriate to Petruchio's newly-married state.
127 *Where are those* –. The Folio reads: 'Where are those?'
128 *Food, food, food, food!* The Folio reads: 'Soud, soud, soud, soud.', which makes no sense whatever. 'Food', however, is exactly what Petruchio wants, and if it were spelled 'foud' in the manuscript, as it well may have been, the mistake is easily intelligible, since the letter 'f' and the 'long s' [ſ] closely resembled each other.
129 *when, I say* (common expression denoting impatience)

He sings

It was the friar of orders grey,
As he forth walkèd on his way –

Out, you rogue! You pluck my foot awry.
He strikes the Servant
Take that, and mend the plucking off the other.
Be merry, Kate. Some water here. What ho!
Enter one with water
Where's my spaniel Troilus? Sirrah, get you hence,
And bid my cousin Ferdinand come hither.

Exit another Servingman
One, Kate, that you must kiss and be acquainted with.
Where are my slippers? Shall I have some water?
Come, Kate, and wash, and welcome heartily.   140
He knocks the basin out of the Servant's hands
You whoreson villain, will you let it fall?
He strikes the Servant

KATHERINA
Patience, I pray you, 'twas a fault unwilling.

PETRUCHIO
A whoreson, beetle-headed, flap-eared knave!

---

131 *It was the friar of orders grey . . . way.*
These lines are the beginning of another lost ballad. The friar in question is a Grey friar or Franciscan.
133 *Out* (expression of anger)
134 *mend* make a better job of
135 *Some water here.* Washing of the
hands before meals, especially important at a time when people ate with
their fingers, was carried out at table
in Shakespeare's England.
(stage direction) *Enter one with water.*
The direction is rightly placed at this
point in the Folio, and there is no
need to move it, as many editors
have done, four lines down to make
it follow Petruchio's second demand.

The house is admirably organized
and runs like clock-work, so making
all his complaints doubly ridiculous;
which is, of course, exactly how he
wants them to appear, since the essence of his plan is to bring Katherina over to the side of order by
showing her the folly of ill-tempered
outbursts of choler.
137 *my cousin Ferdinand.* This looks like a
loose end, for the cousin never turns
up.
143 *beetle-headed* thick-headed. A 'beetle'
is a heavy wooden mallet.
flap-eared with heavy pendulous
ears

Come, Kate, sit down, I know you have a stomach.
Will you give thanks, sweet Kate, or else shall I?
What's this? Mutton?

FIRST SERVINGMAN Ay.

PETRUCHIO   Who brought it?

PETER   I

PETRUCHIO
'Tis burnt, and so is all the meat.
What dogs are these! Where is the rascal cook?
How durst you, villains, bring it from the dresser
150   And serve it thus to me that love it not?
There, take it to you, trenchers, cups, and all.

He throws the food and dishes at them

You heedless joltheads and unmannered slaves!
What, do you grumble? I'll be with you straight.

Exeunt Servants hurriedly

KATHERINA
I pray you, husband, be not so disquiet.
The meat was well, if you were so contented.

PETRUCHIO
I tell thee, Kate, 'twas burnt and dried away,
And I expressly am forbid to touch it,
For it engenders choler, planteth anger;
And better 'twere that both of us did fast,
160   Since, of ourselves, ourselves are choleric,

144 *stomach* appetite
145 *give thanks* say grace
149 *dresser* (kitchen-table on which food was prepared)
151 *trenchers* (wooden platters used for serving up meat)
152 *heedless joltheads* careless blockheads
153 *I'll be with you straight* I'll be after you, I'll chastise you
(stage direction) *Exeunt Servants hurriedly.* The Folio provides no direction here, but one is plainly needed both as a consequence of Petruchio's threat and so that the Servants can

'*Enter severally*' at line 164.
154 *disquiet* upset, in a temper
155 *well* good, satisfactory
158 *For it engenders choler.* For the belief that over-cooked meat produced an excess of choler, and so stimulated anger, see *The Comedy of Errors*, II.2.59–62, where Dromio of Syracuse begs his master not to eat dry unbasted meat, 'Lest it make you choleric, and purchase me another dry basting'.
160 *of ourselves* by nature

Than feed it with such over-roasted flesh.
Be patient, tomorrow't shall be mended,
And for this night we'll fast for company.
Come, I will bring thee to thy bridal chamber.   *Exeunt*
    Enter Servants severally
NATHANIEL Peter, didst ever see the like?
PETER He kills her in her own humour.
    Enter Curtis
GRUMIO Where is he?
CURTIS
In her chamber,
Making a sermon of continency to her,
And rails, and swears, and rates, that she, poor soul,   170
Knows not which way to stand, to look, to speak,
And sits as one new-risen from a dream.
Away, away, for he is coming hither.   *Exeunt*
    Enter Petruchio
PETRUCHIO
Thus have I politicly begun my reign,
And 'tis my hope to end successfully.
My falcon now is sharp and passing empty,

162 *mended* put right
163 *for company* together
164 (stage direction) *severally* one by one
166 *He kills her in her own humour* he
   outdoes her (and so masters her) in
   her own special line of tantrums
169 *Making a sermon of continency to her*
   giving her a lecture on the virtues of
   moderation and restraint
170 *rates* scolds, lays down the law
   that so that
174–97 *Thus have I politicly begun my reign
   . . . to show.* This speech, addressed
   direct to the audience, is central to
   the play, because in it Petruchio explains his plan for taming Katherina
   and, at the same time, through the
   image of the falcon, gives his estimate of her character.

174 *politicly* prudently, like a clever
   statesman
   begun my reign. This is an allusion to
   the idea that the wife was the husband's subject. Compare v.2.145–6,
   'Thy husband is thy lord . . . thy
   sovereign.'
176–82 *My falcon now is sharp and passing
   empty . . . obedient.* The methods used
   in the training of a wild hawk or
   haggard, as she was called, in order
   to make her 'meek, and loving to the
   man', are thus described by a contemporary of Shakespeare:

'All hawks generally are manned
after one manner, that is to say, by
watching and keeping them from
sleep, by a continual carrying of them

And till she stoop she must not be full-gorged,
For then she never looks upon her lure.
Another way I have to man my haggard,
180　To make her come and know her keeper's call,
That is, to watch her, as we watch these kites
That bate and beat and will not be obedient.
She eat no meat today, nor none shall eat.
Last night she slept not, nor tonight she shall not.
As with the meat, some undeserved fault
I'll find about the making of the bed,
And here I'll fling the pillow, there the bolster,
This way the coverlet, another way the sheets.
Ay, and amid this hurly I intend
190　That all is done in reverend care of her.
And, in conclusion, she shall watch all night,
And if she chance to nod I'll rail and brawl,
And with the clamour keep her still awake.
This is a way to kill a wife with kindness,
And thus I'll curb her mad and headstrong humour.

upon your fist, and by a most familiar stroking and playing with them, with the wing of a dead fowl or such like, and by often gazing and looking of them in the face, with a loving and gentle countenance, and so making them acquainted with the man.' Gervase Markham, *Country Contentments* (1615), fourth edition, London, 1631, pages 36–7.

176 *sharp* sharp-set, famished
　passing extremely
177 *stoop* fly to the lure
　full-gorged allowed to feed her fill
178 *looks upon* regards, takes notice of
　lure (apparatus used by falconers to recall their hawks, being a bunch of feathers attached to a cord, within which, during its training, the hawk finds its food)

179 *man my haggard* tame my wild hawk
181 *watch her* keep her awake
　these kites those falcons
182 *bate and beat* flutter and flap their wings
189 *hurly* commotion
　intend pretend, try to make out
190 *reverend* reverent, respectful
191 *watch* stay awake
193 *still* constantly
194 *to kill a wife with kindness*. To 'kill with kindness' was a proverbial phrase for harming someone by excessive and mistaken indulgence. Petruchio is using it ironically for 'to give her a taste of her own medicine'.

He that knows better how to tame a shrew,
Now let him speak – 'tis charity to show.   *Exit*

Enter Tranio as Lucentio, and Hortensio as Licio   IV.2

TRANIO

Is't possible, friend Licio, that Mistress Bianca
Doth fancy any other but Lucentio?
I tell you, sir, she bears me fair in hand.

HORTENSIO

Sir, to satisfy you in what I have said,
Stand by and mark the manner of his teaching.
          They stand aside
          Enter Bianca, and Lucentio as Cambio

LUCENTIO

Now, mistress, profit you in what you read?

BIANCA

What, master, read you? First resolve me that.

LUCENTIO

I read that I profess, *The Art to Love*.

BIANCA

And may you prove, sir, master of your art.

LUCENTIO

While you, sweet dear, prove mistress of my heart.   10
          They court each other

197 *charity to show* to show public spirit.
The rhyme 'shrew – show' indicates
how 'shrew' was pronounced.

IV.2.3. *she bears me fair in hand* she deceives me in a very convincing
fashion
4–8 *Sir, to satisfy you in what I have said
. . . Love*. The Folio distributes these
lines wrongly, giving lines 4–5 to
Lucentio, line 6 to Hortensio, line 7
correctly to Bianca, and line 8 to
Hortensio. For a possible explanation

of how the confusion may have
arisen see the note to III.1.146–56.
4 *to satisfy you in* to convince you of
5 (stage direction) *Enter Bianca, and Lucentio as Cambio*.
          The Folio reads: 'Enter Bianca.' –
a consequence of the mistaken attri-
bution of the previous speech to
Lucentio.
8 *that I profess* that which I practise
The Art to Love (Ovid's witty poem
the *Ars Amatoria* in which love is
presented as a science)

HORTENSIO

Quick proceeders, marry! Now tell me, I pray,
You that durst swear that your mistress Bianca
Loved none in the world so well as Lucentio.

TRANIO

O despiteful love, unconstant womankind!
I tell thee, Licio, this is wonderful.

HORTENSIO

Mistake no more, I am not Licio,
Nor a musician as I seem to be,
But one that scorn to live in this disguise
For such a one as leaves a gentleman
20 And makes a god of such a cullion.
Know, sir, that I am called Hortensio.

TRANIO

Signor Hortensio, I have often heard
Of your entire affection to Bianca,
And since mine eyes are witness of her lightness,
I will with you, if you be so contented,
Forswear Bianca and her love for ever.

HORTENSIO

See how they kiss and court! Signor Lucentio,
Here is my hand, and here I firmly vow
Never to woo her more, but do forswear her,
30 As one unworthy all the former favours
That I have fondly flattered her withal.

TRANIO

And here I take the like unfeignèd oath,
Never to marry with her though she would entreat.

---

11 *Quick proceeders* apt students. The allusion is to 'proceeding' from B.A. to M.A. — compare 'master of your art' in line 9.
15 *wonderful* surprising, incredible
18 *scorn* scorns. The verb agrees with the antecedent 'I' instead of with the relative 'that'.

20 *cullion* base fellow, rascal
23 *entire affection to* pure unalloyed love for
24 *lightness* wantonness, loose behaviour
31 *fondly* foolishly
withal with

Fie on her! See how beastly she doth court him.

HORTENSIO

Would all the world but he had quite forsworn!
For me, that I may surely keep mine oath,
I will be married to a wealthy widow
Ere three days pass, which hath as long loved me
As I have loved this proud disdainful haggard.
And so farewell, Signor Lucentio.   40
Kindness in women, not their beauteous looks,
Shall win my love – and so I take my leave,
In resolution as I swore before.   *Exit*

          Tranio joins Lucentio and Bianca

TRANIO

Mistress Bianca, bless you with such grace
As 'longeth to a lover's blessèd case!
Nay, I have ta'en you napping, gentle love,
And have forsworn you with Hortensio.

BIANCA

Tranio, you jest – but have you both forsworn me?

TRANIO

Mistress, we have.

LUCENTIO   Then we are rid of Licio.

TRANIO

I'faith, he'll have a lusty widow now,   50
That shall be wooed and wedded in a day.

---

34 *how beastly* in what animal fashion
35 *Would all the world but he had quite
    forsworn!* Hortensio spitefully wishes
    that Cambio were Bianca's only
    suitor. It does not occur to him that
    she could ever think of marrying the
    apparent menial.
37 *a wealthy widow.* The sudden mention
    of this new character, of whom there
    has not been a word so far, is another
    sign that the part of Hortensio has
    undergone some cobbling.

38 *which* who. The two words are often
    interchanged in Shakespeare.
39 *haggard* wild intractable hawk – used
    metaphorically here for a light
    woman. Compare *Othello*, III.3.257,
    'If I do prove her haggard', meaning
    'unfaithful'.
43 *In resolution* with fixed purpose, fully
    determined
45 *'longeth to* belongs to, suits with
46 *ta'en you napping* caught you in the act
    (of billing and cooing)

BIANCA
God give him joy!

TRANIO
Ay, and he'll tame her.

BIANCA   He says so, Tranio.

TRANIO
Faith, he is gone unto the taming-school.

BIANCA
The taming-school? What, is there such a place?

TRANIO
Ay, mistress, and Petruchio is the master,
That teacheth tricks eleven and twenty long,
To tame a shrew and charm her chattering tongue.

Enter Biondello

BIONDELLO
O master, master, I have watched so long

60   That I'm dog-weary, but at last I spied
An ancient angel coming down the hill
Will serve the turn.

TRANIO   What is he, Biondello?

BIONDELLO
Master, a marcantant or a pedant,
I know not what – but formal in apparel,
In gait and countenance surely like a father.

LUCENTIO
And what of him, Tranio?

53–8 *Ay, and he'll tame her . . . chattering tongue.* Tranio knows far more about Hortensio's plans than Hortensio has just told him. This passage is yet more evidence that the part of Hortensio has been much altered.

57 *tricks eleven and twenty long* tricks of exactly the right kind. The allusion is to the game of cards called 'one-and-thirty' that Grumio refers to at 1.2.32.

58 *charm* use a magic spell in order to silence (compare 1.1.206)

60 *dog-weary* dog-tired, worn out

61 *An ancient angel* a fellow of the good old stamp. An *angel* was a gold coin, worth ten shillings, carrying as its device the archangel Michael and the dragon. Biondello may also be thinking of the Pedant as the angel who has come in answer to his prayer.

62 *Will serve the turn* who will serve our purpose

63 *marcantant* (Biondello's version of 'mercatante', the Italian for 'merchant')

TRANIO

If he be credulous and trust my tale,
I'll make him glad to seem Vincentio,
And give assurance to Baptista Minola
As if he were the right Vincentio.   70
Take in your love, and then let me alone.

Exeunt Lucentio and Bianca

Enter a Pedant

PEDANT

God save you, sir.

TRANIO   And you, sir. You are welcome.
Travel you farrer on, or are you at the farthest?

PEDANT

Sir, at the farthest for a week or two,
But then up farther, and as far as Rome,
And so to Tripoli, if God lend me life.

TRANIO

What countryman, I pray?

PEDANT   Of Mantua.

TRANIO

Of Mantua? Sir, marry, God forbid!
And come to Padua, careless of your life?

PEDANT

My life, sir? How, I pray? For that goes hard.   80

TRANIO

'Tis death for any one in Mantua

---

67 *trust my tale* believe my story
71 *let me alone* rely on me
73 *farrer* farther. The Folio reads 'farre',
which editors render as 'far', but
'farrer' makes better sense and is supported by Shakespeare's use of this
old form of the comparative in *The
Winter's Tale*, where Polixenes tells
Florizel, in the Folio text:

    wee'l barre thee from succession,
Not hold thee of our blood, no not our
    Kin,

Farre then Deucalion *off . . .*
                IV.4.421–4

77 *What countryman . . .?* where do you
live?
79 *careless of* regardless of
80 *that goes hard* that's a serious matter
81–7 *'Tis death for any one in Mantua . . .
proclaimed about.* Tranio's story looks
to be borrowed from Shakespeare's
own *The Comedy of Errors*, I.1.16–20.

To come to Padua. Know you not the cause?
Your ships are stayed at Venice, and the Duke,
For private quarrel 'twixt your Duke and him,
Hath published and proclaimed it openly.
'Tis marvel – but that you are newly come,
You might have heard it else proclaimed about.

PEDANT

Alas, sir, it is worse for me than so!
For I have bills for money by exchange
90   From Florence, and must here deliver them.

TRANIO

Well, sir, to do you courtesy,
This will I do, and this I will advise you –
First tell me, have you ever been at Pisa?

PEDANT

Ay, sir, in Pisa have I often been,
Pisa renownèd for grave citizens.

TRANIO

Among them know you one Vincentio?

PEDANT

I know him not, but I have heard of him,
A merchant of incomparable wealth.

TRANIO

He is my father, sir, and sooth to say,
100   In countenance somewhat doth resemble you.

BIONDELLO (aside) As much as an apple doth an oyster,
and all one.

---

83 *stayed* held up
84 *For private quarrel* on account of personal dissension
86 *'Tis marvel* it's strange. Two constructions are involved here. Tranio begins to say 'It's strange you haven't heard', but then changes abruptly to another way of putting it, as people often do in speech.
but that you are newly come but for the

fact that you have only just arrived
87 *about* up and down the city
88 *than so* than you think
89 *bills for money by exchange* bills of exchange, promissory notes
95 *Pisa renownèd for grave citizens* (a repetition of I.1.10)
101 *As much as an apple doth an oyster* (a well known proverb)
102 *and all one* just the very same

TRANIO

To save your life in this extremity,
This favour will I do you for his sake –
And think it not the worst of all your fortunes
That you are like to Sir Vincentio –
His name and credit shall you undertake,
And in my house you shall be friendly lodged.
Look that you take upon you as you should.
You understand me, sir. So shall you stay   110
Till you have done your business in the city.
If this be courtesy, sir, accept of it.

PEDANT

O, sir, I do, and will repute you ever
The patron of my life and liberty.

TRANIO

Then go with me to make the matter good.
This, by the way, I let you understand –
My father is here looked for every day
To pass assurance of a dower in marriage
'Twixt me and one Baptista's daughter here.
In all these circumstances I'll instruct you.   120
Go with me, sir, to clothe you as becomes you.

Exeunt

Enter Katherina and Grumio   IV.3

GRUMIO

No, no, forsooth, I dare not for my life.

107 *credit* reputation
    undertake assume, take on you
109 *Look that you take upon you as you
    should* see that you play your part
    properly
112 *accept of* accept
113 *repute* consider, think of
115 *make the matter good* put the plan
    into effect

117 *looked for* expected
118 *pass assurance of* settle, make a bind-
    ing promise of

IV.3 The Folio marks the beginning of
this scene as the opening of Act Four,
heading it 'Actus Quartus. Scena Prima.'
See the head-note to IV.1.

KATHERINA

    The more my wrong, the more his spite appears.
    What, did he marry me to famish me?
    Beggars that come unto my father's door
    Upon entreaty have a present alms,
    If not, elsewhere they meet with charity.
    But I, who never knew how to entreat,
    Nor never needed that I should entreat,
    Am starved for meat, giddy for lack of sleep,
10   With oaths kept waking, and with brawling fed.
    And that which spites me more than all these wants,
    He does it under name of perfect love,
    As who should say, if I should sleep or eat,
    'Twere deadly sickness or else present death.
    I prithee go and get me some repast,
    I care not what, so it be wholesome food.

GRUMIO

    What say you to a neat's foot?

KATHERINA

    'Tis passing good, I prithee let me have it.

GRUMIO

    I fear it is too choleric a meat.
20   How say you to a fat tripe finely broiled?

KATHERINA

    I like it well. Good Grumio, fetch it me.

GRUMIO

    I cannot tell, I fear 'tis choleric.
    What say you to a piece of beef and mustard?

---

2 *The more my wrong* the greater the injustice done to me
5 *Upon entreaty have a present alms* have only to ask and they receive alms immediately
9 *meat* food in general
11 *spites* mortifies, vexes
13 *As who should say* as if to say, as though he were saying
14 *present* immediate
15 *some repast* something to eat
16 *so* so long as, provided that
17 *a neat's foot* the foot of an ox
19 *choleric* productive of anger, prone to make one irascible
20 *broiled* grilled, cooked over the coals
22 *I cannot tell* I don't know what to say

KATHERINA
A dish that I do love to feed upon.

GRUMIO
Ay, but the mustard is too hot a little.

KATHERINA
Why then, the beef, and let the mustard rest.

GRUMIO
Nay then, I will not. You shall have the mustard,
Or else you get no beef of Grumio.

KATHERINA
Then both, or one, or anything thou wilt.

GRUMIO
Why then, the mustard without the beef.   30

KATHERINA
Go, get thee gone, thou false deluding slave,
            She beats him
That feed'st me with the very name of meat.
Sorrow on thee and all the pack of you
That triumph thus upon my misery!
Go, get thee gone, I say.
            Enter Petruchio and Hortensio with meat

PETRUCHIO
How fares my Kate? What, sweeting, all amort?

HORTENSIO
Mistress, what cheer?

KATHERINA   Faith, as cold as can be.

PETRUCHIO
Pluck up thy spirits, look cheerfully upon me.
Here, love, thou seest how diligent I am,

---

26 *let the mustard rest* don't worry about
the mustard
32 *the very name* the mere name, the name
and nothing else
36 *sweeting* darling, sweetheart
all amort down in the dumps, sick to
death (French *à la mort*)

37 *what cheer?* how is it with you?
as cold as can be as cold a reception, as
poor entertainment, as can be imagined (quibbling on the other sense of
'cheer')

40   To dress thy meat myself, and bring it thee.
                He sets the dish down
        I am sure, sweet Kate, this kindness merits thanks.
        What, not a word? Nay then, thou lov'st it not,
        And all my pains is sorted to no proof.
        Here, take away this dish.

KATHERINA   I pray you, let it stand.

PETRUCHIO
        The poorest service is repaid with thanks,
        And so shall mine before you touch the meat.

KATHERINA
        I thank you, sir.

HORTENSIO
        Signor Petruchio, fie, you are to blame.
        Come, Mistress Kate, I'll bear you company.

PETRUCHIO (*aside to Hortensio*)
50   Eat it up all, Hortensio, if thou lovest me.
        (*to Katherina*) Much good do it unto thy gentle heart!
        Kate, eat apace. And now, my honey love,
        Will we return unto thy father's house
        And revel it as bravely as the best,
        With silken coats and caps, and golden rings,
        With ruffs and cuffs and farthingales and things,
        With scarfs and fans and double change of bravery,
        With amber bracelets, beads, and all this knavery.

---

43 *all my pains is sorted to no proof* all my
labour has been in vain, has been
taken to no purpose. 'Pains' is always
singular in Shakespeare.

45 *poorest* slightest, most insignificant

46 *mine before.* The ellipse of the verb
'be' is common in Shakespeare, otherwise 'mine be 'fore' would be an
attractive reading.

48 *to blame* too blameworthy, too much
at fault. This use of 'to blame' as
though it were 'too blame' was
common in Shakespeare's day. Compare the Nurse's reproof to Old Capu-
let, 'You are to blame, my lord, to
rate her so' (*Romeo and Juliet*,
III.5.169).

51 *do it* may it do

52 *apace* quickly

54 *as bravely* in as splendidly dressed a
manner

56 *ruffs* (articles of neckwear elaborately
fluted and stiffly starched)
farthingales hooped petticoats

57 *bravery* finery

58 *this knavery* tricks of dress like those,
that sort of trumpery

What, hast thou dined? The tailor stays thy leisure,
To deck thy body with his ruffling treasure.   60

    Enter Tailor

Come, tailor, let us see these ornaments.
Lay forth the gown.

    Enter Haberdasher

                    What news with you, sir?

HABERDASHER
Here is the cap your worship did bespeak.

PETRUCHIO
Why, this was moulded on a porringer –
A velvet dish. Fie, fie, 'tis lewd and filthy!
Why, 'tis a cockle or a walnut-shell,
A knack, a toy, a trick, a baby's cap.
Away with it! Come, let me have a bigger.

KATHERINA
I'll have no bigger. This doth fit the time,
And gentlewomen wear such caps as these.   70

PETRUCHIO
When you are gentle, you shall have one too,
And not till then.

HORTENSIO (*aside*) That will not be in haste.

KATHERINA
Why sir, I trust I may have leave to speak,
And speak I will. I am no child, no babe.
Your betters have endured me say my mind,

---

59 *stays* awaits
60 *ruffling* swaggering, gay
62–140 *Lay forth the gown . . . Ay, there's
the villainy.* Some interesting parallels
to this attack on fashions in dress are
to be found in *Life in Shakespeare's
England*, ed. J. Dover Wilson, Penguin Books edition, 1968, pp.161–73.
63 HABERDASHER. The Folio heads
this speech '*Fel.*'
bespeak order
64 *moulded on* modelled on, shaped like

porringer (small basin from which
soup, porridge, and the like were
eaten)
65 *A velvet dish* a dish made of velvet
lewd and filthy (Elizabethan equivalent of 'cheap and nasty')
66 *cockle* cockle-shell
67 *knack* knick-knack, silly contrivance
toy piece of nonsense
trick bauble, practical joke
69 *fit the time* suit the fashion
75 *endured me say* suffered me to say

And if you cannot, best you stop your ears.
My tongue will tell the anger of my heart,
Or else my heart concealing it will break,
And rather than it shall, I will be free
80   Even to the uttermost, as I please, in words.

PETRUCHIO

Why, thou say'st true — it is a paltry cap,
A custard-coffin, a bauble, a silken pie.
I love thee well in that thou lik'st it not.

KATHERINA

Love me or love me not, I like the cap,
And it I will have, or I will have none.

PETRUCHIO

Thy gown? Why, ay. Come, tailor, let us see't.

                   Exit Haberdasher

O mercy, God! What masquing stuff is here?
What's this? A sleeve? 'Tis like a demi-cannon.
What, up and down carved like an apple-tart?
90   Here's snip and nip and cut and slish and slash,
Like to a censer in a barber's shop.
Why, what a devil's name, tailor, call'st thou this?

HORTENSIO (*aside*)

I see she's like to have neither cap nor gown.

---

76 *best you stop* it were best for you to stop

82 *custard-coffin* (crust of pastry in which a custard was baked)

83 *in that* because, inasmuch as

86 (stage direction) *Exit Haberdasher*. The Folio gives the Haberdasher no exit, but now that the business of the cap is over there is no reason for his remaining.

87 *masquing stuff* clothes that look suitable for use in a masque. Strange and elaborate costumes were a feature of the masque.

88 *demi-cannon* large gun with a bore of about six and a half inches. The sleeve in question is of the leg-of-mutton variety that became popular around 1580. It was often slashed, as well as being padded and stiffened with embroidery — hence Petruchio's subsequent attacks. Men's dress, it should be added, was equally elaborate.

91 *censer*. The usual explanation of this rare word — that it was a fumigator, consisting of a brazier with a perforated lid to emit the smoke of burning perfumes — is not very satisfactory in this context, but until a better is found it must serve.

92 *a devil's name* in the name of the devil

TAILOR

  You bid me make it orderly and well,
  According to the fashion and the time.

PETRUCHIO

  Marry, and did. But if you be remembered,
  I did not bid you mar it to the time.
  Go, hop me over every kennel home,
  For you shall hop without my custom, sir.
  I'll none of it. Hence, make your best of it.   100

KATHERINA

  I never saw a better-fashioned gown,
  More quaint, more pleasing, nor more commendable.
  Belike you mean to make a puppet of me.

PETRUCHIO

  Why, true, he means to make a puppet of thee.

TAILOR

  She says your worship means to make a puppet of her.

PETRUCHIO

  O monstrous arrogance! Thou liest, thou thread, thou
    thimble,
  Thou yard, three-quarters, half-yard, quarter, nail,
  Thou flea, thou nit, thou winter-cricket thou!
  Braved in mine own house with a skein of thread?

94 *bid* (past tense)
96 *Marry, and did* indeed I did
  be remembered recollect
97 *mar it to the time* ruin it for ever
98 *hop me* hop, I say
  kennel gutter, surface-drain of a street
99 *hop without* lose. Compare *2 Henry VI*, 1.3.133–5:

  Thy sale of offices and towns in France,
  If they were known, as the suspect is great,
  Would make thee quickly hop without thy head.

100 *make your best of it* do what you like with it

102 *quaint* artfully made, elegant
107 *nail* (a measure of length for cloth, being one sixteenth of a yard)
108 *nit* egg of a louse. There is no need to assume from these abusive terms, as some editors have done, that the part of the tailor was played by a small man or by a boy. Petruchio is practising the rhetorical art of diminution, encouraged, no doubt, by the common proverb 'Nine tailors make a man'.
109 *Braved* defied, challenged
  with by

110   Away, thou rag, thou quantity, thou remnant,
            Or I shall so bemete thee with thy yard
            As thou shalt think on prating whilst thou liv'st.
            I tell thee, I, that thou hast marred her gown.

TAILOR
            Your worship is deceived — the gown is made
            Just as my master had direction.
            Grumio gave order how it should be done.

GRUMIO I gave him no order, I gave him the stuff.

TAILOR
            But how did you desire it should be made?

GRUMIO Marry, sir, with needle and thread.

TAILOR
120   But did you not request to have it cut?

GRUMIO Thou hast faced many things.

TAILOR I have.

GRUMIO Face not me. Thou hast braved many men, brave
            not me. I will neither be faced nor braved. I say unto
            thee, I bid thy master cut out the gown, but I did not
            bid him cut it to pieces. Ergo, thou liest.

TAILOR Why, here is the note of the fashion to testify.

PETRUCHIO Read it.

GRUMIO The note lies in's throat, if he say I said so.

130 TAILOR (reads) 'Imprimis, a loose-bodied gown.'

GRUMIO Master, if ever I said loose-bodied gown, sew me

---

110 *rag* (1) tattered bit of cloth; (2)
    shabby person
    quantity scrap
111 *bemete* measure (with a quibble on
    'mete out punishment')
112 *As thou shalt think on* that you will
    think twice about
121 *faced* (1) trimmed with braid, velvet,
    or some other material; (2) impudently
    confronted, bullied

123 *braved* (1) provided fine clothes for;
    (2) defied, set yourself up against
126 *Ergo* therefore, consequently (term
    much used in logic)
129 *The note lies in's throat* (1) the note
    tells a black lie; (2) the musical note
    is in his throat, meaning 'the words
    come from his mouth'
130–31 *loose-bodied* (1) loosely fitting; (2)
    of the kind worn by 'loose bodies',
    meaning 'harlots'

in the skirts of it and beat me to death with a bottom of
brown thread. I said a gown.

PETRUCHIO Proceed.

TAILOR 'With a small compassed cape.'

GRUMIO I confess the cape.

TAILOR 'With a trunk sleeve.'

GRUMIO I confess two sleeves.

TAILOR 'The sleeves curiously cut.'

PETRUCHIO Ay, there's the villainy.   140

GRUMIO Error i'th'bill, sir, error i'th'bill! I commanded
the sleeves should be cut out, and sewed up again; and
that I'll prove upon thee, though thy little finger be
armed in a thimble.

TAILOR This is true that I say; an I had thee in place
where, thou shouldst know it.

GRUMIO I am for thee straight. Take thou the bill, give
me thy mete-yard, and spare not me.

HORTENSIO God-a-mercy, Grumio, then he shall have no
odds.   150

PETRUCHIO Well sir, in brief, the gown is not for me.

GRUMIO You are i'th'right, sir, 'tis for my mistress.

132–3 *bottom of brown thread* ball of
   brown thread. *The bottom* was really
   the core or bobbin on which thread
   was wound.

135 *compassed* cut so as to fall in a circle

137 *trunk sleeve* large wide sleeve

139 *curiously* (1) carefully, accurately; (2)
   elaborately. Petruchio takes the word
   in the second sense, of course.

141 *bill* (1) the 'note' of line 127; (2) bill
   of indictment, accusation

143 *prove upon thee* establish by fighting
   you. The allusion is to trial by
   combat. Compare *Richard II*,
   IV.1.44–8;

   *Aumerle, thou liest; his honour is as true
   In this appeal as thou art all unjust;*

   *And that thou art so, there I throw my
     gage,
   To prove it on thee to the extremest point
   Of mortal breathing.*

145 *an* if

145–6 *in place where* in a fit place, in the
   right spot

147 *for thee straight* ready to do battle
   with you at once
   bill (1) note; (2) kind of pike or
   halbert used by watchmen

148 *mete-yard* measuring yard

149 *God-a-mercy* God have mercy!

150 *odds* advantage, superiority (probably with a quibble on the odds and
   ends left over from a garment which
   were the tailor's perquisites)

PETRUCHIO Go, take it up unto thy master's use.

GRUMIO Villain, not for thy life! Take up my mistress'
gown for thy master's use!

PETRUCHIO Why sir, what's your conceit in that?

GRUMIO

O sir, the conceit is deeper than you think for.

Take up my mistress' gown to his master's use!

O fie, fie, fie!

PETRUCHIO (aside)

160   Hortensio, say thou wilt see the tailor paid.

(to the Tailor) Go take it hence, be gone, and say no more.

HORTENSIO (aside)

Tailor, I'll pay thee for thy gown tomorrow.

Take no unkindness of his hasty words.

Away, I say, commend me to thy master.   *Exit Tailor*

PETRUCHIO

Well, come my Kate, we will unto your father's

Even in these honest mean habiliments.

Our purses shall be proud, our garments poor,

For 'tis the mind that makes the body rich,

And as the sun breaks through the darkest clouds,

170   So honour peereth in the meanest habit.

What, is the jay more precious than the lark

Because his feathers are more beautiful?

Or is the adder better than the eel

Because his painted skin contents the eye?

O no, good Kate, neither art thou the worse

For this poor furniture and mean array.

If thou account'st it shame, lay it on me.

153 *take it up unto thy master's use* take it
away and let your master make what
use he can of it
154-5 *Take up my mistress' gown for thy
master's use!* See note on III.2.164.
155 *use* sexual purposes
156 *conceit* idea, notion, innuendo
157 *think for* imagine
163 *Take no unkindness of* don't imagine

there is any ill-will in
166 *mean habiliments* poor clothes
167 *proud* puffed up
170 *peereth in* can be seen peeping
through
174 *painted* richly coloured
contents pleases, delights
176 *furniture* outfit, dress
array attire

And therefore frolic. We will hence forthwith
To feast and sport us at thy father's house.
(to Grumio) Go call my men, and let us straight to him,   180
And bring our horses unto Long-lane end,
There will we mount, and thither walk on foot.
Let's see, I think 'tis now some seven o'clock,
And well we may come there by dinner-time.

KATHERINA

I dare assure you, sir, 'tis almost two,
And 'twill be supper-time ere you come there.

PETRUCHIO

It shall be seven ere I go to horse.
Look what I speak, or do, or think to do,
You are still crossing it. Sirs, let't alone,
I will not go today, and ere I do,   190
It shall be what o'clock I say it is.

HORTENSIO

Why, so this gallant will command the sun.

Exeunt

Enter Tranio as Lucentio, and the Pedant, booted, and   IV.4
dressed like Vincentio

TRANIO

Sir, this is the house – please it you that I call?

178 *frolic* be merry
180 (stage direction) *(to Grumio)*. This is
   not in the Folio, but Petruchio would
   never give an order of the kind that
   follows to Katherina.
184 *dinner-time* (between eleven o'clock
   and noon)
186 *supper-time* (between half-past five
   and half-past six. Petruchio and Katherina are substantially agreed, if on
   nothing else, that it takes about four
   hours to get to her father's.)
188 *Look what* whatever, no matter what

think to do intend to do, think of
   doing
189 *still crossing* always contradicting,
   constantly thwarting
   let't alone forbear, take no further
   action about the matter
192 *so* apparently, according to what he
   has said. This line leads on very
   neatly to the opening of IV.5, the
   next scene in which Petruchio and
   Katherina appear.

IV.4 (stage direction) *Enter Tranio as Lu-*

PEDANT

Ay, what else? And but I be deceived
Signor Baptista may remember me
Near twenty years ago in Genoa,
Where we were lodgers at the Pegasus.

TRANIO

'Tis well, and hold your own, in any case,
With such austerity as 'longeth to a father.
    Enter Biondello

PEDANT

I warrant you. But sir, here comes your boy.
'Twere good he were schooled.

TRANIO

10   Fear you not him. Sirrah Biondello,
Now do your duty throughly, I advise you.
Imagine 'twere the right Vincentio.

BIONDELLO

Tut, fear not me.

TRANIO

But hast thou done thy errand to Baptista?

BIONDELLO

I told him that your father was at Venice,
And that you looked for him this day in Padua.

---

*centio, and the Pedant, booted, and dressed
like Vincentio.* The Folio reads: 'Enter
Tranio, and the Pedant drest like Vincentio.' For the addition of the word
booted, meaning 'wearing riding
boots', see the note to line 17.
1 *please it you* may it please you
2 *what else?* of course
  but unless
4 *Near* nearly
5 *Where we were lodgers at the Pegasus.* The
Folio prints this as the first line of
Tranio's speech – the result of a
careless alignment of the speech heading in the manuscript, or, perhaps,

to indicate that the line is to be
spoken by the Pedant and Tranio
simultaneously as a sign of their com-
plicity.
at the Pegasus. Pegasus, the winged
horse of classical mythology, was a
popular inn-sign in Shakespeare's
London.
6 *hold your own* play your part well
9 *schooled* instructed in his part
10 *Fear you not him* don't be worried
about him
11 *throughly* thoroughly, properly
  advise instruct, caution
12 *right* real, true
16 *looked for* expected

TRANIO

 Th'art a tall fellow, hold thee that to drink.
   Enter Baptista, and Lucentio as Cambio
 Here comes Baptista. Set your countenance, sir.
 Signor Baptista, you are happily met.
 (*to the Pedant*) Sir, this is the gentleman I told you of.   20
 I pray you stand good father to me now,
 Give me Bianca for my patrimony.

PEDANT

 Soft, son!
 Sir, by your leave, having come to Padua
 To gather in some debts, my son Lucentio
 Made me acquainted with a weighty cause
 Of love between your daughter and himself.
 And – for the good report I hear of you,
 And for the love he beareth to your daughter,
 And she to him – to stay him not too long,   30
 I am content, in a good father's care,
 To have him matched; and, if you please to like
 No worse than I, upon some agreement
 Me shall you find ready and willing
 With one consent to have her so bestowed.
 For curious I cannot be with you,

---

17 *Th'art a tall fellow, hold thee that to drink* you're an able chap, take that to get yourself a drink
(stage direction) *Enter Baptista, and Lucentio as Cambio.* The Folio reads: '*Enter Baptista and Lucentio: Pedant booted and bare headed.*' As the Pedant is already on stage at this point, it looks as though this direction may well be something left over from an earlier version in which the scene began here.
18 *Set your countenance* look like a grave father
21 *stand* be, show yourself
23 *Soft* gently, just a moment
24 *having come* I having come. The omis-

sion of the noun or pronoun on which a participle depends.is fairly common in Shakespeare. Compare 'Coming from Sardis, on our former ensign | Two mighty eagles fell ...' (*Julius Caesar*, v.i.79–80).
26 *weighty cause* serious matter
28 *for* because of
30 *to stay him not* in order not to keep him waiting
32–3 *to like | No worse than I* to be no less satisfied than I
35 *With one consent* in entire agreement
bestowed matched, married
36 *curious* over-particular in a matter of business, niggling

Signor Baptista, of whom I hear so well.

BAPTISTA
Sir, pardon me in what I have to say.
Your plainness and your shortness please me well.
40   Right true it is your son Lucentio here
Doth love my daughter, and she loveth him,
Or both dissemble deeply their affections.
And therefore if you say no more than this,
That like a father you will deal with him,
And pass my daughter a sufficient dower,
The match is made, and all is done —
Your son shall have my daughter with consent.

TRANIO
I thank you, sir. Where then do you know best
We be affied and such assurance ta'en
50   As shall with either part's agreement stand?

BAPTISTA
Not in my house, Lucentio, for you know
Pitchers have ears, and I have many servants.
Besides, old Gremio is hearkening still,
And happily we might be interrupted.

TRANIO
Then at my lodging, an it like you.
There doth my father lie; and there this night
We'll pass the business privately and well.
Send for your daughter by your servant here.

45 *pass* settle upon
46 *done* settled
48–50 *Where then do you know best | We
be affied and such assurance ta'en |
As shall with either part's agreement
stand?* where, in your opinion, may
we best be betrothed and such legal
arrangements be made as will be
agreeable to both parties?
52 *Pitchers have ears.* This proverb, which

Shakespeare uses again in *Richard III*,
II.4.37, puns on the 'ears' or handles
by which water-vessels were lifted,
and means 'there may be listeners'.
53 *hearkening still* still watching his
opportunity
54 *happily* haply, perchance
55 *an it like* if it please
56 *lie* lodge
57 *pass* settle

He winks at Lucentio
My boy shall fetch the scrivener presently.
The worst is this, that at so slender warning   60
You are like to have a thin and slender pittance.

BAPTISTA
It likes me well. Cambio, hie you home,
And bid Bianca make her ready straight.
And, if you will, tell what hath happenèd –
Lucentio's father is arrived in Padua,
And how she's like to be Lucentio's wife. *Exit Lucentio*

BIONDELLO
I pray the gods she may, with all my heart.

TRANIO
Dally not with the gods, but get thee gone.
                                                        Exit Biondello

Enter Peter, a Servingman
Signor Baptista, shall I lead the way?
Welcome! One mess is like to be your cheer.   70
Come sir, we will better it in Pisa.

BAPTISTA
I follow you.   *Exeunt*
Enter Lucentio and Biondello

BIONDELLO
Cambio.

LUCENTIO What say'st thou, Biondello?

BIONDELLO
You saw my master wink and laugh upon you?

---

58 (stage direction) *He winks at Lucentio.*
This is not in the Folio, but clearly
demanded by Biondello's remark at
line 74.
59 *scrivener* (notary, one publicly author-
ized to draw up contracts)
60 *slender* slight, insufficient
61 *pittance* fare, diet
62 *hie you* get you, hurry off
63 *straight* immediately, straightway

68 (stage direction) *Enter Peter, a Servingman.* This direction is based on the
Folio, which reads: 'Enter Peter.' Although Peter says nothing, his purpose is almost certainly to indicate to
Tranio, by a gesture, that the meal is
ready.
70 *One mess is like to be your cheer* one
dish is likely to be your fare

LUCENTIO Biondello, what of that?

BIONDELLO Faith, nothing – but 'has left me here behind
to expound the meaning or moral of his signs and tokens.

LUCENTIO I pray thee moralize them.

BIONDELLO Then thus – Baptista is safe, talking with the
deceiving father of a deceitful son.

LUCENTIO And what of him?

BIONDELLO His daughter is to be brought by you to the
supper.

LUCENTIO And then?

BIONDELLO The old priest at Saint Luke's church is at
your command at all hours.

LUCENTIO And what of all this?

BIONDELLO I cannot tell, except they are busied about a
counterfeit assurance. Take you assurance of her, *cum
privilegio ad imprimendum solum*. To th'church! Take
the priest, clerk, and some sufficient honest witnesses.
If this be not that you look for, I have no more to say,
But bid Bianca farewell for ever and a day.

He turns to go

LUCENTIO Hear'st thou, Biondello?

BIONDELLO I cannot tarry. I knew a wench married in an
afternoon as she went to the garden for parsley to stuff a
rabbit. And so may you, sir; and so adieu, sir. My master
hath appointed me to go to Saint Luke's to bid the

---

76 *'has* he has
78 *moralize* explain the meaning of
79 *safe* safely out of the way
80 *deceiving* sham
   deceitful sham
86 *command* service
89 *assurance* legal settlement
   Take you assurance make sure
89–90 *cum privilegio ad imprimendum
   solum*. This inscription, frequently
   found on the title-pages of books
   printed in Shakespeare's time, meant
   originally 'with the privilege for

printing only', but it was later taken
to mean 'with the sole right to
print', which is the significance
Biondello has in mind here. There is
a pun on printing in the sense
of 'stamping one's own image on
a person by getting her with
child'.
91 *some sufficient* enough, the right
   number required by law
92 *that you look for* that which you long
   for

priest be ready to come against you come with your
appendix.   *Exit*   100

LUCENTIO

I may and will, if she be so contented.
She will be pleased, then wherefore should I doubt?
Hap what hap may, I'll roundly go about her.
It shall go hard if Cambio go without her.

Exit

Enter Petruchio, Katherina, Hortensio and Servants   IV.5

PETRUCHIO

Come on, a God's name, once more toward our father's.
Good Lord, how bright and goodly shines the moon!

KATHERINA

The moon? The sun! It is not moonlight now.

PETRUCHIO

I say it is the moon that shines so bright.

KATHERINA

I know it is the sun that shines so bright.

PETRUCHIO

Now by my mother's son, and that's myself,
It shall be moon, or star, or what I list,
Or e'er I journey to your father's house.
(*to the Servants*) Go on and fetch our horses back again.
Evermore crossed and crossed, nothing but crossed!   10

99 *against you come* in preparation for
your coming
100 *appendix* appendage (meaning
Bianca)
103 *I'll roundly go about her* I'll approach
her without ceremony
104 *It shall go hard if Cambio go without
her* Cambio is not going to lose her if
he can possibly help it

IV.5 The location of this scene, established in the first two lines, is somewhere
on the road between Petruchio's house

and Padua. No Elizabethan audience
would trouble its head over whether the
travellers are in that 'Long-lane', mentioned by Petruchio at IV.3.181, or
whether they are somewhere further
along the main road, walking up a hill
to rest their horses. The audience would
know that the characters must be on
foot, because horses did not appear on
the Elizabethan stage.
7 *list* please, choose
8 *Or e'er* before ever

HORTENSIO
Say as he says, or we shall never go.

KATHERINA
Forward, I pray, since we have come so far,
And be it moon, or sun, or what you please.
And if you please to call it a rush-candle,
Henceforth I vow it shall be so for me.

PETRUCHIO
I say it is the moon.

KATHERINA   I know it is the moon.

PETRUCHIO
Nay, then you lie. It is the blessèd sun.

KATHERINA
Then, God be blessed, it is the blessèd sun.
But sun it is not, when you say it is not,
And the moon changes even as your mind.
What you will have it named, even that it is,
And so it shall be so for Katherine.

HORTENSIO (*aside*)
Petruchio, go thy ways, the field is won.

PETRUCHIO
Well, forward, forward! Thus the bowl should run,
And not unluckily against the bias.
But soft, company is coming here.

    Enter Vincentio

(*to Vincentio*) Good morrow, gentle mistress, where away?
Tell me, sweet Kate, and tell me truly too,
Hast thou beheld a fresher gentlewoman?
Such war of white and red within her cheeks!

20

30

14 *rush-candle* (candle of feeble power made by dipping a rush in grease)
20 *And the moon changes even as your mind* (a nice touch showing that Katherina has lost neither her spirit nor her sense of humour)
23 *go thy ways* go on, carry on (used as a term of approbation)
25 *against the bias* against its natural inclination. The bias is the weight lodged on one side of the wooden ball, or bowl, used in the game of bowls, in order to make it swerve when rolled.
27 *where away?* where are you going?
29 *fresher* more youthful

What stars do spangle heaven with such beauty
As those two eyes become that heavenly face?
Fair lovely maid, once more good day to thee.
Sweet Kate, embrace her for her beauty's sake.

HORTENSIO (*aside*) 'A will make the man mad, to make
the woman of him.

KATHERINA
Young budding virgin, fair and fresh and sweet,
Whither away, or where is thy abode?
Happy the parents of so fair a child,
Happier the man whom favourable stars   40
Allots thee for his lovely bedfellow.

PETRUCHIO
Why, how now, Kate, I hope thou art not mad!
This is a man, old, wrinkled, faded, withered,
And not a maiden, as thou say'st he is.

KATHERINA
Pardon, old father, my mistaking eyes,
That have been so bedazzled with the sun
That everything I look on seemeth green.
Now I perceive thou art a reverend father.
Pardon, I pray thee, for my mad mistaking.

PETRUCHIO
Do, good old grandsire, and withal make known   50

31 *spangle* brightly adorn

35 *'A* he (colloquial)

36 *the woman.* So the First Folio, though
most editors prefer to follow the
Second and read 'a woman'. The
allusion is, however, to the theatre,
where the part of the woman was
played by a boy. Petruchio, says Hortensio, is assigning the old man
the woman's role in the little play he
is staging. Compare *Coriolanus*,
II.2.93–5:

> In that day's feats,
> When he might act the woman in the
>   scene,
> He proved best man i'th' field . . .

38 *Whither away, or where.* This is the
reading of the Second Folio; the First
has 'Whether away, or whether'.
Since 'where' was a contracted form
of 'whether', the mistake is easily
understood.

41 *Allots* (the old plural)

47 *green* (1) green in colour; (2) fresh,
new, youthful

Which way thou travellest — if along with us,
We shall be joyful of thy company.

VINCENTIO
Fair sir, and you my merry mistress,
That with your strange encounter much amazed me,
My name is called Vincentio, my dwelling Pisa,
And bound I am to Padua, there to visit
A son of mine, which long I have not seen.

PETRUCHIO
What is his name?

VINCENTIO   Lucentio, gentle sir.

PETRUCHIO
Happily met — the happier for thy son.
60   And now by law, as well as reverend age,
I may entitle thee my loving father.
The sister to my wife, this gentlewoman,
Thy son by this hath married. Wonder not,
Nor be not grieved — she is of good esteem,
Her dowry wealthy, and of worthy birth,
Beside, so qualified as may beseem
The spouse of any noble gentleman.
Let me embrace with old Vincentio,
And wander we to see thy honest son,
70   Who will of thy arrival be full joyous.

VINCENTIO
But is this true, or is it else your pleasure,

---

54 *encounter* manner of address, greeting
61 *father* father-in-law. Petruchio is
rather stretching the meaning.
62–3 *The sister to my wife, this
gentlewoman, | Thy son by this hath mar-
ried.* Neither Petruchio nor Hortensio, who adds his assurance at line
74, can possibly know this, since it
has not yet happened. Moreover,
Hortensio has every reason to think
it never will, because Tranio, who
for him, as for Petruchio, is Lucen-

tio, joined with him in forswearing
Bianca for ever. Though these discrepancies are likely to go unnoticed
in the theatre, they do point, nevertheless, to the same kind of cobbling
that is evident in the conduct of so
much of the subplot.
64 *of good esteem* of good reputation,
highly respected
66 *qualified* endowed with good qualities
beseem befit
71 *or is it else* or else is it

Like pleasant travellers, to break a jest
Upon the company you overtake?

HORTENSIO
I do assure thee, father, so it is.

PETRUCHIO
Come, go along and see the truth hereof,
For our first merriment hath made thee jealous.

Exeunt all but Hortensio

HORTENSIO
Well, Petruchio, this has put me in heart.
Have to my widow! And if she be froward,
Then hast thou taught Hortensio to be untoward.

Exit

Enter Biondello, Lucentio as himself, and Bianca. V.I
Gremio is out before

BIONDELLO Softly and swiftly, sir, for the priest is ready.
LUCENTIO I fly, Biondello. But they may chance to need
thee at home, therefore leave us.

Exeunt Lucentio and Bianca

BIONDELLO Nay, faith, I'll see the church a your back,

---

72 *pleasant* merry, facetious
    break a jest play a practical joke
76 *jealous* suspicious
77 *put me in heart* encouraged me
78 *froward* difficult, refractory
79 *untoward* unmannerly, unforthcoming

v.1 The Folio marks no Act division at this point, but since the action has now moved back to Padua, where it will remain for the rest of the play, this is obviously the right place for the last Act to begin

        (stage direction) *Enter Biondello, Lucentio as himself, and Bianca, Gremio is out before.* So the Folio, except that

it fails to indicate that Lucentio is no longer in disguise. The very unusual direction '*Gremio is out before*', which has all the appearance of an afterthought, means that Gremio comes on first, and the rest follow after a brief interval. Why he is waiting for Cambio (see line 6) is never made clear, but his failure to notice him when he does come on is accounted for by the fact that Lucentio is not now 'in the habit of a mean man'.

4 *I'll see the church a your back* I'll see the church at your back (meaning 'I'll see you safely married')

and then come back to my master's as soon as I can.

Exit

GREMIO
    I marvel Cambio comes not all this while.

Enter Petruchio, Katherina, Vincentio and Grumio,
with attendants

PETRUCHIO
    Sir, here's the door, this is Lucentio's house.
    My father's bears more toward the market-place.
    Thither must I, and here I leave you, sir.

VINCENTIO
10   You shall not choose but drink before you go.
    I think I shall command your welcome here,
    And by all likelihood some cheer is toward.

He knocks

GREMIO They're busy within. You were best knock louder.

More knocking

Pedant looks out of the window

PEDANT What's he that knocks as he would beat down
    the gate?

VINCENTIO Is Signor Lucentio within, sir?

PEDANT He's within, sir, but not to be spoken withal.

VINCENTIO What if a man bring him a hundred pound
    or two to make merry withal?

20   PEDANT Keep your hundred pounds to yourself. He shall
    need none so long as I live.

7–8 *Sir, here's the door, this is Lucentio's house . . . market-place.* These two lines are a strong indication that for the part of the action that takes place in Padua one of the main doors leading on to the stage is thought of as the entrance to Lucentio's house and the other as the entrance to Baptista's house.

10 *You shall not choose but* you must
11 *your welcome* a welcome for you
12 *some cheer is toward* some good cheer is to be expected

13 (stage direction) *Pedant looks out of the window.* This stage direction has been adapted from a similar one in Gascoigne's *Supposes*, where in the corresponding scene (IV.3) Dalio, the cook in the house of Dulipo (Tranio), 'cometh to the window, and there maketh them answer' when the true father of the hero turns up. The window in question was probably above the stage door that served as the entrance to Lucentio's house.

17 *withal* with

PETRUCHIO Nay, I told you your son was well beloved
in Padua. Do you hear, sir? To leave frivolous circumstances, I pray you tell Signor Lucentio that his father is
come from Pisa, and is here at the door to speak with
him.

PEDANT Thou liest. His father is come from Mantua, and
here looking out at the window.

VINCENTIO Art thou his father?

PEDANT Ay sir, so his mother says, if I may believe her. 30

PETRUCHIO (*to Vincentio*) Why how now, gentleman!
Why, this is flat knavery, to take upon you another man's
name.

PEDANT Lay hands on the villain. I believe 'a means to
cozen somebody in this city under my countenance.

    Enter Biondello

BIONDELLO (aside) I have seen them in the church together. God send 'em good shipping! But who is here?
Mine old master Vincentio! Now we are undone and
brought to nothing.

VINCENTIO (*seeing Biondello*) Come hither, crack-hemp. 40

BIONDELLO I hope I may choose, sir.

VINCENTIO Come hither, you rogue. What, have you forgot me?

BIONDELLO Forgot you? No, sir. I could not forget you,
for I never saw you before in all my life.

23–4 *To leave frivolous circumstances* to
have done with pointless talk, to cut
the cackle

27 *from Mantua.* The Folio reads: 'from
Padua' which does not make very
good sense, since they are in Padua.
A much better comic effect is produced by letting the Pedant forget
his role for a moment and give the
name of the place he has really come
from.

32 *flat* downright, bare-faced

34–5 *'a means to cozen* he plans to cheat

35 *under my countenance* by pretending to
be me

37 *God send 'em good shipping* may God
grant them a good voyage (a proverbial phrase for wishing someone
good luck)

38 *undone* ruined

40 *crack-hemp* rogue deserving to be
hanged, gallows-bird

41 *I hope I may choose* I trust I may suit
myself (meaning 'be allowed to go
on my way')

VINCENTIO What, you notorious villain, didst thou never see thy master's father, Vincentio?

BIONDELLO What, my old worshipful old master? Yes, marry, sir – see where he looks out of the window.

50   VINCENTIO Is't so, indeed?

He beats Biondello

BIONDELLO Help, help, help! Here's a madman will murder me.   *Exit*

PEDANT Help, son! Help, Signor Baptista!

Exit from the window

PETRUCHIO Prithee, Kate, let's stand aside and see the end of this controversy.

They stand aside
Enter Pedant below, with Servants, Baptista, and Tranio

TRANIO Sir, what are you that offer to beat my servant?

VINCENTIO What am I, sir? Nay, what are you, sir? O immortal gods! O fine villain! A silken doublet, a velvet hose, a scarlet cloak, and a copatain hat! O, I am undone, I am undone! While I play the good husband at home, my son and my servant spend all at the university.

60   TRANIO How now, what's the matter?

BAPTISTA What, is the man lunatic?

TRANIO Sir, you seem a sober ancient gentleman by your habit, but your words show you a madman. Why, sir, what 'cerns it you if I wear pearl and gold? I thank my good father, I am able to maintain it.

VINCENTIO Thy father? O villain, he is a sail-maker in Bergamo.

56 *offer* dare, have the effrontery
58 *fine* richly dressed
59 *copatain hat* sugar-loaf hat
60 *good husband* careful economical manager
65 *habit* appearance
66 *what 'cerns it you ...?* how does it concern you, what business of yours is it?
67 *maintain* afford
69 *Bergamo*. This town, some twenty-five miles to the north-east of Milan, is an improbable place for a sail-maker to live, but it is exactly the right place for Tranio to come from, since it was the traditional home of Harlequin, the facetious servant of the Italian *Commedia dell'arte*.

BAPTISTA You mistake, sir, you mistake, sir. Pray, what   70
do you think is his name?

VINCENTIO His name? As if I knew not his name! I have
brought him up ever since he was three years old, and
his name is Tranio.

PEDANT Away, away, mad ass! His name is Lucentio, and
he is mine only son, and heir to the lands of me, Signor
Vincentio.

VINCENTIO Lucentio? O, he hath murdered his master!
Lay hold on him, I charge you, in the Duke's name. O,
my son, my son! Tell me, thou villain, where is my son   80
Lucentio?

TRANIO Call forth an officer.

Enter an Officer

Carry this mad knave to the gaol. Father Baptista, I
charge you see that he be forthcoming.

VINCENTIO Carry me to the gaol?

GREMIO Stay, officer. He shall not go to prison.

BAPTISTA Talk not, Signor Gremio. I say he shall go to
prison.

GREMIO Take heed, Signor Baptista, lest you be cony-
catched in this business. I dare swear this is the right   90
Vincentio.

PEDANT Swear if thou dar'st.

GREMIO Nay, I dare not swear it.

TRANIO Then thou wert best say that I am not Lucentio.

GREMIO Yes, I know thee to be Signor Lucentio.

BAPTISTA Away with the dotard, to the gaol with him!

VINCENTIO Thus strangers may be haled and abused. O
monstrous villain!

---

82 *an officer* a constable
(stage direction) *Enter an Officer*. Not
in the Folio though required by the
dialogue and the action.
84 *forthcoming* ready to stand his trial
when required

89-90 *cony-catched* cheated, swindled,
made the victim of a confidence-
trick
96 *dotard* drivelling old fool
97 *haled and abused* dragged about and
wrongfully treated

Enter Biondello, with Lucentio and Bianca

BIONDELLO O, we are spoiled, and yonder he is! Deny
him, forswear him, or else we are all undone.

LUCENTIO *(kneeling)*
Pardon, sweet father.

VINCENTIO   Lives my sweet son?

Exeunt Biondello, Tranio and Pedant, as fast as may be

BIANCA
Pardon, dear father.

BAPTISTA   How hast thou offended?
Where is Lucentio?

LUCENTIO   Here's Lucentio,
Right son to the right Vincentio,
That have by marriage made thy daughter mine,
While counterfeit supposes bleared thine eyne.

GREMIO
Here's packing, with a witness, to deceive us all.

VINCENTIO
Where is that damnèd villain, Tranio,
That faced and braved me in this matter so?

BAPTISTA
Why, tell me, is not this my Cambio?

BIANCA
Cambio is changed into Lucentio.

LUCENTIO
Love wrought these miracles. Bianca's love
Made me exchange my state with Tranio,
While he did bear my countenance in the town,

99 *spoiled* ruined
101 (stage direction) *Exeunt ... as fast
as may be.* There is a parallel to this
picturesque bit of description in *The
Comedy of Errors*, IV.4.144, where the
Folio direction reads: 'Exeunt omnes,
as fast as may be, frighted.'

106 *counterfeit supposes* false suppositions
caused by the exchange of identities.
There is an obvious reference here
to Gascoigne's *Supposes*.
bleared thine eyne deceived your eyes
107 *Here's packing, with a witness* here's
plotting, and no mistake

And happily I have arrived at last
Unto the wished haven of my bliss.
What Tranio did, myself enforced him to;
Then pardon him, sweet father, for my sake.

VINCENTIO I'll slit the villain's nose that would have sent
me to the gaol.   120

BAPTISTA (*to Lucentio*) But do you hear, sir? Have you
married my daughter without asking my good will?

VINCENTIO Fear not, Baptista, we will content you, go to.
But I will in to be revenged for this villainy.   *Exit*

BAPTISTA And I to sound the depth of this knavery.

Exit

LUCENTIO Look not pale, Bianca – thy father will not
frown.   *Exeunt Lucentio and Bianca*

GREMIO

My cake is dough, but I'll in among the rest,
Out of hope of all but my share of the feast.   *Exit*

KATHERINA Husband, let's follow to see the end of this   130
ado.

PETRUCHIO First kiss me, Kate, and we will.

KATHERINA What, in the midst of the street?

PETRUCHIO What, art thou ashamed of me?

KATHERINA No, sir, God forbid – but ashamed to kiss.

PETRUCHIO

Why then, let's home again.

(*to Grumio*) Come, sirrah, let's away.

KATHERINA

Nay, I will give thee a kiss.

      She kisses him

Now pray thee, love, stay.

---

119 *I'll slit the villain's nose.* The slitting
or cutting-off of the nose was a recog-
nised form of revenge. Compare Othello's words about Cassio, 'I see that
nose of yours, but not that dog I
shall throw it to' (*Othello*, IV.1.142–3).

123 *go to* come, don't worry
128 *My cake is dough* I have failed. See
note to 1.1.108.
129 *Out of hope of all* with no hope of
anything

PETRUCHIO

140   Is not this well? Come, my sweet Kate.
        Better once than never, for never too late.   *Exeunt*

V.2   *Enter Baptista with Vincentio, Gremio with the*
             Pedant, Lucentio with Bianca, Petruchio with
             Katherina, Hortensio with the Widow; followed
             by Tranio, Biondello, and Grumio, with the Servingmen
             bringing in a banquet

LUCENTIO

        At last, though long, our jarring notes agree,
        And time it is when raging war is done
        To smile at scapes and perils overblown.
        My fair Bianca, bid my father welcome,
        While I with self-same kindness welcome thine.

141 *Better once than never, for never too late.*
Petruchio has rolled two proverbs
into one: 'Better late than never',
and 'It is never too late to mend'.
'Once' here means 'sometime'.

    The last few lines of this scene,
when Petruchio and Katherina have
the stage to themselves, are some of
the most important in the play, for it
is here that Katherina addresses
Petruchio for the first time in an
affectionate manner and gives him
the kiss that sets the seal on their
union.

v.2 The Folio heads this scene '*Actus
Quintus.*', disregarding the change of loca-
tion that has occurred a scene before,
and leaving the last Act rather thin.
    (stage direction) *Enter Baptista ...
banquet.* The Folio reads: '*Enter
Baptista, Vincentio, Gremio, the Pedant,
Lucentio, and Bianca. Tranio, Biondello
Grumio, and Widdow: The Seruingmen*

with Tranio bringing in a Banquet.'
Tranio, it will be noticed, is mentioned twice, while Petruchio, Katherina, and Hortensio are not mentioned at all. A direction such as this
can hardly be the work of the author,
and it would certainly not have
passed muster in the theatre.
    (stage direction) *banquet* (dessert of
fruits, sweetmeats and wine, served
after supper)

1 *long* late, after a long time
  agree harmonize

3 *scapes* escapes
  overblown gone by, that have blown
  over

4–5 *My fair Bianca, bid my father welcome
    ... thine.* Lucentio is giving the ban-
    quet at his house, to which they
    have all adjourned after enjoying the
    wedding feast at Baptista's.

5 *kindness* the feelings proper to kinship,
  goodwill

Brother Petruchio, sister Katherina,
And thou, Hortensio, with thy loving widow,
Feast with the best, and welcome to my house.
My banquet is to close our stomachs up
After our great good cheer. Pray you, sit down,   10
For now we sit to chat as well as eat.
     They sit

PETRUCHIO
Nothing but sit and sit, and eat and eat!

BAPTISTA
Padua affords this kindness, son Petruchio

PETRUCHIO
Padua affords nothing but what is kind.

HORTENSIO
For both our sakes I would that word were true.

PETRUCHIO
Now, for my life, Hortensio fears his widow.

WIDOW
Then never trust me if I be afeard.

PETRUCHIO
You are very sensible, and yet you miss my sense:
I mean Hortensio is afeard of you.

WIDOW
He that is giddy thinks the world turns round.   20

PETRUCHIO
Roundly replied.

8 *Feast with* feast on
9 *close our stomachs up* put the finishing
touches to our meal. Cheese is normally used for this purpose today,
but our ancestors had different ideas.
13 *affords this kindness* offers this as the
natural thing
14 *kind* affectionate, kindly. Petruchio is
thinking of Katherina.
16 *fears* (1) is afraid of (the sense in
which Petruchio uses it); (2) frightens

(the sense in which the Widow takes
it)
17 *Then never trust me if I be* I can tell
you I am not
18 *sensible* judicious, discriminating
sense meaning
20 *He that is giddy thinks the world turns
round* people are prone to attribute
their misfortunes to others. The saying was proverbial.
21 *Roundly* (1) outspokenly; (2) glibly

KATHERINA   Mistress, how mean you that?

WIDOW
Thus I conceive by him.

PETRUCHIO
Conceives by me! How likes Hortensio that?

HORTENSIO
My widow says thus she conceives her tale.

PETRUCHIO
Very well mended. Kiss him for that, good widow.

KATHERINA
'He that is giddy thinks the world turns round' –
I pray you tell me what you meant by that.

WIDOW
Your husband, being troubled with a shrew,
Measures my husband's sorrow by his woe.

30   And now you know my meaning.

KATHERINA
A very mean meaning.

WIDOW   Right, I mean you.

KATHERINA
And I am mean, indeed, respecting you.

PETRUCHIO
To her, Kate!

HORTENSIO
To her, widow!

PETRUCHIO
A hundred marks, my Kate does put her down.

HORTENSIO
That's my office.

---

22 *Thus I conceive by him* that's the state I
   think he's in
23 *Conceives by me!* (the obvious quibble)
24 *conceives her tale* interprets her remark
25 *mended* rectified
31 *mean* petty, trivial
32 *I am mean, indeed, respecting you* I am
   moderate in behaviour by comparison with you

33 *To her* have at her, assail her
35 *marks.* A mark was worth thirteen
   shillings and four pence.
   put her down (1) get the better of her;
   (2) have sexual relations with her –
   the sense Hortensio gives the phrase.
   There is a similar quibbling exchange
   between Don Pedro and Beatrice in
   Much Ado About Nothing, II.1.259–62.

PETRUCHIO

Spoke like an officer – ha' to thee, lad.

He drinks to Hortensio

BAPTISTA

How likes Gremio these quick-witted folks?

GREMIO

Believe me, sir, they butt together well.

BIANCA

Head and butt! An hasty-witted body   40
Would say your head and butt were head and horn.

VINCENTIO

Ay, mistress bride, hath that awakened you?

BIANCA

Ay, but not frighted me, therefore I'll sleep again.

PETRUCHIO

Nay, that you shall not. Since you have begun,
Have at you for a bitter jest or two.

BIANCA

Am I your bird? I mean to shift my bush,
And then pursue me as you draw your bow.

36 *office* employment
37 *like an officer* like one who does his
duty
39 *butt together* butt each other. The
Folio reads: 'But together', which
many editors change to 'butt heads
together' in order to prepare the way
for Bianca's retort. This, however,
makes the line unmetrical, and is not
strictly necessary, since the use of
the head is implicit in the act of
butting. Shakespeare employs the
same analogy between young people
exchanging witticisms and cattle butting each other in *Love's Labour's Lost*,
where Longaville tells Katharine:

Look how you butt yourself in these sharp
mocks!

*Will you give horns, chaste
lady?*   V.2.251–2

40 *Head and butt!* head and tail! 'Butt'
here means 'bottom'.
hasty-witted body quick-witted person
41 *your head and butt were head and horn*
your butting head was a horned head
(a reference to the cuckold's horns)
45 *bitter* shrewd. The Folio reads:
'better'.
46–7 *Am I your bird? I mean to shift my
bush,* | *And then pursue me as you
draw your bow.* The reference is to
the Elizabethan method of fowling
with bow and arrows. The target
had to be a sitting one; therefore, if
the bird moved to another tree or
bush, the fowler had to follow.

You are welcome all.

Exeunt Bianca, Katherina, and Widow

PETRUCHIO

She hath prevented me. Here, Signor Tranio,
This bird you aimed at, though you hit her not –
Therefore a health to all that shot and missed

TRANIO

O sir, Lucentio slipped me like his greyhound,
Which runs himself, and catches for his master.

PETRUCHIO

A good swift simile, but something currish.

TRANIO

'Tis well, sir, that you hunted for yourself.
'Tis thought your deer does hold you at a bay.

BAPTISTA

O, O, Petruchio! Tranio hits you now.

LUCENTIO

I thank thee for that gird, good Tranio.

HORTENSIO

Confess, confess, hath he not hit you here?

PETRUCHIO

'A has a little galled me, I confess;
And as the jest did glance away from me,
'Tis ten to one it maimed you two outright.

BAPTISTA

Now, in good sadness, son Petruchio,
I think thou hast the veriest shrew of all.

49 *prevented* forestalled, escaped from
52 *slipped* unleashed
54 *swift* prompt, quick
56 *your deer does hold you at a bay* your deer (with a quibble on 'dear') shows fight and holds you off. A stag is said to be 'at bay' when it turns on the dogs and defends itself with its horns.
57 *hits you* gives you a shrewd blow, catches you on the raw
58 *gird* taunt, gibe
60 *'A* he (colloquial)
   galled me scratched me, given me a surface wound
61 *did glance away from* ricocheted off
63 *in good sadness* in sober earnest

PETRUCHIO

    Well, I say no. And therefore for assurance
    Let's each one send unto his wife,
    And he whose wife is most obedient,
    To come at first when he doth send for her,
    Shall win the wager which we will propose.

HORTENSIO

    Content. What's the wager?

LUCENTIO   Twenty crowns.   70

PETRUCHIO

    Twenty crowns?
    I'll venture so much of my hawk or hound,
    But twenty times so much upon my wife.

LUCENTIO

    A hundred then.

HORTENSIO   Content.

PETRUCHIO   A match! 'Tis done.

HORTENSIO

    Who shall begin?

LUCENTIO   That will I. Biondello,
    Go bid your mistress come to me.

BIONDELLO   I go.   *Exit*

BAPTISTA

    Son, I'll be your half Bianca comes.

LUCENTIO

    I'll have no halves. I'll bear it all myself.

    Enter Biondello

    How now, what news?

BIONDELLO   Sir, my mistress sends you word
    That she is busy and she cannot come.   80

---

65 *for assurance* to make sure
72 *of* on
75–6 *That will I. Biondello,* | *Go* . . . The
    Folio reads: 'That will I. | Goe Bion-
    dello . . .', which is metrically unsatis-
    factory. The transposition of the two

words, 'Biondello' and 'Go', puts the
metre right, while leaving the sense
unaltered.
77 *I'll be your half* I'll go half-shares with
    you in the risk and the profit of
    betting that

PETRUCHIO
How? She's busy, and she cannot come!
Is that an answer?

GREMIO   Ay, and a kind one too.
Pray God, sir, your wife send you not a worse.

PETRUCHIO
I hope better.

HORTENSIO
Sirrah Biondello, go and entreat my wife
To come to me forthwith.   *Exit Biondello*

PETRUCHIO   O ho, entreat her!
Nay, then she must needs come.

HORTENSIO   I am afraid, sir,
Do what you can, yours will not be entreated.
    Enter Biondello
Now, where's my wife?

BIONDELLO
She says you have some goodly jest in hand.
She will not come. She bids you come to her.

PETRUCHIO
Worse and worse, she will not come! O vile,
Intolerable, not to be endured!
Sirrah Grumio, go to your mistress,
Say I command her come to me.   *Exit Grumio*

HORTENSIO
I know her answer.

PETRUCHIO   What?

HORTENSIO   She will not.

PETRUCHIO
The fouler fortune mine, and there an end.
    Enter Katherina

90

---

81 *How?* really? (expression of surprise)
84 *I hope better* I have better expectations

97 *The fouler fortune mine, and there an end*
the worse my luck, and that's that

BAPTISTA

Now, by my holidame, here comes Katherina.

KATHERINA

What is your will, sir, that you send for me?

PETRUCHIO

Where is your sister, and Hortensio's wife?   100

KATHERINA

They sit conferring by the parlour fire.

PETRUCHIO

Go fetch them hither. If they deny to come,
Swinge me them soundly forth unto their husbands.
Away, I say, and bring them hither straight.

Exit Katherina

LUCENTIO

Here is a wonder, if you talk of a wonder.

HORTENSIO

And so it is. I wonder what it bodes.

PETRUCHIO

Marry, peace it bodes, and love, and quiet life,
An awful rule, and right supremacy,
And, to be short, what not that's sweet and happy.

BAPTISTA

Now fair befall thee, good Petruchio!   110
The wager thou hast won, and I will add
Unto their losses twenty thousand crowns –
Another dowry to another daughter,
For she is changed, as she had never been.

PETRUCHIO

Nay, I will win my wager better yet,

98 *by my holidame* by all I hold sacred, by
my halidom
101 *conferring* chatting
102 *deny* refuse
103 *Swinge me them soundly forth* beat them
soundly, I tell you, and make them
come hither
105 *wonder* miracle

106 *bodes* portends, presages
108 *awful* commanding due respect
right supremacy supremacy that deserves the name
110 *fair befall thee* good luck to you,
congratulations to you
114 *as she had never been* as if she had
never existed, out of all recognition

And show more sign of her obedience,
Her new-built virtue and obedience.

Enter Katherina with Bianca and Widow

See where she comes, and brings your froward wives
As prisoners to her womanly persuasion.

120 Katherine, that cap of yours becomes you not.
Off with that bauble, throw it under foot.

She obeys

WIDOW

Lord, let me never have a cause to sigh
Till I be brought to such a silly pass!

BIANCA

Fie, what a foolish duty call you this?

LUCENTIO

I would your duty were as foolish too!
The wisdom of your duty, fair Bianca,
Hath cost me a hundred crowns since supper-time.

BIANCA

The more fool you for laying on my duty.

PETRUCHIO

Katherine, I charge thee, tell these headstrong women

130 What duty they do owe their lords and husbands.

WIDOW

Come, come, you're mocking. We will have no telling.

PETRUCHIO

Come on, I say, and first begin with her.

WIDOW

She shall not.

PETRUCHIO

I say she shall. And first begin with her.

117 *obedience*. So the Folio, but the repetition of the word is suspicious. It has probably been caught by the compositor from the end of the previous line.

127 *a hundred crowns*. The Folio reads: 'Fiue hundred crownes', though Lu-

centio's bet, made at line 74, was only for one hundred. The best explanation of the mistake is C. J. Sisson's; he thinks that the manuscript read 'a hundred', which the compositor took as 'v hundred'.

128 *laying* laying a bet, wagering

KATHERINA

Fie, fie, unknit that threatening unkind brow,
And dart not scornful glances from those eyes
To wound thy lord, thy king, thy governor.
It blots thy beauty as frosts do bite the meads,
Confounds thy fame as whirlwinds shake fair buds,
And in no sense is meet or amiable.   140
A woman moved is like a fountain troubled,
Muddy, ill-seeming, thick, bereft of beauty,
And while it is so, none so dry or thirsty
Will deign to sip or touch one drop of it.
Thy husband is thy lord, thy life, thy keeper,
Thy head, thy sovereign; one that cares for thee,
And for thy maintenance; commits his body
To painful labour both by sea and land,
To watch the night in storms, the day in cold,
Whilst thou liest warm at home, secure and safe;   150
And craves no other tribute at thy hands
But love, fair looks, and true obedience –
Too little payment for so great a debt.
Such duty as the subject owes the prince,
Even such a woman oweth to her husband.
And when she is froward, peevish, sullen, sour,

135 *unkind* harsh, in a manner contrary to nature
138 *blots* disfigures, destroys
   meads meadows
139 *Confounds thy fame* ruins your reputation
   shake shake to pieces
141 *moved* annoyed, in a bad temper
142 *ill-seeming* unpleasant to look at
   thick turbid
143 *none so dry* no one no matter how dry, no one however dry
147 *maintenance; commits.* The Folio reads: 'maintenance. Commits', which many editors change to 'maintenance commits', assuming that it is in order to maintain his wife that the husband 'commits his body | To painful labour'. In this edition the punctuation of the Folio is substantially adhered to, because it brings out a general contrast between the life of the husband and the life of the wife, the one exposed to the dangers of the world, the other safe at home.
148 *painful* hard, toilsome
149 *watch* be on guard through, be on the alert through

And not obedient to his honest will,
What is she but a foul contending rebel
And graceless traitor to her loving lord?
160 I am ashamed that women are so simple
To offer war where they should kneel for peace,
Or seek for rule, supremacy, and sway,
When they are bound to serve, love, and obey.
Why are our bodies soft, and weak, and smooth,
Unapt to toil and trouble in the world,
But that our soft conditions and our hearts
Should well agree with our external parts?
Come, come, you froward and unable worms,
My mind hath been as big as one of yours,
170 My heart as great, my reason haply more,
To bandy word for word and frown for frown.
But now I see our lances are but straws,
Our strength as weak, our weakness past compare,
That seeming to be most which we indeed least are.
Then vail your stomachs, for it is no boot,
And place your hands below your husband's foot.
In token of which duty, if he please,

158 *foul* wicked
159 *graceless* depraved, sinful
160 *simple* foolish, unintelligent
161 *offer* begin, declare
165 *Unapt to* unfit for
166 *conditions* qualities, temperaments
168 *unable* weak, impotent
169 *My mind hath been as big as one of yours*
my inclination has been as strong as
that of either of you
170 *heart* courage
haply perhaps, maybe
171 *bandy* exchange (as a ball is hit to
and fro in tennis)
173 *as weak* (as weak as straws)
174 *That seeming to be most which* seeming
to be that in the highest degree
which

175 *vail your stomachs* lower your pride
it is no boot it is of no avail, there is
no help for it
176 *And place your hands below your husband's foot.* There may well be a reference here to some traditional act of
allegiance, but the basic idea is clearly
set out in the Homily entitled 'Of
the State of Matrimony', where wives
are advised to submit to their husbands 'in respect of the commandment of God, as St Paul expresseth it
in this form of words: *Let women be
subject to their husbands, as to the Lord;
for the husband is the head of the woman,
as Christ is the head of the church.*
Ephes. v' (*Sermons or Homilies,*
London, no date, pp. 553–4).

My hand is ready, may it do him ease.

PETRUCHIO

Why, there's a wench! Come on, and kiss me, Kate.

LUCENTIO

Well, go thy ways, old lad, for thou shalt ha't.   180

VINCENTIO

'Tis a good hearing when children are toward.

LUCENTIO

But a harsh hearing when women are froward.

PETRUCHIO

Come, Kate, we'll to bed.

We three are married, but you two are sped.

(*to Lucentio*) 'Twas I won the wager, though you hit the
      white,

And being a winner, God give you good night!

Exeunt Petruchio and Katherina

HORTENSIO

Now go thy ways, thou hast tamed a curst shrew.

LUCENTIO

'Tis a wonder, by your leave, she will be tamed so.

Exeunt

---

178 *do him ease* give him satisfaction
180 *go thy ways* well done
      ha't have it, meaning 'have the prize', 'be acknowledged as the winner'
181 *a good hearing* a nice thing to hear, a pleasant spectacle
      toward docile, tractable (the exact opposite of 'froward')

184 *sped* done for, defeated
185 *the white* the white ring at the centre of the target (with a quibble on the name Bianca, the Italian for white)
186 *being* since I am. Petruchio, like a successful gamester, goes off while his luck still holds.

The Sly Scenes in 'A Shrew'

In *The Taming of a Shrew* Christopher Sly is involved in the action, after the Induction is over, on five subsequent occasions. Pope inserted these passages into his edition of Shakespeare's play, and many producers have found them irresistible. They are, therefore, given here.

(i) Occurring at a point for which there is no precise equivalent in *The Taming of the Shrew*, this intervention by Sly would, if used in a modern production of Shakespeare's play, best come at the end of II.1.

SLY Sim, when will the fool [Sander, the equivalent of Grumio] come again?

LORD He'll come again, my lord, anon.

SLY Gi's some more drink here. Zounds, where's the tapster? Here, Sim, eat some of these things.

LORD So I do, my lord.

SLY Here, Sim, I drink to thee.

LORD My lord, here comes the players again.

SLY O brave! Here's two fine gentlewomen.

(ii) Sly's next intervention comes between the end of IV.4 and the beginning of IV.5, the scene in which Petruchio and Katherina dispute about the sun and the moon. Polidor and Aurelius have just gone off to marry Emelia and Phylema.

SLY Sim, must they be married now?

LORD Ay, my lord.

   Enter Ferando and Kate and Sander

SLY Look, Sim, the fool is come again now.

(iii) Sly is at his most lordly on the final occasion that he intrudes on the play that is being performed for his benefit. This happens at v.1.101 of Shakespeare's play, the stage direction with which the passage opens coinciding exactly with his direction *Exeunt Biondello, Tranio and Pedant, as fast as may be.* The Duke of Cestus has just given orders that the impostors, Phylotus and Valeria, should be sent to prison.

Phylotus and Valeria runs away
   Then Sly speaks

SLY I say we'll have no sending to prison.

LORD My lord, this is but the play, they're but in jest.

SLY I tell thee, Sim, we'll have no sending to prison, that's flat. Why, Sim, am I not Don Christo Vary? Therefore I say they shall not go to prison.

LORD No more they shall not, my lord. They be run away.

SLY Are they run away, Sim? That's well. Then gi's some more drink, and let them play again.

LORD Here, my lord.

  Sly drinks and then falls asleep

(iv) Between the end of v.1 and the beginning of v.2 Sly is removed.

          Exeunt omnes
  Sly sleeps

LORD
Who's within there? Come hither, sirs.

  Enter Servants

           My lord's
Asleep again. Go take him easily up,
And put him in his own apparel again,
And lay him in the place where we did find him,
Just underneath the alehouse side below,
But see you wake him not in any case.

BOY It shall be done, my lord. Come help to bear him hence.

(v) When the play proper is over, and all the characters have left the stage, this follows:

> *Then enter two bearing of Sly in his own apparel again,*
> *and leaves him where they found him, and then goes out.*
> *Then enter the Tapster*

TAPSTER

Now that the darksome night is overpast,
And dawning day appears in crystal sky,
Now must I haste abroad. But soft, who's this?
What, Sly? O wondrous! Hath he lain here all night?
I'll wake him. I think he's starved by this,
But that his belly was so stuffed with ale.
What ho, Sly! Awake for shame.

SLY Sim, gi's some more wine. What's all the players gone?
Am not I a lord?

TAPSTER A lord, with a murrain. Come, art thou drunken still?

SLY Who's this? Tapster! O Lord, sirrah, I have had the bravest dream tonight that ever thou heardest in all thy life.

TAPSTER Ay, marry, but you had best get you home, for your wife will course [thrash] you for dreaming here tonight.

SLY Will she? I know now how to tame a shrew. I dreamt upon it all this night till now, and thou hast waked me out of the best dream that ever I had in my life. But I'll to my wife presently, and tame her too an if she anger me.

TAPSTER

Nay tarry, Sly, for I'll go home with thee,
And hear the rest that thou hast dreamt tonight.

> *Exeunt omnes*

A MIDSUMMER NIGHT'S DREAM

Introduction

During the interval of a performance – which was not going too well – of one of Shakespeare's other plays, I once heard a schoolboy say plaintively, 'I wish it was *A Midsummer Night's Dream.*' His was not a subtle form of theatre criticism; but the remark illustrates the affection in which this play is held, and the general confidence in its power to entertain. For many people it forms their first introduction to Shakespeare, whether in reading round the class or performance in village hall, school grounds, or professional theatre. And it continues to please many who would not normally enjoy a Shakespeare play. Much of its appeal comes from the scenes in which the 'mechanicals' – the rustic figures of Bully Bottom, Peter Quince, and their fellows – appear. These are among the few comic roles in Shakespeare which are quite often taken by professional comedians rather than 'straight' actors. The roles permit, and may gain from, the display of natural comic talent. A performer whose mere face is enough to set the audience laughing can do much with the silences of Bottom; a doleful clown can amuse and touch us in Moonshine's sad exasperation at his failure to persuade his stage-audience to take him seriously; the actor who plays Wall with blank inanity can give us amusement that does not spring directly from Shakespeare's lines.

Other parts of the play, too, can give theatrical pleasure of a kind that does not imply a sophisticated response. The fairy world provides the visual appeal of youthful figures moving with elegant stylization and costumed with delicacy and charm. The forest scenes are apt to provoke designers to create richly romantic stage pictures. Music and dance are required by the action at various points, and can without too much violence be interpolated elsewhere. It is understandable that the most famous of all incidental music for Shakespeare should have been written for *A Midsummer Night's Dream*. Mendelssohn's exquisite score implies a particular style of production, a style that is now out-of-date. What modern producer would permit the introduction at the beginning of Act Five of a procession lasting as long as Mendelssohn's famous wedding march? Yet the quality of the music itself has been enough to provoke in our own time the reconstruction of the kind of presentation to which it would have been appropriate. Here the play was used as a setting for the music.

The variety of appeal inherent in *A Midsummer Night's Dream* is part of the source of its popularity, but has also caused it often to be reduced from its true stature. In the theatre it has been distorted by an over-emphasis on both its broad comedy and the opportunities it gives for stage spectacle. As early as 1661 was published *The Merry Conceited Humours of Bottom the Weaver*, in which the only characters other than the clowns are Oberon, Titania, Theseus, Hippolyta, and Puck. In Charles Johnson's *Love in a Forest* of 1723, an adaptation of *As You Like It*, the Pyramus and Thisbe episodes were incorporated as an entertainment for the banished Duke and his followers in the forest. America has seen a version called *Swinging the Dream* (1939), in which the Bottom who roared as gently as any sucking-dove was Louis Armstrong.

Over-exploitation of the play's opportunities for spectacle has too a long history. When Samuel Pepys saw it in 1662 only its incidental features appealed to him. He wrote in his diary: 'We saw *Midsummer Night's Dream*, which I had never seen before, nor shall ever again, for it is the most insipid ridiculous play that ever I saw in my life. I saw, I confess, some good dancing, and some handsome women, which was all my pleasure.' Thirty years later appeared *The Fairy Queen*, a lavish spectacle with a fine elaborate score by Henry Purcell. Though this is based on *A Midsummer Night's Dream*, Purcell set no line

of Shakespeare. Another operatic version is Frederick Rey-
nolds's (with music by Henry Bishop) of 1816, which provoked
a violent attack by William Hazlitt. He wrote in a review:

We have found to our cost, once for all, that the regions of
fancy and the boards of Covent Garden are not the same thing.
All that is fine in the play, was lost in the representation. The
spirit was evaporated, the genius was fled; but the spectacle
was fine: it was that which saved the play. Oh, ye scene-
shifters, ye scene-painters, ye machinists and dress-makers, ye
manufacturers of moon and stars that give no light, ye musical
composers, ye men in the orchestra, fiddlers and trumpeters
and players on the double drum and loud bassoon, rejoice!
This is your triumph; it is not ours.

He tells how, after seeing the performance, he read the play
again and 'completely forgot all the noise we have heard and
the sights we have seen'. He concluded that 'Poetry and the
stage do not agree together.' The verdict is understandable
from a critic of the time, when the play was presented in an
unsympathetic adaptation performed in a vast theatre; but it is
not permanently valid.

It was not till 1840 that the play was produced in something
approximating to its original form. Samuel Phelps's production
at Sadler's Wells in 1853 had great visual appeal, but seems
nevertheless to have been a faithful attempt at least to translate
into visual terms features that are a genuine part of the original
play, rather than merely superimposing upon it extraneous
spectacle. Later productions have not always avoided this
danger. Shaw wrote of Augustin Daly's (1895):

He certainly has no suspicion of the fact that every accessory he
employs is brought in at the deadliest risk of destroying the
magic spell woven by the poet. He swings Puck away on a
clumsy trapeze with a ridiculous clash of the cymbals in the
orchestra, in the fullest belief that he is thereby completing
instead of destroying the effect of Puck's lines. His 'panoramic

illusion of the passage of Theseus's barge to Athens' is more absurd than anything that occurs in the tragedy of Pyramus and Thisbe in the last act.

The pictorial, quasi-operatic style of production lasted well into this century, influencing for instance Max Reinhardt's film of 1935, but Harley Granville-Barker's Savoy Theatre perform-ances in 1914 represented a thorough rethinking of the play which effected a healthy clearance of conventional accretions. Thus, Mendelssohn's music was abandoned in favour of Eng-lish folk-tunes, and Puck and Oberon were no longer played by women, as had been the practice. Since Granville-Barker's time the desire for simplicity of presentation has slowly won ground over the desire for visual elaboration. The move has been assisted by the frequency of open-air performances, for which this play is particularly suitable. The development of the histori-cal sense, at least in matters of theatrical taste, during the past hundred years has combined with studies of Shakespeare's verbal and theatrical artistry to encourage presentation of his plays in something approaching their own terms, rather than in adaptations that either grossly misrepresent their originals, or represent only a limited part of them. *A Midsummer Night's Dream* has benefited from this development. But the passage of time creates problems, and it is not surprising that producers frequently fail to maintain a total equilibrium in their presenta-tion of Shakespeare's delicately balanced structure. It is some measure of the play's strength that it is almost infallibly enter-taining under any circumstances; but inadequacies of presenta-tion can cause us to underestimate the artistry with which it is composed. It is not simply by a happy accident that *A Midsum-mer Night's Dream* has retained for close on four centuries its power to entertain. Rather it is because this is a highly articu-lated structure, the product of a genius working with total mastery of his poetic and theatrical craft – a craft which was, of course, intimately bound up with the circumstances of the age.

*

The play was first printed in 1600. We do not know exactly when Shakespeare wrote it, though it is referred to in *Palladis Tamia*, a book by Francis Meres printed in 1598. It is generally thought of as more mature, and therefore probably later, than four other comedies – *The Two Gentlemen of Verona, The Taming of the Shrew, The Comedy of Errors*, and *Love's Labour's Lost*. These too cannot be firmly dated. *The Merchant of Venice*, also mentioned in Meres's book, is noticeably broader in range than *A Midsummer Night's Dream* (which is not to say that it is as assured a success in its own terms), and is reasonably thought of as later in date. Certainty would perhaps be most welcome as to whether *A Midsummer Night's Dream* came before or after *Romeo and Juliet*. It is tempting to imagine Shakespeare glancing at his own tragedy in the burlesque of *Pyramus and Thisbe*, with which it has features in common. This is a permissible speculation, but no more. The richness and complexity of *Romeo and Juliet* cause it to be more usually regarded as the later work.

Topical allusions have been sought in *A Midsummer Night's Dream*. Above all, Titania's lines (II.1.81–117) describing meteorological confusion have been taken as a reference to the bad summer of 1594. But bad summers were, we may suppose, no less common then than now. In any case, Titania speaks of unusually fine winters as well as bad summers; she is concerned with disorder in general. Her lines are thematically of high importance. To regard them as an attempt to win the audience's sympathy by causing her to drag in an irrelevant topical allusion is to take an insultingly low view of Shakespeare's artistry. It would be equally reasonable to argue that the lines were written in a year of perfectly normal weather in which they would have aroused no extra-dramatic response. The theatres were closed because of plague during most of 1593 and 1594. Probably *A Midsummer Night's Dream* was written either shortly before, during, or fairly soon after this period.

More important than the question of the play's exact date is the matter of whether, as has often been assumed, it was written for private performance on some particular occasion such as the marriage of a nobleman. Many attempts have been made to find a suitable wedding. Some of those who hold this theory patronize the play as an 'occasional' piece, commissioned for an audience of specialized taste. The suggestion has been offered that the play as we have it is a revision made for public performance, and even that Theseus and Hippolyta are 'stand-ins' for the pair whose wedding is supposed to have been celebrated. The belief that the wedding blessing of the last Act had some extra-dramatic significance encourages a loose assumption that it is superfluous, and has been used to justify its omission in performance. Interpretative arguments have been based upon the theory.

There is no outside evidence with any bearing on the matter. The theory has arisen from various features of the play itself. It is, certainly, much concerned with marriage; but so are many comedies. It ends with the fairies' blessing upon the married couples; but this is perfectly appropriate to Shakespeare's artistic scheme, and requires no other explanation. It includes a complimentary reference to Queen Elizabeth (II.1.157-8):

> *A certain aim he took*
> *At a fair vestal thronèd by the west . . .*

Admittedly the Queen did not attend the public theatres; but an allusion to her does not imply that she was expected to be present at the play's first, or any other, performance. *A Midsummer Night's Dream* (like *Love's Labour's Lost*) appears to require an unusually large number of boy actors. Hippolyta, Hermia, Helena, Titania, Peaseblossom, Cobweb, Moth, and Mustardseed would all have been boys' parts. Puck and Oberon too may have been played by boys or young men. But the title page of the first edition, printed in 1600, tells us that the play was 'sundry times publicly acted by the Right Honourable the Lord Chamberlain his servants'. If Shakespeare's company could at any time muster enough boys for public performances, we have no reason to doubt that it could have done so from the start.

Thus the suggestion that the roles of the fairies were intended to be taken by children of the hypothetical noble house seems purely whimsical. The stage directions of the first edition, which was probably printed from Shakespeare's manuscript, show no essential differences from those in his other plays; a direction such as 'Enter a Fairie *at one doore, and* Robin goodfellow *at another*' (II.1.0) suggests that he had in mind the structure of the public theatres. Furthermore, although noble weddings in Shakespeare's time were sometimes graced with formal entertainments, usually of the nature of a masque, the first play certainly known to have been written for such an occasion is Samuel Daniel's *Hymen's Triumph*. This was performed in 1614, some twenty years after the composition of *A Midsummer Night's Dream*. By this time the tradition of courtly entertainments had developed greatly; and *Hymen's Triumph* does not appear to have been played in a public theatre.

To me, then, it seems credible that *A Midsummer Night's Dream* was always intended for the public theatres.

A Midsummer Night's Dream is one of the small group of plays in which Shakespeare appears not to have depended upon already existing narrative material. Whereas in *The Comedy of Errors*, for example, he worked from a Latin comedy (Plautus's *Menaechmi*), and in *As You Like It* he was to dramatize an English prose tale (Thomas Lodge's *Rosalind*), we know of nothing that would have provided the main story of *A Midsummer Night's Dream*. In this, as in other respects, it is one of his most individual creations. Inevitably, however, his reading played some part in its genesis. He could have read about Theseus and Hippolyta in the first few pages of Sir Thomas North's great translation (first published in 1579) of Plutarch's *Lives of the Noble Grecians and Romans*, later to become one of his most important source works. He may also have found a few hints about the same characters in Chaucer's *The Knight's Tale*. But he can scarcely be said to have gleaned more than the names and a few general suggestions for characterization from these sources. Similarly with Oberon: the old romance of *Huon of Bordeaux* gave him a few hints, no more. Titania's name seems to have come from Ovid's *Metamorphoses*, where it is used as an adjective for more than one goddess descended of the Titans. Shakespeare knew his Ovid well, in both Latin and English. Several details of the play are influenced by the *Metamorphoses*, and Shakespeare's whole treatment of the Pyramus and Thisbe story may have been sparked off by his reading of it in Arthur Golding's translation of Ovid, published in 1567. The verse medium is that of the fourteener, which often results in a drab, monotonous style. Golding's lines almost parody themselves:

> *The wall that parted house from house had riven therein a cranny*
> *Which shrunk at making of the wall; this fault not marked of any*
> *Of many hundred years before (what doth not love espy!)*
> *These lovers first of all found out, and made a way whereby*
> *To talk together secretly, and through the same did go*
> *Their loving whisperings very light and safely to and fro.*

Finding Thisbe's mantle stained with blood, Pyramus thinks she is dead:

> *And when he had bewept and kissed the garment which he knew,*
> *'Receive thou my blood too,' quoth he, and therewithal he drew*
> *His sword, the which among his guts he thrust, and by and by*
> *Did draw it from the bleeding wound beginning for to die,*
> *And cast himself upon his back. The blood did spin on high*
> *As when a conduit pipe is cracked, the water bursting out*
> *Doth shoot itself a great way off and pierce the air about.*

Then Thisbe, alive after all, comes upon her dying lover, crying:

> *'Alas, what chance, my Pyramus, hath parted thee and me?*
> *Make answer, O my Pyramus; it is thy Thisb', even she*
> *Whom thou dost love most heartily, that speaketh unto thee.*
> *Give ear and raise thy heavy head.' He, hearing Thisbe's name,*
> *Lift up his dying eyes, and having seen her closed the same.*

> *But when she knew her mantle there and saw his scabbard lie*
> *Without the sword: 'Unhappy man, thy love hath made thee die.'*

This tale was very popular in the late sixteenth century. Many versions of it written in the sort of poetic style that must have seemed old-fashioned in the 1590s have survived, and Shakespeare probably read several of them in preparation for his own dramatization of the story.

There are a number of writings which may have suggested Bottom's translation into an ass, just as there are others which may have provided details for the portrayal of the fairy world, but it is difficult to pinpoint precise sources.

One of the most prominent characteristics of Shakespeare's playwriting career is a constant striving not to repeat himself, at any rate in essentials. Each of his plays creates its own world. At the same time, there are close relationships between many of them. He seems to have enjoyed playing variations on a theme, making use of similar material in different ways. Part of the background of *A Midsummer Night's Dream* is his own *Love's Labour's Lost*, written only a short time before. Both are highly patterned plays, concerning the exploits in wooing of pairs of lovers. Both reach their climax in an entertainment given by characters of the sub-plot for the benefit of their social superiors. In both plays the entertainments are punctuated by sarcastic comments from their stage audiences. The link between the plays, and a difference between them, is pointed by a verbal echo. 'Our wooing doth not end like an old play,' says Berowne in *Love's Labour's Lost*; 'Jack hath not Jill.' The happy ending of *A Midsummer Night's Dream* is foretold by Puck (III.2.461–3) with

> *Jack shall have Jill;*
> *Naught shall go ill.*
> *The man shall have his mare again, and all shall be well.*

No doubt Shakespeare was conscious of the relationship. But it would be false to suggest that the later play was simply a more successful attempt to do something which had not quite come off in the earlier. Each is successful in its own way, and the differences between them are as important as the resemblances. It is worth noticing that for *Love's Labour's Lost*, as for *A Midsummer Night's Dream*, there is no known main source. The other play of which this is true is *The Tempest*, which has significant resemblances to *A Midsummer Night's Dream*.

In *A Midsummer Night's Dream* Shakespeare was concerned to create characters that would serve his own purposes, not to portray historical or mythical figures. It would be false to stress Theseus's origins in classical legend. Shakespeare uses the classical hero's name, and a few of his attributes, giving him the medieval title of Duke (instead of King) of Athens. Theseus carries with him some suggestion of the classical world, with his dignified manner, his references to his kinsman Hercules, and the allusions to his love affairs. Yet to the Elizabethan audience he cannot have been far removed from a nobleman – perhaps a duke – of their own times. The opening scene shows him (like Timon of Athens in the first scene of his play) exercising the function of a benevolent landlord called upon to solve his tenants' personal problems. Nor has his Hippolyta many of the characteristics of a Queen of the Amazons. Shakespeare gives them enough non-Elizabethan traits to suggest a certain ideal quality, but leaves them as figures that would in essentials be recognizable to his audience. They have a maturity and self-command which set them off from the young lovers.

The young people are not far removed in social standing from the Duke and Duchess. The Duke knows something of their affairs before the play begins, and at the wedding festivities their easy sharing in their host's conversation suggests no awe of him. And the workmen (or mechanicals), obviously on a much lower level of society, associate them with the Duke and Duchess: 'Masters,' says Snug (IV.2.15–16), 'the Duke is coming from the temple, and there is two or three lords and ladies more married.' The characterization of the young people is deliberately slight. Shakespeare is not anxious to suggest particu-

larity; they are representative figures, practically interchangeable, as the play's action shows. In the theatre, of course, their
anonymity is less noticeable than in reading.

Oberon and Titania, too, are of calculatedly mixed origin.
Oberon smacks of medieval romance: he wants the changeling
boy to be a 'Knight of his train, to trace the forests wild'
(II.1.25). Both he and Titania are more than once associated
with India, which adds an exotic touch. They are also strongly
reminiscent of classical deities, though no precise identification
is suggested. Both have had love affairs with mortals, and
Titania has had a human 'votaress' of her order – the mother of
her changeling boy. The exact nature of their power is left
uncertain; but it is considerable. Their dissension is responsible
for the disorder of the seasons. On the whole they exercise
their power for beneficent ends, and there is a sense in which
they are projections of forces of nature favourable to humanity
just as their human counterparts, Theseus and Hippolyta, exercise a benevolent rule over the citizens of Athens.

Oberon and Titania appear to be thought of as a fully-grown
man and woman. Their attendants, however, are imagined as
tiny creatures, able to creep into acorn cups, and in danger of
being drowned if a bee's honey bag breaks. Their tininess is
something that Shakespeare derived from traditional beliefs
and to which, both here and in the Queen Mab speech in *Romeo
and Juliet*, he gave such memorable expression as to start a
literary tradition that still survives. That the fairies cannot be
thus represented on the stage is not merely obvious; it is also a
point of some importance in the scheme of the play. Shakespeare seems deliberately to draw attention to the discrepancies
between what we see and what is described. Here the audience
is required to use its imagination in order to make the play
possible. The same is true of the stage audience in the final
scene. The other inhabitant of the play's fairy world, Robin
Goodfellow, or Puck, was a well-known figure in folk-lore,
though Shakespeare adds some hints of the classical Mercury.
Obviously he is without the ethereal quality of the Fairy King

and Queen's attendants. As Oberon's agent his function is ultimately beneficent, but he has an independent love of mischief. His characteristics are described in the dialogue between himself and a fairy in Act Two, Scene One.

The other group of characters, the workmen or mechanicals, Shakespeare makes no attempt to portray as Athenians, though he gives his actors ample scope for individual characterization. As with the fairies, he lightly exploits the discrepancy between what we hear and what we see: the 'hard-handed men of Athens' are countrymen of England, through and through. To his original audience they would have suggested a group of amateur actors, perhaps with ambitions of turning professional, such as flourished some twenty or thirty years before the play was written. There are six actors in Peter Quince's company, and this would have been a normal number in a popular troupe of the mid sixteenth century. It is the plays such as these troupes performed that are burlesqued in the last Act.

Shakespeare introduces his groups of characters and organizes his narrative material with great skill. The matter of the opening interchange, between Theseus and Hippolyta, indicates the course the play is to take, looking forward to its culmination in marriage and celebration. These noble lovers provide a comparatively static framework for the play. After this opening episode, they will not reappear till the first scene of Act Four. Their relationship with each other is to remain constant, suggesting a basis of maturity and common sense which serves as a foil to the instability of the young lovers. The nature of their relationship, ardent but controlled, is suggested in the play's opening lines in terms of the normal operation of nature:

> Four days will quickly steep themselves in night;
> Four nights will quickly dream away the time:
> And then the moon — like to a silver bow
> New-bent in heaven — shall behold the night
> Of our solemnities.

The swift purposefulness of the style establishes a mood of harmony and pleasurable anticipation. Stress is laid already on the moon, an image whose recurrence will help to create the play's unity of poetic style. It sheds its radiance throughout, lingering on Theseus's desires, beholding the night of his solemnities, providing a setting for the meeting of the Fairy King and Queen, quenching Cupid's arrow in its beams, looking with a watery eye upon Titania and Bottom, and making a personal appearance in the interlude of Pyramus and Thisbe.

Into this opening harmony comes a harsh interruption. Hermia is at odds with her father. Theseus presents her an alternative if she continues to refuse to obey; and he does so in terms of natural imagery:

> *Either to die the death, or to abjure*
> *For ever the society of men . . .*
> *Thrice blessèd they that master so their blood*
> *To undergo such maiden pilgrimage;*
> *But earthlier happy is the rose distilled*
> *Than that which, withering on the virgin thorn,*
> *Grows, lives, and dies in single blessedness.*

When Hermia and Lysander are left alone, the same image recurs:

> *How now, my love? Why is your cheek so pale?*
> *How chance the roses there do fade so fast?*

The situation as it stands could issue in either tragedy (as a similar situation does in *Romeo and Juliet*) or comedy. As he is here choosing comedy, Shakespeare adopts a style that does not involve us too closely in the lovers' emotions. But he gives it enough body, enough reference to larger concepts, both to keep our sympathetic interest and to enable us to see the lovers' dilemma as an image of universal human experience. It is important to establish such a sympathy early, before the farcical confusions develop, so Lysander is given a lyrical expression of the fragility of love:

> Or if there were a sympathy in choice,
> War, death, or sickness did lay siege to it,
> Making it momentany as a sound,
> Swift as a shadow, short as any dream,
> Brief as the lightning in the collied night,
> That in a spleen unfolds both heaven and earth,
> And – ere a man hath power to say 'Behold!' –
> The jaws of darkness do devour it up.
> So quick bright things come to confusion.

There is pathos here; even a hint of the possibility of tragedy. The same imagery recurs in a premonitory passage in *Romeo and Juliet* (II.2.117–20), where Juliet says:

> I have no joy of this contract tonight.
> It is too rash, too unadvised, too sudden;
> Too like the lightning, which doth cease to be
> Ere one can say 'It lightens'.

Yet Lysander's lines are not out of place in a romantic comedy, because they are generalized: a reflection on what might be rather than what is – and because soon after them he brings forward a plan by which he and Hermia may get out of their difficult situation. They will leave Athens and make for his widowed aunt's house, seven leagues away. And they will meet 'in the wood, a league without the town'.

Helena's entrance gives scope for a comically touching demonstration of her jealousy. Her soliloquy which closes the scene states an important idea, already hinted at, with which Shakespeare is to be concerned: the irrationality of love, the tension between what people ought reasonably to feel and what in fact they do feel. Demetrius, she says,

> . . . errs, doting on Hermia's eyes,
> So I, admiring of his qualities.

> *Things base and vile, holding no quantity,*
> *Love can transpose to form and dignity.*

We may remember this later, especially when we see Bottom adored by Titania. Helena goes on to speak of the irrationality of love, suggesting a dislocation between the eyes and the mind, in which however the eyes are regarded as the objective force.

> *Love looks not with the eyes, but with the mind,*
> *And therefore is winged Cupid painted blind.*
> *Nor hath love's mind of any judgement taste;*
> *Wings and no eyes figure unheedy haste.*
> *And therefore is love said to be a child*
> *Because in choice he is so oft beguiled.*

The first scene, then, has introduced us to two related sets of characters – the Duke and Duchess and the young lovers – and set the romantic plot in motion by presenting the conflict between the young people and their elders. Helena ends the scene with a threat of treachery to Hermia and Lysander. She will reveal their plot to Demetrius, who will then pursue Hermia to the wood.

The second scene, which introduces the mechanicals, also opens by looking forward to the end of the play, as Peter Quince shows 'the scroll of every man's name which is thought fit through all Athens to play in our interlude before the Duke and the Duchess on his wedding day at night.' The interlude will concern characters resembling those we have just seen: young lovers whose romance is thwarted by parental opposition. Roles are decided, parts distributed, and the actors arrange to meet the next night for a rehearsal – in the wood.

With the third scene (Act Two, Scene One) we reach the wood, which has its own function in the play. As in, for instance, *As You Like It*, and even a play as different from *A Midsummer Night's Dream* as *King Lear*, the movement from town to country, from the control of organized society to the freedom of nature, is appropriate to the emotional experiences of the persons involved. The wood is a place of liberation, of reassessment, leading through a stage of disorganization to a finally increased stability. Here we meet the remaining group of characters. Oberon and Titania's mutual recriminations recall the jealousies of the mortal lovers. Again we have a pointer to the last Act – this time to the very end of the play: Titania is jealous that Oberon has come all the way from India only because his 'warrior love' Hippolyta is marrying Theseus, and Oberon wishes 'To give their bed joy and prosperity'. Titania defends herself against Oberon's jealous accusations in the great speech beginning 'These are the forgeries of jealousy'. Most of it has no relevance to the plot, nor is it important in characterizing Titania. It is sometimes thought of as no more than an extended topical reference. It can also be regarded simply as a piece of poetry – Shakespeare indulging his poetic talent at the expense of the drama. The speech has, of course, great poetic merit, and gives the audience pleasure in its own right. If this were its only point it would be expendable; and indeed it has often been severely cut in performance. But to dismiss it as irrelevant, or as mere decoration, is to fail to give proper allowance to the nature of poetic drama. Several major speeches in this play are important not because they further the action or elaborate a character, but because they represent an explicit verbal development of ideas hinted at in other parts of the play. They are as it were arias in which snatches of melody heard elsewhere are fully developed. Titania's lines present a poetic image of confusion in the world of nature, occasioned by Oberon's attacks upon herself and her followers. The 'distemperature' in nature is such that 'The seasons alter'. Behind this lies a notion of the proper order of things, based on the rhythm of the seasons and the workings of nature. The fairy characters have a specially close relationship with nature. They are the wood-dwellers. They have a function as guardians of things natural. They are frequently associated with flowers – 'I know a bank where the wild thyme blows . . .', says Oberon (II.1.249); and the first fairy to enter is busy hanging pearls in cowslips' ears. The disruption in the natural order of things which we see in Titania's speech is caused by the quasi-human passions of the fairies. In this respect the speech may be seen as an image of the construction and movement of the whole play. Many other things relate to it. Just as the quarrel between these lovers causes confusion in the seasons, so later (II.1.231–3) Helena (in more comic terms) will represent her pursuit of the man she loves by a similar reversal:

> *Apollo flies, and Daphne holds the chase;*
> *The dove pursues the griffin; the mild hind*
> *Makes speed to catch the tiger . . .*

Titania's speech is without any comic tinge, though (like Lysander's lines mentioned earlier) it is rendered appropriate to a comedy by its generalized, somewhat distancing style. It presents seriously the danger of disaster when control is lost and the malevolent forces of nature gain the upper hand. The presence of such forces is frequently suggested. Quick bright things can come to confusion. The fairies sing (II.2.22–3):

> *Beetles black, approach not near,*
> *Worm nor snail, do no offence.*

Hermia dreams that a serpent is eating her heart away. Oberon and his fellows are contrasted (III.2.386–7) with the spirits who

> *wilfully themselves exile from light,*
> *And must for aye consort with black-browed night . . .*

and Oberon's final benediction is also an exorcism of 'the blots of nature's hand'.

Titania and Oberon part, still in enmity, and he prepares his plot to avenge his wrong. The character groups of the play begin to interact. For the first time we see two of the lovers – Helena and Demetrius – in the wood; and we have an immediate hint of some of the irrationality of what is going to happen there in Demetrius's pun (II.1.192) on an Elizabethan sense of 'wood', which could also mean 'mad', he is

> *wood within this wood*
> *Because I cannot meet my Hermia*

Shakespeare uses the flower that Puck fetches as the linking force between the plots; for Oberon decides that besides dropping some of the juice on Titania's eyes, he will have Puck drop some of it too upon Demetrius's, making him requite Helena's passion. In fact Puck anoints Lysander's eyes and he falls madly in love with Helena. Ironically he attributes this new affection to his reason (II.2.121–8), whereas we know that the change has been effected by Puck's juice.

> *The will of man is by his reason swayed,*
> *And reason says you are the worthier maid.*
> *Things growing are not ripe until their season;*
> *So I, being young, till now ripe not to reason.*
> *And touching now the point of human skill,*
> *Reason becomes the marshal to my will,*
> *And leads me to your eyes, where I o'erlook*
> *Love's stories written in love's richest book.*

We shall remember the antithesis between love and reason at a later point.

The comic confusions of the lovers are caused by the failure of their reason to keep pace with their emotions. They are in an adolescent whirl. Under the spell of an illusion, they – very understandably – mistake it for reality. Now (Act Three, Scene One) in the midst of their troubles come the mechanicals to rehearse their play. They are in somewhat similar case. They are attempting to cope with a world of illusion, the stage presentation of the classical legend of Pyramus and Thisbe. It is not a world in which they feel comfortable. They too are unable to distinguish between the imaginary and the real, and they fear that others will share their inability. Lion must tell the

audience that he is really Snug the joiner; Bottom must explain
that he is not really killed as Pyramus. Their confusions find
expression in a way similar to those of the lovers. Puck's juice,
applied to the lovers' eyes, distorts their point of view. In the
forthcoming scene in the forest where the confusion is at its
height, Demetrius and Lysander cannot see each other, and are
misled by Puck into thinking they hear each other's voice. The
mechanicals, too, have their senses confused; 'he goes but to
see a noise that he heard', says Quince of Pyramus; Bottom, as he
awakes, becomes similarly muddled. In the last Act Pyramus says:

> *I see a voice. Now will I to the chink*
> *To spy an I can hear my Thisbe's face . . .*

and Bottom invites his audience either to see an epilogue or
hear a dance. The notion of a dislocation between the senses,
and between the senses and the brain, is recurrent.

Throughout the play Shakespeare brilliantly reconciles opposites.

> *How shall we find the concord of this discord?*

asks Theseus (v.1.60); Shakespeare shows us. Classical Athens
is brought into contact with sixteenth-century Warwickshire.
The dignity of Theseus and Hippolyta coexists with the youthful silliness of the younger lovers. Verse in a style of the most
delicate fantasy is juxtaposed with comic prose of earthy robust-
ness. Hard-handed working men enact a classical story of tragic
love. The climax of this method comes when the ethereal
Titania, who had been lulled to sleep by the lullaby of her
attendant fairies, is aroused by Bottom's rustic song. He is now
literally asinine. But under the influence of Puck's magic juice
she is enthralled. Her ear and eye are both enamoured. Even
Bottom, fool that he is, and metamorphosed into an ass, can
see that her love for him is unreasonable; but he is not such a
fool as to reject it:

TITANIA
> *I pray thee, gentle mortal, sing again!*

Mine ear is much enamoured of thy note,
So is mine eye enthrallèd to thy shape,
And thy fair virtue's force perforce doth move me
On the first view to say, to swear, I love thee.

BOTTOM *Methinks, mistress, you should have little reason for that.*
And yet, to say the truth, reason and love keep little company
together nowadays — the more the pity that some honest neighbours
will not make them friends.

III.1.130–38

The comedy of Bottom and Titania is of the sort most admired by Sir Philip Sidney, in which there is both laughter and delight. In *An Apology for Poetry*, of about 1581–3, Sidney wrote:

Delight hath a joy in it, either permanent or present. Laughter hath only a scornful tickling . . . for as in Alexander's picture well set out we delight without laughter, and in twenty mad antics we laugh without delight; so in Hercules, painted with his great beard and furious countenance, in woman's attire, spinning at Omphale's commandment, it breedeth both delight and laughter. For the representing of so strange a power in love procureth delight: and the scornfulness of the action stirreth laughter.

Shakespeare might almost have been playing a deliberate variation upon the situation portrayed by Sidney.

The first edition of this play has no Act divisions, and it seems unlikely that Shakespeare, as he wrote, had an act-structure in mind. The scenes flow smoothly into each other till the end of that between Titania and Bottom (III.1). Here there is a natural break. The next scene begins with something of a recapitulatory episode; for a few moments the dialogue, between Oberon and Puck, looks back upon the preceding action. Then the plot involving the lovers is resumed. In the subsequent episode Hermia speaks significantly of the effect of night on the senses:

Dark night that from the eye his function takes
The ear more quick of apprehension makes.

> *Wherein it doth impair the seeing sense*
> *It pays the hearing double recompense.*
> *Thou art not by mine eye, Lysander, found;*
> *Mine ear — I thank it — brought me to thy sound.*

The stage is set for the full exploitation of the lovers' confusions, and Shakespeare develops the situation with fertile invention. The action has not quite reached the point of maximum complexity when Oberon gives Puck the instruction that shows us how the resolution is to be effected:

> *Then crush this herb into Lysander's eye —*
> *Whose liquor hath this virtuous property,*
> *To take from thence all error with his might,*
> *And make his eyeballs roll with wonted sight.*
> *When they next wake, all this derision*
> *Shall seem a dream and fruitless vision . . .*

The night is ending, and Puck and Oberon forecast the approach of day in a passage of poetic expansiveness (III.2.378–93) which superbly effects a transition of mood. Puck brings the lovers together, sends them to sleep, and squeezes the herb on Lysander's eyes. That the movement of the play is gradually changing direction is further subtly indicated by the fact that each of the lovers, falling asleep, speaks of the approach of day. When Titania and Bottom too fall asleep in each other's arms the action has reached its most complex moment. Oberon begins to feel pity for Titania, who has given up to him the changeling boy. He instructs Puck to remove Bottom's ass's head, and himself releases Titania from her spell. To the sound of music the Fairy King and Queen are reconciled, and the symbolic significance of their reunion is emphasized by the dance with which it is celebrated. Again we look forward to the events to come:

> *Now thou and I are new in amity,*
> *And will tomorrow midnight solemnly*
> *Dance in Duke Theseus' house triumphantly,*
> *And bless it to all fair prosperity.*

The reconciliation of Oberon and Titania makes possible the clarification of the lovers' problems. The night is ending. Day approaches, and with it there re-enter the play's symbols of sanity and maturity – Theseus and Hippolyta, who have been celebrating a rite of May in the early morning. Their entrance is marked by another poetic passage of more than immediate significance. They are going to enjoy hearing the baying of their pack of dogs

> *matched in mouth like bells,*
> *Each under each.*

It is the theme of concord, the notion of a harmony which permits the existence of diversity. It is a symbol of the possibility of a unity that is not sameness, an agreement that can include disagreement:

> *So musical a discord, such sweet thunder.*

And before us is an emblem of at least the temporary existence of such a concord, as the four lovers, last seen in violent rivalry, sleep quietly close by each other. Theseus, having them woken by his hunting horns, points the paradox:

> *I know you two are rival enemies.*
> *How comes this gentle concord in the world,*
> *That hatred is so far from jealousy*
> *To sleep by hate, and fear no enmity?*

As the two young men explain themselves to the Duke, it becomes clear that their problems are nearing a solution. Demetrius's love for Hermia is 'Melted as the snow'; now he loves Helena. So she is satisfied. And Egeus's renewed objections to the marriage of Lysander and Hermia are authoritatively overcome by Theseus. The bewildering confusions of the dream are dissolving into a satisfying order of reality. The lovers, left together, give expression to their sense of wonder in a passage (IV.I.186–98) remarkable for a poetic quality deriving from an awareness of the tension between illusion and reality, between the visions of dreamland and the facts of the morning light.

> *These things seem small and undistinguishable,*
> *Like far-off mountains turnèd into clouds . . .*

says Demetrius, formulating a curious characteristic of the play, which itself has the quality of something looked at from a distance. It is an effect at once of the jewelled delicacy of its style, its controlled neatness of structure, the sense in the fairy scenes of great distances rapidly traversed, and also perhaps of the many passages in which characters describe events of the past: passages such as Titania's description (II.1.123–37) of her friendship with the changeling boy's mother, and Oberon's about the time when Cupid shot his arrow at the imperial votaress (II.1.148–68).

The lovers' feeling of wonder includes a sense of relief that a bad dream is over, and their problems are solved. But Oberon and Puck have made possible another wakening into reality: Bottom's. It might have seemed less desirable than that which precedes it. Bottom's was a pleasant dream: 'a most rare vision' translating him from mundane reality into an ideal world of love and beauty. For him, as for Caliban in *The Tempest*, the clouds have opened and shown riches. Bottom might well have anticipated Caliban also in crying to dream again. Yet he does not regret his awakening, but rather endears himself to us by the typical dislocations in his savouring of it: 'The eye of man hath not heard, the ear of man hath not seen, man's hand is not able to taste, his tongue to conceive, nor his heart to report what my dream was!' His speech of awakening is as masterly a piece of prose as the lovers' episode is of verse; and his irruption into the company of his fellows, grieving over his absence, is a great moment for the actor.

By now all the complications of the plot are resolved. But the play is not over. From the start we have been kept aware that it is to culminate in marriage, celebration, and benediction.

We know too that the tragedy of Pyramus and Thisbe has yet to be enacted. The impetus that carries us forward into the final scenes is that of expectation, not of plot tension. Before the celebrations begin we are allowed a moment of reflection as Theseus and Hippolyta think over what 'these lovers' speak of. To Hippolyta it seems strange; to Theseus, 'More strange than true.' In another speech of poetic recapitulation he compares the imaginations of lovers with those of madmen and poets. All of them are apt to confuse the illusory with the real. This is a splendid expression of a point of view which it would be unwise to identify with Shakespeare's. There is something scoffing and dismissive in Theseus's attitude; he is here the plain, blunt man who prides himself on knowing what's what, on the exercise of 'cool reason'. Hippolyta supplies the necessary corrective:

> But all the story of the night told over,
> And all their minds transfigured so together,
> More witnesseth than fancy's images,
> And grows to something of great constancy;
> But howsoever, strange and admirable.

She can conceive what the lovers have been through; and her use of the word 'transfigured' helps to suggest that the woodland scenes represent for them a genuine shaping experience. Looked at coldly, the adventures of the night are simply a mechanical set of misunderstandings, which to Theseus seem like a complete delusion. But Hippolyta is struck by the fact that 'all their minds' were affected. She can see some hint of a power beyond that of fancy. Unlike Theseus, Hippolyta, or indeed the lovers, we of the audience have seen into the fairy world that has been influencing human actions, and can sympathize with Hippolyta. We are, too, made to feel that the events of the night have been a significant experience for the lovers, teaching them something about themselves; that they come out of the wood more mature than when they went into it.

It is difficult to rationalize this impression. The change in Demetrius's attitude to Helena has been brought about by purely external means. No profound psychological process has been portrayed. The lovers' wanderings in the wood have occupied only one night. But it has been an enchanted, timeless night. As the lovers go off to marriage, we are likely to feel that they have been through a necessary but profoundly disturb-. ing experience, and that now they are safely on the other side of it. The experience has grown 'to something of great constancy', enriching their lives just as Bottom's 'rare vision' enriches his. They bring back into the ordinary world something that they learned in the world of imagination. The illusory has its part in the total experience of reality.

The performance that Bottom and his fellows give before the wedding couples is of course marvellously funny. Shakespeare's verbal virtuosity here is employed in the art of parody, and his target is the interludes, which mixed human characters with personifications, and which flourished two or three decades before he was writing. Those decades had seen a phenomenal development in verse style, and the old modes were ripe for mockery. But these episodes have their place too in the more serious scheme of the play. We have seen already that the lovers needed the tolerance and understanding indulgence of other people to achieve their happiness. The play scene extends this idea outside the world of the lovers to other groups of society too. Theseus is clearly warned that the mechanicals' play is 'nothing, nothing in the world', but insists that he will hear it, since

> *never anything can be amiss*
> *When simpleness and duty tender it.*

The suggestion that for us the interest of the performance should lie partly in the relationship between the amateur actors and their audience is given in Theseus's lines beginning 'The kinder we, to give them thanks for nothing.' He is willing to give credit to his subjects for their good intentions even if the result is not very successful:

> *And what poor duty cannot do, noble respect*
> *Takes it in might, not merit.*

He is willing, in fact, to exert his imagination in the attempt to pierce to the reality behind illusory appearances, to find the 'concord of this discord' (v.1.60). He shows here something of the understanding that previously seemed to belong rather to Hippolyta. The shift in attitudes is interesting. Shakespeare seems to be hinting at the infinite adjustments necessary in the establishment of social and emotional harmony.

The performance of the interlude itself shows literal-minded men trying to cope with a world of illusion, and failing to do so. The discrepancy is so severe that the performance might well have seemed silly, were it not rescued by our knowledge of the good intentions of the performers, and our predisposition to make allowances for them. But the line between charitable acceptance and exasperated rejection is thin, and there are times when the stage-audience is in danger of crossing it:

HIPPOLYTA *This is the silliest stuff that ever I heard.*

THESEUS *The best in this kind are but shadows; and the worst are no worse, if imagination amend them.*

HIPPOLYTA *It must be your imagination, then, and not theirs.*

THESEUS *If we imagine no worse of them than they of themselves, they may pass for excellent men.*

The performance continues with other comments, not all complimentary, from the stage-audience. Fiasco is prevented only by the imaginative indulgence of the spectators, which never seems at all sentimental, since Shakespeare gives a cutting edge to many of their comments.

The play's last scene, then, is not a mere comic appendage. Rather does it serve as an emblem of both the possibility and the precariousness of happiness in human relationships; of the fact that this can be achieved only through a constant openness of the imagination, by the exercise of a charitable understanding, a willingness to accept people as they are rather than rejecting them for their inadequacies, even if this means feeding what one knows to be their illusions. We all pass for excellent men by what we imagine of ourselves. The scene becomes a dancing vision of an achieved unity, a musical discord. Like the baying of the hounds in Theseus's pack, each voice has full expression, moving freely and joyously in a passage of perfect counterpoint. The actors of the interlude need the imaginative participation of their stage-audience if they are to succeed. This is as true of the play itself as of the play within the play. It is all unreal; yet, if we too bring our imaginations to it, it may grow to something of great constancy, a universal harmony, a music of the spheres in which each sings its own song. On these images of concord – the marriage festivity, the dance, the music – the forces of nature shower their blessings:

> So shall all the couples three
> Ever true in loving be . . .

It remains only for Puck to suggest to the real audience that it too has a part to perform. If the spectators have disliked the play they need regard it as no more than an illusion, a dream action performed by shadows. But if they have enjoyed it they can confer a sort of reality upon the poet's and the actors' world, and make their contact with it:

> Give me your hands if we be friends,
> And Robin shall restore amends.

Further Reading

Background Material

E. K. Chambers has an article 'On the Occasion of *A Mid-summer Night's Dream*' (1916, reprinted in *Shakespearian Gleanings*, 1946). W. J. Lawrence states the case against the theory that this is a wedding-play in 'A Plummet for Bottom's Dream' (1922, reprinted in *Shakespeare's Workshop*, Oxford, 1928). The edition by Sir Arthur Quiller-Couch and John Dover Wilson (Cambridge, 1924 etc.) includes Quiller-Couch's introduction, Dover Wilson's discussion of the text, and Harold Child's summary of the stage history. Harold F. Brook's new Arden edition (1979) has a long introduction and a valuably detailed commentary. Sources are discussed in Kenneth Muir's *The Sources of Shakespeare's Plays* (1977); Geoffrey Bullough reprints and discusses sources and analogues in *Narrative and Dramatic Sources of Shakespeare*, Vol. 1 (1957). Background to the fairies is provided by M. W. Latham in *The Elizabethan Fairies* (New York, 1930), and K. M. Briggs in *The Anatomy of Puck* (1959). They are more critically discussed in Ernest Schanzer's 'The Moon and the Fairies in *A Midsummer Night's Dream*' (*University of Toronto Quarterly* XXIV, 3, April 1955). J. W. Robinson's 'Palpable Hot Ice: Dramatic Burlesque in *A Midsummer Night's Dream*' (*Studies in Philology* LXI, No. 2, Part 1, April 1964) is a helpful examination of the targets and methods of burlesque in the Pyramus and Thisbe episodes.

Criticism

Harley Granville-Barker's Preface to the Players' Shakespeare edition (1924) is reprinted in his *Prefaces to Shakespeare*, Vol. VI

(1974). Enid Welsford has a section on the play in *The Court Masque* (1927). G. Wilson Knight, in *The Shakespearian Tempest* (1932), approaches it mainly through an examination of its imagery. M. C. Bradbrook has some perceptive comments in *Shakespeare and Elizabethan Poetry* (1951). Georges A. Bonnard's 'Shakespeare's Purpose in *A Midsummer Night's Dream*' (*Shakespeare Jahrbuch*, XCII, 1956) is particularly good on the relationship between the mechanicals and the lovers. Paul A. Olson's '*A Midsummer Night's Dream* and the Meaning of Court Marriage' (*ELH*, XXIV, 1957) is an interpretation, conducted with much learning, based on the 'wedding-play' theory. John Russell Brown (*Shakespeare and his Comedies*, 1957), C. L. Barber (*Shakespeare's Festive Comedy*, Princeton, 1959), Bertrand Evans (*Shakespeare's Comedies*, 1960), Glynne Wickham (*Shakespeare's Dramatic Heritage*, 1969), and Alexander Leggatt (*Shakespeare's Comedy of Love*, 1974) all have variously interesting chapters on the play. W. M. Merchant, in '*A Midsummer Night's Dream*, a visual recreation' (*Early Shakespeare*, Stratford-upon-Avon Studies, 3, 1961), is much concerned with the history of its presentation on the stage. Peter Brook's famous Stratford-upon-Avon production (1970) is discussed in two articles in *Shakespeare Survey 24* (1971), and an acting edition of it has been edited by Glenn Loney (Chicago, 1974). There are brief but suggestive sections on the play in Frank Kermode's 'The Mature Comedies' (*Early Shakespeare*, Stratford-upon-Avon Studies, 3, 1961), G. K. Hunter's *Shakespeare: The Late Comedies* (1962), and Nevill Coghill's *Shakespeare's Professional Skills* (Cambridge, 1964). David P. Young has written a valuable full-length study called *Something of Great Constancy: The Art of 'A Midsummer Night's Dream'* (1966), and Stephen Fender's *Shakespeare: 'A Midsummer Night's Dream'* (Arnold's Studies in English Literature, No. 35, 1968) is a thoughtful short book about the play.

An Account of the Text

A Midsummer Night's Dream was first published by Thomas Fisher in 1600 in an edition believed to have been printed from a manuscript written by Shakespeare himself. This edition is known as the first Quarto. It was reprinted in 1619 in an edition falsely dated 1600; this is the second Quarto, a reprint of the first, with only minor differences. The play was also included in the collected edition of Shakespeare's plays published in 1623, known as the first Folio. Here it appears to have been printed from a copy of the second Quarto in which some alterations had been made from a theatrical copy. The alterations correct some errors in the original text, and add some information about its staging.

The edition closest to Shakespeare's manuscript, then, is the first Quarto, on which the present edition is based. However, like most editions of Elizabethan plays, the first Quarto was not well printed. A modern editor is obliged to clear up inconsistencies and correct certain errors made in the printing-house. Some are extremely obvious. For example, at II.2.49 the first Quarto has 'Nay god Lysander'. This is corrected in the second Quarto and the Folio to 'Nay good Lysander'. Occasionally the Folio happily provides a solution for a serious misprint in the first Quarto. For example, at v.1.188 the Quarto reads, nonsensically, 'Thy stones with lime and hair knit now againe'. This is corrected in the Folio to 'knit vp in thee'. Other difficulties are less easily solved. There are times when the Quartos and the Folio make good but different sense, and the editor has to decide whether he thinks the Folio's reading may reasonably be considered to be a correction of, or Shakespeare's own improvement on, that of the Quartos. An example is at v.1.122 where the Quartos have 'he hath plaid on this Prologue' and the Folio 'hee hath plaid on his Prologue'. There is very little to choose between these two readings. There are also some difficulties which cannot be certainly solved. Examples are mentioned in the Commentary to III.1.75–7 and v.1.203.

The alterations made in the Folio which affect the staging of the play are slight but interesting. Obviously they reflect stage practice in Shakespeare's lifetime, or shortly after. One can see a real advantage to the actors in having v.1.44–60 broken up between Lysander and Theseus as in the Folio, instead of being spoken by Theseus alone, as indicated in the Quartos. We cannot tell whether such alterations were made by Shakespeare, or with his approval. The division into Acts is first made in the Folio. It is worth remembering that in writing the play Shakespeare does not seem to have had these Act divisions in mind.

A Midsummer Night's Dream is sometimes thought to have undergone revision after its first performance. This theory is connected with the belief that it was written for a special occasion. There is no certain evidence to support it. However, Professor John Dover Wilson, in the New Cambridge edition, brilliantly demonstrated that Shakespeare made additions to the play at the beginning of Act Five. Dover Wilson believed that the interval between the original composition and the rewriting was 'a matter of years rather than of hours or days', but this judgement is based only on considerations of style and is not universally accepted. The additions may well have been made during the process of composition. The demonstration depends on the fact that in the first Quarto some of the verse is printed irregularly. The following well-known passage (v.1.4–22) is printed here as it appears in the Quarto except that the disarranged verse is printed in roman type, and strokes indicate the true ends of the verse lines:

> *Lovers, and mad men haue such seething braines,*
> Such shaping phantasies, that apprehend | more,

Then coole reason euer comprehends. | The lunatick,
The louer, and the Poet | are of imagination all compact. |
One sees more diuels, then vast hell can holde:
That is the mad man. The louer, all as frantick,
Sees Helens beauty in a brow of Ægypt.
The Poets eye, in a fine frenzy, rolling, | doth glance
From heauen to earth, from earth to heauen. | And as
Imagination bodies forth | the formes of things
Vnknowne: the Poets penne | turnes them to shapes,
And giues to ayery nothing, | a locall habitation,
And a name. | *Such trickes hath strong imagination,*
That if it would but apprehend some ioy,
It comprehends some bringer of that ioy.
Or in the night, imagining some feare,
How easie is a bush suppos'd a Beare?

The regularly divided lines form a consecutive passage, complete in itself. It appears that the lines in italics were written, perhaps in the margin of the manuscript, in such a way that the compositor was not clear how they should have been divided. Altogether there are twenty-nine lines, all at the beginning of Act Five, which seem to have been added.

The following notes record the points in the text of the play at which the present edition departs significantly from the first Quarto. Simple misprints, mislineations, and so on are not recorded. Quotations from the Quartos and the Folio are printed as they appear in those editions, that is, in old spelling and so on, though minor typographical differences from one edition to another are not noted. The more interesting textual points are discussed in the notes.

The first Quarto (1600) is referred to as Q1, the second Quarto (1619) as Q2, both Quartos as Q, and the first Folio (1623) as F. In quotations from the Quartos and the Folio the 'long s' (∫) has been replaced by 's'.

COLLATIONS

I

The following is a list of readings in the present text of *A Midsummer Night's Dream* which differ from Q1 and were first made in Q2, followed by F. Most of them are corrections of obvious misprints.(Q1's reading is printed on the right of the square bracket.)

I.I.	4	wanes] waues	
II.2.	36	Be it] bet it	
	49	good] god	
	53	is] it	
III.I.	50	BOTTOM] *Cet.*	
III.2.	299	gentlemen] gentleman	
	426	shalt] shat	
IV.I.	127	is] (not in Q1)	
	205	to expound] expound	
V.I.	303	and prove] and yet prooue	

2

The following readings in the present text of *A Midsummer Night's Dream* depart from those of both Quartos and are first found in the Folio. (The reading of the Quartos is given on the right of the square bracket.)

II.I.	158	the] (not in Q)	
	201	nor] not	
III.I.	76	Odours – odours! (Odours, odours, F)] Odours, odorous.	
	81	PUCK] *Quin.*	
III.2.	19	mimic (Mimmick F)] Minnick Q1; Minnock Q2	

         220   passionate] (not in Q)
IV.I. 207   a patched] patcht a
IV.2.   3   STARVELING] *Flut.*
 V.I.   34   our] Or
        122   his] this
        154   Snout] *Flute*
        188   up in thee] now againe
        342   BOTTOM] *Lyon.*

3

The following readings in the present text of *A Midsummer
Night's Dream* differ from those of both Quartos and the Folio.
Most of these alterations were first made by eighteenth-century
editors. Those that are of special interest are discussed in the
textual notes. (The reading on the right of the square bracket is
common to Q and F unless otherwise indicated.)

The Characters in the Play] (this list is not in Q and F)
  I.I.   10   New-bent] Now bent
         24, 26   ('Stand forth, Demetrius' and 'Stand forth, Ly-
                   sander' are printed as stage directions in Q and F.)
         136   low] loue
         187   Yours would] Your words
         191   I'd] (ile Q1; Ile Q2, F)
         216   sweet] sweld
         219   stranger companies] strange companions
  I.2. 24–5   To the rest. – Yet] To the rest yet
         26–7   split: | The] split the
  II.I.   79   Aegles] Eagles
         101   cheer] heere
         109   thin] chinne
         190   slay . . . slayeth] stay . . . stayeth
  II.2.   9   FIRST FAIRY] (not in Q, F)
         13, 24   CHORUS] (not marked in Q,F)

III.1.   63   and let] or let

         97   fair, fair Thisbe] faire, *Thysby*

     118   ousel] Woosell

  154–8   PEASEBLOSSOM ... go?] *Fairies.* Readie: and I, and I, and I. Where shall we goe?

 170–73   PEASEBLOSSOM ... MUSTARDSEED Hail!] 1. *Fai.* Haile mortall, haile. | 2. *Fai.* Hale. | 3. *Fai.* Haile. your more] you more

III.2.   80   so] (not in Q. F)

     213   first, like] first life

     250   prayers] praise

  257–8   No, no. He'll | Seem to break loose] No, no: heele | Seeme to breake loose; Q1; No, no, Sir, seeme to breake loose; F. (The present edition follows C. J. Sisson's interpretation of this passage.)

     258   he] you

     406   Speak. In some bush?] Speake in some bush

     451   To] (not in Q, F)

IV.1.   40   all ways] alwaies

      72   o'er] or

      81   sleep of all these five] sleepe: of all these, fine

     116   Seemed] Seeme

     132   rite] right

     171   saw] see

V.1.   191   My love! Thou art my love] My loue thou art, my loue

     203   mural down] Moon vsed Q; morall downe F

     214   beasts in: a] beasts, in a

  304–5   How chance Moonshine is gone before Thisbe comes back and finds her lover?] How chance Moone-shine is gone before? *Thisby* comes backe, and findes her louer.

     362   behowls] beholds

 409–10   (The second of these lines is printed before the first in Q and F.)

4

Stage Directions

The stage directions of the present edition are based on those of the first Quarto, though with reference to those of the second Quarto and the Folio. Certain clarifications and regularizations have been made; for example, at the beginning of Act Three, Scene One, the first Quarto has '*Enter the Clownes*'. The names of the mechanicals (or 'clowns') have been substituted. Also some directions for stage business required by the dialogue have been added. The more interesting stage directions of the Quartos and Folio that have been altered are given below in their original form. Also listed are the more important editorial additions.

I.I.　　o　*Enter Theseus, Hippolyta, Philostrate, and Attendants*] *Enter* Theseus, Hippolita, *with others.* Q and F

　　　15　*Exit Philostrate*] (not in Q and F)

　　　19　*Enter Egeus and his daughter Hermia, and Lysander, and Demetrius*] *Enter* Egeus *and his daughter* Hermia, *and* Lysander *and* Helena, *and* Demetrius. Q1

III.I.　　o　*Enter the clowns: Bottom, Quince, Snout, Starveling, Flute, and Snug*] *Enter the Clownes.* Q and F

III.2. 404, 412 (Lysander's exit and re-entry are not in Q and F.)

IV.I.　　83　(*to Bottom, removing the ass's head*)] (not in Q and F)

　　137　*Horns sound; the lovers wake; shout within; the lovers start up*] *Shoute within: they all start vp. Winde hornes.* Q; *Hornes and they wake.* | *Shout within, they all start vp.* F

V.I.　　o　*Enter Theseus, Hippolyta, Philostrate, Lords, and Attendants*] *Enter* Theseus, Hippolita, *and* Philostrate. Q; *Enter Theseus, Hippolita, Egeus and his Lords.* F

　　107　*Flourish of trumpets*] *Flor. Trum.* F (not in Q)

　　125　*Enter Bottom as Pyramus, Flute as Thisbe, Snout as Wall, Starveling as Moonshine, and Snug as Lion; a trumpeter before them*] *Enter* Pyramus, *and* Thysby, *and*

Wall, *and* Moone-shine, *and* Lyon. Q1; *Enter Pyramus and Thisby, Wall, Moone-shine, and Lyon.* Q2; *Tawyer with a Trumpet before them. Enter Pyramus and Thisby, Wall, Moone-shine, and Lyon.* F

150 *Exeunt Quince, Bottom, Flute, Snug, and Starveling*] *Exit* Lyon, Thysby, *and* Mooneshine. Q and F, after line 152; F adds '*Exit all but Wall.*' after line 150.

174 *Wall holds up his fingers*] (not in Q and F)

256 *Lion roars. Flute as Thisbe runs off*] *The Lion roares, Thisby runs off.* F (not in Q)

260 *Lion tears Thisbe's mantle. Exit*] (not in Q and F)

352 *A dance. Exeunt Bottom and his fellows*] (not in Q and F)

390 *Song and dance*] (not in Q and F)

A MIDSUMMER NIGHT'S DREAM
The Characters in the Play

THESEUS, Duke of Athens
HIPPOLYTA, Queen of the Amazons, betrothed to Theseus
EGEUS, Hermia's father
HERMIA, Egeus's daughter, in love with Lysander
LYSANDER, loved by Hermia
DEMETRIUS, suitor of Hermia
HELENA, in love with Demetrius
PHILOSTRATE, Theseus's Master of the Revels

OBERON, King of the Fairies
TITANIA, Queen of the Fairies
PUCK, or Robin Goodfellow
PEASEBLOSSOM ⎫
COBWEB ⎪
         ⎬ Fairies
MOTH ⎪
MUSTARDSEED ⎭

The Act and scene divisions are those of Peter Alexander's edition of the *Complete Works*, London, 1951. All references to other plays by Shakespeare are to this edition.

    Throughout the notes, the first Quarto (1600) is referred to as Q1, the second Quarto (1619) as Q2, both Quartos as Q, and the first Folio (1623) as F. For further details, see the Account of the Text. In quotations from the Quartos and the Folio the 'long s' (ʃ) has been replaced by 's'.

The title 'Midsummer Night' is 23 June.

In Act Four, Theseus suggests that the lovers 'rose up early to observe | The rite/of May' (IV.I.131–2). 'Maying' was not confined to 1 May; it could happen at various times. The title suggests the traditional magic associations of midsummer, and also perhaps the fact that then were practised folk-customs by which young people were supposed to be able to discover whom they were going to marry. The play's action is spread over only two days, though Shakespeare suggests at the start that it will last four days.

PETER QUINCE, a carpenter; Prologue in the interlude
NICK BOTTOM, a weaver; Pyramus in the interlude
FRANCIS FLUTE, a bellows-mender; Thisbe in the interlude
TOM SNOUT, a tinker; Wall in the interlude
SNUG, a joiner; Lion in the interlude
ROBIN STARVELING, a tailor; Moonshine in the interlude

Other fairies attending on Oberon and Titania
Lords and Attendants to Theseus and Hippolyta

Enter Theseus, Hippolyta, Philostrate,
and Attendants   I.I

THESEUS

Now, fair Hippolyta, our nuptial hour
Draws on apace. Four happy days bring in
Another moon – but O, methinks how slow
This old moon wanes! She lingers my desires,
Like to a stepdame or a dowager
Long withering out a young man's revenue.

HIPPOLYTA

Four days will quickly steep themselves in night;
Four nights will quickly dream away the time:
And then the moon – like to a silver bow
New-bent in heaven – shall behold the night   10
Of our solemnities.

THESEUS   Go, Philostrate,
Stir up the Athenian youth to merriments.
Awake the pert and nimble spirit of mirth.

1.1 The Elizabethan stage used little or
no scenery. The dramatist could specify
the location of a scene if he wished, but
could also leave it unmentioned. Many
of Shakespeare's scenes depend for their
effect partly on our consciousness that
they are being enacted on a stage, rather
than on our succumbing totally to the
illusion that they happen in the place
mentioned. With this reservation, the

first scene takes place somewhere in
Athens.
4 *lingers* delays
6 *withering out* causing to dwindle. The
   idea is that the young man has inherited his father's estate, but has to
   go on paying some of the income to
   the widow.
7 *steep themselves* be absorbed
13 *pert* lively, brisk

Turn melancholy forth to funerals:
The pale companion is not for our pomp.

Exit Philostrate

Hippolyta, I wooed thee with my sword,
And won thy love doing thee injuries;
But I will wed thee in another key:
With pomp, with triumph, and with revelling.

*Enter Egeus and his daughter Hermia, and Lysander,
and Demetrius*

EGEUS

20   Happy be Theseus, our renownèd Duke.

THESEUS

Thanks, good Egeus. What's the news with thee?

EGEUS

Full of vexation come I, with complaint
Against my child, my daughter Hermia.
Stand forth, Demetrius! My noble lord,
This man hath my consent to marry her.
Stand forth, Lysander! – And, my gracious Duke,
This man hath bewitched the bosom of my child.
Thou, thou, Lysander, thou hast given her rhymes,
And interchanged love-tokens with my child.

30   Thou hast by moonlight at her window sung
With feigning voice verses of feigning love,
And stolen the impression of her fantasy.
With bracelets of thy hair, rings, gauds, conceits,
Knacks, trifles, nosegays, sweetmeats – messengers

---

15 *companion* fellow (used contemptuously)
pomp procession, pageant, ceremony
16–17 *Hippolyta, I wooed thee with my
sword, | And won thy love doing
thee injuries.* Theseus captured Hippolyta in conquering the Amazons.
19 *triumph* public festivity and show of
rejoicing
(stage direction) *Egeus* (pronounced

Egee-us: three syllables)
Hermia. We learn from III.2.257 and
288 that Hermia is short and dark.
24,26 *Stand forth, Demetrius!* and *Stand
forth, Lysander!* are printed as stage
directions in the early editions. The
fact that they complete the verse lines
shows that they should be spoken.
32 *stolen the impression of her fantasy* craft-
ily impressed yourself on her fancy.

Of strong prevailment in unhardened youth –
With cunning hast thou filched my daughter's heart,
Turned her obedience which is due to me
To stubborn harshness. And, my gracious Duke,
Be it so she will not here before your grace
Consent to marry with Demetrius,
I beg the ancient privilege of Athens: 40
As she is mine, I may dispose of her;
Which shall be either to this gentleman
Or to her death, according to our law
Immediately provided in that case.

THESEUS

What say you, Hermia? Be advised, fair maid:
To you your father should be as a god;
One that composed your beauties – yea, and one
To whom you are but as a form in wax
By him imprinted, and within his power   50
To leave the figure or disfigure it.
Demetrius is a worthy gentleman.

Obviously the metre demands some elision. The actor is likely to pronounce 'stolen' as one syllable ('stol'n') and 'the impression' as three ('th'impression'). There are many other examples in the play of unaccented or lightly accented syllables in verse lines. Editors frequently mark such syllables with an apostrophe. But Shakespeare's verse does not conform to a mathematically exact system of versification, and we cannot always be sure whether for instance an unaccented syllable at the end of a line should be sounded or not (III.2.345: 'This is thy negligence. Still thou mistakest'). Also the marking of such syllables may suggest an abruptness of speaking which is neither necessary nor desirable. For instance, II.1.191 reads 'Thou toldest me they were stolen unto this wood'. Obviously the second syllable in 'toldest' and 'stolen' will be very lightly stressed. Yet an actor may find it easier to sound the syllables while preserving the rhythm rather than try to pronounce something printed as 'told'st' and 'stol'n'. For these reasons, unaccented syllables that may have been elided for metrical reasons are generally printed in full in the present edition.

33 *gauds* playthings, toys
   conceits fancy things, trinkets
34 *Knacks* knick-knacks
35 *prevailment* power
39 *Be it so* if
45 *Immediately* expressly

HERMIA
So is Lysander.

THESEUS   In himself he is;
But in this kind, wanting your father's voice,
The other must be held the worthier.

HERMIA
I would my father looked but with my eyes.

THESEUS
Rather your eyes must with his judgement look.

HERMIA
I do entreat your grace to pardon me.
I know not by what power I am made bold,
60 Nor how it may concern my modesty
In such a presence here to plead my thoughts;
But I beseech your grace that I may know
The worst that may befall me in this case
If I refuse to wed Demetrius.

THESEUS
Either to die the death, or to abjure
For ever the society of men.
Therefore, fair Hermia, question your desires,
Know of your youth, examine well your blood,
Whether, if you yield not to your father's choice,
70 You can endure the livery of a nun,
For aye to be in shady cloister mewed,
To live a barren sister all your life,
Chanting faint hymns to the cold fruitless moon.
Thrice blessèd they that master so their blood

54 *in this kind* in this respect
 voice approval, favour
56–7 *my eyes ... his judgement*. The play
 is to be much concerned with troubles caused by a dislocation between
 the evidence of the senses and the
 reasoning power. See Introduction,
 pages 224–9.

60 *concern* befit
65 *die the death* be put to death by legal
 process
68,74 *blood* passions, feelings
70 *livery* habit, costume
71 *For aye* for ever
 mewed confined
73 *moon* (as Diana, goddess of chastity)

To undergo such maiden pilgrimage;
But earthlier happy is the rose distilled
Than that which, withering on the virgin thorn,
Grows, lives, and dies in single blessedness.

HERMIA

So will I grow, so live, so die, my lord,
Ere I will yield my virgin patent up   80
Unto his lordship whose unwishèd yoke
My soul consents not to give sovereignty.

THESEUS

Take time to pause, and by the next new moon –
The sealing day betwixt my love and me
For everlasting bond of fellowship –
Upon that day either prepare to die
For disobedience to your father's will,
Or else to wed Demetrius, as he would,
Or on Diana's altar to protest
For aye austerity and single life.   90

DEMETRIUS

Relent, sweet Hermia; and, Lysander, yield
Thy crazèd title to my certain right.

LYSANDER

You have her father's love, Demetrius –
Let me have Hermia's. Do you marry him.

EGEUS

Scornful Lysander – true, he hath my love;
And what is mine my love shall render him;
And she is mine, and all my right of her
I do estate unto Demetrius.

LYSANDER

I am, my lord, as well derived as he,

---

76 *earthlier happy* happier on earth
rose distilled. Roses were distilled to
make perfumes.
80 *patent* privilege
81 *his lordship* (that is, the lordship of

him; the metrical stress is on 'his')
92 *crazèd title* flawed, unsound claim
98 *estate unto* settle, bestow upon
99–110 *I am, my lord* . . . Shaw, in the
review quoted from in the Introduc-

100   As well possessed. My love is more than his,
      My fortunes every way as fairly ranked —
      If not with vantage — as Demetrius'.
      And — which is more than all these boasts can be —
      I am beloved of beauteous Hermia.
      Why should not I then prosecute my right?
      Demetrius — I'll avouch it to his head —
      Made love to Nedar's daughter, Helena,
      And won her soul; and she, sweet lady, dotes,
      Devoutly dotes, dotes in idolatry
110   Upon this spotted and inconstant man.

   THESEUS
      I must confess that I have heard so much,
      And with Demetrius thought to have spoke thereof;
      But, being overfull of self affairs,
      My mind did lose it. But Demetrius, come;
      And come, Egeus. You shall go with me.
      I have some private schooling for you both.
      For you, fair Hermia, look you arm yourself
      To fit your fancies to your father's will;
      Or else the law of Athens yields you up —
120   Which by no means we may extenuate —
      To death or to a vow of single life.
      Come, my Hippolyta. What cheer, my love?
      Demetrius and Egeus, go along;
      I must employ you in some business

tion (page 209), writes: 'it should be
clear to any stage manager that Lysander's speech, beginning "I am,
my lord, as well derived as he",
should be spoken privately and not
publicly to Theseus.'
99 *derived* descended
100 *well possessed* rich
101 *My fortunes every way as fairly ranked*
   my fortunes [are] of as good a rank.
   (Abbreviation was not always clearly

indicated by Elizabethan printers,
so it may be that we should read
My fortune's.)
102 *with vantage* better
106 *to his head* to his face, in his teeth
110 *spotted* stained, polluted
117 *arm* prepare
120 *extenuate* mitigate, relax
123 *go along* come along with me
124 *business* (pronounced with three
   syllables)

Against our nuptial, and confer with you
Of something nearly that concerns yourselves.

EGEUS

With duty and desire we follow you.

Exeunt all but Lysander and Hermia

LYSANDER

How now, my love? Why is your cheek so pale?
How chance the roses there do fade so fast?

HERMIA

Belike for want of rain, which I could well   130
Beteem them from the tempest of my eyes.

LYSANDER

Ay me! For aught that I could ever read,
Could ever hear by tale or history,
The course of true love never did run smooth;
But either it was different in blood –

HERMIA

O cross! – too high to be enthralled to low.

LYSANDER

Or else misgraffèd in respect of years –

HERMIA

O spite! – too old to be engaged to young.

LYSANDER

Or else it stood upon the choice of friends –

HERMIA

O hell! – to choose love by another's eyes.   140

LYSANDER

Or if there were a sympathy in choice,
War, death, or sickness did lay siege to it,

125 *Against* in preparation for
126 *nearly that concerns* that closely
   concerns
130 *Belike* perhaps
131 *Beteem* allow
134–40 *The course of true love ...* Shaw,
   in the review quoted from in the
   Introduction (page 209), comments:

'Shakespeare makes the two star-
crossed lovers speak in alternate lines
with an effect which sets the whole
scene throbbing with their absorp-
tion in one another.'
135 *blood* birth, rank
137 *misgraffèd* badly matched

Making it momentany as a sound,
Swift as a shadow, short as any dream,
Brief as the lightning in the collied night,
That in a spleen unfolds both heaven and earth,
And – ere a man hath power to say 'Behold! –
The jaws of darkness do devour it up.
So quick bright things come to confusion.

HERMIA

150   If then true lovers have been ever crossed
It stands as an edict in destiny.
Then let us teach our trial patience,
Because it is a customary cross,
As due to love as thoughts, and dreams, and sighs,
Wishes, and tears – poor fancy's followers.

LYSANDER

A good persuasion. Therefore hear me, Hermia:
I have a widow aunt, a dowager,
Of great revenue; and she hath no child.
From Athens is her house remote seven leagues;
160   And she respects me as her only son.
There, gentle Hermia, may I marry thee;
And to that place the sharp Athenian law
Cannot pursue us. If thou lovest me, then
Steal forth thy father's house tomorrow night,
And in the wood, a league without the town –
Where I did meet thee once with Helena

---

143 *momentany* (an obsolete form of 'momentary')

145 *collied* blackened, darkened

146 *spleen* impulse; fit of anger or passion

149 *quick.* This may be taken either as an adjective (alive, vital) or an adverb (quickly).

155 *fancy* love

156 *persuasion* principle, doctrine

158 *revenue* (pronounced here with the accent on the second syllable)

159–60 *From Athens is her house remote seven leagues; | And she respects me as her only son.* Dr Johnson and some later editors reverse the order of these lines. This may be an improvement in fluency, but it brings together two clauses beginning with 'and', which seems clumsy. There is no need for the alteration.

165 *without* outside

To do observance to a morn of May —
There will I stay for thee.

HERMIA   My good Lysander,
I swear to thee by Cupid's strongest bow,
By his best arrow with the golden head,   170
By the simplicity of Venus' doves,
By that which knitteth souls and prospers loves,
And by that fire which burned the Carthage queen
When the false Trojan under sail was seen,
By all the vows that ever men have broke —
In number more than ever women spoke, —
In that same place thou hast appointed me
Tomorrow truly will I meet with thee.

LYSANDER
Keep promise, love. Look — here comes Helena.
     Enter Helena

167 *To do observance to a morn of May* to
    celebrate May-day. The celebrations,
    common in Elizabethan times, if not
    in the classical ones in which the
    action is ostensibly set, generally
    took place in the woods outside a
    town.
170 *his best arrow with the golden head.*
    Cupid was said to carry arrows of
    lead to repel love, and arrows of
    gold to cause it. The legend is given
    in Ovid's *Metamorphoses*, well known
    to Shakespeare, and anyhow was
    common knowledge.
171 *By the simplicity of Venus' doves ...*
    Hermia moves from blank verse into
    rhyming couplets for her vow. The
    remainder of the scene is in couplets.
    simplicity innocence, guilelessness
    Venus' doves. Doves were sacred to
    Venus, and drew her car. The last
    stanza of Shakespeare's *Venus and
    Adonis*, written in 1593, within a year
    or two of *A Midsummer Night's*

Dream, is:

*Thus weary of the world, away she hies,
And yokes her silver doves, by whose
        swift aid
Their mistress, mounted, through the
        empty skies
In her light chariot quickly is conveyed;
    Holding their course to Paphos, where
    their queen
    Means to immure herself and not be
    seen.*

173–4 *fire which burned the Carthage queen
    | When the false Trojan under sail
    was seen.* Dido, Queen of Carthage,
    burned herself on a funeral pyre
    when her lover, the Trojan Aeneas,
    sailed away. The story is told by
    Virgil in the *Aeneid*, and is the sub-
    ject of a play by Marlowe and Nashe
    dating probably from a few years
    before *A Midsummer Night's Dream.*
179 *Helena.* We learn from III.2.187 and
    291–3 that Helena is tall and fair.

HERMIA

180   God speed, fair Helena! Whither away?

HELENA

Call you me fair? That 'fair' again unsay.
Demetrius loves your fair. O happy fair!
Your eyes are lodestars, and your tongue's sweet air
More tuneable than lark to shepherd's ear
When wheat is green, when hawthorn buds appear.
Sickness is catching. O, were favour so,
Yours would I catch, fair Hermia, ere I go.
My ear should catch your voice, my eye your eye,
My tongue should catch your tongue's sweet melody.
190   Were the world mine, Demetrius being bated,
The rest I'd give to be to you translated.
O, teach me how you look, and with what art
You sway the motion of Demetrius' heart.

HERMIA

I frown upon him, yet he loves me still.

HELENA

O that your frowns would teach my smiles such skill!

HERMIA

I give him curses, yet he gives me love.

HELENA

O that my prayers could such affection move!

HERMIA

The more I hate, the more he follows me.

HELENA

The more I love, the more he hateth me.

HERMIA

200   His folly, Helena, is no fault of mine.

182 *fair* beauty, kind of beauty. The   183 *lodestars* leading or guiding stars
Folio reads 'you fair', which makes   184 *tuneable* tuneful, musical
equally good sense; but the Quarto   186 *favour* good looks
reading is more likely to be   190 *bated* excepted
Shakespeare's.   191 *translated* transformed

HELENA

None but your beauty. Would that fault were mine!

HERMIA

Take comfort. He no more shall see my face.
Lysander and myself will fly this place.
Before the time I did Lysander see
Seemed Athens as a paradise to me.
O then, what graces in my love do dwell
That he hath turned a heaven unto a hell?

LYSANDER

Helen, to you our minds we will unfold.
Tomorrow night, when Phoebe doth behold
Her silver visage in the watery glass,   210
Decking with liquid pearl the bladed grass –
A time that lovers' flights doth still conceal –
Through Athens gates have we devised to steal.

HERMIA

And in the wood, where often you and I
Upon faint primrose beds were wont to lie,
Emptying our bosoms of their counsel sweet,
There my Lysander and myself shall meet,
And thence from Athens turn away our eyes
To seek new friends and stranger companies.
Farewell, sweet playfellow. Pray thou for us;   220
And good luck grant thee thy Demetrius.
Keep word, Lysander. We must starve our sight

207 *That he hath turned a heaven unto a
hell?* This notion is varied at
II.1.243–4, when Helena says of
Demetrius:

*I'll follow thee, and make a heaven of
hell,*
To die upon the hand I love so well.

209 *Phoebe* (the moon)
212 *still* always
213 *Athens.* The noun is used as an adjec-

tive, as in 'the Carthage queen' (line
173).

214–21 *where often you and I* . . . The reference to the girlhood friendship of
Hermia and Helena looks forward to
the scene of their quarrel, to which it
is an ironic background.

219 *stranger companies* the company of
strangers. The early editions read
'strange companions'. A rhyme to
'eyes' is required.

From lovers' food till morrow deep midnight.

LYSANDER

I will, my Hermia.   *Exit Hermia*

Helena, adieu!

As you on him, Demetrius dote on you.   *Exit Lysander*

HELENA

How happy some o'er other some can be!

Through Athens I am thought as fair as she.

But what of that? Demetrius thinks not so;

He will not know what all but he do know.

230   And as he errs, doting on Hermia's eyes,

So I, admiring of his qualities.

Things base and vile, holding no quantity,

Love can transpose to form and dignity.

Love looks not with the eyes, but with the mind,

And therefore is winged Cupid painted blind.

Nor hath love's mind of any judgement taste;

Wings and no eyes figure unheedy haste.

And therefore is love said to be a child

Because in choice he is so oft beguiled.

240   As waggish boys in game themselves forswear,

So the boy love is perjured everywhere;

For ere Demetrius looked on Hermia's eyne

He hailed down oaths that he was only mine,

And when this hail some heat from Hermia felt,

So he dissolved, and showers of oaths did melt.

I will go tell him of fair Hermia's flight.

---

223 *lovers' food* (the sight of each other)

226 *other some* some others

232–3 *Things base and vile, holding no quantity, | Love can transpose to form and dignity.* This looks forward especially to Titania's infatuation with Bottom.

232 *quantity* proportion

234 *Love looks not with the eyes, but with*

the mind. That is, love is prompted not by the objective evidence of the senses, but by the fancies of the mind.

237 *figure* symbolize, represent

240 *waggish* playful

242 *eyne* eyes (an old form, common in Shakespeare, especially in rhymed passages)

Then to the wood will he tomorrow night
Pursue her; and for this intelligence
If I have thanks it is a dear expense.
But herein mean I to enrich my pain,   250
To have his sight thither, and back again.   *Exit*

Enter Quince the carpenter, and Snug the joiner, and   I.2
Bottom the weaver, and Flute the bellows-mender, and
Snout the tinker, and Starveling the tailor

QUINCE Is all our company here?

BOTTOM You were best to call them generally, man by
man, according to the scrip.

QUINCE Here is the scroll of every man's name which is
thought fit through all Athens to play in our interlude
before the Duke and the Duchess on his wedding day at
night.

BOTTOM First, good Peter Quince, say what the play treats
on; then read the names of the actors; and so grow to a
point.   10

QUINCE Marry, our play is *The most lamentable comedy
and most cruel death of Pyramus and Thisbe.*

248 *intelligence* news, information

249 *a dear expense* (perhaps 'an expense
of trouble worth making', or possibly 'it will cost him dear', that is,
'merely to thank me will be painful
to him')

I.2 As is common in Shakespeare and in
Elizabethan plays generally, the characters of low social standing speak in
prose. No particular location for this
scene is suggested. It takes place somewhere in Athens.
　　(stage direction). *Bottom.* As a
　　weaver's term, a bottom was the
　　object on which thread was wound.
　　'Bottom' as 'posterior' is not re-

corded till late in the eighteenth century, but the name 'Mistress Frigbot-
tom' in Thomas Dekker's *The Shoe-
maker's Holiday* (1600) shows that this
sense existed in Shakespeare's time.
Starveling. Tailors were proverbially
thin.

2 *generally* (Bottom's mistaken way of
saying 'severally', that is, individu-
ally)

5 *interlude* play

11–12 *The most lamentable comedy . . .* The
title of the mechanicals' play parodies
ones such as *A lamentable tragedy
mixed full of pleasant mirth, containing
the life of Cambyses, King of Persia,*
published about 1570. See also

BOTTOM A very good piece of work, I assure you, and a merry. Now, good Peter Quince, call forth your actors by the scroll. Masters, spread yourselves.

QUINCE Answer as I call you. Nick Bottom, the weaver?

BOTTOM Ready! – Name what part I am for, and proceed.

QUINCE You, Nick Bottom, are set down for Pyramus.

20 BOTTOM What is Pyramus? – a lover or a tyrant?

QUINCE A lover that kills himself, most gallant, for love.

BOTTOM That will ask some tears in the true performing of it. If I do it, let the audience look to their eyes! I will move storms. I will condole, in some measure. To the rest. – Yet my chief humour is for a tyrant. I could play Ercles rarely, or a part to tear a cat in, to make all split:

> The raging rocks
> And shivering shocks
> Shall break the locks
>   Of prison gates,
> And Phibbus' car
> Shall shine from far

30

v.1.56–7 where the play is described as 'A tedious brief scene of young Pyramus | And his love Thisbe; "very tragical mirth"'.

15 Masters, spread yourselves. It is not clear exactly what action is intended here. Some producers have the mechanicals seated on a bench.

24 condole lament, express grief

25 humour inclination, fancy

26 Ercles Hercules. This may allude to a ranting role in a particular play, now lost.
part to tear a cat in. The phrase, proverbial now for a ranting role, may have been so in Shakespeare's time.

27–34 The raging rocks . . . This may be a quotation from a lost play. More probably it is Shakespeare's bur-

lesque of the kind of writing found in two somewhat similar passages of John Studley's translation (1581) of Seneca's Hercules Oetaeus:

> O lord of ghosts, whose fiery flash
>   That forth thy hand doth shake
> Doth cause the trembling lodges twain
>   Of Phoebus' car to quake . . .
> The roaring rocks have quaking stirred,
>   And none thereat hath pushed;
> Hell gloomy gates I have brast ope
>   Where grisly ghosts all hushed
> Have stood.

31 Phibbus' car the chariot of Phoebus, the sun-god. 'Phibbus', Q1's spelling, may represent Bottom's idiosyncratic pronunciation.

> *And make and mar*
> *The foolish Fates.*

This was lofty! – Now name the rest of the players. – This is Ercles' vein, a tyrant's vein. A lover is more condoling.

QUINCE Francis Flute, the bellows-mender?

FLUTE Here, Peter Quince.

QUINCE Flute, you must take Thisbe on you.   40

FLUTE What is Thisbe? – a wandering knight?

QUINCE It is the lady that Pyramus must love.

FLUTE Nay, faith, let not me play a woman – I have a beard coming.

QUINCE That's all one: you shall play it in a mask, and you may speak as small as you will.

BOTTOM An I may hide my face, let me play Thisbe too. I'll speak in a monstrous little voice: 'Thisne, Thisne!' 'Ah, Pyramus, my lover dear; thy Thisbe dear, and lady dear.'

QUINCE No, no; you must play Pyramus; and Flute, you   50
Thisbe.

BOTTOM Well, proceed.

QUINCE Robin Starveling, the tailor?

STARVELING Here, Peter Quince.

QUINCE Robin Starveling, you must play Thisbe's mother. Tom Snout, the tinker?

SNOUT Here, Peter Quince.

---

37 *condoling* pathetic
41 *a wandering knight* a knight-errant (a typical role in a play)
43 *let not me play a woman* (a reminder that women's parts were played by boys and young men in Shakespeare's time)
45 *mask* (a customary item of ladies' costume in Shakespeare's time)
47 *An* if
48 *Thisne.* Probably the spelling represents Bottom's pronunciation. But some commentators believe that Shakespeare wrote *thisne*, meaning 'in this manner'. The word is not found elsewhere in Shakespeare's writings.
56–9 *Thisbe's mother ... Pyramus' father ... Thisbe's father.* These characters do not appear in the play as acted. There are other discrepancies between the play as projected and as performed. A realistic explanation should not be sought.

QUINCE You, Pyramus' father; myself, Thisbe's father;
Snug, the joiner, you the lion's part; and I hope here is
a play fitted.

SNUG Have you the lion's part written? Pray you, if it be,
give it me; for I am slow of study.

QUINCE You may do it extempore; for it is nothing but
roaring.

BOTTOM Let me play the lion too. I will roar that I will
do any man's heart good to hear me. I will roar that I
will make the Duke say 'Let him roar again; let him
roar again!'

QUINCE An you should do it too terribly you would fright
the Duchess and the ladies that they would shriek; and
that were enough to hang us all.

ALL That would hang us, every mother's son.

BOTTOM I grant you, friends, if you should fright the
ladies out of their wits they would have no more discretion but to hang us. But I will aggravate my voice so
that I will roar you as gently as any sucking dove. I will
roar you an 'twere any nightingale.

QUINCE You can play no part but Pyramus; for Pyramus
is a sweet-faced man; a proper man as one shall see in a
summer's day; a most lovely, gentlemanlike man. Therefore you must needs play Pyramus.

BOTTOM Well, I will undertake it. What beard were I
best to play it in?

QUINCE Why, what you will.

BOTTOM I will discharge it in either your straw-colour
beard, your orange-tawny beard, your purple-in-grain

76 *aggravate*. Bottom means 'moderate'. Mistress Quickly makes the same error (*2 Henry IV*, II.4.153): 'I beseek you now, aggravate your choler.'

77 *roar you* (a colloquialism: 'roar for you', or simply 'roar')
sucking unweaned

78 *an'twere* as if it were

80 *proper* handsome

83–9 *What beard were I best to play it in?* ... Bottom's interest in the colour of beards is perhaps appropriate to his craft of weaver.

87 *orange-tawny* dark yellow

beard, or your French-crown-colour beard, your perfect
yellow.

QUINCE Some of your French crowns have no hair at all;   90
and then you will play bare-faced! But, masters, here
are your parts, and I am to entreat you, request you, and
desire you to con them by tomorrow night, and meet me
in the palace wood a mile without the town by moonlight. There will we rehearse; for if we meet in the city
we shall be dogged with company, and our devices
known. In the meantime I will draw a bill of properties
such as our play wants. I pray you, fail me not.

BOTTOM We will meet, and there we may rehearse most
obscenely and courageously. Take pains, be perfect.   100
Adieu!

QUINCE At the Duke's oak we meet.

BOTTOM Enough; hold, or cut bowstrings.

Exeunt Bottom and his fellows

Enter a Fairy at one door, and Puck (Robin Good-   II.I
fellow) at another

PUCK

How now, spirit; whither wander you?

88 *French-crown-colour* light yellow like a
gold coin. (The French *écu* seems to
be alluded to mainly for the sake of
the joke that follows.)

90 *crowns* heads. 'French crown' refers
to the baldness produced by venereal
disease, particularly associated by the
English with France.

97 *properties* stage requisites

100 *obscenely*. The point lies rather in the
unfitness of this word than in what
Bottom intended. He may have
meant 'seemly'. Compare Costard in
Love's Labour Lost, IV.1.136: 'When
it comes so smoothly off, so obscenely, as it were, so fit.'

be perfect know your lines.

103 *hold, or cut bowstrings*. This is an expression in archery of uncertain meaning. It is reasonably interpreted as
'Keep your promise or be disgraced.'

II.1 With this scene the play moves into
the wood. It is the night of Lysander's
and Hermia's attempt to escape from
Athens, that is, 'tomorrow night' in relation to the first scene. The rhyming
verse used for the opening conversation
between Puck and the Fairy forms an
immediate contrast with the mechanicals'
prose.

FAIRY

Over hill, over dale,
   Thorough bush, thorough briar,
Over park, over pale,
   Thorough flood, thorough fire –
I do wander everywhere
Swifter than the moon's sphere,
And I serve the Fairy Queen,
To dew her orbs upon the green.
The cowslips tall her pensioners be;
In their gold coats spots you see –
Those be rubies, fairy favours;
In those freckles live their savours.
I must go seek some dewdrops here,
And hang a pearl in every cowslip's ear.

10

(stage direction) *at one door . . . at another* (a common direction in Elizabethan plays, referring to the doors at the sides of the stage)

Puck. Puck is often referred to in stage directions and speech prefixes of the early editions as Robin Goodfellow, and is so spoken of and addressed in the dialogue. A 'puck' is a devil or an imp. Properly the character in the play is Robin Goodfellow, a puck.

Robin Goodfellow's appearance is described in a stage direction of *Grim the Collier of Croydon*, a play of unknown authorship written about 1600: 'Enter Robin Goodfellow, in a suit of leather close to his body; his face and hands coloured russet-colour, with a flail.'

2 *Over hill, over dale . . .* The Fairy (com-

monly played by a young woman in modern productions, but presumably by a boy in Shakespeare's time) is given a new verse form.

4 *pale* fenced land, park. (That is, the fairies wander over both public and private land.)

7 *moon's sphere.* According to the astronomical notions of Shakespeare's day, the moon was fixed in a hollow crystalline sphere or globe which itself revolved round the earth each twenty-four hours.

9 *orbs* fairy rings – circles of darker grass

10 *pensioners.* Queen Elizabeth was attended by fifty handsome young gentlemen-pensioners, her royal bodyguard, who were splendidly dressed. The word carries no implications of poverty.

Farewell, thou lob of spirits; I'll be gone.
Our Queen and all her elves come here anon.

PUCK

The King doth keep his revels here tonight.
Take heed the Queen come not within his sight,
For Oberon is passing fell and wrath   20
Because that she as her attendant hath
A lovely boy stolen from an Indian king.
She never had so sweet a changeling,
And jealous Oberon would have the child
Knight of his train, to trace the forests wild.
But she perforce withholds the lovèd boy,
Crowns him with flowers, and makes him all her joy.
And now they never meet — in grove or green,
By fountain clear or spangled starlight sheen —
But they do square, that all their elves for fear   30
Creep into acorn cups and hide them there.

FAIRY

Either I mistake your shape and making quite,
Or else you are that shrewd and knavish sprite
Called Robin Goodfellow. Are not you he
That frights the maidens of the villagery,
Skim milk, and sometimes labour in the quern,
And bootless make the breathless housewife churn,

16 *lob* clown, lout. (Puck is clearly among the least ethereal of fairies.)
17 *elves* fairy boys. (That is, presumably, Cobweb, Peaseblossom, Moth, and Mustardseed.)
20 *passing* exceedingly
   fell fierce, angry
22 *Indian.* Oberon and Tìtania are again associated with India at lines 69 and 124.
   Titania gives a different account of the boy (lines 123–37).
23 *changeling* (usually a child left by fairies in exchange for one stolen, but here, the stolen child. The word has three syllables.)
25 *trace* range, track through
26 *perforce* by force
29 *starlight sheen* shining light of the stars
30 *square* quarrel
32 *making* form, shape, build
33 *shrewd* mischievous
35 *villagery* villages
36 *Skim milk* steal cream
   quern hand-mill for grinding corn. Puck is either grinding meal himself or mischievously labouring to cause the grinding to fail.
37 *bootless* fruitlessly. (Puck prevents the milk from turning to butter.)

And sometime make the drink to bear no barm,
Mislead night-wanderers, laughing at their harm?
40   Those that 'Hobgoblin' call you, and 'Sweet Puck',
You do their work, and they shall have good luck.
Are not you he?

PUCK   Thou speakest aright:
I am that merry wanderer of the night.
I jest to Oberon, and make him smile
When I a fat and bean-fed horse beguile,
Neighing in likeness of a filly foal;
And sometime lurk I in a gossip's bowl
In very likeness of a roasted crab;
And when she drinks, against her lips I bob,
50   And on her withered dewlap pour the ale.
The wisest aunt telling the saddest tale
Sometime for threefoot stool mistaketh me;
Then slip I from her bum. Down topples she,
And 'Tailor' cries, and falls into a cough;
And then the whole choir hold their hips and laugh,
And waxen in their mirth, and neeze, and swear
A merrier hour was never wasted there.
But room, Fairy: here comes Oberon.

FAIRY
And here my mistress. Would that he were gone!

38 *barm* froth on ale
39 *Mislead* (that is, with false fire. Puck later (III.1.103–5) *declares* his intention of doing this to the mechanicals.)
40 *Hobgoblin* (another name for Robin Goodfellow)
45 *bean-fed*. Field beans were used as food for horses, and were also known as horse-beans.
    beguile trick
47 *gossip* old woman, crony
48 *crab* crab-apple; an ingredient in a drink
50 *dewlap* skin hanging from the neck; or (possibly) breasts
51 *aunt* old woman, gossip
    saddest most serious
54 *And 'Tailor' cries.* The exact meaning is unknown. Dr Johnson writes: 'The custom of crying "tailor" at a sudden fall backwards I think I remember to have observed. He that slips beside his chair falls as a tailor squats upon his board.' *Tailor* may mean 'posterior'.
55 *choir* company
56 *waxen* increase
    neeze sneeze
57 *wasted* spent

Enter Oberon, the King of Fairies, at one door, with
his train; and Titania, the Queen, at another with hers

OBERON

Ill met by moonlight, proud Titania!   60

TITANIA

What, jealous Oberon? Fairy, skip hence.
I have forsworn his bed and company.

OBERON

Tarry, rash wanton! Am not I thy lord?

TITANIA

Then I must be thy lady. But I know
When thou hast stolen away from Fairyland
And in the shape of Corin sat all day
Playing on pipes of corn, and versing love
To amorous Phillida. Why art thou here
Come from the farthest step of India
But that, forsooth, the bouncing Amazon,   70
Your buskined mistress and your warrior love,
To Theseus must be wedded? – and you come
To give their bed joy and prosperity.

59 (stage direction) *Titania.* In the classical pronunciation (which Shake-
speare probably followed) the first
two vowels would be long: that is,
the first syllable would be pronounced 'tight', and the name would
rhyme with 'mania'.

60 *Ill met by moonlight, proud Titania! . . .*
The entrance of Titania and Oberon
is marked by a change from rhyming
to blank verse.

61 *Fairy, skip hence.* This is often
emended to 'Fairies'; but Titania may
be addressing the Fairy who has been
speaking to Oberon's follower,
Puck.

64–5 *know | When* know of occasions
when

66, 68 *Corin . . . Phillida* (type-names of
the love-sick shepherd and his
beloved)

69 *step.* Perhaps 'limit of travel or ex-
ploration', resembling the phrase in
Much Ado About Nothing (II.1.237): 'I
will fetch you a tooth-picker now
from the furthest inch of Asia.'
'Steppe', meaning a great plain, was
probably not a known word at the
time. Q2 and F read 'steepe', which
may be correct, referring to a mountain, perhaps of the Himalayas.

70 *Amazon* (that is, Hippolyta, Queen
of the Amazons)

71 *buskined* wearing hunting boots. Hippolyta was known as a huntress.

OBERON

How canst thou thus, for shame, Titania,
Glance at my credit with Hippolyta,
Knowing I know thy love to Theseus?
Didst thou not lead him through the glimmering night
From Perigenia, whom he ravishèd,
And make him with fair Aegles break his faith,
80   With Ariadne, and Antiopa?

TITANIA

These are the forgeries of jealousy;
And never since the middle summer's spring
Met we on hill, in dale, forest, or mead,
By pavèd fountain or by rushy brook,
Or in the beachèd margent of the sea
To dance our ringlets to the whistling wind,
But with thy brawls thou hast disturbed our sport.
Therefore the winds, piping to us in vain,
As in revenge have sucked up from the sea
90   Contagious fogs which, falling in the land,
Hath every pelting river made so proud
That they have overborne their continents.
The ox hath therefore stretched his yoke in vain,
The ploughman lost his sweat, and the green corn

75 *Glance at* hit at, reflect upon
78–80 *Perigenia ... Aegles ... Ariadne
... Antiopa.* All loved by Theseus.
Shakespeare seems to have taken the
names from Plutarch's Life of Theseus, where the first appears as
'Perigouna'.
80 *Ariadne.* The legend of Ariadne's
helping Theseus to thread the laby-
rinth in which the Minotaur was confined, and his deserting her, was well
known.
81–117 *These are the forgeries of jealousy
...* This speech is commented on in
the Introduction, pages 211, 222.
82 *middle summer's spring* the beginning
('spring') of midsummer
84 *pavèd* pebbled
85 *in* on
margent shore
86 *ringlets* dances in the form of a ring
(the meaning 'lock of hair' is not
recorded before 1667)
to to the sound of
90 *Contagious* pestilential, harmful
91 *pelting* paltry
92 *continents* banks

Hath rotted ere his youth attained a beard.
The fold stands empty in the drownèd field,
And crows are fatted with the murrion flock.
The nine men's morris is filled up with mud,
And the quaint mazes in the wanton green

100   For lack of tread are undistinguishable.
The human mortals want their winter cheer.
No night is now with hymn or carol blessed.
Therefore the moon, the governess of floods,
Pale in her anger, washes all the air,
That rheumatic diseases do abound;
And thorough this distemperature we see
The seasons alter; hoary-headed frosts
Fall in the fresh lap of the crimson rose,
And on old Hiems' thin and icy crown

110   An odorous chaplet of sweet summer buds
Is as in mockery set. The spring, the summer,
The childing autumn, angry winter change
Their wonted liveries, and the mazèd world
By their increase now knows not which is which.

97 *murrion flock* flock infected with murrion (or 'murrain'), a disease of sheep
and cattle

98 *nine men's morris* area marked out in
squares for the game of the same
name, a sort of open-air draughts, in
which each player has nine pieces

99 *quaint mazes* intricate arrangements of
paths, normally kept visible by being
frequently trodden
wanton green luxuriant grass

101 *cheer* (a commonly accepted emendation for 'here' in the early editions,
which may however be correct.
'Here' seems weak, whereas 'cheer'
would look forward to the following
line)

103 *Therefore.* This repeats the 'Therefore' of line 88.

104 *washes* moistens, wets

105 *rheumatic* characterized by 'rheum',
that is, colds, coughs, etc. (The
accent is on the first syllable.)

106 *distemperature.* The word means both
'ill-humour, discomposure' and 'bad
weather'.

109 *Hiems* winter personified. He is introduced into the closing episode of
Love's Labour's Lost (v.2.878): 'This
side is Hiems, Winter; this Ver, the
Spring'.

112 *childing* fertile, fruitful (autumn as
the season of harvest)
change exchange

113 *wonted* customary
mazèd amazed, bewildered

114 *increase* (seasonal) products

And this same progeny of evils
Comes from our debate, from our dissension.
We are their parents and original.

OBERON
Do you amend it, then! It lies in you.
Why should Titania cross her Oberon?

120 I do but beg a little changeling boy
To be my henchman.

TITANIA   Set your heart at rest.
The fairy land buys not the child of me.
His mother was a votaress of my order,
And in the spicèd Indian air by night
Full often hath she gossiped by my side,
And sat with me on Neptune's yellow sands
Marking th'embarkèd traders on the flood,
When we have laughed to see the sails conceive
And grow big-bellied with the wanton wind;

130 Which she with pretty and with swimming gait
Following – her womb then rich with my young squire –
Would imitate, and sail upon the land
To fetch me trifles, and return again
As from a voyage, rich with merchandise.
But she, being mortal, of that boy did die,
And for her sake do I rear up her boy;
And for her sake I will not part with him.

OBERON
How long within this wood intend you stay?

TITANIA
Perchance till after Theseus' wedding day.

140 If you will patiently dance in our round
And see our moonlight revels, go with us.
If not, shun me, and I will spare your haunts.

116 *debate* quarrel   127 *traders* trading ships
123 *votaress* a woman under vow (in Tita- 140 *round* round dance
nia's 'order')   142 *spare* avoid

OBERON

Give me that boy and I will go with thee.

TITANIA

Not for thy fairy kingdom! Fairies, away.
We shall chide downright if I longer stay.

Exit Titania with her train

OBERON

Well, go thy way. Thou shalt not from this grove
Till I torment thee for this injury.

My gentle Puck, come hither. Thou rememberest
Since once I sat upon a promontory
And heard a mermaid on a dolphin's back   150
Uttering such dulcet and harmonious breath
That the rude sea grew civil at her song,
And certain stars shot madly from their spheres
To hear the sea-maid's music?

PUCK   I remember.

OBERON

That very time I saw – but thou couldst not –
Flying between the cold moon and the earth
Cupid all armed. A certain aim he took
At a fair vestal thronèd by the west,
And loosed his loveshaft smartly from his bow
As it should pierce a hundred thousand hearts;   160
But I might see young Cupid's fiery shaft
Quenched in the chaste beams of the watery moon,
And the imperial votaress passed on

144–5 *Not for thy fairy kingdom!*. . .As
often, a couplet is used to mark the
end of an episode.
145 *chide* quarrel
147 *injury* insult
149 *Since* when
151 *dulcet* sweet
  breath voice, song
152 *rude* rough
157 *certain* sure
158 *vestal* virgin (usually assumed to

refer to Queen Elizabeth)
  by in
159 *loveshaft* the golden arrow (compare
  I.I.170)
163 *And the imperial votaress passed on.*
  The scansion of this line is uncertain.
  The most satisfactory alternatives
  seem to be 'And the imperial vót'ress
  pássèd ón' and 'And the impérial
  vótaréss páss'd on'.
  imperial majestic, imperious, queenly

In maiden meditation, fancy-free.
Yet marked I where the bolt of Cupid fell:
It fell upon a little western flower,
Before, milk-white; now purple with love's wound:
And maidens call it 'love in idleness'.
Fetch me that flower – the herb I showed thee once.
170 The juice of it on sleeping eyelids laid
Will make or man or woman madly dote
Upon the next live creature that it sees.
Fetch me this herb, and be thou here again
Ere the leviathan can swim a league.

PUCK
I'll put a girdle round about the earth
In forty minutes!   *Exit*

OBERON   Having once this juice
I'll watch Titania when she is asleep,
And drop the liquor of it in her eyes.
The next thing then she, waking, looks upon –
180 Be it on lion, bear, or wolf, or bull,
On meddling monkey or on busy ape –
She shall pursue it with the soul of love.
And ere I take this charm from off her sight –
As I can take it with another herb –
I'll make her render up her page to me.
But who comes here? I am invisible,
And I will overhear their conference.
                Enter Demetrius, Helena following him

DEMETRIUS
I love thee not, therefore pursue me not.
Where is Lysander, and fair Hermia?

165 *bolt* arrow
168 *love in idleness* pansy or heart's ease.
The idea that it changed from white
to purple may have been suggested
by Ovid's statement in the Pyramus
and Thisbe story that the mulberry,
once 'white as snow', was turned to
'a deep dark purple colour' by Pyramus's blood.
171 *or. . .or* either. . .or
174 *leviathan* sea-monster; to the Elizabethans, a whale
176–87 *Having once this juice. . . .* Oberon
addresses the audience.

The one I'll slay; the other slayeth me.   190
Thou toldest me they were stolen unto this wood,
And here am I, and wood within this wood
Because I cannot meet my Hermia.
Hence, get thee gone, and follow me no more!

HELENA
You draw me, you hard-hearted adamant!
But yet you draw not iron: for my heart
Is true as steel. Leave you your power to draw,
And I shall have no power to follow you.

DEMETRIUS
Do I entice you? Do I speak you fair?
Or rather do I not in plainest truth   200
Tell you I do not nor I cannot love you?

HELENA
And even for that do I love you the more.
I am your spaniel; and, Demetrius,
The more you beat me I will fawn on you.
Use me but as your spaniel: spurn me, strike me,
Neglect me, lose me; only give me leave,
Unworthy as I am, to follow you.
What worser place can I beg in your love –
And yet a place of high respect with me –
Than to be used as you use your dog?   210

DEMETRIUS
Tempt not too much the hatred of my spirit;
For I am sick when I do look on thee.

HELENA
And I am sick when I look not on you.

---

192 *and wood* and mad
195 *adamant* very hard stone supposed
to have magnetic properties
196–7 *But yet you draw not iron: for my
heart | Is true as steel.* Iron is the obvi-
ous substance to be attracted by ada-

mant; Helena stresses her more-than-
ordinary fidelity to Demetrius. The
conceit is somewhat strained, perhaps with a deliberate effect of
slightly comic inanity.
199 *speak you fair* speak kindly to you

DEMETRIUS

You do impeach your modesty too much,
To leave the city and commit yourself
Into the hands of one that loves you not;
To trust the opportunity of night
And the ill counsel of a desert place
With the rich worth of your virginity.

HELENA

220   Your virtue is my privilege. For that
It is not night when I do see your face,
Therefore I think I am not in the night;
Nor doth this wood lack worlds of company,
For you in my respect are all the world.
Then how can it be said I am alone
When all the world is here to look on me?

DEMETRIUS

I'll run from thee and hide me in the brakes,
And leave thee to the mercy of wild beasts.

HELENA

The wildest hath not such a heart as you.
230   Run when you will. The story shall be changed:
Apollo flies, and Daphne holds the chase;
The dove pursues the griffin; the mild hind
Makes speed to catch the tiger – bootless speed,
When cowardice pursues, and valour flies.

214 *impeach* call in question, discredit
215 *To leave* by leaving
220 *Your virtue is my privilege.* A difficult
expression. *Virtue* probably means
'qualities', 'attractions'. We may paraphrase: 'the effect of your qualities
upon me puts me in a privileged
position' – that is, because when
Demetrius is there the night seems
like day.
   For that because

224 *in my respect* to my mind
231 *Apollo flies, and Daphne holds the
chase.* Daphne, flying from Apollo,
was changed into a laurel tree so as
to escape him. The story was familiar
from Ovid's *Metamorphoses.*
232 *griffin* a fabulous monster with the
body of a lion but the head, wings,
and forehead of an eagle
   hind doe
233 *bootless* useless

DEMETRIUS

I will not stay thy questions. Let me go;
Or if thou follow me, do not believe
But I shall do thee mischief in the wood.

HELENA

Ay – in the temple, in the town, the field,
You do me mischief. Fie, Demetrius,
Your wrongs do set a scandal on my sex.   240
We cannot fight for love, as men may do;
We should be wooed, and were not made to woo.

                                        Exit Demetrius

I'll follow thee, and make a heaven of hell,
To die upon the hand I love so well.

                                        Exit Helena

OBERON

Fare thee well, nymph. Ere he do leave this grove
Thou shalt fly him, and he shall seek thy love.

        Enter Puck

Hast thou the flower there? Welcome, wanderer.

PUCK

Ay, there it is.

OBERON   I pray thee give it me.
I know a bank where the wild thyme blows,
Where oxlips and the nodding violet grows,   250
Quite overcanopied with luscious woodbine,
With sweet muskroses and with eglantine.
There sleeps Titania some time of the night,

---

235 *stay* wait for
240 *Your wrongs do set a scandal on my sex*
    the wrongs that you do me cause me
    to act in a manner that disgraces my
    sex
241 *We cannot fight for love* . . . The scene
    moves into couplets, partly perhaps
    in preparation for Oberon's lyrical
    lines from line 249.
244 *upon* by
245 *Fare thee well, nymph.* Oberon, who

has been an 'invisible' spectator,
now comes forward.
250 *oxlips* flowering herbs, hybrids be-
    tween the cowslip and the primrose
    grows (the singular verb with a plural
    subject was not unusual in Eliza-
    bethan English)
251 *woodbine* honeysuckle
252 *muskroses . . . eglantine* wild roses . . .
    sweet-briar
253 *some time* for some part of

Lulled in these flowers with dances and delight.
And there the snake throws her enamelled skin,
Weed wide enough to wrap a fairy in.
And with the juice of this I'll streak her eyes
And make her full of hateful fantasies.
Take thou some of it, and seek through this grove.
260   A sweet Athenian lady is in love
With a disdainful youth — anoint his eyes;
But do it when the next thing he espies
May be the lady. Thou shalt know the man
By the Athenian garments he hath on.
Effect it with some care, that he may prove
More fond on her than she upon her love.
And look thou meet me ere the first cock crow.

PUCK
Fear not, my lord; your servant shall do so.

Exeunt Oberon and Puck

II.2   *Enter Titania, Queen of Fairies, with her train*

TITANIA
Come, now a roundel and a fairy song,
Then for the third part of a minute hence:
Some to kill cankers in the muskrose buds,
Some war with reremice for their leathern wings
To make my small elves coats, and some keep back
The clamorous owl that nightly hoots and wonders

255 *throws* throws off, casts
256 *Weed* garment
266 *fond on* in love, infatuated with
267 *ere the first cock crow.* Some supernatural beings were thought to be unable to bear daylight. At III.2.386 Oberon is dissociated from the ghosts and spirits who 'wilfully themselves exile from light'. This seems a way of stressing his generally benevolent function.

II.2 This scene follows immediately on the preceding one. The place is the bank mentioned by Oberon at II.1.249.
1 *roundel* round dance, all joining hands
2 *third part of a minute* (suggesting great rapidity of action on the part of the fairies)
4 *reremice* bats

At our quaint spirits. Sing me now asleep;
Then to your offices, and let me rest.
    Fairies sing

FIRST FAIRY
    You spotted snakes with double tongue,
      Thorny hedgehogs, be not seen.   10
    Newts and blindworms, do no wrong,
      Come not near our Fairy Queen.

CHORUS
    Philomel with melody
    Sing in our sweet lullaby,
  Lulla, lulla, lullaby; lulla, lulla, lullaby.
      Never harm
      Nor spell nor charm
    Come our lovely lady nigh.
    So good night, with lullaby.

FIRST FAIRY
    Weaving spiders, come not here;   20
      Hence, you longlegged spinners, hence!
    Beetles black, approach not near,
      Worm nor snail, do no offence.

CHORUS
    Philomel with melody
    Sing in our sweet lullaby,
  Lulla, lulla, lullaby; lulla, lulla, lullaby.
      Never harm
      Nor spell nor charm
    Come our lovely lady nigh.
    So good night, with lullaby.   30

---

7 *quaint* pretty, dainty
9 *double* forked
11 *Newts and blindworms.* Though neither is in fact harmful, they were thought to be so in Shakespeare's time. The witches' cauldron in *Macbeth* includes 'eye of newt' and 'blindworm's sting'.

13 *Philomel* the classical name for the nightingale
20 *spiders* (also thought to be poisonous)
21 *longlegged spinners* (probably daddy-longlegs)

Titania sleeps

SECOND FAIRY
> Hence, away! Now all is well.
> One aloof stand sentinel!

Exeunt Fairies

Enter Oberon
He squeezes the flower on Titania's eyes

OBERON
> What thou seest when thou dost wake,
> Do it for thy true love take;
> Love and languish for his sake.
> Be it ounce or cat or bear,
> Pard, or boar with bristled hair
> In thy eye that shall appear
> When thou wakest, it is thy dear.

40
> Wake when some vile thing is near!   *Exit*

Enter Lysander and Hermia

LYSANDER
> Fair love, you faint with wandering in the wood;

---

30 (stage direction) *Titania sleeps.* There is no break in the action between Titania's falling asleep and her awakening by Bottom at III.1.122. She must apparently remain on stage throughout this time. However, it is not necessary for her to be visible to the audience. It is possible that on the Elizabethan stage she occupied a recess that could be curtained off at the end of Oberon's spell (line 40), and that the curtain was drawn to reveal her during the first verse of Bottom's song (III.1.118).

32 *One aloof stand sentinel!* Perhaps on an Elizabethan stage one fairy would have been stationed on the upper stage ('aloof'). Oberon, whether or not his 'invisibility' was effective with his fellow-fairies, would have been able to outwit the sentinel by confining his movements to the area at the back of the stage where, presumably, Titania sleeps. In stage practice, the sentinel is sometimes kidnapped by Oberon's attendants.

33–40 *What thou seest. . . .* Oberon's spell is distinguished by the use of trochaic, rhyming verse. This tripping measure is used elsewhere by fairy characters, e.g. the Fairy, II.1.6–13; Puck, II.2.72–89; Oberon for other spells at III.2.102–9 and IV.1.70–73, and Puck and Oberon in their following dialogue; Puck at III.2.396–9, 437–41; Puck, Oberon, and Titania at IV.1.92–101, and in the closing speeches, V.1.361–428.

36 *ounce* lynx

37 *Pard* leopard

And – to speak truth – I have forgot our way.
We'll rest us, Hermia, if you think it good,
And tarry for the comfort of the day.

HERMIA
Be it so, Lysander; find you out a bed,
For I upon this bank will rest my head.

LYSANDER
One turf shall serve as pillow for us both;
One heart, one bed, two bosoms, and one troth.

HERMIA
Nay, good Lysander, for my sake, my dear,
Lie further off yet; do not lie so near.   50

LYSANDER
O, take the sense, sweet, of my innocence!
Love takes the meaning in love's conference –
I mean that my heart unto yours is knit,
So that but one heart we can make of it.
Two bosoms interchainèd with an oath –
So then two bosoms and a single troth.
Then by your side no bed-room me deny,
For lying so, Hermia, I do not lie.

HERMIA
Lysander riddles very prettily.
Now much beshrew my manners and my pride   60
If Hermia meant to say Lysander lied.
But, gentle friend, for love and courtesy
Lie further off, in human modesty:
Such separation as may well be said
Becomes a virtuous bachelor and a maid,
So far be distant, and good night, sweet friend;

---

48 *troth* (an old spelling of 'truth', preserved for the rhyme)
51 *take the sense* take the true meaning
52 *Love takes the meaning in love's conference.* In lovers' conversation ('conference') their love enables them truly
to understand each other.
58 *lie* (a pun on the senses 'lie down'
and 'deceive')

Thy love ne'er alter till thy sweet life end.

LYSANDER

Amen, amen, to that fair prayer say I,
And then end life when I end loyalty.
70   Here is my bed: sleep give thee all his rest.

HERMIA

With half that wish the wisher's eyes be pressed.

They sleep
Enter Puck

PUCK

Through the forest have I gone,
But Athenian found I none
On whose eyes I might approve
This flower's force in stirring love.
Night and silence. – Who is here?
Weeds of Athens he doth wear.
This is he my master said
Despisèd the Athenian maid;
80   And here the maiden, sleeping sound
On the dank and dirty ground.
Pretty soul, she durst not lie
Near this lack-love, this kill-courtesy.
Churl, upon thy eyes I throw
All the power this charm doth owe.

He squeezes the flower on Lysander's eyes

When thou wakest let love forbid
Sleep his seat on thy eyelid.
So, awake when I am gone;
For I must now to Oberon.   *Exit*

Enter Demetrius and Helena, running

HELENA

90   Stay though thou kill me, sweet Demetrius!

---

70 *Here is my bed* (that is, at some distance from Hermia)
74 *approve* test
76 *Who is here?* Puck mistakes Lysander

for Demetrius.
78 *he my master said* he that my master
said
85 *owe* own

DEMETRIUS

I charge thee hence; and do not haunt me thus.

HELENA

O, wilt thou darkling leave me? Do not so!

DEMETRIUS

Stay, on thy peril. I alone will go.   *Exit*

HELENA

O, I am out of breath in this fond chase.
The more my prayer, the lesser is my grace.
Happy is Hermia, wheresoe'er she lies,
For she hath blessèd and attractive eyes.
How came her eyes so bright? Not with salt tears –
If so, my eyes are oftener washed than hers.
No, no – I am as ugly as a bear;   100
For beasts that meet me run away for fear.
Therefore no marvel though Demetrius
Do as a monster fly my presence thus.
What wicked and dissembling glass of mine
Made me compare with Hermia's sphery eyne?
But who is here? – Lysander on the ground?
Dead – or asleep? I see no blood, no wound.
Lysander, if you live, good sir, awake!

LYSANDER (*wakes*)

And run through fire I will for thy sweet sake!
Transparent Helena, nature shows art   110
That through thy bosom makes me see thy heart.
Where is Demetrius? O, how fit a word
Is that vile name to perish on my sword!

HELENA

Do not say so, Lysander, say not so.
What though he love your Hermia, lord, what though?
Yet Hermia still loves you. Then be content.

---

92 *darkling* in darkness (the reminder was especially necessary in the open-air Elizabethan theatre)
94 *fond* foolish
95 *grace* answer to prayer

105 *sphery eyne* star-like eyes
110 *Transparent* (means both 'lacking in deceit; able to be seen through' and 'bright')
art magic power

LYSANDER
Content with Hermia? No, I do repent
The tedious minutes I with her have spent.
Not Hermia but Helena I love.
120 Who will not change a raven for a dove?
The will of man is by his reason swayed,
And reason says you are the worthier maid.
Things growing are not ripe until their season;
So I, being young, till now ripe not to reason.
And touching now the point of human skill,
Reason becomes the marshal to my will,
And leads me to your eyes, where I o'erlook
Love's stories written in love's richest book.

HELENA
Wherefore was I to this keen mockery born?
130 When at your hands did I deserve this scorn?
Is't not enough, is't not enough young man
That I did never — no, nor never can —
Deserve a sweet look from Demetrius' eye
But you must flout my insufficiency?
Good troth, you do me wrong — good sooth, you do —
In such disdainful manner me to woo.
But fare you well. Perforce I must confess
I thought you lord of more true gentleness.

120 *raven.* Compare III.2.257, where Lysander calls Hermia 'Ethiope'. She is presumably dark in hair or complexion.
121 *The will of man is by his reason swayed.* Lysander ironically attributes to his reason the change in his affections that has been brought about by Puck; see Introduction, pages 224–5.
  will desire
124 *ripe not* ('ripe' is a verb)
125 *And touching now the point of human skill* and I now reaching the highest

point of human capacity
127–8 *your eyes, where I o'erlook | Love's stories written in love's richest book.* Shakespeare expresses a similar idea in *Love's Labour's Lost* (IV.3.298–300):

From women's eyes this doctrine I derive:
They are the ground, the books, the
  academes,
From whence doth spring the true
  Promethean fire.

127 *o'erlook* look over, read
138 *gentleness* nobility, breeding

O, that a lady of one man refused
Should of another therefore be abused!   *Exit*   140

LYSANDER

She sees not Hermia. Hermia, sleep thou there,
And never mayst thou come Lysander near.
For, as a surfeit of the sweetest things
The deepest loathing to the stomach brings,
Or as the heresies that men do leave
Are hated most of those they did deceive,
So thou, my surfeit and my heresy,
Of all be hated, but the most of me!
And, all my powers, address your love and might
To honour Helen and to be her knight.   *Exit*   150

HERMIA (*wakes*)

Help me, Lysander, help me! Do thy best
To pluck this crawling serpent from my breast!
Ay me, for pity! – What a dream was here
Lysander, look how I do quake with fear!
Methought a serpent ate my heart away,
And you sat smiling at his cruel prey.
Lysander – what, removed? Lysander, lord!
What, out of hearing? Gone? No sound, no word?
Alack, where are you? Speak an if you hear.
Speak, of all loves! I swoon almost with fear.   160
No? Then I well perceive you are not nigh.
Either death or you I'll find immediately.   *Exit*

139,140 *of* by   had been deceived by them
145–6 *as the heresies that men do leave* | 149 *address* direct, apply
    Are hated most of those they did   156 *prey* preying
    deceive as the heresies that men reject 159 *an if* if
    are hated most by the very men who   160 *of all loves* for love's sake

III.1   *Enter the clowns: Bottom, Quince, Snout, Starveling*
            Flute, and Snug

BOTTOM Are we all met?

QUINCE Pat, pat; and here's a marvellous convenient place
for our rehearsal. This green plot shall be our stage, this
hawthorn brake our tiring-house, and we will do it in
action as we will do it before the Duke.

BOTTOM Peter Quince!

QUINCE What sayest thou, Bully Bottom?

BOTTOM There are things in this comedy of Pyramus and
Thisbe that will never please. First, Pyramus must draw
a sword to kill himself, which the ladies cannot abide.
How answer you that?

SNOUT By 'r lakin, a parlous fear!

STARVELING I believe we must leave the killing out,
when all is done.

BOTTOM Not a whit. I have a device to make all well.
Write me a prologue, and let the prologue seem to say
we will do no harm with our swords, and that Pyramus
is not killed indeed; and for the more better assurance,
tell them that I, Pyramus, am not Pyramus, but Bottom
the weaver. This will put them out of fear.

QUINCE Well, we will have such a prologue; and it shall
be written in eight and six.

BOTTOM No, make it two more: let it be written in eight
and eight.

SNOUT Will not the ladies be afeard of the lion?

STARVELING I fear it, I promise you.

10 (margin)
20 (margin)

III.1. There is no break between the preceding scene and this one.
    (Stage direction) *clowns* rustics
2 *Pat* on the dot
4 *tiring-house* the dressing-room of the
    Elizabethan theatre, directly behind
    the stage. On the Elizabethan stage
    Bottom would have indicated the
    'green plot' by pointing to the stage,

and the 'hawthorn brake' by pointing
to the tiring-house.
12 *By 'r lakin* by our Lady (a light oath)
    parlous perilous, terrible
16 *Write me* write (a colloquialism)
22 *eight and six* lines of eight and six
    syllables (a metre common in
    ballads)

BOTTOM Masters, you ought to consider with yourself, to
bring in – God shield us – a lion among ladies is a most
dreadful thing; for there is not a more fearful wildfowl
than your lion living; and we ought to look to't.   30

SNOUT Therefore another prologue must tell he is not a
lion.

BOTTOM Nay, you must name his name, and half his face
must be seen through the lion's neck, and he himself
must speak through, saying thus, or to the same defect:
'Ladies', or 'Fair ladies – I would wish you', or 'I would
request you', or 'I would entreat you – not to fear, not to
tremble. My life for yours: if you think I come hither
as a lion, it were pity of my life. No. I am no such
thing. I am a man, as other men are' – and there indeed   40
let him name his name, and tell them plainly he is Snug
the joiner.

QUINCE Well, it shall be so. But there is two hard things:
that is, to bring the moonlight into a chamber – for, you
know, Pyramus and Thisbe meet by moonlight.

SNUG Doth the moon shine that night we play our play?

BOTTOM A calendar, a calendar! Look in the almanac –
find out moonshine, find out moonshine!

QUINCE Yes, it doth shine that night.

BOTTOM Why, then, may you leave a casement of the   50
Great Chamber window – where we play – open, and
the moon may shine in at the casement.

QUINCE Ay; or else one must come in with a bush of

---

27 *yourself*. The Folio has 'yourselves';
but the Quarto's singular form may
well be a deliberate touch.

39 *it were pity of* it would be a bad thing
for

46 SNUG. In the early editions the speech
prefix is abbreviated to 'Sn.'. The
line may be spoken by either Snug
or Snout.

48 *find out moonshine!* The Folio has the
stage direction 'Enter Puck' here.

This conflicts with the entry given
for him in the Folio and the Quarto
at line 69. But it is possible that the
Folio's apparently superfluous direction represents an early stage-practice
of bringing Puck in to watch the
mechanicals before he speaks.

51 *Great Chamber* state room

53–4 *bush of thorns*. A traditional attribute of the man in the moon, sometimes said to be the man who picked

thorns and a lantern, and say he comes to disfigure or to
present the person of Moonshine. Then there is another
thing. We must have a wall in the Great Chamber; for
Pyramus and Thisbe, says the story, did talk through the
chink of a wall.

SNOUT You can never bring in a wall. What say you,
60   Bottom?

BOTTOM Some man or other must present Wall; and let
him have some plaster, or some loam, or some roughcast
about him to signify Wall; and let him hold his fingers
thus, and through that cranny shall Pyramus and Thisbe
whisper.

QUINCE If that may be, then all is well. Come, sit down
every mother's son, and rehearse your parts. Pyramus,
you begin. When you have spoken your speech, enter
into that brake; and so everyone according to his cue.

    Enter Puck

PUCK
70   What hempen homespuns have we swaggering here
So near the cradle of the Fairy Queen?
What, a play toward? I'll be an auditor –
An actor too, perhaps, if I see cause.

QUINCE
Speak, Pyramus! Thisbe, stand forth!

BOTTOM *as Pyramus*

    Thisbe, the flowers of odious savours sweet –

up a bundle of sticks on the Sabbath
day (Numbers 15.32–6). There are
other explanations. The following
passage from Ben Jonson's masque
News from the New World (1620), in
reply to a report that a traveller from
the moon has arrived on earth, is an
appropriate comment:
FACTOR *Where? Which is he? I must
see his dog at his girdle, and the bush of
thorns at his back, ere I believe it.*
HERALD *These are stale ensigns of the*

stage's man in the moon.
54 *disfigure* figure
71 *So near the cradle of the Fairy Queen?* (a
    reminder of Titania's presence)
72 *toward* in preparation
75–7 *flowers . . . sweet.* This passage is
    textually difficult. The Quartos read
    'Odours, odorous' in line 76. The
    Folio reads 'Odours, odours'. The
    Folio reading, adopted here, may be
    interpreted to mean that Bottom
    ought to say 'the flowers of odours

QUINCE Odours – odours!

BOTTOM *as Pyramus*

> *. . . odours savours sweet.*
> *So hath thy breath, my dearest Thisbe dear.*
> *But hark, a voice. Stay thou but here awhile,*
> *And by and by I will to thee appear.* *Exit* 80

PUCK

A stranger Pyramus than e'er played here. *Exit*

FLUTE Must I speak now?

QUINCE Ay, marry must you; for you must understand he goes but to see a noise that he heard, and is to come again.

FLUTE *as Thisbe*

> *Most radiant Pyramus, most lilywhite of hue,*
> *Of colour like the red rose on triumphant briar,*
> *Most brisky juvenal, and eke most lovely Jew,*
> *As true as truest horse that yet would never tire,*
> *I'll meet thee, Pyramus, at Ninny's tomb –* 90

QUINCE 'Ninus' tomb', man! – Why, you must not speak that yet. That you answer to Pyramus. You speak all your part at once, cues and all. Pyramus, enter – your cue is past. It is 'never tire'.

savours sweet' (taking 'savours' to mean 'savour'; the singular agreement with a plural subject would have been possible in Elizabethan English). Another possible explanation is that 'of' is a colloquialism for 'have'. If this were so, I should read 'Odorous, odorous' for Quince's correction of Bottom's 'odious'. This would have the advantage of fitting in better with 'hath' in 'so hath thy breath'.

81 *A stranger Pyramus than e'er played here*. Puck conceives the trick that he will play on Bottom.

88 *brisky juvenal* brisk youth (the diction is affected)

eke also (an old-fashioned word in Shakespeare's time)

Jew sometimes explained as an abbreviation of 'jewel' or 'juvenal', but perhaps no more than a deliberately inconsequential piece of padding

90 *Ninny's tomb*. A 'ninny' is a 'fool'. In Ovid's version of the story of Pyramus and Thisbe, they met at the tomb of Ninus, mythical founder of Nineveh.

93 *part* the script given to the actor, containing his speeches and cues

FLUTE O!
(*as Thisbe*)

As true as truest horse, that yet would never tire.

Enter Puck, and Bottom with an ass's head
BOTTOM *as Pyramus*

If I were fair, fair Thisbe, I were only thine.

QUINCE O monstrous! O strange! We are haunted! Pray,
masters! Fly, masters! Help!
Exeunt Quince, Snug, Flute, Snout, and Starveling
PUCK
100 I'll follow you, I'll lead you about a round,
Thorough bog, thorough bush, thorough brake,
thorough briar,
Sometime a horse I'll be, sometime a hound,
A hog, a headless bear, sometime a fire,
And neigh, and bark, and grunt and roar and burn
Like horse, hound, hog, bear, fire at every turn. *Exit*
BOTTOM Why do they run away? This is a knavery of
them to make me afeard.

Enter Snout

SNOUT O Bottom, thou art changed. What do I see on
thee?
110 BOTTOM What do you see? You see an ass head of your
own, do you?
Exit Snout

Enter Quince

QUINCE Bless thee, Bottom! Bless thee! Thou art translated! *Exit*

103 *headless bear*. Headless figures,
whether human or animal, were traditional apparitions.
fire will o'the wisp
105 *at every turn*. The Folio has the stage
direction 'Enter Piramus with the
Asse head'. This seems to be a mis-

take; but it may be that Bottom goes
out at the same time as the other
mechanicals, and re-enters at this
point.
112–13 *translated* transformed. This was
a regular meaning; no joke is
intended.

BOTTOM I see their knavery! This is to make an ass of me,
to fright me, if they could; but I will not stir from this
place, do what they can. I will walk up and down here,
and I will sing, that they shall hear I am not afraid.

(sings)   The ousel cock so black of hue,
                        With orange-tawny bill,
                    The throstle with his note so true   120
                        The wren with little quill.

TITANIA (wakes)

What angel wakes me from my flowery bed?

BOTTOM (sings)

                    The finch, the sparrow, and the lark,
                        The plainsong cuckoo grey,
                    Whose note full many a man doth mark
                        And dares not answer 'Nay'
— for indeed, who would set his wit to so foolish a bird?
Who would give a bird the lie, though he cry 'cuckoo'
never so?

TITANIA

I pray thee, gentle mortal, sing again!   130
Mine ear is much enamoured of thy note.
So is mine eye enthralled to thy shape,
And thy fair virtue's force perforce doth move me
On the first view to say, to swear, I love thee.

BOTTOM Methinks, mistress, you should have little reason

118–29 *The ousel cock* ... Titania had
been lulled to sleep with a song of
the nightingale (Philomel). She is
aroused by Bottom's song of more
homely birds.

118 *ousel* blackbird

120 *throstle* thrush

121 *little quill* small voice

122 *What angel wakes me from my flowery
bed?* If Titania has been curtained off
during her sleep, she must reappear,

probably during the first verse of
Bottom's song.

124 *plainsong* having an unadorned song
(normally a noun; here used adject-
ivally). The allusion is to the
cuckoo's repeated call, with its traditional associations of cuckoldry.

127 *set his wit to* use his intelligence to
answer

133 *thy fair virtue's force* the power of
your excellent qualities

for that. And yet, to say the truth, reason and love keep
little company together nowadays – the more the pity
that some honest neighbours will not make them friends.
– Nay, I can gleek upon occasion.

TITANIA

140 Thou art as wise as thou art beautiful.

BOTTOM Not so neither; but if I had wit enough to get
out of this wood, I have enough to serve mine own turn.

TITANIA

Out of this wood do not desire to go!
Thou shalt remain here, whether thou wilt or no.
I am a spirit of no common rate.
The summer still doth tend upon my state,
And I do love thee. Therefore go with me.
I'll give thee fairies to attend on thee,
And they shall fetch thee jewels from the deep,
150 And sing while thou on pressèd flowers dost sleep;
And I will purge thy mortal grossness so
That thou shalt like an airy spirit go.
Peaseblossom, Cobweb, Moth, and Mustardseed!

Enter the four Fairies

PEASEBLOSSOM Ready!

COBWEB And I!

MOTH And I!

MUSTARDSEED And I!

ALL Where shall we go?

TITANIA

Be kind and courteous to this gentleman.

136–8 *reason and love* ... See Introduction, pages 220–21, 225.
139 *gleek* make a satirical joke
146 *still* continually, always
  doth tend upon (that is, waits upon)
149 *jewels from the deep.* There was a
  belief that precious stones were produced on the sea-bed.
153 *Moth.* This is a normal Elizabethan

spelling of 'mote', which may be
what Shakespeare intended. But the
association with 'Cobweb' may support the traditional spelling with the
modern meaning.
159–69 *Be kind and courteous.* ... The
repeated rhymes add to the lyrical
effect of this speech.

Hop in his walks and gambol in his eyes;   160
Feed him with apricocks and dewberries,
With purple grapes, green figs, and mulberries.
The honey bags steal from the humble bees,
And for night-tapers crop their waxen thighs
And light them at the fiery glow-worms' eyes
To have my love to bed and to arise;
And pluck the wings from painted butterflies
To fan the moonbeams from his sleeping eyes.
Nod to him, elves, and do him courtesies.

PEASEBLOSSOM Hail, mortal!   170

COBWEB Hail!

MOTH Hail!

MUSTARDSEED Hail!

BOTTOM I cry your worships mercy, heartily. I beseech
    your worship's name.

COBWEB Cobweb.

BOTTOM I shall desire you of more acquaintance, good
    Master Cobweb — if I cut my finger I shall make bold
    with you! — Your name, honest gentleman?

PEASEBLOSSOM Peaseblossom.   180

BOTTOM I pray you commend me to Mistress Squash,
    your mother, and to Master Peascod, your father. Good
    Master Peaseblossom, I shall desire you of more acquain-
    tance, too. — Your name, I beseech you, sir?

MUSTARDSEED Mustardseed.

---

161 *apricocks* (an old form of 'apricots',
closer to the word from which it is
derived)
dewberries a kind of blackberry

165 *light them at the fiery glow-worms' eyes.*
Dr Johnson tartly comments: 'I
know not how Shakespeare, who
commonly derived his knowledge of
nature from his own observation,
happened to place the glow-worm's
light in his eyes, which is only in his
tail.' (It is not certain whether Shake-

speare intended *glow-worm's* or *glow-
worms'*.)

174 *cry . . . mercy* beg pardon (for asking
you your names)

178 *cut my finger*. Cobwebs were used to
stop bleeding.

181–2 *Squash* an unripe pea-pod. *Peascod*
is a ripe pea-pod. Compare *Twelfth
Night*, 1.5.148: 'Not yet old enough
for a man, nor young enough for a
boy; as a squash is before 'tis a
peascod'.

BOTTOM Good Master Mustardseed, I know your
patience well. That same cowardly, giantlike Oxbeef
hath devoured many a gentleman of your house. I
promise you, your kindred hath made my eyes water
190   ere now. I desire your more acquaintance, good Master
Mustardseed.

TITANIA

Come, wait upon him. Lead him to my bower.
The moon methinks looks with a watery eye;
And when she weeps, weeps every little flower,
Lamenting some enforcèd chastity.
Tie up my lover's tongue; bring him silently.

Exit Titania with Bottom and the Fairies

III.2   *Enter Oberon, King of Fairies*

OBERON

I wonder if Titania be awaked;
Then what it was that next came in her eye,
Which she must dote on, in extremity.
Here comes my messenger.

Enter Puck

How now, mad spirit?

187–90 *That same cowardly, giantlike
Oxbeef ... Mustard*, of course, is
often eaten with beef. Bottom ad-
mires the patience of Mustardseed's
kin in suffering this. By 'made my
eyes water' he may mean both 'I
have wept in sympathy with them'
and 'they have made my eyes smart'.

193–4 *The moon methinks looks with a
watery eye; | And when she weeps,
weeps every little flower*. There was a
belief that dew originated in the
moon.

195 *enforcèd* violated. (The moon is
Diana, the chaste goddess.)

196 *Tie up my lover's tongue*. This suggests
that Bottom may (as he often does in

performance) be making involuntary
asinine noises.

III.2. Again there is no significant break
between the scenes, in either time or
place. However, this scene begins with a
recapitulatory passage between Puck and
Oberon. The end of III.1 would be an
appropriate place for an interval in
performance.

(stage direction) The Quartos read
'Enter King of Fairies, and Robin
Goodfellow.' The Folio reads 'Enter
King of Pharies solus' at the beginning of the scene, and 'Enter Puck'
after line 3. The Folio is probably
closer to stage practice.

When I did him at this advantage take.
An ass's nole I fixèd on his head.
Anon his Thisbe must be answerèd,
And forth my mimic comes. When they him spy –
As wild geese that the creeping fowler eye,   20
Or russet-pated choughs, many in sort,
Rising and cawing at the gun's report,
Sever themselves and madly sweep the sky –
So at his sight away his fellows fly,
And at our stamp here o'er and o'er one falls.
He 'Murder!' cries, and help from Athens calls.
Their sense thus weak, lost with their fears thus strong,
Made senseless things begin to do them wrong.

5 *night-rule* actions (or possibly 'revels', amusements) of the night.
7 *close* private, secret
9 *patches* fools, clowns
  rude mechanicals rough working men
13 *barren sort* stupid group
15 *scene* stage
17 *nole* noddle, head
19 *mimic* burlesque actor
21 *russet-pated choughs.* The chough is a jackdaw. Its head is grey; but *russet* could mean 'grey' as well as 'red-dish'.

many in sort in a great body, in a flock
25 *our stamp.* Some editors, following Dr Johnson, emend to 'a stump'. Fairies, it is argued, do not stamp; and since Puck is alone, there is no reason why he should use the plural 'our'. But Puck is the most robust of the fairies; and 'our' might well be jocular.
26 *He 'Murder!' cries* one of them makes an outcry

Forsook his scene and entered in a brake
Who Pyramus presented, in their sport
The shallowest thickskin of that barren sort,
Intended for great Theseus' nuptial day.
Were met together to rehearse a play
That work for bread upon Athenian stalls,
A crew of patches, rude mechanicals,
While she was in her dull and sleeping hour,
Near to her close and consecrated bower,
My mistress with a monster is in love.

PUCK
What night-rule now about this haunted grove?

Being o...
And kill me too.
The sun was not so true unto the day
As he to me. Would he have stolen away
From sleeping Hermia? I'll believe as soon

30 *From yielders all things catch* everything preys on the timid
32 *translated* transformed
36 *latched* 'moistened' (a rare sense) or

'fastened'
40 *That* so that
48 *o'er shoes* so far gone

This whole earth may be bored, and that the moon
May through the centre creep, and so displease
Her brother's noontide with the Antipodes.
It cannot be but thou hast murdered him.
So should a murderer look; so dead, so grim.

DEMETRIUS

So should the murdered look, and so should I,
Pierced through the heart with your stern cruelty.
Yet you, the murderer, look as bright, as clear,   60
As yonder Venus in her glimmering sphere.

HERMIA

What's this to my Lysander? Where is he?
Ah, good Demetrius, wilt thou give him me?

DEMETRIUS

I had rather give his carcass to my hounds.

HERMIA

Out, dog! Out, cur! Thou drivest me past the bounds
Of maiden's patience. Hast thou slain him then?
Henceforth be never numbered among men.
O, once tell true – tell true, even for my sake.
Durst thou have looked upon him being awake?
And hast thou killed him sleeping? O, brave touch!   70
Could not a worm, an adder do so much?
An adder did it; for with doubler tongue
Than thine, thou serpent, never adder stung.

53–5 *This whole earth ... Antipodes.*
Whole means 'solid'; *centre*, 'the centre
of the earth'. The moon's brother is
the sun. *The Antipodes* means 'those
who live on the other side of the
earth'. Hermia's notion is that the
moon, creeping through the earth,
will displease (by bringing night with
it) the noontide that the sun is experi-
encing among those who live on the
other side of the world. The conceit
is strained, no doubt for comic effect;
but it has its place among the play's
other images of cosmic disorder,

such as those in Titania's speech,
II.1.81–117.
57 *dead* deadly
61 *sphere* orbit
70–73 *And hast thou killed him sleeping?*
... This recalls Hermia's dream that
she herself was attacked by a serpent
(II.2.151–6).
70 *brave touch!* fine stroke! (ironical)
71 *worm* serpent
72 *doubler* (alluding to the adder's forked
tongue, but also including the meaning 'more deceitful')

DEMETRIUS

You spend your passion on a misprised mood.
I am not guilty of Lysander's blood.
Nor is he dead, for aught that I can tell.

HERMIA

I pray thee, tell me then that he is well.

DEMETRIUS

An if I could, what should I get therefore?

HERMIA

A privilege never to see me more;
80   And from thy hated presence part I so.
See me no more, whether he be dead or no.   *Exit*

DEMETRIUS

There is no following her in this fierce vein.
Here therefore for a while I will remain.
So sorrow's heaviness doth heavier grow
For debt that bankrupt sleep doth sorrow owe,
Which now in some slight measure it will pay,
If for his tender here I make some stay.

                He lies down and sleeps

OBERON

What hast thou done? Thou hast mistaken quite,
And laid the love juice on some true love's sight.
90   Of thy misprision must perforce ensue
Some true love turned, and not a false turned true.

PUCK

Then fate o'errules, that, one man holding truth,

---

74 *spend* 'give vent to' or 'waste'
misprised mood. Mood could mean
'anger'. *Misprised* means 'misunder-
stood'. The phrase probably means
'anger based on a misunderstanding'.
78 *An if* even if
therefore for that
81 *whether.* This word seems often to
have been spoken as one syllable —
'whe'er'.

84 *heaviness . . . heavier* (playing on *heavy*
as 'sad, heavy-spirited' and 'drowsy')
85 *For debt that bankrupt sleep doth sorrow
owe* (that is, as a result of the sleeples-
ness caused by sorrow)
87 *tender* offer
make some stay wait awhile
90 *misprision* misunderstanding, mistake
92–3 *Then fate o'errules, that, one man hold-
ing truth,* | *A million fail, confound-*

A million fail, confounding oath on oath.

OBERON

About the wood go swifter than the wind,
And Helena of Athens look thou find.
All fancy-sick she is and pale of cheer
With sighs of love, that costs the fresh blood dear.
By some illusion see thou bring her here.
I'll charm his eyes against she do appear.

PUCK

I go, I go – look how I go –   100
Swifter than arrow from the Tartar's bow.   *Exit*

OBERON

Flower of this purple dye,
Hit with Cupid's archery,
Sink in apple of his eye.

He squeezes the flower on Demetrius's eyes

When his love he doth espy,
Let her shine as gloriously
As the Venus of the sky.
When thou wakest, if she be by,
Beg of her for remedy.

Enter Puck

PUCK

Captain of our fairy band,   110
Helena is here at hand,
And the youth mistook by me,
Pleading for a lover's fee.

---

ing oath on oath. Perhaps: 'If so, fate has taken a hand, since for one man who is true in love there are a million who fail, breaking oath after oath.'

95 *look* be sure to
96 *fancy-sick* love-sick
   cheer face, look
97 *sighs of love, that costs the fresh blood dear.* It was believed that a sigh caused

the loss of a drop of blood.
99 *against* ready for when
101 *Tartar.* The Oriental bow was of special power. The image may have come to Shakespeare by way of Golding's translation of Ovid's *Metamorphoses*, x.686–7, 'she | Did fly as swift as arrow from a Turkey bow'.
104 *apple* pupil
113 *fee* 'payment' or 'perquisite'

Shall we their fond pageant see?
Lord, what fools these mortals be!

OBERON

Stand aside. The noise they make
Will cause Demetrius to awake.

PUCK

Then will two at once woo one –
That must needs be sport alone;
120 And those things do best please me
That befall preposterously.

Enter Lysander and Helena

LYSANDER

Why should you think that I should woo in scorn?
Scorn and derision never come in tears.
Look when I vow, I weep; and vows so born,
In their nativity all truth appears.
How can these things in me seem scorn to you,
Bearing the badge of faith to prove them true?

HELENA

You do advance your cunning more and more.
When truth kills truth, O devilish-holy fray!
130 These vows are Hermia's. Will you give her o'er?
Weigh oath with oath, and you will nothing weigh.
Your vows to her and me, put in two scales,
Will even weigh, and both as light as tales.

LYSANDER

I had no judgement when to her I swore.

---

114 *fond pageant* foolish spectacle
119 *alone* (probably means 'unique', 'un-equalled' rather than 'in itself')
124 *Look when* whenever (a common Elizabethan use)
124–5 *and vows so born,* | In their nativity all truth appears vows being born so (that is, in tears) are certain to be true
127 *badge of faith* (that is, tears)

129 *When truth kills truth.* The 'truth' that Lysander now tells Helena destroys the 'truth' that he formerly told Hermia. The truths conflict to cause a fray that is 'holy' because between truths, but 'devilish' because the truths are incompatible.
131 *nothing weigh* arrive at no weight (because the scales will be equally balanced)

HELENA

Nor none in my mind now you give her o'er.

LYSANDER

Demetrius loves her, and he loves not you.

DEMETRIUS (*wakes*)

O Helen, goddess, nymph, perfect, divine –
To what, my love, shall I compare thine eyne?
Crystal is muddy! O, how ripe in show
Thy lips – those kissing cherries – tempting grow!   140
That pure congealed white, high Taurus' snow,
Fanned with the eastern wind, turns to a crow
When thou holdest up thy hand. O, let me kiss
This princess of pure white, this seal of bliss!

HELENA

O spite! O hell! I see you all are bent
To set against me for your merriment.
If you were civil and knew courtesy
You would not do me thus much injury.
Can you not hate me – as I know you do –
But you must join in souls to mock me too?   150
If you were men – as men you are in show –
You would not use a gentle lady so,
To vow, and swear, and superpraise my parts,
When, I am sure, you hate me with your hearts.
You both are rivals, and love Hermia;
And now both rivals to mock Helena.
A trim exploit, a manly enterprise –
To conjure tears up in a poor maid's eyes
With your derision. None of noble sort
Would so offend a virgin, and extort   160

---

136 *loves not you*. The interruption of the
   rhyme scheme is appropriate to the
   sudden change in situation.
141 *Taurus* a range of mountains in
   Turkey
144 *princess* paragon
   seal pledge

152 *gentle* perhaps 'noble' rather than (or
   as well as) 'kind' or 'mild'
153 *parts* qualities
157 *trim* fine (ironical)
159 *sort* 'quality' or 'rank'
160 *extort* torture

A poor soul's patience, all to make you sport.

LYSANDER

You are unkind, Demetrius. Be not so,
For you love Hermia – this you know I know.
And hear: with all good will, with all my heart,
In Hermia's love I yield you up my part.
And yours of Helena to me bequeath,
Whom I do love, and will do to my death.

HELENA

Never did mockers waste more idle breath.

DEMETRIUS

Lysander, keep thy Hermia. I will none.

170   If e'er I loved her all that love is gone.
My heart to her but as guestwise sojourned,
And now to Helen is it home returned,
There to remain.

LYSANDER   Helen, it is not so.

DEMETRIUS

Disparage not the faith thou dost not know,
Lest to thy peril thou aby it dear.
Look where thy love comes: yonder is thy dear.

        Enter Hermia

HERMIA

Dark night that from the eye his function takes
The ear more quick of apprehension makes.
Wherein it doth impair the seeing sense

180   It pays the hearing double recompense.
Thou art not by mine eye, Lysander, found;
Mine ear – I thank it – brought me to thy sound.
But why unkindly didst thou leave me so?

LYSANDER

Why should he stay whom love doth press to go?

HERMIA

What love could press Lysander from my side?

169 *I will none* I want nothing to do   175 *aby* pay the penalty for, atone for
with her   177 *his* its

LYSANDER

Lysander's love, that would not let him bide:
Fair Helena, who more engilds the night
Than all yon fiery oes and eyes of light,
Why seekest thou me? Could not this make tnee know
The hate I bare thee made me leave thee so?   190

HERMIA

You speak not as you think. It cannot be.

HELENA

Lo, she is one of this confederacy.
Now I perceive they have conjoined all three
To fashion this false sport in spite of me.
Injurious Hermia, most ungrateful maid,
Have you conspired, have you with these contrived
To bait me with this foul derision?
Is all the counsel that we two have shared –
The sisters' vows, the hours that we have spent
When we have chid the hasty-footed time   200
For parting us – O, is all forgot?
All schooldays' friendship, childhood innocence?
We, Hermia, like two artificial gods
Have with our needles created both one flower,
Both on one sampler, sitting on one cushion,
Both warbling of one song, both in one key,
As if our hands, our sides, voices, and minds
Had been incorporate. So we grew together
Like to a double cherry, seeming parted
But yet an union in partition,   210

---

188 *oes and eyes* stars (punningly). An 'o'
seems to have been a silver spangle.
194 *in spite of me* to spite me
197 *bait* torment
203 *artificial* artistically skilful (and, like
gods, 'creating')
204 *needles*. Needle was often pronounced
as a monosyllable – 'neele'.
206 *both in one key*. That two singers of

one song should be in the same musical key is so obviously desirable that
this phrase sometimes causes laughter. But the phrase 'voices and minds'
in the following line shows that for
Shakespeare the 'song' and the 'key'
were distinct and that *in one key* means
'in mental accord'.
208 *incorporate* of one body

Two lovely berries moulded on one stem,
So with two seeming bodies but one heart,
Two of the first, like coats in heraldry,
Due but to one, and crowned with one crest.
And will you rent our ancient love asunder,
To join with men in scorning your poor friend?
It is not friendly, 'tis not maidenly.
Our sex as well as I may chide you for it,
Though I alone do feel the injury.

HERMIA

220   I am amazèd at your passionate words.
I scorn you not; it seems that you scorn me.

HELENA

Have you not set Lysander, as in scorn,
To follow me and praise my eyes and face?
And made your other love, Demetrius –
Who even but now did spurn me with his foot –
To call me goddess, nymph, divine and rare,
Precious, celestial? Wherefore speaks he this
To her he hates? And wherefore doth Lysander
Deny your love, so rich within his soul,
230   And tender me forsooth affection,
But by your setting on, by your consent?
What though I be not so in grace as you,
So hung upon with love, so fortunate,
But miserable most, to love unloved:
This you should pity rather than despise.

HERMIA

I understand not what you mean by this.

213 *Two of the first* (that is, bodies). *First* is a heraldic term, referring back to the divisions of a shield which have already been described. In the shield that Helena is imagining, the same quartering appears more than once, but the whole is 'crowned with one

crest' because it belongs to one person.
215 *rent* rend, tear
225 *spurn me with his foot*. Helena had invited Demetrius to spurn her (II.1.205).

HELENA

    Ay, do! Persever, counterfeit sad looks,
    Make mouths upon me when I turn my back,
    Wink each at other, hold the sweet jest up.
    This sport well carried shall be chronicled.   240
    If you have any pity, grace, or manners,
    You would not make me such an argument.
    But fare ye well. 'Tis partly my own fault,
    Which death or absence soon shall remedy.

LYSANDER

    Stay, gentle Helena, hear my excuse,
    My love, my life, my soul, fair Helena!

HELENA

    O, excellent!

HERMIA (*to Lysander*)
                  Sweet, do not scorn her so

DEMETRIUS

    If she cannot entreat, I can compel.

LYSANDER

    Thou canst compel no more than she entreat.
    Thy threats have no more strength than her weak   250
        prayers.
    Helen, I love thee. By my life, I do.
    I swear by that which I will lose for thee
    To prove him false that says I love thee not.

DEMETRIUS

    I say I love thee more than he can do.

LYSANDER

    If thou say so, withdraw, and prove it too.

237 *Persever* (a form of 'persevere', which in Shakespeare always has the stress on the second syllable)
239 *hold the sweet jest up* keep up the joke
242 *argument* subject of joking
244 *Which death or absence soon shall remedy.* The exaggerated threat helps to preserve the comic tone.
247 *Sweet, do not scorn her so.* Hermia still does not realize that Lysander is in earnest.
255 *withdraw, and prove it too* (that is, 'let us go and decide the matter by duelling')

DEMETRIUS

Quick, come.

HERMIA   Lysander, whereto tends all this?

LYSANDER

Away, you Ethiope!

DEMETRIUS   No, no. He'll

Seem to break loose, take on as he would follow,

But yet come not. (*To Lysander*) You are a tame man, go.

LYSANDER

260   Hang off, thou cat, thou burr! Vile thing, let loose,

Or I will shake thee from me like a serpent.

HERMIA

Why are you grown so rude? What change is this,

Sweet love?

LYSANDER Thy love? – out, tawny Tartar, out;

Out, loathèd medicine! O hated potion, hence!

HERMIA

Do you not jest?

HELENA   Yes, sooth, and so do you.

LYSANDER

Demetrius, I will keep my word with thee.

DEMETRIUS

I would I had your bond; for I perceive

A weak bond holds you. I'll not trust your word.

257 *Ethiope* (used insultingly – Hermia is evidently of dark complexion; compare line 263)

257–8 *No, no. He'll | Seem to break loose, take on as he would follow*. This passage is textually corrupt. The present reading assumes that Demetrius scornfully says that Lysander will seem to break from Hermia's protectively restraining clutches as if to follow Demetrius to fight with him, but in fact will not turn up.

258 *take on as* make a fuss as if (or 'act as if')

263 *tawny Tartar* (another exaggerated reference to Hermia's dark colouring)

264 *medicine* any sort of drug, including poison

potion (also could be used of poison; Q2 and F read 'poison')

267,268 *bond* both 'pledge' and 'tie' (here, Hermia, who is holding Lysander) ·

LYSANDER

What? Should I hurt her, strike her, kill her dead?
Although I hate her, I'll not harm her so.   270

HERMIA

What? Can you do me greater harm than hate?
Hate me? Wherefore? O me, what news, my love?
Am not I Hermia? Are not you Lysander?
I am as fair now as I was erewhile.
Since night you loved me; yet since night you left me.
Why then, you left me – O, the gods forbid! –
In earnest, shall I say?

LYSANDER   Ay, by my life;

And never did desire to see thee more.
Therefore be out of hope, of question, of doubt,
Be certain. Nothing truer – 'tis no jest   280
That I do hate thee and love Helena.

HERMIA

O me, you juggler, you canker-blossom,
You thief of love! What, have you come by night
And stolen my love's heart from him?

HELENA   Fine, i'faith.

Have you no modesty, no maiden shame,
No touch of bashfulness? What, will you tear
Impatient answers from my gentle tongue?
Fie, fie, you counterfeit, you puppet, you!

HERMIA

Puppet? Why so? – Ay, that way goes the game.
Now I perceive that she hath made compare   290
Between our statures. She hath urged her height,
And with her personage, her tall personage,

---

282 *canker-blossom* worm that cankers the
blossom (of love); or, perhaps, 'wild-
rose'

284 *Fine, i'faith* ... Helena still thinks
that Hermia is joining in the men's
derision of her.

Her height, forsooth, she hath prevailed with him.
And are you grown so high in his esteem
Because I am so dwarfish and so low?
How low am I, thou painted maypole? Speak!
How low am I? – I am not yet so low
But that my nails can reach unto thine eyes.

HELENA

I pray you, though you mock me, gentlemen,
300   Let her not hurt me. I was never curst.
I have no gift at all in shrewishness.
I am a right maid for my cowardice!
Let her not strike me. You perhaps may think
Because she is something lower than myself
That I can match her . . .

HERMIA   Lower? Hark, again!

HELENA

Good Hermia, do not be so bitter with me.
I evermore did love you, Hermia;
Did ever keep your counsels, never wronged you,
Save that in love unto Demetrius
310   I told him of your stealth unto this wood.
He followed you. For love I followed him.
But he hath chid me hence, and threatened me
To strike me, spurn me – nay, to kill me too.
And now, so you will let me quiet go,
To Athens will I bear my folly back
And follow you no further. Let me go.
You see how simple and how fond I am.

HERMIA

Why, get you gone! Who is't that hinders you?

HELENA

A foolish heart that I leave here behind.

300 *curst* shrewish, quarrelsome   314 *so* provided that
310 *stealth* stealing away, secret journey

HERMIA

   What, with Lysander? 320

HELENA   With Demetrius.

LYSANDER

   Be not afraid; she shall not harm thee, Helena.

DEMETRIUS

   No, sir. She shall not, though you take her part.

HELENA

   O, when she is angry she is keen and shrewd.

   She was a vixen when she went to school,

   And though she be but little, she is fierce.

HERMIA

   Little again? Nothing but low and little?

   Why will you suffer her to flout me thus?

   Let me come to her.

LYSANDER   Get you gone, you dwarf,

   You minimus of hindering knot-grass made,

   You bead, you acorn. 330

DEMETRIUS   You are too officious

   In her behalf that scorns your services.

   Let her alone. Speak not of Helena,

   Take not her part; for if thou dost intend

   Never so little show of love to her,

   Thou shalt aby it.

LYSANDER   Now she holds me not.

   Now follow – if thou darest – to try whose right   ·

   Of thine or mine is most in Helena.

DEMETRIUS

   Follow? Nay, I'll go with thee, cheek by jowl.

                  Exeunt Demetrius and Lysander

323 *keen* bitter, severe
    shrewd shrewish
329 *minimus* tiny creature
    knot-grass a common, low-creeping

weed. The juice of it was said to
stunt growth.
335 *aby* pay for

HERMIA

You, mistress – all this coil is 'long of you.

340   Nay – go not back.

HELENA   I will not trust you, I,

Nor longer stay in your curst company.

Your hands than mine are quicker for a fray.

My legs are longer, though, to run away!   *Exit*

HERMIA

I am amazed, and know not what to say!   *Exit*

Oberon and Puck come forward

OBERON

This is thy negligence. Still thou mistakest,

Or else committest thy knaveries wilfully.

PUCK

Believe me, King of shadows, I mistook.

Did not you tell me I should know the man

By the Athenian garments he had on?

350   And so far blameless proves my enterprise

That I have 'nointed an Athenian's eyes.

And so far am I glad it so did sort,

As this their jangling I esteem a sport.

OBERON

Thou seest these lovers seek a place to fight.

Hie therefore, Robin, overcast the night.

The starry welkin cover thou anon

With drooping fog as black as Acheron,

And lead these testy rivals so astray

---

339 *coil* trouble, bother
     'long of caused by, on account of
345 *This is thy negligence* ... The change
     into blank verse marks the change in
     speakers and tone, but the rhymed
     verse resumes at line 350.
     Still always, continually
350 *so far* at least to this extent
352 *sort* fall out
353 *As* in that

354–95 *Thou seest these lovers seek a place
        to fight* ... This conversation be-
        tween Oberon and Puck is a
        turning-point in the action of the
        play.
355 *Hie* go
356 *welkin* sky
357 *Acheron* a river of hell, traditionally
     black. In *Macbeth* (III.5.15) Shake-
     speare refers to 'the pit of Acheron'.

As one come not within another's way.
Like to Lysander sometime frame thy tongue,   360
Then stir Demetrius up with bitter wrong,
And sometime rail thou like Demetrius;
And from each other look thou lead them thus
Till o'er their brows death-counterfeiting sleep
With leaden legs and batty wings doth creep.
Then crush this herb into Lysander's eye –
Whose liquor hath this virtuous property,
To take from thence all error with his might,
And make his eyeballs roll with wonted sight.
When they next wake, all this derision   370
Shall seem a dream and fruitless vision,
And back to Athens shall the lovers wend
With league whose date till death shall never end.
Whiles I in this affair do thee employ
I'll to my Queen and beg her Indian boy,
And then I will her charmèd eye release
From monster's view, and all things shall be peace.

PUCK

My fairy lord, this must be done with haste,
For night's swift dragons cut the clouds full fast,
And yonder shines Aurora's harbinger,   380
At whose approach ghosts wandering here and there
Troop home to churchyards. Damnèd spirits all
That in crossways and floods have burial

---

359 *As* that
361 *wrong* insult
365 *batty* bat-like
367 *virtuous* potent
368 *his* its
370–71 *all this derision | Shall seem a dream and fruitless vision.* In the epilogue Puck suggests that the play may have the same effect on its audience.
373 *date* term, duration
376 *charmèd* bewitched

380 *Aurora's harbinger* the herald of the dawn; the morning star
382 *Damnèd spirits* the ghosts of the damned
383 *in crossways and floods have burial.* Suicides were buried at crossroads. *Floods* may refer to those who have killed themselves by drowning, or to those who were accidentally drowned and whose souls, according to ancient belief, could not rest

Already to their wormy beds are gone.
For fear lest day should look their shames upon
They wilfully themselves exile from light,
And must for aye consort with black-browed night.

OBERON
But we are spirits of another sort.
I with the morning's love have oft made sport
390   And like a forester the groves may tread
Even till the eastern gate all fiery red
Opening on Neptune with fair blessèd beams
Turns into yellow gold his salt green streams.
But notwithstanding, haste, make no delay;
We may effect this business yet ere day.   *Exit*

PUCK
Up and down, up and down,
I will lead them up and down.
I am feared in field and town.
Goblin, lead them up and down.
400   Here comes one
Enter Lysander

LYSANDER
Where art thou, proud Demetrius? Speak thou now.
PUCK (*in Demetrius's voice*)
Here, villain, drawn and ready! Where art thou?
LYSANDER
I will be with thee straight.

because no burial rites had been performed.

389 *I with the morning's love have oft made sport.* Some believe Oberon to say that he has often hunted with Cephalus, Aurora's (the dawn's) lover. More probably he is claiming that he has often dallied with Aurora herself. He is pointing out that he can stay up later than the other sort of spirits.

399 *Goblin* hobgoblin (that is, Puck himself)

400 *Here comes one.* In modern performances, artificial smoke is sometimes used to suggest the fog that Oberon has instructed Puck to cause (lines 355–7). But the scene can be equally effective if this is left to the audience's imagination.

402 *drawn* with drawn sword

PUCK (*in Demetrius's voice*)   Follow me then
    To plainer ground.   *Exit Lysander*
        Enter Demetrius
DEMETRIUS   Lysander, speak again.
    Thou runaway, thou coward – art thou fled?
    Speak. In some bush? Where dost thou hide thy head?
PUCK (*in Lysander's voice*)
    Thou coward, art thou bragging to the stars,
    Telling the bushes that thou lookest for wars,
    And wilt not come? Come, recreant. Come, thou child,
    I'll whip thee with a rod. He is defiled   410
    That draws a sword on thee.
DEMETRIUS   Yea, art thou there?
PUCK (*in Lysander's voice*)
    Follow my voice. We'll try no manhood here.
                        Exeunt Puck and Demetrius
        Enter Lysander
LYSANDER
    He goes before me, and still dares me on;
    When I come where he calls, then he is gone.
    The villain is much lighter-heeled than I.
    I followed fast, but faster he did fly,
    That fallen am I in dark uneven way,
    And here will rest me. (*He lies down*) Come, thou gentle
        day,
    For if but once thou show me thy grey light
    I'll find Demetrius and revenge this spite.   420
        He sleeps
        Enter Puck and Demetrius
PUCK (*in Lysander's voice*)
    Ho, ho, ho, coward! Why comest thou not?
DEMETRIUS
    Abide me if thou darest, for well I wot

404 *plainer* smoother, more level
417 *That* with the result that
421 *Ho, ho, ho.* This was Puck's tradi-

tional cry.
422 *Abide* wait for
    wot know

Thou runnest before me, shifting every place,
And darest not stand nor look me in the face.
Where art thou now?

PUCK (*in Lysander's voice*)
                        Come hither; I am here.

DEMETRIUS
Nay, then thou mockest me. Thou shalt buy this dear
If ever I thy face by daylight see.
Now, go thy way. Faintness constraineth me
To measure out my length on this cold bed.

430   By day's approach look to be visited.
              He lies down and sleeps
              Enter Helena

HELENA
O weary night! O long and tedious night,
    Abate thy hours, shine comforts from the East,
That I may back to Athens by daylight
    From these that my poor company detest.
And sleep, that sometimes shuts up sorrow's eye,
Steal me awhile from mine own company.
              She lies down and sleeps

PUCK
              Yet but three? Come one more,
              Two of both kinds makes up four.
              Here she comes, curst and sad.

440   Cupid is a knavish lad
              Thus to make poor females mad.
              Enter Hermia

HERMIA
Never so weary, never so in woe,
    Bedabbled with the dew, and torn with briars –
I can no further crawl, no further go.
    My legs can keep no pace with my desires.
Here will I rest me till the break of day.
Heavens shield Lysander, if they mean a fray.

426 *buy this dear* pay dearly for this   439 *curst* cross

She lies down and sleeps

PUCK

    On the ground
    Sleep sound.
    I'll apply   450
    To your eye,
  Gentle lover, remedy.

  He squeezes the juice on Lysander's eyes
    When thou wakest,
    Thou takest
    True delight
    In the sight
  Of thy former lady's eye.
  And the country proverb known,
  That every man should take his own,
  In your waking shall be shown.   460
      Jack shall have Jill;
      Naught shall go ill.
  The man shall have his mare again, and all shall be well.

                Exit

Enter Titania, and Bottom, and Fairies; and Oberon IV.I
behind them

TITANIA

  Come, sit thee down upon this flowery bed

---

461 *Jack shall have Jill* (a proverb, meaning 'the man shall have his girl')
463 *The man shall have his mare again* (another proverb, meaning 'all will be well')

IV.1 At the end of the previous scene F has the stage direction *They sleepe all the Act.* This seems to imply that in performance there was some sort of a break during which the lovers remained on stage. It is unlikely that Shakespeare intended any break here. The lovers sleep on stage during the scene between Bottom and the fairies, unremarked by them.

In this scene Shakespeare mingles verse for Titania and prose for Bottom.
1 *flowery bed.* It is possible that this would have been represented by a piece of stage-furniture on Shakespeare's stage.

While I thy amiable cheeks do coy,
And stick muskroses in thy sleek, smooth head,
And kiss thy fair large ears, my gentle joy.

BOTTOM Where's Peaseblossom?

PEASEBLOSSOM Ready.

BOTTOM Scratch my head, Peaseblossom. Where's
Monsieur Cobweb?

COBWEB Ready.

BOTTOM Monsieur Cobweb, good Monsieur, get you your
weapons in your hand and kill me a red-hipped humble
bee on the top of a thistle; and, good Monsieur, bring
me the honey bag. Do not fret yourself too much in the
action, Monsieur; and, good Monsieur, have a care the
honey bag break not, I would be loath to have you over-
flown with a honey bag, signor. Where's Monsieur
Mustardseed?

MUSTARDSEED Ready.

BOTTOM Give me your neaf, Monsieur Mustardseed.
Pray you, leave your courtesy, good Monsieur.

MUSTARDSEED What's your will?

BOTTOM Nothing, good Monsieur, but to help Cavalery
Cobweb to scratch. I must to the barber's, Monsieur,
for methinks I am marvellous hairy about the face. And
I am such a tender ass, if my hair do but tickle me, I
must scratch.

TITANIA
What, wilt thou hear some music, my sweet love?

BOTTOM I have a reasonable good ear in music. Let's have
the tongs and the bones.

---

2 *coy* caress
19 *neaf* fist
20 *leave your courtesy* either 'stop bowing'
or 'put on your hat' (if the fairies
wear hats)
22 *Cavalery* Cavalier (perhaps in imitation of the Italian form, *cavaliere*)

23 *Cobweb.* In fact it is Peaseblossom
who has been told to scratch (line 7).
Presumably this is a mistake of Shakespeare's. The alliteration seems
intentional.
29 *tongs and the bones.* These were elementary musical instruments. The tongs

TITANIA

Or say, sweet love, what thou desirest to eat.   30

BOTTOM   Truly, a peck of provender. I could munch your
good dry oats. Methinks I have a great desire to a bottle
of hay. Good hay, sweet hay hath no fellow.

TITANIA

I have a venturous fairy that shall seek
The squirrel's hoard, and fetch thee new nuts.

BOTTOM   I had rather have a handful or two of dried pease.
But, I pray you, let none of your people stir me. I have
an exposition of sleep come upon me.

TITANIA

Sleep thou, and I will wind thee in my arms.
Fairies be gone, and be all ways away.   *Exeunt Fairies*   40
So doth the woodbine the sweet honeysuckle
Gently entwist; the female ivy so

---

were struck by a piece of metal. The
bones were two flat pieces of bone
held between the fingers and rattled
against each other, as by Negro
minstrels.

Here F has a stage direction, *Musicke Tongs, Rurall Musicke*. Music is
not demanded by the line, but there
may have been some sort of musical
comic business at this point.
Granville-Barker comments: 'The
run of the text here almost forbids
any such interruption. The only
likely occasion for it is when Peaseblossom and company have been dismissed. There would be a pleasing,
fantastic irony in little Titania and
her monster being lulled to sleep by
the distant sound of the tongs and
the bones; it would make a properly
dramatic contrast to the "still music"
for which she calls a moment later,
her hand in Oberon's again. A producer might, without offence, ven-

ture on the effect. (But Oberon, by
the way, had better stop the noise
with a disgusted gesture before he
begins to speak.)'

32 *bottle* small bundle

35 *thee new nuts*. Some editors make an
addition (for example, 'thee thence
. . .') to improve the metre. But as it
stands the line gives most effective
stress to 'new nuts', as a special
treat.

36 *pease*. In Shakespeare's time this was
both the singular and the plural
form. It both means and sounds the
same as 'peas'.

38 *exposition*. He means 'disposition',
that is, inclination.

40 *all ways* in all directions

41–2 *So doth the woodbine the sweet honey-
suckle | Gently entwist*. This has caused
difficulty. *Woodbine* can mean 'honeysuckle' (II.1.251, and *Much Ado
About Nothing*, III.1.30). Here it
seems to mean 'bindweed', or 'con-

Enrings the barky fingers of the elm.
O, how I love thee! How I dote on thee!
They sleep. Enter Puck

OBERON *(comes forward)*

Welcome, good Robin. Seest thou this sweet sight?
Her dotage now I do begin to pity.
For, meeting her of late behind the wood
Seeking sweet favours for this hateful fool,
I did upbraid her and fall out with her,
50 For she his hairy temples then had rounded
With coronet of fresh and fragrant flowers.
And that same dew which sometime on the buds
Was wont to swell, like round and orient pearls,
Stood now within the pretty flowerets' eyes
Like tears that did their own disgrace bewail.
When I had at my pleasure taunted her,
And she in mild terms begged my patience,
I then did ask of her her changeling child,
Which straight she gave me, and her fairy sent
60 To bear him to my bower in Fairyland.
And now I have the boy I will undo
This hateful imperfection of her eyes.
And, gentle Puck, take this transformèd scalp
From off the head of this Athenian swain,
That, he awaking when the other do,
May all to Athens back again repair
And think no more of this night's accidents
But as the fierce vexation of a dream.

---

volvulus'. 'The honeysuckle ... always twines in a left-handed helix. The bindweed family ... always twines in a right-handed helix ... The mixed-up violent left-right embrace of the bindweed and honeysuckle ... has long fascinated English poets' (Martin Gardner, *The Am-* *bidextrous Universe*, 1964; Pelican edition, 1970, page 62).

48 *favours* flowers as love-tokens
53 *orient* lustrous
65 *other* others (a common Elizabethanism)
66 *May all* all may
68 *fierce* wild, extravagant

But first I will release the Fairy Queen.

    (to Titania)

    Be as thou wast wont to be;   70

    See as thou wast wont to see.

    Dian's bud o'er Cupid's flower

    Hath such force and blessèd power.

Now, my Titania, wake you, my sweet Queen!

TITANIA *(wakes)*

My Oberon, what visions have I seen!

Methought I was enamoured of an ass.

OBERON

There lies your love.

TITANIA   How came these things to pass?

O, how mine eyes do loathe his visage now!

OBERON

Silence awhile! Robin, take off this head.

Titania, music call, and strike more dead   80

Than common sleep of all these five the sense.

TITANIA

Music, ho! Music such as charmeth sleep.

PUCK *(to Bottom, removing the ass's head)*

Now when thou wakest with thine own fool's eyes peep.

OBERON

Sound, music! *(Music)* Come, my Queen, take hands
    with me,

And rock the ground whereon these sleepers be.

    They dance

---

72 *Dian's bud* (the herb of II.1.184 and III.2.366). There was a herb associated with Diana, the goddess of chastity, and supposed to have the power of preserving chastity, called *agnus castus*.

Cupid's flower (the 'little western flower' of II.1.166 and the stage direction at II.2.32)

79 *Silence awhile!* Presumably Oberon is simply urging his companions not to disturb the sleeping lovers and Bottom.

81 *these five* (the lovers and Bottom)

82 *charmeth* produces as by a charm

85 (stage direction) *They dance.* The dance is not merely an added entertainment. Giving symbolical expression of the reunion of the Fairy King and Queen, it marks a turning-point in the play's action.

> Now thou and I are new in amity,
> And will tomorrow midnight solemnly
> Dance in Duke Theseus' house triumphantly,
> And bless it to all fair prosperity.
90 There shall the pairs of faithful lovers be
> Wedded with Theseus all in jollity.

PUCK
> Fairy king, attend, and mark:
> I do hear the morning lark.

OBERON
> Then, my queen, in silence sad,
> Trip we after night's shade.
> We the globe can compass soon,
> Swifter than the wandering moon.

TITANIA
> Come, my lord, and in our flight
> Tell me how it came this night
100 That I sleeping here was found
> With these mortals on the ground.

> *Exeunt Oberon, Titania, and Puck*
> *Horns sound. Enter Theseus with Hippolyta, Egeus,*
> *and all his train*

THESEUS
> Go, one of you; find out the forester;
> For now our observation is performed.
> And since we have the vaward of the day,

89 *prosperity.* Q2 and F, followed by some editors, read 'posterity'. At II.I.73 we have 'To give their bed joy and prosperity'.
94 *sad* sober, grave
96–7 *We the globe can compass soon,* | *Swifter than the wandering moon.* Compare Puck's claim to 'put a girdle round about the earth | In forty minutes' (II.I.175–6).

101 (stage direction) *Horns.* The horn was a signalling instrument, not used for music.
103 *observation* an 'observance to a morn of May' such as that mentioned at I.I.167
104 *since we have the vaward of the day* since it is still early.
> *Vaward* means 'forepart', 'vanguard'.

My love shall hear the music of my hounds.
Uncouple in the western valley; let them go.
Dispatch, I say, and find the forester. *Exit an Attendant*
We will, fair Queen, up to the mountain's top,
And mark the musical confusion
Of hounds and echo in conjunction   110

HIPPOLYTA

I was with Hercules and Cadmus once,
When in a wood of Crete they bayed the bear
With hounds of Sparta. Never did I hear
Such gallant chiding, for besides the groves,
The skies, the fountains, every region near
Seemed all one mutual cry. I never heard
So musical a discord, such sweet thunder.

THESEUS

My hounds are bred out of the Spartan kind;
So flewed, so sanded; and their heads are hung
With ears that sweep away the morning dew;   120
Crook-kneed; and dewlapped like Thessalian bulls;
Slow in pursuit, but matched in mouth like bells,

---

106 *Uncouple* release the dogs (chained
together in couples)

111–13 *I was with Hercules and Cadmus
once, | When in a wood of Crete they
bayed the bear | With hounds of Sparta.*
There seems to be no basis in legends
for this statement, which presumably
is local colouring.

112–13 *Crete ... Sparta.* The hounds of
both countries were famous, as
Shakespeare could have known from
Golding's translation of Ovid's *Metamorphoses* (III.247):

> *This latter was a hound of Crete, the
> other was of Spart.*

112 *bayed* brought to bay

114 *chiding* barking

117 *musical ... discord ... sweet thunder.*
Theseus's acceptance of the yoking
of opposites here anticipates v.1.60:

> *How shall we find the concord of this
> discord?*

119 *flewed* having flews, that is, the large
chaps of a deep-mouthed hound
sanded of sandy colour

122–3 *matched in mouth like bells, | Each
under each.* The notion is illustrated
by a passage from Gervase Markham's *Country Contentments* (1615):

> *If you would have your kennel for sweetness
> of cry, then you must compound it of some*

Each under each. A cry more tuneable
Was never hallooed to nor cheered with horn
In Crete, in Sparta, nor in Thessaly.
Judge when you hear.
> *He sees the sleepers*
>   But soft, what nymphs are these?

EGEUS

My lord, this is my daughter here asleep,
And this Lysander; this Demetrius is,
This Helena – old Nedar's Helena.
130   I wonder of their being here together.

THESEUS

No doubt they rose up early to observe
The rite of May, and hearing our intent
Came here in grace of our solemnity.
But speak, Egeus: is not this the day
That Hermia should give answer of her choice?

EGEUS It is, my lord.

THESEUS

Go, bid the huntsmen wake them with their horns.
> *Horns sound; the lovers wake; shout within; the lovers*
> *start up*

Good morrow, friends – Saint Valentine is past!
Begin these woodbirds but to couple now?

---

*large dogs, that have deep, solemn mouths
and are swift in spending, which must (as
it were) bear the bass in the consort; then
a double number of roaring and loud ring-
ing mouths, which must bear the counter-
tenor; then some hollow, plain, sweet
mouths, which must bear the mean or
middle part; and so with these three parts
of music you shall make your cry perfect.*

It is unlikely that any pack reached
Markham's ideal.

123 *cry* pack of hounds
126 *soft* 'stop' rather than 'hush'
134–5 *is not this the day | That Hermia
should give answer of her choice?* Theseus
had given Hermia till 'the next new
moon' to make up her mind. See
1.1.83–90.
138–9 *Saint Valentine is past! | Begin
these woodbirds but to couple now?*
It was said that birds chose their
mates on Saint Valentine's Day (14
February).

LYSANDER

Pardon, my lord.

THESEUS   I pray you all, stand up.   140

I know you two are rival enemies.

How comes this gentle concord in the world,

That hatred is so far from jealousy

To sleep by hate, and fear no enmity?

LYSANDER

My lord, I shall reply amazedly,

Half sleep, half waking. But as yet, I swear,

I cannot truly say how I came here.

But as I think – for truly would I speak –

And now I do bethink me, so it is:

I came with Hermia hither. Our intent   150

Was to be gone from Athens where we might

Without the peril of the Athenian law . . .

EGEUS

Enough, enough – my lord, you have enough!

I beg the law, the law upon his head.

They would have stolen away, they would, Demetrius,

Thereby to have defeated you and me –

You of your wife, and me of my consent –

Of my consent that she should be your wife.

DEMETRIUS

My lord, fair Helen told me of their stealth,

Of this their purpose hither to this wood,   160

And I in fury hither followed them,

Fair Helena in fancy following me.

But, my good lord – I wot not by what power,

But by some power it is – my love to Hermia,

Melted as the snow, seems to me now

As the remembrance of an idle gaud

---

140 *Pardon, my lord.* Presumably the lovers kneel, provoking Theseus's 'I pray you all, stand up.'

143 *jealousy* suspicion

162 *in fancy* impelled by love

166 *idle gaud* worthless toy, trinket. Egeus had accused Lysander of using gauds to attract Hermia (1.1.33).

Which in my childhood I did dote upon;
And all the faith, the virtue of my heart,
The object and the pleasure of mine eye,
170   Is only Helena. To her, my lord,
Was I betrothed ere I saw Hermia;
But like a sickness did I loathe this food.
But, as in health come to my natural taste,
Now I do wish it, love it, long for it,
And will for evermore be true to it.

THESEUS
Fair lovers, you are fortunately met.
Of this discourse we more will hear anon.
Egeus, I will overbear your will;
For in the temple by and by with us
180   These couples shall eternally be knit.
And – for the morning now is something worn –
Our purposed hunting shall be set aside.
Away with us to Athens. Three and three,
We'll hold a feast in great solemnity.
Come, Hippolyta.
            Exit Theseus with Hippolyta, Egeus, and his train

DEMETRIUS
These things seem small and undistinguishable,
Like far-off mountains turnèd into clouds.

HERMIA
Methinks I see these things with parted eye,
When everything seems double.

HELENA   So methinks,
190   And I have found Demetrius, like a jewel,
Mine own and not mine own.

---

172 *like a sickness* (probably means 'as in
    sickness')
188 *with parted eye* (that is, with the eyes
    out of focus)

190 *like a jewel* (that is, like a precious
    thing found, and thus of uncertain
    ownership)

DEMETRIUS   Are you sure
That we are awake? It seems to me
That yet we sleep, we dream. Do not you think
The Duke was here, and bid us follow him?

HERMIA
Yea, and my father.

HELENA   And Hippolyta.

LYSANDER
And he did bid us follow to the temple.

DEMETRIUS
Why, then, we are awake. Let's follow him,
And by the way let's recount our dreams.
          Exeunt Demetrius, Helena, Lysander, and Hermia
          Bottom wakes

BOTTOM When my cue comes, call me, and I will answer.
My next is 'Most fair Pyramus'. Heigh ho! Peter   200
Quince! Flute the bellows-mender! Snout the tinker!
Starveling! God's my life — stolen hence and left me
asleep! — I have had a most rare vision. I have had a
dream past the wit of man to say what dream it was. Man
is but an ass if he go about to expound this dream. Methought I was — there is no man can tell what. Methought
I was — and methought I had — but man is but a patched
fool if he will offer to say what methought I had. The

191-2 *Are you sure | That we are awake?*
This sentence is omitted from the
Folio text. It is metrically rather awkward, and its omission may have
been deliberate — whether on Shakespeare's or someone else's part, we
cannot tell.

198 *let's.* Q2 and F read 'let us'. This
regularizes the metre, and may be
correct.

199 *When my cue comes* ... Bottom, too,
is momentarily lost between illusion
and reality. As he awakes his mind
goes back to the moment of his trans-

lation (III.1.95).

200 *Heigh ho!* a yawn, perhaps with a
hint of 'Hee-Haw!'

203 *vision.* The word has been used by
Oberon (III.2.371) and Titania
(IV.1.75), and will be repeated by
Puck (V.1.416).

205 *go about* try

207-8 *patched fool* a fool or jester wearing
a patchwork costume

208-11 *The eye of man hath not heard, the
ear of man hath not seen, man's hand is
not able to taste, his tongue to conceive,
nor his heart to report what my dream*

eye of man hath not heard, the ear of man hath not seen,
man's hand is not able to taste, his tongue to conceive,
nor his heart to report what my dream was! I will get
Peter Quince to write a ballad of this dream. It shall be
called 'Bottom's Dream', because it hath no bottom; and
I will sing it in the latter end of a play before the Duke.
Peradventure, to make it the more gracious, I shall sing
it at her death.

Exit

IV.2   *Enter Quince, Flute, Snout, and Starveling*

QUINCE Have you sent to Bottom's house? Is he come
home yet?

STARVELING He cannot be heard of. Out of doubt he is
transported.

FLUTE If he come not, then the play is marred. It goes not
forward. Doth it?

QUINCE It is not possible. You have not a man in all
Athens able to discharge Pyramus but he.

FLUTE No, he hath simply the best wit of any handicraft
man in Athens.

---

was! The confusion of the functions of senses is used elsewhere in the play for comic effect (for example, v.1.189–90; and see Introduction, page 224). Attention has been drawn to the resemblance to 1 Corinthians 2.9 (Bishops' Bible):

The eye hath not seen, and the ear hath not heard, neither have entered into the heart of man, the things which God hath prepared for them that love him.

213 *hath no bottom* is unfathomable; has no reality
214 *a play* (sometimes emended to 'our play' or 'the play'; 'a' is the reading

of the early editions)
216 *her death* (presumably Thisbe's)

IV.2 With this scene we return to Athens.
4 *transported* 'carried off by the fairies' or (euphemistically) 'killed'
5–6 *It goes not forward* we're not going on with it. F reads 'It goes not forward, doth it?' It is just possible that Q's division into two sentences represents a deliberate pointing of the words.
8 *discharge* perform
9 *wit* intellect

QUINCE Yea, and the best person, too; and he is a very
paramour for a sweet voice.

FLUTE You must say 'paragon'. A paramour is – God bless
us – a thing of naught.

Enter Snug the joiner

SNUG Masters, the Duke is coming from the temple, and
there is two or three lords and ladies more married. If
our sport had gone forward, we had all been made men.

FLUTE O, sweet Bully Bottom! Thus hath he lost sixpence
a day during his life. He could not have scaped sixpence
a day. An the Duke had not given him sixpence a day for   20
playing Pyramus, I'll be hanged. He would have deserved it. Sixpence a day in Pyramus, or nothing.

Enter Bottom

BOTTOM Where are these lads? Where are these hearts?

QUINCE Bottom! O most courageous day! O most happy
hour!

BOTTOM Masters, I am to discourse wonders – but ask
me not what; for if I tell you, I am not true Athenian. – I
will tell you everything, right as it fell out!

QUINCE Let us hear, sweet Bottom!

BOTTOM Not a word of me! All that I will tell you is – that   30
the Duke hath dined. Get your apparel together, good
strings to your beards, new ribbons to your pumps.
Meet presently at the palace. Every man look o'er his
part. For the short and the long is, our play is preferred.
In any case, let Thisbe have clean linen; and let not him
that plays the lion pare his nails, for they shall hang out
for the lion's claws. And, most dear actors, eat no onions
nor garlic; for we are to utter sweet breath, and I do

---

11 *person* figure, appearance
14 *thing of naught* something evil
17 *we had all been made men* our fortunes
would have been made
18–19 *sixpence a day.* This would have
been a princely reward.
20 *An* if

24 *courageous* perhaps 'encouraging'; or
perhaps Quince's blunder for
'auspicious'
33 *presently* immediately; very soon
34 *preferred* recommended, put forward
35 *In any case* whatever happens

not doubt but to hear them say it is a sweet comedy. No
40   more words. Away – go, away!

Exeunt Bottom and his fellows

V.I.   *Enter Theseus, Hippolyta, Philostrate, Lords, and
            Attendants*

HIPPOLYTA
    'Tis strange, my Theseus, that these lovers speak of.
THESEUS
    More strange than true. I never may believe
    These antique fables, nor these fairy toys.
    Lovers and madmen have such seething brains,
    Such shaping fantasies, that apprehend
    More than cool reason ever comprehends.
    The lunatic, the lover, and the poet
    Are of imagination all compact.
    One sees more devils than vast hell can hold.
10 That is the madman. The lover, all as frantic,

V.i This scene (which forms the complete Act) follows in the evening of the
same day. Theseus, Hippolyta, and the
two pairs of young lovers have been
married, and come to a celebration.

This Act demonstrates Shakespeare's
mastery of varied styles of both prose
and verse. The verse in particular has
great range, including the dignified and
imaginative blank verse of the opening
dialogue, the rather more familiar, somewhat humorous blank verse of Theseus's
conversation with Philostrate, the many
different measures parodied in the play-
within-the-play, and the rhyming trochaic verses of the closing section.

(stage direction) In the Folio 'Philos-

trate' here and elsewhere in Act Five
is changed to 'Egeus'. Philostrate's
only other appearance is at 1.1.11,
where he has nothing to say. The
Folio text seems to be economizing
on actors. It seems desirable that the
roles should be kept distinct.

1 *'Tis strange, my Theseus. . . .* These opening speeches are referred to in the
Introduction, pages 230–31.
3 *antique* both 'grotesque' and 'old-
fashioned'
fairy toys idle tales about fairies
5 *fantasies* imaginations
apprehend imagine, conceive
6 *comprehends* understands
8 *compact* composed

Sees Helen's beauty in a brow of Egypt.
The poet's eye, in a fine frenzy rolling,
Doth glance from heaven to earth, from earth to heaven.
And as imagination bodies forth
The forms of things unknown, the poet's pen
Turns them to shapes, and gives to airy nothing
A local habitation and a name.
Such tricks hath strong imagination
That if it would but apprehend some joy,
It comprehends some bringer of that joy.   20
Or in the night, imagining some fear,
How easy is a bush supposed a bear?

HIPPOLYTA

But all the story of the night told over,
And all their minds transfigured so together,
More witnesseth than fancy's images,
And grows to something of great constancy;
But howsoever, strange and admirable.

> *Enter the lovers: Lysander, Demetrius, Hermia, and
> Helena*

THESEUS

Here come the lovers, full of joy and mirth.
Joy, gentle friends, joy and fresh days of love
Accompany your hearts.

LYSANDER   More than to us   30
Wait in your royal walks, your board, your bed.

THESEUS

Come now, what masques, what dances shall we have
To wear away this long age of three hours
Between our after-supper and bedtime?

---

11 *Helen* (of Troy)
    a brow of Egypt a gypsy's face
20 *comprehends* includes
25 *More witnesseth than fancy's images* gives
    evidence of more than the creations
    of the imagination
27 *admirable* to be wondered at

32 *masques* courtly entertainments, cen-
    tred on a dance but also having some
    dramatic content
34 *after-supper* the dessert, or 'banquet',
    of fruits and sweetmeats taken to
    round off the evening meal

Where is our usual manager of mirth?
What revels are in hand? Is there no play
To ease the anguish of a torturing hour?
Call Philostrate.

PHILOSTRATE   Here, mighty Theseus.

THESEUS

Say, what abridgement have you for this evening?
40   What masque, what music? How shall we beguile
The lazy time if not with some delight?

PHILOSTRATE (*giving a paper*)

There is a brief how many sports are ripe.
Make choice of which your highness will see first.

THESEUS

The Battle with the Centaurs, 'to be sung
By an Athenian eunuch to the harp'.
We'll none of that. That have I told my love
In glory of my kinsman, Hercules.
The riot of the tipsy Bacchanals,
Tearing the Thracian singer in their rage.
50   That is an old device, and it was played
When I from Thebes came last a conqueror.
The thrice three Muses mourning for the death

39 *abridgement*. This may mean both 'a
shortened version of a longer work'
and 'something which will make the
time seem shorter'.
42 *brief* short account, summary
44–60 *The Battle with the Centaurs* ... In
the Folio, Lysander reads the 'brief'
and Theseus comments. This may
well represent the practice of Shakespeare's company.
44–7 *The Battle with the Centaurs* ... *Her-*
cules. Theseus himself had taken part
in a battle with the Centaurs at which
Hercules also was present. The story
is told in Book XII of Ovid's
Metamorphoses.
47 *my kinsman, Hercules*. That Theseus
and Hercules 'were near kinsmen,

being cousins removed by the
mother's side' is mentioned in the
Life of Theseus in Shakespeare's
great source-book, North's translation of Plutarch's *Lives*.
48–9 *The riot of the tipsy Bacchanals,* |
Tearing the Thracian singer in their rage.
'The Thracian singer' is Orpheus.
The story of his being torn to pieces
by the Thracian women under the
influence of Bacchic rites is told at
the beginning of Book XI of Ovid's
Metamorphoses.
50 *device* show, performance
52–3 *The thrice three Muses mourning for*
the death | *Of learning, late deceased in*
beggary. It has been suggested that
this refers to the death of some par-

Of learning, late deceased in beggary.
That is some satire keen and critical,
Not sorting with a nuptial ceremony.
A tedious brief scene of young Pyramus
And his love Thisbe; 'very tragical mirth'.
Merry and tragical? Tedious and brief?
That is, hot ice and wondrous strange snow.
How shall we find the concord of this discord?   60

PHILOSTRATE

A play there is, my lord, some ten words long,
Which is as 'brief' as I have known a play.
But by ten words, my lord, it is too long,
Which makes it 'tedious'. For in all the play
There is not one word apt, one player fitted.
And 'tragical', my noble lord, it is,
For Pyramus therein doth kill himself,
Which when I saw rehearsed, I must confess,
Made mine eyes water: but more 'merry' tears
The passion of loud laughter never shed.   70

THESEUS

What are they that do play it?

PHILOSTRATE

Hard-handed men that work in Athens here,
Which never laboured in their minds till now,
And now have toiled their unbreathed memories
With this same play against your nuptial.

ticular man of learning, variously identified. But there were many complaints in Shakespeare's time of the neglect of scholarship and the arts, and it is not likely that Shakespeare refers to anything more specifically topical than this literary theme.
55 *sorting with* befitting
59 *strange*. Many editors have felt that emendation is necessary and have provided an adjective bearing to 'snow' the relationship of 'hot' to 'ice'. The

passage seems perfectly satisfactory as it stands.
70 *passion*. The word could be used generally of any strong feeling, for example, 'idle merriment, | A passion hateful to my purposes' (*King John*, III.3.46–7). Its associations with grief as well make it appropriate in this context of antithesis.
74 *unbreathed* unexercised
75 *against* in preparation for

THESEUS
    And we will hear it.

PHILOSTRATE   No, my noble lord,
    It is not for you. I have heard it over,
    And it is nothing, nothing in the world,
    Unless you can find sport in their intents,
80 Extremely stretched, and conned with cruel pain,
    To do you service.

THESEUS   I will hear that play,
    For never anything can be amiss
    When simpleness and duty tender it.
    Go bring them in; and take your places, ladies.

                                    Exit Philostrate

HIPPOLYTA
    I love not to see wretchedness o'ercharged,
    And duty in his service perishing.

THESEUS
    Why, gentle sweet, you shall see no such thing.

HIPPOLYTA
    He says they can do nothing in this kind.

THESEUS
    The kinder we, to give them thanks for nothing.
90 Our sport shall be to take what they mistake;
    And what poor duty cannot do, noble respect
    Takes it in might, not merit.
    Where I have come, great clerks have purposèd
    To greet me with premeditated welcomes,
    Where I have seen them shiver and look pale,
    Make periods in the midst of sentences,
    Throttle their practised accent in their fears,

---

77 *I have heard it over.* When Philostrate
heard the play is not a matter that
will bear inquiry.

83 *simpleness* simplicity, innocence

85 *wretchedness* the lowly in both social
position and intellect

91 *respect* consideration

92 *Takes it in might, not merit.* The mean-

ing is clearly 'takes the will for the
deed'. Presumably 'in might' means
'according to their capability'. The
irregularity of metre suggests the possibility of corruption.

93 *clerks* scholars

96 *Make periods in the midst of sentences* (as
Prologue is to do, lines 108–17)

And in conclusion dumbly have broke off,
Not paying me a welcome. Trust me, sweet,
Out of this silence yet I picked a welcome,   100
And in the modesty of fearful duty
I read as much as from the rattling tongue
Of saucy and audacious eloquence.
Love, therefore, and tongue-tied simplicity
In least speak most, to my capacity.

   Enter Philostrate

PHILOSTRATE
So please your grace, the Prologue is addressed.
THESEUS Let him approach.
   Flourish of trumpets
   Enter Quince as Prologue

QUINCE

If we offend it is with our good will.
 That you should think we come not to offend
But with good will. To show our simple skill,   110
 That is the true beginning of our end.
Consider then we come but in despite.
 We do not come as minding to content you,
Our true intent is. All for your delight
 We are not here. That you should here repent you
The actors are at hand, and by their show
You shall know all that you are like to know.

---

104 *simplicity* sincerity, artlessness
105 *to my capacity* as far as I can understand, in my opinion
106 *addressed* ready
107 (stage direction) *Flourish of trumpets.*
 This direction is not in the Quartos.
 It comes from F, and probably represents the stage practice of Shakespeare's company.
108 *If we offend* . . . Presumably Quince
 reads from a scroll. The comic device
 by which a bad reader reverses the
 sense of what he is reading occurs in
 an earlier play, Nicholas Udall's

Ralph Roister Doister (*c.* 1553, III.4).
Quince's prologue is not in either
'eight and six' or 'eight and eight'
(see III.1. 22–4). Its form is that of a
sonnet without the first four lines.
Shakespeare uses the sonnet form for
his prologue (or chorus) to *Romeo
and Juliet* (Acts One and Two).
116,126 *show*. This may refer simply to
the appearance of the characters in
the play; but it is quite likely that they
should adopt attitudes or even perform
a mime, in the fashion of a dumb-
show, suggestive of what is to come.

THESEUS This fellow doth not stand upon points.

LYSANDER He hath rid his prologue like a rough colt; he
knows not the stop. A good moral, my lord: it is not
enough to speak, but to speak true.

HIPPOLYTA Indeed, he hath played on his prologue like a
child on a recorder – a sound, but not in government.

THESEUS His speech was like a tangled chain: nothing
impaired, but all disordered. Who is next?

*Enter Bottom as Pyramus, Flute as Thisbe, Snout as
Wall, Starveling as Moonshine, and Snug as Lion; a
trumpeter before them*

QUINCE

Gentles, perchance you wonder at this show;
But wonder on, till truth make all things plain.
This man is Pyramus, if you would know;
This beauteous lady Thisbe is, certain.
This man with lime and roughcast doth present
Wall – that vile wall which did these lovers sunder;
And through Wall's chink, poor souls, they are content
To whisper. At the which let no man wonder.
This man with lantern, dog, and bush of thorn
Presenteth Moonshine. For if you will know
By moonshine did these lovers think no scorn
To meet at Ninus' tomb, there, there to woo.
This grisly beast – which Lion hight by name –
The trusty Thisbe coming first by night
Did scare away, or rather did affright.
And as she fled, her mantle she did fall,
Which Lion vile with bloody mouth did stain.
Anon comes Pyramus – sweet youth and tall –

118 *stand upon* bother about
 points both 'trifles' and 'marks of
 punctuation'
119 *rid* both 'rid himself of' and 'ridden'
120 *stop* in horsemanship, a sudden
 check in a horse's career; also the
 mark of punctuation
123 *government* control

125 (stage direction) *a trumpeter*. The
 trumpeter is mentioned in F, not in Q.
 He probably appeared in performances
 given by Shakespeare's company.
138 *hight* is called (an old-fashioned
 word in Shakespeare's time)
141 *fall* drop
143 *tall* brave

And finds his trusty Thisbe's mantle slain.
Whereat with blade — with bloody, blameful blade —
He bravely broached his boiling bloody breast.
And Thisbe, tarrying in mulberry shade,
His dagger drew, and died. For all the rest,
Let Lion, Moonshine, Wall, and lovers twain
At large discourse while here they do remain.   150

　　　　　Exeunt Quince, Bottom, Flute, Snug, and Starveling
THESEUS
　　I wonder if the lion be to speak.
DEMETRIUS
　　No wonder, my lord — one lion may, when many asses do.
SNOUT *as Wall*

　　In this same interlude it doth befall
　　That I — one Snout by name — present a wall.
　　And such a wall as I would have you think
　　That had in it a crannied hole or chink,
　　Through which the lovers, Pyramus and Thisbe,
　　Did whisper often, very secretly.
　　This loam, this roughcast, and this stone doth show
　　That I am that same wall; the truth is so.   160
　　And this the cranny is, right and sinister,
　　Through which the fearful lovers are to whisper.

THESEUS Would you desire lime and hair to speak better?
DEMETRIUS It is the wittiest partition that ever I heard
　　discourse, my lord.
　　　　　Enter Bottom as Pyramus
THESEUS Pyramus draws near the wall. Silence!

---

150 *At large* at length
152 *asses* (a subtly chosen word)
153 *interlude* play
161 *right and sinster* right and left;
　　horizontal
161-2 *sinister ... whisper.* The inexact-
　　ness of the rhyme is of course part of
　　the parody. An actor has been known

to show Snout realizing the fault,
and confusedly pronouncing 'whip-
ister'. The effect was amusing. Shakespeare regularly accents 'sinister' on
the second syllable.
164 *wittiest* most intelligent
　　partition wall *and* section of a speech
　　or 'discourse'

BOTTOM *as Pyramus*

> O grim-looked night, O night with hue so black,
>   O night which ever art when day is not!
> O night, O night, alack, alack, alack,
>   I fear my Thisbe's promise is forgot.
> And thou, O wall, O sweet, O lovely wall,
>   That standest between her father's ground and mine,
> Thou wall, O wall, O sweet and lovely wall,
>   Show me thy chink to blink through with mine eyne.

170

> *Wall holds up his fingers*

> Thanks, courteous wall; Jove shield thee well for this.
> But what see I? No Thisbe do I see.
> O wicked wall, through whom I see no bliss:
>   Cursed be thy stones for thus deceiving me!

THESEUS The wall, methinks, being sensible, should curse again.

180

BOTTOM No, in truth sir, he should not. 'Deceiving me' is Thisbe's cue. She is to enter now, and I am to spy her through the wall. You shall see – it will fall pat as I told you. Yonder she comes.

> *Enter Flute as Thisbe*

FLUTE *as Thisbe*

> O wall, full often hast thou heard my moans
>   For parting my fair Pyramus and me.
> My cherry lips have often kissed thy stones,
>   Thy stones with lime and hair knit up in thee.

BOTTOM *as Pyramus*

> I see a voice. Now will I to the chink

179 *sensible* capable of sensation   183 *pat* precisely
180 *again* back, in return   189–90 *see a voice ... spy an I can hear my*

To spy an I can hear my Thisbe's face.   190
Thisbe!

FLUTE *as Thisbe*

My love! Thou art my love, I think?

BOTTOM *as Pyramus*

Think what thou wilt, I am thy lover's grace,
And like Limander am I trusty still.

FLUTE *as Thisbe*

And I like Helen till the Fates me kill.

BOTTOM *as Pyramus*

Not Shafalus to Procrus was so true.

FLUTE *as Thisbe*

As Shafalus to Procrus, I to you.

BOTTOM *as Pyramus*

O, kiss me through the hole of this vile wall!

FLUTE *as Thisbe*

I kiss the wall's hole, not your lips at all.

BOTTOM *as Pyramus*

Wilt thou at Ninny's tomb meet me straight way?

Thisbe's face (another example of the comic dislocation of the senses; see Introduction, page 224–5)
190 *an* if
192 *thy lover's grace* thy gracious lover
193–4 *Limander ... Helen.* Presumably 'Limander' is a mistake for 'Leander', Hero's lover; possibly it is influenced by Alexander, another name for

Paris, lover of Helen of Troy.
195 *Shafalus ... Procrus.* Mispronunciations of 'Cephalus' and 'Procris', a legendary pair of tragic lovers whose story is told in Ovid's *Metamorphoses*, Book VII. An English poem about them, by Thomas Edwards, was in existence by 1593 and survives in an edition of 1595.

FLUTE *as Thisbe*

200   *Tide life, tide death, I come without delay.*

Exeunt Bottom and Flute

SNOUT *as Wall*

Thus have I, Wall, my part dischargèd so;
And being done, thus Wall away doth go.   *Exit*

THESEUS Now is the mural down between the two neighbours.

DEMETRIUS No remedy, my lord, when walls are so wilful to hear without warning.

HIPPOLYTA This is the silliest stuff that ever I heard.

THESEUS The best in this kind are but shadows; and the worst are no worse, if imagination amend them.

210   HIPPOLYTA It must be your imagination, then, and not theirs.

THESEUS If we imagine no worse of them than they of themselves, they may pass for excellent men. Here come two noble beasts in: a man and a lion.

Enter Snug as Lion and Starveling as Moonshine

SNUG *as Lion*

You, ladies — you whose gentle hearts do fear
The smallest monstrous mouse that creeps on floor —

200 *Tide life, tide death* come life, come death

203 *mural down* wall down. A conjectural emendation (by Pope) of a difficult passage. See the Collations, page 241.

208 *in this kind* (that is, actors)

215-22 *You, ladies — you whose gentle hearts do fear*. . . . This passage (anticipated at I.2.70-78 and III.1.25-42) has provoked comparisons with an account of a happening at the Scottish Court on 30 August 1594. King James and his queen were celebrating the baptism of their son, Prince Henry, when a triumphal car was drawn into the hall by a blackamoor. 'This chariot should have been drawn in by a lion, but because his presence might have brought some fear to the nearest, or that the sight of the lights and torches might have commoved his tameness, it was thought meet that the Moor should supply that room' (from John Nichols's *Progresses of Elizabeth*, III.365). This is an interesting parallel with Shakespeare's play, though not necessarily an influence upon it.

May now, perchance, both quake and tremble here,
  When Lion rough in wildest rage doth roar.
Then know that I as Snug the joiner am
A lion fell, nor else no lion's dam,   220
For if I should as lion come in strife
Into this place, 'twere pity on my life.

THESEUS A very gentle beast, and of a good conscience.

DEMETRIUS The very best at a beast, my lord, that e'er I
  saw.

LYSANDER This lion is a very fox for his valour.

THESEUS True; and a goose for his discretion.

DEMETRIUS Not so, my lord; for his valour cannot carry
  his discretion; and the fox carries the goose.

THESEUS His discretion, I am sure, cannot carry his   230
  valour; for the goose carries not the fox. It is well: leave
  it to his discretion, and let us listen to the moon.

STARVELING *as Moonshine*

  This lanthorn doth the hornèd moon present.

DEMETRIUS He should have worn the horns on his head.

THESEUS He is no crescent, and his horns are invisible
  within the circumference.

STARVELING *as Moonshine*

  This lanthorn doth the hornèd moon present;
    Myself the man i' th' moon do seem to be.

THESEUS This is the greatest error of all the rest; the man
  should be put into the lantern. How is it else the man   240
  i'th'moon?

DEMETRIUS He dares not come there, for the candle. For,
  you see, it is already in snuff.

---

220 *fell* fierce (also 'skin')

233 *lanthorn* (a variant form of 'lantern',
  preserved here for the sake of the
  pun)

234 *He should have worn the horns on his
  head* (a waggish remark at Moon-

shine's expense; horns were the mark
  of the cuckold)

235 *crescent* a waxing moon

242 *for the candle* for fear of the candle

243 *in snuff* 'in need of snuffing' and 'in
  a rage'

HIPPOLYTA I am aweary of this moon. Would he would
change.

THESEUS It appears by his small light of discretion that
he is in the wane. But yet in courtesy, in all reason, we
must stay the time.

LYSANDER Proceed, Moon.

250 STARVELING All that I have to say is to tell you that the
lantern is the moon, I the man i'th'moon, this thorn
bush my thorn bush, and this dog my dog.

DEMETRIUS Why, all these should be in the lantern; for
all these are in the moon. But silence: here comes Thisbe.

Enter Flute as Thisbe

FLUTE *as Thisbe*

This is old Ninny's tomb. Where is my love?

SNUG *as Lion*

O!

Lion roars. Flute as Thisbe runs off

DEMETRIUS Well roared, Lion!

THESEUS Well run, Thisbe!

HIPPOLYTA Well shone, Moon! Truly, the moon shines

260 with a good grace.

Lion tears Thisbe's mantle. Exit

THESEUS Well moused, Lion!

DEMETRIUS And then came Pyramus.

LYSANDER And so the lion vanished.

Enter Bottom as Pyramus

BOTTOM *as Pyramus*

Sweet moon, I thank thee for thy sunny beams;
I thank thee, moon, for shining now so bright;

250-52 *All ... my dog.* Moonshine, in
exasperation, lapses into prose

255 *This is old Ninny's tomb* (indicating a
change of scene. No further indication is necessary, though producers

have been known to employ a tomb
inscribed *Hic iacet Ninus.* Thisbe gets
the name wrong again (compare
III.I.90–91).)

For by thy gracious, golden, glittering beams
I trust to take of truest Thisbe sight.
  But stay — O spite!
  But mark, poor Knight,
 What dreadful dole is here?   270
   Eyes, do you see? —
   How can it be?
 O dainty duck, O dear!
  Thy mantle good —
 What, stained with blood!
 Approach, ye Furies fell.
  O Fates, come, come,
  Cut thread and thrum,
 Quail, crush, conclude, and quell.

THESEUS This passion, and the death of a dear friend,   280
would go near to make a man look sad.

HIPPOLYTA Beshrew my heart, but I pity the man.

BOTTOM *as Pyramus*

O wherefore, nature, didst thou lions frame,
 Since lion vile hath here deflowered my dear?
Which is — no, no, which was — the fairest dame
 That lived, that loved, that liked, that looked with cheer.
  Come tears, confound;
  Out sword, and wound
  The pap of Pyramus.
  Ay, that left pap,   290

---

266 *beams.* So Q and F; often emended to 'gleams', both to avoid the repeated rhyming word, and to fit the alliterative scheme. But 'beams' may be a deliberate comic touch.

270 *dole* cause of grief

277 *Fates.* The three Fates in Greek mythology were Clotho, who carried a distaff; Lachesis, who wove the web of a man's life; and Atropos, whose shears cut the thread when the web was complete.

278 *Cut thread and thrum. Thread* is the warp in weaving; *thrum* the tufted end of the warp. *Thread and thrum* means 'good and bad together'; 'everything'. The image is ingeniously related both to the fates and to Bottom's trade.

279 *Quail* overpower
 quell kill

280 *passion* both 'suffering' and 'violent speech'

286 *cheer* face

> *Where heart doth hop.*
> *Thus die I — thus, thus, thus.*

He stabs himself

> *Now am I dead,*
> *Now am I fled;*
> *My soul is in the sky.*
> *Tongue, lose thy light;*
> *Moon, take thy flight;*

Exit Starveling as Moonshine

Now die, die, die, die, die.   *He dies*

DEMETRIUS No die, but an ace for him; for he is but one.

300 LYSANDER Less than an ace, man; for he is dead. He is nothing.

THESEUS With the help of a surgeon he might yet recover, and prove an ass.

HIPPOLYTA How chance Moonshine is gone before Thisbe comes back and finds her lover?

THESEUS She will find him by starlight. Here she comes; and her passion ends the play.

Enter Flute as Thisbe

HIPPOLYTA Methinks she should not use a long one for such a Pyramus. I hope she will be brief.

310 DEMETRIUS A mote will turn the balance which Pyramus, which Thisbe is the better — he for a man, God warrant us; she for a woman, God bless us.

LYSANDER She hath spied him already, with those sweet eyes.

299 *die* one of a pair of dice
ace a single spot on a die. *Ace* was near enough in prounciation to 'ass' to justify the pun in line 303.

307 *passion* formal, or passionate, speech.

310 *mote* (in early editions 'moth', a common spelling for 'mote')

311–12 *he for a man, God warrant us; she for a woman, God bless us.* This was omitted from the Folio text, presumably because of a statute of James I forbidding profanity on the stage.

DEMETRIUS *And thus she means, videlicet:*
FLUTE *as Thisbe*

> *Asleep, my love?*
> *What, dead, my dove?*
> *O Pyramus, arise.*
> *Speak, speak. Quite dumb?*
> *Dead, dead? A tomb*   320
> *Must cover thy sweet eyes.*
> *These lily lips,*
> *This cherry nose,*
> *These yellow cowslip cheeks*
> *Are gone, are gone.*
> *Lovers, make moan —*
> *His eyes were green as leeks.*
> *O sisters three,*
> *Come, come to me*
> *With hands as pale as milk;*   330
> *Lay them in gore,*
> *Since you have shore*
> *With shears his thread of silk.*
> *Tongue, not a word!*
> *Come, trusty sword,*

315 *means.* To *mean* was both a dialect word meaning to 'lament' and a legal term meaning to 'lodge a formal complaint'. The legal term *videlicet* ('you may see') may suggest that both senses are felt here.

320 *tomb* (at this date, a true rhyme with 'dumb')

322–7 *These lily lips ... green as leeks.* The parodic derangement of epithets here recalls the confusions of the senses in earlier scenes.

328 *sisters three* the Fates. This passage resembles the prologue to Thomas Preston's *Cambyses* (1569), a play of the kind that Shakespeare is burlesquing here:

> *But he when sisters three had wrought to*
>   *shear his vital thread*
> *As heir due to take up the crown*
>   *Cambyses did proceed.*

332 *shore* (that is, 'shorn' — a comic misuse for the sake of rhyme)

335 *Come, trusty sword.* In a comedy of 1607 called *The Fleire*, by Edward Sharpham, occurs the following passage:

KNIGHT *And how lives he with 'em?*
FLEIRE *Faith, like Thisbe in the play, 'a has almost killed himself with the scabbard.*

This appears to record a piece of comic business in early performances of the play.

> *Come blade, my breast imbrue.*

She stabs herself

> *And farewell friends.*
> *Thus Thisbe ends.*
> *Adieu, adieu, adieu!*

She dies

340 THESEUS Moonshine and Lion are left to bury the dead.

DEMETRIUS Ay, and Wall, too.

BOTTOM (*starting up*) No, I assure you, the wall is down that parted their fathers. Will it please you to see the epilogue, or to hear a Bergomask dance between two of our company?

THESEUS No epilogue, I pray you; for your play needs no excuse. Never excuse; for when the players are all dead, there need none to be blamed. Marry, if he that writ it had played Pyramus and hanged himself in Thisbe's

350 garter, it would have been a fine tragedy. And so it is, truly, and very notably discharged. But come, your Bergomask; let your epilogue alone.

> *A dance. Exeunt Bottom and his fellows*

The iron tongue of midnight hath told twelve.
Lovers, to bed; 'tis almost fairy time.
I fear we shall outsleep the coming morn
As much as we this night have overwatched.
This palpable-gross play hath well beguiled

---

336 *imbrue* pierce; stain with blood

342 BOTTOM. This speech is given to Bottom in the Folio, but to Lion (that is, Snug) in the Quartos. Shakespeare may have intended Snug to speak it.

343–4 *see the epilogue, or to hear a Bergomask dance* (a last touch of Bottom's characteristic verbal confusion)

344 *Bergomask* a rustic dance after the manner of Bergamo, in Italy

352 (stage direction) *A dance.* No distinct exeunt for the mechanicals is provided in the early editions. They obviously should leave after the dance, before Theseus's reference to their 'palpable-gross play'.

356 *overwatched* stayed up late

357 *palpable-gross* obviously crude

The heavy gait of night. Sweet friends, to bed.
A fortnight hold we this solemnity
In nightly revels and new jollity.   360

Exeunt Theseus, Hippolyta, Philostrate,
Demetrius, Helena, Lysander, Hermia,
Lords, and Attendants

Enter Puck

PUCK

Now the hungry lion roars
    And the wolf behowls the moon,
Whilst the heavy ploughman snores
    All with weary task foredone.
Now the wasted brands do glow
    Whilst the screech-owl, screeching loud,
Puts the wretch that lies in woe
    In remembrance of a shroud.
Now it is the time of night
    That the graves, all gaping wide,   370
Every one lets forth his sprite
    In the churchway paths to glide.
And we fairies, that do run
    By the triple Hecate's team,
From the presence of the sun
    Following darkness like a dream,
Now are frolic. Not a mouse
Shall disturb this hallowed house.
I am sent with broom before

---

360 (stage direction) *Enter Puck*. Puck's
entry is often made through a trap
door.
362 *behowls*. The original texts read 'be-
holds'. The notion of wolves howling against the moon was proverbial;
compare *As You Like It* (V.2.103):
''tis like the howling of Irish wolves
against the moon'.
363 *heavy* weary
364 *foredone* exhausted

365 *wasted* used-up, burnt-out
371 *Every one lets forth his* each grave lets
forth its
374 *triple Hecate*. The goddess Hecate
ruled as Luna and Cynthia in heaven,
as Diana on earth, and as Proserpine
and Hecate in hell. Puck refers to
her as goddess of the moon and night.
377 *frolic* frolicsome, merry
379–80 *I am sent with broom before | To*
sweep the dust behind the door. Robin

380

To sweep the dust behind the door.
Enter Oberon and Titania, with all their train

OBERON

Through the house give glimmering light
    By the dead and drowsy fire;
Every elf and fairy sprite
    Hop as light as bird from briar,
And this ditty after me
Sing, and dance it trippingly.

TITANIA

First rehearse your song by rote,
To each word a warbling note.
Hand in hand with fairy grace

390

Will we sing and bless this place.
Song and dance

OBERON

Now until the break of day
Through this house each fairy stray.
To the best bride bed will we,
Which by us shall blessèd be;
And the issue there create
Ever shall be fortunate.
So shall all the couples three
Ever true in loving be,
And the blots of nature's hand

Goodfellow traditionally had the duty of keeping the house clean, and was often represented with a broom.

387 *rehearse ... by rote* repeat from memory

390 (stage direction) *Song and dance*. Some editors believe that the song has been lost, with perhaps a separate 'ditty' referred to in line 385. Granville-Barker introduced 'Roses, their sharp spines being gone' from *The Two Noble Kinsmen*. The lines beginning 'Now until the break of day' are headed 'Ob.' in Q1. The Folio gives no speech-heading, prints the lines in italics, and heads them 'The song'. It is possible that these lines were sung, perhaps by Oberon, with a chorus of fairies. But there are objections. The lines are not particularly lyrical: Oberon is giving a set of instructions. Also Shakespeare tends to differentiate his lyrics by writing them in a metre different from what comes before and after, whereas this is the same.

Shall not in their issue stand.   400
Never mole, harelip, nor scar,
Nor mark prodigious, such as are
Despisèd in nativity,
Shall upon their children be.
With this field dew consecrate
Every fairy take his gait,
And each several chamber bless
Through this palace with sweet peace;
And the owner of it blessed
Ever shall in safety rest.   410
Trip away; make no stay.
Meet me all by break of day.

Exeunt Oberon, Titania, and their train

PUCK (*to the audience*)

If we shadows have offended,
Think but this, and all is mended:
That you have but slumbered here
While these visions did appear.
And this weak and idle theme,
No more yielding but a dream,
Gentles, do not reprehend.
If you pardon, we will mend.   420
And, as I am an honest Puck,
If we have unearnèd luck
Now to scape the serpent's tongue
We will make amends ere long,
Else the Puck a liar call.
So, good night unto you all.
Give me your hands if we be friends,
And Robin shall restore amends.   *Exit*

402 *mark prodigious* ominous, portentous birthmark
405 *consecrate* consecrated, blessed
406 *take his gait* take his way
407 *several* separate
413–28 *If we shadows have offended* ... These lines form an epilogue, addressed directly to the audience.
418 *No more yielding but* yielding no more than
423 *serpent's tongue* hisses (from the audience)
427 *hands* (that is, in applause)

AS YOU LIKE IT

Introduction

As You Like It is one of the plays in the Shakespeare canon of
which it would be easy to give a completely misleading account
– and to give it not by inventing what is not there but merely
by stressing selected features rather than others. By some such
method, one could even argue that this was an unsophisticated
play.

What, for example, could be more blatant than the exposi-
tion: 'As I remember, Adam, it was upon this fashion be-
queathed me by will, but poor a thousand crowns, and, as thou
sayest, charged my brother on his blessing to breed me well'?
(One even wonders whether Sheridan had this in mind in *The
Critic* when Dangle complains that Sir Walter Raleigh, in
Puff's dreadful play, is telling Sir Christopher Hatton what
Hatton already knows: 'Mr Puff, as he *knows* all this, why does
Sir Walter go on telling him?' – to which Puff replies ''Fore
Gad, now, that is one of the most ungrateful observations I
ever heard – for the less inducement he has to tell all this, the
more I think you ought to be oblig'd to him; for I am sure
you'd know nothing of the matter without it'.) And as if
Orlando's speech were not exposition enough, there soon
follows Oliver's cross-examination of the wrestler Charles,
including the obviously 'unnatural' and, at the time, irrelevant
question 'Can you tell if Rosalind, the Duke's daughter, be
banished with her father?' Only in the 'Romances' of his last
years was Shakespeare quite as casual as this.

What, similarly, could be more unsophisticated than the
unashamed melodrama of the snake and the lioness from which
Orlando rescues his brother Oliver – 'natural' dangers no less

unnatural in the Forest of Arden, in Warwickshire, than they would be in the Forest of the Ardennes in France? What could be more melodramatic than the earlier character of Oliver, so villainous that he proposes to burn the lodging where Orlando customarily lies, and burn it with Orlando inside it? What could be more improbable than the conversion to goodness of this same Oliver –

> *'Twas I, but 'tis not I: I do not shame*
> *To tell you what I was, since my conversion*
> *So sweetly tastes, being the thing I am –*

converted because his brother saved him from the lioness? Only, surely, the conversion of the wicked usurping Duke, converted to the religious life because he met and had 'some question' with an 'old religious man' (v.4.151–62) – while advancing with an army

> *to take*
> *His brother here and put him to the sword.*

But just as the man confident in his truth can afford to joke, so Shakespeare, when the important things he has to say are most subtle, can be most casual about his method of saying other things; he gets them said and, as it were, out of the way. Writing, probably, in 1599, with the experience of many comedies behind him (including not only *The Two Gentlemen of Verona, Love's Labour's Lost,* and *The Taming of the Shrew* but also *A Midsummer Night's Dream, The Merry Wives of Windsor,* and perhaps even *Much Ado About Nothing*), he is already master of his technique and, as Mackail once put it, writes with 'relaxed art'; because the mere story of the play is relatively unimportant, he gives it little attention and concentrates on his lovers and his pastoral theme. Moreover, the play that in many eyes is still the best statement in English literature of that pastoral theme, of the beauties of life free from 'painted pomp' and far from the madding crowd, proves to be anything but simple statement: it may be the finest pastoral drama in English but it is also the most amusing comment on those works of earlier and Elizabethan literature that began and ended with the premise that the country life,

> *exempt from public haunt,*
> *Finds tongues in trees, books in the running brooks,*
> *Sermons in stones, and good in everything.*

Shakespeare's immediate source was just such a work, the one that Thomas Lodge wrote 'to beguile the time with labour' on a voyage to the Canaries, *Rosalynde* (or *Euphues' Golden Legacy*), published in 1590. This in turn was based on the medieval *Tale of Gamelyn*, which was once ascribed to Chaucer and even appeared in editions of *The Canterbury Tales*. *Rosalynde* is a true pastoral, in a mode very popular during the 1580s and for years afterwards, and still enjoyed by modern readers in the poetry of Spenser's *Shepherd's Calendar*, in plays such as Fletcher's *The Faithful Shepherdess* and Ben Jonson's unfinished *The Sad Shepherd*, and in Sir Philip Sidney's *Arcadia*. *Rosalynde* is set, theoretically, in the woods of the Ardennes (curiously placed somewhere between Bordeaux and Lyons, the latter being on the way to Germany and so to Italy!), but in practice these are Arcadian lands and resemble neither French woods nor any others of human experience. Lodge's characters, both the noble lords and ladies – like Rosader and Saladyne (Orlando and Oliver), Rosalynde and Alinda (Celia) – and the shepherds and shepherdesses – like Montanus (Silvius) and Phoebe – are little better than conventional types. Their life is unreal, their conversation artificial and, indeed, mostly Euphuistic; and the story of their loves is told ostensibly to point the moral

that such as neglect their fathers' precepts, incur much prejudice; that division in nature, as it is a blemish in nurture, so 'tis a breach of good fortunes; that virtue is not measured by birth but by action; that younger brethren, though inferior in years, yet may be superior to honours; that concord is the sweetest conclusion, and amity betwixt brothers more forceable than fortune.

Presumably no reader believed a word of it, or was intended to believe it, but it is all completely delightful, and not least so for its pretence that sensible men and women, given the choice, would live under the greenwood tree. Or, as Lodge's Coridon expresses it:

For a shepherd's life, O Mistress, did you but live a while in their content, you would say the court were rather a place of sorrow than of solace. Here, Mistress, shall not Fortune thwart you but in mean misfortunes, as the loss of a few sheep, which, as it breeds no beggary, so it can be no extreme prejudice: the next year may mend all with a fresh increase. Envy stirs not us; we covet not to climb; our desires mount not above our degrees, nor our thoughts above our fortunes. Care cannot harbour in our cottages, nor do our homely couches know broken slumbers: as we exceed not in diet, so we have enough to satisfy: and, Mistress, I have so much Latin, Satis est quod sufficit.

Rosalynde, in short, was a notable example of what we have learned to call 'escapist literature'.

Shakespeare was fully sensitive to the charm of Lodge's romance; he could also see its unreality. The greatness of *As You Like It* is – if one may risk so pretentious a statement – that he retained, and enhanced, the charming artifice of his original and at the same time smilingly revealed its conventionality and unreality.

He retained the charm of *Rosalynde* – and perhaps met what seems to have been a demand for plays on Robin Hood and similar subjects – by taking over both Lodge's basic story (although he omitted all the violent deaths) and its setting (although the European woods of the Ardennes perhaps became conflated with his own Warwickshire Forest of Arden). His banished king, Rosalind's father, 'is already in the Forest of Arden, and a many merry men with him; and there they live like the old Robin Hood of England: they say many young gentlemen flock to him every day, and fleet the time carelessly as they did in the golden world'. The Duke (unlike the banished king in *Rosalynde* in this) duly expounds the pastoral philosophy – so well that his phrases have become proverbial:

Now my co-mates and brothers in exile,
Hath not old custom made this life more sweet
Than that of painted pomp? Are not these woods
More free from peril than the envious court?
Here feel we not the penalty of Adam,
The seasons' difference . . .?
Sweet are the uses of adversity,
Which, like the toad, ugly and venomous,
Wears yet a precious jewel in his head;
And this our life, exempt from public haunt,
Finds tongues in trees, books in the running brooks,
Sermons in stones, and good in everything

and Amiens adds 'I would not change it'. As soon as they have
the chance, however, they do change it: the Duke, hearing that
his brother has become converted to a religious life and has
abandoned all claims to the crown and lands, waits only to
complete the nuptial ceremonies before going back to the
envious court, to 'the good of our returned fortune'. And his
co-mates and brothers in exile are apparently just as ready to
abandon their pastoral principles – with one notable exception,
Jaques.

It is significant that in Lodge's romance there was no character corresponding to Jaques. Shakespeare created him, and
created him, obviously, for a function similar to that of Mercutio in *Romeo and Juliet*: not to 'debunk' romance, so that there
was nothing to be said for it, but to cast the eye of a likeable
cynic on romance, and, in *As You Like It*, on pastoralism and
other such 'romantic' convention as well, so that the audience,
seeing from more than one point of view, could smile and
tolerate. Jaques, in fact, is Shakespeare's main method of
keeping romanticism and pastoralism in their place.

This function is not confined to the conclusion of the play,
when Jaques alone remains true to the philosophy 'Sweet are
the uses of adversity' and refuses to engage in mere 'pastime':
his place is now with the converted Duke, who in his turn has

'thrown into neglect the pompous court', with the further advantage for Jaques that

> *out of these convertites*
> *There is much matter to be heard and learned.*

In exactly the same way Jaques has previously tried to show up the shallowness of the greenwood philosophy, and to the song

> *Who doth ambition shun,*
> *And loves to live i' th' sun,*
> *Seeking the food he eats,*
> *And pleased with what he gets:*
> *Come hither, come hither, come hither.*
> *Here shall he see*
> *No enemy*
> *But winter and rough weather*

he has added a third stanza:

> *If it do come to pass*
> *That any man turn ass,*
> *Leaving his wealth and ease,*
> *A stubborn will to please:*
> *Ducdame, ducdame, ducdame.*
> *Here shall he see*
> *Gross fools as he,*
> *An if he will come to me.*   II.5.47–54

He has not only affirmed what the exiled Duke has himself suspected, that for exiled courtiers to live on venison is all very well, except that it is rather hard on the deer –

> *And, in that kind, swears you do more usurp*
> *Than doth your brother that hath banished you –*

but has also pointed out that Orlando does mar the trees 'with writing love-songs in their barks'; that Touchstone's country wife will soon lose her charms; and that a joke can go too far.

Hence the important scene (III.3) of his interference when Touchstone proposes to perpetrate matrimony with Audrey in unseemly haste:

And will you, being a man of your breeding, be married under a bush like a beggar? Get you to church, and have a good priest that can tell you what marriage is. This fellow will but join you together as they join wainscot; then one of you will prove a shrunk panel and, like green timber, warp, warp.

It is a curious reading of the play that prefers to sentiments such as these Touchstone's lame answer: 'he is not like to marry me well; and not being well married, it will be a good excuse for me hereafter to leave my wife'; and one wonders how many misreadings of the play derive from such an unwillingness to give Jaques his due.

To give him his due, however, is not to give him the last word, and it is certainly not to consider him Shakespeare's mouthpiece or 'chorus'. In particular it is unfortunate that his famous 'seven ages of man' speech is so often quoted as if it expressed Shakespeare's philosophy of life, and that an admirable one. The speech is a variation on another well-known theme, and it is not Shakespeare's only variation on that theme; but just as Antonio's lines in *The Merchant of Venice* —

> *I hold the world but as the world, Gratiano,*
> *A stage, where every man must play a part,*
> *And mine a sad one* —   I.1.77–9

express his particular melancholy, and Macbeth's lines —

> *Out, out, brief candle!*
> *Life's but a walking shadow, a poor player*
> *That struts and frets his hour upon the stage*
> *And then is heard no more. It is a tale*
> *Told by an idiot, full of sound and fury,*
> *Signifying nothing* —   V.5.23–8

express the depths of his acquired despair, so Jaques's lines give one impression of human life – according to which the only significant thing about a baby is its 'mewling and puking'; honour or reputation is a 'bubble'; justices are creatures overfed (probably on food given as bribes) and cannot rise above platitudes; and old age is 'second childishness' and complete forgetfulness. As many a commentator has noted, if Shakespeare's opinion is expressed at all, it is by bringing on the stage at this moment Adam – an old man whose courage and loyalty completely contradict what Jaques has just said. If Shakespeare had chosen to speak in his own person, then, on the theme of what is thought to have been the motto of the Globe Theatre ('*totus mundus agit histrionem*', from Petronius), it is reasonably certain that he would have written something different again from Jaques's speech, or Antonio's, or Macbeth's.

Accordingly we shall not, if we are wise, equate Jaques with the chorus or accept him as an oracle; we shall not join George Sand who, in her version of the play, married him off to Celia (describing this as 'my own romance inserted in that of Shakespeare . . . I have always tenderly loved Jacques'); we shall allow the cynic his cynicism and recognize with the Duke that it is probably the cynicism of the rake reformed and one who takes rather too much pleasure in his chiding of others. But we shall not therefore brand him the 'malcontent type' (though he may have something in common with other cynical commentators in plays written at this time). We shall not say that he is inevitably worsted in argument with Orlando and Rosalind, but shall recognize that he holds his own with them in the art of insult, playing a game of which they all understand the rules, and in the process scoring many a good hit ('Nay then, God buy you, an you talk in blank verse'). We shall probably put aside theories that he is in the play for purposes of personal satire – of Ben Jonson or Jonson's enemy John Marston or anybody else of whose self-confident railing his lines occasionally remind us – and maintain for one thing that he is essentially too likeable, and too often right in his opinions, to be meant as a caricature of anybody. Above all, we shall not think of him as a 'man seeking wisdom by abjuring its first principles' but shall insist that, even if he parades the fashionable melancholy, he is often wise, and that he too is a touchstone – not least when he is serving as a touchstone for Touchstone himself.

It is by no means certain that Shakespeare meant 'Touchstone' to be the name of the character so known to modern readers and theatregoers. In the early scenes in which the character appears, he is dubbed 'Clown'; 'Touchstone' first occurs in the curious stage direction at the beginning of Act II, scene 4, '*Enter Rosalind for Ganimed, Celia for Aliena, and Clowne, alias Touchstone*'. This may mean either that Touchstone was intended as the clown's name all the time or that Touchstone is the name he assumes in the forest. There is no proof, however, that the clown assumes any disguise in the forest; we learn that he there wears the motley of the professional fool or court jester, but jesting seems to be his profession from the beginning, even when Rosalind and Celia call him a 'natural' in 1.2 and 'a clownish fool' in 1.3.

Whatever his name, one of his roles in the Forest of Arden is indubitably that of the 'touchstone' – the stone on which alloys were rubbed, to test their quality or their degree of genuineness, and so, figuratively, the test or criterion of the genuineness of anything. Accordingly, when in Act III, scene 2, Corin sings the praises of the shepherd's life (in words clearly derived from Coridon's in *Rosalynde* – quoted on page 352)

Sir, I am a true labourer: I earn that I eat, get that I wear, owe no man hate, envy no man's happiness, glad of other men's good, content with my harm; and the greatest of my pride is to see my ewes graze and my lambs suck

the words have a different effect from Lodge's, not only because of Touchstone's reply 'That is another simple sin in you, to bring the ewes and the rams together and to offer to get your living by the copulation of cattle' but also because

Touchstone a few minutes earlier has given Corin his assessment of the shepherd's occupation:

Truly, shepherd, in respect of itself, it is a good life; but in respect that it is a shepherd's life, it is naught. In respect that it is solitary, I like it very well; but in respect that it is private, it is a very vile life. Now in respect it is in the fields, it pleaseth me well; but in respect it is not in the court, it is tedious. As it is a spare life, look you, it fits my humour well; but as there is no more plenty in it, it goes much against my stomach.

In passages like these, one can see how far Shakespeare has developed the dramatic function of his fool. In the early romantic comedy *The Two Gentlemen of Verona*, the jester Speed may occasionally make a comment on the main story that helps to keep that story in perspective, such as

> *O excellent device! Was there ever heard a better,*
> *That my master, being scribe, to himself should write the letter?*
>
> II.1.128–9

(and if anything the effect of the comment is *too* damaging, in that it makes the romantic hero look foolish), but for most of the time the jesting is strictly irrelevant and is there only for its own sake. In *As You Like It*, however, Touchstone's jests, like those of Jaques, are for the most part closely related to the main themes, on which they give us yet another point of view; and if only William Cartwright had seen this relevance, he could hardly have written in his 1647 verses to John Fletcher:

> *Shakespeare to thee was dull whose best jest lies*
> *I' the ladies' questions, and the fool's replies;*
> *Old-fashioned wit, which walked from town to town,*
> *In turned hose, which our fathers called the clown,*
> *Whose wit our nice times would obsceneness call.*

The technique was to be developed even further, of course, in the Fool in *King Lear*.

It has often been said that the characters of Shakespeare's

fools changed about the time of *As You Like It* because Robert
Armin had joined the company to play these parts, his skill
being in a more intellectual and perhaps semi-pathetic kind of
humour than the skill of his predecessor, the famous comedian
William Kemp. In fact Touchstone is not as different from
earlier Shakespearian fools as some have claimed (and Armin
records that he, like Kemp, played the part of Dogberry);
moreover Touchstone's singing is confined to a few bars,
although Armin was an excellent singer. *As You Like It* may
well have preceded Armin's arrival by a few months (in 1600,
according to the title page of *Fool upon Fool*, Armin was still
playing at the Curtain); *Twelfth Night* no doubt came after it,
and it may well be that this was why some of the songs were
transferred from Viola to Feste.

What is certain is that Touchstone, like Jaques, has the
function of casting a cynical eye on romanticism run riot, even
when Rosalind herself is at fault ('You have said; but whether
wisely or no, let the forest judge'); yet he does not have the last
word either, and Jaques, for one, is always there to keep *him* in
his place:

> *for thy loving voyage*
> *Is but for two months victualled.*

Shakespeare's method, then, may be called theme and variations
– unless one prefers to call it point counterpoint. Perhaps it is
seen even more clearly in his treatment of the rustic inhabitants
of Arden. He took over from Lodge the conventional pretty
shepherdess, Phoebe, disdainful of her lover Montanus, and he
remembered Rosalynde's rebuke of her coyness:

*What, Shepherdess, so fair and so cruel? . . . Because thou art beautiful,
be not so coy: as there is nothing more fair, so there is nothing more
fading . . . be ruled by me, love while thou art young, lest thou be
disdained when thou art old. Beauty nor time cannot be recalled, and if
thou love, like of Montanus: for as his desires are many, so his deserts
are great.*

But, using the very metaphor Lodge's Phoebe had used to Montanus, 'if your market may be made nowhere else, home again, for your mart is at the fairest', he transformed Rosalynde's mild rebuke into the stinging lines in which Rosalind censures Phebe (III.5.35–9, 57–60):

> *Who might be your mother,*
> *That you insult, exult and all at once*
> *Over the wretched? What, though you have no beauty –*
> *As, by my faith, I see no more in you*
> *Than without candle may go dark to bed . . .*
> *. . . mistress, know yourself; down on your knees*
> *And thank heaven, fasting, for a good man's love!*
> *For I must tell you friendly in your ear,*
> *Sell when you can, you are not for all markets.*

The pastoral love-game is not, after all, as admirable or as amiable as it had been made to seem; and the object of the swain's devotion is herself just as far from the ideal: *her* 'touch' is not so 'sweet', but she has

> *a leathern hand,*
> *A freestone-coloured hand; I verily did think*
> *That her old gloves were on, but 'twas her hands;*
> *She has a housewife's hand – but that's no matter.*

To add yet another variation, Shakespeare invented a 'real' country girl – Audrey – watching (so much for romance!) her *goats*, and ignorant even of the word 'poetical' ('Is it honest in deed and word? Is it a true thing?'). She is only too willing to abandon her country lover, and marry – Touchstone; and her ideals do not rise above 'I am not a slut, though I thank the gods I am foul'.

The rustic swain of Lodge's *Rosalynde*, Montanus, is taken over by Shakespeare as Silvius, similarly sighing for, and victimized by, his Phebe; but whereas in Lodge 'it amazed both Aliena and Ganimede to see the resolution of his loves: so that they pitied his passions and commended his patience', Shakespeare's Rosalind tells us exactly what the status of such pining lovers is: 'I see love hath made thee a tame snake'. And as Audrey is to Phebe, so William is to Silvius: the country boor as Shakespeare probably knew him only too well, set against the shepherd of literature; and William's cross-examination by Touchstone (in Act v, scene 1) leaves the country man only his simple honesty. It is vaguely reminiscent of the cross-examination of another dull William – the Latin 'lesson' in *The Merry Wives of Windsor* (iv.1) – and it is the descendant of many a witbout between professional jester and natural fool in earlier Shakespeare and other Elizabethan comedy, such as the meetings of Speed and Launce in *The Two Gentlemen of Verona* (for example, ii.5 and iii.1.276 ff.). Again the difference is that the earlier quibbling ('Well, your old vice still: mistake the word') has been transformed into an exchange that develops the theme of the play. Perhaps nobody was ever further from understanding *As You Like It* than the commentator who regretted the sub-plot of Silvius and Phebe but allowed it because it 'enhances the pastoral and woodland element' and said that the episode of Touchstone and Audrey should have been omitted because it is 'disagreeable' and not in the true pastoral spirit – unless it be the commentator who argued that Jaques was not in the play as originally written, because he has nothing to do with the plot.

One character whom Shakespeare did not need to develop much from her original in Lodge is his Celia, based on Lodge's Alinda (each taking the greenwood name 'Aliena'). Already in the prose romance Alinda is a staunch friend, treating Rosalynde as an equal (although Rosalynde goes to the Forest as her page, not her brother, and in Lodge Alinda too is banished, but not before she has told her father that she is determined to share Rosalynde's exile); already too she is an amused commentator on any undue solemnity in love. In *As You Like It*, of course, one of her functions is to laugh even at Rosalind if, exceptionally, that normally gay heroine threatens to take herself too seriously; and where Lodge's Alinda says to Rosalynde–

Ganimede 'I pray you, if your robes were off, what metal are you made of that you are so satirical against women? Is it not a foul bird defiles the own nest?', Shakespeare's Celia, in a slightly different context, is even franker: 'You have simply misused our sex in your love-prate. We must have your doublet and hose plucked over your head, and show the world what the bird hath done to her own nest.' To Rosalind's claim that her affection 'hath an unknown bottom, like the Bay of Portugal', Celia retorts 'Or rather, bottomless, that as fast as you pour affection in, it runs out'; and to the perhaps only half-serious 'I'll tell thee, Aliena, I cannot be out of the sight of Orlando: I'll go find a shadow and sigh till he come', she gives the only right answer, 'And I'll sleep'.

Not the least of the tributes to be paid to Shakespeare's portrait of Rosalind is that she is not overshadowed by this pert cousin. One reason for this, though not the main one, is that Shakespeare was not willing to give Celia the same proportion of his time as Lodge gave to Alinda, particularly as the story drew closer to its end. In *Rosalynde*, Aliena (Celia) is rescued by Saladyne (Oliver) from a band of outlaws who were attempting to carry her and Rosalynde off and had already wounded Rosader (Orlando); this naturally leads her to look on her rescuer 'with favour', and Saladyne is in turn impressed by her. Or, in Lodge's unsmiling words:

Saladyne hearing this shepherdess speak so wisely began more narrowly to pry into her perfection, and to survey all her lineaments with a curious insight; so long dallying in the flame of her beauty that to his cost he found her to be most excellent: for Love, that lurked in all these broils to have a blow or two, seeing the parties at the gaze, encountered them both with such a veny that the stroke pierced to the heart so deep as it could never after be razed out.

Perhaps because Shakespeare did not wish to give minor characters an equal prominence; perhaps because he had already written a comedy in which a heroine was rescued from a band of outlaws (*The Two Gentlemen of Verona*) – and had vowed never to try it again (Quiller-Couch was to compare Shakespeare's outlaws with Gilbert and Sullivan's Pirates of Penzance and say that the difference was that Gilbert meant his to be funny); probably because the tone of the play demanded that even these romantic lovers must not be taken too seriously, he abandoned Lodge's story, risked the charge of inadequate motivation, and gave us instead Rosalind's delightful:

... there was never anything so sudden but the fight of two rams, and Caesar's thrasonical brag of 'I came, saw, and overcame'. For your brother and my sister no sooner met but they looked; no sooner looked but they loved; no sooner loved but they sighed; no sooner sighed but they asked one another the reason; no sooner knew the reason but they sought the remedy: and in these degrees have they made a pair of stairs to marriage which they will climb incontinent or else be incontinent before marriage. They are in the very wrath of love and they will together; clubs cannot part them.

It is obvious that Rosalind in turn is a touchstone for Celia. She is, of course, much more than that; and indeed it has been claimed that *As You Like It* is one of only four Shakespeare plays in which the woman has the leading part. (The others are said to be *Cymbeline, The Merchant of Venice*, and *All's Well That Ends Well* – though some of us might wish to add *Romeo and Juliet* or *Antony and Cleopatra*.) He would not ask too much of the boy apprentices who had to play the female roles, capable as those boys must have been; and one of the most fascinating aspects of *As You Like It* is the skill with which even the part of Rosalind is kept within the compass of the boy actor – who can more easily play the part of a girl who for much of the time is disguised as a youth (Ganymede), even though 'she' is sometimes 'pretending' to be a girl! To the modern actress, as George Bernard Shaw has said, the role is 'what Hamlet is to the actor – a part in which, reasonable presentability being granted, failure is hardly possible'.

The Rosalind of the early scenes is a dignified and reserved young lady, as befits one who has been allowed to stay in her uncle's court, with a doubtful status, after that uncle has banished her father and usurped the dukedom. She may try in all goodwill to 'forget the condition of' her own 'estate' and rejoice in Celia's, but obviously the task is difficult, and it is Celia rather than Rosalind who bandies wit with the clown (Touchstone) on his first appearance. The pompous absurdity of Le Beau, however, draws Rosalind out; and she is the first to cry 'Alas' in pity of the old man whose sons have been badly hurt by Charles the wrestler.

The tone of her first exchange of words with Orlando (1.2) is best shown by the terms of address chosen: '*Young man*, have you challenged Charles the wrestler?'; 'Do, *young sir*, your reputation shall not therefore be misprized'; 'Now Hercules be thy speed, *young man*!' The boy actor would have no difficulty here or with the restraint of 'the little strength that I have, I would it were with you'. Then to Orlando's success in the wrestling is added another claim to Rosalind's attention – that his father, Sir Rowland de Boys, was beloved of her father (this being another of Shakespeare's additions to Lodge) – and her growing interest is shown by a simple gesture, when she presents him with a chain she had worn round her neck:

> *Gentleman,*
> *Wear this for me – one out of suits with fortune,*
> *That could give more but that her hand lacks means.*

A small textual point best illustrates the difficulty that some commentators have had with Shakespeare's presentation of his heroine thereafter. In the next scene (1.3), Rosalind's depression has deepened, and Celia again tries to cheer her: 'Why cousin, why Rosalind, Cupid have mercy, not a word?', only to be told 'Not one to throw at a dog'. Then to Celia's later question 'But is all this for your father?' the reply, as given in the text of the First Folio, is 'No, some of it is for my childes Father' – that is, Rosalind's concern is not all for her banished

father; some of it is for the man she would wish to be the
father of any child she may have. It is a remark that Shakespeare could have written for any one of his many heroines
who combine with a true modesty a frankness that refuses to
beat around the bush once feelings are known to be genuine
(which is not to say that Middleton Murry was correct when
he rashly wrote: 'Rosaline, Portia, Beatrice, Rosalind – it is
hard to recollect them apart'). Shakespeare's first editor, Rowe,
however, presumably found the remark unmaidenly, and
emended it to 'No, some of it is for my father's child' – a
reading that was followed by Pope and most of the
eighteenth- and nineteenth-century editors (Theobald being a
notable exception) and duly approved by Coleridge, who complained of the Folio text: 'This is putting a very indelicate
anticipation in the mouth of Rosalind, without reason; not to
speak of the strangeness of the phrase'. Most modern editors
find no strangeness in the phrase and prefer a frank (and not
'indelicate') Rosalind, in love at first sight, to one too much
concerned about her own griefs; and they note that Shakespeare would not follow Lodge in having his heroine begin
by toying with the hero.

If the Folio text is preserved, some of the comments of the
'Victorian' editors are seen to be very wide of the mark indeed.
One example may suffice, Hudson's: 'Rosalind's ... occasional
freedoms of speech are manifestly intended as part of her
disguise, and spring from the feeling that it is far less indelicate
to go a little out of her character, in order to prevent any
suspicion of her sex, than it would be to hazard such a
suspicion by keeping strictly within her character'. One rewrites
Shakespeare at one's peril! His conception of ideal love is
neither prudish nor sentimental; like Swift, he would presumably have refused to identify felicity with 'the possession of
being well deceived'.

The scene that begins with discussion of the 'child's father'
ends with Rosalind's banishment. The second part of the scene,
however, is in verse; and Rosalind's speeches are dignified,

simple (both in sentence-construction and in vocabulary), and free from rhetoric, so that the audience is in no doubt who is in the right: the Duke is completely unable to answer the direct plea

> *I do beseech your grace,*
> *Let me the knowledge of my fault bear with me.*

Thereafter, until the last scene of all that ends this strange eventful history, Rosalind is in disguise — and the actor's problem is largely that of suggesting the feminine modesty, and the occasional timidity, beneath the playful exterior: 'I could find in my heart to disgrace my man's apparel, and to cry like a woman'. The playfulness presumably presented no problem to the pert Elizabethan boy; it certainly presents none to an actress (and one remembers with some amusement the film critics of the 1930s who so solemnly rebuked Elisabeth Bergner for enjoying herself so much in the part). The key phrase could be said to be 'Come, woo me, woo me: for now I am in a holiday humour, and like enough to consent'. Once Orlando has been identified as the writer of the bad sonnets on trees, and once the first misgivings have passed ('Alas the day, what shall I do with my doublet and hose?'), he is sure to be mercilessly teased by this gay young lady; it has been well said that Shakespeare's Rosalind is 'a sort of universal image of Woman as Sweetheart'. It is, then, Rosalind who speaks the famous epigram 'men are April when they woo, December when they wed'; and it is Rosalind who pricks the bubble of the traditional story of tragic love:

The poor world is almost six thousand years old, and in all this time there was not any man died in his own person, videlicet, in a love-cause. Troilus had his brains dashed out with a Grecian club, yet he did what he could to die before, and he is one of the patterns of love. Leander, he would have lived many a fair year though Hero had turned nun, if it had not been for a hot midsummer night: for, good youth, he went but forth to wash him in the Hellespont and being taken with the cramp was drowned, and the foolish chroniclers of that age found it was 'Hero of Sestos'. But these are all lies; men have died from time to time and worms have eaten them, but not for love.

Indeed, Shakespeare would seem to have gone further and to have laughed at his own earlier concept of the romantic hero. Valentine in *The Two Gentlemen of Verona* is known to be in love by, and apparently not considered less admirable for, the traditional gestures of the sighing male:

VALENTINE *Why, how know you that I am in love?*
SPEED *Marry, by these special marks: first, you have learned, like Sir Proteus, to wreathe your arms like a malcontent; to relish a love-song, like a robin-redbreast; to walk alone, like one that had the pestilence; to sigh, like a schoolboy that had lost his A.B.C.; to weep, like a young wench that had buried her grandam; to fast, like one that takes diet; to watch, like one that fears robbing; to speak puling, like a beggar at Hallowmas. You were wont, when you laughed, to crow like a cock; when you walked, to walk like one of the lions; when you fasted, it was presently after dinner; when you looked sadly, it was for want of money. And now you are metamorphosed with a mistress, that, when I look on you, I can hardly think you my master.*

II.1.15—28

Orlando, on the other hand, is mocked for *not* having the 'marks' by which Rosalind has been 'taught' to know a man in love:

A lean cheek, which you have not; a blue eye and sunken, which you have not; an unquestionable spirit, which you have not; a beard neglected, which you have not – but I pardon you for that, for simply your having in beard is a younger brother's revenue. Then your hose should be ungartered, your bonnet unbanded, your sleeve unbuttoned, your shoe untied, and everything about you demonstrating a careless desolation. But you are no such man: you are rather point-device in your accoutrements, as loving yourself, than seeming the lover of any other.

The heroine is completely in charge of the situation and of the action of the play; it is Rosalind, needless to say, who extorts the necessary promises from all concerned, so that the right knots can be tied, or untied, at the end, and every Jack may have his Jill; and it can only be Rosalind who must speak the epilogue.

Perhaps it is the actor who plays Orlando who has the more difficult task; indeed more than one producer has thought that Orlando was the perfect 'part for a stick'. M. R. Ridley has stated the difficulty as being that 'Orlando in Arden suffers from that air of doubtless excusable fatuity that is liable to envelop the best of men when they fall in love'; and various commentators have endeavoured, as it were, to strengthen the part, in various ways. Some have seen topical allusion or even personal portraiture in it and have suggested that the interest of the Elizabethan audience in the character could have been heightened by their recognizing in it comment on a man 'in the public eye'. C. J. Sisson, for example, once advanced the theory that in Orlando Shakespeare was glancing at the real-life story of Thomas Lodge himself, who in 1593 was involved in a lawsuit concerning shares in his father's estate (but on the evidence given it is hard to believe that the resemblance would have been apparent); J. W. Draper thought Shakespeare was retelling the story of 'Belted Will' Howard and writing the play as a plea for the restoration to him of his ancestral estates (but the alleged connexion with the family of de Boys is not nearly enough to justify so curious a reading). Sir Arthur Quiller-Couch went further, and in a different direction: he thought the play could be read – and presumably that the part ought to be played – to imply that Orlando recognized Rosalind all the time. Oddly enough, he did not quote the few lines that might conceivably give support to his theory.

These are in Act v, scene 2, when the various lovers are proclaiming their virtues as lovers ('And so am I for Phebe', 'And I for Ganymede', 'And I for Rosalind', 'And I for no woman'), modulating into Phebe's 'If this be so, why blame

you me to love you?' (presumably to Rosalind); Silvius's 'If
this be so, why blame you me to love you?' (presumably to
Phebe); and Orlando's 'If this be so, why blame you me to love
you?' – which so startles Rosalind that she asks quickly 'Why
do you speak too "Why blame you me to love you?"' only to
be told 'To her that is not here, nor doth not hear'. Rosalind
lets it go with 'Pray you no more of this, 'tis like the howling
of Irish wolves against the moon'; and perhaps we must let it
go too, on the supposition either that Orlando's reply is sincere
or that he is for the minute embarrassing 'Ganymede' by
carrying on the Rosalind pretence in public. We must let it go
because the alternative is to believe that Shakespeare cheated us
and cheated himself. If he had wished even to leave open the
possibility of Orlando's having recognized Rosalind in disguise,
he could surely not have made the Duke say

> *I do remember in this shepherd boy*
> *Some lively touches of my daughter's favour*

and have made Orlando rule the possibility out with

> *My lord, the first time that I ever saw him*
> *Methought he was a brother to your daugher.*
> *But, my good lord, this boy is forest-born,*
> *And hath been tutored in the rudiments*
> *Of many desperate studies by his uncle.*

(Nor is it necessary to believe that Oliver has learnt the truth
'between Acts IV and V'. When in Act V, scene 2, he replies to
Rosalind's 'God save you, brother' with 'And you, fair sister',
it is in Orlando's presence and immediately after Orlando has
said 'Here comes my Rosalind'; Oliver is fitting into the spirit
of the accepted pretence that Ganymede is Rosalind, both here
and at IV.3.179.)

Modern audiences, and commentators, can hardly be blamed
for feeling uncomfortable about this convention that a character
in a play cannot be recognized in disguise, and indeed some of
Shakespeare's contemporaries were unhappy about it. The intel-

lectual George Chapman, for example, may even have been thinking of *As You Like It*, among other plays, when he had a character in his *May-Day* (1601) say to one who was contemplating the donning of disguise to solve a problem:

Out upon't, that disguise [a friar] is worn threadbare upon every stage, and so much villainy committed under that habit that 'tis grown as suspicious as the vilest . . . For though it be the stale refuge of miserable poets by a change of a hat or a cloak to alter the whole state of a comedy, so as the father must not know his own child, forsooth, nor the wife her husband, yet you must not think they do in earnest carry it away so; . . . and therefore unless your disguise be such that your face bear as great a part in it as the rest, the rest is nothing.

Disguise, however, was a convention, and Shakespeare did not break through it.

His solution to the problem of the part of Orlando, if it is a problem, seems to have been different. In a theatre the most important impression of a character may be the first one; and, conceivably because Shakespeare thought it possible that Orlando would seem weak in the later parts of the play, he has put all the initial emphasis on Orlando's strength. Perhaps this is why he risked the obviousness of the exposition – because he wanted to open the play with the hero's justifiable complaints and determination that he will 'no longer endure it'. He then gives Orlando all the better of the quarrel with Oliver, both morally and physically; and, of course, the stress is on Orlando's manliness and valour in the scene of the wrestling. (Shaw said he always enjoyed watching this scene in the theatre – because it is easier to find somebody who can wrestle than somebody who can act!) Nor is Orlando's courage allowed to drop out of sight; if it turns out to be unnecessary, it is none the less *there* when he demands of the exiled Duke food for Adam; and it is still there when he saves Oliver from that fearsome lioness. Although this last incident is merely reported by Oliver to Rosalind, and to the audience, already the actor playing Orlando has had adequate material to work with, and need not be completely outshone even by his heavenly Rosalind.

The characterization, then, is all that it ought to be and, allowing for the difference between 'history' and comedy, should not be regarded as inferior to that of, say, *Henry IV*, probably written at much the same time or a little earlier. Examination of the 'style' of *As You Like It* similarly suggests the skill of the mature and practised playwright.

Somewhat surprisingly to some readers, much of the play is in prose. Verse is frequently used: for example, in the scene in which the usurping Duke dismisses Orlando and that in which he banishes Rosalind; in the scenes involving the banished Duke in the Forest of Arden; in the Silvius–Phebe interludes; and for Oliver's announcement that Orlando has been wounded by the lioness – in short, for the more formal or solemn parts of the play. Nearly all the Rosalind–Celia–Orlando section, however, is in prose, as befits a light-hearted comedy.

The prose is more artfully balanced and formal than one might think on first reading or first hearing it. Phrases and clauses often run parallel, as in 'for my part, he keeps me rustically at home, or, to speak more properly, stays me here at home unkept'; or 'unless you could teach me to forget a banished father, you must not learn me how to remember any extraordinary pleasure'. Indeed, some of the longer passages are built up from a series of parallels; examples are 'I have neither the scholar's melancholy, which is emulation; nor the musician's, which is fantastical; nor the courtier's, which is proud . . .' and the paragraphs previously quoted on pages 358 and 363. Such prose is descended from Euphuism or Arcadianism, but it is not Euphuistic, for the balance is never allowed to become mathematical for too long. (If the parallels are piled up momentarily, it is to portray a character's state of mind, and to provide another subject for laughter – as when Rosalind's 'What did he when thou sawest him? What said he?

How looked he? Wherein went he? What makes he here? Did he ask for me? Where remains he? How parted he with thee? And when shalt thou see him again? Answer me in one word' earns Celia's mocking reply 'You must borrow me Gargantua's mouth first: 'tis a word too great for any mouth of this age's size. To say "ay" and "no" to these particulars is more than to answer in a catechism.')

Even when the prose is formal in construction, the conversational tone, except in the last scenes, is preserved by such phrases as 'to speak more properly' (in the first sentence quoted in the previous paragraph) or by terms of address: 'Good Monsieur Charles, what's the new news at the new court?' 'There's no news at the court, sir, but the old news.' Celia's 'sweet my coz' or Rosalind's 'O coz, coz, coz, my pretty little coz' are among the many greetings that help similarly to establish the informality; yet because of the tightness of construction (and, of course, the vocabulary) the prose never becomes merely colloquial. Even such a minor point of usage as Shakespeare's choice of 'you' or 'thou' will help to demonstrate the trouble he takes to establish 'tone': the more formal 'you' is used not only by the wrestler Charles to the Duke, by Adam to Orlando, and by Touchstone to Celia but also, originally, by Rosalind (still on her guard, as daughter of the banished Duke) to Celia; 'thou' is used by superior to inferior (the Duke to Charles, Orlando to Adam, and Celia to Touchstone) and, as a mark of affection, by Celia, particularly when trying to put Rosalind at her ease.

The imagery is not obtrusive but is none the less effective for that. It ranges from the flood and the ark, through the English seasons and the Bay of Portugal, to the pearl in the oyster and back to the penalty of Adam; but perhaps the most constant feature, as Caroline Spurgeon noticed many years ago, is the tendency to refer to animals and other aspects of country living: Jaques 'can suck melancholy out of a song, as a weasel sucks eggs'; Rosalind is 'native' to the forest 'as the cony that you see dwell where she is kindled'; Touchstone will be married 'as the ox hath his bow, sir, the horse his curb, and the falcon her bells'; and Rosalind will be more jealous of Orlando 'than a Barbary cock-pigeon over his hen, more clamorous than a parrot against rain, more new-fangled than an ape', and 'more giddy' in her desires 'than a monkey'. This last sentence is followed by a reference to 'Diana in the fountain' that perhaps turned the thoughts of Shakespeare's audience temporarily to the City of London, but the cumulative effect of all the allusions to 'nature' must be to build up the rural 'atmosphere'. As Miss Spurgeon further noted, there is surprisingly little actual description of the forest. The exiled Duke's first speech in Act II, finding tongues in trees, books in the running brooks and sermons in stones, sets the 'scene', but after this the audience must be content with an occasional reference to

> *an oak whose antick root peeps out*
> *Upon the brook that brawls along this wood*

or to sheepcotes, and must rely on its imagination, unconsciously prompted by the imagery, to piece out the 'imperfections' of the bare Elizabethan stage.

One's imagination also has the assistance given by the songs. These – though they are perfect simply as songs and have no greater complexity of language than a song can easily bear – are related even more closely to the themes of the play than, possibly, are the songs in any of Shakespeare's earlier work. 'Under the greenwood tree', for example, helps to establish both the pastoral setting and the tone – and Jaques's third stanza of the song is an important statement of the opposite side of the case; and in much the same way 'What shall he have that killed the deer?' 'enhances the woodland element' but also, with its references to horns and the probability of cuckoldry, maintains the spirit of mocking fun.

> *Blow, blow, thou winter wind,*
> *Thou art not so unkind*
> *As man's ingratitude,*

while still reminding us of 'nature', points up the problem of Adam and Orlando, starving because they are victims of Oliver's 'ingratitude' (nor should one overlook the neat piece of stagecraft that has the song sung at this moment, by Amiens, to give Adam and Orlando time and opportunity to eat). Most magical of all, in the theatre, is the singing by the two Pages of 'It was a lover and his lass' – after Rosalind has arranged the meeting when the couples will be paired off, each lover to his lass as romance decrees. Characteristically, the dramatist introduces the song light-heartedly: 'Shall we clap into't roundly, without hawking, or spitting, or saying we are hoarse, which are the only prologues to a bad voice?' – and again the song has a second theatrical purpose, in that it gives the illusion of the passing of time until the day when Rosalind will present the masque of Hymen.

The wedding masque itself (v.4) is another interesting use of a convention to help round a play off happily (as the Herne the Hunter episode is used to turn *The Merry Wives of Windsor* into a good-humoured joke in which all, even Falstaff, can join). Some commentators have thought that the masque indicates that the Folio text of *As You Like It* represents a revised version performed as part of a wedding celebration, but the hypothesis hardly seems necessary. Elizabethans were accustomed to most forms of 'disguisings', and there are masques in many Elizabethan plays. A masque is a natural and at the same time appropriately formal method of ensuring that

> eight . . . *must take hands,*
> *To join in Hymen's bands.*

The entrance of Jaques de Boys stops the revelling in mid-career, much after the manner of the famous entrance of Mercade to the lovers in *Love's Labour's Lost* with the news that the Princess's father is dead; in *As You Like It*, however, the tidings brought are not chilling but announce the 'conversion' of the usurper and so make possible the completely happy

ending, though not without the touch of acid provided by
Jaques. Another convention, the epilogue, enables Shakespeare
to bring the play to a close, after the stage has been cleared for
the boy playing the part of Rosalind; taking advantage both of
his true male sex and of his assumed female one, the player
appeals to the audience for approval, all but saying to them, in
the words of Lodge's address 'To the Gentlemen Readers' of
Rosalynde that probably gave Shakespeare his title, 'If you like
it, so'.

It is difficult to believe that artistry of this order would have
been possible even for Shakespeare as early as 1593, the year in
which some scholars have placed the composition of the play.
There is, to be sure, one passage that may well refer to an
important event in that year: Touchstone's 'When a man's
verses cannot be understood, nor a man's good wit seconded
with the forward child Understanding, it strikes a man more
dead than a great reckoning in a little room' (III.3.10–13).
Particularly if the last phrase is agreed to be an allusion to
Christopher Marlowe's 'infinite riches in a little room' in *The
Jew of Malta* (already well-known on the stage, but not published
until 1633), there may also be reference to the death of Marlowe
in a private room of the inn at Deptford, on 30 May 1593,
following a quarrel over a bill or 'reckoning'. It has been
suggested, however, by J. H. Walter, that, especially since the
preceding lines in *As You Like It* refer to Ovid, Shakespeare
may rather have had in mind lines from Chapman's poem *Ovid's
Banquet of Sense* (1595): Ovid, seeing Corinna naked, is said to see

> *The fair of beauty, as whole countries come*
> *And show their riches in a little room*

and later Chapman writes that

> *Ovid's muse as in her tropic shined*
> *And he, struck dead, was mere heaven-born become.*

Nor, of course, need a reference to Marlowe's death necessarily have been made immediately after it; Marlowe may have been in Shakespeare's mind following the publication of *Hero and Leander* in 1598. Phebe quotes from that poem:

> *Dead Shepherd, now I find thy saw of might,*
> *'Who ever loved that loved not at first sight?'*

and even though the poem may well have circulated in manuscript, the quotation could hardly have been appreciated by the Elizabethan audience unless the poem had also been published.

Rosalind's words 'I will weep for nothing, like Diana in the fountain' may, but do not necessarily, refer to the fountain with a statue of Diana erected in Cheapside in 1596; Celia's 'since the little wit that fools have was silenced, the little foolery that wise men have makes a great show', in reply to Touchstone's similar sentiments, may, but does not necessarily, refer to a decision of the Privy Council in mid-1599 that Nashe's and Harvey's satirical pamphlets should be burnt and none published thereafter. Jaques's 'seven ages of man' speech may or may not have been prompted by the motto of the new Globe Theatre, probably finished by September 1599. The suggestion, however, that the exiled Duke's opening lines in Act II, in praise of the woodland life, owe something to Robin Hood's words (lines 1365–81) in *The Downfall of Robert Earl of Huntington*, acted in 1598–9, although not conclusive, is tempting (there is no 'source' for these lines in *Rosalynde*); and those who favour an early date for *As You Like It* must also get over the difficulty that it is not included in Meres's list of Shakespeare's well-known plays in 1598 (unless, to be sure, they maintain that *As You Like It*, perhaps in some earlier version, is to be identified with Meres's mysterious *Love's Labour's Won*).

To these possibilities, or probabilities, and the more important evidence of the mature general style of the play, both in verse and in prose, one must add that *As You Like It* was first entered on the Stationers' Register on 4 August 1600; and along with *Henry V and Much Ado About Nothing* and Ben

Jonson's *Every Man in his Humour* it was entered with the direction 'to be staied' – a phrase almost certainly indicating a move by Shakespeare and his company to prevent 'pirated' or unauthorized publication of a new and popular play. It is surely difficult to reach any other conclusion than that *As You Like It* was written in 1599.

It is still possible, of course, that the play as we have it (it was first published in the First Folio of 1623) was a revision in 1599 of an earlier play – or even that it was revised between 1599 and 1623. There is, however, no good reason for thinking so. Professor Dover Wilson himself later withdrew in great part the theory he had advanced in 1926 that sections of *As You Like It* now in prose must have been originally written in verse. The 'verse-fossils' that he found in the prose – prose that he reduced to verse (sometimes bad verse) by what he called 'a little innocent faking' – could be found by the same method in almost any prose; and, as has been suggested above, when Shakespeare modulates from prose to verse or verse to prose, he generally seems to do so for good dramatic reason. Nor, for that matter, is the verse of *As You Like It* such as even Shakespeare is likely to have been capable of writing in 1593.

The minor inconsistencies that Dover Wilson and others have found in *As You Like It* do exist – or some of them do. But it is not necessary to infer that they betray two stages of composition.

One of them may be of the commentators' own making: for while it is true that Celia says she was 'too young' to value Rosalind when Rosalind's father was banished, this does not necessarily mean that she is thinking of the event as more than, say, a year or eighteen months in the past; a year would be more than long enough for 'old custom' to have made the greenwood life 'more sweet than that of painted pomp'; and while Oliver asks Charles for the 'new news at the new court', Charles gives it to him expressly as 'no news ... but the old news', of the banishment, and one need assume no more than that Oliver, not living in the new court, has taken a while to catch up with the full details of life there. There is also the convention of 'double time': in many an Elizabethan play time passes more quickly for some purposes of the plot than for others.

Another of the inconsistencies may be removed – and generally has been removed – by a slight textual emendation that seems reasonable enough. In the speech headings of the Folio, the usurping Duke is called simply 'Duke', and his banished brother is 'Duke Senior'; we learn from Orlando in the dialogue, however, at 1.2.220–22 that the usurper's name is Frederick, and this is confirmed by Jaques de Boys at v.4.151. Earlier in Act 1, scene 2, however, Celia asks Touchstone whom he refers to in his story of the knight who swore by his honour and yet was not forsworn, and Touchstone replies 'One that old Frederick, your father, loves' – to which the Folio allows *Rosalind* to retort: 'My father's love is enough to honour him enough'. Yet it is odd that Touchstone should reply to Celia's question by addressing himself to Rosalind (with 'your father'). 'Old' is not necessarily a reference to age; it was (and still is) a term of half-affectionate familiarity, and Celia would be well entitled to resent a clown's use of it. On the whole, then, it seems more likely that there has been a slip in the speech heading, whether Shakespeare's or the compositor's, and that therefore Celia should be allowed to carry on her exchange with Touchstone, than that Touchstone should turn awkwardly from her to Rosalind and that Shakespeare should thereby name Rosalind's father 'Frederick' as well as Celia's. (Even if the contradiction is permitted to remain, it does not imply that Shakespeare was rewriting the play after a period of time, when he had forgotten the names of his characters: he forgot names during the composition of other plays too.)

The third inconsistency concerns the height of Rosalind and Celia. In Act 1, scene 3, Rosalind decides to assume the disguise of the 'man' because she is 'more than common tall', and Celia is content to put herself in mean attire as a girl; and in Act IV, scene 3, Oliver describes 'the boy' (Rosalind) as 'fair', 'the woman' (Celia) as

> *low*
> *And browner than her brother —*

which almost certainly means 'lower and browner' but in any case confirms that Celia is *not* tall. In the source, *Rosalynde*, it is Rosalynde who is the taller; and of course in a whole series of Shakespeare's comedies (including *A Midsummer Night's Dream, The Merchant of Venice, Much Ado About Nothing,* and *Twelfth Night*) we have one heroine who is tall and fair while the second is short and dark. The problem is that when Orlando in Act I, scene 2, asks Le Beau:

> *and pray you tell me this,*
> *Which of the two was daughter of the Duke*
> *That here was at the wrestling?*

Le Beau replies:

> *Neither his daughter, if we judge by manners,*
> *But yet indeed the taller is his daughter;*
> *The other is daughter to the banished Duke,*
> *And here detained by her usurping uncle*
> *To keep his daughter company.*

This is a plain contradiction, and many editors solve the problem by emending 'taller' to 'smaller' or 'shorter' or 'lesser', thereby setting themselves up as judges of the word that Shakespeare would have used had he said what he is thought to have meant. It seems better to leave the text alone and to assume with Sir Walter Greg and others that for some perform-ance of the play there had been a change of cast, and that the text had been adapted for this at one point and not elsewhere. (Such things still happen in the best organized of playhouses.)

It remains to admit that there are two characters called Jaques in *As You Like It* — one the confessed cynic, the other the second son of Sir Rowland de Boys, Oliver's and Orlando's brother, who is called Jaques in the first scene and is simply 'Second Brother' in the Folio, when he appears in person in

Act v. Quite possibly the two Jaqueses were at first intended to be the one character (the second son in *Rosalynde* is a scholar and a student of philosophy) but if so Shakespeare changed his mind. Again we need not assume that he changed it long after he had forgotten his original plan: a mere duplication of name would hardly have worried the playwright who, not satisfied with all the other complications of *The Taming of the Shrew*, wilfully called one character Gremio and another Grumio.

These are minor matters and do not affect the fact that the Folio text of *As You Like It* is one of the best in the Shakespeare canon. Even if an editor cannot quite, in Sir Arthur Quiller-Couch's optimistic words, 'take holiday', he can certainly 'enjoy his while in Arden'. It is to be hoped that the reader can do so too – and 'fleet the time carelessly' as well.

Further Reading

Of the many editions of *As You Like It* since the First Folio, those by H. H. Furness (the New Variorum, 1890), J. W. Holme (the original Arden, 1914), Sir Arthur Quiller-Couch and J. Dover Wilson (the New Cambridge, 1926; reprinted with an added note, 1959), G. L. Kittredge (*Sixteen Plays of Shakespeare*, 1946), Agnes Latham (the 'new' Arden, 1975) and Richard Knowles (A New Variorum, 1977) are perhaps the most helpfully annotated. The major cruxes in the text are discussed not only in the various editions but also in C. J. Sisson's *New Readings in Shakespeare* (Cambridge University Press, 1956); and the First Folio itself is examined in W. W. Greg's *The Shakespeare First Folio* (Oxford University Press, 1955) and, more fully, in Charlton Hinman's *The Printing and Proof-Reading of the First Folio of Shakespeare* (Clarendon Press, 1963), where the work of each of the compositors and the variant readings of different copies are tabulated.

There are critical studies in most of the standard books on Shakespeare and those on the comedies, such as H. B. Charlton's *Shakespearian Comedy* (Methuen, 1938), T. M. Parrott's *Shakespearean Comedy* (Oxford University Press, 1949), and G. K. Hunter's *Shakespeare: The Late Comedies* (British Council and Longmans Green, 1962), but the best essay on the play is Harold Jenkins's, in Volume 8 of *Shakespeare Survey* (edited by Allardyce Nicoll, 1955). Helen Gardner's well-known essay, first published in *More Talking of Shakespeare* (Longmans Green, 1959), is republished in *Shakespeare's Comedies: An Anthology of Modern Criticism* (edited by Laurence Lerner, Penguin Shakespeare Library, 1967), as is the relevant chapter of C. L.

Barber's *Shakespeare's Festive Comedy* (Princeton University Press, 1959).

The major source, Lodge's *Rosalynde*, is analysed, and reprinted, in Geoffrey Bullough's *Narrative and Dramatic Sources of Shakespeare* (Volume 2, Routledge & Kegan Paul, 1958). The standard work on the pastoral tradition is W. W. Greg's *Pastoral Poetry and Pastoral Drama* (Bullen, 1906); and another tradition to which the play belongs is the subject of D. L. Stevenson's *The Love-Game Comedy* (Oxford University Press, 1946).

Essays on single characters include O. J. Campbell's on Jaques in *Huntington Library Bulletin* No. 8 (October 1935) and John Palmer's on Touchstone in his *Comic Characters of Shakespeare* (Macmillan, 1946). Books on the fool include Enid Welsford's *The Fool* (Faber & Faber, 1935) and Leslie Hotson's *Shakespeare's Motley* (Hart-Davis, 1952), although some of the conclusions of the latter have been questioned, for example by E. W. Ives in *Shakespeare Survey* Volume 13 (1960). C. S. Felver's *Robert Armin, Shakespeare's Fool* (Kent State University Press, 1961) also wins only qualified assent.

Shakespeare's imagery was first studied, with some particular reference to *As You Like It*, in Walter Whiter's *A Specimen of a Commentary on Shakespeare* (1794; edited by A. Over and M. Bell, Methuen, 1967); the study was resumed, in different contexts, in Caroline Spurgeon's standard *Shakespeare's Imagery* (Cambridge University Press, 1935) and Edward A. Armstrong's *Shakespeare's Imagination* (Drummond, 1946).

Other specialized treatments of problems relevant to the play include Richmond Noble's *Shakespeare's Biblical Knowledge* (S.P.C.K., 1935) and *Shakespeare's Use of Song* (Humphrey Milford, 1923); E. W. Naylor's *Shakespeare and Music* (1896; revised 1931); J. H. Long's *Shakespeare's Use of Music* (University of Florida Press, 1955); and C. G. Smith's *Shakespeare's Proverb Lore* (Harvard University Press, 1963), which adds to the information given in M. P. Tilley's invaluable *Dictionary of the Proverbs in England in the Sixteenth and Seventeenth Centuries* (Uni-

versity of Michigan Press, 1950). The note by J. H. Walter
referred to in the Introduction, page 375, is in *Notes and Queries*
N.S. 12, 3 (March 1965).

The most stimulating of all reviewers who have written on
performances of *As You Like It* is undoubtedly George Bernard
Shaw. The comments quoted in the Introduction and Commentary are from his collected *Dramatic Opinions and Essays* (Constable, 1907), and are reprinted in *Shaw on Shakespeare* (edited by
Edwin Wilson, Cassell, 1962; Penguin Shakespeare Library,
1969). George Sand's discussion of her adaptation of the play is
in *A Letter to M. Regnier, of the théâtre français* (1856).

An Account of the Text

As You Like It was first published in the great collection of Shakespeare's plays made after his death, the First Folio of 1623 (hereafter called 'F'). The entry of the play on the Stationers' Register on 4 August 1600 'to be staied' may indicate an intention to prevent publication by others rather than an intention by Shakespeare's company to print it themselves; certainly no publication followed, and the play was duly entered on the Register again on 8 November 1623, among the F plays 'not formerly entred to other men'.

The F text was probably based on an authorial manuscript (or a transcript of one) that had been used in the theatre and then prepared for publication (hence the division into Acts and Scenes). As Charlton Hinman has demonstrated in *The Printing and Proof-Reading of the First Folio of Shakespeare*, the text was set up by no fewer than three different compositors ('B', 'C', and 'D'), probably setting copy simultaneously for much of the time. (The evidence is from differing spelling habits as well as typography.) Accordingly the copy had to be 'cast off' (that is, calculation had to be made in advance of how much printed space a certain amount of the manuscript would take); and if the calculation was wrong, prose could be spun out to look like verse (as seems to have happened in II.6 and III.4) or verse could be printed as prose.

There was some sporadic proof-correcting, on three of the twenty-three pages, as the sheets were being run off; and, in the usual Elizabethan fashion, the incorrect sheets were retained and used as well as those corrected. Hence different copies of F have different readings on three pages (193, 204, and 207), but none of the nine alterations would have required reference to copy. The only two variants of even minor interest are the speech ascriptions of v.1.20 and 21, originally given in error to *Orl.* and *Clo.* (Touchstone) and corrected to *Clo.* and *Will.* respectively.

The emendations made in the Second, Third, and Fourth Folios (all in the seventeenth century) are sometimes correct but have no more authority than the emendations of later editors (beginning with Rowe in 1709). Accordingly they are not listed separately here.

COLLATIONS

I

The following emendations of F have been accepted in this edition (the F reading is given after the square bracket, in the original spelling, except that the 'long s' [ʃ] has been replaced by 's'). Obvious printer's errors and mislineation (such as that in II.6 and III.4) are not listed; stage directions are treated separately on pages 388–90.

I.1. 103 she] hee
      152 OLIVER] *not in* F
I.2.   51 and hath] hath
       79 CELIA] *Ros.*
      278 Rosalind] *Rosaline.*
II.1. 49 much] must
II.3. 10 some] seeme
       16 ORLANDO] *not in* F
       29 ORLANDO] *Ad.*
       71 seventeen] seauentie
II.4.   1 weary] merry
    16–17 Ay . . . here: | A . . . talk] *prose in* F
       40 thy wound] they would

66   you, friend] your friend
91–2   And ... place, | And ... it.] And ... wages: | I
      ... could | Waste ... it.
II.5.   1   AMIENS (*sings*)] Song (*above the first line*)
6–7   Here ... see | No enemy] *one line in* F
11–13 (*prose*)] I ... prethee more, | I ... song, | As ...
      more.
15–17 (*prose*)] I ... me, | I ... sing: | Come ... stanzo's?
31–4   (*prose*)] And ... him: | He ... companie: | I ...
      giue | Heauen ... them. | Come ... come.
43–4   (*prose*)] Ile ... note, | That ... Inuention.
46   JAQUES] *Amy.*
52–3   Here ... see | Gross ... he] *one line in* F
59–60 (*prose*)] And ... Duke, | His ... prepar'd.
II.7. 36   A worthy] O worthie
55   Not to seem] Seeme
101–2 (*prose*)] And ... reason, | I ... dye.
103–4 What ... force, | More ... gentleness.] What ...
      haue? | Your ... your force | Moue ... gentlenesse.
168–9 Welcome ... burden, | And ... feed] *prose in* F
175   AMIENS (*sings*)] Song.
183   Then hey-ho] *The heigh ho*
III.2. 121   *a desert*] Desert
      be?] bee,
141   her] his
230   such] forth F1; forth such F2
237   thy] the
246–7 (*prose*)] I ... faith | I ... alone.
248–9 (*prose*)] And ... sake | I ... societie.
348   deifying] defying
III.3. 2   now] how
51   Horns ? Even so. Poor men alone?] hornes, euen so
      poore men alone:
85   (*prose*)] Go ... mee, | And ... thee.
86–95 Come ... *with thee*] Come ... *Audrey,* | We ...
      baudrey: | Farewel ... Not O ... *Oliuer,* O ...

> *Oliuer* leaue . . . thee: But winde away, bee . . . say, I
> . . . with thee.

III.5. 128   I have] Haue

IV.1.   1   me be] me

17–18   my often] by often

195   in, it] in, in

IV.2.   10   LORDS] *not in* F

12–13   Then . . . bear | This burden] *one line in* F

IV.3.   5   *Enter Silvius*] *after 'brain' in line 3*

105   oak] old Oake

V.1.   55   policy] police

V.2.   7   nor her] nor

13–16   (*prose*)] You . . . consent. | Let . . . I | Inuite . . .
followers: | Go . . . looke you, | Heere . . . *Rosalinde.*

V.3.   15   PAGES] *not in* F

18   ring] *rang*

33–8   And therefore . . . spring] *follows first stanza (lines
15–20)*

V.4. 111   her hand] *his hand*

112   her bosom] *his bosome*

117–18   If . . . true, | Why . . . adieu!] *one line in* F

161   them] him

2

The following emendations of F are plausible enough or popular enough to be worthy of record although they have not been
accepted here. The F reading is given first, as modernized in
this edition. There have been many other emendations (those
of the earlier editions are listed in the New Variorum edition).

I.2.   3   would you yet were merrier] would you yet I were
merrier?

87   the Beu] le Beau

155   them] her

232   all promise] promise
261   taller] shorter (*Rowe*); smaller (*Malone*); lesser (*Spedding*)
I.3.   11   child's father] father's child
24   try] cry
135   in we] we in
II.1.   5   not] but
50   friend] friends
II.3.   58   meed] need
II.4.   71   travail] travel
II.7.   73   weary] wearer's
III.2.   101   Wintered] Winter
151   Jupiter] pulpiter
III.3.   19   may] it may
46   horn-beasts] horned beasts
III.4.   14   cast] chaste
27   lover] a lover
IV.1.   124   ROSALIND] CELIA
IV.2.   7   LORD] AMIENS
IV.3.   8   did bid] bid
88   sister] forester
156   this] his
V.2. 91 or 93 observance] obedience
V.3.   18   the spring time] spring time
41   untuneable] untimeable

3

The following are the principal additions to, or alterations of, the stage directions in F. The F reading is given second, in the original spelling.

I.1.   26   *Adam stands aside*] *not in* F
49   *threatening him*] *not in* F
50   *seizing him by the throat*] *not in* F

	59	*coming forward] not in* F
	88	*Exit Dennis] not in* F
1.2.	41	*Enter Touchstone] Enter Clowne.*
138 etc.		*Duke Frederick] Duke (similarly elsewhere)*
	152	*He stands aside] not in* F
	199	*Orlando and Charles wrestle] Wrastle.*
	202	*A shout as Charles is thrown] Shout.*
	203	*coming forward] not in* F
	208	*Attendants carry Charles off] not in* F
	218	*Exit Duke, with Lords, Le Beau, and Touchstone]*
		Exit Duke.
	233	*taking a chain from her neck] not in* F
	236	*to Celia] not in* F
	237	*Rosalind and Celia begin to withdraw] not in* F
	245	*To Orlando] not in* F
		Exeunt Rosalind and Celia] Exit.
	275	*Exit Le Beau] not in* F
1.3.	87	*Exit Duke, with Lords] Exit Duke, &c.*
II.1.	0	*dressed like foresters] like Forresters*
II.3.	0	*from opposite sides] not in* F
II.4.	0	*Enter . . . Touchstone] Enter Rosaline for Ganimed,*
		Celia for Aliena, and Clowne, alias Touchstone.
II.5.	35	ALL TOGETHER (*sing*)] *Song. Altogether heere.*
II.6.	8	*Raising him] not in* F
II.7.	0	*Enter . . . outlaws] Enter Duke Sen. & Lord, like*
		Out-lawes.
	136	*Exit] not in* F
III.2.	10	*and Touchstone] & Clowne.*
	158	*Exit Touchstone, with Corin] Exit.*
	245	*Celia and Rosalind stand back] not in* F
	286	*Exit Jaques] not in* F
	287	*to Celia] not in* F
III.3.	0	*Enter Touchstone and Audrey, followed by Jaques]*
		Enter Clowne, Audrey, & Iaques:
8, 29, 42		*aside] not in* F
	66	*coming forward] not in* F

	96	*aside*] *not in* F
III.5.	7	*unobserved*] *not in* F
	35	*coming forward*] *not in* F
	66	*to Phebe*] *not in* F
	67	*to Silvius*] *not in* F
	69	*To Phebe*] *not in* F
	74	*To Silvius*] *not in* F
	80	*Exit Rosalind, with Celia and Corin*] *Exit.*
IV.1.	28	*Going*] *not in* F
	29	*as he goes*] *not in* F
IV.2.	0	*Enter Jaques, and Lords dressed as foresters*] *Enter Iaques and Lords, Forresters.*
IV.3.	8	*He gives Rosalind a letter, which she reads*] *not in* F
	157	*Rosalind faints*] *not in* F
V.1.	0	*Touchstone and Audrey*] *Clowne and Awdrie.*
V.2.	18	*Exit*] *not in* F
	98–113	*to Rosalind (etc.)*] *These (nine) S.D.s are not in* F.
V.3.	0	*Touchstone*] *Clowne*
V.4.6–16		*to the Duke (etc.)*] *These (four) S.D.s are not in* F.
	33	*Touchstone*] *Clowne*
	104	*Enter . . . themselves*] *Enter Hymen, Rosalind, and Celia.*
	113–46	*to the Duke (etc.)*] *These (ten) S.D.s are not in* F.
	147	*Second Brother, Jaques de Boys*] *Second Brother.*
	183–8	*to the Duke (etc.)*] *These (five) S.D.s are not in* F.
	195	*Exeunt all except Rosalind*] *Exit*

The Songs

There are no early settings of 'Under the greenwood tree' (II.5) or 'Blow, blow, thou winter wind' (II.7). 'O sweet Oliver', from which Touchstone sings fragments (III.3), appears to have been sung to the tune of 'In peascod time', also known as 'The hunt is up'. The version printed below adapts Touchstone's words to the tune.

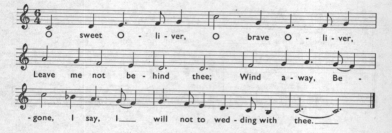

The earliest known setting of 'What shall he have that killed the deer?' (IV.2) is in an arrangement as a catch for four voices made by John Hilton (1599–1657), not published till 1672. The tune may be related to that sung in early performances of the play or it may have been independently composed. It is printed in John H. Long's *Shakespeare's Use of Music* (University of Florida Press, Gainesville, 1955), page 151.

Thomas Morley's well-known setting of 'It was a lover and his lass' (V.3) appeared in his *First Book of Airs, or Little Short Songs* (1600). Its relation to the play is discussed in the note to V.3.15–38. The version given below is from E. H. Fellowes's edition of Morley's book (Stainer & Bell, 1932). The accompaniment is an exact transcription for piano of the lute tablature.

It was a lov-er and his lass, With a

hey, with a ho, and a hey no-ni-

-no, and a hey no-ni no-ni no,

That o'er the green corn-fields did pass, In

spring time, in spring time, in spring time, the

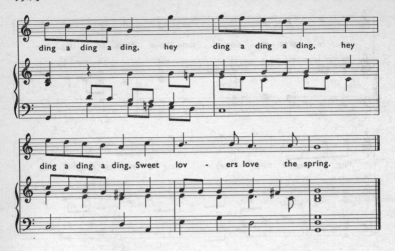

ding a ding a ding, hey ding a ding a ding, hey

ding a ding a ding, Sweet lov - ers love the spring.

2

Between the acres of the rye,
　With a hey, with a ho, and a hey nonino,
These pretty country fools would lie,
　In spring time, the only pretty ring time,
When birds do sing, hey ding a ding a ding,
Sweet lovers love the spring.

3

This carol they began that hour,
　With a hey, with a ho, and a hey nonino,
How that a life was but a flower,
　In spring time, the only pretty ring time,
When birds do sing, hey ding a ding a ding,
Sweet lovers love the spring.

4

Then pretty lovers take the time,
　With a hey, with a ho, and a hey nonino,
For love is crowned with the prime,

In spring time, the only pretty ring time,
When birds do sing, hey ding a ding a ding,
Sweet lovers love the spring.

AS YOU LIKE IT

The Characters in the Play

DUKE SENIOR, a banished duke

AMIENS
JAQUES } noblemen in attendance on him

DUKE FREDERICK, his brother, the usurper

LE BEAU, a courtier

CHARLES, a wrestler

OLIVER
JAQUES } sons of Sir Rowland de Boys
ORLANDO

ADAM
DENNIS } servants of Oliver

In these notes no attempt has been made to 'explain' characteristics of Elizabethan syntax that present no difficulties in comprehension. Accordingly there are no separate notes on, for example, the so-called third-person plural in '-s' (*the Destinies decrees*), the 'attraction' of the verb to the nearer subject (*thou and I am*), the double negatives, the subjunctives, or such constructions as *better than him I am before knows me*. These are all described in E. A. Abbott's *A Shakespearian Grammar*, which, even if in some ways old-fashioned (it was first published in 1869), is still extremely helpful; and in G. L. Brook, *The Language of Shakespeare* (London, 1976).

Throughout the notes, the abbreviation 'F' is used for the First Folio of 1623, in which the play was first published. References to other plays by Shakespeare not yet available in the New Penguin Shakespeare edition are to Peter Alexander's edition of the Complete Works (London, 1951).

The Characters in the Play This list is not in F. For comment on the naming of the two Dukes and on the two characters named Jaques, see Introduction, pages 378 and 380. That *Jaques* was almost certainly two syllables (pronounced 'Jak-es' or, more probably, 'Jake-wes', in either case with a pun on 'jakes') is suggested by lines like 'The melancholy Jaques grieves at that' or (from Robert Greene's *Friar Bacon and Friar Bungay*) 'Whose surname is Don Jaques Vandermast' and 'Bestir thee, Jaques, tak e not now the foil'. Jaques was also an English family name, as was de Boys.

THE CLOWN, alias TOUCHSTONE

SIR OLIVER MARTEXT, a country vicar
CORIN   ⎫
           ⎬ shepherds
SILVIUS   ⎭
WILLIAM, a country youth, in love with Audrey

ROSALIND, daughter of Duke Senior, later disguised as
    GANYMEDE
CELIA, daughter of Duke Frederick, later disguised as
    ALIENA

PHEBE, a shepherdess
AUDREY, a country wench

A masquer representing HYMEN

Lords, pages, and attendants

Enter Orlando and Adam

ORLANDO As I remember, Adam, it was upon this fashion
bequeathed me by will, but poor a thousand crowns, and,
as thou sayest, charged my brother on his blessing to
breed me well; and there begins my sadness. My
brother Jaques he keeps at school, and report speaks
goldenly of his profit: for my part, he keeps me rustically
at home, or, to speak more properly, stays me here at
home unkept – for call you that 'keeping' for a gentleman of my birth, that differs not from the stalling of an
ox? His horses are bred better, for, besides that they   10
are fair with their feeding, they are taught their manage,
and to that end riders dearly hired; but I, his brother,
gain nothing under him but growth, for the which his
animals on his dunghills are as much bound to him as I.

As You Like It is one of the few Shakespeare texts fully divided in the original
editions into Acts and Scenes (the for-
mula used in F being '*Actus primus. Scæna
Prima*' etc.). Since it is improbable that
such divisions were observed on the
Elizabethan public stage where, except
perhaps for one interval, the action
seems to have been continuous, the text
of this play may have been specially
prepared for publication.

1.1.2 *but poor a thousand* a mere (or, in
modern idiom, a 'miserable') thousand. Compare *a many* in line 109.

3 *charged* it was charged, order was given
to
on his blessing as a condition of obtaining, or retaining, his (our father's)
blessing
4 *breed* raise, educate
5 *school* (probably) university
6 *his profit* his progress, the way in
which he benefits
7 *stays* retains (or 'detains')
11 *fair with* healthy as a result of
manage. This was the technical term
for the training of a horse in its
paces, particularly for military purposes (from French *manège*, itself now
used as an English word).

Besides this nothing that he so plentifully gives me, the something that nature gave me his countenance seems to take from me: he lets me feed with his hinds, bars me the place of a brother, and, as much as in him lies, mines my gentility with my education. This is it, Adam, that grieves me, and the spirit of my father, which I think is within me, begins to mutiny against this servitude. I will no longer endure it, though yet I know no wise remedy how to avoid it.

Enter Oliver

ADAM Yonder comes my master, your brother.

ORLANDO Go apart, Adam, and thou shalt hear how he will shake me up.

Adam stands aside

OLIVER Now, sir, what make you here?

ORLANDO Nothing: I am not taught to make anything.

OLIVER What mar you then, sir?

ORLANDO Marry, sir, I am helping you to mar that which God made, a poor unworthy brother of yours, with idleness.

OLIVER Marry, sir, be better employed, and be naught a while.

ORLANDO Shall I keep your hogs and eat husks with them? What prodigal portion have I spent, that I should come to such penury?

---

16 *countenance* demeanour, bearing; or style of living (as allowed to Orlando)

17 *hinds* servants, farm labourers
bars me excludes me from

18–19 *as much as in him lies, mines my gentility with my education* to the best of his ability undermines the advantages I have from my gentle birth, by the poor kind of education he allows me

26 *shake me up* abuse me violently

27 *make* do (but Orlando's reply involves a pun on the word)

30 *Marry* by Mary (with a pun on *mar*, just used by Oliver)

33–4 *be naught a while* leave me, 'make yourself scarce', or (possibly) be quiet

36 *prodigal portion* (with reference to the parable of the prodigal son, Luke 15.11 ff., and particularly 15–17)

OLIVER Know you where you are, sir?

ORLANDO O, sir, very well: here in your orchard.

OLIVER Know you before whom, sir?   40

ORLANDO Ay, better than him I am before knows me: I
know you are my eldest brother, and in the gentle
condition of blood you should so know me. The courtesy
of nations allows you my better, in that you are the first
born, but the same tradition takes not away my blood,
were there twenty brothers betwixt us: I have as much
of my father in me as you, albeit I confess your coming
before me is nearer to his reverence.

OLIVER (*threatening him*) What, boy!

ORLANDO (*seizing him by the throat*) Come, come, elder   50
brother, you are too young in this.

OLIVER Wilt thou lay hands on me, villain?

ORLANDO I am no villain: I am the youngest son of Sir
Rowland de Boys; he was my father, and he is thrice a
villain that says such a father begot villains. Wert thou
not my brother, I would not take this hand from thy
throat till this other had pulled out thy tongue for saying

39 *orchard*. The commonest Elizabethan
meaning was 'garden', although
sometimes the distinction was drawn
between orchard and garden.

42–3 *in the gentle condition of blood* if your
behaviour was what that of a
brother, of gentle blood, should be

48 *nearer to his reverence* more worthy of
the respect due to him (the father),
because as eldest son 'closest' to him
in blood. Oliver's anger is more convincingly explained by Orlando's
tone than by anything in the single
phrase.

49, 50 *threatening him; seizing him by the
throat*. These are not in F, but
the action is made clear by lines 56–
7.

49 *boy*. The word is suggested by Or-

lando's being younger but was a general term of contempt. Compare Coriolanus's anger when it is used of
him, v.6.101–17, and *Romeo and Juliet*,
III.1.65 and 130.

51 *young* inexperienced, immature. Perhaps there is also a pun on *elder* in
the previous line: the elder tree, associated with Judas, may have had connotations of unreliability and deceit.

52 *villain*. Orlando chooses to take the
word in its other sense of 'serf' (our
'villein'). His and Oliver's use for
the first time of the contemptuous
second-person singular indicates that
the quarrel has become ill-tempered.
On its use elsewhere in the play, see
Introduction, page 372.

so; thou hast railed on thyself.

ADAM (*coming forward*) Sweet masters, be patient; for your
father's remembrance, be at accord.

60 OLIVER Let me go, I say.

ORLANDO I will not till I please: you shall hear me. My
father charged you in his will to give me good education:
you have trained me like a peasant, obscuring and hiding
from me all gentleman-like qualities. The spirit of my
father grows strong in me, and I will no longer endure it.
Therefore allow me such exercises as may become a
gentleman, or give me the poor allottery my father left
me by testament; with that I will go buy my fortunes.

70 OLIVER And what wilt thou do, beg when that is spent?
Well, sir, get you in. I will not long be troubled with
you: you shall have some part of your will. I pray you,
leave me.

ORLANDO I will no further offend you than becomes me
for my good.

OLIVER Get you with him, you old dog.

ADAM Is 'old dog' my reward? Most true, I have lost my
teeth in your service. God be with my old master! He
would not have spoke such a word.

Exeunt Orlando and Adam

80 OLIVER Is it even so? Begin you to grow upon me? I will
physic your rankness, and yet give no thousand crowns
neither. Holla, Dennis!

Enter Dennis

DENNIS Calls your worship?

OLIVER Was not Charles, the Duke's wrestler, here to
speak with me?

---

65 *qualities*. In addition to its modern
senses, the word could mean 'accom-
plishments', 'occupations', 'ranks'.

67 *exercises* employments, occupations

68 *allottery* allocation, share

72 *will* (1) desire; (2) portion from the
will or testament

80 *grow upon me* (probably another quibble) grow up too fast for my liking;
take liberties with me; grow rank
(hence *rankness* in line 81)

81 *physic* cure (by a dose of physic),
correct

DENNIS So please you, he is here at the door, and im-
portunes access to you.

OLIVER Call him in.   *Exit Dennis*

'Twill be a good way — and tomorrow the wrestling is.

Enter Charles

CHARLES Good morrow to your worship.   90

OLIVER Good Monsieur Charles, what's the new news at
the new court?

CHARLES There's no news at the court, sir, but the old
news: that is, the old Duke is banished by his younger
brother the new Duke, and three or four loving lords
have put themselves into voluntary exile with him,
whose lands and revenues enrich the new Duke; therefore he gives them good leave to wander.

OLIVER Can you tell if Rosalind, the Duke's daughter, be
banished with her father?   100

CHARLES O, no; for the Duke's daughter, her cousin, so
loves her, being ever from their cradles bred together,
that she would have followed her exile, or have died to
stay behind her; she is at the court, and no less beloved
of her uncle than his own daughter, and never two ladies
loved as they do.

OLIVER Where will the old Duke live?

CHARLES They say he is already in the Forest of Arden,
and a many merry men with him; and there they live
like the old Robin Hood of England: they say many   110
young gentlemen flock to him every day, and fleet the
time carelessly as they did in the golden world.

OLIVER What, you wrestle tomorrow before the new
Duke?

CHARLES Marry do I, sir; and I came to acquaint you

---

91 *new news*. See Introduction, page 378.
103–4 *to stay* if forced to stay
111–12 *fleet the time carelessly as they did in the golden world* while away the time in a carefree way as men did in the Golden Age. *Fleet* is normally an intransitive verb, meaning to 'float', 'pass quickly' or 'glide away'; Shakespeare perhaps invents this use of it to mean 'cause to pass quickly'.

with a matter. I am given, sir, secretly to understand
that your younger brother, Orlando, hath a disposition
to come in disguised against me to try a fall. Tomorrow,
sir, I wrestle for my credit, and he that escapes me
without some broken limb shall acquit him well. Your
brother is but young and tender, and for your love I
would be loath to foil him, as I must for my own honour
if he come in. Therefore, out of my love to you, I came
hither to acquaint you withal, that either you might
stay him from his intendment, or brook such disgrace
well as he shall run into, in that it is a thing of his own
search, and altogether against my will.

OLIVER Charles, I thank thee for thy love to me, which
thou shalt find I will most kindly requite. I had myself
notice of my brother's purpose herein, and have by
underhand means laboured to dissuade him from it;
but he is resolute. I'll tell thee, Charles, it is the stub-
bornest young fellow of France, full of ambition, an
envious emulator of every man's good parts, a secret and
villainous contriver against me, his natural brother.
Therefore use thy discretion; I had as lief thou didst
break his neck as his finger. And thou wert best look
to't; for if thou dost him any slight disgrace, or if he
do not mightily grace himself on thee, he will practise
against thee by poison, entrap thee by some treacherous
device, and never leave thee till he hath ta'en thy life
by some indirect means or other: for, I assure thee —

120 *shall* must, will need to
121 *tender* undeveloped
122 *foil*. This may mean only 'defeat',
but the noun was also a technical
term used in wrestling for a successful throwing of the opponent that
yet did not result in a formal 'fall'.
Foil is used again thus at II.2.14.
124 *withal* with it
125 *brook* endure

131 *underhand* secret, unobtrusive. The
derogatory implication was not yet
inevitable. (Compare *natural* in line
135.)
133–4 *an envious emulator of* one who
hates and is jealous of
139 *grace himself on thee* gain honour at
your expense by defeating you
practise plot

and almost with tears I speak it – there is not one so young and so villainous this day living. I speak but brotherly of him, but should I anatomize him to thee as he is, I must blush and weep, and thou must look pale and wonder.

CHARLES I am heartily glad I came hither to you. If he come tomorrow, I'll give him his payment: if ever he go alone again, I'll never wrestle for prize more. And so God keep your worship! *Exit* 150

OLIVER Farewell, good Charles. Now will I stir this gamester. I hope I shall see an end of him, for my soul – yet I know not why – hates nothing more than he. Yet he's gentle, never schooled and yet learned, full of noble device, of all sorts enchantingly beloved, and indeed so much in the heart of the world, and especially of my own people, who best know him, that I am altogether misprized. But it shall not be so long; this wrestler shall clear all. Nothing remains but that I 160 kindle the boy thither, which now I'll go about. *Exit*

Enter Rosalind and Celia 1.2

CELIA I pray thee, Rosalind, sweet my coz, be merry.

ROSALIND Dear Celia, I show more mirth than I am

---

145 *anatomize* dissect (in the surgical sense, and so it came to mean 'analyse' and 'reveal')

149–50 *go alone* walk without a support (he will be crippled and will need a crutch)

153 *gamester* athlete (but often with derogatory, sometimes with favourable, connotations – like Synge's, and indeed the frequent Irish, use of 'playboy')

156 *device.* Perhaps this means here 'aspiration' rather than 'invention' or 'manner of thinking'.
sorts classes

enchantingly as if by a real process of enchanting or bewitching

159 *misprized* despised or (possibly) underrated.

160 *clear all* solve all problems

1.2.1 *coz.* An abbreviation of 'cousin' (which itself could be used of any relative, as the Duke later in 1.3.40 uses it to Rosalind) but here and throughout the play probably used rather as a term of affection than strictly of the blood relationship of Rosalind and Celia.

mistress of, and would you yet were merrier. Unless you could teach me to forget a banished father, you must not learn me how to remember any extraordinary pleasure.

CELIA Herein I see thou lovest me not with the full weight that I love thee. If my uncle, thy banished father, had banished thy uncle, the Duke my father, so thou hadst been still with me, I could have taught my love to take thy father for mine; so wouldst thou, if the truth of thy love to me were so righteously tempered as mine is to thee.

ROSALIND Well, I will forget the condition of my estate, to rejoice in yours.

CELIA You know my father hath no child but I, nor none is like to have; and truly, when he dies, thou shalt be his heir: for what he hath taken away from thy father perforce, I will render thee again in affection, by mine honour I will, and when I break that oath, let me turn monster. Therefore, my sweet Rose, my dear Rose, be merry.

ROSALIND From henceforth I will, coz, and devise sports. Let me see — what think you of falling in love?

CELIA Marry, I prithee do, to make sport withal; but love no man in good earnest, nor no further in sport neither, than with safety of a pure blush thou mayst in honour

---

3 *would you yet were.* The emendation to 'would you yet I were' turns the phrase into a question 'do you want me to be even merrier than that?'; the F text, preserved here, means 'I wish you at least were merrier, whatever be my feelings'.

5 *learn* teach (not then only a dialectal or 'incorrect' use)

9 *so* provided that

12 *righteously tempered* correctly compounded, blended (an unusual sense of 'righteous')

16 *nor none.* Double negative is common in Shakespeare and does not even necessarily imply emphatic statement. Compare line 26.

18–19 *perforce* forcibly

19 *render* give back to

27–8 *than with safety of a pure blush thou mayst in honour come off again* than will enable you to come out of the affair (or escape) with your honour safe and at no more expense than a pure blush (not the blush of shame)

come off again.

ROSALIND What shall be our sport then?

CELIA Let us sit and mock the good housewife Fortune   30
from her wheel, that her gifts may henceforth be bestowed equally.

ROSALIND I would we could do so; for her benefits are
mightily misplaced, and the bountiful blind woman doth
most mistake in her gifts to women.

CELIA 'Tis true, for those that she makes fair she scarce
makes honest, and those that she makes honest she
makes very ill-favouredly.

ROSALIND Nay, now thou goest from Fortune's office
to Nature's: Fortune reigns in gifts of the world, not in   40
the lineaments of Nature.

        Enter Touchstone

CELIA No; when Nature hath made a fair creature, may
she not by Fortune fall into the fire? Though Nature
hath given us wit to flout at Fortune, hath not Fortune
sent in this fool to cut off the argument?

ROSALIND Indeed, there is Fortune too hard for Nature,
when Fortune makes Nature's natural the cutter-off of
Nature's wit.

30 *housewife*. This is used here as a half-derogatory term: the goddess Fortune, turning her wheel (the symbol of chance, inconstancy), is compared with a mere housewife, spinning. Compare 'Dame Fortune'.

37 *honest* chaste

39–40 *Fortune's office to Nature's*. Some commentators place great stress on this conventional contrast between Nature (responsible for beauty and such lasting gifts as intelligence or *wit*) and Fortune (responsible for wealth and position, which can easily be changed), and elevate it into the major 'theme' of the play; the usurper's court is even equated with Fortune, the Forest of Arden with Nature. Shakespeare has other, subtler, things to say.

41 (stage direction) *Enter Touchstone*. The F stage direction is '*Enter Clowne*', and Shakespeare may have intended 'Touchstone' to be only the name that the clown adopts in the Forest. See Introduction, page 357, and note on line 53 below.

44 *flout* mock

47 *Nature's natural* one who by nature is deficient in intelligence: the 'natural' as opposed to the professional fool.

CELIA Peradventure this is not Fortune's work neither,
but Nature's, who perceiveth our natural wits too dull
to reason of such goddesses and hath sent this natural
for our whetstone: for always the dullness of the fool is
the whetstone of the wits. How now, wit, whither
wander you?

TOUCHSTONE Mistress, you must come away to your
father.

CELIA Were you made the messenger?

TOUCHSTONE No, by mine honour, but I was bid to
come for you.

ROSALIND Where learned you that oath, fool?

TOUCHSTONE Of a certain knight that swore by his
honour they were good pancakes and swore by his
honour the mustard was naught: now I'll stand to it
the pancakes were naught and the mustard was good,
and yet was not the knight forsworn.

CELIA How prove you that, in the great heap of your
knowledge?

ROSALIND Ay, marry, now unmuzzle your wisdom.

TOUCHSTONE Stand you both forth now: stroke your
chins and swear by your beards that I am a knave.

CELIA By our beards — if we had them — thou art.

Touchstone, however, immediately
assumes the role of the latter (see
Introduction, page 357) and Celia
is presumably jesting at his expense.
52 *whetstone.* Although the whetstone
(for sharpening tools) is not the same
as a touchstone (for testing metals),
the jest has more point if Celia (or
Shakespeare) already thinks of Touchstone as the clown's name.
53-4 *How now, wit, whither wander you?*
'Wit, whither wilt?' was proverbial,
addressed to one who was romanc-

ing; and there is a further pun on the
'wandering' of the clown's 'wit'.
57 *messenger* (used not only of one bringing a message but also of the official
employed to arrest a state prisoner)
62 *pancakes* meat-cakes, fritters
63 *naught* worthless
stand to it swear to it, justify the
statement that. Of these passages of
wit, Shaw complained 'Who would
endure such humor from any one
but Shakespeare? — an Eskimo would
demand his money back if a modern
author offered him such fare'.

TOUCHSTONE By my knavery – if I had it – then I were; but if you swear by that that is not, you are not forsworn: no more was this knight, swearing by his honour, for he never had any; or if he had, he had sworn it away before ever he saw those pancakes or that mustard.

CELIA Prithee, who is't that thou meanest?

TOUCHSTONE One that old Frederick, your father, loves.

CELIA My father's love is enough to honour him enough. Speak no more of him; you'll be whipped for taxation   80
one of these days.

TOUCHSTONE The more pity that fools may not speak wisely what wise men do foolishly.

CELIA By my troth, thou sayest true: for since the little wit that fools have was silenced, the little foolery that wise men have makes a great show. Here comes Monsieur the Beu.

Enter Le Beau

ROSALIND With his mouth full of news.

CELIA Which he will put on us, as pigeons feed their young.   90

79–81 *My father's love ... these days.* F gives these lines to Rosalind. For comment, see Introduction, page 378. The F compositor who set these lines (Compositor 'B') made similar errors with other speech prefixes in v.1 (on R6ᵛ of F), but they were discovered during proof-reading and corrected; and another of the compositors ('D') made similar errors in II.3 (on Q 5ᵛ) that were not corrected until the Second Folio years later. See also the Account of the Text, pages 384–5.

80 *taxation* criticism, satire. The theory that a secondary meaning is involved, because the Latin 'tax' means 'the sound of a whip stroke', is not fully convincing.

84–6 *since the little wit ... a great show.* For the possible topical allusion, see Introduction, page 376.

87 *the Beu.* The F reading is preserved here (most editors emend to 'Le Beau') on the assumption that Celia is mocking Le Beau and his mincing speech. (The F spelling 'Boon-iour' in line 93 perhaps has the same intention.) Only in the following stage direction, however, is the name ever spelt '*Beau*' in F; elsewhere it is '*Beu*'.

89 *put on us* force on us, ram down our throats. Possibly Celia purses her lips in mimicry of Le Beau to make the point clearer.

ROSALIND Then shall we be news-crammed.

CELIA All the better: we shall be the more marketable.
Bon jour, Monsieur Le Beau, what's the news?

LE BEAU Fair princess, you have lost much good sport.

CELIA Sport? Of what colour?

LE BEAU What colour, madam? How shall I answer you?

ROSALIND As wit and fortune will.

TOUCHSTONE Or as the Destinies decrees.

CELIA Well said, that was laid on with a trowel.

100   TOUCHSTONE Nay, if I keep not my rank –

ROSALIND Thou losest thy old smell.

LE BEAU You amaze me, ladies. I would have told you of
good wrestling, which you have lost the sight of.

ROSALIND Yet tell us the manner of the wrestling.

LE BEAU I will tell you the beginning; and, if it please
your ladyships, you may see the end, for the best is yet
to do, and here, where you are, they are coming to
perform it.

CELIA Well, the beginning that is dead and buried.

110   LE BEAU There comes an old man and his three sons –

CELIA I could match this beginning with an old tale.

LE BEAU Three proper young men, of excellent growth
and presence –

ROSALIND With bills on their necks: 'Be it known unto
all men by these presents'.

92 *the more marketable* more easily sold, at a profit, because our weights will have been increased

95 *colour* type, kind (a normal Elizabethan meaning, but Le Beau's reply perhaps suggests that he is incapable of understanding it)

98 *Or as the Destinies decrees.* Touchstone, here and in line 100, is also aping Le Beau and is deliberately pompous: hence Celia's reply.

100 *rank.* The *adjective* can mean 'offensively strong in smell', a meaning that Rosalind seizes on.

102 *amaze* bewilder

106–7 *yet to do* still to come

109 *Well, the beginning that is dead and buried.* This has often been taken as a question but may be a cynical comment on Le Beau's obvious delight in making much of what is already past.

112 *proper* handsome

114 *bills* notices, proclamations (such as

LE BEAU The eldest of the three wrestled with Charles, the Duke's wrestler, which Charles in a moment threw him, and broke three of his ribs, that there is little hope of life in him. So he served the second, and so the third. Yonder they lie, the poor old man their father making 120 such pitiful dole over them that all the beholders take his part with weeping.

ROSALIND Alas!

TOUCHSTONE But what is the sport, Monsieur, that the ladies have lost?

LE BEAU Why, this that I speak of.

TOUCHSTONE Thus men may grow wiser every day. It is the first time that ever I heard breaking of ribs was sport for ladies.

CELIA Or I, I promise thee. 130

ROSALIND But is there any else longs to see this broken music in his sides? Is there yet another dotes upon rib-breaking? Shall we see this wrestling, cousin?

LE BEAU You must if you stay here, for here is the place appointed for the wrestling, and they are ready to perform it.

CELIA Yonder, sure, they are coming. Let us now stay and see it.

Flourish. Enter Duke Frederick, Lords, Orlando, Charles, and attendants

DUKE Come on. Since the youth will not be entreated, his own peril on his forwardness. 140

are sometimes carried on the back, slung from the neck). Conceivably there is a pun on *bills* meaning 'halberds'. Le Beau's over-formal language reminds Rosalind of legal jargon and she replies with a legal phrase and a pun on *presence* ('presents', legal documents).

118 *that* so that

121 *dole* lamentation

131-2 *broken music.* The usual meaning, 'part music', hardly makes sense here. The gloss 'broken instruments' (with broken ribs or frets) is better than this (or than 'broken consort').

138 (stage direction) *Flourish* a fanfare of horns or trumpets (normally to mark the entrance of a king, queen, or other ruler)

140 *forwardness* rashness

ROSALIND Is yonder the man?

LE BEAU Even he, madam.

CELIA Alas, he is too young; yet he looks successfully.

DUKE How now, daughter and cousin? Are you crept hither to see the wrestling?

ROSALIND Ay, my liege, so please you give us leave.

DUKE You will take little delight in it, I can tell you, there is such odds in the man. In pity of the challenger's youth I would fain dissuade him, but he will not be
150 entreated. Speak to him, ladies, see if you can move him.

CELIA Call him hither, good Monsieur Le Beau.

DUKE Do so: I'll not be by.

He stands aside

LE BEAU Monsieur the challenger, the princess calls for you.

ORLANDO I attend them with all respect and duty.

ROSALIND Young man, have you challenged Charles the wrestler?

ORLANDO No, fair Princess. He is the general challenger; I come but in as others do, to try with him the strength
160 of my youth.

CELIA Young gentleman, your spirits are too bold for your years. You have seen cruel proof of this man's strength; if you saw yourself with your eyes, or knew yourself with your judgement, the fear of your adventure would counsel you to a more equal enterprise. We pray you for your own sake to embrace your own safety, and give over this attempt.

ROSALIND Do, young sir, your reputation shall not therefore be misprized: we will make it our suit to the Duke
170 that the wrestling might not go forward.

ORLANDO I beseech you, punish me not with your hard

---

148 *such odds in the man* so marked a superiority in the man (Charles), so much in the man's favour (as against the youth)

163 *with your eyes* clearly, as you really are
168-9 *therefore be misprized* be condemned, or undervalued, on that account

thoughts, wherein I confess me much guilty to deny so
fair and excellent ladies anything. But let your fair eyes
and gentle wishes go with me to my trial: wherein if I be
foiled, there is but one shamed that was never gracious,
if killed, but one dead that is willing to be so. I shall do
my friends no wrong, for I have none to lament me; the
world no injury, for in it I have nothing: only in the
world I fill up a place which may be better supplied
when I have made it empty.   180

ROSALIND The little strength that I have, I would it were
with you.

CELIA And mine, to eke out hers.

ROSALIND Fare you well. Pray heaven, I be deceived in
you!

CELIA Your heart's desires be with you!

CHARLES Come, where is this young gallant that is so
desirous to lie with his mother earth?

ORLANDO Ready, sir, but his will hath in it a more
modest working.   190

DUKE You shall try but one fall.

CHARLES No, I warrant your grace, you shall not entreat
him to a second, that have so mightily persuaded him
from a first.

ORLANDO You mean to mock me after; you should not
have mocked me before. But come your ways!

ROSALIND Now Hercules be thy speed, young man!

CELIA I would I were invisible, to catch the strong fellow
by the leg.

                Orlando and Charles wrestle

ROSALIND O excellent young man!   200

---

172 *wherein* in a matter in which
175 *gracious* graced, lucky enough to
     enjoy favour (including the favours
     of Fortune)
184 *deceived* mistaken, (through underesti-
     mating your strength)

190 *working* aim
196 *come your ways* come on
197 *be thy speed* speed thee, grant thee
     success

CELIA If I had a thunderbolt in mine eye, I can tell who
should down.

A shout as Charles is thrown

DUKE (*coming forward*) No more, no more.

ORLANDO Yes, I beseech your grace, I am not yet well
breathed.

DUKE How dost thou, Charles?

LE BEAU He cannot speak, my lord.

DUKE Bear him away.

Attendants carry Charles off

What is thy name, young man?

210 ORLANDO Orlando, my liege; the youngest son of Sir
Rowland de Boys.

DUKE

I would thou hadst been son to some man else.
The world esteemed thy father honourable,
But I did find him still mine enemy.
Thou shouldst have better pleased me with this deed
Hadst thou descended from another house.
But fare thee well, thou art a gallant youth;
I would thou hadst told me of another father.

Exit Duke, with Lords, Le Beau, and Touchstone

CELIA

Were I my father, coz, would I do this?

ORLANDO

220 I am more proud to be Sir Rowland's son,
His youngest son, and would not change that calling
To be adopted heir to Frederick.

ROSALIND

My father loved Sir Rowland as his soul,
And all the world was of my father's mind.

---

205 *breathed* exercised. The modern
idiom is 'have not yet warmed up'.
214 *still* always
220–22 *I am more proud to be Sir Rowland's
son,* | ... *to Frederick.* Perhaps these

words are spoken, in defiance, as
the Duke leaves the stage.
221 *calling* station in life (rather than
'title', a meaning for which there is
no recorded authority)

Had I before known this young man his son,
I should have given him tears unto entreaties
Ere he should thus have ventured.

CELIA   Gentle cousin,
Let us go thank him, and encourage him.
My father's rough and envious disposition
Sticks me at heart. – Sir, you have well deserved.   230
If you do keep your promises in love
But justly as you have exceeded all promise,
Your mistress shall be happy.

ROSALIND (*taking a chain from her neck*)
                              Gentleman,
Wear this for me – one out of suits with fortune,
That could give more but that her hand lacks means.
(*to Celia*) Shall we go, coz?

CELIA Ay. Fare you well, fair gentleman.
        Rosalind and Celia begin to withdraw

ORLANDO
Can I not say 'I thank you'? My better parts
Are all thrown down, and that which here stands up
Is but a quintain, a mere lifeless block.   240

ROSALIND
He calls us back. My pride fell with my fortunes:
I'll ask him what he would. – Did you call, sir?
Sir, you have wrestled well, and overthrown
More than your enemies.

CELIA   Will you go, coz?

ROSALIND
Have with you. (*To Orlando*) Fare you well.
                    Exeunt Rosalind and Celia

230 *Sticks me at heart* pierces (me in) my
heart
232 *justly* precisely
233 (stage direction) *taking a chain from
her neck*. The warrant for this addition to F is III.2.175.
134 *out of suits with* dismissed from the

favour of (and therefore, like a dismissed servant, deprived of the *suit*
or livery)
240 *quintain* the post, block, or perhaps
figure used for tilting practice
242 *would* wishes
245 *Have with you* I am coming with you

ORLANDO

What passion hangs these weights upon my tongue?
I cannot speak to her, yet she urged conference.
        Enter Le Beau
O poor Orlando, thou art overthrown!
Or Charles or something weaker masters thee.

LE BEAU

250   Good sir, I do in friendship counsel you
To leave this place. Albeit you have deserved
High commendation, true applause, and love,
Yet such is now the Duke's condition,
That he misconsters all that you have done.
The Duke is humorous – what he is, indeed,
More suits you to conceive than I to speak of.

ORLANDO

I thank you, sir; and pray you tell me this,
Which of the two was daughter of the Duke
That here was at the wrestling?

LE BEAU

260   Neither his daughter, if we judge by manners,
But yet indeed the taller is his daughter;
The other is daughter to the banished Duke,
And here detained by her usurping uncle
To keep his daughter company, whose loves
Are dearer than the natural bond of sisters.
But I can tell you that of late this Duke
Hath ta'en displeasure 'gainst his gentle niece,

247 *urged conference* invited conversation
249 *Or* either
253 *condition* temper or mood
254 *misconsters* misconstrues (a variant
    form, with the accent on the second
    syllable)
255 *humorous* the victim of a disproportion of the four 'humours' (which had
    to be in perfect balance in a man's
    make-up if he was to be normal)

261 *taller*. For the complete contradiction between this and all other references to Rosalind's height, and
    Celia's, see Introduction, pages 378–9.
264 *whose*. The general sense, not any
    particular word, provides the antecedent for *whose*, which refers to both
    the daughters just mentioned.

Grounded upon no other argument
But that the people praise her for her virtues
And pity her for her good father's sake;   270
And, on my life, his malice 'gainst the lady
Will suddenly break forth. Sir, fare you well;
Hereafter, in a better world than this,
I shall desire more love and knowledge of you.

ORLANDO

I rest much bounden to you: fare you well.

Exit Le Beau

Thus must I from the smoke into the smother,
From tyrant Duke unto a tyrant brother.
But heavenly Rosalind!   *Exit*

Enter Celia and Rosalind   1.3

CELIA Why cousin, why Rosalind, Cupid have mercy,
not a word?

ROSALIND Not one to throw at a dog.

CELIA No, thy words are too precious to be cast away
upon curs; throw some of them at me. Come, lame me
with reasons.

ROSALIND Then there were two cousins laid up, when the
one should be lamed with reasons, and the other mad
without any.

CELIA But is all this for your father?   10

268 *argument* line of reasoning
273 *in a better world than this* if we should
meet in happier circumstances
275 *bounden* indebted
276 *smother* the dense and more suffocat-
ing smoke of the smouldering fire.
The corresponding modern idiom is
'out of the frying pan into the fire'.
278 *Rosalind.* Here, and in the first stage
direction and the text of 1.3, F has
Rosaline. It is often difficult in Elizabethan ('secretary') handwriting to

distinguish between *e* and *d*; but 'Rosaline' and 'Rosalind' may only be
alternative forms of the one name.
Rosaline is the heroine of *Love's
Labour's Lost,* and Romeo's first love
was Rosaline. The verses of Orlando
and Touchstone in III.2 show that
'Rosalind' is the heroine's 'real' name
here – though pronounced, or joc-
ularly mispronounced, to rhyme with
'lined'.

ROSALIND No, some of it is for my child's father. – O, how full of briars is this working-day world!

CELIA They are but burs, cousin, thrown upon thee in holiday foolery. If we walk not in the trodden paths, our very petticoats will catch them.

ROSALIND I could shake them off my coat; these burs are in my heart.

CELIA Hem them away.

ROSALIND I would try, if I could cry 'hem' and have
20   him.

CELIA Come, come, wrestle with thy affections.

ROSALIND O, they take the part of a better wrestler than myself.

CELIA O, a good wish upon you; you will try in time, in despite of a fall. But turning these jests out of service, let us talk in good earnest: is it possible on such a sudden you should fall into so strong a liking with old Sir Rowland's youngest son?

ROSALIND The Duke my father loved his father dearly.

30   CELIA Doth it therefore ensue that you should love his son dearly? By this kind of chase, I should hate him, for my father hated his father dearly; yet I hate not Orlando.

ROSALIND No, faith, hate him not, for my sake.

CELIA Why should I not? Doth he not deserve well?

Enter Duke, with Lords

1.3.11. *child's father.* For the defence of this F reading, see Introduction, pages 364–5.

14 *trodden paths.* Perhaps Celia is implying that she and Rosalind were unconventional in speaking as they did to Orlando after the wrestling.

18 *Hem.* This is a pun on the two senses, the one from sewing, the other imitating the sound of a cough; it is suggested by *burs* ('bur' could also refer to a choking sensation in the throat).

19–20 *cry 'hem' and have him.* This time the pun is on *hem* and *him*. Some commentators have thought the phrase proverbial but it is not listed in the usual source books.

24 *try* try a bout or wrestling match with Orlando – with the usual sexual pun on *fall*)

29 *dearly* intensely

31 *chase* pursuit, sequence (another pun, from hunting)

ROSALIND Let me love him for that, and do you love him
　　because I do. – Look, here comes the Duke.

CELIA With his eyes full of anger.

DUKE
　　Mistress, dispatch you with your safest haste
　　And get you from our court.

ROSALIND　　　　　　　　　　　　Me, uncle?

DUKE　　　　　　　　　　　　　　　　You, cousin.　　　　40
　　Within these ten days if that thou beest found
　　So near our public court as twenty miles,
　　Thou diest for it.

ROSALIND　　　　　　I do beseech your grace,
　　Let me the knowledge of my fault bear with me.
　　If with myself I hold intelligence
　　Or have acquaintance with mine own desires,
　　If that I do not dream or be not frantic –
　　As I do trust I am not – then, dear uncle,
　　Never so much as in a thought unborn
　　Did I offend your highness.

DUKE　　　　　　　　　　Thus do all traitors:　　　50
　　If their purgation did consist in words,
　　They are as innocent as grace itself.
　　Let it suffice thee that I trust thee not.

ROSALIND
　　Yet your mistrust cannot make me a traitor.
　　Tell me whereon the likelihoods depends.

DUKE
　　Thou art thy father's daughter, there's enough.

39 *your safest haste* all speed possible, in
　the interests of your own safety
40 *cousin* niece
47 *frantic* out of my senses
51 *purgation.* In addition to the medical
　meaning, the word was used in theo-
logy (both of the purification of the
soul in Purgatory and of the declaration of innocence on oath) and as a
legal term, of the proving of innocence, particularly by ordeal. Compare v.4.42–3.

ROSALIND
So was I when your highness took his dukedom,
So was I when your highness banished him.
Treason is not inherited, my lord,
60   Or, if we did derive it from our friends,
What's that to me? My father was no traitor;
Then, good my liege, mistake me not so much
To think my poverty is treacherous.

CELIA
Dear sovereign, hear me speak.

DUKE
Ay, Celia, we stayed her for your sake,
Else had she with her father ranged along.

CELIA
I did not then entreat to have her stay;
It was your pleasure and your own remorse.
I was too young that time to value her,
70   But now I know her. If she be a traitor,
Why so am I: we still have slept together,
Rose at an instant, learned, played, eat together,
And wheresoe'er we went, like Juno's swans
Still we went coupled and inseparable.

DUKE
She is too subtle for thee, and her smoothness,

60 *friends* (apparently used in the now obsolete sense, 'relatives')
61 *What's that to me?* How is that relevant to me?
65 *stayed* retained, kept
68 *remorse.* The word already had its modern meaning of 'compunction' or 'repentance', but also commonly meant 'compassion'.
69 *too young.* For comment on the time-scheme, see Introduction, pages 377–8.
71 *still* always, constantly
73 *Juno's swans*, The author of the anony-

mous play *Soliman and Perseda* (possibly Kyd) also refers to 'Juno's goodly swans | Or Venus' milk-white doves', although most Elizabethans knew and accepted the classical tradition that the swans were Venus's birds (Juno's being peacocks). The 'explanation' that Shakespeare is transferring the symbolic qualities of Venus, goddess of love, to Juno, goddess of marriage (and 'patroness' of this play), seems strained and somewhat desperate.

Her very silence, and her patience
Speak to the people, and they pity her.
Thou art a fool; she robs thee of thy name,
And thou wilt show more bright and seem more
    virtuous
When she is gone. Then open not thy lips: 80
Firm and irrevocable is my doom
Which I have passed upon her; she is banished.

CELIA
Pronounce that sentence then on me, my liege,
I cannot live out of her company.

DUKE
You are a fool. – You, niece, provide yourself.
If you outstay the time, upon mine honour
And in the greatness of my word, you die.

Exit Duke, with Lords

CELIA
O my poor Rosalind, whither wilt thou go?
Wilt thou change fathers? I will give thee mine.
I charge thee, be not thou more grieved than I am.   90

ROSALIND
I have more cause.

CELIA   Thou hast not, cousin.
Prithee, be cheerful; knowest thou not the Duke
Hath banished me, his daughter?

ROSALIND   That he hath not.

CELIA
No, hath not? Rosalind lacks then the love
Which teacheth thee that thou and I am one.
Shall we be sundered? Shall we part, sweet girl?
No, let my father seek another heir.
Therefore devise with me how we may fly,
Whither to go, and what to bear with us,

81 *doom* judgement, sentence

100 And do not seek to take your change upon you,
To bear your griefs yourself and leave me out;
For, by this heaven, now at our sorrows pale,
Say what thou canst, I'll go along with thee.

ROSALIND
Why, whither shall we go?

CELIA
To seek my uncle in the Forest of Arden.

ROSALIND
Alas, what danger will it be to us,
Maids as we are, to travel forth so far?
Beauty provoketh thieves sooner than gold.

CELIA
I'll put myself in poor and mean attire
110 And with a kind of umber smirch my face.
The like do you; so shall we pass along
And never stir assailants.

ROSALIND   Were it not better,
Because that I am more than common tall,
That I did suit me all points like a man?
A gallant curtle-axe upon my thigh,
A boar-spear in my hand, and in my heart
Lie there what hidden woman's fear there will,
We'll have a swashing and a martial outside,
As many other mannish cowards have
120 That do outface it with their semblances.

---

102 *now at our sorrows pale* now pale or overcast in sympathy with our sorrows

110 *umber* yellow-coloured earth (so named from Umbria, in Italy). The point is that Elizabethan ladies of degree took care to protect their complexions from the sun, and their paleness would have been in marked contrast to the complexions of country women.

111 *pass along* go on our way

113 *more than common tall.* This contradicts 1.2.261, which is almost certainly 'wrong'. See Introduction, pages 378–9.

114 *suit me all points* dress and equip myself in all ways

115 *curtle-axe* short sword. This form of the noun 'coutelas' (our 'cutlass') arose by mistaken etymology.

CELIA

What shall I call thee when thou art a man?

ROSALIND

I'll have no worse a name than Jove's own page,
And therefore look you call me 'Ganymede'.
But what will you be called?

CELIA

Something that hath a reference to my state:
No longer 'Celia', but 'Aliena'.

ROSALIND

But, cousin, what if we assayed to steal
The clownish fool out of your father's court:
Would he not be a comfort to our travel?

CELIA

He'll go along o'er the wide world with me.   130
Leave me alone to woo him. Let's away
And get our jewels and our wealth together,
Devise the fittest time and safest way
To hide us from pursuit that will be made
After my flight. Now go in we content
To liberty, and not to banishment.   *Exeunt*

118 *swashing* swaggering. The word (or its variant 'washing') was used also of a blow in fencing, as in *Romeo and Juliet*, 1.1.61–2: *Gregory, remember thy washing blow* outside. Perhaps, but not necessarily, in the tailoring sense (as contrasted with the lining). Similarly, *outface* in line 120 perhaps contains a pun on the tailoring sense of 'face', meaning 'trim'.

119 *mannish* masculine

120 *outface it with their semblances* bluff it out (the 'indefinite *it*'), relying on their mere appearance of strength

126 *Aliena* the stranger, or one who is 'not herself'. The accentuation is in doubt, but a stress on the second syllable seems possible in this line.

127 *assayed* attempted

131 *woo* win over, persuade

II.1   *Enter Duke Senior, Amiens, and two or three Lords*
           dressed like foresters

DUKE

Now my co-mates and brothers in exile,
Hath not old custom made this life more sweet
Than that of painted pomp? Are not these woods
More free from peril than the envious court?
Here feel we not the penalty of Adam,
The seasons' difference, as the icy fang
And churlish chiding of the winter's wind,
Which when it bites and blows upon my body
Even till I shrink with cold, I smile and say
10   'This is no flattery; these are counsellors
That feelingly persuade me what I am'?
Sweet are the uses of adversity,
Which, like the toad, ugly and venomous,
Wears yet a precious jewel in his head;
And this our life, exempt from public haunt,
Finds tongues in trees, books in the running brooks,
Sermons in stones, and good in everything.

AMIENS

I would not change it. Happy is your grace

II.1 (stage direction) *like foresters* (probably) in 'Kentish green'

4 *envious* given to enmity or hatred

5 *the penalty of Adam.* According to the traditional view, in Eden there was perpetual spring; the change of seasons, with the hardships of winter, was a consequence of Adam's fall. Apparently, the Duke asks a third question, 'Do we not feel?', and goes on to imply that it is nevertheless a good thing so to feel, for the reasons he gives.

11 *feelingly* by making themselves felt

12 *uses* of (perhaps both 'ways of life associated with' and 'profits to be had from')

13–14 *the toad . . . | . . . head.* Two superstitions of natural history are alluded to here: that the toad was poisonous and that it had a precious stone (alternatively, a bone) in its head that had magical properties and was an antidote against poison.

15 *exempt from public haunt* not exposed to, or visited by, people generally

18 *I would not change it.* Some editors unnecessarily transfer these words to the Duke. As Furness said, 'The Duke has asked a question. Is no one to answer?'

That can translate the stubbornness of fortune
Into so quiet and so sweet a style.   20

DUKE
Come, shall we go and kill us venison?
And yet it irks me the poor dappled fools,
Being native burghers of this desert city,
Should in their own confines with forkèd heads
Have their round haunches gored.

FIRST LORD   Indeed, my lord,
The melancholy Jaques grieves at that
And, in that kind, swears you do more usurp
Than doth your brother that hath banished you.
Today my lord of Amiens and myself
Did steal behind him as he lay along   30
Under an oak whose antick root peeps out
Upon the brook that brawls along this wood,
To the which place a poor sequestered stag
That from the hunter's aim had ta'en a hurt
Did come to languish; and indeed, my lord,
The wretched animal heaved forth such groans
That their discharge did stretch his leathern coat
Almost to bursting, and the big round tears
Coursed one another down his innocent nose
In piteous chase; and thus the hairy fool,   40
Much markèd of the melancholy Jaques,
Stood on th'extremest verge of the swift brook
Augmenting it with tears.

DUKE   But what said Jaques?
Did he not moralize this spectacle?

22 *fools*. This means 'simple creatures', not 'idiots'.

23 *burghers* citizens, of the woods, their own territories (*confines*)

24 *forkèd heads* barbed arrows

27 *kind* respect

31 *antick*. Possibly only 'old' (our 'antique'), but possibly 'antic' in the sense of 'contorted', 'queerly shaped'. The word is to be stressed on the first syllable.

33 *sequestered* separated

41 *of* by

44 *moralize* draw morals from, or explicate

FIRST LORD

O, yes, into a thousand similes.
First, for his weeping into the needless stream:
'Poor deer,' quoth he, 'thou makest a testament
As worldlings do, giving thy sum of more
To that which had too much.' Then, being there
     alone,
Left and abandoned of his velvet friend,
''Tis right,' quoth he, 'thus misery doth part
The flux of company.' Anon a careless herd,
Full of the pasture, jumps along by him
And never stays to greet him: 'Ay,' quoth Jaques,
'Sweep on, you fat and greasy citizens,
'Tis just the fashion! Wherefore do you look
Upon that poor and broken bankrupt there?'
Thus most invectively he pierceth through
The body of country, city, court,
Yea, and of this our life, swearing that we
Are mere usurpers, tyrants, and what's worse
To fright the animals and to kill them up
In their assigned and native dwelling place.

DUKE

And did you leave him in this contemplation?

SECOND LORD

We did, my lord, weeping and commenting
Upon the sobbing deer.

DUKE   Show me the place;

50

60

46 *needless* unneeding (the stream had water enough already)
50 *of* by
   velvet friend. Velvet must refer to the coat of the deer, although it is also the technical term for the covering of the developing horns of a stag; *friend* has been altered by some editors to 'friends'. In any case, it is the deer that is abandoned, not Jaques;
the pronouns create some confusion throughout this speech.
51–2 *part | The flux* separate (or 'separate the miserable one *from*') the flood. The phrase may be basically proverbial.
52 *careless* carefree
58 *invectively* vehemently
61 *and what's worse* and everything that is even worse

I love to cope him in these sullen fits,
For then he's full of matter.

FIRST LORD

I'll bring you to him straight.   *Exeunt*

Enter Duke Frederick, with Lords   II.2

DUKE

Can it be possible that no man saw them?
It cannot be; some villains of my court
Are of consent and sufferance in this.

FIRST LORD

I cannot hear of any that did see her.
The ladies her attendants of her chamber
Saw her abed, and in the morning early
They found the bed untreasured of their mistress.

SECOND LORD

My lord, the roynish clown at whom so oft
Your grace was wont to laugh is also missing.
Hisperia, the princess' gentlewoman,   10
Confesses that she secretly o'erheard
Your daughter and her cousin much commend
The parts and graces of the wrestler
That did but lately foil the sinewy Charles,
And she believes wherever they are gone
That youth is surely in their company.

DUKE

Send to his brother; fetch that gallant hither.
If he be absent, bring his brother to me;
I'll make him find him. Do this suddenly,
And let not search and inquisition quail   20
To bring again these foolish runaways.   *Exeunt*

---

67 *cope* encounter and engage with (in
combat or debate)

11.2.3 *Are of consent and sufferance in*
have agreed and been accessory to
8 *roynish* scurvy
13 *wrestler* (probably three syllables)

17 *that gallant* (Orlando)
19 *suddenly* immediately
20 *quail* (usually explained as 'slacken'
but may well retain its usual meaning
of 'cower', 'shrink back because
afraid')

II.3   *Enter Orlando and Adam from opposite sides*

ORLANDO Who's there?

ADAM

What, my young master? O my gentle master,
O my sweet master, O you memory
Of old Sir Rowland, why, what make you here?
Why are you virtuous? Why do people love you?
And wherefore are you gentle, strong, and valiant?
Why would you be so fond to overcome
The bonny prizer of the humorous Duke?
Your praise is come too swiftly home before you.
Know you not, master, to some kind of men
Their graces serve them but as enemies?
No more do yours; your virtues, gentle master,
Are sanctified and holy traitors to you.
O, what a world is this, when what is comely
Envenoms him that bears it!

10

ORLANDO

Why, what's the matter?

ADAM   O unhappy youth,
Come not within these doors; within this roof
The enemy of all your graces lives.
Your brother – no, no brother – yet the son –
Yet not the son, I will not call him son
Of him I was about to call his father –
Hath heard your praises, and this night he means
To burn the lodging where you use to lie,
And you within it. If he fail of that,

20

II.3.3 *memory* memorial
4 *make you* are you doing
7 *so fond to* so foolish as to
8 *bonny prizer* big (or strong) prize-
fighter
15 *Envenoms* poisons; but Adam seems
to mean that Orlando's bravery has
led people like the Duke to treat him
as if he were poisonous or dangerous. There is probably a reference to
the poisoned garment that Deianira
was tricked into giving to Hercules.
(The story is told by Ovid in the
Metamorphoses, Book IX, lines 138
ff.)
23 *use* are accustomed

He will have other means to cut you off.
I overheard him, and his practices.
This is no place, this house is but a butchery;
Abhor it, fear it, do not enter it.

ORLANDO

Why, whither, Adam, wouldst thou have me go?

ADAM

No matter whither, so you come not here.   30

ORLANDO

What, wouldst thou have me go and beg my food,
Or with a base and boisterous sword enforce
A thievish living on the common road?
This I must do, or know not what to do:
Yet this I will not do, do how I can.
I rather will subject me to the malice
Of a diverted blood and bloody brother.

ADAM

But do not so. I have five hundred crowns,
The thrifty hire I saved under your father,
Which I did store to be my foster-nurse   40
When service should in my old limbs lie lame
And unregarded age in corners thrown.
Take that, and He that doth the ravens feed,
Yea, providently caters for the sparrow,
Be comfort to my age. Here is the gold;
All this I give you. Let me be your servant.
Though I look old, yet I am strong and lusty,

---

26 *practices* plots
27 *place* dwelling, home. (Shakespeare's
own house in Stratford was called
'New Place'.)
30 *so* provided that
32 *boisterous* violent
enforce gain by force
37 *diverted blood* a relationship turned
away from its natural course (perhaps
a kind of pun, for physicians also
'diverted' real blood)

39 *thrifty hire I saved* wages I, thriftily,
saved
42 *thrown* lie thrown, or be thrown
43, 44 *He that doth the ravens feed,* | ...
the sparrow. Shakespeare may be thinking of any one of a number of Biblical passages (for example, Psalms
147.9, Matthew 10.29, Luke 12.6–7).
Compare Hamlet's *there is a special
providence in the fall of a sparrow*
(v.2.212–13).
47 *lusty* vigorous (*not* 'lustful')

For in my youth I never did apply
Hot and rebellious liquors in my blood,
50   Nor did not with unbashful forehead woo
The means of weakness and debility;
Therefore my age is as a lusty winter,
Frosty, but kindly. Let me go with you,
I'll do the service of a younger man
In all your business and necessities.

ORLANDO

O good old man, how well in thee appears
The constant service of the antique world,
When service sweat for duty, not for meed!
Thou art not for the fashion of these times,
60   Where none will sweat but for promotion,
And having that do choke their service up
Even with the having; it is not so with thee.
But, poor old man, thou prunest a rotten tree
That cannot so much as a blossom yield
In lieu of all thy pains and husbandry.
But come thy ways, we'll go along together,
And ere we have thy youthful wages spent
We'll light upon some settled low content.

49 *rebellious* (probably) causing rebellion (in the body)

53 *kindly*. This means either 'beneficial' or '(only insofar) as it ought to be in the ordinary course of nature'.

57 *antique* ancient, former. This is perhaps not the same word as *antick* in II.1.31, although the variation in the F spellings – 'anticke', 'antique' – may be due merely to the two different compositors ('C' and 'D') who set up the sections.

58 *sweat* (the past tense)
meed reward. Furness recorded that his copy of F read 'neede', which also makes good sense; but inspec-

tion reveals that somebody (probably a previous owner) had altered the word by erasing a minim.

61 *choke their service up*. This somewhat unusual phrase probably has a Biblical origin, in Matthew 13.22: the Bishops' Bible reads 'the care of this world, and the deceitfulness of riches, choke up the word', where a gardening metaphor is being used. The meaning would thus be that the services are choked out of existence by the promotion gained. Another gardening metaphor follows in lines 63–5.

65 *lieu of* return for

ADAM

Master, go on, and I will follow thee
To the last gasp with truth and loyalty.   70
From seventeen years till now almost fourscore
Here lived I, but now live here no more.
At seventeen years many their fortunes seek,
But at fourscore it is too late a week.
Yet fortune cannot recompense me better
Than to die well, and not my master's debtor.   *Exeunt*

Enter Rosalind as Ganymede, Celia as Aliena, and   II.4
the Clown, alias Touchstone

ROSALIND O Jupiter, how weary are my spirits!

TOUCHSTONE I care not for my spirits, if my legs were
not weary.

ROSALIND I could find in my heart to disgrace my man's
apparel, and to cry like a woman, but I must comfort the
weaker vessel, as doublet-and-hose ought to show itself
courageous to petticoat: therefore courage, good Aliena!

CELIA I pray you, bear with me, I cannot go no further.

TOUCHSTONE For my part, I had rather bear with you
than bear you: yet I should bear no cross if I did bear   10

68 *low* humble
69 *thee.* This is the first time Adam pre-
sumes to use the familiar form. See
Introduction, page 372.
71 *seventeen.* F's 'seauentie' is an obvious
slip, for it has 'seauenteene' in line 73.
74 *a week.* The modern idiom is 'in the
day'. Alternatively the phrase may
mean, in ironic understatement, 'too
late by a week'.

II.4 (stage direction) *alias Touchstone.* See
Introduction, page 357.
1 *weary.* F's 'merry' must be an error
(perhaps the manuscript read 'wery').
Rosalind can hardly be pretending to
be merry, to encourage Celia, for

Touchstone seems to catch up the
word *weary* in his reply.
6 *weaker vessel.* The phrase is, of course,
Biblical (1 Peter 3.7) and indeed Rosalind's following words are a kind
of jocular paraphrase of that verse.
doublet-and-hose jacket and knee-
breeches (normal Elizabethan male
dress)
10 *no cross.* A pun and not an original
one: (1) no trouble;
    (2) no coin (some coins had a
cross on one side). There may, however, be a further pun on Matthew
10.38 ('And he that taketh not his
cross, and followeth, is not worthy
of me') or the comparable Luke 14.27.

you, for I think you have no money in your purse.

ROSALIND Well, this is the Forest of Arden.

TOUCHSTONE Ay, now am I in Arden, the more fool I.
When I was at home I was in a better place, but travellers must be content.

Enter Corin and Silvius

ROSALIND

Ay, be so, good Touchstone. – Look you, who comes
here:

A young man and an old in solemn talk.

CORIN

That is the way to make her scorn you still.

SILVIUS

O Corin, that thou knewest how I do love her!

CORIN

20   I partly guess, for I have loved ere now.

SILVIUS

No, Corin, being old thou canst not guess,
Though in thy youth thou wast as true a lover
As ever sighed upon a midnight pillow.
But if thy love were ever like to mine –
As sure I think did never man love so –
How many actions most ridiculous
Hast thou been drawn to by thy fantasy?

CORIN

Into a thousand that I have forgotten.

SILVIUS

O, thou didst then never love so heartily.

30   If thou rememberest not the slightest folly

16–17 *Ay, be so ...* | *... solemn talk.*
The lines are printed as prose in F
but (if *Ay* is treated as extrametrical,
in the normal way) make good verse.
They mark the modulation to the
verse of the Corin–Silvius exchange,
and Rosalind's lines 40–41 modulate
from that verse back to Touchstone's
prose.

27 *fantasy* fancy, affection (not used
pejoratively)

That ever love did make thee run into,
Thou hast not loved.
Or if thou hast not sat as I do now,
Wearing thy hearer in thy mistress' praise,
Thou hast not loved.
Or if thou hast not broke from company
Abruptly, as my passion now makes me,
Thou hast not loved.
O Phebe, Phebe, Phebe!   *Exit*

ROSALIND

Alas, poor shepherd, searching of thy wound,   40
I have by hard adventure found mine own.

TOUCHSTONE And I mine. I remember when I was in love
I broke my sword upon a stone and bid him take that for
coming a-night to Jane Smile, and I remember the
kissing of her batler and the cow's dugs that her pretty
chopt hands had milked; and I remember the wooing of
a peascod instead of her, from whom I took two cods
and, giving her them again, said with weeping tears,
'Wear these for my sake.' We that are true lovers run
into strange capers; but as all is mortal in nature, so is   50
all nature in love mortal in folly.

ROSALIND Thou speakest wiser than thou art ware of.

34 *Wearing*. Perhaps this was a variant of 'wearying', perhaps it was a Shakespearian, or Warwickshire, spelling of 'wearying'; more probably it *means* 'wearing (out)'.

40 *searching of* (in) probing (a medical term)

41 *hard adventure* painful experience

45 *batler* (the wooden club used for beating clothes in the process of washing them)

46 *chopt* chapped

47 *peascod*. The peascod or pea-pod was associated with several rustic superstitions in connexion with wooing and was an appropriate 'lucky' gift. No doubt there are the usual quibbles throughout this passage on 'peas', 'cods' (compare 'codpiece') and possibly 'sword' and 'stone'.

51 *mortal in folly* foolish as only a mortal can be – unless it means 'mortally, extremely, foolish' (but that would seem to be a later use). Perhaps Rosalind takes *mortal* in the sense of 'fatal'.

52, 53 *ware*. Another pun: (1) aware; (2) wary, frightened.

TOUCHSTONE Nay, I shall ne'er be ware of mine own wit
till I break my shins against it.

ROSALIND

Jove, Jove! This shepherd's passion
Is much upon my fashion.

TOUCHSTONE

And mine, but it grows something stale with me.

CELIA

I pray you, one of you question yond man
If he for gold will give us any food;

60   I faint almost to death.

TOUCHSTONE Holla, you clown!

ROSALIND Peace, fool, he's not thy kinsman.

CORIN Who calls?

TOUCHSTONE Your betters, sir.

CORIN Else are they very wretched.

ROSALIND Peace, I say. Good even to you, friend.

CORIN

And to you, gentle sir, and to you all.

ROSALIND

I prithee, shepherd, if that love or gold
Can in this desert place buy entertainment,

70   Bring us where we may rest ourselves and feed.
Here's a young maid with travail much oppressed,
And faints for succour.

CORIN   Fair sir, I pity her,
And wish, for her sake more than for mine own,
My fortunes were more able to relieve her;
But I am shepherd to another man,
And do not shear the fleeces that I graze.
My master is of churlish disposition,

53 *Nay* indeed (not implying contradiction)

55–6 *passion* | ... *fashion*. The rhyme
suggests that Rosalind is quoting,
perhaps from a ballad, unless she is
parodying Silvius's style.

57 *something* somewhat

69 *entertainment* provision for the needs
of a guest

And little recks to find the way to heaven
By doing deeds of hospitality.
Besides, his cote, his flocks, and bounds of feed   80
Are now on sale, and at our sheepcote now,
By reason of his absence, there is nothing
That you will feed on. But what is, come see,
And in my voice most welcome shall you be.

ROSALIND
What is he that shall buy his flock and pasture?

CORIN
That young swain that you saw here but erewhile,
That little cares for buying anything.

ROSALIND
I pray thee, if it stand with honesty,
Buy thou the cottage, pasture, and the flock,
And thou shalt have to pay for it of us.   90

CELIA
And we will mend thy wages: I like this place,
And willingly could waste my time in it.

CORIN
Assuredly the thing is to be sold.
Go with me. If you like upon report
The soil, the profit, and this kind of life,
I will your very faithful feeder be,
And buy it with your gold right suddenly.   *Exeunt*

78 *recks to find* cares about finding. (F's 'wreakes' probably signifies only a different pronunciation.) In lines 77–9 Shakespeare may be thinking of the story of Nabal in 1 Samuel 25.
80 *cote* cottage
bounds of feed full extent of his pastures
81 *on sale* in the process of being sold (as lines 85–7 make clear)
84 *in my voice* so far as my voice or decision is concerned
85 *What* who
86 *but erewhile* only a short time ago
88 *stand with honesty* is not inconsistent with fair dealing
90 *to pay for it* something with which to pay for it
91 *mend* amend, improve
92 *waste* pass
94 *upon report* after hearing details
96 *feeder* servant

II.5   *Enter Amiens, Jaques and others*

AMIENS (*sings*)
              Under the greenwood tree,
              Who loves to lie with me,
              And turn his merry note
              Unto the sweet bird's throat:
       Come hither, come hither, come hither.
                    Here shall he see
                    No enemy
              But winter and rough weather.

JAQUES More, more, I prithee, more.

10 AMIENS It will make you melancholy, Monsieur Jaques.

JAQUES I thank it. More, I prithee, more. I can suck
melancholy out of a song, as a weasel sucks eggs. More,
I prithee, more.

AMIENS My voice is ragged, I know I cannot please you.

JAQUES I do not desire you to please me, I do desire you
to sing. Come, more, another stanzo. Call you 'em
'stanzos'?

AMIENS What you will, Monsieur Jaques.

JAQUES Nay, I care not for their names, they owe me
20   nothing. Will you sing?

AMIENS More at your request than to please myself.

JAQUES Well then, if ever I thank any man, I'll thank you;
but that they call 'compliment' is like th'encounter of
two dog-apes, and when a man thanks me heartily,
methinks I have given him a penny and he renders me

II.5 (stage direction) *others* (in stage practice, usually a group of attendant
lords)

1 AMIENS. F has the simple heading
'Song' but the following dialogue
leaves no doubt that Amiens is the
singer.

3 *turn* adapt

14 *ragged* hoarse

19–20 *I care not for their names, they owe
me nothing.* This is normally taken as
a quibble on *names*, in the sense of
signatures on a legal document ac-
knowledging a debt.

23 *that* that which

24 *dog-apes* dog-faced baboons

the beggarly thanks. Come, sing; and you that will not,
hold your tongues.

AMIENS Well, I'll end the song. – Sirs, cover the while:
the Duke will drink under this tree. – He hath been all
this day to look you.   30

JAQUES And I have been all this day to avoid him. He is
too disputable for my company: I think of as many
matters as he, but I give heaven thanks, and make no
boast of them. Come, warble, come.

ALL TOGETHER (*sing*)

           Who doth ambition shun,
           And loves to live i'th'sun,
           Seeking the food he eats,
           And pleased with what he gets:
    Come hither, come hither, come hither.
                Here shall he see   40
                No enemy
           But winter and rough weather.

JAQUES I'll give you a verse to this note, that I made
yesterday in despite of my invention.

AMIENS And I'll sing it.

JAQUES Thus it goes:

           If it do come to pass
           That any man turn ass,
           Leaving his wealth and ease,
           A stubborn will to please: 50

26 *beggarly* to be expected from a beggar

28 *cover the while* in the meantime lay the
covers (the utensils for a meal), 'set
the table'

30 *look you* seek you, look for you (not
an error but a regular transitive use
of the verb)

32 *disputable* argumentative, disputa-
tious

36 *to live i'th'sun* to live the free, irrespon-
sible life of 'nature'

43 *note* melody

44 *in despite of my invention* to spite my
(lack of) inventiveness, to prove
that 'invention' isn't necessary for
the composition of nonsense

46 JAQUES. F heads this speech also
'*Amy*.' (Amiens) – but he can hardly
have three consecutive speeches. It
would be possible for Jaques to say
only *Thus it goes*, handing Amiens a
sheet of paper, and for Amiens both
to sing Jaques's words and to ask
about *ducdame*.

Ducdame, ducdame, ducdame.
            Here shall he see
            Gross fools as he,
        An if he will come to me.

AMIENS What's that 'ducdame'?

JAQUES 'Tis a Greek invocation, to call fools into a circle.
I'll go sleep, if I can; if I cannot, I'll rail against all the
first-born of Egypt.

AMIENS And I'll go seek the Duke; his banquet is pre-
60   pared.   *Exeunt*

II.6   *Enter Orlando and Adam*

ADAM Dear master, I can go no further. O, I die for food.
Here lie I down and measure out my grave. Farewell,
kind master.

ORLANDO Why, how now, Adam, no greater heart in thee?
Live a little, comfort a little, cheer thyself a little. If
this uncouth forest yield anything savage, I will either
be food for it or bring it for food to thee. Thy conceit is
nearer death than thy powers. (*Raising him*) For my sake
be comfortable; hold death a while at the arm's end. I

51 *Ducdame.* 'Explanations' range from a Latin phrase to an Italian to a Welsh to a Romani (all of course slightly adjusted) but Jaques gives the best explanation: the word is deliberate nonsense, which will incite fools to form a circle ('go into a huddle'!).

54 *An if* if

56 *Greek* meaningless ('it's all Greek to me')

58 *first-born of Egypt.* The words are, of course, from Exodus 11.5 and 12.12 and 29, but their relevance is not obvious, even if Jaques is comparing the Duke's banishment with the journey of the Israelites into the wilderness after the first-born of Egypt

had been slain by the Lord.

59 *banquet.* This is probably used in the alternative sense of a light meal, particularly of fruit etc. The meal may have been laid out in the inner stage, if any, or at the rear or side of the stage; no Elizabethan audience would have been worried that Orlando and Adam do not see it in the next 'scene'.

II.6.5 *comfort* comfort thyself, take comfort

6 *uncouth* unknown, or wild, desolate

7 *conceit* imagination

9 *comfortable* comforted, of good comfort

will here be with thee presently, and if I bring thee not   10
something to eat, I will give thee leave to die; but if
thou diest before I come, thou art a mocker of my
labour. Well said! Thou lookest cheerly, and I'll be with
thee quickly. Yet thou liest in the bleak air. Come, I
will bear thee to some shelter, and thou shalt not die
for lack of a dinner, if there live anything in this desert.
Cheerly, good Adam!   *Exeunt*

Enter Duke Senior, Amiens, and Lords, dressed as   II.7
foresters, or outlaws

DUKE

I think he be transformed into a beast,
For I can nowhere find him like a man.

FIRST LORD

My lord, he is but even now gone hence.
Here was he merry, hearing of a song.

DUKE

If he, compact of jars, grow musical,
We shall have shortly discord in the spheres.

---

10 *presently* immediately
13 *Well said!* Well done!
    cheerly cheerful. F's 'cheerely' may
    conceivably be 'cheerily'.

II.7 (stage direction) *Enter Duke Senior,
    Amiens ... outlaws.* F has '*Enter
    Duke Sen. & Lord, like Out-lawes*'.
    One assumes that 'Lords' is intended,
    and that they include Amiens, who
    went off to find the Duke at the end
    of II.5 and who, as the singer of the
    company, presumably sings *Blow,
    blow, thou winter wind*. But though the
    Duke says *Give us some music and, good
    cousin, sing*, the song is simply headed
    'Song', with no name, so that all this
    is mere inference. It is improbable

that '*like Out-lawes*' here points to a
different costume from the '*like Forresters*' of II.1.
3 *but even now* only a moment ago
5 *compact of jars* made up of discords
6 *discord in the spheres.* This alludes to the
    Pythagorean belief, beautifully ex-
    pounded in *The Merchant of Venice*
    v.i.60 ff.: *There's not the smallest orb
    which thou beholdest | But in his motion
    like an angel sings . . .*, the notes of the
    individual planets, or of their
    spheres, combining to form the heav-
    enly 'harmony'. Such harmony was
    one of the basic principles of the
    universe – and would need to be
    reversed before Jaques could become
    'musical'.

Go, seek him, tell him I would speak with him.

Enter Jaques

FIRST LORD

He saves my labour by his own approach.

DUKE

Why, how now, Monsieur, what a life is this,

10   That your poor friends must woo your company?

What, you look merrily?

JAQUES

A fool, a fool, I met a fool i'th'forest,

A motley fool – a miserable world! –

As I do live by food, I met a fool,

Who laid him down, and basked him in the sun,

And railed on Lady Fortune in good terms,

In good set terms, and yet a motley fool.

'Good morrow, fool,' quoth I. 'No, sir,' quoth he,

'Call me not fool till heaven hath sent me fortune.'

20   And then he drew a dial from his poke,

And looking on it, with lack-lustre eye,

Says, very wisely, 'It is ten o'clock.'

'Thus we may see', quoth he, 'how the world wags:

'Tis but an hour ago since it was nine,

And after one hour more 'twill be eleven,

And so from hour to hour we ripe, and ripe,

And then from hour to hour we rot, and rot,

---

13 *motley.* Leslie Hotson has argued that the motley of the Elizabethan fool, including the professional fool, was not, as modern producers believe, breeches and hose quartered like racing colours, but the long robe or petticoat, made of cloth woven from threads of mixed colours, and most often basically green or brown. Alternatively, each robe may have had a small design woven in colour. *a miserable world.* Emendation of this natural parenthesis to 'ah' or 'word' is hardly necessary, even on the theory that *world* is a variant Elizabethan spelling of 'word'.

19 *Call me not fool till heaven hath sent me fortune* (a development of the proverbial 'fortune favours fools')

20 *dial* (either a watch or the common pocket sun-dial)
poke pocket, wallet or bag. Hotson sees a reference to a standard joke that the fool's coat was itself his cloakbag, in which he could conveniently be carried off.

And thereby hangs a tale.' When I did hear
The motley fool thus moral on the time,
My lungs began to crow like Chanticleer   30
That fools should be so deep-contemplative;
And I did laugh, sans intermission,
An hour by his dial. O noble fool!
A worthy fool: motley's the only wear!

DUKE
What fool is this?

JAQUES
A worthy fool: one that hath been a courtier,
And says, if ladies be but young and fair,
They have the gift to know it: and in his brain,
Which is as dry as the remainder biscuit
After a voyage, he hath strange places crammed   40
With observation, the which he vents
In mangled forms. O that I were a fool!
I am ambitious for a motley coat.

DUKE
Thou shalt have one.

JAQUES   It is my only suit –
Provided that you weed your better judgements

28 *And thereby hangs a tale* and more could be said. (The phrase was a cliché.) Some critics have read this passage to mean that Touchstone was parodying Jaques, who does not see that the joke is on him, but there is no good reason for thinking so. What is quite likely is that Jaques is enjoying indecent puns by Touchstone on *hour* (pronounced like 'whore') and 'tail'.
29 *moral.* Perhaps a verb ('moralize'), more probably an adjective ('moralistic').
30 *Chanticleer* (the cock in the traditional story of Reynard the Fox)
32 *sans intermission* without pause. *Inter-*

mission is to be pronounced as five syllables, and *sans* probably as if it were an English word.
39 *dry as the remainder biscuit.* The brain of an idiot was thought to be hard and dry; and nothing could be harder than would have been the seamen's biscuits left over after a long Elizabethan voyage. Compare III.2. 190–91.
40 *places.* Perhaps a kind of pun, with the second meaning of 'extracts', quotations learned off by heart.
41 *observation* (again five syllables, and probably has the older sense of 'maxim' or 'comment')
44 *suit.* Another pun: (1) petition; (2)

Of all opinion that grows rank in them
That I am wise. I must have liberty
Withal, as large a charter as the wind,
To blow on whom I please, for so fools have;
50 And they that are most galled with my folly
They most must laugh. And why, sir, must they so?
The why is plain as way to parish church.
He that a fool doth very wisely hit
Doth very foolishly, although he smart,
Not to seem senseless of the bob: if not,
The wise man's folly is anatomized
Even by the squandering glances of the fool.
Invest me in my motley; give me leave
To speak my mind, and I will through and through
60 Cleanse the foul body of th'infected world,
If they will patiently receive my medicine.

DUKE

Fie on thee! I can tell what thou wouldst do.

clothing; and this in turn suggests the pun in the next line on *weed*. This is one of the image sequences that occur several times in Shakespeare's plays. (It was first noticed by Walter Whiter.)

52 *why . . . way* (perhaps another atrocious pun)

53–5 *He that a fool doth very wisely hit | . . . of the bob.* If Theobald's emendation of F is adopted (the addition of *Not to* to line 55, to complete both metre and sense) the lines mean: 'a man on whom a fool, in his fool's wisdom, scores a hit, is very foolish – even if he smarts under the criticism – if he does not pretend to be insensible of it'. Other bare possibilities are to punctuate 'Doth, very foolishly although he smart, | Seem . . .' or to explain 'the *wise* man appears to be foolish *and to be* insensitive'.

Bob meant 'bitter jest', 'gibe' but may also be used metaphorically: 'rap over the fingers'.

56 *anatomized* dissected

57 *squandering glances* random hits

58–61 *Invest me in my motley . . . | . . . my medicine.* These are the lines, together with 47–9 and 70–87, that have been thought by some to allude to Ben Jonson (see Introduction, page 356). Jonson's boast in the Induction to *Every Man out of his Humour*, 'With an armèd and resolvèd hand, | I'll strip the raggèd follies of the time | Naked as at their birth', is certainly similar in tone. There are other parallels not only in Jonson's work but also in Marston's. Jaques is, then, speaking in the language of the best satirists of the period, and in lines 70–87 is making the satirist's usual defence of his satire.

JAQUES

  What, for a counter, would I do, but good?

DUKE

  Most mischievous foul sin, in chiding sin:
  For thou thyself hast been a libertine,
  As sensual as the brutish sting itself,
  And all th'embossèd sores and headed evils
  That thou with licence of free foot hast caught
  Wouldst thou disgorge into the general world.

JAQUES

  Why, who cries out on pride   70
  That can therein tax any private party?
  Doth it not flow as hugely as the sea,
  Till that the weary very means do ebb?
  What woman in the city do I name
  When that I say the city woman bears
  The cost of princes on unworthy shoulders?
  Who can come in and say that I mean her
  When such a one as she, such is her neighbour?
  Or what is he of basest function,
  That says his bravery is not on my cost,   80
  Thinking that I mean him, but therein suits

---

63 *for a counter* in exchange for a mere imitation coin (which I will give you for telling me)

66 *sting* sexual lust

67 *embossèd* protuberant
headed having come to a head, like boils (and *evils* may mean 'carbuncles' or 'eruptions of the skin': the 'King's evil' was scrofula)

68 *caught* (almost a pun: 'caught' as one catches a cold and as one catches a bur in clothing. Compare 1.3.14–15.)

70–87 For the topical relevance of this speech, see note on lines 58–61 above. The 'incompleteness' of line 70 does not point to textual corruption: there are many other such lines in Shakespeare.

73 *Till that the weary very means do ebb.* This is a notorious crux but no satisfactory emendation has been proposed. A meaning can be extracted: 'Until the very means (wealth, on which pride is based), being exhausted, may be said to run out as the tide does'.

76 *cost of* wealth needed to maintain

79 *function* office, occupation

80 *That says his bravery is not on my cost* who says his fine clothes are not bought at my expense (that is, tells me to mind my own business and not criticize him). The image link of *bravery* and *suits* is again worthy of note.

His folly to the mettle of my speech?
There then, how then, what then? Let me see wherein
My tongue hath wronged him: if it do him right,
Then he hath wronged himself; if he be free,
Why then my taxing like a wild-goose flies,
Unclaimed of any man. But who come here?

Enter Orlando

ORLANDO Forbear, and eat no more.

JAQUES Why, I have eat none yet.

ORLANDO

90 Nor shalt not, till necessity be served.

JAQUES
Of what kind should this cock come of?

DUKE
Art thou thus boldened, man, by thy distress
Or else a rude despiser of good manners,
That in civility thou seemest so empty?

ORLANDO
You touched my vein at first: the thorny point
Of bare distress hath ta'en from me the show
Of smooth civility; yet am I inland bred
And know some nurture. But forbear, I say,
He dies that touches any of this fruit

100 Till I and my affairs are answerèd.

JAQUES An you will not be answered with reason, I
must die.

---

82 *mettle* substance, spirit
84 *do him right* describes him correctly
85 *free* guiltless
86 *taxing* criticism
95 *touched my vein* diagnosed my motive
   or state of mind
97 *inland* near the centre of civilization
   (as opposed to 'country bred')
98 *nurture* manners, culture
101–2 *An you will not be answered with
   reason, I must die.* The attempt to

make these lines scan as verse is mis-
guided: the drop into prose emphasizes the laconic nature of Jaques's
reply. It is customary on the stage
for him to nibble something as he
says these words – an apple, or even
a date, grape, or raisin in deference
to the editors who have suspected
the 'reason' – 'raisin' quibble, as in
Falstaff's *If reasons were as plentiful as
blackberries* (*1 Henry IV*, II.4.231).

DUKE

What would you have? Your gentleness shall force,
More than your force move us to gentleness.

ORLANDO

I almost die for food, and let me have it.

DUKE

Sit down and feed, and welcome to our table.

ORLANDO

Speak you so gently? Pardon me, I pray you.
I thought that all things had been savage here,
And therefore put I on the countenance
Of stern commandment. But whate'er you are   110
That in this desert inaccessible,
Under the shade of melancholy boughs,
Lose and neglect the creeping hours of time:
If ever you have looked on better days;
If ever been where bells have knolled to church;
If ever sat at any good man's feast;
If ever from your eyelids wiped a tear,
And know what 'tis to pity and be pitied,
Let gentleness my strong enforcement be,
In the which hope I blush, and hide my sword.   120

DUKE

True is it that we have seen better days,
And have with holy bell been knolled to church,
And sat at good men's feasts, and wiped our eyes
Of drops that sacred pity hath engendered:
And therefore sit you down in gentleness
And take upon command what help we have
That to your wanting may be ministered.

103–4 *Your gentleness shall force,* | . . . *to gentleness.* The phrase is probably proverbial; a similar one has been found in Publilius Syrus's *Sententiae.*

112 *melancholy* (because they shut out the sunshine)

113 *Lose and neglect* pass, without worry-ing about them

115 *knolled* rung, pealed (but with no implication of mournfulness)

126 *upon command* at your will or pleasure

127 *wanting* needs

ORLANDO
  Then but forbear your food a little while
  Whiles, like a doe, I go to find my fawn
130 And give it food. There is an old poor man
  Who after me hath many a weary step
  Limped in pure love; till he be first sufficed,
  Oppressed with two weak evils, age and hunger,
  I will not touch a bit.
DUKE   Go find him out
  And we will nothing waste till you return.

ORLANDO
  I thank ye, and be blessed for your good comfort! *Exit*
DUKE
  Thou seest we are not all alone unhappy.
  This wide and universal theatre
  Presents more woeful pageants than the scene
  Wherein we play in.
140 JAQUES   All the world's a stage,
  And all the men and women merely players;
  They have their exits and their entrances,
  And one man in his time plays many parts,
  His Acts being seven ages. At first the infant,
  Mewling and puking in the nurse's arms;
  Then, the whining schoolboy, with his satchel
  And shining morning face, creeping like snail

133 *weak* weakening, causing weakness
136 *your good comfort* the goodness and
  kindness you have shown
140–67 *All the world's a stage,* | . . . *sans
  everything.* On the background to this
  famous speech, see Introduction,
  pages 355–6. There is even a passage
  in the old play of *Damon and Pithias*,
  'Pythagoras said, that this world was
  like a stage, | Whereon many play
  their parts'. Shakespeare's originality
  is in the development of the idea and
  in the tone, appropriate to Jaques.
145 *Mewling.* Not just 'whimpering' (a
  meaning that may derive from misun-

derstanding of this passage) but
'mewing like a cat'.

147 *creeping like snail.* This image may
  not have come from Shakespeare's
  memories of Warwickshire after all,
  even if he was thinking of his schooldays, for Nashe has in *The First Part
  of Pasquil's Apology* (1590), speaking
  of contemporary scholars, 'I wonder
  how these silly snails, creeping but
  yesterday out of shops and
  Grammar-schools, dare thrust out
  their feeble horns, against so tough
  and mighty adversaries' (as their
  predecessors).

Unwillingly to school; and then the lover,
Sighing like furnace, with a woeful ballad
Made to his mistress' eyebrow; then, a soldier,   150
Full of strange oaths, and bearded like the pard,
Jealous in honour, sudden and quick in quarrel,
Seeking the bubble reputation
Even in the cannon's mouth; and then, the justice,
In fair round belly, with good capon lined,
With eyes severe, and beard of formal cut,
Full of wise saws and modern instances,
And so he plays his part; the sixth age shifts
Into the lean and slippered pantaloon,
With spectacles on nose and pouch on side,   160
His youthful hose, well saved, a world too wide
For his shrunk shank, and his big manly voice,
Turning again toward childish treble, pipes
And whistles in his sound; last Scene of all,
That ends this strange eventful history,
Is second childishness, and mere oblivion,
Sans teeth, sans eyes, sans taste, sans everything.
        Enter Orlando with Adam

DUKE
Welcome. Set down your venerable burden,
And let him feed.

ORLANDO
I thank you most for him.

ADAM   So had you need;   170
I scarce can speak to thank you for myself.

149 *woeful* full of woe
151 *pard* panther or leopard
152 *Jealous in honour* quick to take offence in matters thought to concern his honour
155 *capon* chicken (and 'capon-justice' was the regular term for one who could be bribed with such a gift)
157 *saws* sayings
    modern instances trite or commonplace (*not* 'up-to-date') illustrations

159 *pantaloon* (the dotard of Italian comedy)
161 *hose* breeches
165 *history* history-play, chronicle
166 *mere* complete
167 (stage direction) *Enter Orlando with Adam*. Capell first recorded the tradition that a contemporary remembered Shakespeare's having played a part, presumably Adam, in which he was carried on the stage on another's back.

DUKE

    Welcome, fall to. I will not trouble you
    As yet to question you about your fortunes.
    Give us some music and, good cousin, sing.

AMIENS (*sings*)

      Blow, blow, thou winter wind,
      Thou art not so unkind
        As man's ingratitude.
      Thy tooth is not so keen,
      Because thou art not seen,
180   Although thy breath be rude.
    Hey-ho, sing hey-ho, unto the green holly,
    Most friendship is feigning, most loving mere folly;
      Then hey-ho, the holly,
        This life is most jolly.

      Freeze, freeze, thou bitter sky
      That dost not bite so nigh
        As benefits forgot.
      Though thou the waters warp,
      Thy sting is not so sharp
190   As friend remembered not.
    Hey-ho, sing hey-ho, unto the green holly,
    Most friendship is feigning, most loving mere folly;
      Then hey-ho, the holly,
        This life is most jolly.

  DUKE

    If that you were the good Sir Rowland's son,
    As you have whispered faithfully you were,
    And as mine eye doth his effigies witness

180 *rude* rough
181 *Hey-ho*. This is common in refrains and though spelt 'Heigh ho' in F does not necessarily refer to a sigh.
    holly (associated with rejoicing and festivities)

182 *Most friendship . . . mere folly*. Perhaps this too is a proverb.
197 *effigies*. This is an alternative, singular, form of 'effigy' (meaning 'image') and is stressed on the second syllable.

Most truly limned and living in your face,
Be truly welcome hither. I am the Duke
That loved your father. The residue of your fortune,   200
Go to my cave and tell me. – Good old man,
Thou art right welcome as thy master is. –
Support him by the arm. Give me your hand,
And let me all your fortunes understand.   *Exeunt*

Enter Duke Frederick, Lords, and Oliver   III.I

DUKE

Not see him since? Sir, sir, that cannot be.
But were I not the better part made mercy,
I should not seek an absent argument
Of my revenge, thou present. But look to it,
Find out thy brother wheresoe'er he is,
Seek him with candle, bring him dead or living
Within this twelvemonth, or turn thou no more
To seek a living in our territory.
Thy lands and all things that thou dost call thine
Worth seizure do we seize into our hands   10
Till thou canst quit thee by thy brother's mouth
Of what we think against thee.

198 *limned* portrayed, or reproduced

III.I.2 *the better part made mercy* for the greater part so merciful by disposition
3 *argument* subject
6 *Seek him with candle.* The reference (coming ironically from the Duke) is to Luke 15.8, 'What woman, having ten pieces of silver, if she lose one, doth not light a candle, and sweep the house, and seek diligently till she find it?' (the verse that follows 'joy shall be in heaven over one sinner that repenteth . . .').
7 *turn* return
10 *seize.* Perhaps in the sense of 'seise' (take legal possession of); *extent* in line 17 is the legal term for a writ for taking the initial steps in the seising of land as security for debt etc.
11 *quit* acquit
mouth (that is, words, evidence)

OLIVER

O that your highness knew my heart in this!
I never loved my brother in my life.

DUKE

More villain thou. — Well, push him out of doors,
And let my officers of such a nature
Make an extent upon his house and lands.
Do this expediently, and turn him going.   *Exeunt*

III.2   *Enter Orlando*

ORLANDO

Hang there, my verse, in witness of my love,
    And thou, thrice-crownèd queen of night, survey
With thy chaste eye, from thy pale sphere above,
    Thy huntress' name that my full life doth sway.
O Rosalind, these trees shall be my books
    And in their barks my thoughts I'll character
That every eye which in this forest looks
    Shall see thy virtue witnessed everywhere.
Run, run, Orlando, carve on every tree
10 The fair, the chaste, and unexpressive she.   *Exit*
          Enter Corin and Touchstone

CORIN And how like you this shepherd's life, Master
Touchstone?

16 *of such a nature* whose duty it is to do this
18 *expediently* in haste, expeditiously
   turn him going 'set him packing'

III.2.1 *Hang there.* No doubt one of the pillars supporting the 'heavens' over the bare Elizabethan public stage would serve well enough for a tree (Rosalind says later that she found Orlando's poem *on a tree*). Hanging love poems (or carving names) on trees was part of the traditional behaviour of the pastoral lover.

2 *thrice-crownèd.* Diana (Artemis), the goddess of chastity, was identified with Proserpina (Hecate) in the underworld and with Luna (Selene) in the sky; alternatively, the passage suggests three functions of Diana: goddess of the moon (line 2), of chastity (line 3), and of the hunt (line 4).
4 *Thy huntress' name.* Rosalind is thought of as a nymph in Diana's train because she too is chaste.
   sway control
6 *character* inscribe
10 *unexpressive* inexpressible

TOUCHSTONE Truly, shepherd, in respect of itself, it is a good life; but in respect that it is a shepherd's life, it is naught. In respect that it is solitary, I like it very well; but in respect that it is private, it is a very vile life. Now in respect it is in the fields, it pleaseth me well; but in respect it is not in the court, it is tedious. As it is a spare life, look you, it fits my humour well; but as there is no more plenty in it, it goes much against my stomach. Hast any philosophy in thee, shepherd? 20

CORIN No more but that I know the more one sickens, the worse at ease he is, and that he that wants money, means, and content is without three good friends; that the property of rain is to wet and fire to burn; that good pasture makes fat sheep; and that a great cause of the night is lack of the sun; that he that hath learned no wit by nature nor art may complain of good breeding, or comes of a very dull kindred.

TOUCHSTONE Such a one is a natural philosopher. Wast 30 ever in court, shepherd?

CORIN No, truly.

TOUCHSTONE Then thou art damned.

CORIN Nay, I hope.

TOUCHSTONE Truly thou art damned, like an ill-roasted egg all on one side.

CORIN For not being at court? Your reason.

TOUCHSTONE Why, if thou never wast at court, thou never sawest good manners; if thou never sawest good manners, then thy manners must be wicked, and wicked- 40

---

15 *naught* worthless

16 *private* secluded; not public. (The contrast between *solitary* and *private* is none too clear.)

18 *spare* frugal

19 *humour* temperament, or mood. (Compare 'I am not in the humour'.)

23 *wants* lacks

28 *complain of good breeding* complain that he has been denied good upbringing

or birth

30 *natural philosopher* (1) a philosopher who studies nature; (2) a foolish pretender to thought

35–6 *damned . . . on one side.* A comparable modern idiom is 'half-baked'.

39 *manners.* Another quibble: (1) forms of polite behaviour; (2) morals.

ness is sin, and sin is damnation. Thou art in a parlous
state, shepherd.

CORIN Not a whit, Touchstone. Those that are good
manners at the court are as ridiculous in the country
as the behaviour of the country is most mockable at the
court. You told me you salute not at the court but you
kiss your hands; that courtesy would be uncleanly if
courtiers were shepherds.

TOUCHSTONE Instance, briefly; come, instance.

50 CORIN Why, we are still handling our ewes, and their fells
you know are greasy.

TOUCHSTONE Why, do not your courtier's hands sweat?
And is not the grease of a mutton as wholesome as the
sweat of a man? Shallow, shallow. A better instance, I
say; come.

CORIN Besides, our hands are hard.

TOUCHSTONE Your lips will feel them the sooner. Shallow,
again. A more sounder instance; come.

CORIN And they are often tarred over with the surgery of
60 our sheep; and would you have us kiss tar? The
courtier's hands are perfumed with civet.

TOUCHSTONE Most shallow man! Thou worms' meat, in
respect of a good piece of flesh indeed! Learn of the
wise and perpend: civet is of a baser birth than tar, the
very uncleanly flux of a cat. Mend the instance, shepherd.

CORIN You have too courtly a wit for me; I'll rest.

TOUCHSTONE Wilt thou rest damned? God help thee,
shallow man! God make incision in thee, thou art raw!

46 *salute* greet
but unless
49 *Instance* (give an) example
50 *still* constantly
fells fleeces
61 *civet* the perfume obtained (as Touchstone is quick to point out) from the
flux or glandular secretion of the
civet cat
62 *worms' meat* food for worms, a mere
corpse. (Mercutio in *Romeo and Juliet*,

III.1.107, when stabbed, says *They
have made worms' meat of me*.)
62-3 *in respect of* in comparison with
64 *perpend* consider, weigh the facts
68 *God make incision . . . raw!* Two explanations have been offered, one from surgery (blood-letting to cure soreness or
sickness), one from gardening (graft-
ing to improve what is *raw* or wild).

CORIN Sir, I am a true labourer: I earn that I eat, get
that I wear, owe no man hate, envy no man's happiness, 70
glad of other men's good, content with my harm; and
the greatest of my pride is to see my ewes graze and my
lambs suck.

TOUCHSTONE That is another simple sin in you, to bring
the ewes and the rams together and to offer to get your
living by the copulation of cattle; to be bawd to a bell-
wether, and to betray a she-lamb of a twelvemonth to a
crooked-pated, old, cuckoldly ram, out of all reasonable
match. If thou beest not damned for this, the devil
himself will have no shepherds. I cannot see else how 80
thou shouldst 'scape.

CORIN Here comes young Master Ganymede, my new
mistress's brother.

    Enter Rosalind

ROSALIND (*reads*)
      From the east to western Ind,
      No jewel is like Rosalind.
      Her worth being mounted on the wind
      Through all the world bears Rosalind.
      All the pictures fairest lined
      Are but black to Rosalind.
      Let no face be kept in mind 90
      But the fair of Rosalind.

TOUCHSTONE I'll rhyme you so eight years together,
dinners and suppers and sleeping-hours excepted: it is
the right butter-women's rank to market.

---

69 *get* earn
71 *content with my harm* patient under my misfortunes
76-7 *bell-wether* the leading sheep of the flock (obviously here a ram, *not* a castrated male) on whose neck a bell was hung
84 *Ind* Indies. It was, often at least, pronounced to rhyme with 'lined'. But the suggestion may be that Orlando is straining for rhymes.

88 *lined* drawn (but the word is also used, as Touchstone uses it in line 101, of the male dog covering the bitch)
94 *right butter-women's rank to market* the genuine movement of the butter-women jogging along to the market. Perhaps there is also a picture of the butter-women in a rank or line, at regular intervals, but the later phrase

ROSALIND Out, fool!

TOUCHSTONE For a taste:

> If a hart do lack a hind,
> Let him seek out Rosalind.
> If the cat will after kind,
> So be sure will Rosalind.
> Wintered garments must be lined,
> So must slender Rosalind.
> They that reap must sheaf and bind,
> Then to cart with Rosalind.
> Sweetest nut hath sourest rind,
> Such a nut is Rosalind.
> He that sweetest rose will find,
> Must find love's prick and Rosalind.

This is the very false gallop of verses. Why do you infect yourself with them?

ROSALIND Peace, you dull fool, I found them on a tree.

TOUCHSTONE Truly, the tree yields bad fruit.

ROSALIND I'll graff it with you, and then I shall graff it with a medlar; then it will be the earliest fruit

---

false gallop makes it probable that *rank* here means 'pace' or 'jog-trot'. Both phrases may be reminiscences of a passage in Nashe's *Strange News* (1592): 'I would trot a false gallop through the rest of his ragged verses, but that if I should report his rhyme doggerel aright I must make my verses, as he doth his, run hobbling like a brewer's cart upon the stones, and observe no length in their feet.'

99 *kind* its own kin or species

101 *Wintered* used in winter

103–4 *They that reap ... cart with Rosalind.* Touchstone's parody is far from genteel: 'Those that sow must reap, and so Rosalind must pay the cost of what she has done – by being carted like a prostitute'.

Public exposure in, and whipping at the rear of, a cart was the regular punishment.

113 *graff* graft (which is a later form of the word). Perhaps there is a pun on *you* and 'yew', and reference to Matthew 7.17–18: '. . . a corrupt tree bringeth forth evil fruit . . .'

114 *medlar* the tree bearing the apple-like fruit which is fit for eating only when decayed. There is also a pun, of course, on 'meddler': Touchstone is interfering.

114–15 *then it will be the earliest fruit i'th' country* the fruit of the medlar (which normally bears late in the season) will then be rotten far sooner (and rottenness is the *right virtue* or true merit of the medlar)

i'th'country: for you'll be rotten ere you be half ripe,
and that's the right virtue of the medlar.

TOUCHSTONE You have said; but whether wisely or no,
let the forest judge.

Enter Celia with a writing

ROSALIND Peace, here comes my sister, reading. Stand
aside.   120

CELIA (*reads*)

    Why should this a desert be?
      For it is unpeopled? No,
    Tongues I'll hang on every tree,
      That shall civil sayings show.
    Some, how brief the life of man
      Runs his erring pilgrimage,
    That the stretching of a span
      Buckles in his sum of age;
    Some, of violated vows
      'Twixt the souls of friend and friend;   130
    But upon the fairest boughs,
      Or at every sentence end,
    Will I 'Rosalinda' write,
      Teaching all that read to know
    The quintessence of every sprite

121–2 *Why should this . . . unpeopled? No.* Some editors have defended F's 'Desert' against Rowe's emendation 'a desert', but Orlando's versification is mostly jingle. F has a comma after *be*, but probably a question is intended: 'Why should this be a desert? Because it is unpeopled? No.' It could be argued, however, that the comma makes slightly better sense of Orlando's lame poem as a whole: 'Why should lack of people make this a desert? I'll put tongues on every tree and solve that difficulty.'

124 *civil sayings* maxims appropriate to civilization (as against deserts)

126 *erring* wandering (with no sense of error)

127–8 *the stretching of a span . . . sum of age.* A span is the distance measured by thumb and little finger, and Shakespeare is no doubt alluding to Psalm 39.5, 'Thou hast made my days as it were an hand breadth long' ('span' in the Prayer Book).

128 *Buckles in* encloses

135 *quintessence.* The quintessence was the fifth 'essence' (additional to the four elements) of which heavenly bodies were thought to be composed and which was latent in everything; astrologers aimed at isolating

Heaven would in little show.
Therefore Heaven Nature charged
That one body should be filled
With all graces wide-enlarged.
140   *Nature presently distilled*
Helen's cheek, but not her heart,
Cleopatra's majesty,
Atalanta's better part,
Sad Lucretia's modesty.
Thus Rosalind of many parts
By heavenly synod was devised,
Of many faces, eyes, and hearts,
To have the touches dearest prized.
Heaven would that she these gifts should have,
150   *And I to live and die her slave.*

ROSALIND O most gentle Jupiter, what tedious homily of
love have you wearied your parishioners withal, and
never cried 'Have patience, good people!'
CELIA How now? Back, friends. – Shepherd, go off a little.

it by distillation (line 140), in a
search for the secrets of transmutation.
sprite spirit
136 *in little* in the little world of man,
the microcosm, of which every part
corresponded to something in the
universe, or macrocosm
137 *Heaven Nature charged* Heaven gave
orders to Nature
139 *wide-enlarged* endowed in fullest
measure
140 *presently* immediately
141 *Helen's cheek* the beautiful complexion or face of Helen of Troy
143 *better part.* Probably Atalanta's
'grace' or her 'physique' (since she
was such a splendid runner – compare lines 268–9), but the meaning is
in dispute. Another suggestion is Ata-

lanta's 'determination to remain
chaste'.
144 *Sad Lucretia's modesty.* Lucretia killed
herself after she was violated by Tarquin. *Sad* means 'serious'.
146 *synod* (probably used here in its astrological sense of 'conjunction')
148 *touches* traits
151 *Jupiter.* The generally accepted emendation to 'pulpiter' (preacher) is gra-
tuitous. Rosalind swears by Jupiter
and by Jove in II.2 and is no doubt
comparing and contrasting the
poet, or Celia who reads his poem,
with the not-so-gentle voice of Jupiter speaking from Heaven.
154 *How now? Back, friends.* It seems
more likely that Celia is telling Corin
and Touchstone to stand back than
that she puns on 'back-friends' – (1)

– Go with him, sirrah.

TOUCHSTONE Come, shepherd, let us make an honourable retreat, though not with bag and baggage, yet with
scrip and scrippage.

Exit Touchstone, with Corin

CELIA Didst thou hear these verses?

ROSALIND O, yes, I heard them all, and more too, for   160
some of them had in them more feet than the verses
would bear.

CELIA That's no matter: the feet might bear the verses.

ROSALIND Ay, but the feet were lame, and could not bear
themselves without the verse, and therefore stood lamely
in the verse.

CELIA But didst thou hear without wondering how thy
name should be hanged and carved upon these trees?

ROSALIND I was seven of the nine days out of the wonder
before you came; for look here what I found on a palm-   170
tree. I was never so be-rhymed since Pythagoras' time
that I was an Irish rat, which I can hardly remember.

CELIA Trow you who hath done this?

ROSALIND Is it a man?

CELIA And a chain that you once wore about his neck!
Change you colour?

false friends; (2) people standing
behind her back, whom she now sees
for the first time.

157–8 *bag and baggage . . . scrip and scrippage.* To be allowed to depart with
one's bags and their contents was an
honourable condition on which to
surrender; Touchstone and Corin
may have no bags, but Corin has
the shepherd's pouch (the *scrip*) and
Touchstone, presumably, the fool's
wallet. *Baggage* already meant also a
strumpet (and Touchstone has just
made his uncomplimentary comparison of Rosalind with a prostitute)
and so *scrippage* (a word he invents

for the contents of the scrip) may
be better worth having than baggage.

168 *should be* came to be

169 *seven of the nine days.* The phrase depends on the proverbial 'a nine days'
wonder'.

171–2 *I was never . . . hardly remember.*
Rosalind jokingly pretends to accept
two wild beliefs: Pythagoras's doctrine of the transmigration of souls,
and the Irish superstition that rats
could be killed with rhymes used as
spells.

172 *that* in that; when

173 *Trow you* do you know

ROSALIND I prithee, who?

CELIA O Lord, Lord, it is a hard matter for friends to meet; but mountains may be removed with earthquakes and so encounter.

ROSALIND Nay, but who is it?

CELIA Is it possible?

ROSALIND Nay, I prithee now with most petitionary vehemence, tell me who it is.

CELIA O wonderful, wonderful, and most wonderful wonderful, and yet again wonderful, and after that out of all whooping!

ROSALIND Good my complexion! Dost thou think, though I am caparisoned like a man, I have a doublet and hose in my disposition? One inch of delay more is a South Sea of discovery. I prithee tell me who is it quickly, and speak apace. I would thou couldst stammer, that thou mightst pour this concealed man out of thy mouth as wine comes out of a narrow-mouthed bottle: either too much at once, or none at all. I prithee take the cork out of thy mouth, that I may drink thy tidings.

CELIA So you may put a man in your belly.

ROSALIND Is he of God's making? What manner of man? Is his head worth a hat? Or his chin worth a beard?

CELIA Nay, he hath but a little beard.

ROSALIND Why, God will send more, if the man will be thankful. Let me stay the growth of his beard, if thou delay me not the knowledge of his chin.

178–80 *it is a hard matter ... so encounter*. There is an old proverb 'Friends may meet but mountains never greet'.

182 *Is it possible?* (that is, possible that you don't know)

186–7 *out of all whooping* far beyond what all cries of astonishment can express

188 *Good my complexion!* pardon my blushes

189 *caparisoned* dressed, decked out

190–91 *a South Sea of discovery* as tedious as a voyage of discovery in the interminable South Seas

192 *apace* rapidly, or immediately

203 *stay* wait for

CELIA It is young Orlando, that tripped up the wrestler's heels and your heart, both in an instant.

ROSALIND Nay, but the devil take mocking; speak sad brow and true maid.

CELIA I'faith, coz, 'tis he.

ROSALIND Orlando?   210

CELIA Orlando.

ROSALIND Alas the day, what shall I do with my doublet and hose? What did he when thou sawest him? What said he? How looked he? Wherein went he? What makes he here? Did he ask for me? Where remains he? How parted he with thee? And when shalt thou see him again? Answer me in one word.

CELIA You must borrow me Gargantua's mouth first: 'tis a word too great for any mouth of this age's size. To say 'ay' and 'no' to these particulars is more than to   220 answer in a catechism.

ROSALIND But doth he know that I am in this forest and in man's apparel? Looks he as freshly as he did the day he wrestled?

CELIA It is as easy to count atomies as to resolve the propositions of a lover; but take a taste of my finding him, and relish it with good observance. I found him under a tree like a dropped acorn.

ROSALIND It may well be called Jove's tree, when it drops such fruit.   230

CELIA Give me audience, good madam.

207–8 *sad brow and true maid* with a serious face and on your honour as a virgin
214 *Wherein went he?* in what clothes was he dressed?
215 *makes he* is he doing
218 *Gargantua* the giant of fairy-tale (and of Rabelais's famous story)
225 *atomies* motes, specks

225–6 *resolve the propositions of* solve the problems put forward for solution by
227 *relish it with good observance* sauce it and make it more palatable, by paying respectful attention
229 *Jove's tree* the oak (sacred to Jove)
231 *Give me audience* let me do the talking

240 *burden.* The word was used both of the refrain and of the bass or undersong. Compare IV.2.13 and note.
244 *bring me out* put me out
250 *God buy you* God be with you (our 'good-bye')
254 *moe* more. It is not clear why Orlando is given this older form when Jaques uses *more*.
255 *ill-favouredly* badly; or with a disapproving expression

JAQUES Rosalind is your love's name?

ORLANDO Yes, just.

JAQUES I do not like her name.

ORLANDO There was no thought of pleasing you when she was christened.

260

JAQUES What stature is she of?

ORLANDO Just as high as my heart.

JAQUES You are full of pretty answers: have you not been acquainted with goldsmiths' wives, and conned them out of rings?

ORLANDO Not so; but I answer you right painted cloth, from whence you have studied your questions.

JAQUES You have a nimble wit; I think 'twas made of Atalanta's heels. Will you sit down with me, and we two will rail against our mistress the world, and all our misery?

270

ORLANDO I will chide no breather in the world but myself, against whom I know most faults.

JAQUES The worst fault you have is to be in love.

ORLANDO 'Tis a fault I will not change for your best virtue. I am weary of you.

JAQUES By my troth, I was seeking for a fool when I found you.

ORLANDO He is drowned in the brook; look but in and you shall see him.

280

JAQUES There I shall see mine own figure.

ORLANDO Which I take to be either a fool or a cipher.

JAQUES I'll tarry no longer with you. Farewell, good Signor Love.

---

257 *just* exactly, quite so

264–5 *conned them out of rings* learned them by heart from rings (in which posies were inscribed)

266 *right painted cloth* in the authentic manner of painted cloth (the cheaper alternative to tapestry), on which were painted scriptural and other texts

272 *breather* ('man alive' in modern idiom)

281 *There I shall see mine own figure.* As Furness said, the line is unworthy of Jaques!

ORLANDO I am glad of your departure. Adieu, good
Monsieur Melancholy.

Exit Jaques

ROSALIND [*to Celia*] I will speak to him like a saucy lackey,
and under that habit play the knave with him. – Do you
hear, forester?

290 ORLANDO Very well. What would you?

ROSALIND I pray you, what is't o'clock?

ORLANDO You should ask me what time o'day : there's no
clock in the forest.

ROSALIND Then there is no true lover in the forest, else
sighing every minute and groaning every hour would
detect the lazy foot of Time as well as a clock.

ORLANDO And why not the swift foot of Time? Had not
that been as proper?

ROSALIND By no means, sir: Time travels in divers
300 paces with divers persons. I'll tell you who Time
ambles withal, who Time trots withal, who Time
gallops withal, and who he stands still withal.

ORLANDO I prithee, who doth he trot withal?

ROSALIND Marry, he trots hard with a young maid
between the contract of her marriage and the day it is
solemnized. If the interim be but a se'nnight, Time's
pace is so hard that it seems the length of seven year.

ORLANDO Who ambles Time withal?

ROSALIND With a priest that lacks Latin, and a rich man
310 that hath not the gout: for the one sleeps easily because
he cannot study, and the other lives merrily because he
feels no pain, the one lacking the burden of lean and
wasteful learning, the other knowing no burden of
heavy tedious penury. These Time ambles withal.

ORLANDO Who doth he gallop withal?

ROSALIND With a thief to the gallows: for though he go

---

304 *trots hard* moves at an uncomfortable
jog-trot

313 *wasteful* (perhaps) causing to waste
away

316–17 *go as softly* walk as slowly

as softly as foot can fall, he thinks himself too soon
there.

ORLANDO Who stays it still withal?

ROSALIND With lawyers in the vacation: for they sleep   320
between term and term, and then they perceive not how
Time moves.

ORLANDO Where dwell you, pretty youth?

ROSALIND With this shepherdess, my sister, here in the
skirts of the forest, like fringe upon a petticoat.

ORLANDO Are you native of this place?

ROSALIND As the cony that you see dwell where she is
kindled.

ORLANDO Your accent is something finer than you could
purchase in so removed a dwelling.   330

ROSALIND I have been told so of many; but indeed an old
religious uncle of mine taught me to speak, who was in
his youth an inland man – one that knew courtship too
well, for there he fell in love. I have heard him read
many lectures against it, and I thank God I am not a
woman, to be touched with so many giddy offences as
he hath generally taxed their whole sex withal.

ORLANDO Can you remember any of the principal evils
that he laid to the charge of women?

ROSALIND There were none principal, they were all like   340
one another as halfpence are, every one fault seeming
monstrous till his fellow-fault came to match it.

ORLANDO I prithee, recount some of them.

ROSALIND No, I will not cast away my physic but on

---

319 *stays* stands
327 *cony* rabbit
328 *kindled* born
330 *purchase* acquire
removed remote
332 *religious uncle* uncle who was a
member of a religious order. Some
editors, implausibly, have suggested
some connexion between this supposed *religious uncle* and the *old reli-*

gious man of v.4.157.
333 *inland* city, cultured. Compare
II.7.97 and note.
courtship (1) court life; (2) wooing
336 *touched with* stained with; or accused
of
344–5 *I will not cast away ... are sick.*
There may be an allusion to Matthew
9.12: 'They that be whole need not
the physician, but they that are sick'.

those that are sick. There is a man haunts the forest
that abuses our young plants with carving 'Rosalind' on
their barks; hangs odes upon hawthorns, and elegies on
brambles; all, forsooth, deifying the name of Rosalind.
If I could meet that fancy-monger, I would give him
350 some good counsel, for he seems to have the quotidian
of love upon him.

ORLANDO I am he that is so love-shaked. I pray you, tell
me your remedy.

ROSALIND There is none of my uncle's marks upon you.
He taught me how to know a man in love; in which cage
of rushes I am sure you are not prisoner.

ORLANDO What were his marks?

ROSALIND A lean cheek, which you have not; a blue eye
and sunken, which you have not; an unquestionable
360 spirit, which you have not; a beard neglected, which
you have not – but I pardon you for that, for simply
your having in beard is a younger brother's revenue.
Then your hose should be ungartered, your bonnet
unbanded, your sleeve unbuttoned, your shoe untied,
and everything about you demonstrating a careless
desolation. But you are no such man: you are rather
point-device in your accoutrements, as loving yourself,
than seeming the lover of any other.

ORLANDO Fair youth, I would I could make thee believe
370 I love.

ROSALIND Me believe it? You may as soon make her that

---

349 *fancy-monger* one who deals in love
(as a woodmonger deals in wood)

350 *quotidian* daily, recurrent fever

356 *rushes* reeds. Rosalind is implying
that it is easy to escape from the cage
of love.

358 *blue eye* eye with dark rings around
it. On this paragraph, see Introduction, pages 367–8.

359 *unquestionable* not to be spoken to

361–2 *simply your having* the little you
have

364 *unbanded* without a coloured hat-band

365–6 *careless desolation* despondency
beyond caring

367 *point-device* fastidiously precise (shortened from 'at point device', from
French *à point devis*)

you love believe it, which I warrant she is apter to do than to confess she does: that is one of the points in the which women still give the lie to their consciences. But in good sooth, are you he that hangs the verses on the trees, wherein Rosalind is so admired?

ORLANDO I swear to thee, youth, by the white hand of Rosalind, I am that he, that unfortunate he.

ROSALIND But are you so much in love as your rhymes speak?   380

ORLANDO Neither rhyme nor reason can express how much.

ROSALIND Love is merely a madness and, I tell you, deserves as well a dark house and a whip as madmen do; and the reason why they are not so punished and cured is that the lunacy is so ordinary that the whippers are in love too. Yet I profess curing it by counsel.

ORLANDO Did you ever cure any so?

ROSALIND Yes, one, and in this manner. He was to imagine me his love, his mistress; and I set him every   390 day to woo me. At which time would I, being but a moonish youth, grieve, be effeminate, changeable, longing and liking, proud, fantastical, apish, shallow, inconstant, full of tears, full of smiles; for every passion something, and for no passion truly anything, as boys and women are for the most part cattle of this colour; would now like him, now loathe him; then entertain him, then forswear him; now weep for him, then spit at him; that I drave my suitor from his mad humour of

374 *still* always
376 *admired* marvelled at
383 *merely* completely (similarly in line 402, and compare *mere oblivion* in II.7.166)
384 *dark house and a whip.* Rosalind is not inventing the punishment. This was a common Elizabethan treatment for the insane, as the trick played on Malvolio in *Twelfth Night* shows.
386 *ordinary* common, frequent
392 *moonish* changeable (like the moon)
397 *entertain* receive kindly
399 *that* with the result that
drave drove (a common form of the past tense)

love to a living humour of madness – which was, to forswear the full stream of the world and to live in a nook merely monastic. And thus I cured him, and this way will I take upon me to wash your liver as clean as a sound sheep's heart, that there shall not be one spot of love in't.

ORLANDO I would not be cured, youth.

ROSALIND I would cure you, if you would but call me 'Rosalind', and come every day to my cote, and woo me.

ORLANDO Now, by the faith of my love, I will. Tell me
410   where it is.

ROSALIND Go with me to it and I'll show it you: and by the way you shall tell me where in the forest you live. Will you go?

ORLANDO With all my heart, good youth.

ROSALIND Nay, you must call me 'Rosalind'. – Come, sister, will you go?   *Exeunt*

III.3   *Enter Touchstone and Audrey, followed by Jaques*

TOUCHSTONE Come apace, good Audrey. I will fetch up your goats, Audrey. And now, Audrey, am I the man yet? Doth my simple feature content you?

AUDREY Your features, Lord warrant us! What features?

TOUCHSTONE I am here with thee and thy goats, as the most capricious poet, honest Ovid, was among the Goths.

400 *living* real, authentic, not put on for the occasion. (Othello asks for *a living reason* of Desdemona's guilt.)

403 *liver*. This was thought to be the seat of the passions.

411–12 *by the way* on the way

III.3.3 *feature* form (or, judging by Touchstone's next lines, 'conduct'); but presumably Audrey suspects an innuendo

4 *warrant* protect

6–7 *capricious . . . Goths*. There is a series of learned puns here. *Capricious* is derived from the Latin word *caper* (goat) and originally meant 'goat-like' and 'lascivious'; *Goths* was pronounced like 'goats'; and Ovid, who was exiled from Rome and forced to live among the Goths, was renowned not for being *honest* (pure) but as the author of some very licentious poems: indeed, his banishment was possibly due either to his *Ars Ama-*

JAQUES (*aside*) O knowledge ill-inhabited, worse than Jove
in a thatched house!

TOUCHSTONE When a man's verses cannot be understood,   10
nor a man's good wit seconded with the forward child
Understanding, it strikes a man more dead than a great
reckoning in a little room. Truly, I would the gods had
made thee poetical.

AUDREY I do not know what 'poetical' is. Is it honest in
deed and word? Is it a true thing?

TOUCHSTONE No, truly: for the truest poetry is the most
feigning; and lovers are given to poetry; and what they
swear in poetry may be said as lovers they do feign.

AUDREY Do you wish then that the gods had made me   20
poetical?

TOUCHSTONE I do, truly: for thou swearest to me thou art
honest; now, if thou wert a poet, I might have some hope
thou didst feign.

AUDREY Would you not have me honest?

TOUCHSTONE No, truly: unless thou wert hard-favoured:
for honesty coupled to beauty is to have honey a sauce
to sugar.

JAQUES (*aside*) A material fool!

AUDREY Well, I am not fair, and therefore I pray the gods   30
make me honest.

toria or to his liaison with the Emperor's daughter Julia. All this is wasted on Audrey, of course, but not on Jaques.

8 *ill-inhabited* badly housed

8–9 *Jove in a thatched house.* Jaques also has his classical learning. He refers to the time when Jove, in disguise, visited the earth and was warmly entertained by the poor old couple Baucis and Philemon, in their humble cottage.

11 *seconded with* supported by

12–13 *it strikes . . . in a little room.* For the possible reference to the death of

Marlowe, see Introduction, pages 375–6 A *little room* may mean a private one in an inn, in which the *reckoning* ('bill for a meal') would be more likely to be unreasonable.

19 *may be said.* Mason's emendation 'it may be said' perhaps makes the sense a little clearer, but Touchstone is merely playing with words. There may be a pun on *feign* meaning 'pretend' and 'fain' meaning 'desire'.

26 *hard-favoured* ugly

29 *material* full of matter; or practical, unromantic

TOUCHSTONE Truly, and to cast away honesty upon a foul slut were to put good meat into an unclean dish.

AUDREY I am not a slut, though I thank the gods I am foul.

TOUCHSTONE Well, praised be the gods for thy foulness; sluttishness may come hereafter. But be it as it may be, I will marry thee; and to that end, I have been with Sir Oliver Martext, the vicar of the next village, who hath
40 promised to meet me in this place of the forest and to couple us.

JAQUES (aside) I would fain see this meeting.

AUDREY Well, the gods give us joy.

TOUCHSTONE Amen. A man may, if he were of a fearful heart, stagger in this attempt; for here we have no temple but the wood, no assembly but horn-beasts. But what though? Courage! As horns are odious, they are necessary. It is said, 'Many a man knows no end of his goods'. Right! Many a man has good horns, and knows no end
50 of them. Well, that is the dowry of his wife, 'tis none of his own getting. Horns? Even so. Poor men alone? No, no, the noblest deer hath them as huge as the rascal. Is the single man therefore blessed? No. As a walled town is more worthier than a village, so is the forehead of a married man more honourable than the bare brow of a bachelor; and by how much defence is better than

---

35 *foul.* Perhaps to Audrey the word means only 'plain' ('homely' in the current American usage).

38-9 *Sir Oliver Martext. Martext* is a type-name, of the kind frequently used in anti-Puritan pamphlets; and *Sir* seems to have been the normal 'title' for an unlettered country clergyman.

46 *horn-beasts.* There is the usual quibble on 'animals with horns' and 'cuckolds'. F's 'horne' may be a misread-ing of 'hornd', but the sense is not affected.

46-7 *what though?* what of it?

51 *Poor men alone?* Whether one retains the F punctuation ('euen so poore men alone:') or interprets as in the given text, the sense is clear: Touchstone himself raises, and rejects, the supposition that only poor men's wives are unfaithful.

52 *rascal* poorer deer of the herd

no skill, by so much is a horn more precious than to
want.

   Enter Sir Oliver Martext

Here comes Sir Oliver. – Sir Oliver Martext, you are
well met. Will you dispatch us here under this tree, or 60
shall we go with you to your chapel?

SIR OLIVER Is there none here to give the woman?

TOUCHSTONE I will not take her on gift of any man.

SIR OLIVER Truly, she must be given, or the marriage is
not lawful.

JAQUES (*coming forward*) Proceed, proceed; I'll give her.

TOUCHSTONE Good even, good Master What-ye-call't:
how do you, sir? You are very well met. God 'ild you
for your last company, I am very glad to see you.
Even a toy in hand here, sir. Nay, pray be covered. 70

JAQUES Will you be married, motley?

TOUCHSTONE As the ox hath his bow, sir, the horse his
curb, and the falcon her bells, so man hath his desires;
and as pigeons bill, so wedlock would be nibbling.

JAQUES And will you, being a man of your breeding, be
married under a bush like a beggar? Get you to church,
and have a good priest that can tell you what marriage
is. This fellow will but join you together as they join
wainscot; then one of you will prove a shrunk panel and,
like green timber, warp, warp. 80

58 *want* be without (but there is another
learned quibble because of the 'horn
of plenty')

68 *'ild* reward (abbreviation of 'yield' in
its original meaning). So too in
v.4.53.

69 *your last company* your latest company
('your action in joining us now')

70 *toy* matter of no great importance
be covered replace your hat. Here, and to
William in v.1.16–17, Touchstone
condescendingly speaks as the mon-

arch or nobleman normally speaks to
the inferior who has thus shown a
mark of respect – but the respect
was being paid by Jaques to the
clergyman's office, not to Touchstone.

72 *bow* yoke (or part inserted in it)

79 *wainscot* wooden panelling
panel. If, as has been suggested, *panel*
could also mean 'prostitute', *warp*
may also have the secondary meaning
of 'go wrong'.

TOUCHSTONE I am not in the mind but I were better to be married of him than of another, for he is not like to marry me well; and not being well married, it will be a good excuse for me hereafter to leave my wife.

JAQUES Go thou with me, and let me counsel thee.

TOUCHSTONE Come, sweet Audrey, we must be married, or we must live in bawdry. Farewell, good Master Oliver. Not

> *O sweet Oliver,*
> *O brave Oliver,*
> *Leave me not behind thee*

but

> *Wind away,*
> *Be gone, I say,*
> *I will not to wedding with thee.*

SIR OLIVER (aside) 'Tis no matter; ne'er a fantastical knave of them all shall flout me out of my calling.

Exeunt

III.4   *Enter Rosalind and Celia*

ROSALIND Never talk to me, I will weep.

CELIA Do, I prithee, but yet have the grace to consider that tears do not become a man.

ROSALIND But have I not cause to weep?

CELIA As good cause as one would desire; therefore weep.

ROSALIND His very hair is of the dissembling colour.

CELIA Something browner than Judas's. Marry, his kisses are Judas's own children.

81 *not in the mind but.* This must be the double negative that does make an affirmative: 'inclined to think that'.

85 *me ... thee.* Jaques's internal rhyme may be unintentional, but Touchstone caps it with a deliberate one *Audrey ... bawdry.* F sets the lines out as verse.

89-95 *O Sweet Oliver.* Touchstone sings part of, and parodies, a popular ballad, which is believed to have been sung to the tune of 'In peascod time'. See 'The Songs', page 391.

III.4.6 *dissembling colour* (red; or, as line 10 has it, *chestnut*: the traditional colour of Judas's hair and therefore the sign of hypocrisy)

ROSALIND I'faith, his hair is of a good colour.

CELIA An excellent colour: your chestnut was ever the 10
only colour.

ROSALIND And his kissing is as full of sanctity as the
touch of holy bread.

CELIA He hath bought a pair of cast lips of Diana. A nun
of winter's sisterhood kisses not more religiously; the
very ice of chastity is in them.

ROSALIND But why did he swear he would come this
morning, and comes not?

CELIA Nay, certainly, there is no truth in him.

ROSALIND Do you think so? 20

CELIA Yes, I think he is not a pick-purse nor a horse-
stealer, but for his verity in love I do think him as
concave as a covered goblet or a worm-eaten nut.

ROSALIND Not true in love?

CELIA Yes, when he is in – but I think he is not in.

ROSALIND You have heard him swear downright he was.

CELIA 'Was' is not 'is'. Besides, the oath of lover is no
stronger than the word of a tapster: they are both the
confirmer of false reckonings. He attends here in the
forest on the Duke your father. 30

ROSALIND I met the Duke yesterday and had much
question with him. He asked me of what parentage I
was. I told him, of as good as he – so he laughed and let
me go. But what talk we of fathers, when there is such a
man as Orlando?

10 *your chestnut* (*not* Rosalind's, but 'the chestnut we are talking about')

13 *holy bread.* This was originally the bread that was blessed and distributed to those who had *not* taken Communion, but after the Reformation it came to mean sacramental bread. (Interestingly the phrase was expunged by a seventeenth-century Catholic priest censoring a copy of the Second Folio to be used by English students at Valladolid in Spain.)

14 *cast lips of Diana* lips cast for a statue of Diana, the goddess of chastity. (The alternative interpretation, 'cast off', seems almost ludicrous.)

15 *of winter's sisterhood.* That is to say, extremely 'cold' or chaste

23 *concave* hollow

28 *tapster* waiter, or drawer of ale, in an inn, who would also make up the *reckonings* ('bills')

32 *question* conversation

34 *what* why

CELIA O, that's a brave man! He writes brave verses, speaks brave words, swears brave oaths and breaks them bravely, quite traverse, athwart the heart of his lover, as a puisny tilter that spurs his horse but on one side breaks his staff like a noble goose. But all's brave that youth mounts and folly guides. Who comes here?

Enter Corin

CORIN
Mistress and master, you have oft inquired
After the shepherd that complained of love,
Who you saw sitting by me on the turf,
Praising the proud disdainful shepherdess
That was his mistress.

CELIA   Well: and what of him?

CORIN
If you will see a pageant truly played,
Between the pale complexion of true love
And the red glow of scorn and proud disdain,
Go hence a little and I shall conduct you,
If you will mark it.

ROSALIND   O come, let us remove;
The sight of lovers feedeth those in love.
Bring us to this sight, and you shall say
I'll prove a busy actor in their play.   *Exeunt*

III.5   *Enter Silvius and Phebe*

SILVIUS
Sweet Phebe, do not scorn me, do not, Phebe.
Say that you love me not, but say not so

---

36 *brave* fine
36–40 *He . . . swears brave oaths . . . noble goose.* Orlando's oaths merely glance off the heart of his loved one, just as an insignificant (or, perhaps, 'unskilled') knight, who in tilting spurs his horse only on one side, breaks his lance like a coward, with a glancing blow (instead of hitting his target in the centre)
43 *complained of* uttered his lament about
51 *remove* go, move off

In bitterness. The common executioner,
Whose heart th'accustomed sight of death makes hard,
Falls not the axe upon the humbled neck
But first begs pardon: will you sterner be
Than he that dies and lives by bloody drops?

Enter Rosalind, Celia, and Corin, unobserved

PHEBE
I would not be thy executioner.
I fly thee, for I would not injure thee.
Thou tellest me there is murder in mine eye: 10
'Tis pretty, sure, and very probable,
That eyes, that are the frail'st and softest things,
Who shut their coward gates on atomies,
Should be called tyrants, butchers, murderers!
Now I do frown on thee with all my heart,
And if mine eyes can wound, now let them kill thee.
Now counterfeit to swoon, why now fall down,
Or if thou canst not, O for shame, for shame,
Lie not, to say mine eyes are murderers!
Now show the wound mine eye hath made in thee.   20
Scratch thee but with a pin, and there remains
Some scar of it; lean upon a rush,
The cicatrice and capable impressure
Thy palm some moment keeps; but now mine eyes,
Which I have darted at thee, hurt thee not,
Nor, I am sure, there is no force in eyes
That can do hurt.
SILVIUS   O dear Phebe,
If ever – as that ever may be near –
You meet in some fresh cheek the power of fancy,
Then shall you know the wounds invisible   30

III.5.5 *Falls* drops
6 *But first begs* without first begging
11 *sure* surely
13 *atomies* motes (as before in III.2.225)

23 *cicatrice and capable impressure* scar-like
mark and perceptible imprint
29 *fancy* love

That love's keen arrows make.

PHEBE   But till that time
Come not thou near me; and when that time comes,
Afflict me with thy mocks, pity me not,
As till that time I shall not pity thee.

ROSALIND (*coming forward*)
And why, I pray you? Who might be your mother,
That you insult, exult and all at once
Over the wretched? What, though you have no beauty –
As, by my faith, I see no more in you
Than without candle may go dark to bed –
40   Must you be therefore proud and pitiless?
Why, what means this? Why do you look on me?
I see no more in you than in the ordinary
Of nature's sale-work. 'Od's my little life,
I think she means to tangle my eyes too!
No, faith, proud mistress, hope not after it:
'Tis not your inky brows, your black silk hair,
Your bugle eyeballs, nor your cheek of cream
That can entame my spirits to your worship.
You foolish shepherd, wherefore do you follow her,
50   Like foggy south, puffing with wind and rain?
You are a thousand times a properer man
Than she a woman. 'Tis such fools as you
That makes the world full of ill-favoured children.
'Tis not her glass but you that flatters her,
And out of you she sees herself more proper
Than any of her lineaments can show her.
But, mistress, know yourself; down on your knees

38–9 *no more in you* | . . . *to bed*. Rosalind
   means that Phebe's beauty alone
   would not light up the room and
   make a candle unnecessary.
42 *ordinary* ordinary run
43 *sale-work* ready-made goods (inferior
   to more careful work)
   '*Od's* (an abbreviation of 'may God

   save')
47 *bugle* bead-like. A bugle was a glass
   bead, usually black (and Phebe's eyes
   are black according to line 130).
50 *south* south wind
51 *properer* more handsome (as again in
   line 55)
53 *ill-favoured* ugly

And thank heaven, fasting, for a good man's love!
For I must tell you friendly in your ear,
Sell when you can, you are not for all markets.   60
Cry the man mercy, love him, take his offer.
Foul is most foul, being foul to be a scoffer.
So take her to thee, shepherd. Fare you well.

PHEBE

Sweet youth, I pray you chide a year together;
I had rather hear you chide than this man woo.

ROSALIND (*to Phebe*) He's fallen in love with your foulness,
(*to Silvius*) and she'll fall in love with my anger. If it
be so, as fast as she answers thee with frowning looks,
I'll sauce her with bitter words. (*To Phebe*) Why look
you so upon me?   70

PHEBE

For no ill will I bear you.

ROSALIND

I pray you, do not fall in love with me,
For I am falser than vows made in wine.
Besides, I like you not. (*To Silvius*) If you will know
    my house,
'Tis at the tuft of olives here hard by. –
Will you go, sister? – Shepherd, ply her hard. –
Come, sister. – Shepherdess, look on him better,
And be not proud, though all the world could see,
None could be so abused in sight as he.
Come, to our flock.   80

Exit Rosalind, with Celia and Corin

61 *Cry the man mercy* beg the man's
    forgiveness
62 *Foul is most foul . . . a scoffer* ugliness
    is most ugly when the ugliness is in
    being a scoffer (with 'wicked' as a
    secondary meaning of *foul*)
66–7 *He's fallen . . . my anger.* Some editors think these lines are an aside,
but Rosalind is not concerned to
spare Phebe's feelings.
69 *sauce* rebuke, sting
78 *see* see you
79 *abused* deceived

PHEBE

Dead Shepherd, now I find thy saw of might,
'Who ever loved that loved not at first sight?'

SILVIUS

Sweet Phebe —

PHEBE   Ha, what sayest thou, Silvius?

SILVIUS

Sweet Phebe, pity me.

PHEBE

Why, I am sorry for thee, gentle Silvius.

SILVIUS

Wherever sorrow is, relief would be.
If you do sorrow at my grief in love,
By giving love, your sorrow and my grief
Were both extermined.

PHEBE

90   Thou hast my love; is not that neighbourly?

SILVIUS

I would have you.

PHEBE   Why, that were covetousness.
Silvius, the time was that I hated thee,
And yet it is not that I bear thee love;
But since that thou canst talk of love so well,
Thy company, which erst was irksome to me,
I will endure, and I'll employ thee too.
But do not look for further recompense
Than thine own gladness that thou art employed.

SILVIUS

So holy and so perfect is my love,
100   And I in such a poverty of grace,

81 *saw* maxim. For this quotation from
Marlowe's *Hero and Leander*, see Introduction, page 376.
89 *extermined* destroyed, ended
90 *neighbourly* (in accordance with the injunction to love one's neighbour as
oneself)

93 *it is not that* the time has not yet
come
95 *erst* not long ago
irksome hateful, offensive
100 *in such a poverty of grace.* That is,
because so little grace has been
shown, or given, to him.

That I shall think it a most plenteous crop
To glean the broken ears after the man
That the main harvest reaps. Loose now and then
A scattered smile, and that I'll live upon.

PHEBE

Knowest thou the youth that spoke to me erewhile?

SILVIUS

Not very well, but I have met him oft,
And he hath bought the cottage and the bounds
That the old carlot once was master of.

PHEBE

Think not I love him, though I ask for him.
'Tis but a peevish boy. Yet he talks well.   110
But what care I for words? Yet words do well
When he that speaks them pleases those that hear.
It is a pretty youth – not very pretty –
But, sure, he's proud – and yet his pride becomes him.
He'll make a proper man. The best thing in him
Is his complexion; and faster than his tongue
Did make offence, his eye did heal it up.
He is not very tall – yet for his years he's tall.
His leg is but so so – and yet 'tis well.
There was a pretty redness in his lip,   120
A little riper and more lusty red
Than that mixed in his cheek; 'twas just the difference
Betwixt the constant red and mingled damask.
There be some women, Silvius, had they marked him
In parcels, as I did, would have gone near
To fall in love with him: but, for my part,
I love him not, nor hate him not; and yet
I have more cause to hate him than to love him,

104 *scattered* random
107 *bounds* lands (on which he had the right of pasturage)
108 *carlot* peasant, churl. (The word is not recorded elsewhere, but 'carl' is,
in the same sense.)
123 *damask.* The reference may be to the damask rose or to the woven fabric.
125 *In parcels* feature by feature

For what had he to do to chide at me?

130 He said mine eyes were black and my hair black,
And, now I am remembered, scorned at me;
I marvel why I answered not again.
But that's all one: omittance is no quittance;
I'll write to him a very taunting letter,
And thou shalt bear it — wilt thou, Silvius?

SILVIUS
Phebe, with all my heart.

PHEBE   I'll write it straight:
The matter's in my head and in my heart.
I will be bitter with him and passing short.
Go with me, Silvius.   *Exeunt*

IV.I   *Enter Rosalind, Celia, and Jaques*

JAQUES I prithee, pretty youth, let me be better acquainted
with thee.

ROSALIND They say you are a melancholy fellow.

JAQUES I am so: I do love it better than laughing.

ROSALIND Those that are in extremity of either are
abominable fellows, and betray themselves to every
modern censure worse than drunkards.

132 *answered not again* did not answer
back
133 *omittance is no quittance.* This is a
proverb: 'failure to do something at
the time is not a full discharge from
the responsibility of doing it in the
long run'.
136 *straight* immediately
138 *passing short* extremely curt

IV.I.3 *melancholy fellow.* There is, no
doubt, topical humour here: a pose
of melancholy seems to have been
fashionable in the 1590s and early

seventeenth century, and many
dramatists refer to it. The man who
adopted the pose could always claim
that black bile predominated in his
make-up and made his 'humour' inevitable. (Compare *humorous* in line
18.) Fashionable modern 'complexes'
provide the perfect parallel.
6 *abominable.* The F spelling 'abhomina-
ble' probably preserves the false etymology *ab homine* and so the second
sense of 'not human'.
7 *modern* everyday (as in II.7.157)

JAQUES Why, 'tis good to be sad and say nothing.

ROSALIND Why then, 'tis good to be a post.

JAQUES I have neither the scholar's melancholy, which is   10
emulation; nor the musician's, which is fantastical; nor
the courtier's, which is proud; nor the soldier's, which is
ambitious; nor the lawyer's, which is politic; nor the
lady's, which is nice; nor the lover's, which is all these:
but it is a melancholy of mine own, compounded of
many simples, extracted from many objects, and indeed
the sundry contemplation of my travels, in which my
often rumination wraps me in a most humorous sadness.

ROSALIND A traveller! By my faith, you have great
reason to be sad. I fear you have sold your own lands to   20
see other men's; then, to have seen much and to have
nothing is to have rich eyes and poor hands.

JAQUES Yes, I have gained my experience.

Enter Orlando

ROSALIND And your experience makes you sad. I had
rather have a fool to make me merry than experience to
make me sad — and to travail for it too!

ORLANDO
Good day, and happiness, dear Rosalind!

JAQUES Nay then, God buy you, an you talk in blank verse.
(Going)

ROSALIND (*as he goes*) Farewell, Monsieur Traveller. Look
you lisp and wear strange suits; disable all the benefits   30
of your own country; be out of love with your nativity,
and almost chide God for making you that countenance

8 *sad* solemn
13 *politic* crafty, guided by considerations only of expediency
14 *nice* (pretending to be) fastidious
16 *simples* ingredients
26 *travail* (1) work hard; (2) travel
28 (stage direction) *Going*. F does not
mark an 'exit' for Jaques, but obviously Rosalind should not deign to
notice Orlando, who has come late

for his appointment, until Jaques,
who has begun to leave as he
speaks his farewell, is off stage; she
continues talking to Jaques as he
goes.
30 *lisp* affect a foreign accent (Rosalind's
list of complaints against returned
travellers echoes many others in
Elizabethan writing)
disable belittle

you are; or I will scarce think you have swam in a gondola. – Why, how now, Orlando, where have you been all this while? You a lover! An you serve me such another trick, never come in my sight more.

ORLANDO My fair Rosalind, I come within an hour of my promise.

ROSALIND Break an hour's promise in love? He that will
40   divide a minute into a thousand parts, and break but a part of the thousandth part of a minute in the affairs of love, it may be said of him that Cupid hath clapped him o'th'shoulder, but I'll warrant him heart-whole.

ORLANDO Pardon me, dear Rosalind.

ROSALIND Nay, an you be so tardy come no more in my sight; I had as lief be wooed of a snail.

ORLANDO Of a snail?

ROSALIND Ay, of a snail: for though he comes slowly, he carries his house on his head – a better jointure, I think,
50   than you make a woman. Besides, he brings his destiny with him.

ORLANDO What's that?

ROSALIND Why, horns; which such as you are fain to be beholding to your wives for. But he comes armed in his fortune, and prevents the slander of his wife.

ORLANDO Virtue is no horn-maker; and my Rosalind is virtuous.

ROSALIND And I am your Rosalind.

CELIA It pleases him to call you so; but he hath a Rosalind
60   of a better leer than you.

ROSALIND Come, woo me, woo me: for now I am in a

---

33 *swam* floated (an alternative form of the past participle). The gibe has the further point that Venice was the goal of many Elizabethan travellers, partly because it was notorious for its prostitutes.

42–3 *clapped him o'th'shoulder* arrested him or claimed him as his own

49 *jointure* marriage-settlement
55 *prevents* anticipates
    slander disgrace (rather than 'evil report' in the modern sense)
60 *leer* complexion (the restricted meaning 'sly look' seems to have developed later)

holiday humour, and like enough to consent. What
would you say to me now, an I were your very, very
Rosalind?

ORLANDO I would kiss before I spoke.

ROSALIND Nay, you were better speak first, and when you
were gravelled for lack of matter, you might take occasion
to kiss. Very good orators, when they are out, they will
spit, and for lovers lacking – God warn us! – matter, the
cleanliest shift is to kiss.   70

ORLANDO How if the kiss be denied?

ROSALIND Then she puts you to entreaty, and there
begins new matter.

ORLANDO Who could be out, being before his beloved
mistress?

ROSALIND Marry, that should you if I were your mistress,
or I should think my honesty ranker than my wit.

ORLANDO What, of my suit?

ROSALIND Not out of your apparel, and yet out of your
suit. Am not I your Rosalind?   80

ORLANDO I take some joy to say you are, because I would
be talking of her.

ROSALIND Well, in her person, I say I will not have you.

ORLANDO Then, in mine own person, I die.

ROSALIND No, faith, die by attorney. The poor world is
almost six thousand years old, and in all this time there
was not any man died in his own person, videlicet, in a
love-cause. Troilus had his brains dashed out with a

---

67 *gravelled* perplexed, at a loss (a similar
modern image is 'stranded')

68 *out* at a loss

69 *warn* summon (although Onions and
others believe it to be a variant of
'warrant')

77 *honesty* virtue, chastity
ranker more suspect (but some editors
paraphrase as 'stronger')

78 *of* out of (and Rosalind proceeds to
pun on *suit* in the senses of 'suit of
clothes' and 'courting' and possibly
even 'law suit')

85 *by attorney* by proxy (as in 'power of
attorney')

87 *videlicet* namely (Rosalind is continuing the legal language begun by *attorney* or *suit*)

Grecian club, yet he did what he could to die before, and he is one of the patterns of love. Leander, he would
90   have lived many a fair year though Hero had turned nun, if it had not been for a hot midsummer night: for, good youth, he went but forth to wash him in the Hellespont and being taken with the cramp was drowned, and the foolish chroniclers of that age found it was 'Hero of Sestos'. But these are all lies; men have died from time to time and worms have eaten them, but not for love.

ORLANDO I would not have my right Rosalind of this
100   mind, for I protest her frown might kill me.

ROSALIND By this hand, it will not kill a fly. But come, now I will be your Rosalind in a more coming-on disposition; and ask me what you will, I will grant it.

ORLANDO Then love me, Rosalind.

ROSALIND Yes, faith will I, Fridays and Saturdays and all.

ORLANDO And wilt thou have me?

ROSALIND Ay, and twenty such.

ORLANDO What sayest thou?

110   ROSALIND Are you not good?

ORLANDO I hope so.

ROSALIND Why then, can one desire too much of a good thing? Come, sister, you shall be the priest and marry us. – Give me your hand, Orlando. – What do you say, sister ?

ORLANDO Pray thee, marry us.

CELIA I cannot say the words.

ROSALIND You must begin 'Will you, Orlando'.

---

89 *Grecian club*. There are various versions of how Troilus, the prototype of the true lover, met his death; this is Rosalind's own. (Shakespeare's *Troilus and Cressida* does not carry the story to the death of Troilus but has him fling himself recklessly into battle when he discovers Cressida to be false.)
90 *Leander*. According to the accepted version of the story, he swam the Hellespont every night to visit Hero in Sestos (and was drowned).

CELIA Go to. – Will you, Orlando, have to wife this Rosalind? 120

ORLANDO I will.

ROSALIND Ay, but when?

ORLANDO Why, now, as fast as she can marry us.

ROSALIND Then you must say 'I take thee, Rosalind, for wife.'

ORLANDO I take thee, Rosalind, for wife.

ROSALIND I might ask you for your commission, but I do take thee, Orlando, for my husband. There's a girl goes before the priest, and certainly a woman's thought runs before her actions. 130

ORLANDO So do all thoughts, they are winged.

ROSALIND Now tell me how long you would have her after you have possessed her.

ORLANDO For ever and a day.

ROSALIND Say 'a day' without the 'ever'. No, no, Orlando, men are April when they woo, December when they wed; maids are May when they are maids, but the sky changes when they are wives. I will be more jealous of thee than a Barbary cock-pigeon over his hen, more clamorous than a parrot against rain, more new-fangled 140 than an ape, more giddy in my desires than a monkey; I will weep for nothing, like Diana in the fountain, and I will do that when you are disposed to be merry; I will laugh like a hyen, and that when thou art inclined to sleep.

119 *Go to* (not an abbreviation, but an exclamation of mild or simulated impatience)

127 *commission* authority. This exchange of vows may have had even greater significance for an Elizabethan audience, since such a declaration, before a third party, constituted one kind of legal marriage contract.

129 *goes before* anticipates (because, for one thing, she has not waited to be asked 'Will you . . .?')

139 *Barbary* a breed introduced from Barbary, the 'Barb' (apparently its origin is enough to imply jealousy)

140 *against* anticipating, predicting
new-fangled readily distracted by every novelty

142 *Diana in the fountain*. A figure of Diana was the centre of more than one fountain. Shakespeare may or may not have been thinking of the one erected in London in 1596 (it does not seem to have had a *weeping* Diana).

ORLANDO But will my Rosalind do so?

ROSALIND By my life, she will do as I do.

ORLANDO O, but she is wise.

ROSALIND Or else she could not have the wit to do this.
150   The wiser, the waywarder. Make the doors upon a
        woman's wit, and it will out at the casement; shut that,
        and 'twill out at the key-hole; stop that, 'twill fly with
        the smoke out at the chimney.

ORLANDO A man that had a wife with such a wit, he might
        say 'Wit, whither wilt?'

ROSALIND Nay, you might keep that check for it, till you
        met your wife's wit going to your neighbour's bed.

ORLANDO And what wit could wit have to excuse that?

ROSALIND Marry, to say she came to seek you there. You
160   shall never take her without her answer, unless you take
        her without her tongue. O, that woman that cannot make
        her fault her husband's occasion, let her never nurse her
        child herself, for she will breed it like a fool.

ORLANDO For these two hours, Rosalind, I will leave thee.

ROSALIND Alas, dear love, I cannot lack thee two hours!

ORLANDO I must attend the Duke at dinner. By two
        o'clock I will be with thee again.

ROSALIND Ay, go your ways, go your ways: I knew what
        you would prove, my friends told me as much, and I
170   thought no less. That flattering tongue of yours won
        me. 'Tis but one cast away, and so, come death. Two
        o'clock is your hour?

ORLANDO Ay, sweet Rosalind.

ROSALIND By my troth, and in good earnest, and so God
        mend me, and by all pretty oaths that are not dangerous,
        if you break one jot of your promise, or come one minute

---

150 *Make* close (a use still found in
    dialect)
155 *Wit, whither wilt?* For the same joke,
    see 1.2.53–5 and note.
162 *her husband's occasion* the opportunity

of finding fault
171 *but one cast away* only one woman
    cast off. (Editors have suspected a
    proverb or quotation from a popular
    ballad.)

behind your hour, I will think you the most pathetical break-promise, and the most hollow lover, and the most unworthy of her you call Rosalind, that may be chosen out of the gross band of the unfaithful. Therefore, 180 beware my censure, and keep your promise.

ORLANDO With no less religion than if thou wert indeed my Rosalind. So, adieu.

ROSALIND Well, Time is the old justice that examines all such offenders, and let Time try. Adieu!   *Exit Orlando*

CELIA You have simply misused our sex in your love-prate. We must have your doublet and hose plucked over your head, and show the world what the bird hath done to her own nest.

ROSALIND O coz, coz, coz, my pretty little coz, that thou 190 didst know how many fathom deep I am in love! But it cannot be sounded: my affection hath an unknown bottom, like the Bay of Portugal.

CELIA Or rather, bottomless, that as fast as you pour affection in, it runs out.

ROSALIND No, that same wicked bastard of Venus, that was begot of thought, conceived of spleen, and born of madness, that blind rascally boy that abuses everyone's eyes because his own are out, let him be judge how deep I am in love. I'll tell thee, Aliena, I cannot be out 200 of the sight of Orlando: I'll go find a shadow and sigh till he come.

CELIA And I'll sleep.   *Exeunt*

177 *pathetical* affecting; producing strong emotion (not only pity)
180 *gross* whole; or large
185 *try* judge the case
186 *simply misused* completely disgraced
187-9 *We must . . . her own nest.* For the adaptation from Lodge, see Introduction, page 362.
196 *bastard of Venus* Cupid (son of

Venus but by Mercury, not by her husband Vulcan)
197 *thought.* It is difficult to say which of many possible shades of meaning the word has here: probably 'fancy' rather than 'melancholy'.
spleen caprice, waywardness
198 *abuses* deceives

IV.2   *Enter Jaques, and Lords dressed as foresters*

JAQUES Which is he that killed the deer?

LORD Sir, it was I.

JAQUES Let's present him to the Duke like a Roman
    conqueror. And it would do well to set the deer's horns
    upon his head for a branch of victory. Have you no song,
    forester, for this purpose?

LORD Yes, sir.

JAQUES Sing it. 'Tis no matter how it be in tune, so it
    make noise enough.
                    Music

LORDS   SONG

10 What shall he have that killed the deer?
    His leather skin and horns to wear.
    Then sing him home, the rest shall bear
    This burden.
    Take thou no scorn to wear the horn,
    It was a crest ere thou wast born,
        Thy father's father wore it,
        And thy father bore it,
    The horn, the horn, the lusty horn,
    Is not a thing to laugh to scorn.
                                                    Exeu.

IV.2 This charming interlude, which contributes to the pastoral atmosphere (and mocks it), has the added function of marking the passing of the two hours specified in the previous scene.

(stage direction) *Lords dressed as foresters.* The F stage direction is 'Enter Iaques and Lords, Forresters'. Lines 2 and 7 are given to 'Lord' and the song is headed simply 'Musicke, Song' with no singer named. Perhaps this time foresters were intended to appear and even to sing, but there would seem to be no need for variation from II.1 and II.7: the Lords would have done the hunting and Jaques could address one of them as *forester* because of the costume. It is not necessary to give

Amiens either line 7 or the song, for Jaques's lines 8–9 may envisage singing by the whole group.

12–13 *the rest shall bear | This burden.* Burden does also mean 'chorus' (compare III.2.240 and note) and some editors take these words to be a direction to *the rest* to sing the refrain. But F prints the words in italic, as part of the song; *bear* rhymes with *wear* although F prints 'Then sing . . . burthen' as one line; and the point of the song is that *all* must run the risk of cuckoldry.

18 *lusty.* This time there is reference to 'lust' in the modern sense: the horn is *lusty* because it is the symbol of the wife's lust as well as the husband's shame.

Enter Rosalind and Celia   IV.3

ROSALIND How say you now? Is it not past two o'clock?
  And here much Orlando!

CELIA I warrant you, with pure love and troubled brain
  he hath ta'en his bow and arrows, and is gone forth to
  sleep.

      Enter Silvius
  Look who comes here.

SILVIUS
  My errand is to you, fair youth:
  My gentle Phebe did bid me give you this.

      He gives Rosalind a letter, which she reads
  I know not the contents, but as I guess
  By the stern brow and waspish action   10
  Which she did use as she was writing of it,
  It bears an angry tenor. Pardon me,
  I am but as a guiltless messenger.

ROSALIND
  Patience herself would startle at this letter,
  And play the swaggerer. Bear this, bear all.
  She says I am not fair, that I lack manners,
  She calls me proud, and that she could not love me
  Were man as rare as phoenix. 'Od's my will,
  Her love is not the hare that I do hunt!
  Why writes she so to me? Well, shepherd, well,   20
  This is a letter of your own device.

SILVIUS
  No, I protest, I know not the contents;
  Phebe did write it.

ROSALIND   Come, come, you are a fool,
  And turned into the extremity of love.

IV.3.2 *much* (used ironically: compare   new bird rose from the ashes of its
the modern colloquialism 'a fat lot   predecessor.
of . . .')   '*Od's my will* as God's is my will (or
18 *phoenix*. The point is that only one   'God save my will')
phoenix, according to the myth,   24 *turned* brought
could be alive at any one time; the

I saw her hand: she has a leathern hand,
A freestone-coloured hand; I verily did think
That her old gloves were on, but 'twas her hands;
She has a housewife's hand – but that's no matter.
I say she never did invent this letter;

30   This is a man's invention, and his hand.

SILVIUS

Sure, it is hers.

ROSALIND

Why, 'tis a boisterous and a cruel style,
A style for challengers. Why, she defies me,
Like Turk to Christian; women's gentle brain
Could not drop forth such giant rude invention,
Such Ethiop words, blacker in their effect
Than in their countenance. Will you hear the letter?

SILVIUS

So please you, for I never heard it yet;
Yet heard too much of Phebe's cruelty.

ROSALIND

40   She Phebes me; mark how the tyrant writes:

    Art thou god to shepherd turned,
    That a maiden's heart hath burned?

Can a woman rail thus?

SILVIUS Call you this railing?

ROSALIND

    Why, thy godhead laid apart,
    Warrest thou with a woman's heart?

Did you ever hear such railing?

    Whiles the eye of man did woo me,
    That could do no vengeance to me.

---

26 *freestone* (a fine-grained limestone or sandstone, between brown and yellow in colour)

35 *giant rude.* This is probably a compound adjective: 'incredibly barbarous, on the scale of a giant'.

40 *Phebes me* addresses me in her own style

45 *laid apart* doffed for the time being

49 *vengeance* damage

Meaning me a beast.   50

> *If the scorn of your bright eyne*
> *Have power to raise such love in mine,*
> *Alack, in me what strange effect*
> *Would they work in mild aspect?*
> *Whiles you chid me, I did love,*
> *How then might your prayers move?*
> *He that brings this love to thee*
> *Little knows this love in me;*
> *And by him seal up thy mind,*
> *Whether that thy youth and kind*   60
> *Will the faithful offer take*
> *Of me and all that I can make,*
> *Or else by him my love deny,*
> *And then I'll study how to die.*

SILVIUS Call you this chiding?

CELIA Alas, poor shepherd!

ROSALIND Do you pity him? No, he deserves no pity. – Wilt thou love such a woman? What, to make thee an instrument and play false strains upon thee? Not to be endured! Well, go your way to her – for I see love hath   70 made thee a tame snake – and say this to her: that if she love me, I charge her to love thee; if she will not, I will never have her, unless thou entreat for her. If you be a true lover, hence, and not a word, for here comes more company.

Exit Silvius

50 *Meaning me a beast* thereby making me into a beast (since my eye has a different effect from a man's)

51 *eyne* eyes (an old form, used by Shakespeare here as a 'poeticism')

54 *aspect.* Possibly 'look' but more probably this is the astrological term, meaning, roughly, 'phase'.

59 *by him seal up thy mind* use him as messenger to carry a sealed letter in which you state your decision. The alternative explanation, 'make your final decision', hardly explains *by him.*

60 *kind* disposition

62 *make* bring with me; or do

Enter Oliver

OLIVER

Good morrow, fair ones. Pray you, if you know,
Where in the purlieus of this forest stands
A sheepcote fenced about with olive trees?

CELIA

West of this place, down in the neighbour bottom,
80 The rank of osiers by the murmuring stream
Left on your right hand brings you to the place.
But at this hour the house doth keep itself,
There's none within.

OLIVER

If that an eye may profit by a tongue,
Then should I know you by description.
Such garments and such years: 'The boy is fair,
Of female favour, and bestows himself
Like a ripe sister; the woman low
And browner than her brother'. Are not you
90 The owner of the house I did inquire for?

CELIA

It is no boast, being asked, to say we are.

OLIVER

Orlando doth commend him to you both,
And to that youth he calls his 'Rosalind'
He sends this bloody napkin. Are you he?

ROSALIND

I am. What must we understand by this?

79 *bottom* valley
80 *rank of osiers* row of willows
81 *Left* passed
87 *favour* complexion; or countenance
  bestows himself carries himself, has the manner
88 *ripe sister* mature older sister (of the girl Celia). Some editors emend *sister*

to 'forester', not very plausibly.
low short (or 'shorter' if *low and browner* is to be construed, in a normal Elizabethan way, as 'lower and browner'). See too Introduction, pages 378–9.
94 *napkin* handkerchief

OLIVER
> Some of my shame, if you will know of me
> What man I am, and how, and why, and where
> This handkercher was stained.

CELIA   I pray you, tell it.

OLIVER
> When last the young Orlando parted from you,
> He left a promise to return again   100
> Within an hour; and pacing through the forest,
> Chewing the food of sweet and bitter fancy,
> Lo, what befell! He threw his eye aside,
> And mark what object did present itself!
> Under an oak, whose boughs were mossed with age
> And high top bald with dry antiquity,
> A wretched ragged man, o'ergrown with hair,
> Lay sleeping on his back. About his neck
> A green and gilded snake had wreathed itself,
> Who with her head nimble in threats approached   110
> The opening of his mouth; but suddenly,
> Seeing Orlando, it unlinked itself
> And with indented glides did slip away
> Into a bush: under which bush's shade
> A lioness, with udders all drawn dry,
> Lay couching, head on ground, with catlike watch
> When that the sleeping man should stir; for 'tis
> The royal disposition of that beast
> To prey on nothing that doth seem as dead.
> This seen, Orlando did approach the man,   120
> And found it was his brother, his elder brother.

CELIA
> O, I have heard him speak of that same brother,
> And he did render him the most unnatural
> That lived amongst men.

---

102 *fancy* love
113 *indented* zigzagging, undulating

117 *When that* for the time when
123 *render* declare, describe (as)

OLIVER   And well he might so do,
For well I know he was unnatural.

ROSALIND
But to Orlando: did he leave him there,
Food to the sucked and hungry lioness?

OLIVER
Twice did he turn his back and purposed so.
But kindness, nobler ever than revenge,
130   And nature, stronger than his just occasion,
Made him give battle to the lioness,
Who quickly fell before him; in which hurtling
From miserable slumber I awaked.

CELIA
Are you his brother?

ROSALIND   Was't you he rescued?

CELIA
Was't you that did so oft contrive to kill him?

OLIVER
'Twas I, but 'tis not I: I do not shame
To tell you what I was, since my conversion
So sweetly tastes, being the thing I am.

ROSALIND
But, for the bloody napkin?

OLIVER   By and by.
140   When from the first to last betwixt us two
Tears our recountments had most kindly bathed,
As how I came into that desert place –
I'brief, he led me to the gentle Duke,
Who gave me fresh array and entertainment,
Committing me unto my brother's love,

---

129 *kindness* (probably in both senses:
   (1) kinship; (2) generosity)
130 *just occasion* legitimate excuse, or perfect opportunity
132 *hurtling* tumult, violent conflict
135 *contrive* scheme

139 *By and by* immediately (the sense is
   much weaker now)
141 *recountments* narratives of our adventures (the word is the grammatical
   object of *bathed*)
144 *entertainment* hospitality

Who led me instantly unto his cave,
There stripped himself, and here upon his arm
The lioness had torn some flesh away,
Which all this while had bled; and now he fainted,
And cried, in fainting, upon Rosalind.   150
Brief, I recovered him, bound up his wound,
And after some small space, being strong at heart,
He sent me hither, stranger as I am,
To tell this story, that you might excuse
His broken promise, and to give this napkin,
Dyed in this blood, unto the shepherd youth
That he in sport doth call his 'Rosalind'.
        Rosalind faints

CELIA
Why, how now, Ganymede, sweet Ganymede!

OLIVER
Many will swoon when they do look on blood.

CELIA
There is more in it. – Cousin Ganymede!   160

OLIVER
Look, he recovers.

ROSALIND
I would I were at home.

CELIA   We'll lead you thither. –
I pray you, will you take him by the arm?

OLIVER Be of good cheer, youth! You a man? You lack
a man's heart.

ROSALIND I do so, I confess it. Ah, sirrah, a body would
think this was well counterfeited. I pray you, tell your
brother how well I counterfeited. Heigh-ho!

OLIVER This was not counterfeit, there is too great testimony in your complexion that it was a passion of earnest.   170

151 *Brief* in brief (as in line 143)   170 *passion of earnest* genuine emotion or
    recovered revived   suffering
166 *a body* anybody, one

ROSALIND Counterfeit, I assure you.

OLIVER Well then, take a good heart, and counterfeit to
be a man.

ROSALIND So I do; but, i'faith, I should have been a
woman by right.

CELIA Come, you look paler and paler. Pray you, draw
homewards. – Good sir, go with us.

OLIVER

That will I: for I must bear answer back
How you excuse my brother, Rosalind.

180   ROSALIND I shall devise something. But I pray you
commend my counterfeiting to him. Will you go?

Exeunt

V.I   *Enter Touchstone and Audrey*

TOUCHSTONE We shall find a time, Audrey. Patience,
gentle Audrey.

AUDREY Faith, the priest was good enough, for all the old
gentleman's saying.

TOUCHSTONE A most wicked Sir Oliver, Audrey, a most
vile Martext. But, Audrey, there is a youth here in the
forest lays claim to you.

AUDREY Ay, I know who 'tis: he hath no interest in me in
the world. Here comes the man you mean.

Enter William

10   TOUCHSTONE It is meat and drink to me to see a clown.
By my troth, we that have good wits have much to answer
for: we shall be flouting, we cannot hold.

WILLIAM Good even, Audrey.

AUDREY God ye good even, William.

---

v.I.10 *clown yokel*, country bumpkin   a rustic speech, which Touchstone
12 *shall be flouting* must jeer *hold* refrain   imitates.
13 *even*. F's spelling 'eu'n' may represent   14 *God ye* God give you

WILLIAM And good even to you, sir.

TOUCHSTONE Good even, gentle friend. Cover thy head, cover thy head; nay, prithee, be covered. How old are you, friend?

WILLIAM Five-and-twenty, sir.

TOUCHSTONE A ripe age. Is thy name William? 20

WILLIAM William, sir.

TOUCHSTONE A fair name. Wast born i'th'forest here?

WILLIAM Ay, sir, I thank God.

TOUCHSTONE 'Thank God': a good answer. Art rich?

WILLIAM Faith, sir, so so.

TOUCHSTONE 'So so' is good, very good, very excellent good; and yet it is not, it is but so so. Art thou wise?

WILLIAM Ay, sir, I have a pretty wit.

TOUCHSTONE Why, thou sayest well. I do now remember a saying: 'The fool doth think he is wise, but the wise 30 man knows himself to be a fool'. The heathen philosopher, when he had a desire to eat a grape, would open his lips when he put it into his mouth, meaning thereby that grapes were made to eat and lips to open. You do love this maid?

WILLIAM I do, sir.

TOUCHSTONE Give me your hand. Art thou learned?

WILLIAM No, sir.

TOUCHSTONE Then learn this of me. To have is to have. For it is a figure in rhetoric that drink, being poured out 40 of a cup into a glass, by filling the one doth empty the other; for all your writers do consent that 'ipse' is he. Now, you are not 'ipse', for I am he.

---

34 *lips to open.* Perhaps William's mouth is similarly wide open, but with astonishment.

40 *figure* accepted device (such as hyperbole). Touchstone's illustration, of course, is deliberate nonsense.

42 *consent* agree

ipse (Latin for 'he himself')

WILLIAM Which he, sir?

TOUCHSTONE He, sir, that must marry this woman. Therefore, you clown, abandon – which is in the vulgar 'leave' – the society – which in the boorish is 'company' – of this female – which in the common is 'woman' – which, together, is 'abandon the society of this female', or, clown, thou perishest; or, to thy better understanding, diest; or, to wit, I kill thee, make thee away, translate thy life into death, thy liberty into bondage. I will deal in poison with thee, or in bastinado, or in steel; I will bandy with thee in faction; I will o'er-run thee with policy; I will kill thee a hundred and fifty ways – therefore tremble and depart.

AUDREY Do, good William.

WILLIAM God rest you merry, sir.   *Exit*

           Enter Corin

CORIN Our master and mistress seeks you: come away, away.

TOUCHSTONE Trip, Audrey, trip, Audrey. I attend, I attend.   *Exeunt*

V.2   *Enter Orlando and Oliver*

ORLANDO Is't possible, that on so little acquaintance you should like her? That, but seeing, you should love her? And loving woo? And, wooing, she should grant? And will you persever to enjoy her?

OLIVER Neither call the giddiness of it in question: the

51 *to wit* that is to say (a legal phrase)
53 *bastinado* beating with a cudgel (as against fencing with *steel*)
54 *bandy with thee in faction* compete against you in insults and other forms of dissension
55 *policy* 'Machiavellian' policy (using

any means to achieve the desired end)

v.2.4 *persever* (an obsolete form of 'persevere', stressed on the second syllable)
5 *giddiness* rashness

poverty of her, the small acquaintance, my sudden
wooing, nor her sudden consenting; but say with me
'I love Aliena'; say with her that she loves me; consent
with both that we may enjoy each other. It shall be to
your good, for my father's house and all the revenue   10
that was old Sir Rowland's will I estate upon you, and
here live and die a shepherd.

    Enter Rosalind

ORLANDO You have my consent. Let your wedding be
tomorrow. Thither will I invite the Duke and all's
contented followers. Go you and prepare Aliena; for,
look you, here comes my Rosalind.

ROSALIND God save you, brother.

OLIVER And you, fair sister.   *Exit*

ROSALIND O my dear Orlando, how it grieves me to see
thee wear thy heart in a scarf.   20

ORLANDO It is my arm.

ROSALIND I thought thy heart had been wounded with
the claws of a lion.

ORLANDO Wounded it is, but with the eyes of a lady.

ROSALIND Did your brother tell you how I counterfeited
to sound, when he showed me your handkercher?

ORLANDO Ay, and greater wonders than that.

ROSALIND O, I know where you are. Nay, 'tis true; there
was never anything so sudden but the fight of two rams,
and Caesar's thrasonical brag of 'I came, saw, and over-   30
came'. For your brother and my sister no sooner met

---

11 *estate* settle
14 *all's* all his
18 *sister.* For comment on Oliver's acceptance of the pretence that
'Ganymede' is Rosalind, see Introduction, pages 369–70.
26 *sound* swoon
28 *where you are* what you are referring to

28–39 *there was never anything so sudden
... part them.* For comment on this
passage as an element in the plot, see
Introduction, page 363.
30 *thrasonical* in the bragging style of the
soldier Thraso, in Terence's *Eunuch*
(Shakespeare was certainly not the
first to use the word)

but they looked; no sooner looked but they loved; no
sooner loved but they sighed; no sooner sighed but they
asked one another the reason; no sooner knew the
reason but they sought the remedy: and in these
degrees have they made a pair of stairs to marriage
which they will climb incontinent or else be incontinent
before marriage. They are in the very wrath of love and
they will together; clubs cannot part them.

40 ORLANDO They shall be married tomorrow; and I will
bid the Duke to the nuptial. But, O, how bitter a thing
it is to look into happiness through another man's eyes!
By so much the more shall I tomorrow be at the height
of heart-heaviness, by how much I shall think my
brother happy in having what he wishes for.

ROSALIND Why, then, tomorrow I cannot serve your
turn for Rosalind?

ORLANDO I can live no longer by thinking.

ROSALIND I will weary you then no longer with idle
50 talking. Know of me then, for now I speak to some
purpose, that I know you are a gentleman of good conceit. I speak not this that you should bear a good
opinion of my knowledge, insomuch I say I know you
are; neither do I labour for a greater esteem than may
in some little measure draw a belief from you to do
yourself good, and not to grace me. Believe then, if you
please, that I can do strange things: I have, since I was

36 *degrees.* There is a quibble on *degrees*
meaning also flight (*pair*) of stairs,
and another on *incontinent*: (1) in
haste; (2) unchaste.
39 *clubs.* Some editors see a reference to
the Elizabethan custom of calling
'clubs' when summoning help to
break up a street brawl.
50 *Know of me then* ... Although some
wrong conclusions have been drawn,
it has rightly been noted that Rosalind's style changes here to a

manner much more formal – some
would no doubt say 'ritualistic' – as
she begins to adopt the role of ma-
nipulator of events. The syntax becomes more involved, the sentences
longer – and the audience knows
that the time for joking is now
over.
51-2 *conceit* understanding
53 *insomuch* in as much as
56 *grace me* add to my own merits or
reputation

three year old, conversed with a magician, most profound in his art, and yet not damnable. If you do love
Rosalind so near the heart as your gesture cries it out,   60
when your brother marries Aliena, shall you marry her.
I know into what straits of fortune she is driven, and it
is not impossible to me, if it appear not inconvenient
to you, to set her before your eyes tomorrow, human as
she is, and without any danger.

ORLANDO Speakest thou in sober meanings?

ROSALIND By my life I do, which I tender dearly though
I say I am a magician. Therefore, put you in your best
array, bid your friends; for if you will be married tomorrow, you shall; and to Rosalind, if you will.   70

    Enter Silvius and Phebe

Look, here comes a lover of mine and a lover of hers.

PHEBE

Youth, you have done me much ungentleness,
To show the letter that I writ to you.

ROSALIND

I care not if I have: it is my study
To seem despiteful and ungentle to you.
You are there followed by a faithful shepherd;
Look upon him, love him: he worships you.

PHEBE

Good shepherd, tell this youth what 'tis to love.

SILVIUS

It is to be all made of sighs and tears,
And so am I for Phebe.   80

58 *conversed* associated (or even
   'studied')
59 *not damnable* not eligible for damnation (his is not 'black' magic, involving the devil). A magician of the
   wrong kind might be condemned to
   death too (hence lines 67–8).
60 *gesture* demeanour
63 *inconvenient* inappropriate, out of place

64–5 *human as she is* in the flesh ('the real
   Rosalind, not the mere phantom or
   spirit that you might expect a magician to conjure up')
67 *tender* value
69 *bid* invite
74 *study* aim
75 *despiteful* contemptuous

PHEBE
>And I for Ganymede.

ORLANDO
>And I for Rosalind.

ROSALIND
>And I for no woman.

SILVIUS
>It is to be made of faith and service,
>And so am I for Phebe.

PHEBE
>And I for Ganymede.

ORLANDO
>And I for Rosalind.

ROSALIND
>And I for no woman.

SILVIUS
>It is to be all made of fantasy,
>All made of passion, and all made of wishes,
>All adoration, duty and observance,
>All humbleness, all patience, and impatience,
>All purity, all trial, all observance;
>And so am I for Phebe.

90

PHEBE
>And so am I for Ganymede.

ORLANDO
>And so am I for Rosalind.

ROSALIND
>And so am I for no woman.

PHEBE (*to Rosalind*)
>If this be so, why blame you me to love you?

---

89 *fantasy* imagination not controlled by
reason

91 *observance* humble attention. The repetition of the word in line 93 may be
an error, compositor's or author's
(in which case one has the hopeless

task of guessing what Shakespeare
may have written or intended to
write); but it is just possible that
all observance is the best Silvius can
do to sum up what he has been
saying.

SILVIUS (*to Phebe*)

    If this be so, why blame you me to love you?

ORLANDO

    If this be so, why blame you me to love you?   100

ROSALIND Why do you speak too 'Why blame you me to love you?'

ORLANDO

    To her that is not here, nor doth not hear.

ROSALIND Pray you no more of this, 'tis like the howling of Irish wolves against the moon. (*To Silvius*) I will help you, if I can. (*To Phebe*) I would love you, if I could. – Tomorrow meet me all together. (*To Phebe*) I will marry you if ever I marry woman, and I'll be married tomorrow. (*To Orlando*) I will satisfy you, if ever I satisfied man, and you shall be married tomorrow.   110 (*To Silvius*) I will content you, if what pleases you contents you, and you shall be married tomorrow. (*To Orlando*) As you love Rosalind, meet. (*To Silvius*) As you love Phebe, meet. – And as I love no woman, I'll meet. So, fare you well; I have left you commands.

SILVIUS I'll not fail, if I live.

PHEBE Nor I.

ORLANDO Nor I.   *Exeunt*

    Enter Touchstone and Audrey   V.3

TOUCHSTONE Tomorrow is the joyful day, Audrey. Tomorrow will we be married.

101–2 *Why do you . . . you?* For the possible plot implications of these lines, and of the modulating into prose, see Introduction, page 369.

104–5 *howling of Irish wolves.* The phrase is perhaps an adaptation of one in Lodge, where Rosalynde tells Montanus that in courting Phoebe he barks 'with the wolves of Syria against the moon' (that is, in vain). Perhaps Shakespeare's wolves are Irish because of the tradition that once a year the Irish were turned into wolves.

v.3 On the dramatic functions of this scene, see Introduction, page 374.

AUDREY I do desire it with all my heart; and I hope it
is no dishonest desire to desire to be a woman of the
world? Here come two of the banished Duke's pages.

Enter two Pages

FIRST PAGE Well met, honest gentleman.

TOUCHSTONE By my troth, well met. Come, sit, sit, and
a song.

SECOND PAGE We are for you. Sit i'th'middle.

10 FIRST PAGE Shall we clap into't roundly, without hawking, or spitting, or saying we are hoarse, which are the
only prologues to a bad voice?

SECOND PAGE I'faith, i'faith; and both in a tune, like two
gypsies on a horse.

PAGES   SONG
It was a lover and his lass,
  With a hey, and a ho, and a hey nonino,
That o'er the green corn field did pass,
  In the spring time, the only pretty ring time,
When birds do sing, hey ding a ding, ding,
20   Sweet lovers love the spring.

4 *dishonest* unchaste – with a pun, not intended by Audrey, on *woman of the world*, which she uses in its other meaning of 'married woman'. Perhaps there are subtle allusions to Genesis 19.31 and Luke 20.34. *Dishonest* is the opposite of *honest* as used two lines later to mean 'honourable'.

10 *clap into't roundly* strike into it without unnecessary preliminaries

10–11 *hawking* making the customary noises to clear the throat

11–12 *the only prologues* merely the prologues

13 *in a tune.* This may mean either 'keeping time with one another' or 'in unison'.

15–38 *It was a lover ...* The best known

setting for this song is that by Shakespeare's famous contemporary Thomas Morley (published in his *First Book of Airs*, 1600, of which there is a unique copy in the Folger Shakespeare Library). It is printed on pages 392–5. If Morley wrote the music especially for Shakespeare's words (as seems likely from his statement in the Dedication that the airs 'were made this vacation time'), this would be the only known occasion when a Shakespeare song was so set by one of the great school of Elizabethan lutenists; but it is possible that Morley's music (and even the words) preceded the play. The Morley version justifies the re-ordering of the stanzas as in the text (F

Between the acres of the rye,
 With a hey, and a ho, and a hey nonino,
These pretty country folks would lie,
 In spring time, the only pretty ring time,
When birds do sing, hey ding a ding, ding,
Sweet lovers love the spring.

This carol they began that hour,
 With a hey, and a ho, and a hey nonino,
How that a life was but a flower,
 In spring time, the only pretty ring time,   30
When birds do sing, hey ding a ding, ding,
Sweet lovers love the spring.

And therefore take the present time,
 With a hey, and a ho, and a hey nonino,
For love is crownèd with the prime,
 In spring time, the only pretty ring time,
When birds do sing, hey ding a ding, ding,
Sweet lovers love the spring.

TOUCHSTONE Truly, young gentlemen, though there was
no great matter in the ditty, yet the note was very   40
untuneable.

---

prints the present last stanza as the second) and the emending of F's 'rang time' to ring time; perhaps it would also justify the omitting of the in line 18 (In the spring time) to make that part of the first stanza identical with the others (Morley has notes of music only for In and spring). In line 23 it reads not country folks but 'Countrie fooles' and in line 17 has the tempting reading 'corne fields'; on the other hand, it confirms a life (as against the emendation 'life') in line 29.

18 ring time time for giving or exchanging rings

21 Between the acres of the rye (presumably) on the unploughed strips dividing the fields of rye

35 the prime perfection (but 'the prime' also meant 'the spring')

40 the ditty the words (as opposed to the note or music)

41 untuneable. Touchstone probably means 'unmusical, even though the words weren't hard to set' or 'ill fitted to the words, insignificant as they were'; but the Pages reply as if he meant either that they both failed to keep proper time or that they did not sing in tune with each other.

FIRST PAGE You are deceived, sir; we kept time, we lost not our time.

TOUCHSTONE By my troth, yes: I count it but time lost to hear such a foolish song. God buy you, and God mend your voices! Come, Audrey.   *Exeunt*

V.4   *Enter Duke Senior, Amiens, Jaques, Orlando, Oliver, and Celia*

DUKE
Dost thou believe, Orlando, that the boy
Can do all this that he hath promised?

ORLANDO
I sometimes do believe, and sometimes do not,
As those that fear they hope, and know they fear.
         Enter Rosalind, Silvius, and Phebe

ROSALIND
Patience once more, whiles our compact is urged.
(*to the Duke*) You say, if I bring in your Rosalind,
You will bestow her on Orlando here?

DUKE
That would I, had I kingdoms to give with her.

ROSALIND (*to Orlando*)
And you say you will have her, when I bring her?

ORLANDO
10   That would I, were I of all kingdoms king.

ROSALIND (*to Phebe*)
You say you'll marry me, if I be willing?

PHEBE
That will I, should I die the hour after.

ROSALIND
But if you do refuse to marry me,

---

v.4.4 *fear they hope, and know they fear* fear   5 *urged* stated formally, and clarified
that they are only hoping against
hope, and know in their hearts that
they are afraid

You'll give yourself to this most faithful shepherd?

PHEBE

So is the bargain.

ROSALIND (*to Silvius*)

You say that you'll have Phebe, if she will?

SILVIUS

Though to have her and death were both one thing.

ROSALIND

I have promised to make all this matter even.
Keep you your word, O Duke, to give your daughter;
You yours, Orlando, to receive his daughter;   20
Keep you your word, Phebe, that you'll marry me
Or else, refusing me, to wed this shepherd;
Keep your word, Silvius, that you'll marry her,
If she refuse me – and from hence I go,
To make these doubts all even.

Exeunt Rosalind and Celia

DUKE

I do remember in this shepherd boy
Some lively touches of my daughter's favour.

ORLANDO

My lord, the first time that I ever saw him
Methought he was a brother to your daughter.
But, my good lord, this boy is forest-born,   30
And hath been tutored in the rudiments
Of many desperate studies by his uncle,

18 *make all this matter even* smooth everything out (perhaps with an implied contrast between even and odd). The phrase is curiously echoed in line 25 and again by Hymen in line 106.

21 *Keep you ... marry me.* It is not true that one has to pronounce *Phebe* as one syllable in order to scan this line, which may be basically trochaic,

with a stress on *your*.

26–34 *I do remember ... this forest.* For comment on the significance of these lines to the plot, see Introduction, page 369.

27 *lively* lifelike; or vivid
touches traits; or strokes (a metaphor from painting)
favour appearance, features, look

32 *desperate* dangerous

Whom he reports to be a great magician,
> *Enter Touchstone and Audrey*

Obscurèd in the circle of this forest.

JAQUES There is sure another flood toward, and these couples are coming to the ark. Here comes a pair of very strange beasts, which in all tongues are called fools.

TOUCHSTONE Salutation and greeting to you all!

JAQUES Good my lord, bid him welcome: this is the motley-minded gentleman that I have so often met in the forest. He hath been a courtier, he swears.

TOUCHSTONE If any man doubt that, let him put me to my purgation. I have trod a measure, I have flattered a lady, I have been politic with my friend, smooth with mine enemy, I have undone three tailors, I have had four quarrels, and like to have fought one.

JAQUES And how was that ta'en up?

TOUCHSTONE Faith, we met, and found the quarrel was upon the seventh cause.

JAQUES How seventh cause? — Good my lord, like this fellow.

DUKE I like him very well.

TOUCHSTONE God 'ild you, sir, I desire you of the like. I

---

34 *Obscurèd* concealed, and protected (as the magician is protected from interference by devils while he is within his magic circle)

35 *toward* on the way

36 *a pair*. The reference is to Genesis 7.2: the Lord told Noah to take with him into the ark seven of each species of 'clean' beast — 'but of unclean cattle two, the male and his female'.

40 *motley-minded* with mind as mixed as the thread of his coat

42–3 *put me to my purgation* give me the chance of clearing myself (compare I.3.51 and note)

43 *measure* a formal aristocratic dance

44 *politic* Machiavellian (compare *policy* in V.1.55)

45 *undone* (by not paying them)

46 *like to have fought* almost fought (the joke being, of course, that courtiers seldom stand to their words when a quarrel becomes serious)

47 *ta'en up* made up (with the consequent avoiding of the duel). The phrase is used again in lines 95–6.

53 *'ild* reward (as in III.3.68)
   desire you of the like. This has been variously interpreted: 'I ask permission to return the compliment' or 'I sincerely hope you do think so (and will continue to think so)'.

press in here, sir, amongst the rest of the country copulatives, to swear and to forswear, according as marriage
binds and blood breaks. A poor virgin, sir, an ill-
favoured thing, sir, but mine own, a poor humour of
mine, sir, to take that that no man else will. Rich honesty
dwells like a miser, sir, in a poor house, as your pearl in
your foul oyster.   60

DUKE By my faith, he is very swift and sententious.

TOUCHSTONE According to the fool's bolt, sir, and such
dulcet diseases.

JAQUES But for the seventh cause. How did you find the
quarrel on the seventh cause?

TOUCHSTONE Upon a lie seven times removed. – Bear
your body more seeming, Audrey. – As thus, sir. I did
dislike the cut of a certain courtier's beard. He sent me
word, if I said his beard was not cut well, he was in the
mind it was: this is called the Retort Courteous. If I   70
sent him word again it was not well cut, he would send
me word he cut it to please himself: this is called the
Quip Modest. If again 'it was not well cut', he disabled
my judgement: this is called the Reply Churlish. If
again 'it was not well cut', he would answer, I spake not
true: this is called the Reproof Valiant. If again 'it was
not well cut', he would say, I lie: this is called the
Countercheck Quarrelsome: and so to Lie Circumstantial and the Lie Direct.

54-5 *copulatives* those about to be joined, in marriage and carnally
56 *blood breaks* passion wanes
58 *honesty* chastity
61 *swift and sententious* quick-witted and full of wisdom
62 *fool's bolt*. There is a proverb 'a fool's bolt is soon shot'; and perhaps Touchstone is even alluding to the form of bolt or short arrow that was known as a 'quarrel'.
63 *dulcet diseases*. Commentators have tripped over the phrase, but it probably means 'mild or pleasant weaknesses' and refers to the fool's inability to forbear from gibes.
67 *seeming* becomingly
68 *dislike* express disapproval of
69-70 *in the mind* of the opinion that
73 *disabled* belittled (as in IV.1.30)
78-9 *Circumstantial* indirect, the product of circumstance only

80   JAQUES   And how oft did you say his beard was not well cut?

TOUCHSTONE   I durst go no further than the Lie Circumstantial, nor he durst not give me the Lie Direct. And so we measured swords and parted.

JAQUES   Can you nominate in order now the degrees of the lie?

TOUCHSTONE   O sir, we quarrel in print, by the book, as you have books for good manners. I will name you the degrees. The first, the Retort Courteous; the second,
90   the Quip Modest; the third, the Reply Churlish; the fourth, the Reproof Valiant; the fifth, the Countercheck Quarrelsome; the sixth, the Lie with Circumstance; the seventh, the Lie Direct. All these you may avoid but the Lie Direct; and you may avoid that too, with an 'If'. I knew when seven justices could not take up a quarrel, but when the parties were met themselves, one of them thought but of an 'If': as, 'If you said so, then I said so'; and they shook hands and swore brothers. Your 'If' is the only peace-maker; much
100   virtue in 'If'.

JAQUES   Is not this a rare fellow, my lord? He's as good at anything, and yet a fool.

DUKE   He uses his folly like a stalking-horse, and under the presentation of that he shoots his wit.

---

84   *measured.* That is, to see that one was not longer than the other (a necessary precaution before the duel).

87   *in print.* There is a quibble here. The phrase also meant 'in a precise way', as did 'by the book': according to the textbook, 'according to Hoyle'. There were textbooks setting out the justifications for duelling, and Shakespeare possibly has a particular one in mind.

95–6   *take up* settle

98–9   *swore brothers* pledged themselves to act like brothers, ever after

103   *stalking-horse* (the horse or, more frequently, imitation horse behind which the hunter sheltered without disturbing the quarry)

104   *presentation. The Oxford English Dictionary* takes this as an example of *presentation* meaning a theatrical or symbolic representation or show. It could also mean 'inferior representation', 'mere shadow of the real thing'

Enter a masquer representing Hymen, and Rosalind
and Celia as themselves. Still music

HYMEN

> Then is there mirth in heaven,
> When earthly things, made even,
>   Atone together.
> Good Duke, receive thy daughter,
> Hymen from heaven brought her,
>   Yea, brought her hither   110
> That thou mightst join her hand with his
> Whose heart within her bosom is.

ROSALIND (*to the Duke*)

> To you I give myself, for I am yours.
> (*to Orlando*)
> To you I give myself, for I am yours.

DUKE

> If there be truth in sight, you are my daughter.

ORLANDO

> If there be truth in sight, you are my Rosalind.

– and the Duke is saying that Touchstone's folly is only pretended.

(stage direction) *Hymen* (the god of marriage, who was frequently represented in masques). F has simply 'Enter Hymen . . .' and the producer must make up his mind who plays the part. Some editors think it should be given to the singer who earlier plays Amiens (F does not specify that Hymen's first words are to be sung but does print them in italic). If, as others have maintained, although unnecessarily, the masque was written into the play for a special performance at a wedding, one of the distinguished guests may have been brought in as Hymen. But too much fuss altogether has been made over the masque: it is an appropriate way of arranging weddings, and the stilted verse is not un-Shakespearian but is in the manner of his other masques and interludes, in, for example, *Cymbeline* and *Timon of Athens*. *Still music* quiet, peaceful music (such as that of recorders and flutes, not drums and trumpets)

106 *made even.* See line 18 and note.

107 *Atone together* are joined as one, come into accord

111–12 *her hand ... her bosom.* The F reading, '*his*' in both places, can be justified, if at all, on the ground that Rosalind is still being referred to as a boy. F does not *say* that Rosalind appears in female dress here but the Duke and Orlando – and Phebe – obviously now first see her as a woman.

PHEBE

> If sight and shape be true,
> Why then, my love adieu!

ROSALIND (*to the Duke*)

> I'll have no father, if you be not he;
> (*to Orlando*)

120

> I'll have no husband, if you be not he;
> (*to Phebe*)
> Nor ne'er wed woman, if you be not she.

HYMEN

> Peace, ho! I bar confusion.
> 'Tis I must make conclusion
>> Of these most strange events.
> Here's eight that must take hands,
> To join in Hymen's bands,
>> If truth holds true contents.
> (*to Orlando and Rosalind*)
> You and you no cross shall part;
> (*to Oliver and Celia*)
> You and you are heart in heart;
> (*to Phebe*)

130

> You to his love must accord,
> Or have a woman to your lord;
> (*to Touchstone and Audrey*)
> You and you are sure together,
> As the winter to foul weather.
> Whiles a wedlock-hymn we sing,
> Feed yourselves with questioning,
> That reason wonder may diminish
> How thus we met, and these things finish.

---

122 *bar* stop

127 *holds true contents.* Commentators find the phrase feeble, or incomprehensible, but presumably it means 'if the couples are to remain true to their vows, to what they have alleged to be true'.

128 *cross* trial or affliction

130 *accord* consent

132 *sure together* bound fast

SONG

Wedding is great Juno's crown,
  O blessèd bond of board and bed;
'Tis Hymen peoples every town,   140
  High wedlock then be honourèd;
Honour, high honour and renown
To Hymen, god of every town!

DUKE

O my dear niece, welcome thou art to me,
Even daughter, welcome, in no less degree.

PHEBE (*to Silvius*)

I will not eat my word, now thou art mine,
Thy faith my fancy to thee doth combine.

  Enter Second Brother, Jaques de Boys

JAQUES DE BOYS

Let me have audience for a word or two.
I am the second son of old Sir Rowland
That bring these tidings to this fair assembly.   150
Duke Frederick, hearing how that every day
Men of great worth resorted to this forest,
Addressed a mighty power, which were on foot,
In his own conduct, purposely to take
His brother here and put him to the sword;
And to the skirts of this wild wood he came,
Where, meeting with an old religious man,
After some question with him, was converted
Both from his enterprise and from the world,
His crown bequeathing to his banished brother,   160
And all their lands restored to them again

---

141 *High.* Line 142 suggests that this may mean 'highly' rather than 'true'.

145 *Even daughter.* The phrase is unusual, whether addressed to Celia ('even as a daughter', 'no less than a daughter') or to Rosalind ('and you, my true daughter').

153 *Addressed* gathered, prepared
power armed force

154 *In his own conduct* under his own leadership

157 *religious man* man of some religious function or intent (probably a hermit)

158 *question* discussion

161 *them.* The F reading is 'him', which has been defended on the ground that it was for Duke Senior to restore the lands to the owners if he wished.

That were with him exiled. This to be true,
I do engage my life.
DUKE   Welcome, young man.
Thou offerest fairly to thy brothers' wedding:
To one his lands withheld, and to the other
A land itself at large, a potent dukedom.
First, in this forest, let us do those ends
That here were well begun and well begot;
And after, every of this happy number
170   That have endured shrewd days and nights with us
Shall share the good of our returnèd fortune
According to the measure of their states.
Meantime, forget this new-fallen dignity,
And fall into our rustic revelry:
Play, music, and you brides and bridegrooms all,
With measure heaped in joy, to th'measures fall.

JAQUES
Sir, by your patience. – If I heard you rightly,
The Duke hath put on a religious life,
And thrown into neglect the pompous court?

JAQUES DE BOYS
180   He hath.

JAQUES
To him will I: out of these convertites
There is much matter to be heard and learned.

163 *engage* pledge
164 *offerest fairly* bringest splendid gifts
and offerings
166 *potent* (perhaps not 'powerful' but
'potential': Orlando will inherit it)
167 *do those ends* achieve the aims
170 *shrewd* sharp (a possible reference
back to the winter wind and its *icy
fang*)
172 *states* status, rank
176 *measures* stately dances (as in line 43

and again in line 190), but with a
quibble on *with measure* earlier in the
line, where it means 'in good measure', 'liberally'. (In line 172 *measure*
has one of its normal modern
meanings.)
177 *Sir*. Jaques addresses the Duke,
asking his pardon for interrupting
and for addressing another directly.
179 *thrown into neglect* rejected as
worthless

(to the Duke)
You to your former honour I bequeath:
Your patience and your virtue well deserves it;
(to Orlando)
You to a love that your true faith doth merit;
(to Oliver)
You to your land, and love, and great allies;
(to Silvius)
You to a long and well deservèd bed;
(to Touchstone)
And you to wrangling, for thy loving voyage
Is but for two months victualled. – So to your pleasures:
I am for other than for dancing measures.   190

DUKE

Stay, Jaques, stay.

JAQUES

To see no pastime, I. What you would have
I'll stay to know at your abandoned cave.   *Exit*

DUKE

Proceed, proceed. We'll begin these rites
As we do trust they'll end, in true delights.

Exeunt all except Rosalind

ROSALIND   It is not the fashion to see the lady the epilogue,
but it is no more unhandsome than to see the lord the
prologue. If it be true that good wine needs no bush, 'tis
true that a good play needs no epilogue. Yet to good
wine they do use good bushes, and good plays prove   200
the better by the help of good epilogues. What a case am
I in, then, that am neither a good epilogue nor cannot
insinuate with you in the behalf of a good play? I am
not furnished like a beggar; therefore to beg will not

198 *good wine needs no bush.* This is a
proverb ('what is good needs no ad-
vertisement') alluding to the vint-
ner's practice of hanging a 'bush'
(generally, some ivy) outside his
shop.

203 *insinuate with you* subtly work on you
and win you over
204 *furnished* dressed (as also in
III.2.238)

become me. My way is to conjure you, and I'll begin with the women. I charge you, O women, for the love you bear to men, to like as much of this play as please you; and I charge you, O men, for the love you bear to women — as I perceive by your simpering, none of you hates them — that between you and the women the play may please. If I were a woman, I would kiss as many of you as had beards that pleased me, complexions that liked me, and breaths that I defied not; and, I am sure, as many as have good beards, or good faces, or sweet breaths, will, for my kind offer, when I make curtsy, bid me farewell.   *Exit*

210

205 *conjure you* work on you by charms or spells, like a magician
211 *If I were a woman.* The part of Rosalind was, of course, played by a boy — and, characteristically, Shakespeare takes advantage of the fact.

213 *liked* appealed to, pleased
defied disdained
216 *bid me farewell* grant the applause that will allow me to leave the stage in good spirits

TWELFTH NIGHT

Introduction

Among the high-rise buildings and packed car parks of present-day London there are a very few places where it is possible to stand, look round, and say 'This is what Shakespeare saw.' The hall of the Middle Temple is one such place. True, much of the decoration of its beautiful interior is only a replica of what was destroyed in the Second World War. Yet a sense of the past is very strong here. The reason is perhaps that for four centuries Middle Temple Hall has continued to be put to the use for which it was built. Benchers and law-students still eat their dinners under its hammerbeam roof, as they did in Elizabethan days, when the Inns of Court were the country's third university, attended by hundreds of young men who had come to London to learn as much of the law as was required for the administration of the Queen's affairs and of their own estates.

On 2 February 1951, the restoration of Middle Temple Hall was celebrated by a performance of *Twelfth Night*. The date chosen was an anniversary. All but three and a half centuries earlier, on 2 February 1602 – Candlemas Day – Shakespeare's company, and presumably Shakespeare among them, had acted *Twelfth Night* in the same hall. Regrettably, we know nothing of the way the play was staged on that occasion. The actors may have taken advantage of the magnificent screen, already darkening after thirty years of use, which stood across the entrance to the hall and which would have afforded them a setting very similar to the back wall of the Elizabethan public playhouse. A platform stage could have been built to the height of the base of the screen's pilasters, leaving ample room for entrance through the two lofty arched doorways. These were presumably curtained – the present doors date from the Restoration – and may have served not only for entrances and exits but also for the box-tree (with three heads bobbing up above the curtain rail) in Act II, scene 5, and for the dark house, with Malvolio's hand groping pathetically through the opening, in Act IV, scene 2 – unless, that is, the company brought a box-tree and a solid property 'dark house' with them. We have no way of knowing; but we do know how the play was received on that night in 1602 by one member of the audience, a barrister called John Manningham:

At our feast (Manningham noted in his diary), *we had a play called* Twelfth Night *or* What You Will; *much like the* Comedy of Errors, *or* Menaechmi *in Plautus, but most like and near to that in Italian called* Inganni. *A good practice in it to make the steward believe his lady widow was in love with him, by counterfeiting a letter as from his lady in general terms, telling him what she liked best in him, and prescribing his gesture in smiling, his apparel, etc. And then when he came to practise, making him believe they took him to be mad.*

No spectator can relish the effect of a comedy in isolation from the rest of the audience round him, and Manningham's enjoyment must have been widely shared. The players had brought to the feast a thoroughly festive play. *Twelfth Night* was conceived for a time of pleasure: this is the clue to the play's special mood and flavour which set it apart from – many would say above – Shakespeare's other comedies.

Masques and revels, such as the plays Sir Andrew delights in 'altogether', were a feature of life at Court, the Inns of Court, and the Universities for some three months of the year. This tradition of winter feasting was older than Christianity, but by Shakespeare's time it had become associated with a number of Church festivals extending from St Andrew's Day, or even from Hallowe'en a month earlier, through the twelve days of Christmas to Candlemas and so on to Shrovetide, just before Lent. Special private performances of plays were often a part of these festivities. Between Christmas Day 1597 and Candlemas

1598, for example, the students of the Middle Temple enjoyed two comedies – one of them followed by dancing – three masques, and a number of other entertainments of a make-believe kind. Sometimes the make-believe embraced the whole feast: a Lord of Misrule, attended by a fool or jester, could usurp all normal authority in the social group – as he did at St John's College, Oxford, in the winter of 1607 to 1608. So at the Middle Temple in 1602, feast and farce must have blended together in the 'civil misrule' of Sir Toby and his companions; the killjoy upstart Malvolio was placed at the mercy of Sir Toby much in the same way as crusty benchers had to submit, during the feasting, to the caprices of young law-students. Even the music with which the play opens could have been part of the after-dinner music provided by a consort, or small orchestra, in the gallery of the hall; and the song with which it ends is in the nature of a jig and could lead on to further music.

The music of *Twelfth Night* provides much more than the festive framework to the play. Two kinds of music are integral to the comedy itself. On the one hand, there are the straight love songs, 'O mistress mine' and 'Come away, death'; on the other, snatches of songs that satirize love or are sung in a way that burlesques sentiment: 'My lady is unkind, perdy'; 'Farewell, dear heart, since I must needs be gone'; and the ballad of Susanna and the Elders, which reflects the impropriety of Malvolio's passion for Olivia. This is a deliberate contrast, basic to the nature of a festive play. The union of romance and satire, of poetry and wit, in *Twelfth Night*, corresponds to a union found in festive rites wherever they are performed in the world: a union between the invocation of nature's plenty and the ritual abuse of powers that may work against her blessings. *Twelfth Night* is a festive play not just because it was written for a feast and has a high-spirited plot, but rather because it is in itself a kind of saturnalia to invoke the festive virtues and to exorcize the killjoy powers.

Chief among these festive virtues is the capacity to enjoy oneself. John Donne once told a Jacobean congregation that

God loved a cheerful taker quite as much as He loved a cheerful giver. This would have struck Shakespeare's audience as sound doctrine; any spoilsport who, at a time when food was getting short, days cold, and work burdensome, refused the opportunities for plentiful food and drink, fires and entertainment, which were offered by the Church's calendar deserved, in their view, to be baited like Malvolio. At its simplest level, then, *Twelfth Night* defends people's right to cakes and ale. But it has a deeper concern with present mirth. When Olivia vows to season a brother's dead love with her tears for seven years – the very image suggests winter, since the Elizabethans had to make do with salted food until the spring pastures were ready – she is failing to understand that there is a time for everything: 'A time to weep, and a time to laugh; a time to mourn and a time to dance.' Human life, like nature's, has its due seasons (11.4. 38–9) –

> *For women are as roses whose fair flower,*
> *Being once displayed, doth fall that very hour.*

So too when Feste tries to rally Olivia out of her melancholy (1.5.46–7) with the words

> *As there is no true cuckold but calamity, so beauty's a*
> *flower,*

he deftly hints at her folly in mourning when she should be marrying. And Orsino, for his part, also fails to seize the present time when he lies back on sweet beds of flowers and performs his wooing by proxy.

In contrast to such misusers of time, Viola and Sebastian grasp him by the forelock. We first hear of Sebastian in the story of how he survived shipwreck – 'Courage and hope both teaching him the practice' (1.2.13). Viola is just as tenacious of life. As soon as she reaches land she begins to make resourceful plans for her survival and safety. The whole-hearted zest with which she flings herself into the role of Orsino's page is just the frame of mind that masques and revels call for. And when

Olivia becomes infatuated, Viola adjusts rapidly to the new situation, simply trusting that an opportunity will present itself (II.2.40) for setting matters to rights:

O time, thou must untangle this, not I!

This willingness to trust all to time has another aspect. It is not only a readiness to seize opportunities when they offer themselves, but it is also a readiness to bide the time when it is necessary to do so. In this connexion it is interesting to notice that both Viola's longsuffering and her image of Patience on a monument are foreshadowed in the Prologue to the Italian play of *Gl'Ingannati*, which we shall see was one of Shakespeare's sources for his plot: 'Two lessons above all you will take away with you: how great is the power of chance and good fortune in affairs of love; and how great too in them is the value of long-enduring patience accompanied by good counsel.' As Shakespeare dispensed with all the parents and mentors in his source, good counsel in the play comes only from Feste; but patience, and the readiness to take whatever opportunities time offers, are Viola's shining virtues. They are her brother's virtues too. Sebastian's sprint to the altar with Olivia is not, as is sometimes suggested, a crude device for making the broad plots of Shakespeare's sources 'respectable'; it shows rather that Sebastian recognizes 'the power of chance and good fortune in affairs of love', and is as ready as his sister to make the best of opportunity.

Twelfth Night extols the cheerful giver as well as the cheerful taker: generosity is celebrated alongside the festive virtue of a right opportunism. From antiquity onwards, present-giving has been an important part of most festivities, and a surprising number of presents, in the form of money and jewels, change hands during the play's action. In all these benefactions, Shakespeare maintains a distinction of which 'under-developed' societies are much more aware than are developed ones, between the gift that is a real love-token – like the Roman honey and gold – and the gift that is mere payment or bribe. There is no generosity, nothing indicative of the *generosus*, or man of breeding, about Sir Andrew's attempt to buy off his opponent with the gift of his horse, or about Malvolio's promise of reward if Feste will help him to pen, paper, and a candle. Feste is especially sensitive to the spirit in which gifts are bestowed. When the Duke Orsino, whose appetite for Feste's music is quickly surfeited, drops a coin into his hand with a cool 'There's for thy pains' (II.4.66), he gets from Feste, the artist to whom payment is at once a necessity and an unreality, the equally cool retort: 'No pains, sir. I take pleasure in singing, sir.'

In contrast to such ungenerous giving stands the generosity of Sebastian, Antonio, Viola, and ultimately of Olivia. Sebastian does not know how he can repay Antonio for his goodness; he dreads making him a 'bad recompense' or shuffling him off 'with such uncurrent pay' as mere thanks. For Sebastian is himself a warm-hearted enough person to see that Antonio's entrustment to him of all his money is the least part of his generosity. Antonio gives himself away with his gold, and in consequence Sebastian's apparent ingratitude wounds him deeply. But of course what has really happened is that Antonio has mistaken the disguised Viola for Sebastian; and she rebuffs his appeal with what seems to him the ultimate hypocrisy – a speech in condemnation of ingratitude. This speech is very much in character. First among Viola's unrehearsed words to Olivia (I.5.181) is a protest at Olivia's miserly hoarding of her natural gifts – 'what is yours to bestow is not yours to reserve'. Nor can Viola understand the temperament that (lines 231–2)

> *will lead these graces to the grave,*
> *And leave the world no copy.*

The warmth of her protestations on Orsino's behalf (lines 241–2) –

> *O, such love*
> *Could be but recompensed!*

awakens at last a warmth of feeling in Olivia and then of

course the complications of comedy begin; but through them all Shakespeare keeps before us the two festive virtues of opportunism and generosity, as they are epitomized in Olivia's own words (III.1.153):

> Love sought, is good; but given unsought, is better.

The play evokes the festive virtues without preaching them. Nor is there any Christmas Book bonhomie, any exhortation to be jolly and join in, about this play with a Christmas title. In trying to define the mood of *Twelfth Night* as a festive play we should not look forward, anachronistically, to the cosy merry-making of Dingley Dell, but rather backwards in time to the Feast of Fools and other medieval revels. For in these survived, almost to Shakespeare's own day, the second main aspect of ancient festivities: their 'ritual abuse of hostile spirits'. Once we have grasped the spell-like, incantatory nature of such abuse, we can perhaps begin to respond to the baiting of Malvolio as an Elizabethan audience may have responded. It is not to be thought of as heartless practical joking, but as a form of exorcism; and this response lends piquancy to the scenes in which Malvolio is actually treated as a man 'possessed'.

The device used against Olivia's steward is only one aspect of the play's satirical character. Everywhere in *Twelfth Night* we find the topsyturvy inversions typical of the Feast of Fools, when folly reigned in the seat of wisdom in order to show up the foolishness of those who counted themselves wise, and when the confusions of the masquerade brought home to all the truth that, in sober daily life, we know neither our own identities nor the identities of our neighbours. Folly, which walks the orb like the sun, permeates the language of the play: Sir Andrew, a bumpkin knight, recalls the good country saying that fools have wit enough to keep themselves dry; and every fool, according to Feste's song, knows how to make use of opportunity when it calls. Much of the play sustains Blake's belief that if the fool would persist in his folly he would become wise. Olivia runs mad for the love of 'Cesario', yet this alienation is really a discovery of her own repressed instincts. The behaviour of Feste and Sir Andrew, and finally of Olivia herself, seems sheer lunacy to Sebastian, but he decides to do as the rest in this mad place – and immediately finds happiness as Olivia's husband. Malvolio is led a long dance through midsummer madness to the sober, reproachful letter he writes, not as Count Malvolio, but as Olivia's faithful steward. Significantly, Feste has no part in Malvolio's gulling until the point at which he can begin to lead him back to normalcy.

Just as in *Much Ado About Nothing*, where the 'shallow fools' bring to light what wisdom could not discover, clarification is reached in *Twelfth Night* through massive delusions. This is very much in keeping with the spirit of Elizabethan Christmas revels, with their masquerades and carnival-like disguises. Shakespeare perhaps saw in such mummery a process at work similar to the illusions of the theatre which help us to discover the truth of what we are. Accordingly, *Twelfth Night* is a play composed of deceptions – *inganni*. Olivia and Orsino are self-deceivers: the one in her delusion that she can live like an imperial votaress, the other in thinking he really loves Olivia; in fact, the first time in the play he comes face to face with her he is so disconcerted that he immediately starts to quarrel with her. Malvolio thinks Olivia is in love with him, Sir Andrew thinks he can marry Olivia, Olivia thinks she can marry 'Cesario'. Antonio thinks Viola is Sebastian, Sir Andrew and Sir Toby think Sebastian is Viola, Malvolio thinks Feste is Sir Topas. Viola thinks Sir Andrew a redoubtable swordsman and he thinks the same of her. And yet through all these confusions clarification and self-knowledge are reached, just as a masquerade releases people from their everyday inhibitions and enables them to discover themselves.

Twelfth Night, or the Feast of the Epiphany, itself symbolic of the readiness to bring gifts and to receive a great joy, was also the last feasting day of the Christmas season. At Oxford, in 1603, the Prologue to a 'Twelfth Night merriment' pleaded with his audience –

This is the night, night latest of the twelve;
Now give us leave for to be blithe and frolic.
Tomorrow we must fall to dig and delve . . .

Shakespeare's *Twelfth Night* too is a holiday entertainment in
which we are made aware of the proximity of the non-holiday
world. This is the last of Shakespeare's happy comedies, and
when he creates another Fool, it is to drive him out into the
wind and the rain. In *King Lear*, the worst cruelty is found
withindoors. In *Twelfth Night*, however, we are still secure in
the festive hall, in what has been called an evergreen world in
contrast to the self-renewing green world of a pastoral comedy
such as *As You Like It*. Yet even here the leader of the revels,
Feste, is threatened (1.5.105): 'your fooling grows old'. The
fear of being turned away causes Malvolio's sneer (lines 71–2) –
'Infirmity, that decays the wise, doth ever make the better fool'
– to rankle for a long time in Feste's thoughts. Nor does
Feste's 'love of having', the workaday virtue of prudence,
belong by right to the holiday world; but then patrons will not
always be expansive and generous. And outside the holiday
world, love is not always generous either: there are images of a
love which builds a Hell in Heaven's despite – the fell hounds
of Orsino's desire, the unmuzzled thoughts spoken of by
Olivia. Such feelings intrude directly into the play for a short
time in Act v, when Orsino threatens to kill the thing he loves.
And though Sebastian's supposed treachery towards Antonio
turns out to be one more delusion, there lingers an awareness
that such things are possible. A surprising number of references
to plague and corruption in the imagery of the play cast a deep
shadow beyond its brilliance. There are reminders, too, of a
time that can't be fleeted as they did in the golden world: the
clock upbraids Olivia with the waste of time, and the priest
measures time by the distance it carries him towards his grave.
There is even something a little sepulchral about the free maids
who weave their thread with bones, and the song they sing is a
mournful one about love's cruelty, instead of that kindness of

love which is celebrated in the play itself. By invoking the bounty of man and nature the revellers of the Christmas season tried to keep out the winter wind and man's ingratitude. They could not wholly forget them, and their presence is never quite forgotten in *Twelfth Night*.

The mood of *Twelfth Night* is so subtle and at the same time so unified that it comes as a surprise to the producer or to the careful reader to discover how many minor confusions and inconsistencies there are in the play's construction. The second scene, for example, raises expectations which are never satisfied. Viola's remarks about the Captain's reliable appearance are so pointed that we expect him to have a fairly influential part in the plot. But he fades out of the play at once. Shakespeare himself seems uneasy about his disappearance, because he suddenly informs us in the last scene that the Captain is detained on a charge brought against him by Malvolio. But this fresh evidence of Malvolio's ill will towards men is used only to bring him back himself on to the stage, and when he finally stalks off we are still – as Orsino exclaims – in the dark about the Captain. A further puzzle created by the second scene is that it leads us to expect Viola will sing to the Duke, but she never does so. Other mysterious features of the action are the unexplained substitution of Fabian for Feste in the trick played on Malvolio, and the sudden entrance in Act v of Sir Toby and Sir Andrew bleeding from a second encounter with Sebastian of which we have been told nothing. In the same scene, events which seem to have happened in a couple of days are said to have occupied three months. This kind of double time is so common in Shakespeare's plays that it is of no significance in itself, but here it does contribute to the general effect that *Twelfth Night*, for all its harmony of mood, is far from being a conventionally well-made play.

There are two ways of explaining these inconsistencies. One explanation is that the text of the play as we now have it represents a revision made some years after the first performance. Another is that the play was written at speed without having been thought out and planned in consistent detail. A test case for deciding, however tentatively, between these two views is offered by the scene that seems to bear the most obvious signs of revision, that between Viola and the Duke Orsino in the second Act. This starts with Orsino calling, in verse, for 'That old and antique song we heard last night'. He is told, in prose, that the singer is not present but can be found, and while Feste is fetched the tune is played and Orsino explains to Viola that the song is 'old and plain'. The song that Feste sings, however, is not a ballad or folk-song, but an up-to-date 'air'.

The explanation usually offered for all this is that, when the play was revived, perhaps about 1606, Feste had to be substituted for Viola as the singer because the voice of the boy who played Viola in the revival was breaking; and that Feste chose to sing a different song from the one Viola had sung in the original production. A similar theory has been used to explain the omission of the willow song in *Othello* as it was printed in 1622 – much more plausibly, for there we seem to have a genuine and rather obvious acting cut. But there are no awkwardnesses that suggest revision in Act II, scene 4 of *Twelfth Night*. The scene is a dramatic climax, perfectly conceived and perfectly executed. Viola, in her disguise as Cesario, is· no longer the Duke Orsino's singer, but has been 'much advanced' to someone who summons others to sing for him – a sort of Master of the Duke's Music. Feste's entrance is delayed in order that background music may be used to stress the stagy melancholy of Orsino's love, and in order to draw the audience's attention to Viola's feelings for Orsino. Feste not only furnishes the song but also, by his slight asperity and mockery of Orsino, separates the Duke's more shallow feelings from the scene's final statement of Viola's double sorrow: her unspoken, hopeless love for Orsino and her grief for her missing brother.

Shakespeare in fact speaks 'masterly' in this scene, and it is hard to believe that the writing of it was not part of his original inspiration. If we are to call it a revised scene we need perhaps first to revise our own notions of what constitutes a revision. A playwright can revise his intentions while he is actually writing a play, and the practice of Brecht and other modern dramatists has shown how much further revision can go on in rehearsals, as the author improves on his script, or adapts it to the abilities of his actors. All such revisions will be incorporated into the acting copy, or promptbook, and precede the play's first performance. Other revisions may be carried out later by the playwright to meet the theatrical exigencies of a revival; it is fairly clear that 'God' was replaced by 'Jove' at several points in the text of *Twelfth Night* which has come down to us, in order to make the play conform with the 1606 statute against profanity in the theatre. Yet other changes in a play may be made years later and without the playwright's knowledge. Shakespeare's fellow actors presumably saw no harm in adding the odd topical joke to his plays from time to time. The mysterious allusion in Act II, scene 5 to the lady of the Strachy who married the yeoman of the wardrobe may well be a piece of Blackfriars gossip current after Shakespeare's death; perhaps it was slipped in for the Court performance of 1623.

But most of the other so-called revisions of *Twelfth Night* could be of the kind that precede the first performance. Shakespeare at first meant Viola to sing to Orsino, and tells us as much in the second scene; later, when he came to write Act II, scene 4, he realized that he could create an enthralling effect by having Viola sit listening beside her master, as moved as he by the music but able to give only indirect expression to her feelings. Having written this scene as it now stands, Shakespeare perhaps realized that Feste's part was becoming very heavy, and accordingly substituted Fabian for him in the plot against Malvolio. A sound dramatic instinct was also at work in this change of plan. The box-tree episode was Malvolio's big scene, and the Fool's popularity with the audience might have detracted from the effect Shakespeare was aiming at here. So the main encounter between Malvolio and Feste is deferred until the dark house scene in Act IV, in which Malvolio is heard but not seen and in which Feste can therefore be given full scope.

Shakespeare's admirers have often been reluctant to see in the inconsistencies of his texts the result of rapid *ad hoc* decisions by the playwright in the very course of composition. But a degree of improvisation is natural to drama; and the tradition that Shakespeare wrote *The Merry Wives of Windsor* in a fortnight at Queen Elizabeth's request, whether it is true or not, at least suggests that plays could be commissioned at very short notice. As a brilliant improvisation, *Twelfth Night* offers us the pleasure of tracing the artist's hand at work. It is no less an achievement for having been written at speed and perhaps for a special occasion.

The play's sprinkling of legal jokes suggests that this special occasion was the Middle Temple performance watched by Manningham on Candlemas night, 1602. But two arguments have been advanced for dating the play a year earlier than this. The first of these is based on two allusions, in the course of the dialogue, to the Shah of Persia. As the infatuated Malvolio, clutching Maria's letter and practising smiles, moves out of earshot of the plotters, Fabian (II.5.173–4) exclaims: 'I will not give my part of this sport for a pension of thousands to be paid from the Sophy.' Later on, Sir Andrew's fears of Cesario as a duelling opponent are doubled when he is told (III.4.272) that the youth 'has been fencer to the Sophy'. The Sophy or Shah of the time, Abbas the Great, was known about in England as the result of an expedition to Persia in 1599 led by two adventurers, Sir Anthony Shirley and his brother Sir Robert Shirley. The leaders of the expedition did not return to England. Sir Robert Shirley stayed in Persia, virtually as 'fencer to the Sophy', in order to reorganize the Persian army, while Sir Anthony, after receiving gifts which included sixteen thousand pistolets – 'a pension of thousands' – prevailed on the Shah to appoint him ambassador to the Christian Princes of Europe. But two other members of the expedition who did return to

England published anonymously in the autumn of 1600 a small pamphlet called *The True Report of Sir Anthony Shirley's Journey*. It has been suggested that Shakespeare saw in this story of the expedition a way of drawing attention to the plight of the Shirleys' patron, the Earl of Essex, whose life had been in jeopardy since his attempted palace revolution of the previous summer; and that the allusions to the Shah therefore fix the date of *Twelfth Night* as somewhere between the publication of *The True Report* and Essex's execution in February 1601.

There is nothing, however, in these two slight allusions to suggest that Shakespeare thought of the Shirley expedition as a diplomatic triumph. The government certainly did not see it in this light. They were thoroughly embarrassed by it, and quickly suppressed *The True Report*. A year later, however, Shakespeare could have heard a great deal about the Shirleys from his former close associate in the Lord Chamberlain's company of actors, Will Kemp, who in the late summer of 1601 returned from a continental tour which had included a meeting in Rome with Sir Anthony Shirley. Kemp's account of this, which was common talk at the time, together with a fuller account of the expedition published legitimately in September 1601, are the most likely sources for Shakespeare's two allusions to the Shah, and therefore support a date in the acting season 1601–1602 for *Twelfth Night*.

The second argument for the date 1600/1601 is based on the name of the play's leading male part. Orsino, Duke of Bracciano, was the name of a Florentine nobleman who visited England that winter and who was entertained by Queen Elizabeth on Twelfth Night – 6 January 1601 – with festivities that included the performance of a play in the Great Chamber of Whitehall Palace. In his memorandum of the many things to be done for the occasion, the Lord Chamberlain noted down that he had to confer with the Master of the Revels about the choice of a play 'that shall be best furnished with rich apparel, have great variety and change of music and dances, and of a subject that may be most pleasing to her majesty'. This memorandum, together with the title of the play and the name 'Orsino', have been taken as proof that *Twelfth Night* had its first night at Whitehall on 6 January 1601.

Queen Elizabeth's requirements would, however, have been better met by many other extant plays. *Twelfth Night* has no dances other than Sir Andrew's brief capers. Besides, only a threadbare inventiveness would give the title *Twelfth Night* to a play written for performance on the sixth of January. *A Midsummer Night's Dream* was not written for 24 June nor Chapman's *All Fools* for 1 April. All three titles indicate, not the date of performance, but a mood of licensed jesting. Finally, Shakespeare's choice of the name Orsino makes it virtually impossible for *Twelfth Night* to have been the play acted before the Duke of Bracciano. We only have to translate the episode into modern terms – a Royal Command performance on the occasion of a State Visit – to see how unthinkable it would be to use the important visitor's name for the chief character in a comedy. The rigid etiquette of Queen Elizabeth's court would have rendered such a joke impossible. On this very occasion a play by Ben Jonson which a company of child actors, the Children of the Revels, had hoped to perform before the Queen was rejected because – Jonson's modern editors argue – it contained a tactless reference to the disgrace of Essex. It is hard to believe that it would have been 'most pleasing to her majesty' to see her guest portrayed as Orsino or herself as Olivia.

If, though, Shakespeare was among the actors of an unidentified play performed by the Lord Chamberlain's Men in the Great Chamber on 6 January 1601, he must have been struck by the appearance of the guest of honour: the slight but splendid figure of the Duke Orsino as he stood by the Queen's side throughout the performance. And when, a year later, he was called upon to write a festive comedy either for one of the three Christmas performances that his company gave at Court or for the Middle Temple feast in February, it would be natural for him to remember the name Orsino and to use it for his leading character. He may even have recalled the real Duke's reputation for hotheaded family pride when he came to write Act v, in which Orsino reacts so bitterly to the favour shown by Olivia towards his page Cesario.

A sign of Shakespeare's rapid writing in *Twelfth Night* is the freedom with which he borrows from his own work. When he was pressed for time it was inevitable that his thoughts should fly to incidents and characters which had gone down well with the audiences for his earlier comedies. Indeed there are so many self-borrowings in *Twelfth Night* that the play has been called 'a masterpiece of recapitulation'. The deeply loyal friend Antonio comes without so much as a change of name from *The Merchant of Venice*; Slender of *The Merry Wives of Windsor* brings his mincing oaths with him when he becomes Sir Andrew Aguecheek, and Shakespeare was counting on his fellow-shareholder in the company, Richard Cowley, to repeat his success in interpreting this 'silly ass' type of role. The comic possibilities of eavesdropping, explored in *Much Ado About Nothing*, and of girl disguised as boy, exploited in *As You Like It*, are stretched yet further in *Twelfth Night*, the one in the box-tree scene and the other in the duel.

Two situations in particular Shakespeare knew from experience to be ready sources of laughter. One was the arrival of a stranger in a town where he was immediately mistaken for his twin brother. As Manningham noticed, Shakespeare had already borrowed this unfailingly funny device from Plautus when writing *The Comedy of Errors* – a play which had entertained another Inn of Court at their feast eight years previously. Equally attractive was the Polly Oliver theme: the girl who follows her lover disguised as a page. Shakespeare had tried this out in *The Two Gentlemen of Verona*, a play which appears to have left him discontented since he kept trying to find new uses for its components. The inherent liveliness of the plot of *Twelfth Night* owes a great deal to the skill with which Shakespeare has combined these two comic situations. But he was not the first to combine them. A whole family group of plays and stories merging the twin situation with the Polly Oliver situation already existed by 1602, and Shakespeare certainly knew some of this group. If we follow Manningham's clue, we find among them two Italian plays called *Gl'Inganni* – the Deceptions – but these are less close to *Twelfth Night* than is an earlier play which was a source for both of them, *Gl'Ingannati* – the Deceived – acted at Siena in 1531.

Discussions of a literary source are often hard or tedious to follow because of the differences in names to be met with in two versions of the same plot. The use of generic names may help us to keep things clear here: the lover, for the character corresponding to Orsino; the brother, for Sebastian's counterpart; the lady, for Olivia's; and the heroine, for the character in Viola's situation. In *Gl'Ingannati*, the heroine assumes her disguise in order to follow and serve a lover who has apparently forgotten all about her during her temporary absence from Modena, the scene of the play, and who in fact now woos a lady to whom he sends the heroine as emissary. The lady promptly falls in love with the disguised heroine. Next the heroine's father and his friend, the ageing father of the lady (himself a suitor to the heroine), hear of her disguise, intercept her – or so they think – and shut her up with the lady. Actually they have seized the heroine's long-lost brother, who has just arrived in the city. On discovering what has occurred, the lover flies into a rage of jealousy and frustration; but he is brought to realize, through the eloquence of the heroine's old nurse, what a treasure he already has in the heroine's devotion.

This bald narration of its plot makes *Gl'Ingannati* sound very much as if it were the direct source of *Twelfth Night*. Actually the two plays are quite different in spirit. The Italian comedy has a realistic background of recent history. Its heroine was raped in the sack of Rome in 1527; in Modena she has had the good fortune to find a lover who belongs 'to the same political party' as herself. This is a long way from Shakespeare's Illyria; and in her heartless amusement at the lady's predicament, the heroine of *Gl'Ingannati* is a very long way from Viola. The whole play is in fact a heartless work; a bright, bustling, and often salacious comedy of intrigue. But it must have been very popular: French and Spanish translations soon appeared, and the plot was adapted for short stories by the Italian Bandello, the Frenchman Belleforest, and the Englishman Barnaby Rich. Each of these narrative versions carries us a little farther away from the harsh topicality of *Gl'Ingannati*, towards the Illyrian world represented in the sixteenth century by many translations of late Greek romances. Barnaby Rich's version, for example, which he called 'Apolonius and Silla', and published in 1581 as the second story in a volume entitled *Farewell to Military Profession* (he was a retired soldier), starts where many such romances start, with a shipwreck. This disaster brings the heroine to Constantinople, where she assumes her disguise in order to seek service with the lover, who is now raised to a dukedom and who, unlike the lover in the Italian versions of the tale, has not previously plighted his troth to the heroine. The lover sends the heroine to the lady, here a widow, and his messages are loyally delivered. Meanwhile the heroine's brother arrives in Constantinople and is entertained by the lady in mistake for the disguised heroine, with whom she has become infatuated. The brother shortly afterwards leaves. The lover now makes a direct approach to the lady, who tells him that she is promised to another. From servants' talk, the lover discovers that this rival is his own page. He immediately throws the heroine into prison. Next the lady discovers herself to be pregnant, and in desperation comes to the lover and tells him that his supposed page is the child's father. This compels the heroine to reveal that she is a girl. Overcome by gratitude for her devotion, the lover marries her; the lady's reputation is saved by the return of the brother and by their subsequent marriage.

For all its absurdity, this story is clearly closer to *Twelfth Night* than is any previous version. Several verbal echoes confirm Shakespeare's debt to Rich's story, which had the advantage of being in English and being easily available –

another dramatist had made a play out of the first story in Rich's collection only a couple of years earlier. At the same time, Shakespeare knew and used some foreign versions of the tale. What happened may have been something like this. Asked for a comedy, Shakespeare recalled and almost certainly re-read Rich's 'Apolonius and Silla' because he liked its blend of two themes that he had already used with success. Then he must have remembered or discovered that there were in fact dramatic versions of this tale already extant. One, a Latin translation of *Gl'Ingannati*, had been acted at Cambridge before the Earl of Essex as recently as 1595, and Shakespeare could have borrowed a manuscript of this from his Stratford acquaintance and future son-in-law John Hall, who had been at Cambridge at the time. Or he could have glanced through a copy of the original Italian play; or come across the close translation of it into French, which had the distinction of being the first prose comedy in that language. He certainly knew *Gl'Ingannati* in the original or translation, since some details in *Twelfth Night* derive from no other source: the brother's sightseeing in the city, the heroine's hopeless passion described as though (II.4.106) it were experienced by someone else —

My father had a daughter loved a man . . .

— and the servant's invitation to the brother, whom he mistakes for the disguised heroine, to come and visit the lady. Moreover, Shakespeare was familiar with the tale in the collections of Bandello and Belleforest. Not only are their re-tellings echoed verbally several times in *Twelfth Night*, but both writers place the emotional climax of the story in the heroine's attempt to dissuade the lover from his pursuit of the lady; and we have already seen that the episode in *Twelfth Night* which corresponds to this, Act II, scene 4, is a highlight of the play. It has no counterpart in Rich's story.

All these recollections did not prevent Shakespeare from handling the tale in his own way. His Viola does not assume her disguise in pursuit of the man she loves; she falls in love with Orsino only after she has found service with him. Olivia is not a widow (her mourning must have misled Manningham) but a young girl who repels the Duke Orsino's suit because she is stricken with grief for her brother's death. Viola too loves a brother she believes to be dead; and the brother himself is not brought in merely to complicate the plot and then disappear, but is a positive and likeable character whose impetuous marriage to Olivia establishes, in a world of fantasies, one irrefutable fact from which the dénouement can be swiftly and gaily reached. All these changes help to normalize and humanize Rich's melodramatic tale. However many versions of the story may have been known to Shakespeare, he succeeded in shaping it afresh with deftness and confidence.

What Rich calls 'a leash of lovers' derives, then, from 'Apolonius and Silla' and from some of the tales and plays that preceded it. But there are no hints in these earlier versions of Antonio, nor of Malvolio and his tormentors. Yet for Manningham, the memorable scenes were those in which Malvolio figured, and his response was typical of its time. When the play was acted at Court in 1623, it was called *Malvolio*, and Charles I changed the title to this in his own copy of the second edition of Shakespeare's works.

A suggestion for the baiting of Malvolio could have come from Rich's book. One of his tales is about a man who married a scold. Driven to desperation by her clamour, he shut her up

in a dark house that was on his back side; and then, calling his neighbours about her, he would seem with great sorrow to lament his wife's distress, telling them that she was suddenly become lunatic; whereas, by his gesture, he took so great grief as though he would likewise have run mad for company. But his wife (as he had attired her) seemed indeed not to be well in her wits but, seeing her husband's manners, showed herself in her conditions to be a right Bedlam. She used no other words but curses and bannings, crying for the plague and the pestilence, and that the devil would tear her husband in pieces. The company that were about her, they would exhort her, 'Good neighbour,

forget these speeches which doth so much distemper you, and call upon
God, and he will surely help you.'

In just the same way, Feste exhorts Malvolio to leave his vain
bibble-babble and Maria bids him remember his prayers. But if
this passage gave Shakespeare his first idea for the trick played
on Malvolio, Malvolio himself quickly grew far beyond the
stature of a mere dupe in his creator's mind. In fact he is so
sharply particularized that there is a strong likelihood that
when he appeared 'in the habit of some sir of note' he was
recognized as the caricature of some unpopular figure of the
time, well known to a Court, or Middle Temple, audience.
Malvolio's alleged Puritanism, his dislike of bear-baiting, his
'august regard of control', and his interruption of a noisy revel,
have all been taken to point to Sir William Knollys, the
Controller of the Queen's Household. Even the name Malvolio
has been read as a reference to Knollys's notorious infatuation
with his ward Mary Fitton ('I-want-Mall'), whose disgrace at
Court in the winter of 1600–1601 may be alluded to when Sir
Toby speaks of the picture of Mistress Mall which has taken
dust.

   Whether or not this and other identifications of characters in
Twelfth Night with real people are correct, they help to remind
us of one aspect of the play which stage designers, eager to
hoist sail for the Mediterranean, too easily overlook: its English-
ness. Shakespeare's Illyria is within hailing distance of the
Thames watermen, and the visitor from Messaline puts up in
the south suburbs, at the Elephant – as did many other visitors
to London. Shakespeare had learned a good deal about the
possibilities of realistic social comedy when he had acted in Ben
Jonson's *Every Man in His Humour* some three years before
Twelfth Night was written. The oddities of Jonson's Stephano
were still vivid in Shakespeare's memory when he invented the
part of Sir Andrew Aguecheek. Both are typical English
country 'gulls' – the Elizabethan word for anyone easily taken
in – both echo the phrases of more inventive characters, both

demean themselves by abusing their social inferiors, both waver between bluster and timidity, both are convinced they have a very pretty leg worth clothing in fine hose. Yet to speak of *Every Man in His Humour* as a 'source' for *Twelfth Night* is to be reminded once more of Shakespeare's skill in subjugating all the elements that go to make up the play to its dominant mood of festivity. Stephano is an object of real contempt to Jonson; but such is the spirit of *Twelfth Night* that Shakespeare, a bad hater at all times, enjoys his Sir Andrew and endears him to us as somebody who 'was adored once, too'.

This introduction has been more concerned with the mood and atmosphere of *Twelfth Night* than with an interpretation of its characters. Actors and producers must of course give much thought to such interpretations, but these are necessarily conditioned by their grasp of the play's own character. Moreover, their readings of characters in the play are bound to be still further modified by the way the actors' abilities interact in the company as a whole. For example, a sympathetic, or simply pathetic, Sir Andrew presupposes a Sir Toby whose dark, rascally side must be exposed to the audience long before his final repudiation of his fellow-knight. Contrast in itself is not enough; a tomboyish Viola, who enjoys scrapping with Olivia's attendants, does not sort well with a mournfully infatuated Olivia. In fact an almost operatic principle of contrast is too often seen at work in the play's casting, and this is especially true of the age of the characters. Sixty years ago, Orsino was a part for the greying matinée idol, and even Harley Granville-Barker, who did so much to free Shakespeare production from its nineteenth-century conventions, spoke of him as 'your middle-aged romantic'. True, Olivia thinks Orsino no match for her in years, but at eighteen or so – and Olivia should be no more – five or six years constitute a great gap. Elsewhere she speaks of his 'fresh and stainless youth', and this accords with the way the lover is presented in earlier versions of the tale. Bandello describes him as not yet twenty.

The trend in productions at the present is away from a straight to a satiric playing of Orsino. Unfortunately in the process he has sometimes been transformed into what one critic calls the Moony Duke. A little absurd he must be; but his absurdity can well consist in his eagerness, the zest with which he plays the role of the romantic lover. He is like Romeo before he has met Juliet and while he still fancies himself in love with Rosalind: changeful and moody, his mind a very opal. Just as Romeo forgets he can feed off his love and starts asking about dinner, so Orsino forgets his generalization that men's fancies are more giddy and infirm than women's are; five minutes later, he is insisting that there is no comparison between the love a woman can bear him and that he owes Olivia. Yet this absurdity must never submerge what is genuinely 'romantic' in the role, the appeal, as C. S. Lewis has described it, of a foreign duke 'speaking golden syllables, wearing rich clothes, and standing in the centre of the stage'.

Olivia for her part is too often played as — in the words of a modern producer — 'the stately contralto whom a sudden bereavement has distracted from the organization of the Hunt Ball'. Shakespeare deliberately turned the widow he found in his chief source into a young girl; perhaps a young girl rather like Queen Victoria at her accession, awed by her responsibilities and determined to be good. She can be prim, circumspect, shyly severe with the extraordinary household left at her command. She wants to do the right thing, and is appalled when she finds the fair young man at the gate has been intercepted by Sir Toby, a most embarrassing relation to have about the house. Then, when the fair young man appears, we watch the awakening of the Sleeping Beauty, from her firm denial (1.5.246) 'I cannot love him' — to lively, responsive repartee, then (guided by Shakespeare's internal stage direction) to her speaking in starts, distractedly, and so finally to the admission that she, hitherto so self-possessed, has caught the plague: 'ourselves we do not owe'. Her big scene with Viola in Act III gives the actress a splendid chance to show the audience how Olivia has grown up. It is important to control the comedy of this scene, so that Olivia does not appear ludicrous because she is in love, but only because she has fallen in love with a girl disguised as a boy. Her frankness in love should be as attractive as Juliet's, and make her the embodiment of a festive generosity. Her love is madness only in its lack of a true object; as soon as Viola is replaced by Sebastian it becomes reasonable love as that is defined by Barnaby Rich in 'Apolonius and Silla': 'If a question might be asked, "What is the ground indeed of reasonable love, whereby the knot is knit of true and perfect friendship?" I think those that be wise would answer, "Desert"; that is, where the party beloved doth requite us with the like.'

The actress who takes on the part of Viola also has to resist the temptation to play for the wrong kind of laughs. The Victorians, who gave us the Principal Boy, expected their actresses to make fun of the equivocations of Viola's disguise. The first producer to rebel against the nineteenth-century style of acting this part was Harley Granville-Barker, whose Savoy Theatre production of 1912 was perhaps the most famous *Twelfth Night* in theatrical history. Granville-Barker's knowledge of Elizabethan stage conditions made him sharply aware of the anachronism of a swaggering and gruff-toned actress in the part. When the Viola of 1602 disguised as Cesario, the boy-actor retained his natural gait and his 'maiden pipe'. The part itself has demands enough, without an additional obligation on the player to slip in and out of the Cesario manner. For example, at the end of Act II, scene 4, Viola's words

> *I am all the daughters of my father's house,*
> *And all the brothers too*

must deepen the melancholy of the scene by adding to her helpless love for Orsino her hopeless grief for her brother. It is catastrophic if, in order to get an easy laugh, the actress at this point gives a start and seems to correct herself in the phrase 'And all the brothers too'. Again there have been Violas who, in the willow-cabin speech in Act I, scene 5, have deliberately stumbled over 'Olivia!' as if they had been on the point of saying 'Orsino!' But Viola's great virtue is the generosity which makes her sink her own feelings in Orsino's, so that here she speaks entirely in her master's voice; any hesitation destroys the moving effect of this utter self-forgetfulness.

Sebastian's role is perhaps more of a problem for the producer than it is for the actor. Stage twins are never easy to cast. One unfortunate Sebastian between the wars had to look like two different Violas at successive performances as two famous actresses alternated in the chief female parts. It is not really surprising that some producers have tried to dispense with Sebastian altogether. Nevertheless, it is shocking. The reunion of brother and sister cannot be left to ventriloquism or to a trick with mirrors. It is the dramatic climax of the play's last Act, and completes its celebration of generous love, by adding the feelings of those whose ties are of blood to the feelings of the friends and of the lovers. Any dissimilarity there may be between the twins goes unnoticed at this point, because Shakespeare quickly diverts our attention from the bystanders' astonishment over this 'natural perspective', and focuses it instead on the exquisitely conveyed emotions of the brother and sister, as they hesitate before the great sea of joys which threatens to overwhelm them. Sebastian must be played as someone who can inspire such feelings in his sister and in his friend, and who will be a worthy husband for the Countess Olivia. He matters very much, that is to say, in the play's total effect. His part is short and relatively simple, but it is a strong one.

If stage interpretations of the lovers in *Twelfth Night* have changed little since Victorian times, the playing of Malvolio has, in some recent productions, been strongly influenced by a twentieth-century sociological reading of the play. According to such a reading, *Twelfth Night* depicts an Elizabethan household in transition from the easy-going paternalism that always kept a place by the fire for people like Feste and Sir Toby, to a new economic order of things dominated by the efficient, utterly uncharitable Malvolio. As an overall interpretation of the play, this view has one serious flaw. *Twelfth Night* is not about Olivia's household. Like every version of the story from *Gl'Ingannati* onwards, it is about Viola and her predicament, and any interpretation that moves Viola from the centre to the periphery of the play's interest is bound to make us cry out: 'I care not for your play of good life: give me a love play.' But this sociological approach has its appeal for actors used to playing Shaw, and modern productions often give Olivia a diligent, self-made steward, socially angular perhaps, but thoroughly responsible; every office and school staff-room contains such a Malvolio. This interpretation is full of hazards and difficulties, in spite of its superficial appeal. The differences between Malvolio and his social betters were plain to the play's first audience: yellow stockings, cross-gartered, were comically unfashionable by 1602, as was Malvolio's use of words like 'element', which the courtly jester Feste knows to be 'over-worn'. But how can it be conveyed to a modern audience, on whom these distinctions are wasted, that Malvolio comes from a class that has lagged behind the fashionable world? Actors who try to get the point across by dropped aitches are guilty of an anachronism as well as a gross vulgarization. And a further danger in this class-conscious presentation of Malvolio is that it makes him much too sympathetic. We live in the world of responsible executives, and if Malvolio is presented to us as one of them the tricks played on him appear cruel and unjusti-fied – the spite of the old and impoverished gentry against the class who were, in the revolution of 1642, to be 'revenged on the whole pack' of them.

The festive mood of the play is much better preserved if Malvolio is presented to us as a psychological rather than a social misfit. He is incapable of the easy give and take of those who are 'generous, guiltless, and of free disposition'. Most of the great stage Malvolios have been stiff as ramrods, and the play's best laughs come from the unexpected rapidity with which the ramrod unbends. There is comic justice in the process; Malvolio, who refuses to acknowledge that there is a time to dance, that people sometimes need cakes and ale, is tricked into the most outrageously untimely skittishness and facetiousness. Act III, scene 4 needs to be played as a transformation scene, perhaps even with Malvolio breaking into song; 'Please one and please all' was, after all, an Elizabethan pop song, though unfortunately the music has not survived. Next there is thrust upon him, by Maria's letter, the further role of being distant with Sir Toby, which produces a delicious exaggeration of his usual manner. What makes this most admirable fooling is that it is completely integrated with the play's main theme. Malvolio hates to give himself away. He won't play spontaneously; but with gain in view – the prospect of being Count Malvolio – he eagerly makes a fool of himself.

A sociological reading of the play has also left its mark on the behaviour of the plotters in the device against Malvolio. On the whole, this has had the good effect of toning down the traditional slapstick playing of these scenes. Maria must of course be small and shrill and the sort of young woman who finds life intensely dramatic. But she is not a hoyden, and the part will probably be played as the kind of waiting-gentlewoman Shakespeare had in mind if the actress conceives of her as a poor relation with no dowry, anxious to find a husband before she is relegated to the shelf. Sir Toby too is often presented nowadays as a character who, it is said, could gain admission to, and be helped out of, the best clubs in London. In fact the reaction against playing some scenes of the play as sheer farce has now gone rather far. There has even been a production without a box-tree, presumably because of some notion of Shakespeare's bare stage. But the Elizabethan public theatre made use of very solid properties, including trees; and it is a pity to deny any audience the fun of watching faces – aghast, apoplectic, or delighted – appear through the foliage. By and large, however, the new restraint has had the welcome effect of restoring the play's balance and its unity of mood, so that the drinking and devising scenes become comic relief in the sense that they heighten the comic effect, and not in the sense that they offer relaxation from more serious matters. For all the characters in the play, with two exceptions, are to some degree absurd. Olivia, by her own admission, is as mad as Malvolio, and Fortune plays some ludicrous tricks on the twins.

The two exceptions are Feste and Antonio. As a character Feste must have owed much to the genius – for one feels it was just that – of Robert Armin, who joined Shakespeare's company when it moved to the Globe Theatre in 1599, and whose creations included Touchstone and the Fool in *King Lear* as well as Feste. Armin played a 'sage fool' or professional jester, whose business was to mock the pedantry of the learned, bandy words skilfully with the witty, moralize on the vanity of womankind, and entertain everyone by his songs. In keeping with this concept, Feste is the source of much of the play's laughter; but he is not, unlike earlier Shakespeare clowns, its object. Indeed many actors have been tempted into playing him as a kind of Pagliacci, half concealing a breaking heart beneath the motley. But though Feste is, as we have seen, a character who from time to time steps out of the play's festive atmosphere, it is his detachment, and not a passionate attachment to Olivia or anyone else, that gives him his special and moving place in the play. Harley Granville-Barker ended his Savoy Theatre production by having the huge golden gates of Olivia's house slowly close on the rejoicing couples, leaving Feste outside to sing plaintively about the wind and the rain. It is perhaps even more effective if Feste sings this song about the ages of man with a certain briskness. Throughout the play Feste has stressed the need to use time wisely; since 'there is a time to everything under the sun', he knows that in the passing of life he now sings about his fooling grows old too. The depth and strength of Feste's character lies not in any tragic dimension, nor even in that pathos which is the invention of Romantic and post-Romantic criticism, but in its solid basis of stoical common sense.

If there is any hint of tragedy in a play written a year or two after *Hamlet*, it is to be found in Antonio rather than in Feste. Antonio's protestation of his love for Sebastian, and his bitter outcry at his supposed betrayal, are the true voice of feeling. They stir us painfully, even though we know all will come right in the end, because they move outside comedy's range of emotions in a way that Orsino's melodramatic outburst in Act v does not. And when the play ends, Antonio, like his name-sake in *The Merchant of Venice*, is odd man out. He has regained his faith in his friend, but that friend can pay little attention to him in the excitement of finding himself restored to Viola and married to Olivia. Although Antonio is inside the golden gate, he does not belong to the golden world. Producers seem uneasily aware of this isolation, and dress him up as a stage pirate in a desperate attempt to make him part of the Illyrian scene. But if Shakespeare has given us in this character a fragment of personal experience – the experience which is expressed in numerous sonnets and which makes betrayal of trust a dominant theme of his tragedies – we must accept this as a rare revelation. One day a producer may be bold enough to free Antonio from his pirate disguise and instead make him up to look like the Droeshout engraving of Shakespeare him-self. To do this would be wholly in the spirit of a play which evokes, and makes us free citizens of, a world of mirth, and yet at the same time keeps us aware of a world where malice is seldom 'sportful', nor time golden.

Further Reading

(1) *Editions*

The best fully-annotated edition of *Twelfth Night* is that by J. M. Lothian and T. W. Craik in the new Arden series (1975). A paperback reprint is available of the fifth edition (1901) of Horace Howard Furness's presentation of the play in the New Variorum Shakespeare; it reproduces the Folio text of the play together with a wealth of eighteenth-and nineteenth-century comments. Sidney Musgrove has produced an 'old-spelling' edition for the general reader (1969).

(2) *Background Material*

Rich's 'Apolonius and Silla' is given in full in *Elizabethan Love Stories*, edited by T. J. B. Spencer (Penguin Shakespeare Library, 1968), as well as in the Variorum edition of *Twelfth Night*, which includes some other source material. An indispensable work on the sources of *Twelfth Night* is volume 2 (*The Comedies, 1597–1603*) of *Narrative and Dramatic Sources of Shakespeare* (1957–), edited by Geoffrey Bullough. This has a lively translation of *Gl'Ingannati* and a full discussion of the many suggested sources of Shakespeare's play. Other discussions are to be found in Kenneth Muir's *Shakespeare's Sources*, volume 1, *Comedies and Tragedies* (1957), and in an article by René Pruvost with the title '*The Two Gentlemen of Verona, Twelfth Night* et *Gl'Ingannati*' which appeared in volume 13 of *Études Anglaises* (1960).

Two views of the play's origins which are briefly discussed in the Introduction are represented by Leslie Hotson's *The First Night of Twelfth Night* (1954, paperback 1961) and John

W. Draper's *The Twelfth Night of Shakespeare's Audience* (1950).
The first of these is questioned in 'Topicality and the Date of
Twelfth Night' by Josephine W. Bennett in the *South Atlantic
Quarterly*, volume 71 (1972), and the second is challenged in
'The *Twelfth Night* of Shakespeare and of Professor Draper' by
N. A. Brittain in *Shakespeare Quarterly*, volume 7 (1956).

(3) *Criticism*

Recent general works on Shakespeare's comedies which form a
good background to *Twelfth Night* are: John Russell Brown's
Shakespeare and his Comedies (1957); C. L. Barber's *Shakespeare's
Festive Comedy* (Princeton, 1959); Northrop Frye's *A Natural
Perspective* (New York, 1965); and the article 'The Mature
Comedies' by Frank Kermode in *Early Shakespeare: Stratford-
upon-Avon Studies*, 3, edited by J. R. Brown and B. Harris
(1961). Special studies of the play include the articles of L. G.
Salingar, 'The Design of *Twelfth Night*', *Shakespeare Quarterly*,
volume 9 (1958), Joseph Summers, 'The Masks of *Twelfth
Night*' in *Shakespeare: Modern Essays in Criticism* edited by L. F.
Dean (New York, 1957), John Russell Brown's 'Directions for
Twelfth Night' in *Shakespeare's Comedies: An Anthology of Criti-
cism* edited by Laurence Lerner (Penguin Books, 1967), the
same writer's admirable close reading of some passages from
Twelfth Night in *Shakespeare's Dramatic Style* (1970), Terence
Eagleton's 'Language and Reality in *Twelfth Night*' in *Critical
Quarterly*, volume 9 (1967), and a book by Clifford Leech,
Twelfth Night and Shakespearean Comedy (Toronto, 1965). Walter
N. King has made a collection of *Twentieth Century Interpretations
of Twelfth Night* (1968), and D. J. Palmer has compiled '*Twelfth
Night*': *A Casebook* (1972). Three good articles published since
these anthologies were made are: Alexander Leggatt's 'Shakespeare and the Borderlines of Comedy' in *Mosaic*, volume 5
(1971); Joan Hartwig's 'Feste's Whirligig and the Comic Providence of *Twelfth Night*' in the *Journal of English Literary History*,
volume 40 (1973); Anne Barton's '*As You Like It* and *Twelfth*

Night: Shakespeare's Sense of an Ending' in *Shakespearian Comedy: Stratford-upon-Avon Studies*, 14, edited by D. J. Palmer and M. Bradbury (1974).

The editors of the new Arden edition give a full account of the play's stage history. Arthur Colby Sprague and J. C. Trewin, in *Shakespeare's Plays Today* (1971), discuss changing theatrical interpretations of the play's roles, while the minor parts are analysed by Dennis R. Preston in *Shakespeare Quarterly*, volume 21 (1969). Feste has always aroused critical interest and scholarly inquiry. Our understanding of him is helped by Andrew Bradley's 'Feste the Jester' in *A Miscellany* (1929), Enid Welsford's *The Fool* (Cambridge, 1935), Leslie Hotson's *Shakespeare's Motley* (1952), R. H. Goldsmith's *Wise Fools in Shakespeare* (Liverpool, 1955), and Charles S. Felver's *Robert Armin* (New York, 1961). Harley Granville-Barker's Preface to his acting edition of the play has been reprinted in *Prefaces to Shakespeare* volume 6 (1974). There is a chapter on the play's music in J. H. Long's *Shakespeare's Use of Music* (Florida, 1955) and a chapter on 'Adult Songs and Robert Armin' in *Music in Shakespearean Tragedy* (1963) by F. W. Sternfeld.

Finally, readers who disagree with my Introduction will enjoy F. H. Langman's onslaught in 'Comedy and Saturnalia: the Case of *Twelfth Night*', *Southern Review* (Adelaide), volume 7 (1974).

An Account of the Text

Twelfth Night was first published in the posthumous collection of Shakespeare's plays known as the Folio (1623). It appears there in a very accurate carefully-punctuated text in which misreadings such as 'coole my nature' (for 'curl by nature', 1.3.94–5) are rare. The play's real puzzles, Mistress Mall's picture and the Lady of the Strachy, are not due to textual corruption but to our ignorance of Elizabethan gossip.

The manuscript of *Twelfth Night* which was sent to the printer in 1623 was either the copy of the play actually used for productions, known as the promptbook, or a copy of this specially made for the printer. This is evident from the theatrical practicality of the text as it stands. Actors' entrances are given at the point where they must begin to move on to the stage. For example, at v.1.186 Sir Toby starts to struggle in, supported by Feste. Sir Andrew speaks a sentence before he becomes aware of Sir Toby's arrival, and it takes another two lines spoken by Sir Andrew for Sir Toby to get well down-stage where Orsino can address him. So, too, the actor playing Malvolio is warned to get ready for the 'dark house' dialogue by the stage direction *Malvolio within*. Exits are not given when it is perfectly plain to the actor that he has to get off the stage. Thus Maria is kept flitting to and fro on errands, but the list of variant stage directions given below shows that most of her exits go unnoted. Nor does Malvolio need any direction to stalk out at 'I'll be revenged on the whole pack of you' (v.1.375), for it is evident from Orsino's next speech that he has done so.

An author's own 'fair copy' could be used as the promptbook

in an Elizabethan theatre. Unfortunately there appears to be no evidence that this was the case with *Twelfth Night*. A small piece of evidence that the promptbook was not Shakespeare's fair copy is afforded by the occurrence of *Uiolenta* for *Viola* at 1.5.160, *Marian* for *Maria* at 11.3.13, and (unless a joke is intended) *Agueface* for *Aguecheek* at 1.3.40. Such uncertainty about names is natural in the first Act or so of an autograph play, especially one that has been written in haste, but it is likely to be eliminated when the author copies out his work for himself. It is reasonably safe to assume that the manuscript of *Twelfth Night* which reached the playhouse presented the play in a finished form but was not tidy enough to be used as the promptbook, so that a copy had to be made. The possibility that Maria's letter is a stage closer to Shakespeare's autograph manuscript than is the rest of the play is briefly discussed in the notes on 11.5.140 and on 111.4.71.

The Act and scene divisions of the Folio are unlikely to be Shakespeare's own. They are quite arbitrary, and the action of the play is in fact continuous between Acts 1 and 11, and between Acts 111 and 1v. Possibly the Act divisions were introduced to give an opportunity for intermission music at Court performances, such as those in 1618 and 1623. In addition to these Act and scene divisions, which are in Latin, the Folio has *Finis Actus primus* (*secundus, Quartus*) at the end of Acts 1, 11, and 1v. Other changes which may have been made in the play while it was in the King's Men's repertory are discussed in the Introduction.

The variants listed below do not include the few lines printed as prose in the Folio and as verse in this edition (for example, the 'Jolly Robin' song in 1v.2) or the few others, such as 111.4.19-22, which were erroneously printed in the Folio as verse but are here restored to prose. Following the practice of the Folio, a number of short verse-lines have been printed on their own, instead of being shown as halves of lines divided between two speakers, the normal practice of eighteenth-and nineteenth-century editions. Metrical continuity is natural only when one character is responding fully to another, either in affection or anger. When a character follows his or her own thoughts independently of the other speaker (as Viola does in 1.2), or when a marked pause or sudden change of mood occurs, Shakespeare does not hesitate to use half-lines, and this edition has tried to preserve his free handling of his poetic medium. On the same principle, no attempt has been made to regularize lines such as 'That – methought – her eyes had lost her tongue' (II.2.20). The slight pause before and after the parenthesis lengthens out the line to a normal blank verse, and similar irregularities in other lines can usually be justified in the same way.

It will be seen from the short list of variants below that this is a very conservative text, preserving the Folio readings wherever they make sense. But what is sense in the study is not always sense on the modern stage. The second list is therefore of emendations which producers may wish to adopt in the theatre for the sake of lucidity.

COLLATIONS

I

The following is a list of readings in the present text which are departures from the Folio text of 1623. The reading on the right of the square bracket is that of the Folio.

Title. TWELFTH] Twelfe
1.1. 11 sea, naught] Sea. Nought
1.2. 15 Arion] *Orion*
1.3. 26 all, most] almost
      49 SIR ANDREW] *Ma.*
   94–5 curl by nature] coole my nature
    128 dun-coloured] dam'd colour'd
         set] sit

	131	That's] That
I.5.	86	guiltless] guitlesse
	142	He's] Ha's
	160	(stage direction) *Viola*] *Uiolenta*
II.2.	31	our frailty] O frailtie
II.3.	2	*diluculo*] *Deliculo*
	24	leman] Lemon
	25	impetticoat] impeticos
	83	O' the twelfth] O the twelfe
	130	a nayword] an ayword
	142	swathes] swarths
II.5.	112	staniel] stallion
	140	born] become
	141	achieve] atcheeues
	154	champain] champian
	169	dear] deero
III.1.	8	king] Kings
	66	wise men, folly-fallen] wisemens folly falne
	88	all ready] already
III.2.	7	see thee the] see the
	50	thy] the
	63	nine] mine
	66	renegado] Renegatho
III.4.	23	OLIVIA] *Mal.*
	71	tang] langer
	289	oath's sake] oath sake
IV.2.	7	student] Studient
	14	Gorboduc] Gorbodacke
	37	clerestories] cleere stores
	51	haply] happily
IV.3.	27	jealous] jealious
V.1.	173	He's] H'as
		he's] has
	193	he's] has
	197	pavin] panyn

2

The following is a list of well-founded emendations which have not been adopted in this edition. The emendation is in each case to the right of the square bracket.

I.I.	5	sound] south
	27	heat] hence
I.2.	40–41	sight | And company] company | And sight
I.3.	39	*vulgo*] *volto*
	128	dun-coloured] flame-coloured
I.4.	33	shrill and sound] shrill of sound
I.5.	191	not mad] but mad
	197–8	Tell me your mind; I am a messenger] OLIVIA Tell me your mind. VIOLA I am a messenger
II.2.	12	of me, I'll none] of me! I'll none
	20	That – methought –] That sure methought
	32	made, if such] made of, such
II.3.	9	lives] life
	144	grounds] ground
II.4.	52	Fie away, fie away] Fly away, fly away
	87	It] I
II.5.	33	SIR TOBY] FABIAN
	37	SIR TOBY] FABIAN
	169–70	dear my sweet] dear, O my sweet
III.2.	50	cubiculo] cubicle
III.3.	15	And thanks. And ever oft] And thanks and ever thanks. And oft
III.4.	88	How is't with you, man?] SIR TOBY How is't with you, man?
	198	unchary on't] unchary out
	203	griefs] grief
	241	computent] competent
	346	lying, vainness] lying vainness
IV.2.	69–70	the upshot] to the upshot
V.I.	112	have] hath
	369	thrown] thrust

3

There follow the chief departures of this edition from the Folio stage-directions. Minor additions such as *aside, reads, sings, to Feste*, are not noted here.

I.I.	I	*Music*] not in F
I.5.	I	*Feste the Clown*] *Clowne* here and elsewhere throughout the Folio
	28	and attendants] not in F
	124	followed by Maria] not in F
	133	*Exit*] not in F
	194	(*showing Viola the way out*)] not in F
	210	*Maria and attendants withdraw*] not in F
	301	*Exit*] *Finis, Actus primus.* F
II.2.	41	*Exit*] not in F
II.4.	14	*Exit Curio*] not in F
	78	*Curio and attendants withdraw*] not in F
II.5.	20	*The men hide. Maria throws down a letter*] not in F
	200	*Exeunt*] *Exeunt. Finis Actus secundus* F
III.I.	I	*at different entrances . . . playing his pipe and tabor*] not in F
	42	*She gives him a coin*] not in F
	52	*She gives another coin*] not in F
	80	*Maria*] *Gentlewoman* F
	90	*Exeunt Sir Toby . . . he, too, leaves*] not in F
III.2.	80	*Exeunt*] *Exeunt Omnes.* F
III.3.	49	*separately*] not in F
III.4.	14	*Exit Maria*] not in F
	15	*and Maria*] not in F
	64	*and Maria different ways*] not in F
	196	*Exit Maria. Sir Toby and Fabian stand aside*] not in F

213 *Sir Toby and Fabian come forward*] *Enter Toby and Fabian.* F

266 F gives direction *Exeunt* for Viola and Fabian

282 (*Aside, as he crosses to Fabian*)] not in F

283 (*To Fabian*)] *Enter Fabian and Viola.*

296 (*crossing to Sir Andrew*)] not in F

301 *He draws*] not in F. So too *She draws* at line 302.

363 *Exeunt Antonio and Officers*] *Exit* F

375 *Exit*] not in F

384 *Exit*] not in F

386 *Exeunt*] *Exit* F

IV.1. 24 *He strikes Sebastian*] not in F

25 *He beats Sir Andrew with the handle of his dagger*] not in F

31 *He grips Sebastian*] not in F

40 *He breaks free and draws his sword*] not in F

43 *He draws*] not in F

50 *Exeunt Sir Toby, Sir Andrew, and Fabian*] not in F

IV.2. 3 *Exit*] not in F

10 *and Maria*] not in F

70 *and Maria*] not in F

95 (*In priest's voice*)] not in F. So in line 101.

99–100 (*In own voice*)] not in F. So in line 101.

IV.3. 35 *Exeunt*] *Exeunt. Finis Actus Quartus.* F

V.1. 140 *Exit an attendant*] not in F

205 *Exeunt Sir Toby and Sir Andrew, helped by Feste and Fabian*] not in F

288 *He reads frantically*] not in F

298 (*snatching the letter and giving it to Fabian*)] not in F

312 *Exit Fabian*] not in F

323 *and Fabian*] not in F

375 *Exit*] not in F

385 *all but Feste*] not in F

405 *Exit*] FINIS F

The Songs

The editor gratefully acknowledges the assistance of F. W. Sternfeld in the transcribing and editing of the songs.

1. 'O mistress mine' (II.3.37)

No contemporary setting has survived, but there exist two instrumental pieces with this title, both based on the same tune. Their exact relationship to the song in the play is not known, but the tune can be fitted to Shakespeare's words. The words, the tune, or both, may be traditional. The song printed below has been transcribed and edited by Sidney Beck from Thomas Morley's *First Book of Consort Lessons*, published in 1599.

1. O mis-tress mine! Where are you roam - ing?
2. What is love? 'Tis not here - af - ter;

O, stay and hear: your true love's co - ming, O, stay and
Pre - sent mirth hath pre - sent laugh-ter, Pre - sent

hear: your true love's co - ming, That can sing both high and
mirth hath pre-sent laugh - ter, What's to come is still un -

low. Trip no fur-ther, pret-ty sweet-ing; Jour-neys end in lov-ers
- sure. In de - lay there lies no plen - ty - Then come kiss me, sweet and

meet - ing, Ev - ery wise man's son doth know.
twen - ty, Youth's a stuff will not en - dure.

2. 'Hold thy peace' (II.3.63)

This round was published in Thomas Ravenscroft's *Deutero-melia*, 1609.

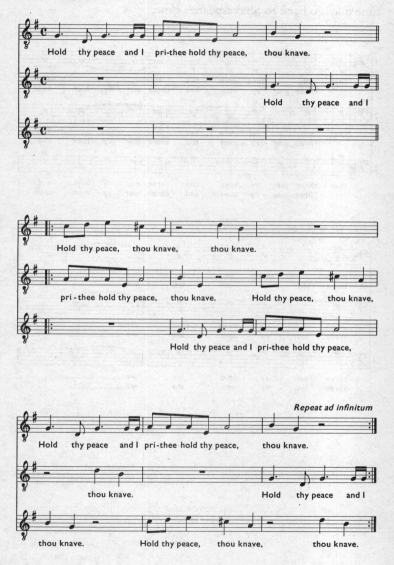

3. 'Three merry men' (II.3.75)

The following version of this catch has been transcribed and edited from William Lawes's *Catch that Catch Can*, 1652. The tune may go back to Shakespeare's time.

4. 'There dwelt a man in Babylon' (II.3.78)

This is the first line of 'The Ballad of Constant Susanna', which was sung to a corrupt version of 'Greensleeves'.

5. 'O' the twelfth day of December' (II.3.83)

No early music is known.

6. 'Farewell, dear heart' (II.3.99)

This song by Robert Jones was printed in his *First Book of Airs*, 1600. It has been transcribed and adapted to the words of the play.

7. 'Come away, come away death' (II.4.50)
  No early music is known.
8. 'Hey Robin' (IV.2.71)
  This is part of a round for three or four voices, probably by
William Corneyshe (*c.* 1465–*c.* 1523), preserved in the British Mu-
seum, Additional MSS. 31922 (sixteenth century; folios 53–4).
The full round, transcribed and edited, is given below. It is
followed by an arrangement suitable for stage performance.

so? She lov'th a - no - ther bet - ter than me, And
true. In faith my la - dy lo - veth me well, She

- bin! Tell me how thy le - man doth, And

- bin! Tell me how thy le - man doth, And

yet she will say no.
will change for no new.

thou shalt know of mine.

thou shalt know of mine.

MIDDLE PART
(as sung by Feste in a stage production)

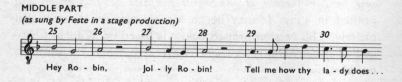

Hey Ro - bin,   Jol - ly Ro - bin!   Tell me how thy   la - dy does . . .

TOP PART

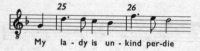

My   la - dy is un - kind per-die

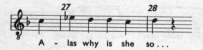

A - las why is she so . . .

She   loves   a - no - ther . . .

9. 'I am gone, sir' (IV.2.121)

No early music has survived.

10. 'When that I was and a little tiny boy' (V.1.386)

The tune to which these lines are traditionally sung first appears in a volume called *The New Songs in the Pantomime of the Witches; the Celebrated Epilogue in the Comedy of Twelfth Night ... sung by Mr Vernon at Vauxhall; composed by J. Vernon,* and printed in 1772. It may be an arrangement of a traditional melody. The version printed below is based on William Chappell's *Popular Music of the Olden Time* (1859), where the source is not identified.

An accompaniment by F. W. Sternfeld is printed in his *Songs from Shakespeare's Tragedies* (Oxford University Press, 1964).

TWELFTH NIGHT; or, *What You Will*

The Characters in the Play

ORSINO, Duke of Illyria
VALENTINE ⎫
CURIO ⎭ gentlemen attending on Orsino
First Officer
Second Officer

VIOLA, a shipwrecked lady, later disguised as Cesario
SEBASTIAN, her twin brother
CAPTAIN of the wrecked ship
ANTONIO, another sea-captain

OLIVIA, a countess
MARIA, her waiting-gentlewoman
SIR TOBY BELCH, her uncle
SIR ANDREW AGUECHEEK, Sir Toby's protégé
MALVOLIO, Olivia's steward
FABIAN, a member of her household
FESTE, her jester
A PRIEST
A SERVANT

Musicians, lords, sailors, attendants

References to plays by Shakespeare not yet available in the New Penguin Shakespeare are to Peter Alexander's edition of the *Complete Works*, London, 1951. 'Folio' (F) means the first collected edition of Shakespeare's plays, published in 1623. *The title* The original spelling of the title, *Twelfe Night*, preserves the form of the ordinal number which was common in Shakespeare's day.

Music. Enter Orsino Duke of Illyria, Curio, and other lords

ORSINO

If music be the food of love, play on,
Give me excess of it, that, surfeiting,
The appetite may sicken, and so die.
That strain again! It had a dying fall.

1.1 The eighteenth-century custom of lo-
calizing scenes ('A street', etc.) has
been dropped in this edition. Shakespeare's audience was interested in
the relation of characters to one another, not in their relation to any
particular place, except when the
place itself was part of the action.
Twelfth Night could have been acted
on a very simple stage in a great hall,
or perhaps even in the floor space in
front of the two big doorways at the
screen end of such a hall. These doorways would soon establish themselves as leading to Olivia's house
and to Orsino's, and the strangers to
the town would arrive by a third
entrance, perhaps through the audience. The doors or the curtained
doorways could also serve for the
box-tree and for the dark house (see
Introduction, page 518) or these
could be brought on as two substantial properties. The only other requirements would be two or three
easily movable seats. No upper stage

is needed. When the play was performed at the Globe, the dark house
could have been represented by the
curtained booth between the two
main entrances to the stage.
(stage direction) *Music.* At the original production in a great hall, this
music may have been provided by a
seated group of performers on the
viol and bass viol, who would have
been playing to the company before
the play started. When the play was
repeated in the public theatre,
Orsino's own group of musicians,
playing portable instruments such as
recorders, a lute, and an arch-lute,
could enter with him.
(stage direction) *Orsino.* The link
which has been suggested between
this character and the historical Vir-
ginio Orsino, Duke of Bracciano, is
discussed in the Introduction, pages
530–32.
3 *appetite* (Orsino's longing for music)
4 *fall* cadence

O, it came o'er my ear like the sweet sound
That breathes upon a bank of violets,
Stealing and giving odour. Enough, no more!
'Tis not so sweet now as it was before.
O spirit of love, how quick and fresh art thou,
That, notwithstanding thy capacity
Receiveth as the sea, naught enters there,
Of what validity and pitch soe'er,
But falls into abatement and low price
Even in a minute. So full of shapes is fancy
That it alone is high fantastical.

CURIO
Will you go hunt, my lord?

ORSINO
What, Curio?

CURIO
The hart.

ORSINO
Why, so I do, the noblest that I have.
O, when mine eyes did see Olivia first,
Methought she purged the air of pestilence.
That instant was I turned into a hart,

9–14 *O spirit of love, how quick and fresh art thou . . . in a minute.* The involved syntax of these lines perhaps led either the playhouse copyist or the compositor to insert a full stop after 'sea' in line 11, but this does not give good sense unless we read 'Receivest' for 'Receiveth'. The general meaning is clear: love is so ravenous that nothing it devours can give it real satisfaction.

9 *quick and fresh* keen and eager (to devour or consume)

12 *validity* value
pitch (1) height; (2) excellence

13 *abatement* depreciation

15 *alone* exceeding all other passions

high fantastical intensely imaginative. 'Fantastical' was a fashionable bit of psychological jargon.

19 *Why, so I do.* Orsino's pun on 'heart' and 'hart' betrays his lordly possessiveness; he thinks he should command where he adores.

23–4 *And my desires, like fell and cruel hounds,* | *E'er since pursue me.* Orsino recalls a classical legend which Shakespeare would know best from Ovid's *Metamorphoses* (III. 138 onwards): the hunter Actaeon, because he saw the goddess Diana naked, was turned into a stag and torn to pieces by his hounds.

And my desires, like fell and cruel hounds,
E'er since pursue me.
      Enter Valentine
                           How now! What news from her?

VALENTINE

So please my lord, I might not be admitted,
But from her handmaid do return this answer:
The element itself, till seven years' heat,
Shall not behold her face at ample view,
But like a cloistress she will veilèd walk,
And water once a day her chamber round   30
With eye-offending brine; all this to season
A brother's dead love, which she would keep fresh
And lasting, in her sad remembrance.

ORSINO

O, she that hath a heart of that fine frame
To pay this debt of love but to a brother –
How will she love, when the rich golden shaft
Hath killed the flock of all affections else
That live in her; when liver, brain, and heart,
These sovereign thrones, are all supplied and filled –
Her sweet perfections – with one self king!   40
Away before me to sweet beds of flowers!
Love thoughts lie rich when canopied with bowers.
                                Exeunt

---

23 *fell* savage
27 *element* sky
heat. This is often emended to 'hence', but *heat* suggests the way the passage of the seasons will destroy Olivia's beauty, if she spends the best years of her life in mourning.
29 *a cloistress* an enclosed nun
31 *eye-offending brine* stinging tears
season preserve by salting
33 *remembrance* (pronounced as four syllables)

34 *frame* construction
36 *shaft* arrow (shot by Cupid)
38 *liver, brain, and heart* (the seats of the passions, judgement, and sentiments)
40 *Her sweet perfections*. Olivia's nature will be completed by Orsino's occupying each of these thrones. The condescension is in character, but the idea that 'woman receiveth perfection by the man' is common in the period.
self sole

I.2   *Enter Viola, a Captain, and sailors*

VIOLA
What country, friends, is this?

CAPTAIN
This is Illyria, lady.

VIOLA
And what should I do in Illyria?
My brother, he is in Elysium.
Perchance he is not drowned. What think you, sailors?

CAPTAIN
It is perchance that you yourself were saved.

VIOLA
O, my poor brother! and so perchance may he be.

CAPTAIN
True, madam, and to comfort you with chance,
Assure yourself, after our ship did split,
10   When you and those poor number saved with you
Hung on our driving boat, I saw your brother,
Most provident in peril, bind himself —
Courage and hope both teaching him the practice —
To a strong mast, that lived upon the sea;
Where, like Arion on the dolphin's back,

I.2 (stage direction) *Viola*. This name probably derives, without Shakespeare being fully aware of the fact, from a romance published in 1598: *The Famous History of Parismus*, by Emanuel Forde. It is set in Thessaly, a country ruled by Queen Olivia. The heroine Violetta disguises as a page and seeks service with the man she loves. But apart from this girl-page theme, *Parismus* had little to interest Shakespeare.

2 *Illyria*. This name for what was Yugoslavia conjures up the world of the late Greek romances, but the local colour of the play is all English.

4 *Elysium* (abode of the happy dead, hence heaven)

6, 7 *perchance*. The Captain and Viola play on the meanings 'perhaps' and 'by good fortune'.

8 *chance* what may have happened

11 *driving* drifting

14 *lived* kept afloat (a nautical term)

15 *Arion*. This was the name of a Greek musician who threw himself overboard to escape being murdered by sailors, and was carried to land by a dolphin which had heard him play on the ship. Ovid tells the legend in the *Fasti*, 11, 79–118.

I saw him hold acquaintance with the waves
So long as I could see.

VIOLA

For saying so, there's gold.
Mine own escape unfoldeth to my hope,
Whereto thy speech serves for authority,   20
The like of him. Knowest thou this country?

CAPTAIN

Ay, madam, well, for I was bred and born
Not three hours' travel from this very place.

VIOLA

Who governs here?

CAPTAIN

A noble Duke, in nature as in name.

VIOLA

What is his name?

CAPTAIN

Orsino.

VIOLA

Orsino . . . I have heard my father name him.
He was a bachelor then.

CAPTAIN

And so is now, or was so, very late;   30
For but a month ago I went from hence,
And then 'twas fresh in murmur – as you know,
What great ones do, the less will prattle of –
That he did seek the love of fair Olivia.

VIOLA

What's she?

CAPTAIN

A virtuous maid, the daughter of a count

16 *hold acquaintance with the waves* 'bob up
and down as if greeting the waves'
or perhaps 'follow every movement
of the waves'
19-21 *Mine own escape unfoldeth to my hope*

| . . . *The like of him* my own escape
encourages me in the hope, which is
warranted by what you have just
said, that he also has escaped
32 *murmur* rumour

That died some twelvemonth since, then leaving her
In the protection of his son, her brother,
Who shortly also died; for whose dear love,
40   They say, she hath abjured the sight
And company of men.

VIOLA
O, that I served that lady,
And might not be delivered to the world –
Till I had made mine own occasion mellow –
What my estate is.

CAPTAIN   That were hard to compass,
Because she will admit no kind of suit,
No, not the Duke's.

VIOLA
There is a fair behaviour in thee, Captain,
And though that nature with a beauteous wall
50   Doth oft close in pollution, yet of thee
I will believe thou hast a mind that suits
With this thy fair and outward character.
I prithee – and I'll pay thee bounteously –
Conceal me what I am, and be my aid
For such disguise as haply shall become
The form of my intent. I'll serve this Duke.
Thou shalt present me as an eunuch to him.
It may be worth thy pains, for I can sing

43 *delivered* revealed
45 *estate* status. Viola does not want her true identity to be disclosed until she has decided the time is ripe for it to be known.
    compass bring about
46 *suit* petition
49–50 *nature with a beauteous wall | Doth oft close in pollution.* Like the reference to Arion's story in line 15, this may be a vestigial remnant of the sea captain's villainy in Rich's 'Apolonius and Silla' (*Elizabethan Love Stories*,

ed. T. J. B. Spencer, pp. 101–3; see Further Reading). It also prepares us for Antonio's bitter reproach of what he takes to be Sebastian's treachery later in the play.
52 *character* appearance and behaviour
55–6 *as haply shall become | The form of my intent* as may be suitable for the purpose I have shaped
58 *I can sing.* For Shakespeare's possible change of plan here, see Introduction, page 528.

And speak to him in many sorts of music
That will allow me very worth his service. 60
What else may hap to time I will commit.
Only shape thou thy silence to my wit.

CAPTAIN

Be you his eunuch, and your mute I'll be.
When my tongue blabs, then let mine eyes not see.

VIOLA

I thank thee. Lead me on. *Exeunt*

Enter Sir Toby Belch and Maria 1.3

SIR TOBY What a plague means my niece to take the death
of her brother thus? I am sure care's an enemy to life.

MARIA Ay my troth, Sir Toby, you must come in earlier
o'nights. Your cousin, my lady, takes great exceptions to
your ill hours.

SIR TOBY Why, let her except before excepted.

MARIA Ay, but you must confine myself within the
modest limits of order.

SIR TOBY Confine! I'll confine myself no finer than I am.
These clothes are good enough to drink in, and so be 10
these boots too; an they be not, let them hang themselves in their own straps.

MARIA That quaffing and drinking will undo you. I heard

---

60 *allow* prove
62 *wit* design
63 *mute*. Dumb attendant, as well as eu-
nuchs, were known by the Elizabethans to be part of the entourage
of oriental monarchs.

1.3.1 *my niece*. On the strength of this
expression, Sir Toby is usually described as Olivia's uncle. Maria and
Olivia herself speak of him as
Olivia's 'cousin', but this term could
be used in Elizabethan English for

any collateral relative other than a
brother or sister.
3 *By my troth* by my faith (an asseveration)
6 *except before excepted* exclude what has
already been excluded (a legal
phrase). Sir Toby may mean that
Olivia has not taken exception to his
'ill hours' in the past and should not
do so now.
8 *modest limits of order* bounds of good
behaviour
11 *an* if

my lady talk of it yesterday, and of a foolish knight that
you brought in one night here, to be her wooer.

SIR TOBY Who? Sir Andrew Aguecheek?

MARIA Ay, he.

SIR TOBY He's as tall a man as any's in Illyria.

MARIA What's that to the purpose?

20   SIR TOBY Why, he has three thousand ducats a year.

MARIA Ay, but he'll have but a year in all these ducats.
He's a very fool and a prodigal.

SIR TOBY Fie, that you'll say so. He plays o'the viol-de-
gamboys, and speaks three or four languages word for
word without book, and hath all the good gifts of nature.

MARIA He hath indeed all, most natural; for besides that
he's a fool, he's a great quarreller; and but that he hath
the gift of a coward to allay the gust he hath in quarrel-
ling, 'tis thought among the prudent he would quickly
30   have the gift of a grave.

SIR TOBY By this hand, they are scoundrels and substractors that say so of him. Who are they?

MARIA They that add, moreover, he's drunk nightly in
your company.

SIR TOBY With drinking healths to my niece. I'll drink to
her as long as there is a passage in my throat and drink
in Illyria. He's a coward and a coistrel that will not

18 *tall* courageous. Maria takes the
word in its usual sense.
any's any who is
20 *ducats.* A ducat was worth a third of
£1.
21 *have but a year in all these ducats.* Maria
means Sir Andrew will get through
his fortune in a year.
22 *very* perfect
23–4 *viol-de-gamboys* bass viol, or *viol da
gamba* (ancestor of the modern
violoncello)
25 *without book* by memory
26 *natural* like an idiot or 'natural'

28–30 *gift of a coward ... gift of a grave*
(with a play on the meanings 'natural
ability' and 'present')
28 *gust* relish
31–2 *substractors* detractors
37 *coistrel* groom, low fellow. The word
does not occur elsewhere in Shakespeare's work, and it has been suggested that he picked it up from
Rich's *Farewell to Military Profession.*
But it is not uncommon in the
period, and still survives in North of
England dialects.

drink to my niece till his brains turn o'the toe, like a
parish top. What, wench! Castiliano, *vulgo* – for here
comes Sir Andrew Agueface! 40

Enter Sir Andrew Aguecheek

SIR ANDREW Sir Toby Belch! How now, Sir Toby
Belch?

SIR TOBY Sweet Sir Andrew!

SIR ANDREW Bless you, fair shrew.

MARIA And you too, sir.

---

39 *parish top.* There are several references to parish tops in Elizabethan
plays, but nothing is known about
them.
Castiliano, vulgo. This is a puzzling
phrase. We would expect it to mean
'Talk of the devil!' (from the proverb
'Talk of the devil and he will
appear'), since Sir Toby has just
caught sight of Sir Andrew. *Castiliano* is in fact the name adopted by
the devil Belphegor when he comes
to earth in *Grim the Collier of Croydon,
or The Devil and his Dame*, a play
written in or before 1600; and Shakespeare may here be alluding to this
play in order to give a new twist to
an old saying. He would have been
reminded of the play in reading
Rich's collection of tales, because
Rich tells the story on which the
play is based – how the devil was
worsted by a woman – in his Conclusion. Sir Toby's mention of a parish
top also connects the two plays. The
scene in *Grim the Collier* which immediately follows Belphegor's assumption of the name Castiliano starts
with Grim complaining 'Every night
I dream I am a town top.' We would
expect '*vulgo*', meaning 'in the
common tongue' to be followed by
'devil', but perhaps Sir Toby, warned
by the proverb, makes the gesture of

horns instead. '*Vulgo*' could also
follow the noun to which it referred,
and if it does here, Shakespeare, by
saying the devil was Castiliano in the
common tongue, or to the common
people, is commenting on the popularity of the old play.
40 *Agueface.* This form of Sir Andrew's
name has led editors to emend '*vulgo*'
to '*volto*' and explain that Sir Toby is
telling Maria to put on a solemn face
like a Castilian, or Spaniard, to suit
with Sir Andrew's expression. Shakespeare is often, however, a little uncertain about the form of a character's name near the beginning of a
play, and there may be no joke
intended.
(stage direction) *Sir Andrew Aguecheek.* This name has been learnedly
explained as being from Spanish '*an-
drajo*', 'a despicable person', or
from '*aguicia chica*' meaning 'little
wit'. But to Shakespeare's audience it
would simply suggest the shaking
cheeks of cowardice.
44 *shrew.* This is usually explained as an
allusion to Maria's mouse-like size.
It could also be another unconscious
recollection of *Grim the Collier*, in
which the devil's human wife is an
untamable shrew called Marian and a
waiting-gentlewoman into the bargain.

SIR TOBY Accost, Sir Andrew, accost.

SIR ANDREW What's that?

SIR TOBY My niece's chambermaid.

SIR ANDREW Good Mistress Accost, I desire better ac-
50   quaintance.

MARIA My name is Mary, sir.

SIR ANDREW Good Mistress Mary Accost —

SIR TOBY (aside) You mistake, knight. 'Accost' is front
      her, board her, woo her, assail her.

SIR ANDREW (aside) By my troth, I would not undertake
      her in this company. Is that the meaning of 'accost'?

MARIA Fare you well, gentlemen.

SIR TOBY (aside) An thou let part so, Sir Andrew, would
      thou mightst never draw sword again.

60   SIR ANDREW An you part so, mistress, I would I might
      never draw sword again. Fair lady, do you think you
      have fools in hand?

MARIA Sir, I have not you by the hand.

SIR ANDREW Marry, but you shall have, and here's my
      hand.

MARIA Now, sir, 'Thought is free.' I pray you, bring your
      hand to the buttery bar and let it drink.

SIR ANDREW Wherefore, sweetheart? What's your meta-
      phor?

46 *accost.* Great play is made with the word '*accostare*' in *Gl'Ingannati*, but plays contemporary with *Twelfth Night* show that it was also fashionable in England, in the form 'accost', at the end of the sixteenth century. Like 'board' (line 54), it was a nautical metaphor, meaning 'address' or 'greet'. Sir Andrew takes both words in a more concrete sense than Sir Toby intends.

48 *chambermaid* (not a menial position; more like the modern 'lady companion')

58 *let part so* let her go thus (without ceremony)

62 *in hand* to deal with

64 *Marry* (a mild oath, originally 'By Mary')

66 *Thought is free.* This was the stock retort to 'Do you think I'm a fool?' and is one of many proverbs and stock phrases to do with fools and folly used in this play.

67 *buttery bar* (ledge in front of the hatch through which drink was handed out from the buttery, or store-room for liquor)

MARIA It's dry, sir. 70

SIR ANDREW Why, I think so. I am not such an ass, but
I can keep my hand dry. But what's your jest?

MARIA A dry jest, sir.

SIR ANDREW Are you full of them?

MARIA Ay, sir. I have them at my fingers' ends. Marry,
now I let go your hand, I am barren. *Exit*

SIR TOBY O knight, thou lack'st a cup of canary. When
did I see thee so put down?

SIR ANDREW Never in your life, I think, unless you see
canary put me down. Methinks sometimes I have no 80
more wit than a Christian or an ordinary man has; but I
am a great eater of beef, and I believe that does harm to
my wit.

SIR TOBY No question.

SIR ANDREW An I thought that, I'd forswear it. I'll ride
home tomorrow, Sir Toby.

SIR TOBY *Pourquoi*, my dear knight?

SIR ANDREW What is *pourquoi*? Do or not do? I would I
had bestowed that time in the tongues that I have in
fencing, dancing, and bear-baiting. O, had I but fol- 90
lowed the arts!

SIR TOBY Then hadst thou had an excellent head of hair.

70 *It's dry*. Maria means 'thirsty', but
hints at a supposed sign of impo-
tence. In *Othello* III.4.38 a moist
palm 'argues fruitfulness and liberal
heart'.

72 *keep my hand dry* (in allusion to the
proverb 'Fools have wit enough to
keep themselves dry')

73 *A dry jest*. Maria puns on the meanings 'stupid' and 'mocking, ironic'.

77 *canary* (a sweet wine, originally from
the Canary Islands)

78 *put down* defeated in repartee. Sir
Andrew plays with the literal
meaning.

81 *a Christian* (any normal man)
an ordinary man. Since *Christian* here
means 'ordinary' in the modern
sense, *an ordinary man* may mean an
eater of court rations. The ordinary
was the common table.

82 *eater of beef*. Medical writers of the
period argued that beef made men
low and melancholy, and 'beef-
witted' is an insult in *Troilus and
Cressida*, II.1.13.

87 *Pourquoi?* why? (French)

SIR ANDREW Why, would that have mended my hair?

SIR TOBY Past question, for thou seest it will not curl by nature.

SIR ANDREW But it becomes me well enough, does't not?

SIR TOBY Excellent, it hangs like flax on a distaff; and I hope to see a huswife take thee between her legs and spin it off.

100 SIR ANDREW Faith, I'll home tomorrow, Sir Toby. Your niece will not be seen, or if she be, it's four to one she'll none of me; the Count himself, here hard by, woos her.

SIR TOBY She'll none o'the Count; she'll not match above her degree, neither in estate, years, nor wit. I have heard her swear't. Tut, there's life in't, man.

SIR ANDREW I'll stay a month longer. I am a fellow o'the strangest mind i'the world. I delight in masques and revels sometimes altogether.

SIR TOBY Art thou good at these kickshawses, knight?

110 SIR ANDREW As any man in Illyria, whatsoever he be, under the degree of my betters, and yet I will not compare with an old man.

SIR TOBY What is thy excellence in a galliard, knight?

SIR ANDREW Faith, I can cut a caper.

SIR TOBY And I can cut the mutton to't.

94–5 *curl by nature*. The Folio reads 'coole my nature'. This skilful emendation by the eighteenth-century editor, Theobald, is confirmed by the pun on 'tongues' and 'tongs', which were pronounced alike in Elizabethan English, and by the antithesis between 'art' and 'nature'.

98 *huswife*. The Folio spelling preserves Sir Toby's pun. 'Housewife' (Middle English 'huswif') and 'hussy' had diverged in meaning, but not in pronunciation, at this time. The Elizabethans believed venereal disease and sexual excess to be among the causes of baldness.

109 *kickshawses* trifles (French *quelque-choses*)

111 *betters* social superiors

112 *old man* old hand, someone experienced

113 *galliard*. This was a lively five-step dance in which the fifth step was a leap, or caper. The puns in the next few lines may owe something to the quibbles on dancing terms in the epistle dedicatory in Rich's *Farewell to Military Profession*.

114 *caper*. Sir Toby quibbles on the meaning 'a spice to season mutton'.

SIR ANDREW And I think I have the back-trick, simply as strong as any man in Illyria.

SIR TOBY Wherefore are these things hid? Wherefore have these gifts a curtain before 'em? Are they like to take dust, like Mistress Mall's picture? Why dost thou not go to church in a galliard and come home in a coranto? My very walk should be a jig. I would not so much as make water but in a sink-apace. What dost thou mean? Is it a world to hide virtues in? I did think by the excellent constitution of thy leg it was formed under the star of a galliard.

SIR ANDREW Ay, 'tis strong, and it does indifferent well in a dun-coloured stock. Shall we set about some revels?

SIR TOBY What shall we do else? Were we not born under Taurus?

SIR ANDREW Taurus? That's sides and heart.

SIR TOBY No, sir, it is legs and thighs. Let me see thee caper. Ha! Higher! Ha! Ha! Excellent! *Exeunt*

116 *back-trick*. Sir Andrew means either the special backward leap called the *riccacciata*, or the reversed series of steps in a galliard; but the audience is meant to catch the sexual meaning of 'trick', following on 'mutton', which could mean 'a loose woman'.

120 *Mistress Mall's picture*. Paintings were frequently protected by curtains. Mistress Mall has been identified as Mary Fitton, a lady-in-waiting who became involved in a court scandal in 1601, and this identification would be probable if we could be sure that Malvolio is a portrait of Mary Fitton's guardian, Sir William Knollys (see Introduction, page 537). But there must have been quite a number of Malls whose pictures took dust – that is, who lost their good name – around 1600. If the allusion is literary, it could be to the sub-plot of Marston's *Jack Drum's Entertain-*

ment (1600), a play which has some interesting verbal parallels with *Twelfth Night*.

122 *coranto* (a fast, skipping dance)

123 *sink-apace*. The French 'cinquepas', or five-step dance, was very similar to the galliard. There is a quibble on 'sink' meaning 'sewer'. Beatrice quibbles differently with the word in *Much Ado About Nothing*, II.1.66–71.

126 *the star of a galliard* a dancing star (another recollection of Beatrice)

128 *dun-coloured stock* brown-coloured stocking. From what is known of Elizabethan handwriting, this is the most convincing of many emendations suggested for the Folio's *dam'd colour'd*.

130 *Taurus*. The twelve constellations, of which Taurus, the Bull, is one, were each held to govern a different part of the body.

1.4   *Enter Valentine, and Viola in man's attire*

VALENTINE If the Duke continue these favours towards
    you, Cesario, you are like to be much advanced. He hath
    known you but three days, and already you are no
    stranger.

VIOLA You either fear his humour or my negligence, that
    you call in question the continuance of his love. Is he
    inconstant, sir, in his favours?

VALENTINE No, believe me.

            Enter Orsino, Curio, and attendants

VIOLA I thank you. Here comes the Count.

10   ORSINO Who saw Cesario, ho?

VIOLA On your attendance, my lord, here.

ORSINO *(to Curio and attendants)*
    Stand you awhile aloof. (*To Viola*) Cesario,
    Thou knowest no less but all. I have unclasped
    To thee the book even of my secret soul.
    Therefore, good youth, address thy gait unto her.
    Be not denied access; stand at her doors,
    And tell them, there thy fixèd foot shall grow
    Till thou have audience.

VIOLA   Sure, my noble lord,
    If she be so abandoned to her sorrow

1.4.2 *Cesario*. Viola's assumed name
could come from Curio Gonzaga's
comedy, *Gl'Inganni*, published in
1592, in which the heroine disguises
as a page and assumes the name of
Cesare. This has been taken as evidence that when Manningham said
Twelfth Night resembled *Gl'Inganni* he
meant Gonzaga's play, and not *Gl'Ingannati*. But there are very few other
resemblances between Shakespeare's
play and Gonzaga's. In the Italian
and French tales based on *Gl'Ingannati* which Shakespeare certainly did

read, the heroine calls herself
Romulo or Romule because she is
from Rome, and in making Viola
call herself Cesario, which has the
same associations, Shakespeare may
be echoing these narrative versions.
5 *his humour* the changefulness of his
    disposition
6–7 *Is he inconstant* . . .? (asked with
    anxiety)
15 *address thy gait* direct your steps
16 *access*. This is accented on the second
    syllable.

As it is spoke, she never will admit me.   20

ORSINO

Be clamorous and leap all civil bounds
Rather than make unprofited return.

VIOLA

Say I do speak with her, my lord, what then?

ORSINO

O, then unfold the passion of my love.
Surprise her with discourse of my dear faith.
It shall become thee well to act my woes;
She will attend it better in thy youth
Than in a nuncio's of more grave aspect.

VIOLA

I think not so, my lord.

ORSINO   Dear lad, believe it.
For they shall yet belie thy happy years   30
That say thou art a man. Diana's lip
Is not more smooth and rubious. Thy small pipe
Is as the maiden's organ, shrill and sound,
And all is semblative a woman's part.
I know thy constellation is right apt
For this affair. Some four or five attend him –
All, if you will; for I myself am best
When least in company. Prosper well in this,
And thou shalt live as freely as thy lord,
To call his fortunes thine.

VIOLA   I'll do my best   40
To woo your lady. [Aside] Yet, a barful strife!
Whoe'er I woo, myself would be his wife.   Exeunt

---

28 *nuncio* messenger
aspect. This is accented on the second
syllable.
32 *rubious* ruby-red
pipe voice
33 *sound* unbroken
34 *semblative* like, resembling
part (a theatrical term; Shakespeare is
thinking of his company's boy actors)

35 *constellation* character (as decided by
the stars)
39–40 *And thou shalt live as freely as thy
lord . . . thine*. Orsino speaks more
truly than he knows.
41 *barful strife* struggle to overcome my
disinclination (to woo on Orsino's
behalf)

I.5   *Enter Maria and Feste the Clown*

MARIA Nay, either tell me where thou hast been, or I will
not open my lips so wide as a bristle may enter, in way of
thy excuse. My lady will hang thee for thy absence.

FESTE Let her hang me. He that is well hanged in this
world needs to fear no colours.

MARIA Make that good.

FESTE He shall see none to fear.

MARIA A good lenten answer! I can tell thee where that
saying was born, of 'I fear no colours'.

10 FESTE Where, good Mistress Mary?

MARIA In the wars; and that may you be bold to say in
your foolery.

FESTE Well, God give them wisdom that have it; and
those that are fools, let them use their talents.

MARIA Yet you will be hanged for being so long absent;
or to be turned away – is not that as good as a hanging
to you?

FESTE Many a good hanging prevents a bad marriage;
and for turning away, let summer bear it out.

20 MARIA You are resolute, then?

FESTE Not so neither, but I am resolved on two points.

I.5 (stage direction) *Feste*. 'Clown' in all
speech-headings of the 1623 text. The
name suggests a feast or festivity.

3 *hang thee* (an exaggeration, like 'You'll
be shot')

5 *fear no colours*. In using this catchphrase
for 'fear nothing' Feste puns on 'colours' and 'collars'. Maria in her reply
reverts to the original meaning of
'colours' in this phrase – 'military
standards'.

6 *Make that good* explain that

8 *good lenten answer* thin joke

13–14 *Well, God give them wisdom that
have it . . . talents.* Feste's special line
in jesting is a mock sanctimonious-

ness, which often gives his speech a
biblical flavour. Here there are
echoes of 'To him that hath shall be
given' and of the parable of the good
steward who put out his talent to
usury. Feste implies that his seeming
foolishness is a God-given insight.

16 *turned away* dismissed

19 *let summer bear it out* may the fine
weather hold! In the same way the
dismissed Fool in *Two Maids of More-
clacke* (printed 1608, acted earlier), a
part played by Armin, says 'the
summer's day is long, the winter's
nights be short'.

21 *points*. Maria seizes on the meaning

MARIA That if one break, the other will hold; or if both break, your gaskins fall.

FESTE Apt, in good faith, very apt. Well, go thy way, if Sir Toby would leave drinking, thou wert as witty a piece of Eve's flesh as any in Illyria.

MARIA Peace, you rogue, no more o'that. Here comes my lady. Make your excuse wisely, you were best. *Exit*
Enter Olivia with Malvolio and attendants

FESTE Wit, an't be thy will, put me into good fooling. Those wits that think they have thee do very oft prove 30 fools; and I that am sure I lack thee may pass for a wise man. For what says Quinapalus? 'Better a witty fool than a foolish wit'. God bless thee, lady!

OLIVIA Take the fool away.

FESTE Do you not hear, fellows? Take away the lady.

OLIVIA Go to, y'are a dry fool. I'll no more of you. Besides, you grow dishonest.

FESTE Two faults, madonna, that drink and good counsel will amend. For give the dry fool drink, then is the fool

'laces to hold up breeches', perhaps with a pun on *resolvo* (Latin), 'untie'.

23 *gaskins* loose breeches

24–6 *if Sir Toby . . . Illyria.* This gives a hint of the marriage which is to occur before the end of the play.

28 *you were best* it would be best for you (stage direction) *Malvolio.* It is just, but only just, conceivable that this name was suggested to Shakespeare by the name of Messer Agnol Malevolti, a lovesick character in the Italian play *Il Sacrificio*, which was acted as a form of curtain-raiser to *Gl'Ingannati*. It is if anything a little less conceivable that the name means 'I-want-Mall' and refers to Sir William Knollys's infatuation with Mary Fitton (see Introduction, page 537, and note on 1.3.120). Shakespeare could have made up this name, sug-

gestive of churlishness and misplaced desire, himself – influenced maybe by the expression '*mala volgia*' which occurs several times in Bandello's Italian version of the tale. But compare 'Benvolio' in *Romeo and Juliet*.

29 *Wit* intelligence

32 *Quinapalus.* Feste takes off the pedantry of quoting obscure authorities. This no longer gets a laugh, and the actor may be grateful for Leslie Hotson's suggestion that Feste here pretends to consult the carved head on his fool's stick, or bauble – even if he cannot accept the explanation that '*quinapalo*' is an italianate nonce-word for 'there on a stick'.

36 *Go to* (an expression of impatience, like our 'Come, come')
dry barren (of jests)

37 *dishonest* unreliable

40   not dry. Bid the dishonest man mend himself: if he
      mend, he is no longer dishonest; if he cannot, let the
      botcher mend him. Anything that's mended, is but
      patched: virtue that transgresses is but patched with
      sin; and sin that amends is but patched with virtue. If
      that this simple syllogism will serve, so; if it will not,
      what remedy? As there is no true cuckold but calamity,
      so beauty's a flower. The lady bade take away the fool;
      therefore I say again – take her away!

OLIVIA Sir, I bade them take away you.

50 FESTE Misprision in the highest degree! Lady, *cucullus
      non facit monachum*; that's as much to say as I wear not
      motley in my brain. Good madonna, give me leave to
      prove you a fool.

OLIVIA Can you do it?

FESTE Dexteriously, good madonna.

OLIVIA Make your proof.

FESTE I must catechize you for it, madonna. Good my
      mouse of virtue, answer me.

OLIVIA Well, sir, for want of other idleness, I'll bide your
60   proof.

FESTE Good madonna, why mourn'st thou?

40–42 *mend*. Feste plays with the meanings 'repair' and 'reform'.

42 *botcher* tailor who does repairs

45 *simple syllogism*. In this quibbling parody of formal deductive reasoning, Feste reminds Olivia that she must not expect too much of her fool, who is a mixture of vices and virtues like the rest of humanity; he then moves easily on to the suggestion that she should not expect her own grief to be unnaturally prolonged.

46 *no true cuckold but calamity*. Olivia seems, like Juliet, to be 'wedded to calamity'; but no one can mourn forever – nor should Olivia try to do

so, since while she tries her beauty will fade. There is probably a pun on *cuckold* and 'cockle' meaning 'weed'.

50 *Misprision* wrongful arrest (with a play on the more common meaning of 'misunderstanding')

50–51 *cucullus non facit monachum* the cowl does not make the monk (Latin proverb)

55 *Dexteriously* (a common Elizabethan variant of 'dexterously')

57–8 *Good my mouse of virtue*. Assuming his Sir Topas voice, Feste speaks to Olivia as a priest catechizing a small girl.

59 *idleness* pastime
    bide abide, wait for

OLIVIA Good fool, for my brother's death.

FESTE I think his soul is in hell, madonna.

OLIVIA I know his soul is in heaven, fool.

FESTE The more fool, madonna, to mourn for your
brother's soul, being in heaven. Take away the fool,
gentlemen.

OLIVIA What think you of this fool, Malvolio? Doth he
not mend?

MALVOLIO Yes, and shall do, till the pangs of death shake   70
him. Infirmity, that decays the wise, doth ever make the
better fool.

FESTE God send you, sir, a speedy infirmity for the better
increasing your folly. Sir Toby will be sworn that I am
no fox, but he will not pass his word for twopence that
you are no fool.

OLIVIA How say you to that, Malvolio?

MALVOLIO I marvel your ladyship takes delight in such a
barren rascal. I saw him put down the other day with an
ordinary fool that has no more brain than a stone. Look   80
you now, he's out of his guard already; unless you laugh
and minister occasion to him, he is gagged. I protest I
take these wise men, that crow so at these set kind of
fools, no better than the fools' zanies.

OLIVIA O, you are sick of self-love, Malvolio, and taste

69 *mend* improve
71–2 *Infirmity, that decays the wise, doth
ever make the better fool.* The bitterness
of Malvolio's reply is due to his
realization that Olivia has forgiven
Feste, and is not going to turn him
away.
75 *no fox* not cunning. By emphasizing
'I', Feste shows he is aware of Malvolio's scheming.
79 *put down* defeated in repartee
80 *ordinary fool ... stone.* If this is a
reference to Stone the Fool, a well-
known Elizabethan jester, *ordinary*

means 'of a tavern or eating-house'.
Stone is called a tavern fool in Ben
Jonson's *Volpone*, II.1.53–4.
81 *he's out of his guard* he has used up all
his retorts (a fencing metaphor)
82 *minister occasion* supply opportunity
83 *set* (not spontaneous)
84 *zanies.* These were the professional
fools' 'stooges' who fed them with
matter for jests and unsuccessfully
imitated their tricks. Olivia naturally
resents this description of her father
and herself.

with a distempered appetite. To be generous, guiltless,
and of free disposition, is to take those things for bird-
bolts that you deem cannon bullets. There is no slander
in an allowed fool, though he do nothing but rail; nor no
90   railing in a known discreet man, though he do nothing
but reprove.

FESTE Now Mercury endue thee with leasing, for thou
speak'st well of fools.

Enter Maria

MARIA Madam, there is at the gate a young gentleman
much desires to speak with you.

OLIVIA From the Count Orsino, is it?

MARIA I know not, madam. 'Tis a fair young man, and
well attended.

OLIVIA Who of my people hold him in delay?

100   MARIA Sir Toby, madam, your kinsman.

OLIVIA Fetch him off, I pray you, he speaks nothing but
madman. Fie on him! Go you, Malvolio. If it be a suit
from the Count, I am sick or not at home — what you
will, to dismiss it.   *Exit Malvolio*
Now you see, sir, how your fooling grows old and people
dislike it?

FESTE Thou hast spoke for us, madonna, as if thy eldest
son should be a fool; whose skull Jove cram with brains,
for — here he comes —

(Enter Sir Toby)

110   one of thy kin has a most weak *pia mater*.

87 *free* magnanimous. Like 'generous',
the word suggests good breeding.
87-8 *bird-bolts* short, blunt arrows
89 *allowed* licensed
90 *known discreet man*. Olivia, regaining
her equanimity, tactfully turns her
reproach into a compliment.
92 *Mercury endue thee with leasing* may the
god of deception make you a good
liar

98 *well attended* with several attendants
108 *Jove*. Here and elsewhere this is
almost certainly a substitution for
'God' in the play's original text, and
must have been made after 27 May
1606, when a statute was passed
against stage profanity.
110 *pia mater* brain (actually the mem-
brane covering the brain)

OLIVIA By mine honour, half drunk! What is he at the
gate, cousin?

SIR TOBY A gentleman.

OLIVIA A gentleman! What gentleman?

SIR TOBY 'Tis a gentleman here – a plague o'these pickle-
herring! (*To Feste*) How now, sot!

FESTE Good Sir Toby!

OLIVIA Cousin, cousin, how have you come so early by
this lethargy?

SIR TOBY Lechery! I defy lechery! There's one at the   120
gate.

OLIVIA Ay, marry, what is he?

SIR TOBY Let him be the devil an he will, I care not. Give
me faith, say I. Well, it's all one.

Exit Sir Toby, followed by Maria

OLIVIA What's a drunken man like, fool?

FESTE Like a drowned man, a fool, and a madman. One
draught above heat makes him a fool, the second mads
him, and a third drowns him.

OLIVIA Go thou and seek the crowner, and let him sit o'
my coz, for he's in the third degree of drink – he's   130
drowned. Go, look after him.

FESTE He is but mad yet, madonna, and the fool shall look
to the madman.   *Exit*

Enter Malvolio

MALVOLIO Madam, yond young fellow swears he will
speak with you. I told him you were sick; he takes on
him to understand so much, and therefore comes to
speak with you. I told him you were asleep; he seems to

---

115 *here*. The Folio 'heere' may represent
a stage direction which indicated a
hiccup.

116 *sot* fool

123 *an* if

124 *faith*. Strengthened more by faith
than works, Sir Toby lurches out to
defy the devil.

(stage direction) *followed by Maria*.
Maria's exit is not marked in the
Folio. The producer may prefer to
make her leave later with Feste.

127 *above heat* above a normal tempera-
ture. Drink was thought to heat the
blood.

129 *crowner* coroner

have a foreknowledge of that too, and therefore comes
to speak with you. What is to be said to him, lady? He's
140 fortified against any denial.

OLIVIA Tell him, he shall not speak with me.

MALVOLIO He's been told so; and he says he'll stand at
your door like a sheriff's post and be the supporter to a
bench, but he'll speak with you.

OLIVIA What kind o'man is he?

MALVOLIO Why, of mankind.

OLIVIA What manner of man?

MALVOLIO Of very ill manner; he'll speak with you, will
you or no.

150 OLIVIA Of what personage and years is he?

MALVOLIO Not yet old enough for a man, nor young
enough for a boy; as a squash is before 'tis a peascod, or
a codling when 'tis almost an apple. 'Tis with him in
standing water between boy and man. He is very well-
favoured, and he speaks very shrewishly. One would
think his mother's milk were scarce out of him.

OLIVIA Let him approach. Call in my gentlewoman.

MALVOLIO Gentlewoman, my lady calls. *Exit*

    Enter Maria

OLIVIA

Give me my veil. Come, throw it o'er my face.

160 We'll once more hear Orsino's embassy.

    Enter Viola

VIOLA The honourable lady of the house, which is she?

OLIVIA Speak to me, I shall answer for her. Your will?

VIOLA Most radiant, exquisite, and unmatchable beauty —

---

143 *sheriff's post.* A post was set up to
mark the house of the civic authority.
The custom persists in Scotland.

146 *of mankind* fierce. Leontes calls
Paulina 'A mankind witch' in *The
Winter's Tale*, II.3.67.

148–9 *will you or no* whether or not you
are willing

150 *personage* appearance

152 *a squash* an unripe peascod

153 *a codling* an unripe apple

153–4 *in standing water* at the turn of the
tide

154–5 *well-favoured* handsome

155 *shrewishly* sharply and like a woman

I pray you, tell me if this be the lady of the house, for I never saw her. I would be loath to cast away my speech; for besides that it is excellently well penned, I have taken great pains to con it. Good beauties, let me sustain no scorn. I am very comptible, even to the least sinister usage.

OLIVIA Whence came you, sir?   170

VIOLA I can say little more than I have studied, and that question's out of my part. Good gentle one, give me modest assurance if you be the lady of the house, that I may proceed in my speech.

OLIVIA Are you a comedian?

VIOLA No, my profound heart; and yet, by the very fangs of malice, I swear I am not that I play. Are you the lady of the house?

OLIVIA If I do not usurp myself, I am.

VIOLA Most certain, if you are she, you do usurp your-   180
self; for what is yours to bestow is not yours to reserve. But this is from my commission. I will on with my speech in your praise, and then show you the heart of my message.

OLIVIA Come to what is important in't. I forgive you the praise.

VIOLA Alas, I took great pains to study it, and 'tis poetical.

OLIVIA It is the more like to be feigned; I pray you, keep it in. I heard you were saucy at my gates, and allowed your

---

167 *con* learn by heart
168–9 *comptible, even to the least sinister usage* sensitive to even the least slight
173 *modest assurance* just enough assurance to satisfy me
175 *a comedian* an actor
176–7 *my profound heart . . . fangs of malice.* Viola acknowledges Olivia's penetration, but protests at her maliciousness.
179 *usurp* conterfeit. Viola takes the

word in a more literal sense, as meaning 'to exercise a power which is not yours by right'.
182 *from my commission* not part of my instructions
185 *forgive* excuse (from delivering)
188 *feigned.* This may be an echo of *As You Like It*, where Touchstone maintains (III.3.17–18) that 'the truest poetry is the most feigning'.

190   approach rather to wonder at you than to hear you. If you be not mad, be gone; if you have reason, be brief. 'Tis not that time of moon with me, to make one in so skipping a dialogue.

MARIA *(showing Viola the way out)* Will you hoist sail, sir? Here lies your way.

VIOLA No, good swabber, I am to hull here a little longer. Some mollification for your giant, sweet lady! Tell me your mind; I am a messenger.

OLIVIA Sure, you have some hideous matter to deliver, 200   when the courtesy of it is so fearful. Speak your office.

VIOLA It alone concerns your ear. I bring no overture of war, no taxation of homage. I hold the olive in my hand; my words are as full of peace as matter.

OLIVIA Yet you began rudely. What are you? What would you?

VIOLA The rudeness that hath appeared in me have I learned from my entertainment. What I am and what I would are as secret as maidenhead; to your ears divinity, to any others profanation.

210   OLIVIA Give us the place alone.

Maria and attendants withdraw

190–91 *If you be not mad . . . if you have reason.* The antithesis here is between partial sanity and complete sanity, or reason. There is no need to emend.

192 *'Tis not that time of moon with me* I am not sufficiently lunatic.

196 *swabber* deckhand. Viola retorts in Maria's own nautical language. *hull* drift with furled sails

197 *Some mollification for* pray pacify *giant* (used ironically of Maria)

197–8 *Tell me your mind.* Nearly all editors give this to Olivia. But Viola thinks she is on the point of being dismissed, and wants at least to be able to take back a message to Orsino. Olivia, however, is becoming increasingly interested in Viola, and asks her to deliver whatever message she has been entrusted with. This emboldens Viola to ask that all bystanders should be sent out of earshot.

200 *courtesy* preliminary greetings (said ironically, either of Viola's behaviour at the gate or of a scuffle at the door with Maria)
fearful alarming
Speak your office tell me what you have been entrusted with

201 *It alone concerns your ear* it is meant to be heard only by you

202 *taxation of homage* demand for money to be paid as an acknowledgement of vassalage

207 *entertainment* reception

208–9 *divinity . . . profanation* (the language of the religion of love)

We will hear this divinity. Now sir, what is your text?

VIOLA Most sweet lady —

OLIVIA A comfortable doctrine, and much may be said of
it. Where lies your text?

VIOLA In Orsino's bosom.

OLIVIA In his bosom! In what chapter of his bosom?

VIOLA To answer by the method, in the first of his heart.

OLIVIA O, I have read it; it is heresy. Have you no more to
say?

VIOLA Good madam, let me see your face.　　　　　　　　220

OLIVIA Have you any commission from your lord to ne-
gotiate with my face? You are now out of your text; but
we will draw the curtain and show you the picture. Look
you, sir, such a one I was this present. Is't not well
done?

VIOLA Excellently done – if God did all.

OLIVIA 'Tis in grain, sir, 'twill endure wind and weather.

VIOLA

'Tis beauty truly blent, whose red and white
Nature's own sweet and cunning hand laid on.
Lady you are the cruellest she alive,　　　　　　　　230
If you will lead these graces to the grave,
And leave the world no copy.

OLIVIA O, sir, I will not be so hard-hearted. I will give
out divers schedules of my beauty. It shall be inven-
toried, and every particle and utensil labelled to my will.
As, item: two lips, indifferent red; item: two grey eyes,
with lids to them; item: one neck, one chin, and so forth.
Were you sent hither to praise me?

213 *comfortable* comforting
217 *by the method* in the same style
222 *are now out of your text* have changed
the subject
224 *such a one I was this present* this is a
recent portrait of me. Olivia throws
back her veil as if she were revealing
a curtained picture of herself.
227 *'Tis in grain* the colour is fast

228 *blent* blended. Viola keeps up the
image of a painting.
229 *cunning* skilful
232 *copy.* Viola means a child, but Olivia
pounces on the literal meaning.
234 *divers schedules* various lists
235 *labelled* attached as a codicil
236 *indifferent* fairly
238 *praise* appraise, estimate

VIOLA

I see you what you are, you are too proud.
240 But if you were the devil, you are fair.
My lord and master loves you – O, such love
Could be but recompensed, though you were crowned
The nonpareil of beauty!

OLIVIA   How does he love me?

VIOLA

With adorations, fertile tears,
With groans that thunder love, with sighs of fire.

OLIVIA

Your lord does know my mind, I cannot love him.
Yet I suppose him virtuous, know him noble,
Of great estate, of fresh and stainless youth,
In voices well divulged, free, learned, and valiant,
250 And in dimension and the shape of nature
A gracious person. But yet I cannot love him.
He might have took his answer long ago.

VIOLA

If I did love you in my master's flame,
With such a suffering, such a deadly life,
In your denial I would find no sense;
I would not understand it.

OLIVIA   Why, what would you?

VIOLA

Make me a willow cabin at your gate,
And call upon my soul within the house;
Write loyal cantons of contemnèd love
260 And sing them loud even in the dead of night;

243 *The nonpareil of beauty* the one un-
matched in beauty
244 *fertile* copious
249 *In voices well divulged* well spoken of
free well bred. Orsino has the
courtier's, scholar's, and soldier's
qualities, and so represents, like
Hamlet, the Renaissance ideal.

251 *A gracious person* endowed with a
good physique
257 *willow* (associated with rejected love,
as in the willow song in *Othello*)
258 *my soul* (Olivia)
259 *cantons* songs (from Italian '*canzone*',
by confusion with 'canto' from Latin
'*cantus*')

Hallow your name to the reverberate hills
And make the babbling gossip of the air
Cry out 'Olivia!' O, you should not rest
Between the elements of air and earth,
But you should pity me.

OLIVIA   You might do much.
What is your parentage?

VIOLA
Above my fortunes, yet my state is well.
I am a gentleman.

OLIVIA   Get you to your lord.
I cannot love him. Let him send no more –
Unless, perchance, you come to me again   270
To tell me how he takes it. Fare you well.
I thank you for your pains. Spend this for me.

VIOLA
I am no fee'd post, lady; keep your purse.
My master, not myself, lacks recompense.
Love make his heart of flint, that you shall love,
And let your fervour like my master's be
Placed in contempt. Farewell, fair cruelty!   *Exit*

OLIVIA
'What is your parentage?'
'Above my fortunes, yet my state is well.
I am a gentleman.' I'll be sworn thou art.   280
Thy tongue, thy face, thy limbs, actions, and spirit
Do give thee fivefold blazon. Not too fast! soft, soft –
Unless the master were the man. How now?
Even so quickly may one catch the plague?

261 *Hallow.* The Folio spelling for 'halloo' is kept, because it conveys also the idea of 'bless'
262 *babbling gossip* (Echo personified)
265 *But* unless
267 *state* social standing

273 *fee'd post* messenger to be tipped
275 *Love make* may the god of love make *that you shall love* (the man) whom you will love
282 *blazon* a coat of arms. Cesario's bearing declares his high birth.

Methinks I feel this youth's perfections,
With an invisible and subtle stealth,
To creep in at mine eyes. Well, let it be!
What ho, Malvolio!

   Enter Malvolio

MALVOLIO
Here, madam, at your service.

OLIVIA
290 Run after that same peevish messenger,
The County's man. He left this ring behind him,
Would I or not. Tell him, I'll none of it.
Desire him not to flatter with his lord,
Nor hold him up with hopes; I am not for him.
If that the youth will come this way tomorrow,
I'll give him reasons for't. Hie thee, Malvolio!

MALVOLIO
Madam, I will.   *Exit*

OLIVIA
I do I know not what, and fear to find
Mine eye too great a flatterer for my mind.
300 Fate, show thy force; ourselves we do not owe.
What is decreed must be, and be this so.   *Exit*

II.1   *Enter Antonio and Sebastian*

ANTONIO Will you stay no longer? Nor will you not that
    I go with you?

285 *perfections* (pronounced as four syllables)

291 *County.* This was a common Elizabethan form of 'count', keeping the two syllables of the Old French 'conté'.

292 *Would I or not* whether I wanted it or not

293 *flatter with* encourage

299 *Mine eye too great a flatterer for my mind* my eye will betray my reason into thinking too well of him (Cesario)

300 *owe* own, control

II.1.1–2 *will you not that I go* do you not want me to go

SEBASTIAN By your patience, no. My stars shine darkly
over me. The malignancy of my fate might perhaps
distemper yours; therefore I shall crave of you your
leave, that I may bear my evils alone. It were a bad recompense for your love to lay any of them on you.

ANTONIO Let me yet know of you whither you are bound.

SEBASTIAN No, sooth, sir; my determinate voyage is mere
extravagancy. But I perceive in you so excellent a touch   10
of modesty, that you will not extort from me what I am
willing to keep in; therefore it charges me in manners
the rather to express myself. You must know of me
then, Antonio, my name is Sebastian which I called
Roderigo. My father was that Sebastian of Messaline
whom I know you have heard of. He left behind him
myself and a sister, both born in an hour – if the
heavens had been pleased, would we had so ended! But
you, sir, altered that, for some hour before you took me
from the breach of the sea was my sister drowned.   20

ANTONIO Alas the day!

SEBASTIAN A lady, sir, though it was said she much resembled me, was yet of many accounted beautiful. But
though I could not with such estimable wonder over-far
believe that, yet thus far I will boldly publish her: she

3 *By your patience* if you will be so
forbearing
4 *malignancy* evil influence (an astrological term)
5 *distemper* disorder, disturb
9 *sooth* indeed
9–10 *my determinate voyage is mere extravagancy* I only intend to wander
12–13 *it charges me in manners the rather to
express myself* courtesy obliges me all
the more to reveal who I am
15 *Messaline.* This is probably the
modern Marseilles. The inhabitants
of Marseilles and of Illyria are mentioned together ('*Massiliensis, Hilu-

rios*') in a speech about one twin looking for another twin in Plautus's *Menaechmi*, line 235. Shakespeare could
also have had the word suggested to
him by the occurrence of Messilina
as a name in the story preceding
'Apolonius and Silla' in Rich's *Farewell to Military Profession.*
17 *in an hour* at the same time
20 *breach* surf, breakers
24 *estimable* appreciative. Sebastian
means that he could not, in modesty,
go so far as to marvel at the beauty
of his twin sister.
25 *publish* speak openly of

bore a mind that envy could not but call fair. She is
drowned already, sir, with salt water, though I seem to
drown her remembrance again with more.

ANTONIO Pardon me, sir, your bad entertainment.

30 SEBASTIAN O good Antonio, forgive me your trouble.

ANTONIO If you will not murder me for my love, let me
be your servant.

SEBASTIAN If you will not undo what you have done –
that is, kill him whom you have recovered – desire it not.
Fare ye well at once; my bosom is full of kindness, and I
am yet so near the manners of my mother that, upon the
least occasion more, mine eyes will tell tales of me. I am
bound to the Count Orsino's court. Farewell.   *Exit*

ANTONIO
The gentleness of all the gods go with thee!
40 I have many enemies in Orsino's court,
Else would I very shortly see thee there –
But come what may, I do adore thee so
That danger shall seem sport, and I will go!   *Exit*

II.2   *Enter Viola and Malvolio at several doors*

MALVOLIO Were not you even now with the Countess
Olivia?

VIOLA Even now, sir; on a moderate pace I have since
arrived but hither.

MALVOLIO She returns this ring to you, sir. You might
have saved me my pains, to have taken it away yourself.

---

28 *with more* with more salt water (that
is, with tears)

29 *entertainment* treatment as my guest

31 *murder me for my love* cause me to die
of grief at leaving you. Sebastian's
reply is just as exaggerated: he would
rather die than let Antonio demean
himself by waiting on him.

34 *desire* request

35 *kindness* tender feelings

37 *tell tales of me* betray my feelings (by
tears)

II.2 (stage direction) *several doors* separate
entrances. The doors are those leading on to the stage or acting area;
the scene itself is unlocalized.

1 *even* just

4 *arrived but hither* come only this far

She adds, moreover, that you should put your lord into
a desperate assurance she will none of him; and one
thing more, that you be never so hardy to come again in
his affairs – unless it be to report your lord's taking of   10
this. Receive it so.

VIOLA She took the ring of me, I'll none of it.

MALVOLIO Come, sir, you peevishly threw it to her, and
her will is it should be so returned. If it be worth stooping for, there it lies in your eye; if not, be it his that finds
it.   *Exit*

VIOLA

I left no ring with her; what means this lady?
Fortune forbid my outside have not charmed her!
She made good view of me, indeed so much
That – methought – her eyes had lost her tongue,   20
For she did speak in starts, distractedly.
She loves me, sure, the cunning of her passion
Invites me in this churlish messenger.
None of my lord's ring? Why, he sent her none.
I am the man! If it be so – as 'tis –
Poor lady, she were better love a dream.
Disguise, I see thou art a wickedness
Wherein the pregnant enemy does much.
How easy is it for the proper false
In women's waxen hearts to set their forms.   30
Alas, our frailty is the cause, not we,

8 *desperate assurance* certainty beyond all
hope
she will none of him she wants nothing
to do with him
12 *She took the ring of me* (a quick-witted
lie to conceal Olivia's indiscretion
from her steward)
of from
15 *in your eye* where you can see it
18 *charmed* cast a spell over
19 *made good view of me* examined me
closely
20 *lost* lost touch with, failed to coordi-
nate with
22 *cunning* craftiness
28 *the pregnant enemy* (Satan)
pregnant wily
29 *proper false* handsome deceivers
31–2 *Alas, our frailty is the cause, not we,* |
For such as we are made, if such we be.
These lines continue the idea of something being formed or made, like a
wax seal: 'Alas, women's frailty is
the cause, not women themselves,
for what happens to us – if we are
like that.' The lines make reasonable
sense, but are not easy to get across

For such as we are made, if such we be.
How will this fadge? My master loves her dearly;
And I, poor monster, fond as much on him;
And she, mistaken, seems to dote on me.
What will become of this? As I am man,
My state is desperate for my master's love.
As I am woman – now, alas the day,
What thriftless sighs shall poor Olivia breathe!
40   O time, thou must untangle this, not I!
It is too hard a knot for me t'untie.   *Exit*

II.3   *Enter Sir Toby and Sir Andrew*

SIR TOBY Approach, Sir Andrew. Not to be abed after
midnight, is to be up betimes, and *diluculo surgere*,
thou knowest –

SIR ANDREW Nay, by my troth, I know not; but I know
to be up late is to be up late.

SIR TOBY A false conclusion! I hate it as an unfilled can.
To be up after midnight and to go to bed then is early;
so that to go to bed after midnight is to go to bed betimes. Does not our lives consist of the four elements?

10   SIR ANDREW Faith, so they say; but I think it rather con-
sists of eating and drinking.

SIR TOBY Thou'rt a scholar. Let us therefore eat and
drink. Marian, I say! A stoup of wine!

                    Enter Feste

SIR ANDREW Here comes the fool, i'faith.

in a theatre, and producers may
prefer the emendation accepted by
many editors: *Alas, our frailty is the
cause, not we!* | *For such as we are
made of, such we be.*
33 *fadge* turn out
34 *monster* (neither man nor woman)
   fond dote
39 *thriftless* wasted, useless

II.3.2 *betimes* early
   diluculo surgere. The adage *dīlūculo
   sūrgere salūberrimum est'* ('to get up at
   dawn is most healthy') occurs in
   Lilly's Latin Grammar, a popular
   sixteenth-century schoolbook.
4 *troth* faith
9 *four elements* (the basic components of
   the world – fire, air, water, earth)
13 *stoup* (pronounced 'stoop') two-pint
   jug

FESTE How now, my hearts! Did you never see the picture of We Three?

SIR TOBY Welcome, ass! Now let's have a catch.

SIR ANDREW By my troth, the fool has an excellent breast.
I had rather than forty shillings I had such a leg, and so
sweet a breath to sing, as the fool has. In sooth, thou   20
wast in very gracious fooling last night, when thou
spok'st of Pigrogromitus, of the Vapians passing the
equinoctial of Queubus. 'Twas very good, i'faith. I sent
thee sixpence for thy leman, hadst it?

FESTE I did impetticoat thy gratillity; for Malvolio's nose
is no whipstock, my lady has a white hand, and the
Myrmidons are no bottle-ale houses.

---

16 *We Three*. Trick pictures, or anamor-
phoses, with this title were common
at the time. One such picture shows
a fool's head if viewed the right way
up and another fool's head if viewed
upside down. The spectator who
asked 'Where's the third?' would be
invited to view the picture from the
side, where it took on the form of a
donkey, and would then be asked (in
Bottom's words) 'You see an ass
head of your own, do you?' Hence
Sir Toby's retort of 'Welcome, ass!'

17 *catch* round (a song with a continuous
melody that could be divided into
parts, each harmonizing with the
others)

18 *breast* singing voice

19 *leg* (the bow with which Feste begins
and ends his songs)

21 *gracious* talented, inspired

22 *Pigrogromitus, of the Vapians passing
the equinoctial of Queubus*. Feste's astronomical patter is mock-learning of
the kind he later displays as Sir
Topas. The names are probably
Shakespeare's invention.

24 *leman* sweetheart

25 *impetticoat* (for Folio 'impeticos')
pocket (in reference to the fool's long

coat; a nonce-word) *gratillity* little tip
(another nonce-word, probably a di-
minutive formed from 'gratuity')

25-7 *Malvolio's nose is no whipstock, my
lady has a white hand, and the Myrmidons
are no bottle-ale houses*. No explanation
satisfactorily connects these three
statements. If *whipstock* means a
wooden post or handle, Feste is
saying Malvolio's nose is sensitive
enough to smell out Sir Andrew's
tip. If it means 'the piece of wood
attached to a ship's tiller', he is saying
much the same thing – that Malvolio
can't be led by the nose. One attractive suggestion is that Malvolio, by
reason of his haughty hooked nose
(not straight like a whipstock), seems
destined for greatness, and Olivia is
ripe for marriage, a meaning of
'white hand' found in several Shakespeare plays; but the conclusion, that
Malvolio is an upstart who as a
Count will abolish cakes and ale, is
less convincing. *My lady* could be
Feste's leman, who likes to be taken
to the most expensive inns such as
the Myrmidons (perhaps with a pun
on 'Mermaidens').

SIR ANDREW Excellent! Why, this is the best fooling,
when all is done. Now, a song!

30 SIR TOBY Come on, there is sixpence for you. Let's have a
song.

SIR ANDREW There's a testril of me, too. If one knight
give a —

FESTE Would you have a love song, or a song of good life?

SIR TOBY A love song! A love song!

SIR ANDREW Ay, ay, I care not for good life.

FESTE (*sings*)

     O mistress mine! Where are you roaming?
     O, stay and hear: your true love's coming,
        That can sing both high and low.
40   Trip no further, pretty sweeting;
     Journeys end in lovers meeting,
        Every wise man's son doth know.

SIR ANDREW Excellent good, i'faith.

SIR TOBY Good, good.

FESTE (*sings*)

     What is love? 'Tis not hereafter;
     Present mirth hath present laughter,
        What's to come is still unsure.
     In delay there lies no plenty —

32 *testril* sixpence (a variant of 'tester')

33 *give a —*. As there is no point here in
an interruption, it appears that a line
was passed over by the compositor.

34 *a song of good life* a drinking song. But
Sir Andrew takes it to be a moral
song or hymn.

37 *O mistress mine!* Two instrumental versions of a tune with this title are
known: one for a small band, by
Thomas Morley, was published in
1599 and the other, for keyboard, by
William Byrd, was published in 1619.
A modern transcription of Morley's

air is given on page 556. Both pieces
may be based on a popular Elizabethan tune to which Armin also
sang Shakespeare's lyric. But we
cannot be sure that Shakespeare intended to use this tune, which also
occurs in an early seventeenth-century commonplace book as the setting for a quite different lyric.

40 *sweeting* darling

42 *Every wise man's son* (in allusion to the
saying that wise men have fools for
their sons)

Then come kiss me, sweet and twenty,
        Youth's a stuff will not endure.   50

SIR ANDREW A mellifluous voice, as I am true knight.

SIR TOBY A contagious breath.

SIR ANDREW Very sweet and contagious, i'faith.

SIR TOBY To hear by the nose, it is dulcet in contagion.
    But shall we make the welkin dance indeed? Shall we
    rouse the night-owl in a catch that will draw three souls
    out of one weaver? Shall we do that?

SIR ANDREW An you love me, let's do't. I am dog at a
    catch.

FESTE By'r lady, sir, and some dogs will catch well.   60

SIR ANDREW Most certain. Let our catch be 'Thou
    knave'.

FESTE 'Hold thy peace, thou knave', knight? I shall be
    constrained in't to call thee knave, knight.

SIR ANDREW 'Tis not the first time I have constrained
    one to call me knave. Begin, fool; it begins (*he sings*)
        'Hold thy peace –'

52 *contagious*. Sir Toby means 'catchy', but Sir Andrew's 'sweet and contagious' sounds so odd, in view of the usual meaning of 'contagious' – 'infectious, evil smelling' – that Sir Toby goes on to echo Sir Andrew ('dulcet in contagion') and say that a phrase like this could be used only if we heard with our noses. Shakespeare may have remembered an equally forced use of 'contagious' in 'Apolonius and Silla': 'But Silla, the further that she saw herself bereaved of all hope ever any more to see her beloved Apolonius, so much the more contagious were her passions . . .' (*Elizabethan Love Stories*, ed. T. J. B. Spencer, p. 100; see Further Reading).

55 *welkin* sky

56–7 *three souls out of one weaver*. Sir Toby boasts that their catch will not only make the sky dance, but will have three times the usual effect of music on a pious weaver. Weavers were often Calvinist refugees from the Low Countries, who would be in ecstasy on hearing a well-sung psalm; and someone in an ecstasy appears to be without movement, feeling, or thought, and so without the three souls – of motion, feeling, and sense – which man was held to possess by the medieval philosophers.

58 *An* if

    dog at clever at

63 *Hold thy peace*. A tune for this round is given on page 557. The effect when it is sung is that of a brawl, with each singer calling the others 'knave'.

FESTE I shall never begin if I hold my peace.

SIR ANDREW Good, i'faith. Come, begin!

Catch sung. Enter Maria

70   MARIA What a caterwauling do you keep here! If my lady
have not called up her steward Malvolio and bid him
turn you out of doors, never trust me.

SIR TOBY My lady's a – Cataian; we are – politicians;
Malvolio's a – Peg-a-Ramsey; and (*he sings*)
        Three merry men be we!
Am not I consanguineous? Am I not of her blood?
Tilly-vally! 'Lady'! (*He sings*)
        There dwelt a man in Babylon, lady, lady –

FESTE Breshrew me, the knight's in admirable fooling.

80   SIR ANDREW Ay, he does well enough if he be disposed,
and so do I too. He does it with a better grace, but I do
it more natural.

73 *Cataian* Chinese. Olivia is inscrutable.
politicians schemers

74 *Peg-a-Ramsey*. A ballad about a jealous, spying wife was sung to this popular Elizabethan dance tune, so Sir Toby, if he is not so drunk that he is talking nonsense, may mean that Malvolio is keeping a watchful eye on the 'politicians'.

75 *Three merry men*. We have the words, but not the music, of several Elizabethan songs ending with this phrase. The music given on page 558 is that of a round in a collection made by the early seventeenth-century composer William Lawes, of which the final line was originally 'And three merry boys, and three merry boys, and three merry boys are we.'

77 *Tilly-vally!* It has been suggested that this is another snatch of song, as a tune has been found with the title 'Tilly-vally, any money'. But it is more probably an exclamation of impatience on Sir Toby's part.

78 *There dwelt a man in Babylon*. In mocking Maria's use of 'lady', Sir Toby recalls a ballad about Susanna and the Elders which has this word for its refrain. The first stanza is quoted in Percy's *Reliques of Ancient English Poetry*, ii. x:

There dwelt a man in Babylon
    Of reputation great by fame;
He took to wife a fair woman,
    Susanna she was called by name:
A woman fair and virtuous;
        Lady, lady:
Why should we not of her learn thus
        To live godly?

79 *Beshrew me* curse me

81-2 *grace . . . natural*. By making use of the theological distinction between grace and nature, Sir Andrew inadvertently calls himself a 'natural' fool.

SIR TOBY (*sings*)
> O' the twelfth day of December –

MARIA For the love o'God, peace!

Enter Malvolio

MALVOLIO My masters, are you mad? Or what are you? Have you no wit, manners, nor honesty, but to gabble like tinkers at this time of night? Do ye make an alehouse of my lady's house, that ye squeak out your coziers' catches without any mitigation or remorse of voice? Is there no respect of place, persons, nor time in   90
you?

SIR TOBY We did keep time, sir, in out catches. Sneck up!

MALVOLIO Sir Toby, I must be round with you. My lady bade me tell you that, though she harbours you as her kinsman, she's nothing allied to your disorders. If you can separate yourself and your misdemeanours, you are welcome to the house. If not, an it would please you to take leave of her, she is very willing to bid you farewell.

SIR TOBY (*sings*)
> Farewell, dear heart, since I must needs be gone –

MARIA Nay, good Sir Toby!   100

---

83 *O' the twelfth day of December.* No song beginning with these words is known. Sir Toby may be misquoting the ballad of 'Musselburgh Field', which starts 'On the tenth day of December'. Or his words could be a misquotation of the first line of the carol called 'The Twelve Days of Christmas', which traditionally begins 'On the twelfth day. . .' and not as it is usually sung nowadays 'On the first day. . .'

86 *wit* sense
honesty decency

87 *tinkers.* These were noted for their songs and their drinking. In *Egregious Popish Impostures* (1603), Richard Harsnet writes about a 'master setter of catches or rounds, used to be sung by tinkers as they sit by the fire with a pot of good ale between their legs'.

89 *coziers* cobblers (who also sang at their work)

89–90 *mitigation or remorse of voice* lowering your voices out of consideration

92 *Sneck up!* buzz off! Originally meaning 'Go and be hanged', this survives in both American and British dialects with the meaning 'Make yourself scarce!'

93 *round* blunt

99 *Farewell, dear heart.* Sir Toby and Feste sing their own version of a song which is given in Robert Jones's *First Book of Airs*, 1600. See page 559.

FESTE (*sings*)
> His eyes do show his days are almost done –

MALVOLIO Is't even so!

SIR TOBY (*sings*)
> But I will never die –

FESTE (*sings*)
> Sir Toby, there you lie –

MALVOLIO This is much credit to you!

SIR TOBY (*sings*)
> Shall I bid him go?

FESTE (*sings*)
> What an if you do?

SIR TOBY (*sings*)
> Shall I bid him go and spare not?

FESTE (*sings*)
> O no, no, no, no, you dare not!

110 SIR TOBY Out o'tune, sir, ye lie. (*To Malvolio*) Art any more than a steward? Dost thou think, because thou art virtuous, there shall be no more cakes and ale?

FESTE Yes, by Saint Anne, and ginger shall be hot i'the mouth, too.

SIR TOBY Th'art i'the right. (*To Malvolio*) Go, sir, rub your chain with crumbs. A stoup of wine, Maria!

MALVOLIO Mistress Mary, if you prized my lady's favour at anything more than contempt, you would not give means for this uncivil rule. She shall know of it, by this
120 hand!   *Exit*

---

104 *there you lie*. Probably Sir Toby has fallen over.

110 *Out o'tune* (a way of refuting Feste's denial and taking his 'dare')

112 *cakes and ale*. These were traditional at Church feasts, and so repugnant to Puritans, who would also be offended at the mention of Saint Anne, mother of the Virgin Mary.

113 *ginger*. This was a favourite Eliza-bethan spice, and the sheep-shearing feast in *The Winter's Tale* calls for a root or two of ginger. Robert Armin liked ginger washed down with ale.

116 *chain* chain of office. There is a reference to this method of cleaning such insignia in Webster's *The Duchess of Malfi*, III.2. Sir Toby is reminding Malvolio of his station in Olivia's household.

MARIA Go, shake your ears.

SIR ANDREW 'Twere as good a deed as to drink when a man's a-hungry, to challenge him the field and then to break promise with him and make a fool of him.

SIR TOBY Do't, knight, I'll write thee a challenge; or I'll deliver thy indignation to him by word of mouth.

MARIA Sweet Sir Toby, be patient for tonight. Since the youth of the Count's was today with my lady, she is much out of quiet. For Monsieur Malvolio, let me alone with him. If I do not gull him into a nayword, and make   130
him a common recreation, do not think I have wit enough to lie straight in my bed. I know I can do it.

SIR TOBY Possess us, possess us, tell us something of him.

MARIA Marry, sir, sometimes he is a kind of puritan –

SIR ANDREW O, if I thought that, I'd beat him like a dog.

SIR TOBY What, for being a puritan? Thy exquisite reason, dear knight?

SIR ANDREW I have no exquisite reason for't, but I have reason good enough.

MARIA The devil a puritan that he is, or anything, con-   140
stantly, but a time-pleaser, an affectioned ass that cons state without book and utters it by great swathes; the best persuaded of himself, so crammed, as he thinks, with excellencies, that it is his grounds of faith that all

---

121 *shake your ears* (a contemptuous dismissal, equivalent to calling Malvolio a donkey)

123 *challenge him the field* challenge him to a duel. The suggestion shows Sir Andrew's ill breeding, as it was a social solecism to challenge an inferior.

130 *gull* trick
nayword byword

131 *common recreation* source of amusement for everyone

133 *Possess us* give us the facts

136 *exquisite* (a difficult word for the drunken knights to get their tongues

round. Shakespeare puts it twice in the mouth of Cassio, to mark his increasing drunkenness, in *Othello*, II.3.18, 93)

141 *time-pleaser* time-server
affectioned affected

141-2 *cons state without book* learns high-sounding phrases by heart

142 *swathes*. A swathe is the grass cut at a single sweep of a scythe. The image is of a huge circuitous period falling like hay about the listener's ears.

142-3 *the best persuaded of himself* thinking better of himself than anyone else does

that look on him love him – and on that vice in him will my revenge find notable cause to work.

SIR TOBY What wilt thou do?

MARIA I will drop in his way some obscure epistles of love; wherein, by the colour of his beard, the shape of his leg, the manner of his gait, the expressure of his eye, forehead, and complexion, he shall find himself most feelingly personated. I can write very like my lady, your niece; on a forgotten matter we can hardly make distinction of our hands.

SIR TOBY Excellent! I smell a device.

SIR ANDREW I have't in my nose too.

SIR TOBY He shall think by the letters that thou wilt drop that they come from my niece, and that she's in love with him.

MARIA My purpose is indeed a horse of that colour.

SIR ANDREW And your horse now would make him an ass.

MARIA Ass, I doubt not.

SIR ANDREW O, 'twill be admirable!

MARIA Sport royal, I warrant you. I know my physic will work with him. I will plant you two, and let the fool make a third, where he shall find the letter. Observe his construction of it. For this night, to bed, and dream on the event. Farewell.   *Exit*

SIR TOBY Good night, Penthesilea.

SIR ANDREW Before me, she's a good wench.

150 *expressure* expression
152 *feelingly personated* vividly described
163 *Ass* (Maria puns on 'as' and 'ass')
165 *physic* medicine (to purge Malvolio's conceit)
166-7 *let the fool make a third.* See Introduction, pages 528-9, on Shakespeare's probable change of plan here. It is odd that Feste himself says nothing in this part of the scene. Producers have sometimes made him exit in the wake of Malvolio, or even fall asleep until the end of the scene.
168 *construction* interpretation
170 *Penthesilea* (an Amazonian queen. Maria's spirit is out of all proportion to her size.)

SIR TOBY She's a beagle true bred, and one that adores
me – what o'that?

SIR ANDREW I was adored once, too.

SIR TOBY Let's to bed, knight. Thou hadst need send for
more money.

SIR ANDREW If I cannot recover your niece, I am a foul
way out.

SIR TOBY Send for money, knight. If thou hast her not
i'the end, call me cut.   180

SIR ANDREW If I do not, never trust me, take it how you
will.

SIR TOBY Come, come, I'll go burn some sack, 'tis too
late to go to bed now. Come, knight; come, knight.

Exeunt

Enter Orsino, Viola, Curio, and others   II.4

ORSINO
Give me some music! Now, good morrow, friends!
Now, good Cesario, but that piece of song,
That old and antique song we heard last night.
Methought it did relieve my passion much,
More than light airs and recollected terms
Of these most brisk and giddy-pacèd times.
Come, but one verse.

172 *beagle* (a small but keen and intelligent hound)

177 *recover* get hold of

178 *out* out of pocket

180 *cut* (a term of contempt, in reference
to a cut horse, or gelding)

183 *burn some sack* warm and spice some
Spanish wine

II.4.1 *good morrow* good morning

2 *good Cesario*. It has been suggested that
Shakespeare altered this scene to

make Feste the singer, and that this
opening indicates his original inten-
tion of having Viola sing the song.
But Orsino may simply be inviting
Viola to listen to the song with him.
See Introduction, pages 526–8.

3 *antique* strange and old-world

5 *recollected terms* studied phrases. New-
fangled words accompanied new-
fangled music: 'airs' were all the rage
around 1601.

CURIO He is not here, so please your lordship, that should
sing it.

10   ORSINO Who was it?

CURIO Feste the jester, my lord, a fool that the Lady
Olivia's father took much delight in. He is about the
house.

ORSINO Seek him out, and play the tune the while.

Exit Curio

Music plays

Come hither, boy. If ever thou shalt love,
In the sweet pangs of it, remember me.
For such as I am, all true lovers are:
Unstaid and skittish in all motions else,
Save in the constant image of the creature
20   That is beloved. How dost thou like this tune?

VIOLA
It gives a very echo to the seat
Where love is throned.

ORSINO   Thou dost speak masterly.
My life upon't, young though thou art, thine eye
Hath stayed upon some favour that it loves.
Hath it not, boy?

VIOLA   A little, by your favour.

ORSINO
What kind of woman is't?

VIOLA   Of your complexion.

ORSINO
She is not worth thee, then. What years, i'faith?

VIOLA
About your years, my lord.

18 *Unstaid* unsteady
   motions emotions
21–2 *It gives a very echo to the seat | Where
   love is throned* it awakens an immediate
   response in the heart
22 *masterly* from experience, as one who
   has mastered the art of love

24 *favour* face
25 *by your favour.* A slight stress on *your*
   shows that Viola is playing with the
   meanings 'if you please' and 'like
   you in feature'.

ORSINO

Too old, by heaven. Let still the woman take
An elder than herself; so wears she to him;   30
So sways she level in her husband's heart.
For, boy, however we do praise ourselves,
Our fancies are more giddy and unfirm,
More longing, wavering, sooner lost and worn,
Than women's are.

VIOLA   I think it well, my lord.

ORSINO

Then let thy love be younger than thyself,
Or thy affection cannot hold the bent.
For women are as roses whose fair flower,
Being once displayed, doth fall that very hour.

VIOLA

And so they are. Alas, that they are so,   40
To die, even when they to perfection grow.
            Enter Curio and Feste

ORSINO

O, fellow, come, the song we had last night.
Mark it, Cesario; it is old and plain.
The spinsters, and the knitters in the sun,
And the free maids that weave their thread with bones,
Do use to chant it. It is silly sooth,
And dallies with the innocence of love
Like the old age.

29 *still* always
30 *wears she* she adapts herself
31 *sways she level in her husband's heart* her husband's love for her remains steady
34 *worn* exhausted. Orsino seems inconstant even to his belief in his own constancy.
35 *I think it well*. Viola says this hesitantly and with mixed feelings, since she both wants and does not want Orsino to be inconstant. The plot unties this particular knot for her.

37 *hold the bent* remain at full stretch (a metaphor from archery)
39 *displayed* unfolded, open (not merely 'shown')
44 *spinsters* spinners
45 *free*. This can mean either 'unattached' or 'free from care'. To Orsino these are one and the same thing.
   weave their thread with bones make lace on bone bobbins
46 *silly sooth* simple truth
47 *dallies with* dwells on
48 *the old age* the good old days

FESTE
    Are you ready, sir?

ORSINO   Ay, prithee sing.

    Music plays

FESTE (*sings*)

50   Come away, come away, death,
       And in sad cypress let me be laid.
    Fie away, fie away, breath!
       I am slain by a fair cruel maid.
    My shroud of white, stuck all with yew,
       O, prepare it!
    My part of death, no one so true
       Did share it.

    Not a flower, not a flower sweet
       On my black coffin let there be strewn.
60   Not a friend, not a friend greet
       My poor corpse, where my bones shall be thrown.
    A thousand thousand sighs to save,
       Lay me, O, where
    Sad true lover never find my grave
       To weep there.

ORSINO There's for thy pains.
    He gives Feste money

FESTE No pains, sir. I take pleasure in singing, sir.

ORSINO I'll pay thy pleasure, then.

FESTE Truly, sir, and pleasure will be paid, one time or
70   another.

---

50 *Come away, come away, death.* No contemporary setting of this has been discovered.
51 *cypress.* This could be either a coffin of cypress wood or a bier decorated with boughs of cypress. There are references to both in the period.
52 *Fie away!* be off!
56–7 *My part of death, no one so true | Did share it* no one so faithful has ever

received his allotted portion, death
60 *greet* bewail. This verb was no longer used transitively in the sixteenth century, but perhaps this is one of the things that give Feste's song its antique flavour.
67 *No pains, sir.* Feste seems to resent Orsino's offhand payment.
69 *pleasure will be paid* (proverbial)

ORSINO Give me now leave, to leave thee.

FESTE Now the melancholy god protect thee, and the tailor make thy doublet of changeable taffeta, for thy mind is a very opal. I would have men of such constancy put to sea, that their business might be everything, and their intent everywhere; for that's it that always makes a good voyage of nothing. Farewell.

Exit Feste

ORSINO

Let all the rest give place.

Curio and attendants withdraw

Once more, Cesario,

Get thee to yond same sovereign cruelty.

Tell her my love, more noble than the world,   80

Prizes not quantity of dirty lands.

The parts that fortune hath bestowed upon her

Tell her I hold as giddily as fortune.

But 'tis that miracle and queen of gems

That nature pranks her in, attracts my soul.

VIOLA

But if she cannot love you, sir?

ORSINO

It cannot be so answered.

VIOLA   Sooth, but you must.

Say that some lady, as perhaps there is,

Hath for your love as great a pang of heart

71 *leave, to leave thee* (a courteous dismissal)

72 *the melancholy god* (Saturn, whose planet ruled those of a melancholy humour)

73 *changeable* shot (having the weft of one colour and the woof of another so that the material shows different colours when viewed from different angles)

74 *opal* (semi-precious stone which changes colour with changes in the light)

74–7 *I would ... nothing.* The captain of a merchant ship with no fixed schedule would be able to pick up cargoes easily.

80 *the world* society

82 *parts* gifts of wealth and position

83 *giddily* lightly, carelessly. Fortune was a fickle goddess.

84 *that miracle* (her beauty)

85 *pranks* adorns

87 *Sooth* in truth

90   As you have for Olivia. You cannot love her.
    You tell her so. Must she not then be answered?

ORSINO
    There is no woman's sides
    Can bide the beating of so strong a passion
    As love doth give my heart; no woman's heart
    So big to hold so much, they lack retention.
    Alas, their love may be called appetite,
    No motion of the liver, but the palate,
    That suffer surfeit, cloyment, and revolt.
    But mine is all as hungry as the sea,
100   And can digest as much. Make no compare
    Between that love a woman can bear me
    And that I owe Olivia.

VIOLA   Ay, but I know —

ORSINO
    What dost thou know?

VIOLA
    Too well what love women to men may owe.
    In faith, they are as true of heart as we.
    My father had a daughter loved a man —
    As it might be perhaps, were I a woman,
    I should your lordship.

ORSINO   And what's her history?

VIOLA
    A blank, my lord. She never told her love,
110   But let concealment, like a worm i'the bud,
    Feed on her damask cheek. She pined in thought,
    And with a green and yellow melancholy,

---

93 *bide* bear
95–8 *retention . . . cloyment, and revolt.* 'Retention' is a medical term meaning 'the power to retain'. Orsino is not speaking metaphorically; in Shakespeare's day, the emotions were held to have physiological origins. Thus the liver (generative of the digestive juices) is not only to the appetite as real passion is to a passing fancy, but is itself the seat of the passions. See also 1.1.38–9.

111 *damask.* The contrast with 'green and yellow melancholy', suggesting the unhealthy pallor of grief, shows that the mingled pink and white of the damask rose is meant here.

She sat like Patience on a monument,
Smiling at grief. Was not this love indeed?
We men may say more, swear more, but indeed
Our shows are more than will; for still we prove
Much in our vows, but little in our love.

ORSINO
But died thy sister of her love, my boy?

VIOLA
I am all the daughters of my father's house,
And all the brothers too; and yet, I know not . . .   120
Sir, shall I to this lady?

ORSINO   Ay, that's the theme.
To her in haste; give her this jewel; say
My love can give no place, bide no denay.   *Exeunt*

Enter Sir Toby, Sir Andrew, and Fabian   II.5
SIR TOBY Come thy ways, Signor Fabian.
FABIAN Nay, I'll come. If I lose a scruple of this sport,
    let me be boiled to death with melancholy.
SIR TOBY Wouldst thou not be glad to have the nig-
    gardly, rascally sheep-biter come by some notable
    shame?

113 *Patience on a monument*. Both here
and in *Pericles* v.1.137–8 – 'Like Patience gazing on kings' graves, and
smiling | Extremity out of act' –
Shakespeare has in mind some such
allegorical figure as the representation
of Patience in *Iconologia* (1593), a popular Elizabethan reference book, where
she is seated on a stone with a yoke on
her shoulders and her feet on thorns.
116 *Our shows are more than will* we display
more passion than we actually feel
120 *And all the brothers too*. Viola remembers Sebastian with these words, and
the thought deepens the scene's
melancholy.

123 *denay* denial

II.5 (stage direction) *Fabian*. This name
may echo 'Fabio', the girl-page's assumed name in *Gl'Ingannati*. On
Feste's replacement by Fabian, see
Introduction, page 528. Fabian's position in Olivia's household seems to
be that of a 'hanger-on', rather than
of a paid servant.
3 *boiled to death* (a piece of facetiousness;
melancholy was a cold humour)
5 *sheep-biter* (originally a dog that attacks
sheep; so a slang word meaning a
sneaking fellow)

FABIAN I would exult, man. You know he brought me out o'favour with my lady about a bear-baiting here.

SIR TOBY To anger him, we'll have the bear again, and we will fool him black and blue – shall we not, Sir Andrew?

SIR ANDREW An we do not, it is pity of our lives.

Enter Maria

SIR TOBY Here comes the little villain. How now, my metal of India?

MARIA Get ye all three into the box-tree. Malvolio's coming down this walk, he has been yonder i'the sun practising behaviour to his own shadow this half-hour. Observe him, for the love of mockery, for I know this letter will make a contemplative idiot of him. Close, in the name of jesting!

The men hide. Maria throws down a letter

Lie thou there – for here comes the trout that must be caught with tickling.   *Exit*

Enter Malvolio

MALVOLIO 'Tis but fortune, all is fortune. Maria once told me she did affect me; and I have heard herself come thus near, that should she fancy, it should be one of my complexion. Besides, she uses me with a more exalted respect than anyone else that follows her. What should I think on't?

SIR TOBY Here's an overweening rogue!

FABIAN O, peace! Contemplation makes a rare turkey cock of him; how he jets under his advanced plumes!

---

8 *bear-baiting.* This explanation of Fabian's presence fits in with the mention of Malvolio as a kind of Puritan; the Puritans were fiercely opposed to bear-baiting.

12 *An* if

14 *metal of India* pure gold (with a pun on 'mettle')

19 *a contemplative idiot* the kind of imbe-cile who gazes into vacuity

Close hide

22 *tickling* flattery. Trout can be caught in shallow pools by rubbing them round the gills.

24 *affect* care for

26 *complexion* temperament

31 *jets* struts

SIR ANDREW 'Slight, I could so beat the rogue!

SIR TOBY Peace, I say!

MALVOLIO To be Count Malvolio . . .

SIR TOBY Ah, rogue!

SIR ANDREW Pistol him, pistol him!

SIR TOBY Peace, peace!

MALVOLIO There is example for't. The lady of the Strachy married the yeoman of the wardrobe.

SIR ANDREW Fie on him! Jezebel!   40

FABIAN O, peace! Now he's deeply in. Look how imagination blows him.

MALVOLIO Having been three months married to her, sitting in my state . . .

SIR TOBY O for a stone-bow to hit him in the eye!

MALVOLIO Calling my officers about me, in my branched velvet gown, having come from a day-bed, where I have left Olivia sleeping . . .

SIR TOBY Fire and brimstone!

FABIAN O, peace, peace!   50

32 *'Slight* (an oath – 'by God's light')

38–9 *The lady of the Strachy married the yeoman of the wardrobe.* One recent explanation of this is that William Strachy was a shareholder in the Children's company at Blackfriars Theatre early in the seventeenth century, and either he or his wife visited the theatre two or three times a week to collect their share of the takings in the presence of David Yeomans, tiresman (wardrobe-keeper) of the company, whom Strachy's widow can be presumed eventually to have married. But if the allusion is in fact to these people, it must have been added to the play a very little time before it was printed in the Folio, as William Strachy did not die till 1621. The two definite articles make it hard to accept this statement as an allusion to Strachy's wife and David Yeomans. 'Yeoman of a wardrobe' was a generic name for a tiresman, but *the* Wardrobe usually meant the Queen's Wardrobe in the Blackfriars precinct – as it does in Shakespeare's will. *The* Strachy sounds like the name of a house rather than a man. Probably the allusion is to a piece of Blackfriars or Court gossip of 1601 or 1602 which is not recorded elsewhere.

40 *Jezebel* (the shameless wife of King Ahab; see I Kings 16.31 onwards)

42 *blows him* puffs him up

44 *state* canopied chair of state

45 *stone-bow* (cross-bow from which small stones could be shot)

46–7 *branched velvet* velvet brocade

MALVOLIO And then to have the humour of state; and after a demure travel of regard – telling them I know my place, as I would they should do theirs – to ask for my kinsman Toby.

SIR TOBY Bolts and shackles!

FABIAN O, peace, peace, peace! Now, now!

MALVOLIO Seven of my people, with an obedient start, make out for him. I frown the while, and perchance wind up my watch, or play with my (*fingering his* 60 *steward's chain of office*) – some rich jewel. Toby approaches, curtsies there to me . . .

SIR TOBY Shall this fellow live?

FABIAN Though our silence be drawn from us with cars, yet peace!

MALVOLIO I extend my hand to him thus – quenching my familiar smile with an austere regard of control . . .

SIR TOBY And does not Toby take you a blow o'the lips then?

MALVOLIO Saying, Cousin Toby, my fortunes having 70 cast me on your niece give me this prerogative of speech . . .

SIR TOBY What, what!

MALVOLIO You must amend your drunkenness.

SIR TOBY Out, scab!

FABIAN Nay, patience, or we break the sinews of our plot.

MALVOLIO Besides, you waste the treasure of your time with a foolish knight . . .

SIR ANDREW That's me, I warrant you.

---

51 *to have the humour of state* to be up on my dignity
52 *demure travel of regard* grave look round the company
58 *make out* go out
59 *with my* –. Malvolio is fingering his steward's chain of office when he suddenly realizes he will no longer be wearing it.

61 *curtsies* bows low
63-4 *Though our silence be drawn from us with cars, yet peace!* This resembles the modern 'Wild horses wouldn't draw it out of me.' Fabian is saying 'Keep quiet, though it is a torment to do so.'
cars chariots
74 *scab* scurvy fellow

MALVOLIO One Sir Andrew.

SIR ANDREW I knew 'twas I, for many do call me fool. 80

MALVOLIO (*picks up the letter*) What employment have we here?

FABIAN Now is the woodcock near the gin.

SIR TOBY O, peace, and the spirit of humours intimate reading aloud to him!

MALVOLIO By my life, this is my lady's hand. These be her very C's, her U's and her T's; and thus makes she her great P's. It is, in contempt of question, her hand.

SIR ANDREW Her C's, her U's and her T's? Why that?

MALVOLIO (*reads*)

To the unknown beloved this, and my good wishes. 90

Her very phrases! By your leave, wax. Soft! and the impressure her Lucrece, with which she uses to seal. 'Tis my lady! To whom should this be?

FABIAN This wins him, liver and all.

MALVOLIO (*reads*)

> *Jove knows I love;*
> *But who?*
> *Lips, do not move;*
> *No man must know.*

'No man must know'! What follows? The numbers altered! 'No man must know'! If this should be thee, 100 Malvolio!

---

81 *employment* business, matter

83 *woodcock* (an easily trapped bird)
gin snare

84-5 *the spirit of humours intimate reading aloud to him* may he take it into his head to read aloud
spirit of humours genius who guides the *capricious*

86-8 *These be her ... great P's.* Not all these letters occur in the superscription, but they are given to Malvolio to make him sound bawdy. 'Cut' is the female organ.

87-8 *makes ... P's* (with a play on the

meaning 'urinates')

88 *in contempt of question* beyond all doubt

91 *Soft!* gently! (as he breaks the seal)

92 *impressure* stamp, seal
Lucrece (seal bearing the image of the Roman matron Lucretia, the model of chastity)

94 *liver and all.* Malvolio is deeply excited.

99-100 *The numbers altered!* the metre is changed!

SIR TOBY   Marry, hang thee, brock!

MALVOLIO   (*reads*)

> *I may command where I adore;*
> *But silence, like a Lucrece' knife,*
> *With bloodless stroke my heart doth gore;*
> *M.O.A.I. doth sway my life.*

FABIAN   A fustian riddle!

SIR TOBY   Excellent wench, say I!

MALVOLIO   'M.O.A.I. doth sway my life.' Nay, but first
110   let me see, let me see, let me see . . .

FABIAN   What dish o'poison has she dressed him!

SIR TOBY   And with what wing the staniel checks at it!

MARVOLIO   'I may command where I adore'. Why, she
may command me. I serve her, she is my lady. Why,
this is evident to any formal capactiy. There is no obstruction in this. And the end: what should that alpha-
betical position portend? If I could make that resemble
something in me . . . Softly, 'M.O.A.I.' . . .

SIR TOBY   O, ay, make up that. He is now at a cold scent.

120   FABIAN   Sowter will cry upon't for all this, thought it be as
rank as a fox.

MALVOLIO   M . . . Malvolio! M! Why, that begins my
name!

FABIAN   Did not I say he would work it out? The cur is
excellent at faults.

---

102   *brock* badger. Malvolio is burrowing for the letter's meaning.

106   *M.O.A.I.* Shakespeare scholars have been no quicker than Malvolio at solving this fustian riddle. An attractive suggestion is that the letters stand for I AM O (I am Olivia and this rules my conduct), but that Malvolio, sick of self-love, immediately applies them to himself thus provoking Sir Toby's remark about a cold scent.

107   *fustian* wretched

112   *staniel* (an   inferior   hawk)

checks at it swerves to pounce on it (a hawking term)

115   *formal capacity* normal intelligence

115–16   *obstruction* difficulty

117   *position* arrangement

120–21   *Sowter will cry . . . rank as a fox.* Malvolio has missed the right meaning and is about to go full cry after his own interpretation, like a hound which has missed the hare's scent and picked up a fox's instead. *Sowter* means 'cobbler' and is presumably a name for an awkward hound.

125   *faults* breaks in the scent .

MALVOLIO M! But then there is no consonancy in the
sequel that suffers under probation. A should follow,
but O does.

FABIAN And O shall end, I hope.

SIR TOBY Ay, or I'll cudgel him and make him cry O.   130

MALVOLIO And then I comes behind.

FABIAN Ay, an you had eye behind you, you might
see more detraction at your heels than fortunes before
you.

MALVOLIO M.O.A.I. This simulation is not as the
former. And yet, to crush this a little, it would bow to
me, for every one of these letters are in my name. Soft!
Here follows prose.

He reads

If this fall into thy hand, revolve. In my stars I am above
thee, but be not afraid of greatness. Some are born great,   140
some achieve greatness, and some have greatness thrust
upon 'em. Thy fates open their hands, let thy blood and
spirit embrace them; and to inure thyself to what thou art
like to be, cast thy humble slough and appear fresh. Be
opposite with a kinsman, surly with servants. Let thy

126 *consonancy* consistency
127 *that suffers under probation* that will
stand up to investigation
129 *O shall end.* 'O' could mean the hang-
man's noose. But if the riddle means
'I AM O', Fabian may be hoping
that Malvolio will work it out.
135 *simulation* disguise
135–6 *the former* (referring to 'I may command where I adore')
139 *revolve* consider
140 *born.* The Folio has 'become'. The
sentence is repeated twice later in the
play, with *born* in each case, so we
must assume the compositor read
'borne' as 'become' – a plausible
error. Maria's letter is not italicized
in the Folio after *revolve*, which suggests that only the beginning of it

was in the promptbook, and that
this had to be supplemented by the
letter read out on the stage. This is
also suggested by the end of the
letter, where the Folio reads 'tht fortunate vnhappy daylight and cham-
pian' with an awkward space after
'vnhappy'. The punctuation of the
letter is also uncertain, by comparison with the careful punctuation of
the rest of the play. A property letter
would be less legible than the promptbook, either because of rough handling or because it was a piece of the
author's manuscript, and this might
explain 'become' as a misreading of
'borne'.
144 *slough* (a snake's old skin)
145 *opposite with* hostile towards

*tongue tang arguments of state. Put thyself into the trick of
singularity. She thus advises thee that sighs for thee.
Remember who commended thy yellow stockings and wished
to see thee ever cross-gartered. I say, remember. Go to, thou*
150   *art made if you desirest to be so. If not, let me see thee a
steward still, the fellow of servants, and not worthy to
touch Fortune's fingers. Farewell. She that would alter
services with thee, The Fortunate Unhappy.*

Daylight and champain discovers not more! This is
open. I will be proud, I will read politic authors, I will
baffle Sir Toby, I will wash off gross acquaintance, I
will be point-devise the very man. I do not now fool
myself, to let imagination jade me; for every reason
excites to this, that my lady loves me. She did commend
160   my yellow stockings of late, she did praise my leg being
cross-gartered; and in this she manifests herself to my
love and with a kind of injunction drives me to these
habits of her liking. I thank my stars, I am happy! I
will be strange, stout, in yellow stockings and cross-
gartered, even with the swiftness of putting on. Jove and
my stars be praised! Here is yet a postcript.

He reads

146 *tang* resound
146–7 *trick of singularity* affectation of
oddness
148 *yellow stockings.* Not only were these
old-fashioned by 1602, but they
would be out of keeping with the
deep mourning of Olivia's household. It is hard to believe that Olivia
ever 'commended' them, if she ab-
horred the colour yellow (line 192
below). Probably the only commendation is in this letter, and Shakespeare
shows us how Malvolio's imagination does the rest.
149 *cross-gartered* wearing garters which

crossed at the back of the knee and
tied above it in front. This custom
was old-fashioned at the date of the
play.
154 *Daylight and champain discovers not
more* broad daylight and open
country couldn't make this more
plain
156 *baffle* disgrace (used of a knight)
157 *point-devise* to the last detail
158 *jade* deceive
163 *habits* clothes
164 *strange* aloof
    stout bold

*Thou canst not choose but know who I am. If thou enter-
tainest my love, let it appear in thy smiling, thy smiles
become thee well. Therefore in my presence still smile, dear
my sweet, I prithee.*   170

Jove, I thank thee! I will smile. I will do everything that
thou wilt have me!   *Exit*

FABIAN I will not give my part of this sport for a pension
of thousands to be paid from the Sophy.

SIR TOBY I could marry this wench for this device.

SIR ANDREW So could I too.

SIR TOBY And ask no other dowry with her but such another jest.

SIR ANDREW Nor I neither.

> *Enter Maria*

FABIAN Here comes my noble gull-catcher.   180

SIR TOBY Wilt thou set thy foot o' my neck?

SIR ANDREW Or o' mine either?

SIR TOBY Shall I play my freedom at tray-trip and become thy bondslave?

SIR ANDREW I'faith, or I either?

SIR TOBY Why, thou hast put him in such a dream, that
when the image of it leaves him, he must run mad.

MARIA Nay, but say true: does it work upon him?

SIR TOBY Like aqua-vitae with a midwife.

MARIA If you will then see the fruits of the sport, mark   190
his first approach before my lady. He will come to her in
yellow stockings, and 'tis a colour she abhors; and cross-
gartered, a fashion she detests; and he will smile upon
her, which will now be so unsuitable to her disposition —
being addicted to a melancholy as she is — that it cannot

---

169 *dear.* Possibly the Folio 'deero' is
not a misprint for 'deere', and we
should read 'dear, O my sweet'.

174 *Sophy* Shah of Persia. This may be
an allusion to the gifts heaped on Sir
Anthony Shirley by the Shah. See

Introduction, page 529.

180 *gull-catcher* one who traps fools

183 *tray-trip* (a dicing game in which
success depends on throwing a
three)

189 *aqua-vitae* spirits

but turn him into a notable contempt. If you will see it, follow me.

SIR TOBY To the gates of Tartar, thou most excellent devil of wit!

200   SIR ANDREW I'll make one too.   *Exeunt*

III.1   *Enter at different entrances Viola, and Feste playing his pipe and tabor*

VIOLA Save thee, friend, and thy music. Dost thou live by thy tabor?

FESTE No, sir, I live by the church.

VIOLA Art thou a Churchman?

FESTE No such matter, sir; I do live by the church. For I do live at my house, and my house doth stand by the church.

VIOLA So thou mayst say the king lies by a beggar, if a beggar dwell near him; or the Church stands by thy
10   tabor, if thy tabor stand by the church.

FESTE You have said, sir. To see this age! A sentence is but a cheveril glove to a good wit; how quickly the wrong side may be turned outward!

VIOLA Nay, that's certain. They that dally nicely with words may quickly make them wanton.

FESTE I would therefore my sister had had no name, sir.

196 *a notable contempt* an infamous disgrace

198 *Tartar* Tartarus (the classical name for hell)

III.1 (stage direction) *tabor*. Queen Elizabeth's jester Tarlton is shown in a famous engraving playing a tabor, or small drum, and a pipe. The only real break in the play's action occurs between Acts II and III, and perhaps Feste has been entertaining the audience in this interval by playing his pipe and tabor.

1 *Save thee* God save thee
  live by make a living by

8 *lies by* dwells near (playing on the meaning 'go to bed with')

9 *stands by* (with a play on the meaning 'is upheld by')

12 *cheveril* kid leather

14 *dally nicely* play subtly

15 *wanton* equivocal. Feste goes on to play with the meaning 'unchaste'.

VIOLA Why, man?

FESTE Why, sir, her name's a word, and to dally with that word might make my sister wanton. But indeed, words are very rascals, since bonds disgraced them.   20

VIOLA Thy reason, man?

FESTE Troth, sir, I can yield you none without words, and words are grown so false, I am loath to prove reason with them.

VIOLA I warrant thou art a merry fellow, and car'st for nothing.

FESTE Not so, sir. I do care for something; but in my conscience, sir, I do not care for you. If that be to care for nothing, sir, I would it would make you invisible.

VIOLA Art not thou the Lady Olivia's fool?   30

FESTE No indeed, sir, the Lady Olivia has no folly. She will keep no fool, sir, till she be married, and fools are as like husbands as pilchers are to herrings; the husband's the bigger. I am indeed not her fool, but her corrupter of words.

VIOLA I saw thee late at the Count Orsino's.

FESTE Foolery, sir, does walk about the orb like the sun, it shines everywhere. I would be sorry, sir, but the fool should be as oft with your master as with my mistress. I think I saw your wisdom there?   40

VIOLA Nay, an thou pass upon me, I'll no more with thee. Hold, there's expenses for thee!

    She gives him a coin

FESTE Now Jove, in his next commodity of hair, send thee a beard!

19–20 *words are very rascals, since bonds disgraced them.* This is often read as an allusion to the Jesuit practice of equivocation. But Feste can simply be moralizing by saying that frequent demands for vows and pledges show that a man's yea is no longer yea, nor his nay, nay.

22–4 *I can yield you . . . reason with them.* Feste, who is a wise fool, here touches on one of the biggest problems in philosophy.

33 *pilchers* pilchards (shoaling fish, similar to herrings)

40 *your wisdom* (an ironic courtesy title)

41 *an* if

    pass upon jest at

43 *commodity* consignment

VIOLA By my troth, I'll tell thee, I am almost sick for one – (*aside*) though I would not have it grow on my chin. Is thy lady within?

FESTE Would not a pair of these have bred, sir?

VIOLA Yes, being kept together and put to use.

50 FESTE I would play Lord Pandarus of Phrygia, sir, to bring a Cressida to this Troilus.

VIOLA I understand you, sir; 'tis well begged.

She gives another coin

FESTE The matter, I hope, is not great, sir, begging but a beggar – Cressida was a beggar. My lady is within, sir. I will conster to them whence you come. Who you are and what you would are out of my welkin – I might say 'element', but the word is overworn.   *Exit*

VIOLA

This fellow is wise enough to play the fool;

And to do that well craves a kind of wit.

60   He must observe their mood on whom he jests,

45 *By my troth* in faith
48 *these* (coins)
49 *use* interest
50 *Pandarus* (the go-between in the medieval story of Troilus and Cressida, on which Shakespeare wrote a tragedy. Feste hints that he will further a meeting between Olivia and Cesario if he is well tipped.)
53–4 *begging but a beggar* (in allusion to the practice of begging the guardianship of rich orphans from the sovereign)
54 *Cressida was a beggar*. She became one in Henryson's fifteenth-century poem, *The Testament of Cresseid*.
55 *conster* construe, explain
56 *out of my welkin* not my affair
56–7 *welkin . . . element*. In substituting a far-fetched word like *welkin*, which means 'sky', for *element*, Shakespeare

may be defending Ben Jonson, whose use of the word 'element' had been satirized in a play by Dekker, *Satiromastix* (1601).

58–9 *This fellow is wise enough to play the fool . . . kind of wit.* This idea about the professional fool is a commonplace of the time, but it is possible that Shakespeare is remembering a set of verses in Robert Armin's *Quips upon Question* (1600):

A merry man is often thought unwise;
Yet mirth in modesty's loved of the
    wise.
Then say, should he for a fool go,
When he's a more fool that accounts
    him so?
Many men descant on another's wit
When they have less themselves in
    doing it.

The quality of persons, and the time,
And, like the haggard, check at every feather
That comes before his eye. This is a practice
As full of labour as a wise man's art.
For folly that he wisely shows is fit;
But wise men, folly-fallen, quite taint their wit.

Enter Sir Toby and Sir Andrew

SIR TOBY Save you, gentleman!

VIOLA And you, sir!

SIR ANDREW *Dieu vous garde, monsieur!*

VIOLA *Et vous aussi; votre serviteur!*   70

SIR ANDREW I hope, sir, you are, and I am yours.

SIR TOBY Will you encounter the house? My niece is desirous you should enter, if your trade be to her.

VIOLA I am bound to your niece, sir. I mean, she is the list of my voyage.

SIR TOBY Taste your legs, sir; put them to motion.

VIOLA My legs do better under-stand me, sir, than I understand what you mean by bidding me taste my legs.

SIR TOBY I mean to go, sir, to enter.

VIOLA I will answer you with gate and entrance.   80

Enter Olivia and Maria

But we are prevented. (*To Olivia*) Most excellent, accomplished lady, the heavens rain odours on you!

SIR ANDREW (*aside*) That youth's a rare courtier. 'Rain odours'! Well!

---

62 *Like the haggard, check at every feather* swoop on every small bird, as the wild hawk does. So Feste seizes every opportunity for a jest.

65 *fit* to the point

66 *folly-fallen, quite taint their wit* stooping to folly, considerably impair their reputation for common sense

69–70 *Dieu vous garde, monsieur! |Et vous aussi; votre serviteur!* God keep you, sir! And you too; your servant!

72 *encounter* approach. Sir Toby speaks affectedly, but Viola is a match for him.

73 *trade* business. Viola picks up the meaning 'a trading voyage'.

75 *list* objective

76 *Taste* try out

80 *gate and entrance.* This phrase has a legal flavour, and *gate* has a special legal meaning – 'the right to pasture'. There is a pun on 'gait'.

81 *prevented* forestalled

VIOLA My matter hath no voice, lady, but to your own
most pregnant and vouchsafed ear.

SIR ANDREW 'Odours'; 'pregnant'; and 'vouchsafed'.
I'll get 'em all three all ready.

OLIVIA Let the garden door be shut and leave me to my
90   hearing.

Exeunt Sir Toby and Maria, Sir Andrew
lingering before he, too, leaves

Give my your hand, sir.

VIOLA

My duty, madam, and most humble service!

OLIVIA

What is your name?

VIOLA

Cesario is your servant's name, fair princess.

OLIVIA

My servant, sir? 'Twas never merry world
Since lowly feigning was called compliment.
Y'are servant to the Count Orsino, youth.

VIOLA

And he is yours, and his must needs be yours.
Your servant's servant is your servant, madam.

OLIVIA

100   For him, I think not on him. For his thoughts,
Would they were blanks rather than filled with me.

VIOLA

Madam, I come to whet your gentle thoughts
On his behalf —

OLIVIA   O, by your leave, I pray you.
I bade you never speak again of him.
But would you undertake another suit,

---

86 *pregnant* quick in understanding, re-
ceptive *vouchsafed* attentive
88 *all ready*. Sir Andrew may write them
down carefully.
95 *'Twas never merry world* (a catchphrase

like the modern 'Things have never
been the same')
96 *lowly feigning* pretended humility (in
allusion to the mistress–servant convention of courtly love)

I had rather hear you to solicit that
Than music from the spheres.

VIOLA   Dear lady —

OLIVIA

Give me leave, beseech you. I did send,
After the last enchantment you did here,
A ring in chase of you. So did I abuse   110
Myself, my servant, and, I fear me, you. ·
Under your hard construction must I sit,
To force that on you in a shameful cunning
Which you knew none of yours. What might you think?
Have you not set mine honour at the stake,
And baited it with all th'unmuzzled thoughts
That tyrannous heart can think? To one of your
    receiving
Enough is shown; a cypress, not a bosom,
Hides my heart. So let me hear you speak.

VIOLA

I pity you.

OLIVIA   That's a degree to love.   120

VIOLA

No, not a grize; for 'tis a vulgar proof
That very oft we pity enemies.

OLIVIA

Why, then, methinks 'tis time to smile again.
O world, how apt the poor are to be proud!

107 *music from the spheres*. In ancient
astronomy, still widely accepted in
Shakespeare's day, the universe was
thought of as being constructed of
crystalline spheres, so tightly fitted
the one inside the other that they
ground together as they turned and
so produced music.
110 *abuse* impose upon
112 *hard construction* harsh interpretation
115 *at the stake* (an image from bear-

baiting)
117 *receiving* perception
118 *cypress* piece of thin black gauze
121 *grize* flight of steps (which is also
the literal meaning of *degree*, line 120)
vulgar proof common experience
124 *how apt the poor are to be proud*. Olivia
refers to herself rather than to Viola
— 'Though you reject me, I've something to be proud of — I have fallen
for a king among men.'

If one should be a prey, how much the better
To fall before the lion than the wolf!
   Clock strikes
The clock upbraids me with the waste of time.
Be not afraid, good youth; I will not have you.
And yet, when wit and youth is come to harvest,
130   Your wife is like to reap a proper man.
There lies your way, due west.

VIOLA   Then westward ho!
Grace and good disposition attend your ladyship.
You'll nothing, madam, to my lord by me?

OLIVIA
Stay.
I prithee, tell me what thou think'st of me?

VIOLA
That you do think you are not what you are.

OLIVIA
If I think so, I think the same of you.

VIOLA
Then think you right; I am not what I am.

OLIVIA
I would you were as I would have you be.

VIOLA
140   Would it be better, madam, than I am?
I wish it might, for now I am your fool.

OLIVIA (*aside*)
O, what a deal of scorn looks beautiful
In the contempt and anger of his lip!

---

130 *proper* handsome

131 *due west*. Olivia is telling Cesario to go and seek his fortunes elsewhere.
   westward ho! (the cry of the Thames watermen seeking passengers for the journey from the City to the Court at Westminster)

132 *good disposition* equanimity (a natural happiness, as distinct from that given by *grace*)

136 *That you do think you are not what you are*. Viola implies that Olivia is forgetting her worldly position.

137 *the same of you* (that you are not in fact what you are in appearance. Olivia suspects Cesario is a high-born youth in disguise.)

A murderous guilt shows not itself more soon
Than love that would seem hid; love's night is noon.
(*To Viola*) Cesario, by the roses of the spring,
By maidhood, honour, truth, and everything,
I love thee so that, maugre all thy pride,
Nor wit nor reason can my passion hide.
Do not extort thy reasons from this clause: 150
For that I woo, thou therefore hast no cause.
But rather reason thus with reason fetter:
Love sought, is good; but given unsought, is better.

VIOLA

By innocence I swear, and by my youth,
I have one heart, one bosom, and one truth.
And that no woman has, nor never none
Shall mistress be of it, save I alone.
And so, adieu, good madam; never more
Will I my master's tears to you deplore.

OLIVIA

Yet come again; for thou perhaps mayst move   160
That heart, which now abhors, to like his love.

Exeunt

Enter Sir Toby, Sir Andrew, and Fabian   III.2

SIR ANDREW No, faith, I'll not stay a jot longer.
SIR TOBY Thy reason, dear venom, give thy reason.
FABIAN You must needs yield your reason, Sir Andrew.
SIR ANDREW Marry, I saw your niece do more favours to

---

145 *love's night is noon* (love cannot be hid)
148 *I love thee so.* Olivia changes to the intimate second person singular. *maugre* in spite of
149 *wit* common sense
150–53 *Do not extort thy reasons from this clause ... is better* do not force your-self to think that because I have declared my love you ought not to love me, but rather restrain this way of thinking with the reflection that love which is freely given is better than love that has been begged
150 *clause* premise
151 *for that* because

the Count's servingman than ever she bestowed upon
me. I saw't i'the orchard.

SIR TOBY Did she see thee the while, old boy, tell me
that?

SIR ANDREW As plain as I see you now.

10 FABIAN This was a great argument of love in her toward
you.

SIR ANDREW 'Slight! Will you make an ass o'me?

FABIAN I will prove it legitimate, sir, upon the oaths of
judgement and reason.

SIR TOBY And they have been grand-jury men since before Noah was a sailor.

FABIAN She did show favour to the youth in your sight
only to exasperate you, to awake your dormouse valour,
to put fire in your heart and brimstone in your liver. You
20 should then have accosted her, and with some excellent
jests fire-new from the mint, you should have banged
the youth into dumbness. This was looked for at your
hand, and this was baulked. The double gilt of this
opportunity you let time wash off, and you are now
sailed into the north of my lady's opinion; where you
will hang like an icicle on a Dutchman's beard, unless you
do redeem it by some laudable attempt either of valour
or policy.

SIR ANDREW An't be any way, it must be with valour, for

III.2.10 *argument* proof

12 *'Slight!* by God's light!

13–14 *oaths of judgement and reason.* Theo-
logians laid down three conditions
for an oath: truth, judgement, reason.
Fabian omits truth.

15 *grand-jury men.* The task of a grand
jury was to decide if the evidence in
particular cases was sufficient to warrant a trial. Fabian goes on to pro-
duce evidence that Olivia is in love
with Sir Andrew.

18 *dormouse* sleeping (but with a further

implied meaning 'timid')

23 *baulked* shirked

23–4 *double gilt of this opportunity.* The
most costly gold plate was twice
gilded. We still speak of a golden
opportunity.

25 *sailed into the north of my lady's opinion*
earned my lady's cold disdain

26 *icicle on a Dutchman's beard.* This is
probably an allusion to William
Barentz's Arctic voyage in 1596–7.

28 *policy* diplomacy

policy I hate. I had as lief be a Brownist as a politician.   30

SIR TOBY Why then, build me thy fortunes upon the basis
of valour. Challenge me the Count's youth to fight with
him; hurt him in eleven places; my niece shall take note
of it – and, assure thyself, there is no love-broker in the
world can more prevail in man's commendation with
woman than report of valour.

FABIAN There is no way but this, Sir Andrew.

SIR ANDREW Will either of you bear me a challenge to
him?

SIR TOBY Go, write it in a martial hand. Be curst and   40
brief. It is no matter how witty, so it be eloquent and
full of invention. Taunt him with the licence of ink. If
thou 'thou'-est him some thrice it shall not be amiss, and
as many lies as will lie in thy sheet of paper – although
the sheet were big enough for the bed of Ware in England, set 'em down, go about it. Let there be gall enough
in thy ink, though thou write with a goose pen, no
matter. About it!

SIR ANDREW Where shall I find you?

SIR TOBY We'll call thee at thy cubiculo. Go!   50

Exit Sir Andrew

FABIAN This is a dear manikin to you, Sir Toby.

SIR TOBY I have been dear to him, lad, some two thousand strong or so.

---

30 *Brownist*. The Brownists were a religious group later called 'Independ-
ents' and (in the nineteenth century)
'Congregationalists'. Their advocacy
of a very democratic form of Church
government seemed highly seditious
and 'political' to the average Elizabethan.
politician schemer

31–2 *build me . . . Challenge me.* 'Me' here
implies 'on my advice'.

40 *curst* petulant

42 *invention* inventiveness, matter
with the licence of ink with things you

dare not say to his face

43 *'thou'-est* address him as 'thou' (that
is, as an inferior)

45 *bed of Ware* (the famous Elizabethan
bed, measuring over ten feet each
way, now in the Victoria and Albert
Museum in London)

46 *gall.* Sir Toby puns on the meanings
'an ingredient of ink' and 'bitterness'.

47 *goose* (symbolic of cowardice)

50 *cubiculo* bedroom (Italian – another
affected term from Sir Toby)

51 *manikin* puppet

FABIAN We shall have a rare letter from him. But you'll not deliver it?

SIR TOBY Never trust me then – and by all means stir on the youth to an answer. I think oxen and wain-ropes cannot hale them together. For Andrew, if he were opened and you find so much blood in his liver as will clog the foot of a flea, I'll eat the rest of the anatomy.

FABIAN And his opposite the youth bears in his visage no great presage of cruelty.

Enter Maria

SIR TOBY Look where the youngest wren of nine comes.

MARIA If you desire the spleen, and will laugh yourselves into stitches, follow me. Yond gull Malvolio is turned heathen, a very renegado; for there is no Christian, that means to be saved by believing rightly, can ever believe such impossible passages of grossness. He's in yellow stockings!

SIR TOBY And cross-gartered?

MARIA Most villainously; like a pedant that keeps a school i'the church. I have dogged him like his murderer. He does obey every point of the letter that I dropped to betray him. He does smile his face into more lines than is in the new map with the augmentation of the Indies. You have not seen such a thing as 'tis. I can hardly forbear hurling things at him; I know my lady

---

57 *wain-ropes* waggon-ropes pulled by oxen

58 *hale* drag

60 *anatomy* cadaver

63 *youngest wren of nine*. A wren lays nine or ten eggs and the last bird hatched is usually the smallest. This justifies the emendation from the Folio 'youngest Wren of mine', which has little meaning.

64 *the spleen* a fit of laughter

68 *impossible passages of grossness* wildly improbable statements (in Maria's letter)

71–2 *pedant that keeps a school i'the church* schoolmaster who, having no schoolhouse of his own, teaches in the church. The practice was oldfashioned by this period.

75–6 *the new map with the augmentation of the Indies*. Emmeric Mollineux's map of the world on a new projection, published in 1599, has a mesh of rhumb lines, and is the first to show the whole of the East Indies, which are therefore 'augmented'.

will strike him. If she do, he'll smile, and take it for a
great favour.

SIR TOBY Come, bring us, bring us where he is.   *Exeunt*   80

Enter Sebastian and Antonio   III.3

SEBASTIAN
  I would not by my will have troubled you.
  But since you make your pleasure of your pains,
  I will no further chide you.

ANTONIO
  I could not stay behind you. My desire,
  More sharp than filèd steel, did spur me forth,
  And not all love to see you – though so much
  As might have drawn one to a longer voyage –
  But jealousy what might befall your travel,
  Being skill-less in these parts; which to a stranger,
  Unguided and unfriended, often prove   10
  Rough and unhospitable. My willing love,
  The rather by these arguments of fear,
  Set forth in your pursuit.

SEBASTIAN   My kind Antonio,
  I can no other answer make but thanks,
  And thanks. And ever oft good turns
  Are shuffled off with such uncurrent pay.
  But were my worth, as is my conscience, firm,
  You should find better dealing. What's to do?
  Shall we go see the reliques of this town?

ANTONIO
  Tomorrow, sir; best first go see your lodging.   20

III.3.1 *troubled you* (to follow me to the
city)
6 *not all* not only
8 *jealousy* concern
9 *skill-less in* unacquainted with
12 *rather* more speedily (the original

meaning of the word)
16 *uncurrent* worthless (like coins out of
currency)
17 *worth* means
   conscience awareness of my debt to you
19 *reliques* antiquities, sights

SEBASTIAN

I am not weary, and 'tis long to night.
I pray you, let us satisfy our eyes
With the memorials and the things of fame
That do renown this city.

ANTONIO

Would you'd pardon me.
I do not without danger walk these streets.
Once in a seafight 'gainst the Count his galleys
I did some service – of such note indeed
That, were I ta'en here, it would scarce be answered.

SEBASTIAN

30   Belike you slew great number of his people?

ANTONIO

Th'offence is not of such a bloody nature,
Albeit the quality of the time and quarrel
Might well have given us bloody argument.
It might have since been answered in repaying
What we took from them, which, for traffic's sake,
Most of our city did. Only myself stood out.
For which, if I be lapsèd in this place,
I shall pay dear.

SEBASTIAN   Do not then walk too open.

ANTONIO

' It doth not fit me. Hold, sir, here's my purse.
40   In the south suburbs, at the Elephant,

---

24 *renown* make famous
27 *the Count his galleys* the Count's galleys
29 *it would scarce be answered* it would be difficult to make reparation
30 *Belike* perhaps
32–3 *Albeit the quality of the time and quarrel | Might well have given us bloody argument* although at that time, and with the cause we had, bloodshed could have been justified

35 *traffic's* trade's
37 *lapsèd* apprehended
40 *Elephant*. At the time this play was written, there was an inn called the Elephant in Southwark, near the Globe Theatre. The more famous Elephant and Castle, still in London's 'south suburbs', is not mentioned in documents until the middle of the seventeenth century.

Is best to lodge. I will bespeak our diet
Whiles you beguile the time, and feed your knowledge
With viewing of the town. There shall you have me.

SEBASTIAN

Why I your purse?

ANTONIO

Haply your eye shall light upon some toy
You have desire to purchase; and your store,
I think, is not for idle markets, sir.

SEBASTIAN

I'll be your purse-bearer, and leave you for
An hour.

ANTONIO To th'Elephant.

SEBASTIAN   I do remember.

Exeunt separately

Enter Olivia and Maria   III.4

OLIVIA (*aside*)

I have sent after him, he says he'll come.
How shall I feast him? What bestow of him?
For youth is bought more oft than begged or borrowed.
I speak too loud.
(*To Maria*) Where's Malvolio? He is sad and civil,
And suits well for a servant with my fortunes.
Where is Malvolio?

MARIA He's coming, madam, but in very strange manner.
He is sure possessed, madam.

OLIVIA Why, what's the matter? Does he rave?   10

MARIA No, madam, he does nothing but smile. Your
ladyship were best to have some guard about you, if he

---

41 *bespeak our diet* order our meals
45 *Haply* perhaps
    toy trifle
47 *idle markets* unnecessary expenditure

III.4.1 *he says he'll come* supposing he says
    he'll come
2 *bestow of* give
5 *sad and civil* grave and sedate
9 *possessed* (by the devil)

come, for sure the man is tainted in's wits.

OLIVIA

Go, call him hither.   *Exit Maria*

    I am as mad as he

If sad and merry madness equal be.

  Enter Malvolio and Maria

How now, Malvolio?

MALVOLIO Sweet lady! Ho! Ho!

OLIVIA Smil'st thou? I sent for thee upon a sad occasion.

MALVOLIO Sad, lady? I could be sad; this does make
some obstruction in the blood, this cross-gartering – but
what of that? If it please the eye of one, it is with me as
the very true sonnet is: 'Please one and please all'.

OLIVIA Why, how dost thou, man? What is the matter
with thee?

MALVOLIO Not black in my mind, though yellow in my
legs. It did come to his hands; and commands shall be
executed. I think we do know the sweet Roman hand.

OLIVIA Wilt thou go to bed, Malvolio?

MALVOLIO To bed! 'Ay, sweetheart, and I'll come to
thee!'

OLIVIA God comfort thee! Why dost thou smile so, and
kiss thy hand so oft?

MARIA How do you, Malvolio?

MALVOLIO At your request? Yes; nightingales answer
daws.

MARIA Why appear you with this ridiculous boldness
before my lady?

---

22 *sonnet* song
 'Please one and please all'. This is the
refrain of a popular song of the time.
Malvolio should perhaps squeak it
out, to mark his transformation.

25–6 *Not black in my mind, though yellow
in my legs* not melancholy (melancholy
being caused by the black bile) in
spite of the melancholy colour of my
stockings. There is a possible allusion
to a ballad tune called 'Black and

Yellow', and perhaps Malvolio hums
a little of it.

26 *It* (Maria's letter)

27 *sweet Roman hand* (fashionable new
italic handwriting)

29–30 *'Ay, sweetheart, and I'll come to thee'*.
This is a quotation from another
popular song, of which the words
are given in *Tarlton's Jests*, 1601.

35 *daws* jackdaws. The remark has more
point if Malvolio has been singing.

MALVOLIO 'Be not afraid of greatness.' 'Twas well writ.

OLIVIA What mean'st thou by that, Malvolio?

MALVOLIO 'Some are born great –'   40

OLIVIA Ha?

MALVOLIO 'Some achieve greatness –'

OLIVIA What sayst thou?

MALVOLIO 'And some have greatness thrust upon them.'

OLIVIA Heaven restore thee!

MALVOLIO 'Remember who commended thy yellow stockings –'

OLIVIA Thy yellow stockings?

MALVOLIO '– and wished to see the cross-gartered.'   50

OLIVIA Cross-gartered?

MALVOLIO 'Go to, thou art made if thou desir'st to be so.'

OLIVIA Am I maid!

MALVOLIO 'If not, let me see thee a servant still.'

OLIVIA Why, this is very midsummer madness.

Enter a Servant

SERVANT Madam, the young gentleman of the Count Orsino's is returned. I could hardly entreat him back. He attends your ladyship's pleasure.

OLIVIA I'll come to him.   *Exit Servant*   60
Good Maria, let this fellow be looked to. Where's my cousin Toby? Let some of my people have a special care of him. I would not have him miscarry for the half of my dowry.   *Exeunt Olivia and Maria different ways*

MALVOLIO O ho! Do you come near me now? No worse man than Sir Toby to look to me! This concurs directly

---

47–8 *thy yellow stockings*. In quoting the letter, Malvolio appears to be calling his mistress 'thou' and she echoes him in shocked surprise at this familiarity.

56 *midsummer madness* (a proverbial phrase; great heat was supposed to make dogs run mad)

58 *hardly* only with difficulty

63 *miscarry* come to harm

65 *come near me* begin to understand who I am

with the letter. She sends him on purpose, that I may appear stubborn to him; for she incites me to that in the letter. 'Cast thy humble slough,' says she. 'Be opposite with a kinsman, surly with servants, let thy tongue tang with arguments of state, put thyself into the trick of singularity' – and consequently sets down the manner how: as, a sad face, a reverend carriage, a slow tongue, in the habit of some sir of note, and so forth. I have limed her! But it is Jove's doing, and Jove make me thankful! And when she went away now – 'let this fellow be looked to'. Fellow! Not 'Malvolio', nor after my degree, but 'fellow'! Why, everything adheres together, that no dram of a scruple, no scruple of a scruple, no obstacle, no incredulous or unsafe circumstance – what can be said? – nothing that can be, can come between me and the full prospect of my hopes. Well, Jove, not I, is the doer of this, and he is to be thanked.

Enter Sir Toby, Fabian, and Maria

SIR TOBY Which way is he, in the name of sanctity? If all the devils of hell be drawn in little and Legion himself possessed him, yet I'll speak to him.

FABIAN Here he is, here he is. How is't with you, sir? How is't with you, man?

71 *tang.* The Folio has 'langer'. The compositor had apparently no difficulty with the rather unusual word 'tang' in II.5.146, which suggests that the letter and this passage were in different handwritings, and that here the word ended with a flourish.

74 *the habit of some sir of note* the way of dressing of some very important personage (perhaps Sir William Knollys)

75 *limed* snared

76 *fellow.* This word originally meant 'companion', but was used to inferiors, with polite condescension, from the fourteenth century onwards. Malvolio flatters himself Olivia uses it of him as an equal.

79 *scruple.* Malvolio plays on the meanings 'doubt' and 'minute quantity'.

80 *incredulous* incredible

84 *in the name of sanctity.* Sir Toby invokes holy powers before his encounter with the possessed Malvolio.

85 *drawn in little* contracted to minute size (like Milton's devils in Pandaemonium)

Legion (used of the many devils possessing the madman described in Saint Mark 5.9)

MALVOLIO Go off, I discard you. Let me enjoy my private. Go off.   90

MARIA Lo, how hollow the fiend speaks within him. Did not I tell you? Sir Toby, my lady prays you to have a care of him.

MALVOLIO Ah ha! Does she so!

SIR TOBY Go to, go to! Peace, peace, we must deal gently with him. Let me alone. How do you, Malvolio? How is't with you? What, man, defy the devil! Consider, he's an enemy to mankind.

MALVOLIO Do you know what you say?

MARIA La you, an you speak ill of the devil, how he takes   100
it at heart! Pray God he be not bewitched!

FABIAN Carry his water to the wisewoman.

MARIA Marry, and it shall be done tomorrow morning, if I live. My lady would not lose him, for more than I'll say.

MALVOLIO How now, mistress?

MARIA O Lord!

SIR TOBY Prithee, hold thy peace, this is not the way. Do you not see you move him? Let me alone with him.

FABIAN No way but gentleness, gently, gently. The fiend   110
is rough, and will not be roughly used.

SIR TOBY Why, how now, my bawcock? How dost thou, chuck?

MALVOLIO Sir!

SIR TOBY Ay, biddy, come with me. What, man, 'tis not for gravity to play at cherry-pit with Satan. Hang him, foul collier!

89–90 *private* privacy
96 *Let me alone* let me deal with this
102 *wisewoman* herbalist
109 *move* upset
111 *rough* violent
112 *bawcock* fine bird
113 *chuck* chicken

115 *biddy* chickabiddy. Sir Toby is clucking encouragingly at Malvolio.
116 *gravity* a sober, mature man
cherry-pit (children's game played with cherry-stones)
117 *collier* coal-vendor (in allusion to the devil's blackness)

MARIA Get him to say his prayers, good Sir Toby; get him to pray.

120 MALVOLIO My prayers, minx!

MARIA No, I warrant you, he will not hear of godliness.

MALVOLIO Go, hang yourselves all. You are idle, shallow things; I am not of your element. You shall know more hereafter.   *Exit Malvolio*

SIR TOBY Is't possible?

FABIAN If this were played upon a stage now, I could condemn it as an improbable fiction.

SIR TOBY His very genius hath taken the infection of the device, man.

130 MARIA Nay, pursue him now, lest the device take air, and taint.

FABIAN Why, we shall make him mad indeed.

MARIA The house will be the quieter.

SIR TOBY Come, we'll have him in a dark room and bound. My niece is already in the belief that he's mad. We may carry it thus for our pleasure and his penance till our very pastime, tired out of breath, prompt us to have mercy on him; at which time, we will bring the device to the bar, and crown thee for a finder of mad-

140 men. But see, but see!

Enter Sir Andrew

123 *element* sphere of existence

126 *played upon a stage*. This kind of theatrical bravado is found also in *Julius Caesar*, III.1.111–16, and *Antony and Cleopatra*, V.2.215–20. It does not imply that *Twelfth Night* was not originally acted on a stage.

128 *genius* soul

130–31 *take air, and taint* be exposed, and so spoilt. The Elizabethans thought fresh air bad for many fevers.

133 *quieter* freer from Malvolio's interference

134–5 *dark room and bound*. This was the usual treatment for insanity in the period. 'Love' (says Rosalind) 'is merely a madness and, I tell you, deserves as well a dark house and a whip as madmen do' (*As You Like It*, III.2.383–4).

139 *to the bar*. This is unexplained. It may mean the bar dividing the benchers from the students in hall in the Inns of Court.

139–40 *a finder of madmen* one of a jury appointed to find out if an accused person was insane

FABIAN More matter for a May morning!

SIR ANDREW Here's the challenge, read it. I warrant there's vinegar and pepper in't.

FABIAN Is't so saucy?

SIR ANDREW Ay, is't, I warrant him. Do but read.

SIR TOBY Give me.

    He reads

    Youth, whatsoever thou art, thou art but a scurvy fellow.

FABIAN Good and valiant.

SIR TOBY (*reads*) *Wonder not, nor admire not in thy mind, why I do call thee so, for I will show thee no reason for't.* 150

FABIAN A good note, that keeps you from the blow of the law.

SIR TOBY (*reads*) *Thou com'st to the Lady Olivia, and in my sight she uses thee kindly. But thou liest in thy throat; that is not the matter I challenge thee for.*

FABIAN Very brief, and to exceeding good sense – (*aside*) less!

SIR TOBY (*reads*) *I will waylay thee going home; where, if it be thy chance to kill me –*

FABIAN Good! 160

SIR TOBY (*reads*) *thou kill'st me like a rogue and a villain.*

FABIAN Still you keep o' the windy side of the law; good.

SIR TOBY (*reads*) *Fare thee well, and God have mercy upon*

141 *matter for a May morning* sport fit for a holiday

144 *saucy* (with a pun on the meanings 'impudent' and 'piquant')

149 *admire* marvel

151–2 *keeps you from the blow of the law* shelters you from the law (that is, from being accused of causing a breach of the peace)

154 *thou liest in thy throat*. If Sir Andrew's letter is not as senseless as Fabian thinks, Sir Andrew is postulating a statement by Cesario: 'You are angry because of the Lady Olivia's attentions to me' in order to have grounds for calling him a liar.

161–2 *thou kill'st me like a rogue and a villain*. Sir Andrew's effort to avoid any actionable abuse, or any threat of violence towards his opponent, would have delighted an audience of law students.

163 *o' the windy side* on the safe side (because you can't be scented out)

one of our souls. He may have mercy upon mine, but my
hope is better — and so, look to thyself. Thy friend as thou
usest him, and thy sworn enemy, Andrew Aguecheek. If
this letter move him not, his legs cannot. I'll give't him.

170 MARIA You may have very fit occasion for't. He is now in
some commerce with my lady, and will by and by
depart.

SIR TOBY Go, Sir Andrew. Scout me for him at the
corner of the orchard like a bum-baily. So soon as ever
thou seest him, draw, and as thou drawest, swear hor-
rible; for it comes to pass oft that a terrible oath, with a
swaggering accent sharply twanged off, gives manhood
more approbation than ever proof itself would have
earned him. Away!

180 SIR ANDREW Nay, let me alone for swearing.   *Exit*
SIR TOBY Now will not I deliver his letter. For the behaviour of the young gentleman gives him out to be of
good capacity and breeding; his employment between
his lord and my niece confirms no less. Therefore this
letter, being so excellently ignorant, will breed no terror
in the youth; he will find it comes from a clodpole. But,
sir, I will deliver his challenge by word of mouth; set
upon Aguecheek a notable report of valour, and drive
the gentleman — as I know his youth will aptly receive it
190   — into a most hideous opinion of his rage, skill, fury, and
impetuosity. This will so fright them both, that they
will kill one another by the look, like cockatrices.

166–7 *my hope* (of winning — but Sir
Andrew is made to appear as if he is
in hope of something better than sal-
vation)
167–8 *as thou usest him* as thy usage of
him deserves (not at all, in fact)
171 *commerce* conference
173 *Scout me for him* I want you to keep
a look-out for him

174 *bum-baily* (bailiff, or sheriff's officer,
who shadowed a debtor in order to
arrest him)
178 *approbation* credit
proof trial, testing
186 *clodpole* blockhead
192 *cockatrices* (mythical monsters able
to kill with a glance)

Enter Olivia and Viola

FABIAN Here he comes with your niece. Give them way
till he take leave, and presently after him.

SIR TOBY I will meditate the while upon some horrid
message for a challenge.

Exit Maria

Sir Toby and Fabian stand aside

OLIVIA

I have said too much unto a heart of stone,
And laid mine honour too unchary on't.
There's something in me that reproves my fault.
But such a headstrong, potent fault it is,   200
That it but mocks reproof.

VIOLA

With the same 'haviour that your passion bears
Goes on my master's griefs.

OLIVIA

Here, wear this jewel for me, 'tis my picture.
Refuse it not, it hath no tongue to vex you.
And, I beseech you, come again tomorrow.
What shall you ask of me that I'll deny,
That honour saved may upon asking give?

VIOLA

Nothing but this: your true love for my master.

OLIVIA

How with mine honour may I give him that   210
Which I have given to you?

VIOLA   I will acquit you.

193 *Give them way* keep out of their way
194 *presently* immediately
195 *horrid* terrifying
198 *unchary* unguardedly
on't (on a heart of stone, in allusion
to the Elizabethan custom of making
payment of a debt on a known stone
in a church)

202 *With the same 'haviour* in the same
manner
204 *jewel* jewel-set miniature
208 *That honour saved may upon asking give*
that honour may grant, when requested, without compromising
itself

OLIVIA

Well, come again tomorrow. Fare thee well.
A fiend like thee might bear my soul to hell. *Exit*
Sir Toby and Fabian come forward

SIR TOBY Gentleman, God save thee!

VIOLA And you, sir.

SIR TOBY That defence thou hast, betake thee to't. Of what nature the wrongs are thou hast done him, I know not; but thy intercepter, full of despite, bloody as the hunter, attends thee at the orchard end. Dismount thy tuck; be yare in thy preparation; for thy assailant is quick, skilful, and deadly.

VIOLA You mistake, sir. I am sure no man hath any quarrel to me. My remembrance is very free and clear from any image of offence done to any man.

SIR TOBY You'll find it otherwise, I assure you. Therefore, if you hold your life at any price, betake you to your guard; for your opposite hath in him what youth, strength, skill, and wrath can furnish man withal.

VIOLA I pray you, sir, what is he?

SIR TOBY He is knight dubbed with unhatched rapier and

212-13 *Well, come again tomorrow. Fare thee well ... bear my soul to hell.* The conclusive-sounding couplet here, and the fact that the action from this point to the end of the Act can be thought of as taking place in the street outside Olivia's garden, would justify a modern producer's treating the remainder of this Act as a separate scene. On the Elizabethan stage, however, the action is continuous. Sir Toby and Fabian come forward and intercept Viola outside the door (or the curtain concealing the back of the stage) by which Olivia has just left. Then Sir Toby crosses the stage and either goes out by the farthest door to bring Sir Andrew back at 'Why man, he's a very devil' (line 267), or, finding him in view of the audience, engages him in conversation and brings him downstage so that 'Why, man' are the first words heard by the audience. Sir Toby and Fabian then coax the duellists into coming face to face, and as soon as they do so Antonio makes his dramatic entry.

218 *despite* defiance

219-20 *Dismount thy tuck* draw thy sword

220 *yare* prompt

223 *remembrance* recollection

227 *opposite* opponent

228 *withal* with

230 *unhatched.* This means either 'not marked in battle' or 'never drawn'.

on carpet consideration – but he is a devil in private brawl. Souls and bodies hath he divorced three; and his incensement at this moment is so implacable, that satisfaction can be none, but by pangs of death, and sepulchre. Hob, nob! is his word: give't or take't.

VIOLA I will return again into the house and desire some conduct of the lady. I am no fighter. I have heard of some kind of men that put quarrels purposely on others to taste their valour. Belike this is a man of that quirk.

SIR TOBY Sir, no. His indignation derives itself out of a very computent injury. Therefore, get you on and give him his desire. Back you shall not to the house, unless you undertake that with me, which with as much safety you might answer him. Therefore on, or strip your sword stark naked; for meddle you must, that's certain, or forswear to wear iron about you.   240

VIOLA This is as uncivil as strange. I beseech you, do me this courteous office, as to know of the knight what my offence to him is. It is something of my negligence, nothing of my purpose.   250

SIR TOBY I will do so. Signor Fabian, stay you by this gentleman till my return.   *Exit*

VIOLA Pray you, sir, do you know of this matter?

FABIAN I know the knight is incensed against you, even to a mortal arbitrement, but nothing of the circumstance more.

VIOLA I beseech you, what manner of man is he?

FABIAN Nothing of that wonderful promise, to read him by his form, as you are like to find him in the proof of his valour. He is indeed, sir, the most skilful, bloody,   260

231 *on carpet consideration* for non-military services to the crown (usually financial ones at that period)
235 *Hob, nob* come what may (literally, have it or have it not)
239 *taste* test
     quirk peculiarity

241 *computent* to be reckoned with
245 *meddle* engage in combat
248 *know of* inquire from
250 *purpose* intention
255 *mortal arbitrement* decision of the matter by mortal combat
259 *form* appearance

and fatal opposite that you could possibly have found in any part of Illyria. Will you walk towards him? I will make your peace with him, if I can.

VIOLA I shall be much bound to you for't. I am one that had rather go with Sir Priest than Sir Knight; I care not who knows so much of my mettle.

Enter Sir Toby and Sir Andrew

SIR TOBY Why, man, he's a very devil. I have not seen such a firago. I had a pass with him, rapier, scabbard and all; and he gives me the stuck-in with such a mortal
270   motion that it is inevitable; and on the answer, he pays you as surely as your feet hits the ground they step on. They say he has been fencer to the Sophy.

SIR ANDREW Pox on't! I'll not meddle with him.

SIR TOBY Ay, but he will not now be pacified. Fabian can scarce hold him yonder.

SIR ANDREW Plague on't! An I thought he had been valiant, and so cunning in fence, I'd have seen him damned ere I'd have challenged him. Let him let the matter slip, and I'll give him my horse, grey Capilet.

280 SIR TOBY I'll make the motion. Stand here, make a good show on't. This shall end without the perdition of souls. (*Aside, as he crosses to Fabian*) Marry, I'll ride your horse as well as I ride you! (*To Fabian*) I have his horse to take up the quarrel. I have persuaded him the youth's a devil.

265 *Sir Priest*. Sir here stands for '*Dominus*', the title given to a graduate and thence used of a clergyman.
268 *firago* virago. The word means a fighting woman, but was used of both sexes in Shakespeare's day.
269 *stuck-in* thrust (from the Italian fencing term, '*stoccata*')
269–70 *mortal motion* deadly movement
270 *it is inevitable* it cannot be averted
270–71 *on the answer, he pays you* he counters your return blow

272 *to the Sophy*. Shakespeare may have learned from his former colleague Kemp, who had met Sir Anthony Shirley on his return from Persia, that Sir Robert Shirley had remained in the Shah's military service. See Introduction, pages 529–30.
276 *An* if
280 *make the motion* put the proposal
281 *perdition of souls* (killing)
282 *Marry* (an asseveration – originally 'By Mary')

FABIAN He is as horribly conceited of him, and pants and
looks pale as if a bear were at his heels.

SIR TOBY (*to Viola*) There's no remedy, sir, he will fight
with you for's oath's sake. Marry, he hath better be-
thought him of his quarrel, and he finds that now scarce　290
to be worth talking of. Therefore, draw for the sup-
portance of his vow. He protests he will not hurt you.

VIOLA (*aside*) Pray God defend me! A little thing would
make me tell them how much I lack of a man.

FABIAN Give ground if you see him furious.

SIR TOBY (*crossing to Sir Andrew*) Come, Sir Andrew,
there's no remedy. The gentleman will, for his honour's
sake, have one bout with you, he cannot by the *duello*
avoid it. But he has promised me, as he is a gentleman
and a soldier, he will not hurt you. Come on, to't!　300

SIR ANDREW Pray God he keep his oath!

> *He draws*
> *Enter Antonio*

VIOLA I do assure you, 'tis against my will.

> *She draws*

ANTONIO
Put up your sword. If this young gentleman
Have done offence, I take the fault on me.
If you offend him, I for him defy you.

SIR TOBY You, sir? Why, what are you?

ANTONIO
One, sir, that for his love dares yet do more
Than you have heard him brag to you he will.

SIR TOBY Nay, if you be an undertaker, I am for you.

> *Enter Officers*

FABIAN O good Sir Toby, hold! Here come the Officers.　310

SIR TOBY (*to Antonio*) I'll be with you anon.

VIOLA (*to Sir Andrew*) Pray sir, put your sword up, if
you please.

---

286 *He is as horribly conceited* he has　309 *an undertaker* one who undertakes
as terrifying an idea　　　　　　　　　　another's quarrel
298 *duello* code of duelling

SIR ANDREW Marry, will I, sir. And for that I promised
you, I'll be as good as my word. He will bear you easily,
and reins well.

FIRST OFFICER This is the man; do thy office.

SECOND OFFICER
Antonio, I arrest thee at the suit
Of Count Orsino.

ANTONIO   You do mistake me, sir.

FIRST OFFICER
320 No, sir, no jot. I know your favour well,
Though now you have no sea-cap on your head.
Take him away; he knows I know him well.

ANTONIO
I must obey. (to Viola) This comes with seeking you.
But there's no remedy, I shall answer it.
What will you do, now my necessity
Makes me to ask you for my purse? It grieves me
Much more for what I cannot do for you
Than what befalls myself. You stand amazed;
But be of comfort.

SECOND OFFICER Come, sir, away!

330 ANTONIO I must entreat of you some of that money.

VIOLA
What money, sir?
For the fair kindness you have showed me here,
And part being prompted by your present trouble,
Out of my lean and low ability,
I'll lend you something. My having is not much.
I'll make division of my present with you.
Hold: there's half my coffer.

314 *that I promised* (the horse)
320 *favour* face
324 *answer* make reparation for
325-6 *What will you do, now my necessity | ... purse?* Antonio's appeal, even in a desperate situation, expresses his concern for Sebastian.
328 *amazed* bewildered, dazed
329 *be of comfort* do not grieve
335 *having* resources
336 *my present* what I have at present
337 *coffer* money (literally, chest)

ANTONIO

Will you deny me now?
Is't possible that my deserts to you
Can lack persuasion? Do not tempt my misery,   340
Lest that it make me so unsound a man
As to upbraid you with those kindnesses
That I have done for you.

VIOLA   I know of none.
Nor know I you by voice or any feature.
I hate ingratitude more in a man
Than lying, vainness, babbling drunkenness,
Or any taint of vice whose strong corruption
Inhabits our frail blood—

ANTONIO   O heavens themselves!

SECOND OFFICER

Come, sir, I pray you go.

ANTONIO

Let me speak a little. This youth that you see here   350
I snatched one half out of the jaws of death;
Relieved him with such sanctity of love;
And to his image, which methought did promise
Most venerable worth, did I devotion.

FIRST OFFICER

What's that to us? The time goes by. Away!

ANTONIO

But O, how vild an idol proves this god!
Thou hast, Sebastian, done good feature shame.
In nature, there's no blemish but the mind;
None can be called deformed, but the unkind.

339–40 *Is't possible that my deserts to you | Can lack persuasion?* is it possible that the claims of my past kindnesses can fail to move you?
346 *vainness* boasting
352 *sanctity of love* love as for a sacred object
354 *venerable* worthy to be venerated

356 *vild* vile (a common Elizabethan form of the word, kept here for euphony)
358–9 *In nature, there's no blemish but the mind; | None can be called deformed, but the unkind* although there may seem to be deformities in nature, the only real deformity is a hard heart

360   Virtue is beauty; but the beauteous evil
      Are empty trunks o'er-flourished by the devil.

FIRST OFFICER
      The man grows mad; away with him. Come, come, sir.

ANTONIO
      Lead me on.   *Exeunt Antonio and Officers*

VIOLA (*aside*)
      Methinks his words do from such passion fly
      That he believes himself; so do not I?
      Prove true, imagination, O, prove true –
      That I, dear brother, be now ta'en for you!

SIR TOBY Come hither, knight; come hither, Fabian.
      We'll whisper o'er a couplet or two of most sage saws.

VIOLA
370   He named Sebastian. I my brother know
      Yet living in my glass. Even such and so
      In favour was my brother; and he went
      Still in this fashion, colour, ornament,
      For him I imitate. O, if it prove,
      Tempests are kind, and salt waves fresh in love!   *Exit*

SIR TOBY A very dishonest, paltry boy, and more a
      coward than a hare. His dishonesty appears in leaving
      his friend here in necessity and denying him; and for his
      cowardship, ask Fabian.

380   FABIAN A coward, a most devout coward, religious in it!
      SIR ANDREW 'Slid! I'll after him again and beat him.

---

361 *o'er-flourished* richly decorated. Elaborately carved or painted chests were
   a feature of prosperous Elizabethan
   homes.
365 *so do not I?* why do I not believe
   myself (my hope that my brother is
   alive)?
368 *Come hither.* Sir Toby and his friends
   draw contemptuously aside, leaving
   Viola to speak her thoughts in coup-
   lets, the common form for adages,
   or 'sage saws'.

369 *sage saws* wise sayings, aphorisms
370–71 *I my brother know | Yet living in
   my glass* I know my brother is the
   image of me
374 *prove* prove to be so
376 *dishonest* dishonourable
380 *religious in it* behaving as if it were a
   principle of his faith (to be cowardly)
381 *'Slid* (a mild oath – originally,
   'God's eyelid')

SIR TOBY Do, cuff him soundly, but never draw thy
    sword.

SIR ANDREW An I do not –   *Exit*

FABIAN Come, let's see the event.

SIR TOBY I dare lay any money, 'twill be nothing yet.
                                  Exeunt

       Enter Sebastian and Feste   IV.I

FESTE Will you make me believe that I am not sent for
    you?

SEBASTIAN Go to, go to, thou art a foolish fellow. Let me
    be clear of thee.

FESTE Well held out, i'faith. No: I do not know you; nor
    I am not sent to you by my lady, to bid you come speak
    with her; nor your name is not Master Cesario; nor this
    is not my nose, neither. Nothing that is so, is so.

SEBASTIAN I prithee, vent thy folly somewhere else; thou
    knowest not me.   10

FESTE Vent my folly! He has heard that word of some
    great man, and now applies it to a fool. Vent my folly!
    I am afraid this great lubber the world will prove a
    cockney. I prithee now, ungird thy strangeness, and
    tell me what I shall vent to my lady? Shall I vent to her
    that thou art coming?

SEBASTIAN I prithee, foolish Greek, depart from me.

385 *event* result
386 *yet* after all

IV.I.5 *held out* kept up
9 *vent* void, get rid of
13 *lubber* overgrown boy
14 *cockney* pampered child. Feste is
    saying 'How affected everyone is get-
    ting, using words like "vent"!'

ungird thy strangeness stop being
stand-offish
15 *vent* utter, say. This meaning, devel-
    oped from the meaning 'get rid of'
    (see line 9 above) was to become
    common in the seventeenth century.
17 *foolish Greek* buffoon. The expression
    is usually found in the form 'merry
    Greek'.

There's money for thee; if you tarry longer, I shall give
worse payment.

20 FESTE By my troth, thou hast an open hand! These wise
men that give fools money get themselves a good report
– after fourteen years' purchase.

Enter Sir Andrew, Sir Toby, and Fabian

SIR ANDREW Now, sir, have I met you again? There's
for you!

He strikes Sebastian

SEBASTIAN Why, there's for thee! And there!

He beats Sir Andrew with the handle of his dagger

And there! Are all the people mad?

SIR TOBY Hold, sir, or I'll throw your dagger o'er the
house.

FESTE This will I tell my lady straight. I would not be in
30 some of your coats, for twopence.   *Exit*

SIR TOBY Come on, sir, hold!

He grips Sebastian

SIR ANDREW Nay, let him alone. I'll go another way to
work with him. I'll have an action of battery against
him, if there be any law in Illyria – though I struck him
first, yet it's no matter for that.

SEBASTIAN Let go thy hand!

SIR TOBY Come, sir, I will not let you go. Come, my
young soldier, put up your iron; you are well fleshed.
Come on!

SEBASTIAN

40 I will be free from thee!

He breaks free and draws his sword

What wouldst thou now?

---

22 *after fourteen years' purchase.* The usual
Elizabethan price of land was the
equivalent of twelve years' rent, so
fourteen years' purchase was a lot of
money, and the phrase means 'at a
price'.

33 *action of battery.* As Sir Andrew struck

the first blow he has, of course, no
case: another joke for the law students.

38 *put up your iron* sheathe your sword
(said ironically; Sebastian has only
used the hilt of his dagger)
fleshed initiated into fighting,
blooded

If thou darest tempt me further, draw thy sword.

SIR TOBY What, what! Nay, then, I must have an ounce
or two of this malapert blood from you.

> *He draws*
> *Enter Olivia*

OLIVIA

Hold, Toby! On thy life, I charge thee hold!

SIR TOBY Madam!

OLIVIA

Will it be ever thus? Ungracious wretch,
Fit for the mountains and the barbarous caves
Where manners ne'er were preached, out of my sight!
Be not offended, dear Cesario.
Rudesby, be gone!   50

> *Exeunt Sir Toby, Sir Andrew, and Fabian*
>   I prithee, gentle friend,

Let thy fair wisdom, not thy passion, sway
In this uncivil and unjust extent
Against thy peace. Go with me to my house,
And hear thou there how many fruitless pranks
This ruffian hath botched up, that thou thereby
Mayst smile at this. Thou shalt not choose but go;
Do not deny. Beshrew his soul for me!
He started one poor heart of mine, in thee.

SEBASTIAN (*aside*)

What relish is in this? How runs the stream?
Or I am mad, or else this is a dream.   60
Let fancy still my sense in Lethe steep;
If it be thus to dream, still let me sleep!

---

43 *malapert* impudent
50 *Rudesby* boor
52 *uncivil* barbarous
 extent assault (originally a legal term)
55 *botched up* crudely contrived
57 *deny* refuse
 Beshrew curse
58 *started* roused (a hunting term)
 heart (with a pun on 'hart' and a use

of the familiar conceit that lovers
exchange hearts)
59 *What relish is in this?* what am I to
make of this?
 relish taste
60 *Or* either
61 *Lethe* (the mythical river of forgetfulness)

OLIVIA
Nay, come, I prithee. Would thou'dst be ruled by me!
SEBASTIAN
Madam, I will.
OLIVIA   O, say so, and so be!   *Exeunt*

IV.2   *Enter Maria and Feste*
MARIA Nay, I prithee, put on this gown and this beard;
make him believe thou art Sir Topas the curate. Do it
quickly. I'll call Sir Toby the whilst.   *Exit*
FESTE Well, I'll put it on and I will dissemble myself in't,
and I would I were the first that ever dissembled in such
a gown. I am not tall enough to become the function
well, nor lean enough to be thought a good student. But
to be said an honest man and a good housekeeper goes as
fairly as to say a careful man and a great scholar. The
10   competitors enter.
            Enter Sir Toby and Maria
SIR TOBY Jove bless thee, Master Parson!
FESTE *Bonos dies*, Sir Toby; for as the old hermit of
Prague that never saw pen and ink very wittily said to
a niece of King Gorboduc: that that is, is. So I, being
Master Parson, am Master Parson; for what is 'that' but
'that'? And 'is' but 'is'?
SIR TOBY To him, Sir Topas.
FESTE What ho, I say! Peace in this prison!
SIR TOBY The knave counterfeits well; a good knave.

63 *Would thou'dst* if only you would

IV.2.2 *Sir* (a title used for clergymen; see
III.4.265, note)
Topas. All precious and semi-precious
stones were supposed to have healing
properties; the topaz cured lunacy.
curate parish priest
8 *said* called *an honest man and a good
housekeeper* a good sort, and hospitable
9 *careful* serious-minded

10 *competitors* confederates
12 *Bonos dies* good day (mock Latin)
12–13 *old hermit of Prague* (an authority
invented in parody of pedantic
name-dropping)
14 *Gorboduc* (legendary early British
king, hero of a famous sixteenth-century play)
that that is, is. Feste takes off the
axioms of medieval philosophy
which often sound absurdly self-evi-
dent to the layman.

MALVOLIO (*within*)Who calls there?   20

FESTE Sir Topas the curate, who comes to visit Malvolio
the lunatic.

MALVOLIO Sir Topas, Sir Topas, good Sir Topas, go to
my lady —

FESTE Out, hyperbolical fiend, how vexest thou this man!
Talkest thou nothing but of ladies?

SIR TOBY Well said, Master Parson.

MALVOLIO Sir Topas, never was man thus wronged.
Good Sir Topas, do not think I am mad. They have laid
me here in hideous darkness —   30

FESTE Fie, thou dishonest Satan! I call thee by the most
modest terms, for I am one of those gentle ones that will
use the devil himself with courtesy. Sayst thou that
house is dark?

MALVOLIO As hell, Sir Topas.

FESTE Why, it hath bay windows transparent as barricadoes, and the clerestories toward the south–north
are as lustrous as ebony. And yet complainest thou of
obstruction!

MALVOLIO I am not mad, Sir Topas. I say to you, this   40
house is dark.

FESTE Madman, thou errest. I say there is no darkness but
ignorance, in which thou art more puzzled than the
Egyptians in their fog.

---

20 (stage direction) *within*. In the Folio,
the stage direction *Maluolio within* precedes the speech-heading *Mal.*, as a
warning to the actor to be ready. See
An Account of the Text, page 549.

25 *hyperbolical* boisterous. Feste is addressing the devil which has possessed Malvolio.

33–4 *that house is dark*. A dark house
was the term for a darkened room
in which a madman was confined.
The expression occurs in the fifth
story of Rich's *Farewell to Military
Profession*.

36 *bay windows*. These were the rage of
the period, when great houses were
laughed at for being 'more glass than
wall'.

36–7 *barricadoes* barricades. These and
ebony wood are the most opaque
things Feste can think of. His joke is
of the 'clear as mud' type.

37 *clerestories* (a range of windows high
up in a wall)

42 *darkness*. A three-day darkness was
one of the plagues of Egypt described in Exodus 10.

MALVOLIO I say this house is as dark as ignorance,
though ignorance were as dark as hell. And I say there
was never man thus abused. I am no more mad than you
are – make the trial of it in any constant question.

FESTE What is the opinion of Pythagoras concerning
50   wildfowl?

MALVOLIO That the soul of our grandam might haply
inhabit a bird.

FESTE What thinkest thou of his opinion?

MALVOLIO I think nobly of the soul, and no way approve
his opinion.

FESTE Fare thee well; remain thou still in darkness. Thou
shalt hold the opinion of Pythagoras ere I will allow of
thy wits, and fear to kill a woodcock lest thou dispossess
the soul of thy grandam. Fare thee well.

60   MALVOLIO Sir Topas, Sir Topas!

SIR TOBY My most exquisite Sir Topas!

FESTE Nay, I am for all waters.

MARIA Thou mightst have done this without thy beard
and gown; he sees thee not.

SIR TOBY To him in thine own voice, and bring me word
how thou findest him. I would we were well rid of this
knavery. If he may be conveniently delivered, I would
he were, for I am now so far in offence with my niece
that I cannot pursue with any safety this sport the up-
70   shot. Come by and by to my chamber.

Exeunt Sir Toby and Maria

---

47 *abused* ill treated
48 *constant question* question and answer
on a normal topic
49 *Pythagoras* (a Greek philosopher who
held the theory of the transmigration
of souls; the same soul could inhabit
in succession the bodies of different
kinds of creatures – fish, birds, and
animals, as well as men)
51 *haply* perhaps
62 *I am for all waters* I can turn my hand

to anything (with a pun on 'water' in
the sense of the brilliance or lustre of
a precious or semi-precious stone
such as a topaz)
63–4 *Thou . . . not.* This suggests an afterthought on Shakespeare's part, and
so, rapid composition. See pages 528–9.
69–70 *the upshot* to its final outcome (an
archery term, meaning 'the decisive
shot')

FESTE (*sings*)

Hey Robin, jolly Robin!
Tell me how thy lady does –

MALVOLIO Fool!

FESTE (*sings*)

My lady is unkind, perdy.

MALVOLIO Fool!

FESTE (*sings*)

Alas, why is she so?

MALVOLIO Fool, I say!

FESTE (*sings*)

She loves another –
Who calls, ha?

MALVOLIO Good fool, as ever thou wilt deserve well at
my hand, help me to a candle, and pen, ink, and paper.
As I am a gentleman, I will live to be thankful to thee
for't.

FESTE Master Malvolio?

MALVOLIO Ay, good fool.

FESTE Alas, sir, how fell you besides your five wits?

MALVOLIO Fool, there was never man so notoriously
abused. I am as well in my wits, fool, as thou art.

FESTE But as well? Then you are mad indeed, if you be
no better in your wits than a fool.

MALVOLIO They have here propertied me; keep me in
darkness, send ministers to me – asses! – and do all they
can to face me out of my wits.

FESTE Advise you what you say. The minister is here.

80

90

71 *Hey Robin, jolly Robin.* An early Tudor
setting to this poem is given on page
560. The words have been attributed
to Sir Thomas Wyatt.
74 *perdy* (an adjuration; French *par Dieu*)
86 *besides your five wits* out of your mind
(the five wits being the five faculties

of the mind: common wit, imagination, fantasy, estimation, and
memory)
91 *propertied me* treated me as a mere
property
93 *face* brazen
94 *Advise you* be careful

(*In priest's voice*) Malvolio, Malvolio, thy wits the heavens restore! Endeavour thyself to sleep and leave thy vain bibble-babble.

MALVOLIO Sir Topas!

FESTE Maintain no words with him, good fellow. (*In own voice*) Who, I, sir? Not I, sir! God buy you, good Sir Topas! (*In priest's voice*) Marry, amen! (*In own voice*) I will, sir, I will.

MALVOLIO Fool! Fool! Fool, I say!

FESTE Alas, sir, be patient. What say you sir? I am shent for speaking to you.

MALVOLIO Good fool, help me to some light and some paper. I tell thee, I am as well in my wits as any man in Illyria.

FESTE Well-a-day, that you were, sir!

MALVOLIO By this hand, I am! Good fool, some ink, paper, and light; and convey what I will set down to my lady. It shall advantage thee more than ever the bearing of letter did.

FESTE I will help you to't. But tell me true, are you not mad indeed, or do you but counterfeit?

MALVOLIO Believe me, I am not. I tell thee true.

FESTE Nay, I'll ne'er believe a madman till I see his brains. I will fetch you light, and paper, and ink.

MALVOLIO Fool, I'll requite it in the highest degree. I prithee, be gone.

---

97 *bibble-babble*. There may be some echo here of a controversy which raged round the preacher John Darrell, who claimed to have successfully cured several people possessed by devils. In 1600 Darrell published *A True Narration*, in which the victims are said on three occasions to have called the Scriptures 'bible-bable'.

But the expression was quite a common one.

100 *God buy you* God be with you

102 *I will, sir, I will* (with a pun on 'marry' used as a mild oath and as meaning 'wed')

104 *shent* scolded

109 *Well-a-day!* alas!

FESTE (*sings*)

> I am gone, sir, and anon, sir,
>> I'll be with you again.
> In a trice, like to the old Vice,
>> Your need to sustain.
> Who with dagger of lath, in his rage and his wrath,
>> Cries 'Ah ha!' to the devil;
> Like a mad lad – 'Pare thy nails, dad?
>> Adieu, goodman devil!'   *Exit*

Enter Sebastian   IV.3

SEBASTIAN

> This is the air; that is the glorious sun;
> This pearl she gave me, I do feel't and see't;
> And though 'tis wonder that enwraps me thus,
> Yet 'tis not madness. Where's Antonio, then?
> I could not find him at the Elephant.
> Yet there he was; and there I found this credit
> That he did range the town to seek me out.
> His counsel now might do me golden service.
> For though my soul disputes well with my sense
> That this may be some error, but no madness,   10
> Yet doth this accident and flood of fortune
> So far exceed all instance, all discourse,
> That I am ready to distrust mine eyes,
> And wrangle with my reason that persuades me

121–8 *I am gone, sir, and anon, sir ... goodman devil.* This may have been recited and not sung.

123 *old Vice* (a character who defied the devil in the early Tudor interludes which developed from the Morality plays. He was one ancestor of the Elizabethan stage fool.)

127 *Pare thy nails.* A passage in *Henry V* – 'this roaring devil i'th'old play, that everyone may pare his nails with a wooden dagger' (IV.4.69–70) – suggests that this was a familiar piece of stage business.

IV.3.6 *there he was* he had been there
  credit report
11 *accident* unexpected happening
12 *instance* example
  discourse reasoning

To any other trust but that I am mad –
Or else the lady's mad; yet if 'twere so,
She could not sway her house, command her followers,
Take and give back affairs and their dispatch,
With such a smooth, discreet, and stable bearing
20   As I perceive she does. There's something in't
That is deceivable. But here the lady comes.

Enter Olivia and a Priest

OLIVIA

Blame not this haste of mine. If you mean well,
Now go with me and with this holy man
Into the chantry by; there before him
And underneath that consecrated roof
Plight me the full assurance of your faith,
That my most jealous and too doubtful soul
May live at peace. He shall conceal it
Whiles you are willing it shall come to note;
30   What time we will our celebration keep
According to my birth. What do you say?

SEBASTIAN

I'll follow this good man, and go with you;
And having sworn truth, ever will be true.

OLIVIA

Then lead the way, good father, and heavens so shine
That they may fairly note this act of mine!

Exeunt

17 *sway* rule
18 *Take and give back affairs and their
dispatch.* Olivia receives reports from
her household and gives them orders
in return.
21 *deceivable* deceptive
24 *chantry by* nearby chapel (a chantry
being an endowed chapel where

masses were said for the soul of the
founder)
26 *Plight me the full assurance.* A
ceremony of betrothal, in the presence of a priest, was as binding a contract as the actual marriage service.
29 *Whiles* until
31 *birth* nobility

Enter Feste and Fabian   V.I

FABIAN Now, as thou lov'st me, let me see his letter.

FESTE Good Master Fabian, grant me another request.

FABIAN Anything!

FESTE Do not desire to see this letter.

FABIAN This is to give a dog, and in recompense desire
my dog again.

Enter Orsino, Viola, Curio, and lords

ORSINO Belong you to the Lady Olivia, friends?

FESTE Ay, sir, we are some of her trappings.

ORSINO I know thee well. How dost thou, my good
fellow?   10

FESTE Truly, sir, the better for my foes, and the worse for
my friends.

ORSINO Just the contrary: the better for thy friends.

FESTE No, sir: the worse.

ORSINO How can that be?

FESTE Marry, sir, they praise me – and make an ass of me.
Now my foes tell me plainly, I am an ass; so that by my
foes, sir, I profit in the knowledge of myself, and by my
friends I am abused. So that, conclusions to be as
kisses, if your four negatives make your two affirma-   20
tives, why then, the worse for my friends and the better
for my foes.

v.i.5–6 *This is to give a dog . . . dog again.*
Manningham's diary, which records
the first known performance of
Twelfth Night, also gives us the
source of this saying: 'Mr Francis
Curle told me how one Doctor Bul-
leyn, the Queen's kinsman, had a
dog which he doted on, so much
that the Queen, understanding of it,
requested he would grant her one
desire, and he should have whatsoever he would ask. She demanded
his dog. He gave it, and – "Now,

Madam," quoth he, "you promised
to give me my desire." "I will,"
quoth she. "Then I pray you, give
me my dog again."'

8 *trappings* bits and pieces. Feste, who
belongs to no one, is irritated by
Orsino's tone.

19–21 *conclusions to be as kisses, if your four
negatives make your two affirmatives.*
Similar jests of the period are based
on the assumption that a girl's 'No,
no, no, no!' could be interpreted as
'Yes, yes!'

ORSINO Why, this is excellent.

FESTE By my troth, sir, no – though it please you to be one of my friends.

ORSINO Thou shalt not be the worse for me: there's gold.

FESTE But that it would be double-dealing, sir, I would you could make it another.

ORSINO O, you give me ill counsel!

30 FESTE Put your grace in your pocket, sir, for this once, and let your flesh and blood obey it.

ORSINO Well, I will be so much a sinner to be a double-dealer; there's another.

FESTE *Primo, secundo, tertio*, is a good play; and the old saying is, the third pays for all; the triplex, sir, is a good tripping measure; or the bells of Saint Bennet, sir, may put you in mind – one, two, three!

ORSINO You can fool no more money out of me at this throw. If you will let your lady know I am here to speak
40 with her, and bring her along with you, it may awake my bounty further.

FESTE Marry, sir, lullaby to your bounty till I come again. I go, sir, but I would not have you to think that my desire of having is the sin of covetousness. But as you say, sir, let your bounty take a nap – I will awake it anon.   *Exit*

Enter Antonio and Officers

27 *double-dealing* (punning on the meanings 'a double donation' and 'duplicity')

30 *your grace*. There is a pun here on (1) the form of address to a duke, and (2) Orsino's share of divine grace which should prevent his listening to 'ill counsel'.

34 *Primo, secundo, tertio* one, two, three (Latin for first, second, third – probably the beginning of a children's counting game)

35 *the third pays for all*. The words 'at this

throw' in Orsino's next speech, meaning 'this throw of the dice', suggest that Feste is here quoting the gambler's proverb which is best known in the form 'third time lucky'.

36 *Saint Bennet* Saint Benedict. Shakespeare may have been thinking of the London church just across the river from the Globe.

lullaby to your bounty may your generosity sleep well (continuing the metaphor used by Orsino)

46 *anon* soon

VIOLA

Here comes the man, sir, that did rescue me.

ORSINO

That face of his I do remember well.
Yet when I saw it last, it was besmeared
As black as Vulcan in the smoke of war.   50
A baubling vessel was he captain of,
For shallow draught and bulk, unprizable;
With which, such scatheful grapple did he make
With the most noble bottom of our fleet,
That very envy and the tongue of loss
Cried fame and honour on him. What's the matter?

FIRST OFFICER

Orsino, this is that Antonio
That took the *Phoenix*, and her fraught from Candy;
And this is he that did the *Tiger* board
When your young nephew Titus lost his leg.   60
Here in the streets, desperate of shame and state,
In private brabble did we apprehend him.

VIOLA

He did me kindness, sir, drew on my side,
But in conclusion put strange speech upon me.
I know not what 'twas, but distraction.

ORSINO

Notable pirate, thou salt-water thief,
What foolish boldness brought thee to their mercies
Whom thou, in terms so bloody and so dear,
Hast made thine enemies?

---

50 *Vulcan* (the smith of the gods in Roman mythology)
51 *baubling* paltry
52 *unprizable* worthless
53 *scatheful* destructive
54 *bottom* ship
55 *loss* the losers
58 *fraught* cargo
   Candy Candia (now Crete)

61 *desperate of shame and state* recklessly disregarding both the harm a quarrel would do to his character and the danger in which it would place him
62 *brabble* brawl
64 *put strange speech upon me* spoke to me in a strange manner
65 *distraction* madness
68 *dear* dire

ANTONIO

70   Orsino, noble sir,
        Be pleased that I shake off these names you give me.
        Antonio never yet was thief or pirate;
        Though, I confess, on base and ground enough,
        Orsino's enemy. A witchcraft drew me hither.
        That most ingrateful boy there by your side
        From the rude sea's enraged and foamy mouth
        Did I redeem; a wrack past hope he was.
        His life I gave him, and did thereto add
        My love without retention or restraint,
80   All his in dedication. For his sake
        Did I expose myself – pure for his love –
        Into the danger of this adverse town;
        Drew to defend him when he was beset;
        Where, being apprehended, his false cunning –
        Not meaning to partake with me in danger –
        Taught him to face me out of his acquaintance,
        And grew a twenty years' removèd thing
        While one would wink; denied me mine own purse
        Which I had recommended to his use
90   Not half an hour before.

VIOLA   How can this be?

ORSINO
        When came he to this town?

ANTONIO
        Today, my lord; and for three months before
        No interim, not a minute's vacancy,
        Both day and night, did we keep company.
                Enter Olivia and attendants

ORSINO
        Here comes the Countess; now heaven walks on earth!

---

77 *wrack* shipwrecked person   86 *face me out of* deny to my face
79 *retention* power of holding back   87 *removèd thing* estranged being
81 *pure* purely, only

But for thee, fellow – fellow, thy words are madness.
Three months this youth hath tended upon me.
But more of that anon. Take him aside.

OLIVIA

What would my lord – but that he may not have –
Wherein Olivia may seem serviceable?   100
Cesario, you do not keep promise with me.

VIOLA

Madam?

ORSINO

Gracious Olivia –

OLIVIA

What do you say, Cesario? [*To Orsino*] Good, my lord.

VIOLA

My lord would speak; my duty hushes me.

OLIVIA

If it be aught to the old tune, my lord,
It is as fat and fulsome to mine ear
As howling after music.

ORSINO

Still so cruel?

OLIVIA   Still so constant, lord.

ORSINO

What, to perverseness? You uncivil lady,   110
To whose ingrate and unauspicious altars
My soul the faithful'st offerings have breathed out
That e'er devotion tendered! What shall I do?

OLIVIA

Even what it please my lord, that shall become him.

ORSINO

Why should I not – had I the heart to do it –

---

97 *Three months*. Actually Viola has been only three days in Orsino's service when she is sent to Olivia, and after that the action is very rapid. But the inconsistency passes unnoticed in the theatre.

104 *Good, my lord* (a polite request to Orsino to let Viola speak first)
107 *fat and fulsome* nauseating
111 *ingrate* ungrateful
114 *become him* be fitting for him

Like to th'Egyptian thief at point of death
Kill what I love – a savage jealousy
That sometime savours nobly? But hear me this:
Since you to non-regardance cast my faith,
120   And that I partly know the instrument
That screws me from my true place in your favour,
Live you the marble-breasted tyrant still.
But this your minion, whom I know you love,
And whom, by heaven, I swear, I tender dearly,
Him will I tear out of that cruel eye
Where he sits crownèd in his master's spite.
Come, boy, with me, my thoughts are ripe in mischief.
I'll sacrifice the lamb that I do love
To spite a raven's heart within a dove.

VIOLA
130   And I, most jocund, apt, and willingly
To do you rest, a thousand deaths would die.

OLIVIA
Where goes Cesario?

VIOLA   After him I love
More than I love these eyes, more than my life,
More by all mores than e'er I shall love wife.
If I do feign, you witnesses above,
Punish my life, for tainting of my love!

OLIVIA
Ay me, detested! How am I beguiled!

VIOLA
Who does beguile you? Who does do you wrong?

---

116 *th'Egyptian thief*. This alludes to a
story told by Heliodorus in his *Ethi-
opica*, which was popular in a translation in Shakespeare's day. The thief
was Thyamis, a brigand who attempted to kill his captive Chariclea
to prevent her falling into the hands
of his own captors.

119 *non-regardance* contempt

121 *screws* wrenches
124 *tender* hold, esteem
126 *in his master's spite* to the mortifica-
tion of his master
134 *More by all mores* more beyond all
comparisons
137 *detested* denounced with an oath, ex-
ecrated

OLIVIA

Hast thou forgot thyself? Is it so long?

Call forth the holy father!   *Exit an attendant*

ORSINO   Come, away!   140

OLIVIA

Whither, my lord? Cesario, husband, stay!

ORSINO

Husband?

OLIVIA   Ay, husband. Can he that deny?

ORSINO

Her husband, sirrah?

VIOLA   No, my lord, not I.

OLIVIA

Alas, it is the baseness of thy fear

That makes thee strangle thy propriety.

Fear not, Cesario, take thy fortunes up.

Be that thou know'st thou art, and then thou art

As great as that thou fear'st.

        Enter Priest

                                O, welcome, Father.

Father, I charge thee, by thy reverence,

Here to unfold – though lately we intended   150

To keep in darkness what occasion now

Reveals before 'tis ripe – what thou dost know

Hath newly passed between this youth and me.

PRIEST

A contract of eternal bond of love,

Confirmed by mutual joinder of your hands,

Attested by the holy close of lips,

Strengthened by interchangement of your rings,

And all the ceremony of this compact

Sealed in my function, by my testimony;

Since when, my watch hath told me, toward my grave   160

143 *sirrah* (a contemptuous mode of ad-
     dress)
145 *strangle thy propriety* suppress your
     identity as my husband (perhaps with

a play on a further meaning of *propriety*, 'ownership' – 'the fact that I am
yours')

I have travelled but two hours.

ORSINO

O thou dissembling cub! What wilt thou be
When time hath sowed a grizzle on thy case?
Or will not else thy craft so quickly grow
That thine own trip shall be thine overthrow?
Farewell, and take her; but direct thy feet
Where thou and I henceforth may never meet.

VIOLA

My lord, I do protest —

OLIVIA   O, do not swear!
Hold little faith, though thou hast too much fear.

Enter Sir Andrew

170 SIR ANDREW For the love of God, a surgeon! Send one
presently to Sir Toby.

OLIVIA What's the matter?

SIR ANDREW He's broke my head across, and he's given
Sir Toby a bloody coxcomb too. For the love of God,
your help! I had rather than forty pound I were at home.

OLIVIA Who has done this, Sir Andrew?

SIR ANDREW The Count's gentleman, one Cesario. We
took him for a coward, but he's the very devil incardinate.

180 ORSINO My gentleman, Cesario?

SIR ANDREW 'Od's lifelings, here he is! You broke my
head for nothing; and that that I did, I was set on to do't
by Sir Toby.

VIOLA

Why do you speak to me? I never hurt you.
You drew your sword upon me without cause,
But I bespake you fair, and hurt you not.

---

163 *a grizzle* grey hairs
    case skin
165 *trip.* This can mean 'headlong speed'
    or 'trap', and probably means both
    here; Orsino calls Cesario both a de-
    ceiver and a fast worker.

169 *little* a little
171 *presently* at once
174 *coxcomb* pate
178–9 *incardinate* (Sir Andrew's error for
    'incarnate')
181 *'Od's lifelings . . .!* God's life!

Enter Sir Toby and Feste

SIR ANDREW If a bloody coxcomb be a hurt, you have
hurt me. I think you set nothing by a bloody coxcomb.
Here comes Sir Toby halting, you shall hear more; but
if he had not been in drink, he would have tickled you   190
othergates than he did.

ORSINO How now, gentleman? How isn't with you?

SIR TOBY That's all one; he's hurt me, and there's the
end on't. [*To Feste*] Sot, didst see Dick Surgeon, sot?

FESTE O, he's drunk, Sir Toby, an hour agone. His eyes
were set at eight i'the morning.

SIR TOBY Then he's a rogue and a passy-measures pavin.
I hate a drunken rogue.

OLIVIA Away with him! Who hath made this havoc with
them?   200

SIR ANDREW I'll help you, Sir Toby, because we'll be
dressed together.

SIR TOBY Will you help? An asshead, and a coxcomb,
and a knave – a thin-faced knave, a gull!

OLIVIA Get him to bed, and let his hurt be looked to.

Exeunt Sir Toby and Sir Andrew,
helped by Feste and Fabian

Enter Sebastian

SEBASTIAN
I am sorry, madam, I have hurt your kinsman.
But had it been the brother of my blood
I must have done no less, with wit and safety.

188 *set nothing by* think nothing of
189 *halting* limping
191 *othergates* otherwise
196 *set* closed
197 *passy-measures pavin.* This was a
stately dance to a strain consisting of
at least eight semibreves, and Sir
Toby, an expert on the dance, is
perhaps reminded of it by mention
of 'eight i' the morning'. He means
that Dick Surgeon's slowness in answering his call passes all measure.

The phrase must have been a little
puzzling to the copyist or compositor, because *pavin* appears as 'panyn'
in the Folio. A more common form
of the word is 'pavane'.
201–2 *be dressed* have our wounds dressed
203 *coxcomb* blockhead
204 *gull* fool
207 *the brother of my blood* my own brother
208 *with wit and safety* having any sense
at all of my own safety

TWELFTH NIGHT   V.1

You throw a strange regard upon me; and by that
210 I do perceive it hath offended you.
Pardon me, sweet one, even for the vows
We made each other but so late ago.

ORSINO
One face, one voice, one habit, and two persons!
A natural perspective, that is and is not.

SEBASTIAN
Antonio! O, my dear Antonio!
How have the hours racked and tortured me
Since I have lost thee!

ANTONIO
Sebastian, are you?

SEBASTIAN   Fear'st thou that, Antonio?

ANTONIO
How have you made division of yourself?
220 An apple cleft in two is not more twin
Than these two creatures. Which is Sebastian?

OLIVIA
Most wonderful!

SEBASTIAN
Do I stand there? I never had a brother;
Nor can there be that deity in my nature
Of here and everywhere. I had a sister
Whom the blind waves and surges have devoured.
Of charity, what kin are you to me?

213 *habit* garb
214 *perspective* optical device. This could
not have been a stereoscopic device,
as these were not invented until the
early eighteenth century. Besides, a
stereoscopic device makes two
images into one, and what Shakespeare has in mind here is something
that makes one image into two. It
could be a trick painting on a surface
folded concertina-wise, so that it appeared to be two different paintings

when viewed from two different
angles. Or it could be a theatrical
illusion of the Pepper's Ghost type
in which, by the use of mirrors, one
figure was turned into two. Such
illusions were known and practised
on the Continent early in the seventeenth century.
218 *Fear'st* do you doubt
224 *that deity in my nature* (ubiquity; only
God can be in two places at once)

What countryman? What name? What parentage?

VIOLA

Of Messaline. Sebastian was my father.
Such a Sebastian was my brother too.   230
So went he suited to his watery tomb.
If spirits can assume both form and suit
You come to fright us.

SEBASTIAN   A spirit I am indeed,
But am in that dimension grossly clad
Which from the womb I did participate.
Were you a woman, as the rest goes even,
I should my tears let fall upon your cheek,
And say, 'Thrice welcome, drownèd Viola.'

VIOLA

My father had a mole upon his brow.

SEBASTIAN

And so had mine.   240

VIOLA

And died that day when Viola from her birth
Had numbered thirteen years.

SEBASTIAN

O, that record is lively in my soul.
He finished indeed his mortal act
That day that made my sister thirteen years.

VIOLA

If nothing lets to make us happy both
But this my masculine usurped attire,
Do not embrace me, till each circumstance
Of place, time, fortune, do cohere and jump

231 *suited* dressed
232–3 *If spirits can assume both form and suit | You come to fright us.* One Elizabethan theory about ghosts was that they were evil spirits assuming the appearance of dead people.
234 *dimension* bodily form
   grossly substantially

235 *participate* have in common with others
236 *as the rest goes even* as everything fits in with your being my sister
243 *record* recollection
246 *lets* hinders
249 *cohere* accord together
   jump agree

250   That I am Viola; which to confirm,
I'll bring you to a captain in this town
Where lie my maiden weeds; by whose gentle help
I was preserved to serve this noble Count.
All the occurence of my fortune since
Hath been between this lady and this lord.

SEBASTIAN (*to Olivia*)
So comes it, lady, you have been mistook.
But nature to her bias drew in that.
You would have been contracted to a maid.
Nor are you therein, by my life, deceived:
260   You are betrothed both to a maid and man.

ORSINO
Be not amazed; right noble is his blood.
If this be so, as yet the glass seems true,
I shall have share in this most happy wrack.
(*To Viola*) Boy, thou hast said to me a thousand times
Thou never shouldst love woman like to me.

VIOLA
And all those sayings will I overswear
And all those swearings keep as true in soul
As doth that orbèd continent the fire
That severs day from night.

ORSINO   Give me thy hand,
270   And let me see thee in thy woman's weeds.

VIOLA
The Captain that did bring me first on shore
Hath my maid's garments. He, upon some action,
Is now in durance at Malvolio's suit,
A gentleman and follower of my lady's.

252 *weeds* clothes
257 *to her bias drew* obeyed her inclination (a metaphor from the game of bowls)
260 *maid and man* virgin youth
262 *as yet the glass seems true* as in fact the 'perspective' turns out not to be an illusion after all
263 *wrack* shipwreck
268 *that orbèd continent* (the sphere of the sun)
272 *action* legal charge
273 *durance* imprisonment

OLIVIA

  He shall enlarge him; fetch Malvolio hither.

  And yet, alas, now I remember me,

  They say, poor gentleman, he's much distract.

      Enter Feste with a letter, and Fabian

  A most extracting frenzy of mine own

  From my remembrance clearly banished his.

  (*To Feste*) How does he, sirrah?   280

FESTE Truly, madam, he holds Beelzebub at the stave's end as well as a man in his case may do. He's here writ a letter to you. I should have given it you today morning. But as a madman's epistles are no gospels, so it skills not much when they are delivered.

OLIVIA Open it, and read it.

FESTE Look, then, to be well edified when the fool delivers the madman.

      He reads frantically

 By the Lord, madam —

OLIVIA How now, art thou mad?   290

FESTE No, madam; I do but read madness. An your ladyship will have it as it ought to be, you must allow *vox*.

OLIVIA Prithee, read i' thy right wits.

FESTE So I do, madonna; but to read his right wits, is to read thus. Therefore, perpend, my princess, and give ear.

---

275 *enlarge* free

277 *distract* disturbed in his mind

278 *extracting* that drew everything else out of my thoughts. Olivia is playing a variation upon 'distract' in the previous line.

281–2 *Beelzebub at the stave's end* the devil at bay

284 *epistles.* Feste puns on the general sense 'letters' and the special sense 'New Testament letters'. There is a reference to the sixteenth-century liturgical controversies about when the gospel for the day should be read, or 'delivered'.

    skills not doesn't matter

287–8 *delivers* speaks the words of

293 *vox* the right voice. This was a technical term of Elizabethan public speaking.

294 *Prithee* I pray thee (equivalent to 'please')

296 *perpend* be attentive

OLIVIA (*snatching the letter and giving it to Fabian*) Read it you, sirrah.

FABIAN (*reads*)

300 *By the Lord, madam, you wrong me, and the world shall know it. Though you have put me into darkness and given your drunken cousin rule over me, yet have I the benefit of my senses as well as your ladyship. I have your own letter that induced me to the semblance I put on; with the which I doubt not but to do myself much right, or you much shame. Think of me as you please, I leave my duty a little unthought-of, and speak out of my injury. The madly-used Malvolio.*

OLIVIA Did he write this?

310 FESTE Ay, madam.

ORSINO This savours not much of distraction.

OLIVIA
See him delivered, Fabian, bring him hither.

Exit Fabian

My lord, so please you, these things further thought on,
To think me as well a sister as a wife,
One day shall crown th'alliance on't, so please you,
Here at my house, and at my proper cost.

ORSINO
Madam, I am most apt t'embrace your offer.
(*To Viola*) Your master quits you; and for your service
done him
So much against the mettle of your sex,
320 So far beneath your soft and tender breeding,
And since you called me master for so long,
Here is my hand; you shall from this time be
Your master's mistress.

OLIVIA   A sister, you are she.

Enter Malvolio and Fabian

---

316 *proper* own   318 *quits you* releases you from service
317 *apt* ready

ORSINO
  Is this the madman?
OLIVIA   Ay, my lord, this same.
  How now, Malvolio?
MALVOLIO
  Madam, you have done me wrong;
  Notorious wrong.
OLIVIA   Have I, Malvolio? No!
MALVOLIO
  Lady, you have; pray you, peruse that letter.
  You must not now deny it is your hand.
  Write from it if you can, in hand or phrase,   330
  Or say 'tis not your seal, not your invention;
  You can say none of this. Well, grant it then,
  And tell me in the modesty of honour,
  Why you have given me such clear lights of favour?
  Bade me come smiling and cross-gartered to you,
  To put on yellow stockings, and to frown
  Upon Sir Toby and the lighter people?
  And, acting this in an obedient hope,
  Why have you suffered me to be imprisoned,
  Kept in a dark house, visited by the priest,   340
  And made the most notorious geck and gull
  That e'er invention played on? Tell me why?
OLIVIA
  Alas, Malvolio, this is not my writing,
  Though, I confess, much like the character.
  But out of question 'tis Maria's hand.
  And now I do bethink me, it was she
  First told me thou wast mad; then, camest in smiling,
  And in such forms which here were presupposed
  Upon thee in the letter. Prithee, be content.

330 *from it* differently   337 *lighter* lesser
331 *invention* composition   341 *geck and gull* butt and dupe
333 *in the modesty of honour* with a modest 344 *character* hand
    regard for your reputation   348 *presupposed* previously enjoined
334 *lights* signals, indications

350   This practice hath most shrewdly passed upon thee;
           But when we know the grounds and authors of it,
           Thou shalt be both the plaintiff and the judge
           Of thine own cause.

FABIAN   Good madam, hear me speak;
           And let no quarrel, nor no brawl to come,
           Taint the condition of this present hour,
           Which I have wondered at. In hope it shall not,
           Most freely I confess, myself and Toby
           Set this device against Malvolio here,
           Upon some stubborn and uncourteous parts
360   We had conceived against him. Maria writ
           The letter at Sir Toby's great importance,
           In recompense whereof, he hath married her.
           How with a sportful malice it was followed
           May rather pluck on laughter than revenge,
           If that the injuries be justly weighed
           That have on both sides passed.

OLIVIA
           Alas, poor fool! How have they baffled thee!

FESTE Why, 'Some are born great, some achieve great
       ness, and some have greatness thrown upon them.' I
370   was one, sir, in this interlude, one Sir Topas, sir – but
       that's all one. 'By the Lord, fool, I am not mad!' But do
       you remember: 'Madam, why laugh you at such a
       barren rascal, an you smile not, he's gagged'? And thus
       the whirligig of time brings in his revenges.

MALVOLIO
           I'll be revenged on the whole pack of you!   Exit

---

350 *This practice hath most shrewdly passed*
    upon thee this trick has been very
    cunningly played on you
359–60 *Upon some stubborn and uncourte-*
    ous parts | We had conceived against him
    in consequence of his stiff-necked
    and unfriendly behaviour to which
    we took exception

361 *importance* importunity
367 *poor fool!* (said affectionately)
    baffled treated shamefully
374 *whirligig* spinning top
375 *pack* (a word used of a group of plot-
    ters)

OLIVIA

He hath been most notoriously abused.

ORSINO

Pursue him and entreat him to a peace.
He hath not told us of the Captain yet.
When that is known, and golden time convents,
A solemn combination shall be made   380
Of our dear souls. Meantime, sweet sister,
We will not part from hence. Cesario, come;
For so you shall be, while you are a man.
But when in other habits you are seen –
Orsino's mistress, and his fancy's queen!

Exeunt all but Feste

FESTE (*sings*)

When that I was and a little tiny boy,
    With hey-ho, the wind and the rain;
A foolish thing was but a toy,
    For the rain it raineth every day.

But when I came to man's estate,   390
    With hey-ho, the wind and the rain;
'Gainst knaves and thieves men shut their gate,
    For the rain it raineth every day.

But when I came, alas, to wive,
    With hey-ho, the wind and the rain;
By swaggering could I never thrive,
    For the rain it raineth every day.

But when I came unto my beds,
    With hey-ho, the wind and the rain;

379 *convents* calls us together
386 *When that I was and a little tiny boy.*
    The confusion of the fourth stanza
    suggests that this was a folk-song.
    Another stanza of it is said or sung
    by the Fool in *King Lear*. Modern
    actors of Feste like to sing it with
pathos, but probably it was intended
as a 'jig' or cheerful conclusion to a
comedy. See page 564 for the tune to
which it is traditionally sung in the
theatre.
388 *toy* trifle

400   With tosspots still had drunken heads,
         For the rain it raineth every day.

    A great while ago the world began,
         With hey-ho, the wind and the rain;
    But that's all one, our play is done,
         And we'll strive to please you every day.   *Exit*

400 *tosspots* sots

READ MORE IN PENGUIN

In every corner of the world, on every subject under the sun, Penguin represents quality and variety – the very best in publishing today.

For complete information about books available from Penguin – including Puffins, Penguin Classics and Arkana – and how to order them, write to us at the appropriate address below. Please note that for copyright reasons the selection of books varies from country to country.

In the United Kingdom: Please write to *Dept. JC, Penguin Books Ltd, FREEPOST, West Drayton, Middlesex UB7 OBR*

If you have any difficulty in obtaining a title, please send your order with the correct money, plus ten per cent for postage and packaging, to *PO Box No. 11, West Drayton, Middlesex UB7 OBR*

In the United States: Please write to *Penguin USA Inc., 375 Hudson Street, New York, NY 10014*

In Canada: Please write to *Penguin Books Canada Ltd, 10 Alcorn Avenue, Suite 300, Toronto, Ontario M4V 3B2*

In Australia: Please write to *Penguin Books Australia Ltd, 487 Maroondah Highway, Ringwood, Victoria 3134*

In New Zealand: Please write to *Penguin Books (NZ) Ltd,182–190 Wairau Road, Private Bag, Takapuna, Auckland 9*

In India: Please write to *Penguin Books India Pvt Ltd, 706 Eros Apartments, 56 Nehru Place, New Delhi 110 019*

In the Netherlands: Please write to *Penguin Books Netherlands B.V., Keizersgracht 231 NL–1016 DV Amsterdam*

In Germany: Please write to *Penguin Books Deutschland GmbH, Friedrichstrasse 10–12, W–6000 Frankfurt/Main 1*

In Spain: Please write to *Penguin Books S. A., C. San Bernardo 117–6° E–28015 Madrid*

In Italy: Please write to *Penguin Italia s.r.l., Via Felice Casati 20, I–20124 Milano*

In France: Please write to *Penguin France S. A., 17 rue Lejeune, F–31000 Toulouse*

In Japan: Please write to *Penguin Books Japan, Ishikiribashi Building, 2–5–4, Suido, Bunkyo-ku, Tokyo 112*

In Greece: Please write to *Penguin Hellas Ltd, Dimocritou 3, GR–106 71 Athens*

In South Africa: Please write to *Longman Penguin Southern Africa (Pty) Ltd, Private Bag X08, Bertsham 2013*

BY THE SAME AUTHOR

Four Histories
Richard II · Henry IV, Part I · Henry IV, Part II · Henry V

This tetralogy of plays – written by Shakespeare *c.* 1595 to *c.* 1599 – inhabits the turbulent period of change from the usurpation of the throne of Richard II by Bolingbroke to the triumph – some would say triumphalism – of heroic kingship under Henry V. Walter Pater, in his famous essay, found the central idea of the *Histories* to be 'the irony of kingship – average human nature, flung with wonderfully pathetic effect into the vortex of great events'.

Four Tragedies
Hamlet · Othello · King Lear · Macbeth

The theme of the great Shakespearian tragedies is the fall from grace of a great man due to a flaw in his nature. Whether it is the ruthless ambition of Macbeth or the folly of Lear, the irresolution of Hamlet or the suspicion of Othello, the cause of the tragedy – even when it is the murder of a king – is trifling compared with the calamity it unleashes.

The four plays in each edition are accompanied by notes and an introduction to each text, making these volumes of particular value to students and theatre-goers.